Hoover, Blacks, and Lily-Whites

The Fred W. Morrison
Series in Southern Studies

HOOVER, BLACKS, &

LILY-WHITES

A Study of Southern Strategies

DONALD J. LISIO

The University of North Carolina Press

Chapel Hill and London

© 1985 The University of North Carolina Press

All rights reserved

Manufactured in the United States of America

Library of Congress Cataloging in Publication Data

Lisio, Donald J.

Hoover, Blacks, and lily-whites.

(The Fred W. Morrison series in Southern studies)

Bibliography: p.

Includes index.

1. Hoover, Herbert, 1874–1964—Views on race relations.
2. Southern States—Race relations. 3. Southern States—
Politics and government—1865–1950. I. Title.

II. Series.

E802.L.56 1985   973.91'6'0924   84-22002

ISBN 0-8078-1645-0

270260

For Suzie, Denise, and Steve

Contents

Illustrations

Preface

Herbert Hoover took quiet pride in finding solutions to problems that defeated men of lesser abilities. He shone especially in organizational matters, whether marshaling aid for victims of the Great War or transforming the placid Commerce Department into a dynamo of innovative government. In the area of economic planning, scholars are recognizing that his ideas were often well ahead of those of many of his contemporaries. Yet as president, when he had to deal with more specific political problems, his sophistication often seemed to abandon him. One notable case was his encounter with racism.

When Hoover made forays into the thickets of southern Republican politics, racism was the most significant human reality that he was unable to penetrate. He was not alone in this failing. In some respects his views of race reflected conventional prejudices. Although he seldom mentioned the subject, he believed that certain races exhibited traits that were inferior to those of whites. However, he differed from most in emphasizing his belief that through education and self-help these inferior traits could be largely overcome. In the sense that, like conventional wisdom, he held blacks inferior to whites, he was a "racist"; in the sense that he attributed to blacks the ability to make great progress and that he wanted to help them and to advance racial goodwill, he was, for his time, racially progressive. Many others with whom he would deal in the South—particularly *lily-white* leaders (that is, white Republicans who were determined to exclude blacks from positions of influence and prominence in the Republican party), and, of course, the white supremacist Democrats—took a much dimmer view of black people. Yet despite his relatively benign racial attitudes and desire to help, Hoover was criticized as a racial bigot both by his contemporaries and later historians. That view, in turn, reinforced the charge that he cared little for the disadvantaged and the downtrodden.

For over fifty years Herbert Hoover has been viewed incorrectly as a lily-white racist who deliberately pursued a "southern strategy" to revitalize Republican fortunes in the South by driving blacks from positions of leadership and influence at all levels of southern Republican politics. According to this prevalent interpretation, which was seemingly supported by many of his public actions at the time, Hoover deliberately stripped southern black Republicans of power and cooperated with lily-whites in an effort to steal the mantle of white supremacy from southern Democrats and thus wrest from them their political hold on the South.

This seemingly blatant effort to win southern white votes without regard for the Republican party's traditional although ineffectual role as the protector of Negro rights understandably appalled and angered blacks and their white allies. Feeling betrayed by their own party, black leaders naturally turned their wrath on Hoover. It would certainly be easier and less demanding to argue this thesis. But although such an interpretation has been plausible, it is nonetheless inaccurate and woefully incomplete. This study separates these misperceptions from historical reality by examining the hitherto unrecognized complexities and contradictions of Hoover's unhappy encounter with racism.

Hoover's ignorance about racism and its central importance in the South—indeed, throughout the United States—generated misconceptions that frustrated and baffled not only him but other participants and later scholars as well. During the disastrous Mississippi flood of 1927 Hoover gained some valuable firsthand knowledge of how southerners treated blacks, but his preconceptions about voluntarism and his consuming effort to capture the Republican nomination for president prevented him from extending this knowledge into an understanding of the nature and extent of racism in American society. In fairness to Hoover it ought to be noted that, given the pervasiveness of racism at all levels of the society, acquiring such an understanding would have been difficult, if not impossible. Yet ironically he thought that his brief exposure to some of racism's manifestations during the flood had enabled him to understand how he might help in overcoming the problems confronting blacks. In reality he understood only enough to generate high hopes among his black supporters.

After the flood and the Republican National Convention, Hoover believed that he had learned much in a short period of time. He had discovered both the desperate plight of black people and the intense criticism directed at him for dealing with patronage-bloated southern state parties that traded convention votes for federal patronage. He came away from the flood wanting to help black people and thereafter actively encouraged their Republican leaders. He came away from the nominating convention repelled by the charges of having bought the southern delegate votes that ensured his first-ballot victory. Thus his early encounters with the South erected for him several goals that he thought were reconcilable. He wanted to act against peonage and other racial problems and to improve the lot of blacks generally. At the same time he wanted to move quickly to combat corruption in the southern Republican state parties. On the surface he appeared to many to be exceptionally knowledgeable about the South, as his electoral victories in seven southern and border states would suggest, yet he was still as ignorant about southern politics as he was about the racism that was central to them. That ignorance about racism, so common at the time and since then, would blight and then destroy his efforts to bring about reform.

Because he did not adequately understand the nature and varied manifestations of racism and because he was eager to remove the taint of having dealt with patronage-seeking southern politicos, two visionary southerners easily convinced the Republican nominee that he could begin an immediate reform and revitalization of the state parties. Their vision was especially attractive to him because it relied upon one of Hoover's favorite agencies for reform—a new elite leadership, which would assume the responsibility and tap the idealism of local citizens. In this way he would promote a political and economic "revolution" throughout the entire South and ultimately provide more help to blacks than Republicans had since the end of Reconstruction.

The prospect of a new South had an irresistible appeal to Hoover. He envisioned a new southern white elite that would set high standards for honesty and efficiency in government and, through genuine political competition with the Democrats, inaugurate a true revolution of southern political life. He accepted the view that if Republicans could field a higher class of white candidates, southern Democrats could no longer rely on their tawdry appeal to white supremacy. At the same time he would create a Republican black elite that would work harmoniously with the new white leaders. With a revitalized southern Republican party, differing economic policies would replace race as the basis of southern politics, and that would further ensure a true two-party system in the South.

Thus, as the two parties became evenly matched, both would be increasingly forced to appeal to black voters. This would eventually bring about real political power for blacks. Because blacks would also divide over economic issues, they would gravitate to either party for philosophical or economic reasons, and as a result, Hoover believed, the old fears generated by racial politics would die out. Then the way would be open for both parties to do more for black people than could the relatively ineffectual existing *black-and-tan* organizations, that is, Republican state parties controlled by blacks and racially moderate white southerners. The idea of this southern "revolution" and the racial progress it seemed to promise excited Hoover with the hope of simultaneously reforming the patronage-corrupt state parties, advancing racial progress, and promoting a new South.

To achieve the utopian vision of a revolution in southern politics, Hoover first would have to outwit the Democrats. To do so southern advisers cautioned him that he must not explain his high hopes for black advancement publicly or make any appeal or even reference to black votes, lest the white supremacist Democrats seize on them as evidence of traditional Republican reliance on Negro votes. If he did not remain silent on matters relating to race and thereby rise above it, he would be unable to attract the new white elite leadership, and Republicans would be unable to dislodge the entrenched Democratic oligarchies.

By embracing this utopian vision, especially with its insistence on silence, Hoover placed himself in an impossible political position. The plan was badly flawed in conception, execution, and timing and ended in bitter misunderstanding and failure. In this context plausible charges of lily-whitism arose, which, when reinforced by his refusal to explain his motives, gained acceptance as historical truth. His policy of silence on race combined with his periodic outbursts of personal pique against critics further reinforced the impression of a cynical lily-white racist who cared nothing for the plight of black Americans.

In effect, Hoover unwittingly compromised with racism without understanding either the extent or the certain consequences of that compromise. Moreover, although he felt that he could not explain his good intentions and high hopes either to blacks or to lily-whites, he expected, indeed insisted, that his followers remain convinced of his honorable intentions and support him despite appearances to the contrary. Finally he stretched these expectations beyond the breaking point in his nomination of Judge John J. Parker to the United States Supreme Court.

In reality, Hoover did try to crack the solid South, but not for the reasons his critics or historians imagined. Rather than implement a single, racist, lily-white southern strategy to exclude blacks and thus challenge the Democrats, as has been the standard interpretation, the new president evolved several southern strategies and pursued them simultaneously, choosing different combinations of policies to fit the varying situations he found. Thus he attempted to replace reputedly dishonest black-and-tan leaders with new lily-white leaders in Mississippi and South Carolina and with a white-black coalition in Georgia. He also supported honest black politicians at the expense of their lily-white rivals in Tennessee and, to a much lesser degree, in Louisiana. He worked with lily-white organizations that he believed were honest and had gained power legally, as in Texas and, with special enthusiasm, in North Carolina. He cooperated with the black-and-tan coalitions in Arkansas, Missouri, and West Virginia; and he encouraged reform-minded lily-whites to oust reputedly corrupt or disreputable lily-whites in Florida and Virginia.

The overriding goals or operating principles of these various southern strategies were his commitment to clean and efficient government and his dream of a southern revolution that would remove race as the traditional basis of southern politics and pave the way for political, economic, and racial progress. However, because he believed that he must outwit the Democrats by a policy of silence and by working behind the scenes, these varied efforts never became publicly known and understood. Instead they remained in the shadow of the more sensational perception of one racist, lily-white southern strategy. In the end Hoover's diverse, unexplained, and thus confusing southern strategies managed to alienate both blacks and lily-whites.

In addition to his plans for southern progress, Hoover also worked behind the scenes to lay what he believed must be the national basis for real black advancement, a long-range goal, which, he insisted, mere politics could never hope to achieve. At the core was his vision of a new, elite black leadership, which he would nourish and sustain through federal appointments and which would help other blacks to take advantage of federal programs. More important, this new leadership would encourage an expanding network of elite leaders throughout the black community who would join in discovering new ways to advance racial progress.

At the same time reputable black leaders in the South would find his high-minded southern Republican white elite cooperative and helpful, and together these exemplary leaders would combat political corruption and racial injustice by enlisting the abundant energies and organizational genius of public-spirited men and women in both races. To this end he appointed new and often politically unknown black leaders to federal posts or as participants in federally sponsored studies of important social problems. He also surreptitiously protected respected black political leaders against lily-white enemies and worked with reputable black-and-tan state parties. In one dramatic gesture to illustrate those hopes, he and Mrs. Hoover invited the wife of a northern black congressman to tea at the White House. The charges of lily-whitism directed against Hoover cannot be reconciled with these intentions, appointments, and actions. But few blacks knew of them, and fewer still understood or agreed with his appointments to federal posts. The gap that developed between his private assurances and his other, seemingly contrary, public actions caused even the members of his own black elite to fall into disappointed silence.

Hoover's devotion to the progressive principles of honest and efficient government and the personal embarrassment he suffered in winning the nomination moved him to end traditional Republican patronage politics in the South. The ideals of clean, effective public service would replace the discredited practices of former Republicans. By eliminating all vestiges of the old patronage politics and appointing only well-qualified candidates to federal posts, he would attract and hold new elite leaders who would prove to their fellow southerners that Republican leadership and their affiliation with the Republican party could work a genuine transformation of their society. Because frontal attacks on the corrupt system of white supremacy only strengthened the Democrats, he would crack the solid South first by earning the respect of the voters and later by tapping the reservoir of unrecognized capacity for genuine racial progress. To Hoover the reform of southern patronage was the indispensable first step toward his cherished goals.

But to black leaders in both the North and South federal patronage had a different and far more important meaning and function. Black Republicans, especially in the South, depended on federal patronage as one of their few effective ways of securing some degree of protection and prestige in an otherwise hostile society. Black influence in the selection of federal marshals, attorneys, and judges, for example, was no small matter. These appointees were not black, to be sure, but their attitude toward blacks could be crucial.

Thus patronage was essential to establish some degree of black protection, to provide a source of status and influence for those black leaders who controlled it, and to demonstrate goodwill and good intentions toward black people generally. Hoover had not articulated any alternative, practical program for blacks, and the one he held privately was so idealistic and complex as to be all but unimaginable to them. Federal patronage, therefore, was real, tangible proof of a genuine desire to help, and ideals and principles which, at best, could take years to implement could not substitute for it. Patronage, to Hoover a path toward a distant goal, was to southern blacks an important, immediate goal itself.

Hoover and his black supporters were men of high principles and goodwill, yet in practice, his methods of achieving the principles of reform government, which he insisted would bring about a southern political revolution and eventual racial progress, were irreconcilable with black needs and principles. Hoover's methods would force blacks to depend even more on the mercy of whites whose idealism could not be trusted in any contest with racism. Black principles and pride forbade their leaders to accept any further compromises with racism, especially not from those who professed to be their friends. Despite his articulation of high principles, his methods of implementing them convinced black critics that these reform "principles" were in reality ill-disguised racist verbiage cynically designed to strip them of their last remaining vestiges of influence and protection.

Ignorant about racism and its workings, Hoover thus unwittingly became its captive. He was not a bigot with a lily-white southern strategy, as the standard interpretation argues. Indeed, southern lily-whites were the first to recognize this fact. Instead a combination of ignorance about racism and his utopian idealism worked against both himself and black Americans. When he attempted to put his southern reforms into practice, his staunch black supporters, who had earlier invested so much of their faith in him, became increasingly dismayed and alienated. Their hopes destroyed, they perceived a tragic and perhaps fatal setback for racial progress under Republican leadership. Old friends became enemies, and as the principles of effective government and racial progress collided, these men of goodwill drew further and further apart. For both Herbert Hoover and his black supporters the experience ended in puzzled disillusionment.

Relatively little has been written about Hoover's relations with blacks and southern lily-whites during his prepresidential and presidential years. General studies about Hoover make reference to his views about race, but his complex relationship with blacks, lily-whites, and the South is not discussed. Several scholars have explored this subject in varying degrees, but each of them accepts the incomplete and therefore erroneous view that Hoover pursued a single southern strategy, which was a lily-white scheme designed to remove blacks from positions of leadership and influence in the South in order to appeal to previously Democratic voters. These interpretations differ significantly from mine, and I discuss them in greater detail in the notes and bibliographical essay.

Rather than concentrate exclusively on Hoover or focus attention primarily on the politics of the southern Republican state parties, I have sought to place their story in its proper, wider national context. Although this work is not primarily a study of racism, I hope nonetheless that it helps to illustrate its importance. Perhaps I may thereby add to our historical knowledge of how ignorance about that phenomenon, as well as the power of racist leaders, effectively separated men of goodwill and frustrated hopes for racial cooperation and progress during the years between 1929 and 1933. In developing this larger context, I hope also to make a contribution to black history and to bring a clearer understanding to an important transitional era in America's past.

Acknowledgments

Thanking the many individuals and institutions that helped to make this book possible is indeed a pleasure. A senior fellowship from the American Council of Learned Societies enabled me to spend an uninterrupted year to write the first draft. A sabbatical leave from Coe College and appointment to the Henrietta Arnold Chair in History contributed significantly. The yearly stipend from the Henrietta Arnold Chair enabled me to make productive use of the summer months, paid for the typing of the manuscript, encouraged me to continue my research in distant collections, and helped in many other ways. I am grateful to Coe for its continuing recognition and support of the crucial interrelatedness of teaching and scholarshsip.

The archivists at the Herbert Hoover Presidential Library in West Branch, Iowa, have been most helpful in suggesting additional sources and by their highly professional and efficient services generally. Thomas T. Thalken, the former director, Robert S. Wood, the present director, and staff members Dale Mayer, Mildred Mather, Shirley Sondergard, and Pat Wildenberg were most cooperative. Other professionals who assisted me include Diane Howard, Laura Brault, Richard Doyle, and Peggy Knott of Coe College; Ken Scheffel of the Bentley Historical Library, the University of Michigan; Ferris Stovall and Mabel E. Deutrich of the National Archives, who aided in obtaining materials under the Freedom of Information Act; George Warren of the State Archives and Public Records, Denver, Colorado; Mary Kim Kennon of Memphis State University; Roberta Church, who granted special permission to use the Robert R. Church, Jr., Papers; and the librarians at the Library of Congress; the Chicago Historical Society; Tuskegee Institute; Howard University; Morgan State University; Yale University; the Ohio Historical Society; the New York Public Library; the Hoover Institution on War, Revolution, and Peace at Stanford University; the Virginia Historical Society; the University of North Carolina; the Franklin D. Roosevelt Library; the University of Florida at Gainesville; Florida State University at Tallahassee; the University of Iowa; and Coe College.

Others who have been supportive in various ways and deserve recognition include the late Violet Swanson Anderson, Arnold and Anne Moore Lisio, Richard and Lila Lisio Walker, Alice Lisio, John Brown, David Burner, J. Preston Cole, Lowry C. Fredrickson, Paul Glad, Diane Hernandez, Joe

McCabe, Roger Nichols, Leo Nussbaum, Theron Schlabach, Mary Thee, and the late Irvin G. Wyllie.

I am happy to acknowledge several colleagues and friends who have helped me at various stages of this study. Charles Cannon and James Randall read the early chapters. Denise Petska typed the first draft of my handwritten notes. Glenn Janus encouraged me in a variety of ways; and Mary Miskimen cheerfully, patiently, and expertly typed the entire manuscript.

I am grateful as well to the University of North Carolina Press, which has been generous in accepting this lengthy analysis without requesting cuts. Lewis Bateman, the Executive Editor, and the staff of the Press have been most cordial and unfailingly supportive in guiding this book through the production process.

Since beginning my study of history at Knox College, David M. Pletcher, now at Indiana University, has been my mentor and good friend. My attempt to offer fair and balanced historical judgments owes much to the example that he has set for his students both in the classroom and as a distinguished historian. His literary precision improved the manuscript's clarity. To him I owe a special debt.

My wife, Suzanne Swanson Lisio, unfailingly provided the special encouragement and support so essential to the completion of this book. She, like my parents, Dorothy and Anthony Lisio, has shared the values that my work represents. Her suggestions, typing, editorial skills, and good cheer, together with the patience and understanding of our children Denise and Steve, enabled me to experience again all of the joys in writing history.

Hoover, Blacks, and Lily-Whites

1. The Mississippi Flood

The year 1927 offered considerable promise for Secretary of Commerce Herbert Hoover. On 2 August President Calvin Coolidge informed the American people that he did not "choose to run" for the Republican nomination in 1928. Coolidge's cryptic comment was welcome news to Hoover, who had long been interested in the presidential nomination. He was already well known as an international hero who was admired by millions of Americans for his extraordinary success in feeding many millions of starving Europeans during and after the Great War, which had been an arduous task complicated by wartime hatreds and mistrust. Overcoming many obstacles, at times only after personal confrontations with powerful political leaders, but always steadfastly supported by a corps of dedicated volunteers, he had earned a reputation as a superb organizer, a skillful problem solver, and a quietly inspirational leader. Few were more keenly schooled in the special difficulties and potential political hazards encountered by humanitarian leaders during periods of great crisis.[1]

In 1917 when the United States entered the war, President Woodrow Wilson asked Hoover to take charge of American food production and distribution. Soon *to Hooverize* became a household expression for food conservation. Following the armistice, Hoover returned to Europe, where he resumed the awesome job of distributing food to additional millions of starving Europeans and Russian citizens. The Great Humanitarian, as he came to be known, had repeatedly demonstrated a desire and ability to serve his fellow man, and Americans were justly proud of him.[2]

Other honors and titles awaited Herbert Hoover. Instead of resuming his highly profitable career as a mining engineer, he entered public service. In many ways he seemed an unlikely politician—shy, round faced, with a high starched collar and an awkward public-speaking manner. Yet his international reputation had made him a contender. At first he stated no party preference, and both the Republican and Democratic leaders, including Franklin D. Roosevelt, courted him. Eventually Hoover decided that he was a Republican, and after a brief boomlet for the presidential nomination in 1920, he busied himself building a new reputation as secretary of commerce during the Harding and Coolidge administrations.[3] His leadership in peacetime more than matched that which he had shown in crisis. The Commerce Department quickly developed from an insignificant, neglected agency into the most dynamic, innovative, and powerful of the federal bureaucracies.[4] Hoover combined an organizing genius with innovative economics, and before long people were referring to him as the Great Engineer as well as the Great Humanitarian.

During the spring of 1927 Hoover gained further admiration and respect from his countrymen. In April, following many weeks of unusually heavy rains, the thousands of tributaries in the 1,240,000-square-mile Mississippi River basin began to dump more than 60 cubic miles of water into the main channel, creating a record flood crest that took two months to reach the Gulf of Mexico. At first officials were confident of their ability to contain the water, but as levees crumbled from southern Illinois all the way to New Orleans, over one and a half million people hastily fled to higher ground. The flood stranded hundreds on portions of levees that threatened to collapse entirely. Staggering property losses rose higher, with some estimates as high as $1 billion. The flooded area extended almost 1,000 miles to the Gulf of Mexico and was approximately 50 miles wide, although in some sections its width reached 150 miles. Several hundred people died, and thousands of dead mules, horses, cows, and wildlife collected on log jams and raised the specter of epidemic. Earth tremors, electrical storms, and tornadoes added to the misery.[5]

President Coolidge recognized Hoover as the logical choice to direct the massive rescue and relief operation and on 22 April 1927 appointed him chairman of the Special Mississippi Flood Committee. The secretary of commerce immediately began developing a successful national effort. Cooperating closely with the American Red Cross, he raised $17 million from private gifts—$15 million of this from a national radio appeal—and secured $10 million more from the federal government. Then he set out by train, with a Pullman car for his headquarters, to organize state and local relief committees throughout the stricken Mississippi valley. These local committees created over 150 tent cities to house the destitute and to distribute food, clothing, medical supplies, and vaccines. At the height of its activity over 33,000 persons, almost all volunteers, worked in Hoover's organization.[6]

During the three months that Hoover directed operations from his Pullman, he secured $1 million from the Rockefeller Foundation to finance a sanitation program, and with the help of the United States Chamber of Commerce he created a nonprofit rehabilitation corporation, which would provide $10 million in low-interest loans.[7] In some respects this new assignment was similar to the great relief effort that he had directed in Europe. The millions of dollars donated by millions of Americans, coupled with the talents of over 30,000 volunteers, inspired Hoover with a great sense of pride. Although federal subsidies were essential, he firmly believed that success had resulted from the initiative and leadership of the private citizens, which proved once again that Americans were truly a great people. Later he would declare, "We rescued Main Street with Main Street."[8]

One of the greatest symbols of the volunteer ethic was the American Red

Cross. Hoover had worked with the Red Cross during the Great War, and he considered it to be the prototype of other future voluntary organizations, which with some assistance from the federal government would tap local initiative and talent in solving many of the nation's problems. Unselfish voluntarism was an ideal to be nurtured, a goal toward which Hoover directed most of his reform efforts while president. With much of the rescue phase successfully completed, Hoover found occasion to praise the organization. At a celebration given in his honor by the black people of Pine Bluff, Arkansas, he focused attention on the crucial role of the Red Cross in the flood and in American life. "In rescue and relief," he stated, "it is the embodiment of helpfulness and compassion." Indeed, according to Hoover, the Red Cross could be considered "the country's mother in times of distress."[9]

Viewed from a different perspective, local voluntarism and leadership was neither as compassionate nor as inspiring as Hoover had claimed. In fact, to judge from reports of black observers in the flooded area, rather than ennobling the American character, the crisis had accentuated one of the great flaws in the southern power structure. On 4 May Claude S. Barnett warned Hoover that Negroes were being forced back into debt peonage by the local leaders and planters who controlled Red Cross relief supplies. Burly, handsome, and hard driving, Barnett was the owner of the Chicago-based Associated Negro Press. He was well known to Hoover as an enthusiastic political supporter and loyal friend whose national news service had enabled him to establish valuable political contacts among Negro Republican leaders throughout the United States. By personally covering the flood story, Barnett had quickly discovered that land-owning white planters were systematically preventing their Negro tenant farmers from leaving the plantations for the promise of a better life in the North. He explained that these "debt-slaves" were victims of the peonage system that had been developed after the Civil War, which kept the Negroes in perpetual debt to the white planter. To discourage escape, local Red Cross relief officers gave the free supplies directly to the planters, to whom the Negro tenants had therefore to turn for survival. The bestowing or withholding of supplies gave the planter a great deal of control over his tenants. In addition, planters required their black workers to pay them the worth of the donated supplies, thus driving the blacks further into debt. Barnett urged that Negro officers and supervisors were needed to put an end to these injustices.[10]

On 7 May, shortly after Barnett's warning to Hoover, national relief leaders were shocked to read sensational headlines in a well-respected black newspaper, the Chicago *Defender*: "Use Troops in Flood Area to Imprison Farm Hands" and "Refugees Herded like Cattle to Stop Escape from Peonage." The *Defender* charged that Negroes were being denied food relief and instead were being forcibly "imprisoned." A *Defender* reporter, J. Winston Harrington, had visited the relief camps in Mississippi, Arkansas, and Tennessee, where he found plantation owners holding their Negro tenants at gunpoint to prevent their escape. Furthermore, like Barnett, he too discovered that these planters, if they passed on supplies at all, charged their Negro tenants for the donated Red Cross relief.[11] One of Hoover's supporters, Sen. Arthur Capper of Kansas, immediately informed the secretary of a formal protest he had received from the Topeka office of the National Association for the Advancement of Colored People. Capper outlined the charges and enclosed a copy of the Chicago *Defender*, which he described as "one of the strongest and most reliable Negro newspapers in the country."[12]

Verification of the charges came from still another source. On 2 May, two days before Barnett wrote Hoover, the Reverend Harold M. Kingsley had reported on the matter to the national leaders of the NAACP. Although Kingsley confirmed that Negroes in the flood area were being held in boxcars at gunpoint,[13] officials of the NAACP were somewhat skeptical of these claims at first. On 10 May James Weldon Johnson, the executive secretary of that organization, wrote to Robert R. Church, Jr., a prominent NAACP leader and Republican political leader in Memphis, Tennessee, and to George W. Lucas, president of the New Orleans branch of the NAACP, to inform them that he was having difficulty authenticating the reports concerning mistreatment of Negroes and to ask them to investigate them personally.[14] Two days later Walter White, who would soon succeed Johnson as NAACP director, cautioned Kingsley that if the mistreatment was "only a temporary condition, it would hardly be worth our while to kick up a row about it."[15] As the reports persisted, however, White finally undertook his own personal inspection and working closely with Robert Church, documented the authenticity of many of the charges. Indeed, in White's considered judgment, the Red Cross was cooperating fully with plantation owners and, as a result of tying food and supplies to peonage, subjecting many black people to exposure and malnutrition.[16]

While Hoover did not yet know about the inquiries being made by the NAACP, he had received reliable information from two different sources whom he trusted, Barnett and Capper. Even so, at first he too could not bring himself to believe the charges. Unlike the leaders of the NAACP who did investigate the allegations before making public pronouncements, Hoover immediately defended the Red Cross. He indignantly denied the truth of the accusations and thereby revealed both his naïveté about race relations and his persistent tendency to reject or parry criticism. The Negroes, he insisted, were not complaining; instead they were "pathetic and overwhelming" in their gratitude. He interpreted the boxcars not as prisons but as safe, dry, and thus highly desirable improvisations. Continuing with his positive perception, Hoover suggested that the Negroes wore tags not to facilitate recovery by the planters, but to prevent repetition in vaccinations and in daily food rations. He refused to believe that it was possible for planters to charge their Negro tenants for Red Cross supplies. Instead he maintained that the lack of Red Cross records indicated that the food and supplies had been given directly to the people. Hoover did concede that some planters might well have established their own camps for tenants before the Red Cross arrived, but he believed that these were exceptions and that they were entirely independent of the relief organizations under his direction.[17]

Hoover's conviction that critics were "overalarmed" stemmed from refutations offered to him by the local Red Cross directors.[18] More important, although he was uneasy about the reports, he would not tolerate any criticism of the Red Cross. Thus, instead of conducting his own investigation, he stubbornly and naively accepted the assurances of the southerners who were responsible for dispensing the Red Cross relief and merely telegraphed all Red Cross representatives, asking them to ensure that none of these conditions existed "either directly or indirectly" in their areas. He cautioned his volunteers that to allow such abuses would be "a negation of the spirit of the Red Cross" and ordered that any such injustice be reported directly to him.[19]

To their credit, Hoover and James L. Fieser, the national Red Cross official in charge of flood relief, issued orders that all relief supplies were to go directly to the needy and that all plantation owners were ineligible to receive the donated supplies. Instead, the planters must borrow any funds they needed from the Agricultural Finance Corporation.[20] Hoover was adamant about refusing the planters access to the relief.[21]

Yet despite Hoover's denials, his admonitions to local Red Cross workers, and his requirement that planters borrow funds to feed their tenants, Negro leaders understandably remained unsatisfied. Thousands of blacks living in the North had only recently arrived from the South in what has been termed the great migration of the 1920s. They knew well the ways of peonage and numerous other types of racial injustice that were routinely practiced in the South. Angry at the absence of forceful action to correct the abuses, black leaders, particularly in the North, intensified the criticism until finally on 24 May Hoover felt compelled to initiate his own inquiry.[22]

Hoover chose a well-known Negro leader, Robert Russa Moton, to select and lead an all-black investigating team. The principal of Tuskegee Institute in Alabama, Moton was a large, impressive man with a broad, handsome face who often expressed his quiet, dignified pride in the abilities of the Negro race and criticized racial injustice, although he rarely spoke out in public. For twenty-five years he had commanded the Army Reserve Officer's Training Corps at Hampton Institute. At the same time he worked closely with Booker T. Washington on a variety of projects, and in 1915, when Washington died, Moton was asked to become his successor.

Long before Washington's death his leadership had come under attack. Newer, more militant black leaders in the North had repeatedly criticized his great political power within the Republican party; his inordinate influence on northern philanthropists who were interested in Negro education; his emphasis on practical, economically remunerative education; and his refusal to fight openly for social and political rights.[23] Throughout long and often vituperative clashes between the newer leaders and the Washington coterie, Moton steadfastly defended Washington, but he also skillfully avoided criticizing the new militants. Instead he sought to mitigate differences. From Moton's perspective, a variety of methods and tactics, both militant and conciliatory, were necessary to combat racial injustice and to promote interracial brotherhood.[24]

Moton was no Uncle Tom, as some critics have occasionally charged.[25] In 1928 his book *What the Negro Thinks* vigorously challenged white stereotypes of blacks and called for an unrelenting drive for equality.[26] Nevertheless, his unwillingness to speak out more forcefully drew fire from some leaders of the NAACP, especially W. E. B. Du Bois, one of its founders and editor of its journal, the *Crisis*.[27] Eventually, in 1932, partly because of the views expressed in Moton's book, the NAACP presented him with its most coveted award, the Joel Spingarn Medal for distinguished service to the Negro race.[28] Although he was clearly respected by many black leaders in both the North and South,[29] Moton differed in some important respects from younger, more politically active northerners, and these differences would contribute to the widening schism in black leadership.[30]

Shrewd and pragmatic, Moton tried to maximize his influence by working through the existing political and economic institutions and customs of his day.[31] As Booker T. Washington's successor, he was not only principal of Tuskegee Institute but also president of the influential National Negro Business League. With financial backing from Andrew Carnegie, Washington had established the league to stimulate Negro business and to spread the philosophy of self-help and racial solidarity. In addition Moton served as one of the sponsors and an active board member of the National Urban League.[32] As a southerner in a southern institution, Moton did not have the same degree of freedom in expressing his opinions as did black leaders in the North. He believed in the great value of the practical, economically oriented education that he, like Washington, saw as the surest, fastest way to economic independence and a rising standard of living. A staunch Republican who used his political contacts to promote black capitalism, he knew Secretary of Commerce Hoover, who shared many of his economic views. Hoover had already taken steps to help promote the economic advancement of black businessmen, and he admired Moton's efforts. It is understandable, therefore, that Hoover turned to Moton to head the investigation of the flood relief in the South.[33]

When Hoover appointed Moton, several leaders of the NAACP were suspicious of the secretary's choice. Moton had not spoken out against the abuse of flood victims, and the leaders of Tuskegee Institute had long enjoyed a special, favored position with the white leaders of the Republican party. Indeed, for many years Booker T. Washington had been the Republicans' principal black patronage adviser.[34] The suspicions of Moton's critics increased when Moton did not appoint a member of the NAACP to join the investigating team. W. E. B. Du Bois, the Harvard history Ph.D., and the caustic editor of the *Crisis*, believed that Hoover might have picked Moton in order to whitewash the evidence.[35] Over the years Du Bois had criticized Moton's leadership, especially in regard to his not speaking out boldly against injustices to Negro troops during World War I.[36] Du Bois used the *Crisis* in an effort to influence the Tuskegee-oriented black leaders and also to end what he considered to be the blind allegiance of blacks to the Republican party. In place of that allegiance he hoped to encourage the development of a politically independent black voting bloc that would use racial criteria in choosing which candidates to support. In a clear departure from the Tuskegee emphasis on improvement through practical education, Du Bois believed that the Negro vote could decide the outcome of elections in the closely contested northern states and thus gain blacks "real" political power in the battle against racial and economic injustice.[37]

Exactly why Moton did not appoint a member of the NAACP to his investigating team is not clear. Perhaps Hoover was irritated and defensive because the NAACP had demanded the investigation, but the evidence does not support such speculation. Prior to 1927 Hoover's contact with blacks was so limited that he probably knew little if anything about the NAACP or of the long ideological battle between the NAACP and the so-called "Tuskegee machine." Certainly there is no evidence that he did. It is more likely that Hoover relied instead on the prestigious Negro leader who was friendly, shared his political and economic outlook, and was thoroughly familiar with conditions in the South.

Moton, in turn, selected black leaders who were well known to him. These included Bishop Robert E. Jones of the Methodist Episcopal Church in New Orleans; Eugene Kinckle Jones, the executive secretary of the National Urban League; and Eva D. Bowles, national secretary of the YMCA. Others were his close personal friends, such as Claude Barnett and Albon Holsey, Moton's secretary. Many of the eighteen engaged in activities related either to education or to the National Negro Business League. As a whole, they were an eminently competent group, representative at least in part of a southern Negro elite. Yet they were an older, less militant generation of Negro educators and professionals who preferred to work within established institutions rather than chart long-term legal and political strategies.[38]

Soon after the Moton commission began its investigation, Hoover learned that the NAACP might publicize highly damaging charges against him. On 9 June Will Irwin, a close friend and a free-lance writer who was actively promoting the secretary's quiet efforts to capture the Republican presidential nomination, informed Hoover that Walter White was going about claiming that Hoover used troops to perpetuate the peonage system. Alarmed by White's claims, Irwin tried to dissuade him, but to no avail. "I have managed to call off most of the dogs I know," he informed Hoover, but White was "literally the nigger in the woodpile." Irwin bluntly called White "a negro who looks like a white man and has set himself up as a champion of his race" and a "fanatic" who insisted that Hoover "was using state militia for the purpose of perpetuating the [peonage] system."[39]

Hoover assured Irwin that he had nothing to hide; yet Irwin's report greatly disturbed the secretary and his associates.[40] White was not the only one making such charges. The Communist party also blamed Hoover. The *Daily Worker* claimed that "the relief machinery, under Hoover's direct control, has vigorously repressed any attempt by the Negro peons to escape from their peonage."[41] Publicly Hoover denied the charges, but he did admit to Irwin, who communicated the response directly to White, that "these things were the actions of irresponsible" but "important national guardsmen," and he insisted that "when the matter was brought to his attention, he stopped it."[42] Irwin worried over White's forthcoming article in the *Nation* and asked him to acknowledge that Hoover had removed the armed guards and stopped the practice of returning tenants to plantation owners.[43]

Despite his strong personal convictions, White refrained from openly attacking the secretary.[44] Moreover, he gave a generally favorable accounting of the Red Cross efforts. Rather than accuse anyone by name, White blamed "selfish persons" who were using the Red Cross in ways that he was certain the Red Cross would not approve. For the most part he was pleased and somewhat surprised by "the essentially fair deal" given to blacks. He noted and protested that Negroes had been forced to work on the levees at gunpoint and that they had been denied freedom to relocate, but he found that "on the whole Negroes were being given food, clothing, shelter, and medical attention little different from that given to whites."[45] Privately, White still complained about Hoover's denial of the shortcomings that he had uncovered, and years later in his autobiography he recalled that his reports had "created my first of many bitter clashes with Herbert Hoover," who "unequivocally and indignantly denied the charges," but who "was forced by public indignation to appoint a committee of Negroes headed by Dr. Robert R. Moton of Tuskegee, to investigate." To "Hoover's great disappointment," White concluded, "the absolution he manifestly expected did not materialize."[46]

If Hoover had not allowed a defensive, scolding tone to dominate his responses to White, and if White had accepted Hoover's invitation to meet with him to discuss plans for improving services to blacks, the growing rift between the two men might not have become as deep as it eventually did.[47] Hoover conceded that "wicked actions" had taken place but insisted that "both colored and whites" were responsible. As White remained convinced that Hoover was principally interested in hiding the facts of peonage and mismanagement, Hoover began to believe that White and the NAACP were more interested in embarrassing him for political purposes than they were in offering "constructive suggestions." In any case, considering Hoover's repeated indignant denials of all criticisms, it is little wonder that White, Du Bois, and Monroe Trotter, head of the Negro Equal Rights League, as well as the editors of the Chicago *Defender* increasingly viewed Hoover with undisguised suspicion and mistrust. Ironically, Moton's commission eventually would offer criticisms much sharper than White's and make recommendations more sweeping than those demanded by the NAACP, but the Moton commission presented its urgings privately.[48]

Moton knew that his assignment would be difficult. As a southerner, he was vitally concerned about improving living conditions for blacks in the South. He knew that he could not expect help from the Democratic party, from prominent southern leaders, or from the national Republicans, who long ago had ceased any meaningful efforts to help blacks. Therefore, Moton also recognized that Hoover and the Red Cross would be crucial to the immediate well-being of 400,000 southern blacks in the months ahead. Indeed much good would result if Moton could educate this powerful northern Republican leader, who might well become the next president of the United States, about racial injustice and peonage in the South.

On 13 June the Moton commission gathered to present its complete report to Hoover and James L. Fieser, the director of Red Cross relief. One after another the members of the investigating team forcefully expressed their dismay at what they had found. Barnett recalled that the investigators were, in fact, "bitter in their comments on conditions in several camps." They had discovered that Negro refugees were reluctant to talk to Negro investigators for fear of subsequent beatings or worse. Their fears appeared to be well founded. Moton angrily cited the "large number of armed white guardsmen" and insisted that they be reduced to the few needed for everyday protection. The commission also recommended sleeping cots for all black refugees, an improved system of clothing distribution, and the hiring of trained Negro social workers and nurses. Most important, they urged that Hoover create colored advisory committees in each camp to ensure the fair treatment of Negroes and the appointment of at least two colored men to each state relief committee with the express power to investigate complaints. In effect, the Moton commission called for the reorganization of the methods of relief distribution to blacks and delegation of authority to black supervisors who could stop abuses.[49]

Hoover listened carefully, and his reaction to the recommendations pleased the black investigators. Rather than becoming defensive, as in his earlier public pronouncements, the secretary revealed to them that he had learned a great deal since the charges of injustice were first raised. He promised to implement all of their recommendations as speedily as possible and assured Moton that all of the organizations assisting the Red Cross had been ordered "to carry out your suggestions at every point to the fullest possible degree."[50]

Within four days Hoover had begun establishing advisory groups, closing undesirable camps, further demobilizing national guardsmen, entirely rebuilding one large camp, and generally attempting to implement all of the commission's recommendations as quickly as he could. He also sought to convince the heads of state relief and rehabilitation commissions to appoint Negro representatives to their state commissions. He insisted that black leaders were essential in such positions "to develop full interracial cooperation on reconstruction questions." State administrators would soon learn what Hoover's white lieutenants already knew: that he was determined to implement the Moton reforms. Jesse O. Thomas, the field secretary of the National Urban League, reported that Hoover "did not countenance any discrimination or injustice that was brought to his attention."[51]

Hoover's experiences during the flood began his education on racism in the South. In his contacts with supportive black leaders he became more sympathetic, positive, and encouraging. He began to delete from his correspondence the earlier, often repeated denial that black refugees had been cruelly exploited. Instead, he now emphasized the work of the Moton commission and the positive benefits that colored advisory committees would exert in each camp.[52] Having worked closely with black leaders for the first time, Hoover had come to believe that "full interracial cooperation" was both desirable and necessary for future progress. He looked to the prestigious voluntary organization, the Commission on Interracial Cooperation, to achieve significant future progress.[53] But his greatest emphasis was on the need to enlarge and strengthen black leadership. "I have gained an appreciation," he told R. E. Malone, superintendent of a black school in Pine Bluff, Arkansas, "of the real leadership which lies in the colored people which I believe if built upon means the complete solution of our problems."[54]

Hoover was well pleased with the work of the Moton commission and by its conclusion that the abuses that they found had occurred where local volunteers and committees had deliberately disregarded the directives of the national Red Cross officials.[55] In turn, Claude Barnett especially approved Hoover's responses to the commission's findings. Barnett had been the first to warn Hoover about the abuses. He had been highly critical and forthright in his reports to the commission, yet he had also been an important interpreter and conciliator in Hoover's meetings with the members of the commission. Now Barnett championed the much-criticized secretary in a series of news articles circulated by his Associated Negro Press and printed by influential black newspapers, such as the New York *Age*, the Pittsburgh *Courier*, and the Baltimore *Afro-American*, which gave the story prominent coverage. "Hoover Orders Militia from Camps" proclaimed the Baltimore *Afro-American*.[56] Hoover's defense of Negro rights and well-being was front-page news. But more important to him were the personal tributes and trust he now began to receive from Negroes.

On 27 June 1927 almost 3,000 Negroes and 1,000 whites from southeastern

Arkansas gathered at Pine Bluff to extend their thanks to "Uncle Sam" Hoover. Gov. John Ellis Martineau of Arkansas; Scipio A. Jones, a lawyer and prominent Republican politician; Harvey C. Couch, chairman of the Arkansas state relief commission; and C. C. Neal, president of the Arkansas Haygood Industrial School for Negroes, praised Hoover for the outstanding relief work he had done to aid black people. The theme struck by all of the speakers was a celebration of the greater understanding and respect that the flood crisis had produced between blacks and whites. The speakers' tributes touched Hoover the man and flattered Hoover the unannounced presidential candidate, and when 200 women students sang "Swing Low, Sweet Chariot," tears filled his eyes. Hoover spoke only briefly, but in those few sentences he conveyed his belief that economic independence for blacks was the key to a better future. He lauded the practically-oriented education offered by Tuskegee Institute as a way to achieve that independence. "In this type of institution lies one of the foremost hopes of the future of the South," he proclaimed. "For education along the lines represented by this school means the economic independence of the negro race—the ownership of its own homes and businesses."[57]

Black ownership of farms and businesses was a conception of society that contrasted sharply with the reality of the southern peonage system. Yet by midsummer Hoover had come to understand better the workings of peonage, and he recognized the need to work toward its destruction. A few years later he privately deplored the staying power of peonage to some intimate friends, lamenting that "the old patrician civilization of pre-slave days" still existed in the South. The planter "lives off the famished agriculture by holding his tenants in practical peonage of constant debt," and he still "controls the activities of the senators and congressmen" as well.[58] He was convinced that the solidly Democratic South controlled by its planter elite was an important part of the problem.

Hoover did not believe that the abolishment of the peonage system and the reconstruction of southern land ownership were merely idealistic or utopian dreams. He had personally visited successful, independent black farms and businesses at Mound Bayou in Mississippi, and he had been very favorably impressed by the community's black leader, Eugene P. Booze and by his wife Mary Booze, Republican national committeewoman from Mississippi.[59] Because Hoover insisted that elected state and federal officials served the interests of the old planter elite, he would not support either federal or Red Cross programs in which funds to eliminate peonage went directly to the state or were in any way controlled by state officials or federal representatives from the state. Instead, he outlined what then might have been considered a visionary plan for establishing a multimillion dollar private land corporation to aid blacks. Rather than depending on local management, the corporation would be controlled by northern philanthropists. Financed initially with surplus Red Cross flood relief funds, it would buy the land made idle by the flood and through a system of long-term, low-interest loans initiate a process that would enable black tenants to become independent yeoman farmers.[60]

The scope of Hoover's flood reconstruction plans and his land scheme surprised and delighted the members of the Moton commission. After speaking with the secretary, Bishop Robert E. Jones confided to Moton, "I was amazed at Mr. Hoover's insight into the difficulties and the problems and the courage with which he was facing them."[61] Hoover's land scheme plan remained a secret, known to only a few of the Moton commission members, and it helps to explain the great enthusiasm of these Negro leaders for Hoover. It is not entirely clear why Hoover failed to publicize his plans for helping black farmers. Aspirations to the presidency and fear of southern whites may have entered his thinking. Or he may have believed that advance publicity could create obstacles. In any event, the secrecy left other, more militant black leaders to draw their own conclusions from his public statements, which had often created quite a different impression of him.

Hoover's education about the injustices experienced by blacks did not, unfortunately, better equip him to deal with black detractors. These leaders knew little about his efforts to correct abuses or about his land distribution plan, and obviously they discounted Barnett's praise in the news releases from the Associated Negro Press. Hoover resented their criticism and remained highly defensive and even haughty toward them, especially toward Walter White and the NAACP. Instead of admitting publicly that the Moton commission had confirmed White's allegations, Hoover again revealed his penchant for irritating rather than conciliating critics. Hoover should have released the Moton committee's report.[62] Instead, to protect the Red Cross, he convinced Moton to keep it secret, apparently relying on the reforms themselves, Barnett's favorable articles, and his own explanations to convey the sincerity of his intentions.

Understandably, northern black leaders wanted some indication that the secretary of commerce would implement reforms or at the very least admit to the nation that abuses had been committed and that the peonage system was exploiting blacks. At the very least Hoover should have attempted to correct the unfavorable impression that he had created among northern black leaders, but he did not. Instead, Hoover added to that unfavorable impression by informing White that neither he nor the Red Cross could do the impossible. "I think you will agree with me," he told White, "that the National agencies have no responsibility for the economic system which exists in the South or for matters which have taken place in recent years; nor can they be charged with responsibility for statements or actions of officers of the state militia, even if such action is improper." He insisted that the Red Cross could not be expected to "undertake either social or economic reforms."[63]

If Hoover had taken White into his confidence rather than scold him, his relations with the NAACP and other black activists might well have been far less damaging to him in the years ahead. White had not asked the Red Cross to "undertake either social or economic reforms," and he correctly and easily rebutted Hoover's inept response.[64] Hoover may well have been angry over Will Irwin's report that White had blamed him for using armed guards to keep blacks in peonage, yet White had not attacked Hoover or the Red Cross publicly. More important, Hoover was allowing his personal pique at White to cut him off from, indeed to alienate, men who were on the threshold of becoming—or were already, as some scholars believe—the most important and influential group of black leaders in the United States.

During the 1920s black leadership was still in a period of transition, marked by a decline in NAACP membership. By 1928 the organization had only 23,500 members. Sale of the *Crisis* had also suffered. From a high of 95,000 copies a month in 1919, the magazine circulated less than 30,000 by 1930, and some of the NAACP national leaders who often disagreed with the more radical ideas that Du Bois put forth in the *Crisis* began to talk about ending the financial drain caused by the publication.[65] Hoover acted as if the NAACP were merely a small band of black militant critics who did not speak for the vast majority of the Negro people. Even if he based his attitude on the NAACP's declining membership rolls and revenue problems, he underestimated its potential. The organization would soon prove how wrong he had been.

If Hoover had his problems communicating with the NAACP, he must have felt particular frustration when dealing with white southern leaders. Reforms to help blacks, like inscriptions in sand, usually disappeared in the tide of recurring custom. Hoover knew that southern blacks were virtually powerless, and he believed that one of the best ways to help them advance was to marshal a new white Republican elite that would work well together with them against the old planter elite and its Democratic allies. Just as Moton felt that he must, of necessity, depend on the goodwill of Hoover and the Red Cross, the secretary of commerce would later attempt to rely upon the goodwill of new southern Republican leaders. Unfortunately, it was not always possible to tell which of the cooperative southern leaders were progressive, and later efforts to implement his ideas often brought either confusing or disastrous results.

One of the white leaders who impressed Hoover as the type of dedicated public servant who could cooperate with black leaders was Harvey C. Couch, president of the Arkansas Power and Light Company. Although not a politician, Couch had accepted the task of administering the Arkansas State Flood Relief Commission and in that capacity had earned so much respect from Hoover that later, as president, he would appoint him to the board of the Reconstruction Finance Corporation. Hoover confided to Couch the details of his plan to combat peonage. He told him that he envisioned twenty-acre farms complete with good housing, equipment, animals, and enough financing to bring in the first crop. He did not consider whether such small farms would be sufficient to provide families with more than mere subsistence, but he regarded them as a good beginning in the fight against peonage. Couch did not reply.

Hoover had also worked with L. O. Crosby, head of the state relief agency in Mississippi. He stressed to Crosby both the economy that would result from placing black supervisors in his organization and in the camps as well as the long-term benefits to the South from his plan to create independent Negro farmers. He assured Crosby that such a "reconstruction will give relief to the whole economic situation by taking some of the land off the market and [it] would also tend to create a more stable social and economic situation through the division of some of the landholders."[66]

The resettlement plan was the type of "practical idealism" that thrilled Hoover. He told Couch and Crosby of his confidence that once initiated, "such a plan would also appeal to some benevolently-minded men in the North who were desirous of doing something substantial for the negro [sic] and that if we could get the nuclei of such an organization, I believe I could build upon its capital from other sources."[67] Hoover had reason for his optimism. Fieser, the vice-chairman of the national Red Cross, who worked with him daily, had already agreed to use whatever Red Cross money remained from the relief operation for the land resettlement scheme.[68]

Despite his planning and initial groundwork, Hoover's vision of creating a class of independent black farmers did not take into account the degree to which white planters and their allies would resist such an effort. A quick, sharp rebuttal came from L. O. Crosby, who urged Hoover to abandon all of his efforts to help black people. Crosby was a loyal Hoover supporter, but he initially resisted appointing blacks to his state relief committee or sanctioning Negro advisory committees in the camps. He explained that Hoover simply did not understand the furious racial hatred that existed in Mississippi and the South. For illustration he pointed to racial tensions during the current primary race. Unfounded charges had proliferated that Negro crime was especially high during the flood, with the result that Governor Murphree had already spent $50,000 for troops to prevent the lynching of Negroes. The same governor had also tried to stop the appointment of Sidney D. Redmond, a prominent black Mississippian who was active in Republican politics, to the Moton commission.[69] Yet rather than advocate measures to combat these problems, Crosby further reasoned that reforms would only make matters worse. According to him, Negroes on the state relief committee would cause "endless trouble," especially as "poisonous literature coming from New York and Chicago had already distorted the state's generous aid to the Negro flood relief victims." In Crosby's view, Hoover's ideas were "beset with much danger."[70]

Bad news also came from the Red Cross. Fieser, who had at first supported Red Cross financing of the land resettlement effort, informed Hoover that it would be "impossible" for the Red Cross to participate in any way. Fieser complained that in introducing him to the National Negro Business League, Moton had promised his audience that Hoover and Fieser were planning to do "something in behalf of the negro [sic] more significant than anything which had happened since emancipation." As a result Negro expectations were running high, but after Fieser had talked with other Red Cross officials, he had come to accept their objections to the land reform scheme as convincing.[71]

Fieser offered two principal reasons why the Red Cross would not participate. First, if it loaned money for the project, it would resurrect the false charges that it was using donated funds improperly. Red Cross officials felt that the resulting publicity would be highly damaging to the organization. Second, Fieser now argued that the whole plan was impractical. Not only was the initial financing totally inadequate, but many white farmers and tenants, who were not so favored by the resettlement corporation, might well resort to "gorilla [sic] warfare or financial persecution or ostracism." Such tactics had already ruined two or three small Negro communities in the South. Even at Mound Bayou, he predicted, Negro ownership would soon be lost.[72]

Resistance to his resettlement plan was a blow to the secretary. Worse still was the resurgence of black criticism over the failure to improve conditions in the refugee camps. By now an active candidate for the Republican presidential nomination, Hoover ignored White's second attack; but complaints from the Colored Unity League and the Negro Women's Council coincided with reports from Moton that desperate conditions had again developed or still existed in the camps and that black supervisory personnel must be appointed to correct the continued injustices and inadequate relief.[73] Hoover responded quickly. He assigned federal Negro agricultural agents to Red Cross organizations and secured more black supervisors who would theoretically constitute independent state advisory committees. These would work "actively in the field to canvass the needs of the colored population" and report directly to the national Red Cross officials.[74]

By the end of September Moton reported that conditions for black refugees had deteriorated, especially in the delta. Local Red Cross officials and the state relief agencies distributing donated relief had largely ignored Hoover's orders. Moton reported that white plantation owners still controlled the donated Red Cross supplies to their tenants, while Negro landowners could not get relief for their own tenants unless white men "vouched" for them. In many places Negroes received inadequate supplies and faced a winter of extreme hardship. Moton demanded "prompt action in order that justice may be done the Negro sufferers."[75]

Despite Hoover's promise "to see that justice is done," blacks knew that intolerable conditions still existed in the camps. By 15 October the Chicago *Defender* was criticizing the Red Cross for the suffering on which Moton had reported privately to Hoover over two weeks earlier. By November conditions had grown worse, and Hoover again sent the members of the Moton commission on a fact-finding expedition. They were appalled by what they found.[76]

Local committees had diverted funds intended for rebuilding from Negro to white housing so that many Negroes faced the coming winter months without adequate shelter. As in previous months, food was again unequally distributed, and living conditions were wretched; many other earlier abuses reappeared, especially the use of force and violence to control black peonage labor. The local committees simply ignored Hoover's reform orders, but proof against the violators was virtually impossible to obtain. "The most depressing condition," Moton informed Hoover, "was the fear on the part of the colored people." They were convinced that if they identified the violators "and somehow it was discovered that they have 'talked too much,' . . . they would be killed." Equally discouraged, Claude Barnett concluded that "rehabilitation" only meant returning blacks to the same miserable conditions that they had endured before the flood.[77]

Hoover and Fieser were badly shaken by the Moton commission's second report. Barnett recorded that Hoover was "startled and chagrined at the condemnation which we gave."[78] Unfortunately Hoover again was irritated that the report should so strongly criticize the national Red Cross, and according to Fieser, he claimed to have " 'laid Dr. Moton out' " for failing to record "some of the fine things the Red Cross had done." After praising the Red Cross, Hoover would not "have cared" what the commission concluded, and with this understanding Moton agreed to recast the report, but his revision did not suit Red Cross officials.[79] Eventually, when the Red Cross published the report, its leaders insisted on deleting Moton's criticisms and substituting their own statement. Barnett urged that no changes be permitted. "Because I realize so keenly the state of mind of the colored people of the country as it affects the flood, as well as the attitude of the critics of the commission," and because the Red Cross and Hoover were so highly praised for their "splendid work," he admonished Fieser to make no changes.[80] Barnett's plea went unheeded.

Hoover substantially increased the number of black supervisors and placed them directly on the Red Cross payroll, and again he set out on his own investigation. The results provoked him further, for he informed Moton that he had quizzed the black inspectors in the state organizations and those who worked in the camps, and their written responses did not support Moton's conclusions. In an angry letter, which he revised and made more temperate, Hoover told Moton, "[Black investigators] had expressed themselves most strongly that except for a small percentage and some exceptional committees, the work has been carried out with great justice and efficiency to the colored people."[81]

It is little wonder that Hoover and Moton received almost totally different impressions. The evidence indicates that in addition to threatening blacks with harm if they should speak to investigators, local officials, at least in Mississippi, had sought deliberately to deceive the investigators. At the time that Hoover was making his inspection, L. O. Crosby, the head of the Mississippi state relief effort, ordered all of his committee chairmen throughout the state to take the inspectors "in charge and supply them with such information as will enable them to make a desirable report." In this way Crosby believed that they could counteract the "propaganda" in northern newspapers.[82] With local white officials covering up abuses and blacks fearful for their lives, it is not surprising that Hoover's personal tour failed to uncover the magnitude of the abuses. The extent of the injustice was not publicly revealed until early 1928, when Du Bois ran a three-part report in the *Crisis*, which had been commissioned by the NAACP and which fully supported the unpublished findings of the Moton commission.[83]

Hoover sincerely believed that he and the Red Cross had accomplished a great deal for the 400,000 Negroes caught in the devastating flood, and even today scholars can agree that this judgment is essentially correct.[84] Nonetheless, well before the onslaught of the Great Depression black critics pointed to serious defects in the voluntaristic basis of Hoover's domestic humanitarianism. While privately critical, Moton and the other black leaders who worked with Hoover had remained silent because they appreciated what he had been able to accomplish and because they knew of the numerous local obstacles to the reforms he had ordered. Most important, they had come to know him as a hardworking, well-intentioned man who had begun to understand the problems faced by black people and who had tried to be fair to the Negro refugees. Because they believed the change in his thinking and that his efforts to help were honest, they would defend him in the months ahead against the growing criticism of other black leaders who were not privy to the secretary's unpublicized thoughts and actions.[85]

Hoover's attempt to help southern blacks brought more frustration than satisfaction. Few of them knew about his efforts to end the abuses or about his land resettlement scheme, and by early 1928 even the attempt by Hoover and Moton to interest northern philanthropists in the land corporation had faltered.[86] His own duties as secretary of commerce and his activities as a vigorous contender for the Republican presidential nomination led him to conclude that he could not assume the personal direction of the corporation. The project virtually collapsed after Julius Rosenwald, the famed benefactor of Negro people, refused to become involved on the grounds that he had already tried several similar ventures in the South in vain. Later, the New Deal's Resettlement and Farm Security Administration would undertake programs similar to that proposed by Hoover.[87]

Hoover's most significant failure was his consistent and steadfast refusal to reveal to the American people the difficulties that he and the Red Cross faced in seeking to improve, much less provide, fair treatment for destitute blacks. Flood stories were often front-page news throughout the United States during the early months of the disaster, and a full disclosure from Hoover of how local officials were managing the relief would have reached many millions of Americans. While Hoover's successful administration of the vast rescue effort added to his already illustrious reputation and no doubt boosted his political candidacy, there is surprisingly little evidence that either his actions or his attitudes during this crisis were governed by political considerations.[88] Political considerations cannot be entirely discounted. He and his advisers were no doubt aware of the advantages of gaining the allegiance of southern Republican delegates to the forthcoming national nominating convention, but all available evidence suggests that politics played a minor role in his thinking. The principal reason why he neglected to publicize abuses to black citizens was because of his devotion to the Red Cross and to the voluntarism that it represented. A candid disclosure of these abuses would certainly have called into question the great virtues of local initiative, leadership, and control that Hoover cherished. Ironically, he may never have realized that the NAACP, although critical of him and the Red Cross on flood relief for blacks, was also a private, voluntary, self-help association.

This blind spot in Hoover's thinking resulted in two different impressions of his leadership: that received by Moton and the commission members, who possessed much information about his intentions and efforts, and that received by most other blacks, who did not. To a growing number of northern and southern black critics, Hoover seemed to be cooperating with, even defending, the white planter at the expense of the human needs and the civil liberties of black people. This impression was certainly consistent with published facts. Hoover had repeatedly denied White's charges, assumed a scolding tone toward him and the NAACP, and refused to sanction the release of the two Moton reports. Given these facts and the extensive report in the *Crisis*, black leaders who did not know of Hoover's efforts and of the obstacles he experienced would naturally conclude that he was no friend of the black people. As winter approached, many impoverished southern blacks, still destitute from the flood, knew only that reforms had been few and fleeting. Meanwhile two groups of black leaders regarded Hoover from opposing impressions and assumptions, and both believed that they had correctly judged the man.

2. Racial Education

In early 1928, after Hoover had announced that he would campaign actively in the state primaries for the Republican presidential nomination, the question of his beliefs about black Americans became a contested issue among Negro leaders. Du Bois was sharply critical. He informed his readers of the *Crisis* that the principal question that black people needed to decide about Herbert Hoover was whether the secretary of commerce believed "that Negroes are men or sub-men."[1] Du Bois was certain that he already knew the answer, but not all leaders of the NAACP were as confident in their responses as Du Bois. When asked about Hoover's attitude toward blacks during the Mississippi flood, James Weldon Johnson, the executive secretary, frankly stated that he did not know Hoover's attitude, but he suggested that Sidney B. Thompson, who was worried about the primary campaign in Ohio, write directly to Robert R. Moton.[2]

The Tuskegee principal, supported by Claude Barnett and his private secretary Albon L. Holsey, tried to counteract the unfavorable impression of Hoover that had spread among many blacks during the flood. Moton was confident that his personal knowledge of Hoover's beliefs and actions toward Negroes would fully "satisfy any reasonable person, even the most radical of our race."[3] Holsey, who had also been a member of the Moton commission, outlined a different type of defense. Hoover, he said, had learned a great deal about black needs during the flood relief campaign, and he hinted that this new understanding would make him a valuable ally to the Negro as president. Holsey pointed out in the Pittsburgh *Courier* on 21 January 1928 that although Hoover had "constructed a perfect machine for handling the flood situation," it had broken down "at the point of conflict between exact justice to the Negro and the perpetuation of the plantation system—and at that point Mr. Hoover discovered the South, which was the greatest blessing of the flood."[4] This theme expressed the dominant hope and belief of Moton, Holsey, Barnett, and other enthusiastic black supporters.[5]

An assessment of the extent to which Holsey's suggestion placed Hoover in a category different from other white leaders depends, at least in part, upon an understanding of the historical context in which Hoover developed his beliefs about race and, in part, on the degree to which he was able to overcome those beliefs. Like other leaders, Hoover had been affected by the dominant ideas and prejudices of his generation. It is not possible in this study to develop fully the historic context of his racial beliefs, but a brief, general account is essential for the understanding of Hoover's development.

By 1877, only three years after Hoover was born in West Branch, Iowa, the Republican party had ended its last lingering efforts to provide and enforce legal and political rights for Negroes. During the next twenty years the people of the United States, proceeding from the widespread assumption that black people were biologically and thus culturally inferior, developed a pervasive ideology that permitted and encouraged society's institutions to exclude blacks from the principal benefits, rights, and protections provided for white people. Between 1873 and 1896, for example, in a long series of legal cases, the Supreme Court of the United States nullified federal enforcement of civil rights laws and declared that racial segregation was constitutionally valid.

Southern leaders who had protected the Negro after the Civil War thereupon joined forces during the 1890s with the Negro-hating elements in the South to intensify the blacks' existing economic peonage and their political and social isolation. Both in the North and in the South newspaper editors, intellectuals, the new social scientists, and those of otherwise liberal or progressive views on social justice either joined with the less enlightened or, by failing to resist, allowed them to formulate, legitimize, and enforce a repressive racial ideology. In effect they denied "biologically inferior" nonwhites access to the benefits of society; deprived them of their rights as citizens and as humans; and forced them to accept political, cultural, social, and economic subjugation. This marshaling of society's institutions to control, exclude, and exploit "inferior" nonwhite peoples is referred to in this study as *racism*.[6]

Although the term racism often has been all too loosely used, and although scholars have had great difficulty in agreeing upon a generally acceptable meaning of the term, there is little dispute among scholars that racism has been one of the most important and dominant characteristics of American society. Perhaps because there have been so many manifestations of racism, so many methods of subjugation, and so many shifting meanings of the word *racism* in different periods of history, an exact, concise definition of the term may never be possible. The one offered here as a guide for evaluating the 1920s is not intended to be definitive or comprehensive. Its purpose is to serve as a perspective from which we may examine and make some distinctions concerning Hoover's understanding of and reactions to that phenomenon.[7]

Racism was more than an attitude or prejudice toward "inferior" races, and it went well beyond specific acts of discrimination against them. It became an all-encompassing ideology that encouraged new forms of exclusion, exploitation, and subjugation. Racists or racist institutions could be passive as well as active; that is, they need not actually promote hatred but might merely fail to challenge the ideology, or condone the discriminatory acts. Thus, racism included both the active, all-encompassing ideology of inequality and subjugation as well as the passive failure to contest that ideology and its institutionalized manifestations.[8] By including passive aspects of racism, few whites can escape some degree of responsibility for it, yet for the Hoover era another important element existed in attempting to understand men's motives and reaction to racism: the widespread ignorance about the nature and extent of racism and how it pervaded all levels of society.

In the sense that he accepted the conventional prejudices of his time, namely, that nonwhite races were inferior, Herbert Hoover was a "racist"; in the sense that he believed that blacks had made great progress, that he enthusiastically foresaw even greater progress through education and self-help, and that he wanted to promote racial progress and goodwill, he was, for his time, racially progressive. It was his tragic ignorance about the nature, resiliency, and pervasiveness of racism that would incapacitate and doom his efforts for reform. That failure would frustrate black hopes for racial cooperation and progress during the years from 1927 to 1933 and destroy the trust and friendship of Hoover and his once-loyal black supporters.

Negroes, of course, were not the only people to suffer from racism. American Indians had long been considered "savages" fit only to be penned in on federal reservations. Chinese and Japanese, indeed all Orientals, were also thought to be inferiors. Hatred of the "yellow races" had been prevalent especially on the West Coast, and by the 1880s it was sufficiently widespread to prompt the United States to prevent further Chinese and later Japanese immigration. State governments also added to the laws discriminating against "inferior" races.

By the late 1890s and throughout the Progressive Era, white middle-class Americans became increasingly optimistic that they could rescue the nation from the evils of industrialism but increasingly apprehensive lest "inferior" races "mongrelize" and destroy American society. World War I brought an end to the Progressive Era and an even greater increase in hatred toward minority groups. During and following the war and partly as a result of war-generated hysterias, the United States entered into one of its most hate-filled decades. Fearful of internal subversives, angered at the influx of southern Negroes who found jobs in northern cities during the war, and alarmed over the increase of immigrants from southern and eastern Europe, many Americans responded with renewed outbursts of hatred. Whites forced blacks out of jobs they coveted, and race riots erupted in northern cities. Patriotic demagogues denounced political radicals as alien subversives and saw to it that many were deported, often illegally. Southern and eastern Europeans were increasingly stigmatized as culturally and even biologically inferior to the "Anglo-Saxon races," and beginning in 1921 Congress passed a series of immigration restriction laws designed to reduce greatly the influx of racially "inferior" whites. Restrictions against "inferior" whites were much less damaging than the racism invoked against nonwhites, but both were all-pervasive, and each tended to reinforce the other. Therefore, by the early 1920s the Ku Klux Klan enjoyed great popularity in both northern and southern states, and because these various hatreds were all too often socially acceptable, few prominent leaders cared to speak out against them.[9]

To understand Hoover's assimilation of the conventional attitudes of his time, one must consider his early encounters with other races and his rare references to the subject.

Orphaned in 1884, young Hoover left Iowa to live with his uncle in Oregon and later entered the newly opened Leland Stanford, Jr. University in Palo Alto, California. While living on the West Coast, he more than likely absorbed some of the intense prejudice directed against Orientals. During the Progressive period Hoover was out of the country amassing a fortune as a mining engineer. In the course of his world travels he came to regard both blacks and Orientals as workers "of a low mental order." In 1909 his book *Principles of Mining* advised his fellow engineers that white workers were better miners than "Asiatics and negroes" because whites possessed a higher "inherent intelligence" and exercised more individual initiative. Later, in 1920 and again in 1924 when he was secretary of commerce, he reiterated his prejudice against nonwhites. Although he highly praised the Japanese culture, he nonetheless supported the exclusion of Japanese, indeed, the exclusion of all Asian immigrants, in order to prevent interracial marriages. It was a "biological fact," he argued, that intermarriage between whites and Orientals, and, by implication, between whites and blacks, resulted in "degenerate" offspring and great racial antagonism. This practice therefore was harmful both to the races involved and to society, which could not assimilate these misfits.[10]

Although the evidence reveals that Hoover shared the conventional prejudices of his day, he made so few references to race that one must wonder how significant these prejudices were in his thinking. Obviously, like most other white Americans, he was influenced by the prevailing racist ideology of his time. Yet more specific questions about his thoughts and actions must also be raised. Aside from its effect on mining productivity, how much importance did Hoover attach to the supposed inferiority of Negroes? How firmly did he hold to his prejudices? Did he believe that blacks could overcome this alleged inferiority? Did his prejudices influence his decisions when in public office? If so, what effect did his policies, both as secretary of commerce and as president, have in fostering or condoning the ideology of racism? If Hoover was not in practice as prejudiced as the available few references suggest, what beliefs did he express, and what actions did he take to overcome or at least contest his heritage and to combat and reduce racism and prejudice?

Precise questions such as these, concerning the depth of Hoover's racial prejudices and the extent to which he allowed them to influence his public leadership, have been difficult to answer. In some cases the evidence has been inconclusive, in others open to various interpretations.[11] Understanding was made even more difficult by Hoover's ignorance of the breadth and depth of racism, by his insistence on personal loyalty, by his self-righteousness, and by his adherence to overarching "principles." At times his principles of good government and reform appeared to contradict his desire to promote better conditions for blacks, and as a result unclear impressions were created and conflicting interpretations of them arose. Thus, what could be interpreted as principle by one could be interpreted as prejudice by another. Understanding has been further confounded by Hoover's political insensitivity, by his often inept leadership, and by the sudden perplexing economic depression that bedeviled him throughout most of his presidency. Nonetheless, while some of the evidence can be interpreted in more than one way, a general pattern of belief and behavior does emerge, which historians may legitimately use in judging his racial attitudes while he was in public service. This pattern becomes clear, however, only after a careful, detailed analysis of his actions and policies as secretary of commerce, Republican nominee, and president of the United States.

In 1921, when Hoover became secretary of commerce, the United States suffered from a severe economic recession in which over 5,000,000 workers were unemployed. To provide solutions to the unemployment problem, Hoover called together a conference of leaders representing all major sections of the economy.[12] Almost immediately, A. L. Jackson, assistant to the president of the Chicago *Defender*, complained to Hoover that although Negroes comprised 10 percent of the population and 7 percent of the labor force, he had not included a black person to represent the interests of the Negro race.[13] Eugene Kinckle Jones, executive secretary of the National Urban League, also objected, as did Emmett J. Scott, the secretary-treasurer of Howard University and for many years a leader in the Republican party.[14] But Hoover refused to consider "groups" in selecting representatives. After repeated protests his secretary, Edward Eyre Hunt, informed James G. Blaine, vice-president of the New York Trust Company, that when he had taken up the matter with "the Chief" again, Hoover had made it clear that "the principle on which the Conference is built does not allow for representation of the negro race per se."[15] Exactly what that principle might have been is not clear. Apparently representatives of economic special interests were legitimate, but representatives of racial interests somehow violated administrative "principle." Indeed, not until President Harding intervened did Hoover inform the protesters that two Negro representatives would attend the conference.

The president's intervention had little positive impact upon his secretary of commerce. Harding supported an antilynching bill, a national interracial commission to improve race relations, withdrawal of the Marines from Haiti, and increased federal patronage to blacks. To prove his good intentions he appointed Walter L. Cohen as collector of customs at New Orleans and Perry W. Howard of Mississippi as special assistant attorney general, and he publicly denounced the Ku Klux Klan. But his patronage appointments were too few to satisfy black leaders, his legislative efforts were either defeated or stymied by southern congressmen, and his plans to expand and strengthen the southern state parties by attracting new white leaders were denounced by blacks as a betrayal of their interests to the antiblack lily-whites. Before long Harding began to complain of the increasingly harsh black criticism directed at him. He felt that black leaders expected more of him than he could realistically achieve and was especially upset over their demands for more federal patronage. "The Negroes are very hard to please," he lamented to a friend.[16]

By contrast Hoover was even less aware of black needs than was Harding. Despite the president's desire to expand the number of blacks appointed to federal posts, Hoover steadfastly refused to cooperate. He defended his rejection of black applicants on the grounds that none of them had the necessary qualifications. He remained oblivious also to the relationship between economic deprivation and racism and to the need for special Department of Commerce programs to help black businessmen. Then in 1925 George Barr Baker, a noted public-relations executive, prominent Republican, and devoted Hoover enthusiast helped to expand Hoover's awareness of the special needs of black people by arranging a meeting between the secretary and Claude Barnett. Baker assured Hoover that Barnett was a loyal, hardworking Republican who had proven very valuable to him when Baker had headed the Republican National Speakers' Bureau during the 1924 campaign.[17] In addition, Barnett was an active leader in the National Negro Business League; owner of the Associated Negro Press; and close friend of Robert R. Moton, principal of Tuskegee Institute.[18]

Barnett was forthright in his complaint to the secretary. The Negro businessman remained at the bottom of the economic ladder, he told Hoover, because the Department of Commerce "was paying too little attention to his problems." Stung by this unexpected criticism, Hoover pointed to his department's numerous publications, which he argued were great aids to the Negro businessman. Not so, Barnett insisted. The literature was written in language that the Negro could not understand. "It's written in English," Hoover retorted. "Does the Negro speak a foreign language?" Momentarily astounded by the vehemence of the reply, Barnett nonetheless refused to accede to Hoover's self-righteous defense of "self-help," and instead he countered with a specific proposal. The National Negro Business League would enthusiastically support the appointment of a Negro information specialist who would make the department's publications more meaningful to Negro businessmen. Hoover appeared unconvinced, and as Barnett moved toward the door to make his exit, he believed that he had failed. Then Hoover asked, "If I agree to make the appointment, can you find me the right man?"[19]

Barnett's criticism had a positive effect on Hoover. During that same year, 1925, the secretary became somewhat more aware and concerned about opportunities for black Americans. He appointed a Negro, James A. Jackson, whose job was to communicate the department's willingness to assist and to explain to Negro businessmen the various ways it could help them.[20] Now fully aware of the private self-help-oriented National Negro Business League, Hoover was eager to promote its goals, and he established frequent and cordial relations with its president, Robert R. Moton, assuring him that he was happy to meet with him at any time.[21] In addition, Negro appointments to federal positions also became a matter of interest to him.[22] He also began to recognize the need for better Negro housing, especially in the South, and in 1926 he used his influence to ensure that a special exhibit featuring inventions by Negroes would become a part of the National Sesquicentennial Exposition. In that same year he refused to sign a neighborhood agreement that excluded blacks.[23]

Hoover also showed an increased awareness of the educational needs of blacks. He visited Hampton Institute in Virginia, and on 20 March 1925 he vigorously supported the campaign for the joint Hampton-Tuskegee Endowment Fund Drive. In his message to those who gathered at Carnegie Hall for the kickoff of the drive, Hoover repeatedly emphasized that the practically oriented education offered by these two institutions had not only "brought constructive results beyond the greatest anticipations of the founders" but had become a model for educating "backward races" throughout the world. "If we are to solve the negro problem this is the direction of its resolution," he concluded, "and the burden of finding that solution rests upon the American people as a whole."[24] Today some of Hoover's language would be highly offensive, but his statements indicated that he was making at least some progress toward sympathetic awareness.

One of the principal themes that Hoover would reiterate over the years in support of Negro education was the thesis that education produced leadership. In a larger sense, Hoover believed that education for all people was vital to a democratic society. In 1926 he told a University of Alabama audience that the ideals of the Declaration of Independence "required a fundamental expansion." He argued forcefully that "it was not enough that all men should be born equal and should have the inalienable rights of life, liberty, and the pursuit of happiness." Beyond those rights individuals "must have also an equal chance in the race of life," so that they could attain whatever position in society to which their intelligence, character, ability, and ambition entitled them. Basic to such an equal chance was the right to the best education that the individual was capable of attaining. Universal free education was "the door of opportunity" in America.

Hoover believed that making an excellent educational system a reality for all people was possible because of the "national instinct for equality of opportunity." Indeed, all of the other factors that made for equality of opportunity "are small in weight compared to an equal chance [for] the highest physical, intellectual, and moral equipment" developed through education. Education was "the major protector of democracy itself . . . the organized search for truth" that "defeated the prophesies of Malthus" and made possible the progress of mankind.[25]

For all of his emphasis upon competition, the "race of life," and the necessity for individual achievement, Hoover was no adherent to Social Darwinism, as some have suggested. Free public education would help defeat the prophecies of the Social Darwinists and assist those who had been greatly disadvantaged to develop their individual potential. Moreover, he believed that it was the moral duty of the state to ensure equality of opportunity. In 1926 Hoover pointed out that blacks had been prevented from developing their talents by the institution of slavery, but since they had been emancipated the "negroes of America have made wonderful progress," and he believed that that progress could be greatly accelerated in the future. Hoover told the Reverend Alfred Williams Anthony of Stover College that "the work of training youth to become Christian teachers and leaders for the future generations is of vital importance."[26] Although he praised the vocational and technical emphasis at Tuskegee, he went well beyond this more limited and controversial attitude toward education. Black leaders, he believed, were needed in all of the professions as well as in business and industry, and this need required access to the fullest range of educational opportunity. When he became president, he doubled the appropriation to Howard University, the federally sponsored black university in Washington, D.C., and in a message to the National Association of Teachers in Colored Schools he reiterated his belief that education "is not only the foundation of personal efficiency but is the solvent of many of the problems which confront us as a nation."[27]

Hoover derived part of his great faith in the value of education from his own experience and part from his Quaker background. Since the 1700s Quakers had been in the forefront of the antislavery efforts, and unlike other abolitionists, they had continued to concern themselves about Negro welfare long after the Civil War. In 1929 when Hoover became president, he convinced Professor Augustus T. Murray, head of the classical literature department at Stanford University and a leading Quaker, to become the resident minister at the Orthodox Friends Congregation in Washington, D.C., where Hoover would worship. Murray was active in promotion of educational opportunities for black Americans, and in 1930 the trustees of Fisk University asked him to make the principal address at the laying of the cornerstone for the new library. When Hoover learned of this, he wrote to Murray asking him to extend his congratulations to the university for its rapid rise "to such high rank among institutions of learning" and to express his belief that the new library "would bring still closer the day when it can offer to the Negroes of this country every opportunity for advanced education that is open to others, and fully equip their best talents for leadership of their race."[28]

Black leadership was the most important theme in Hoover's numerous messages to black educators, but the need for black leaders became even more evident to him during the Mississippi flood of 1927. During the hectic months of work, grappling with myriad problems, Hoover came to believe that Negro leadership would provide "the complete solution to many of our problems." Yet the leaders that Hoover admired were not the southern black Republican politicians, who apparently had not come forth to offer Hoover their help during the crisis, nor the leaders of the NAACP, who had criticized him severely yet had not offered "practical solutions" to the problems he faced. The black leaders he had worked with during the flood were the educators, businessmen, and community leaders, such as those who comprised the vast majority of the Moton commission. As a result of his own education by the members of the Moton commission, Hoover now also emphasized "economic independence" as one of the great goals that black educators and their allies must stress.

Prior to the flood Hoover had not expressed any sense of indignation or urgency about the problems faced by black people. The evidence suggests that, like many other white leaders, he simply did not realize the impact of racism. Peonage helped somewhat to open his eyes. For the first time Hoover began to understand what the black people in the South still had to endure, and he was sincere in his desire to begin an attack on the causes of their suffering. His repeated frustrations and failures to correct the abuses in the camps and to reform the relief system alerted him also to the need for enlisting sympathetic white leaders who would work with and protect the Negro leaders during the long, arduous, and often dangerous task of eradicating peonage and other abuses. Particularly in the South, blacks were justifiably afraid of white reaction to initiatives taken by them, and their weakness and fear seemed likely to prevent any sustained progress until like-minded white and black leaders could join forces in a spirit of interracial brotherhood and self-help. Hoover naively underestimated the magnitude of the task and the obstacles. He was still unaware of racism in any sophisticated sense. But after his land resettlement plan had been rejected as impractical by white northern philanthropists, he recognized that reforms in the South would be more difficult than he had first assumed.[29]

As a result of what he had learned during the flood, the secretary accelerated and expanded his efforts to help blacks. By November 1927 Negro business leaders were congratulating him for creating a new agency within the Department of Commerce, the Division of Colored Industries, headed by "a colored brother," as Hoover privately expressed it. This action indicated that his thinking about blacks had developed well beyond the point in 1921 when his administrative "principle" had not allowed him to concede that Negroes ought to be represented at the unemployment conference.[30] By creating the Division of Colored Industries, Hoover acknowledged that private efforts would not suffice and that education alone could not bring economic independence to the Negro. Some active federal assistance was also needed. In other areas new emphasis upon the need for federal assistance was also especially clear after the flood. Hoover assigned top personnel to help the National Negro Business League identify uneconomical business practices and recommend improvements to its members; and he responded to the need to collect accurate birth and death statistics for blacks, the neglect of which had resulted in extremely high insurance rates for Negroes.[31]

There was even more important evidence that Hoover had gained new understanding of the need to enlist the federal government. This was his decision to attack segregation, one of the most solid bastions of racism, within his own department. Like many Quakers, Hoover believed that one's actions revealed inner convictions. Thus, in late March 1928, after Neville Thomas, president of the Washington, D.C., chapter of the NAACP, criticized the practice of racial segregation of clerks in the Census Bureau, Hoover did not issue ringing denials or sidestep the issue as did other cabinet officers whom Thomas had also accused of condoning segregation. Instead, Hoover ordered an end to the practice.[32]

The desegregation of the Department of Commerce naturally delighted Negro newspaper editors.[33] Hoover had responded to a highly sensitive issue with courage and determination. He seemed to be saying that equality of opportunity for personal advancement could not flourish in a segregated society. According to black supporters, this was proof that Hoover was no racist. His action bore out the faith that Moton and the other members of the commission had repeatedly expressed to the more skeptical black leaders. Alone among the cabinet officers, Hoover had made an important public commitment and had seemingly put his convictions into action.

Understandably, some observers remained skeptical. Because the secretary actively sought the Republican nomination for the presidency, his political opponents were by no means convinced that he had acted out of principle or inner conviction. But such an action had political disadvantages too. Indeed, vocal southern Democrats especially delighted in the desegregation order and lost no opportunity to remind their constituents of the Republican contender's action. The Mississippi flood had made many southern Democratic leaders apprehensive about his political appeal in the coming elections. In an address to a local committee of the United States Chamber of Commerce, Sen. Thaddeus H. Caraway of Arkansas lamented the great popularity that the potential Republican nominee enjoyed in the South. According to Caraway, Hoover "had come among us as a friend and we accepted him as such," but "he just naturally ruined our politics. This is what I hear all over the Valley and even in Louisiana."[34]

Many Democrats now hoped that the desegregation order would weaken his appeal. They were worried also because Alfred E. Smith, a Roman Catholic, Tammany Hall New Yorker, antiprohibitionist, and vigorous opponent of the Ku Klux Klan in the 1924 Democratic convention, was assured of the 1928

Democratic nomination. Smith's candidacy prompted fear among southern Democrats over revolts against Smith within their state organizations. But Hoover's desegregation of the Commerce Department seemed to be the exact ammunition that they needed. As one unidentified southern senator put it, when Hoover received the nomination to run against Al Smith, southern Democrats could say to their people, "Yes, Smith is a Tammany man, a Catholic, and a wet, but would you rather not have him in the White House than a President who compels white men and white women to associate with negroes?"[35]

Sen. Cole L. Blease of South Carolina, an infamous race baiter, openly charged on the Senate floor that Hoover's motive for the desegregation order was political. Citing an article that had appeared in the Washington *Post*, Blease claimed that Hoover had issued his order just in time to please Negro politicians in Ohio, where he faced a tough primary race. It was, Blease charged, nothing less than a "serious attack" upon the white race and "a systematic plan to humiliate white girls" in order to "secure the Negro vote in the doubtful States."[36]

Although there was probably some validity in the belief that Hoover hoped to win black votes in doubtful northern states, it is unlikely that this was his only or even his primary motive for the desegregation order. In fact, the order might well have proven politically disadvantageous to Hoover in both the North and the South, which was a view forcefully expressed by some of his most important and influential advisers who privately responded to inquiries by denying categorically that Hoover had issued any order intended to desegregate the Commerce Department.[37] Moreover, one wonders if such a dramatic and, for the times, politically explosive action was necessary in order to win the black primary vote. Other less risky means of persuasion were readily available to Hoover, including campaigning in northern states by black leaders who had worked closely with him during the Mississippi flood. Given the background for the desegregation order—the education about racism that Hoover had received during the flood and the steps that he had taken to help black Americans prior to the desegregation order—it is more reasonable to argue that he acted from the sincere conviction that racial segregation, like peonage, was an evil that must be combated.

Hoover's desegregation order was not the first indication that he dreamed of a society free of the hatreds that prevented individuals from fully realizing and using their talents. In 1919–20, while most politicians were silent, Hoover denounced the political witch-hunts and deportations directed at alleged foreign radicals by Attorney General A. Mitchell Palmer. Earlier, during his relief efforts in Europe, he became infuriated over the persecution of Jews and threatened to cut off relief to countries that allowed such persecution.[38] These hatreds, which he had witnessed in Europe and which he was beginning to identify in the United States, obviously troubled the secretary of commerce.

He had spent most of the time since his graduation from Stanford University traveling and working throughout the world. As a result of this he lacked a close understanding of his own society, but despite his customary idealistic optimism, he was coming to understand some of America's serious shortcomings as well as its many blessings.

Looking back on Hoover's emerging social philosophy, one is tempted to criticize its racial naïveté and emphasize its limitations. American society in the 1920s had more than its share of severe restrictions on equal opportunity. Social hatreds or restrictions against Jews, Roman Catholics, inferior whites, women, and other minorities were everywhere evident. Racism dominated the thinking of most Americans toward nonwhites. Yet Hoover still spoke in terms of education as the door to opportunity for all as if a good education would unlock all of the closed doors. In *American Individualism*, published in 1922, he spoke glowingly of competition, voluntarism, and economic progress. One not thoroughly familiar with Hoover's developing awareness of social problems may well conclude that his views on race were limited to those popularly understood as the Booker T. Washington philosophy.[39] Actually Hoover's social philosophy was by no means fully expressed in *American Individualism* nor completely formulated when he became president in 1928. Those who hoped that his understanding of racism would grow and deepen based that hope on limited yet nonetheless encouraging evidence.

During his eight years as secretary of commerce, Hoover's thinking about the need to take active, positive steps to help black Americans had steadily, if slowly, become more progressive. There is no evidence that Hoover changed his views about the biological "inferiority" of Asians and Negroes, but there is some evidence to demonstrate that he had begun to overcome the usual racist manifestations that emanated from such views. He believed that black people had made great progress against immense obstacles and that they were entitled to the proper social environment and opportunities to make far greater strides toward better lives. He also believed that, when necessary, the power of the federal government must be utilized to promote equality of opportunity and, in particular, through the nation's educational institutions, to enable the disadvantaged to rise as high as their ability and determination would allow. However, much depended upon developing a broadly based black leadership that, he stressed, was essential to continued advancement. He greatly admired Booker T. Washington and Robert R. Moton because both of them promoted the belief that self-help through education would provide that leadership as well as the economic advances so vital in the long, hard quest for racial progress.[40]

Hoover's education on the evils of racism by no means converted him into a champion for racial equality. He did not envision using federal power to confront and defeat the forces of racism. Prominent white political leaders did not think in those terms in the 1920s.[41] Moreover, he was unsure of how to go about promoting racial progress. When he became president he instituted studies that he hoped would provide the objective information, offer rational objectives, and suggest the best means to improve the quality of life for blacks. Hoover would continue to make mistakes in his dealings with black Americans, just as he continued to make mistakes in his dealings with other groups.

Yet despite his limitations and failures in understanding the deeply rooted nature of racism, he came to view himself as a friend of the Negro people and tried to carry that belief into action. Although as secretary of commerce Hoover refrained from using the power of the federal government either to carry out far-reaching social programs or to attack racism, he did take positive steps in the direction of greater aid and encouragement to black Americans. He attempted to enlist the Red Cross and private philanthropists in a land scheme to combat peonage in the South; he encouraged the expansion of black leadership through higher education; he helped to win national recognition for black inventors; and he tried to alter the institution under his direct control by abolishing segregation in the Census Bureau and creating the Division of Colored Industries. For actions like these, Moton, Barnett, Holsey, and other black leaders close to him came to regard him as the best white hope on the political horizon.

3. Preconvention Infighting

Among Republican leaders Hoover was by no means the overwhelming choice for the presidential nomination. During his eight years as secretary of commerce and "Under-Secretary of all other departments," Hoover's aggressive, wide-ranging leadership had earned him a number of enemies. On the one hand, progressives within the party viewed him as too business oriented. Senators George Norris and Robert La Follette, for example, opposed him for resisting federal development of the Tennessee River valley and federal ownership of the nation's inefficient railroads. On the other hand, Old Guard Republicans called him unacceptably progressive on economic and social issues, while virtually all of the congressional leadership recognized his disdain for politics and politicians in general. Still other enemies included the Midwest farm bloc, alienated by his opposition to the McNary-Haugen export subsidy bill; eastern bankers, angered by his efforts to place greater federal controls on their overseas credit and speculative activities; and isolationists, suspicious because Hoover had supported the League of Nations and the World Court. There were the usual rival candidates: Sen. James B. Watson of Indiana, Sen. Charles Curtis of Kansas, Sen. Frank B. Willis of Ohio, Gov. Frank Lowden of Illinois, and Vice-President Charles Dawes. Most of Hoover's enemies favored a brokered convention in which their delegations could bargain for political advantage.[1]

To win the nomination Hoover knew that he must enter the exhausting and expensive primaries, especially against the favorite son candidates, whom he had little chance of defeating. Some of his friends worried that he lacked experienced politicians in his entourage who could organize his campaign and secure him enough convention delegates to win at Kansas City in June. Edgar Rickard, his investment consultant and one of his closest friends, felt that poor advisers had caused his failure in 1920.[2] But Hoover felt better prepared this time, for since 1920 he had surrounded himself with influential newsmen and amateur enthusiasts. Moreover, he decided not to force his candidacy upon the party's professionals but instead to rely upon his well-placed friends to do the campaigning for him. It was going to be a Republican year, he told Rickard, with no Democrat in sight who could win "and no clearly defined issues between the parties to make people look for a superman to save the country."[3]

To encourage a "national draft," Hoover adopted a strategy for the primaries designed to reinforce the impression of a dedicated public servant who was above politics. The Chief, as his loyalists called him, would remain at his post as secretary of commerce.[4] He would neither formally designate a campaign manager nor establish an official preconvention organization.[5] He did authorize his friends to raise money, a task at which they excelled, and conceded to Rickard that Will Hays and other professional politicians were already "down to hard work getting delegates."[6] This strategy produced a loose, cumbersome, occasionally uncoordinated primary campaign that soon created serious problems for the candidate.

Located in Washington's fashionable new Willard Hotel, the Hoover-for-President Club became the unofficial headquarters for the delegate hunt. James Good, congressman from Iowa, knew the most about the major decisions of the club; and George Lockwood, a Muncie, Indiana, newspaper owner, was its nominal head; but other important strategists included Walter Brown, the assistant secretary of commerce, an experienced political professional from Ohio; and Claudius Huston, a successful businessman and political operative for Coolidge who also had served briefly as an assistant secretary under Hoover, and who was considered by him a "very warm personal friend."[7] Huston brought to Washington Horace Mann, a Tennessee politician about whom surprisingly little is known. More important was Hubert Work, secretary of the interior and Hoover's eventual campaign manager, who wasted no time taking control of the least publicized but most important early strategy of the campaign.[8]

These shrewd hunters for delegates set Hoover on a course that was to influence not only his campaign but his presidency. They knew that delegates were not limited to the hotly contested northern and western primaries, where Hoover would have to face the professional politicians of his party. The eleven states of the former Confederacy held no Republican primaries; yet those Republican state organizations would choose 30 percent of the delegates needed to win the nomination.[9] Work knew that the southern delegations would be easiest to convince and therefore the most important in establishing early campaign momentum. Accordingly, he set out after them at once.

Hoover had become both well known and popular in the South during the Mississippi flood of 1927, especially among a growing number of businessmen. Many of them felt that the South owed Hoover a debt of gratitude for his relief efforts. More important, perhaps, as commerce secretary he had become more familiar with the needs of the South, and these businessmen believed that as president he would promote the region's economic development, a belief that Hoover had encouraged several years earlier. In September 1927, one month after Coolidge's decision not to seek reelection, a leading southern business newspaper, the *Manufacturer's Record*, urged that a two-party system in each of the southern states was crucial to the future prosperity of the South. Hoover boosters used this article to convince other disgruntled Democrats to join them.[10] The industrialization of the South, the diversification of its agriculture, the growth of extractive industries, and the increasing northern migration all stimulated sentiment for Republican policies, especially a high protective tariff.[11] Another factor was the likelihood that Alfred E. Smith, the wet, Tammany Hall, Roman Catholic governor of New York State, would win the Democratic nomination in 1928. Harvey C. Couch, the Arkansas flood commissioner, predicted that if Smith should gain the nomination, "over 90 percent of the Methodists and Baptists in Arkansas would vote for Hoover."[12]

During the flood Hoover had met on at least one occasion with Louisiana Republicans, and he no doubt came into contact with individual southern Republicans from time to time.[13] Except for the Louisiana meeting, there is no evidence that Hoover took advantage of his relief assignment to advance his standing with other southern Republican organizations. For the most part, he remained above, but not too far above, politics. George Akerson, his distinguished-looking private secretary, was a politically experienced newsman who handled many of the political details for Hoover and who seldom missed an opportunity to promote his candidacy.[14]

Despite the relatively few party members in the region, Hoover and his aides understood that the southern Republican delegations to the national nominating convention might well provide the margin of victory. He also knew that he needed those votes as much as his political idol Theodore Roosevelt had needed them in the 1912 convention, where he lost to Taft.[15] As early as December 1927 Hoover expressed his confidence about getting the votes of "several southern delegations."[16] Yet Hoover, like Roosevelt, had little but disdain for the type of politics that had developed in the southern Republican parties since the failure of Reconstruction.

At the close of the Civil War the Republican party had welcomed the new black citizens into its midst as it sought to guarantee their new constitutional rights. As Reconstruction failed, the Democratic party united behind white supremacy based upon the ideology of racism, and the South became a one-party region. Local Republican parties consisted primarily of blacks with a small number of white allies. During the 1890s Republican voters decreased further in number as whites aggressively strengthened and expanded discrimination and exclusion, virtually disenfranchising all black people. Racism in the South reduced the Republican party to cliques of officeholders and patronage seekers who exerted their only remaining influence at the Republican national conventions, where they generally cast their ballots for the likely winner in return for control of patronage in their states.[17]

Thousands of patronage jobs were at stake. Most of these were postal, but the political plums also included appointments of United States attorneys, marshals, and judges, as well as the control of the state organizations. Even though the Republicans held little additional power in the South, patronage was an attractive prize, especially as Republicans controlled the White House and, therefore, the federal appointments for all but four terms from 1865 to 1932. Because the ideology of white supremacy would not allow blacks to accept important patronage positions, black Republican patronage controllers often had to recommend white Democrats for the jobs. Occasionally, therefore, black Republican leaders could trade these appointments for some measure of influence and white cooperation. Eager to have their own workers appointed to the mostly white-only jobs, Democratic politicians actively cooperated with the black Republican chieftains in an "unholy patronage alliance."

The regular Republican, or *black-and-tan*, organizations were headed by blacks and a few sympathetic whites, disparagingly called *tans*, who supported Negro participation in politics. Some white Republicans, irritated by any cooperation between blacks and whites, ironically blamed the Negro Republican leadership rather than racism and the Democrats' white supremacy policies for the inability of Republicans to attract white voters. As long as Negroes retained positions of leadership, these Republican *lily-whites* charged, the party could never hope to build viable state organizations. Many lily-whites would have entirely excluded Negroes from Republican councils. In the 1880s lily-white efforts to "reform" the party by displacing the dominant black-and-tan leadership became more and more common.[18]

Most lily-white factions retained some Negro representatives who believed that they would have a better chance for advancement under all-white leadership than under the ineffective black-and-tan party regulars. In general, black Republicans tended to view any lily-white group as antiblack, but scholars have differed over this interpretation.[19] Some have defined lily-white to mean the total exclusion of the Negro, while others have found that lily-whites wanted Negro votes but not Negro leadership. Still others insist that not all lily-whites were anti-Negro.

Some lily-whites were more sympathetic to blacks than were others. They favored racial reform through granting blacks the vote and improved economic opportunity, but they insisted upon the social and political supremacy of whites. Nonetheless, despite these significant differences it appears clear that the vast majority of lily-white Republicans supported the ideology of racism in the South. Their immediate aim was control of the party, which primarily meant the elimination of black leaders. Indeed, the lily-whites never tired of charging that black leaders "sold" their votes at the national convention and "sold" federal patronage in their states. Only by eliminating these black corruptionists, only by "reforming" the black-and-tan regulars, could the Republican party rise again in the South. In the eyes of the lily-whites, a Negro leader, almost by definition, was a corrupt politician.[20]

Vincent De Santis has skillfully set forth and analyzed the repeated efforts by northern Republicans to "reform" the southern wing of the party by replacing black and tans with white leaders. The desire of Democrats to have their party remain the only white-supremacy party, combined with the weaknesses caused by internal struggles among the lily-white factions and between them and the black-and-tan organizations, successfully thwarted the Republican "reformers."[21] Yet despite repeated setbacks, the lily-whites never abandoned their efforts, and in the 1920s they initiated renewed drives to gain dominance. In some states, notably Virginia, North Carolina, and Arkansas, they were successful, but at the 1924 convention, the credentials committee seated every regular black-and-tan delegation challenged by the lily-whites. Nonetheless, during the next four years, the "reformers" grew stronger, and in 1928 they launched vigorous challenges in every southern state still controlled by black and tans.[22]

Lily-white challenges to black and tans meant little to the secretary of the interior Hubert Work. Thoroughly familiar with the internecine warfare waged in the South, he was not interested in which faction won control but in which one would support Hoover's nomination and therefore should be aided in its fight for dominance. Secretary Work was the most important and influential of Hoover's early supporters and campaign managers. Within two weeks after Coolidge's announcement, he had contacted leading Republicans, arguing that he had spent "many hours" with the president and that as Coolidge really did intend to retire, Herbert Hoover was his logical successor and the certain winner in 1928.[23] In that same month, August 1927, Work contacted at least five southern Republican state chairmen urging Hoover's candidacy.[24]

Although at first Work believed that the South would vote for Al Smith,[25] he busied himself from August to December learning which of the southern parties would support Hoover and which would need to be "reformed."[26] He resolved not to meddle with the local party organization if that organization— either black and tan or lily-white—could be counted on to support Hoover. But if the local organization seemed to be leaning toward another Republican candidate, Work devised strategies for shifting control to more friendly forces. Sometimes the anti-Hoover forces happened to be made up of black and tans, sometimes lily-whites. Work's only concern was gaining power for the pro-Hoover groups, whatever their composition might be.

When possible, Work preferred to deal with the Republican national committeemen, who would organize the delegation and select representatives to the credentials committee.[27] Some, like Oliver D. Street of Alabama, needed constant prodding and encouragement; while others, such as R. B. Creager of Texas and Bascom Slemp of Virginia, Coolidge's former secretary, were easily recruited.[28] To give the Hoover bandwagon early momentum and thus convince northern and western states to climb on, Work insisted on immediate declarations for Hoover. When Street seemed hesitant in January 1928, Work bluntly warned him that the "movement for the Secretary is growing and apparently those who do not get in very soon will be late."[29] Without further urging, Street joined the Hoover forces.

Similar efforts in other southern states to ensure "crystallization of national sentiment" were more difficult. Leaders in Arkansas, Louisiana, Florida, South Carolina, and Mississippi needed considerable additional persuasion.[30] For this difficult task Work assigned a former assistant attorney general, Rush Holland, a close, trusted friend who had specialized in factional squabbles and patronage, to marshal the Hoover forces.[31] The few who were aware of his assignment later denied any knowledge of his activities.[32]

Backed by Work's assurance of "authority . . . to talk confidentially to those who are interested in our campaign," Holland also carried $10,000 supplied by Claudius Huston.[33] Holland was able to save his campaign funds in Arkansas, where Hoover enthusiasts, especially Harvey Couch, had long been at work among the state's lily-white leaders lining up support for Hoover.[34] However, these efforts had been hampered by Hoover's adamant refusal to allow Couch to use patronage promises and by Hoover's eagerness, as one knowledgeable Arkansas politician warned, "to see justice done to the negro race."[35]

For several months after Holland's visit, Hoover's private secretary George Akerson still worried that Arkansas would support Frank Lowden of Illinois, but by March Hoover had succeeded in breaking the impasse. Not sure of the lily-whites, Hoover forces had aided pro-Hoover black and tans to win control of the delegation. Hoover dispatched William J. "Wild Bill" Donovan, an assistant attorney general, to arrange a compromise that allowed the black leader Scipio A. Jones to become a delegate-at-large, thus cementing the entire delegation for Hoover.[36] Jones was the successful black lawyer who in 1927 had given Hoover an enthusiastic introduction to the 3,000 black people attending the ceremony honoring the secretary for his flood relief in Pine Bluff. Hoover placed great emphasis on Jones's election and alerted both Moton and Holsey to his importance in maintaining the loyalty of the Arkansas delegation. Thus the lily-whites had been defeated and a black-and-tan delegation put together for Hoover. Jones was delighted at the help he had received from Hoover and Moton in throwing off "the yoke of lily whitism" and in "being restored to committees and delegations" that gave "proper recognition" to Arkansas Negroes.[37]

In Louisiana the lily-whites quickly gained the upper hand. For several years two men had cooperated in managing a successful black-and-tan coalition: Emile Kuntz, a white national committeeman, and Walter Cohen, a wealthy black insurance executive who had been since 1922 comptroller of customs at New Orleans.[38] However, by 1928 the lily-whites in the party had grown considerably stronger, and Kuntz, assisted by Victor Loisel, the United States marshal at New Orleans, had broken with Cohen and thrown his support to the lily-whites.[39] The Ku Klux Klan also assisted Kuntz, even though he was Jewish. Fearing that Alfred E. Smith, the progressive governor of New York State who had repeatedly supported efforts to drive Klan influence out of the Democratic party, would be the 1928 Democratic nominee, Louisiana Klansmen were eager to ensure the Republican nomination for Hoover as the candidate with the greatest appeal to the South and thus most likely to split the solid South and thereby defeat Smith. Certainly the Klan had no desire to promote a more vital Republican party or to split the solid South permanently—only long enough to teach Smith or any other anti-Klan reformer a lesson. Mabel Walker Willebrandt, a personal friend of the Hoovers and the assistant attorney general best known for her zealous enforcement of Prohibition, obtained firsthand knowledge of the Klan's political activities in Louisiana and other parts of the South. According to Willebrandt, the Klan strategy was very similar to that of the lily-white Republicans. Because the delegates to the Republican state convention were chosen in parish meetings attended by few Republicans, the Klan planned "to get four or five worth-while and responsible men to register Repunlican [sic] so as to vote a reliable delegate from their district to Kuntz's convention, and then throw control of the thing over to Kuntz—providing he would propose that the delegates go instructed for Hoover. Well, I made hay while the sun shone, rapidly and in detail, getting a great many practical suggestions [apparently from the same Klansman, named Sullivan, who had explained the Klan strategy to her] and arranging for a good deal of work in Alabama, Mississippi, and Florida."

Although it is not possible to determine the degree to which the Klan actually became involved in Louisiana, the Klan strategy, like that of the lily-whites generally, was designed to eliminate Cohen as well as Smith. As the most prestigious black federal official in the South and a successful businessman and political leader, Cohen was well known and respected by black leaders throughout the United States. He had survived in the deep South since the 1890s by fighting lily-whites; what was more he had also expanded the black vote in New Orleans and had used his political influence for the welfare of his people. But as Cohen had declared for Sen. Charles Curtis, who had helped him win senate confirmation as comptroller of customs, Work and Holland decided to abandon Cohen and his black followers and to strike a deal with Kuntz.[40]

Holland believed that Kuntz and Loisel could ensure the entire Louisiana delegation for Hoover. At the state convention the Kuntz-Loisel lily-whites soon took control, and Kuntz was certain that the state courts would strike down Cohen's legal action challenging the successful lily-white coup. If this happened, Holland promised that the Hoover forces on the credentials committee at the forthcoming national convention would ensure the seating and thus officially legitimize the Kuntz-Loisel lily-white faction.[41] As Kuntz had predicted, the state courts ruled against Cohen's challenge. Kuntz was jubilant. He immediately reminded Akerson to tell "Work and friend Holland that we have carried out our part and expect aid and support from them."[42] Cohen's last hope was to appeal to other black leaders at the convention, urging them to support him against the seating of the lily-whites.[43]

Work was especially pleased with Holland's success in Florida, where large numbers of northern Republicans had recently settled. Work had earlier contacted C. E. Pitts, chairman of the Florida state central committee, who revealed the need for financial assistance in the effort for Hoover. Holland therefore supplied $500 to Glenn B. Skipper, the lily-white but pro-Hoover vice-chairman of the state central committee. Holland provided the money to defray the expenses involved in Skipper's efforts to overturn the anti-Hoover black-and-tan faction at the party's state convention. At the same time Holland funneled $2,500 through the Protective Tariff League, a group of Florida businessmen who were actively working to get Hoover delegates elected at the state convention. Work believed that Holland had done an excellent job of gathering "several independent organizations into one organization," which defeated the anti-Hoover black and tans led by George Bean, elected Skipper as state chairman, and secured the entire delegation for Hoover.[44]

In Alabama Holland had only to supply the lily-white state chairman Oliver D. Street with $1,000 to cover his convention expenses, but Georgia posed a special problem.[45] Apparently Holland was not the only Hoover agent in the South giving out expense money; for at least two Republicans, reportedly working for Horace Mann, were going about the state soliciting support for Hoover with an unlimited campaign fund. This, in any case, was the complaint of Benjamin J. Davis, the black editor of the Atlanta *Independent*, Republican national committeeman from Georgia, and leader of the black-and-tan faction. Davis might well have uncovered one of Work's covert operations. Nor was he the only one to do so. Willebrandt complained loudly when she discovered that the man to whom money had been sent "to round up delegates" was well known to her as one who "ought to be in a penitentiary." She insisted instead that Ben Davis was the one with whom "decent white folks could work" because "the reputation of Ben Davis is that he stands by his word—at least, he 'stays bought' instead of selling out to the next bidder who comes along with a higher price."

Because Davis favored Coolidge's renomination, and Work had earlier told Secretary of Treasury Andrew Mellon that Georgia was "torn between factions," the situation was certainly ripe for the type of delegation building employed in other states. As Willebrandt admitted, her reference to Davis as one who "stays bought" was "a little harsh on him." Black-and-tan organizations found cash contributions all too scarce. As head of the state party, Davis, like other black-and-tan leaders, was obligated by tradition to pay most convention expenses of the county delegates to the state convention, which selected state delegations to the national convention. Often travel money to the national convention was also necessary. Using his newspaper to good advantage, Davis therefore alerted the black and tans to an apparent lily-white maneuver for electing a Hoover majority to the state convention. If successful, the lily-whites would oust Davis and his followers, elect new officers, and appeal to the credentials committee at the national convention for recognition as the legitimate Republican party in Georgia.[46]

Because Atlanta blacks could vote in municipal elections, Davis had always enjoyed a greater degree of power and independence than most other black politicians in the South. His successful registration drives rallied the black vote and earned him the political respect of his Democratic opponents, so his ire was a cause for concern.[47] To pacify him, Fred Arn, a longtime political lieutenant of Claudius Huston, journeyed to Atlanta in a vain effort to convince Davis that the lily-white money suppliers did not have Hoover's approval. Arn showed Davis a letter signed by Hoover that stated that he would not allow anyone to buy delegates or promise patronage in return for convention support.

Unconvinced, Davis went to Washington, D.C., to see Assistant Attorney General Perry W. Howard, the black Republican national committeeman from Mississippi. Howard put him in touch with Rush Holland, who had been distributing campaign money throughout the South. Alarmed at the lack of coordination among the Hoover precampaign forces in Georgia, Holland moved quickly to smooth over the break. He reassured Davis that Hoover forces supported his state organization and supplied him with $200 to cover his personal expenses in coming to the capital and $2,000 for the expenses of the county and state conventions. Davis remained suspicious, nonetheless.[48]

Perry Howard, the black Republican national committeeman from Mississippi, had more reason to be suspicious than Ben Davis. Since 1915 Howard had been fighting a lily-white Mississippi faction that almost succeeded in wresting control of the party from him and his chief lieutenant, a black physician, Dr. Sidney D. Redmond. By 1920 the Republican national convention had seated both the lily-white and black-and-tan factions with one-half vote for each delegate, but the lily-whites backed the losing candidate, and in 1924 the credentials committee seated only Howard's faction, recognizing him as national committeeman, Mrs. Mary Booze as national committeewoman, and Redmond as Mississippi state chairman. Meanwhile, in 1921 Howard had won appointment as a special assistant attorney general and established his residence in Washington, D.C. Blue eyed, light skinned, articulate, and urbane, Howard became an influential national figure well known to prominent Republicans, both black and white, in the North.[49]

In 1924, after Howard had triumphed at the national convention, A. M. Storer, the United States marshal for the Northern District of Mississippi, filed an affidavit with the attorney general of the United States, John F. Sargent, and with William M. Butler, chairman of the Republican National Committee, alleging that Howard had offered to recommend his reappointment if Storer would pay him $1,500. Storer also sent documents in support of his charge to

Sen. George Norris, chairman of the powerful Senate Judiciary Committee, which passed on all appointments for federal marshals, attorneys, and judges. Norris believed Storer, as did the officials of the National Civic Service Reform League and the editors of the crusading progressive magazine, the *Independent*.[50]

This was not the first time that the lily-whites of Mississippi had accused Howard of patronage corruption. In 1921, immediately after Harding had appointed him special assistant attorney general, Howard had been accused of selling post office appointments. The postmaster general conducted a full investigation of the charges, and on 16 September 1921, postal inspectors reported that "there is no evidence directly connecting Perry W. Howard . . . with the nefarious scheme." The inspectors believed that one of Howard's political associates was probably guilty, and Charles Banks of Mound Bayou was formally charged.[51] Later another of Howard's political allies, Eugene P. Booze, head of the successful black agricultural community of Mound Bayou, which had so impressed Hoover in 1927, would be accused by the aggressive *Independent* magazine of being Howard's "chief collector" in the wholesale of patronage.[52]

As the 1924 investigation continued, Storer complained bitterly to President Coolidge that Howard "and his political gangsters" had "whitewashed" the post office investigations.[53] He also told Coolidge that the FBI's investigation of his own case had been "hushed-up."[54] His message was clear enough. Officials high in the administration had bowed to Howard's political power. In February 1925 Assistant Attorney General Rush Holland, who had investigated the charges, informed Storer that "the Department believes that so far there is not sufficient evidence to justify any affirmative action but the matter is not closed."[55] Storer insisted to Coolidge that as Holland and Howard were good friends, and as Holland handled patronage for the Justice Department, the investigation had been rigged.[56] He also made the same charges to the chairman of the Republican National Committee, William Butler; to the chief justice of the Supreme Court, William Howard Taft; and to Postmaster General Harry New.[57]

Howard denied the charges, complaining that he had had to endure continual allegations of patronage corruption made by his political enemies. He pointed out that Storer was angry at him because Howard was recommending someone else for the marshal's position and because he had apparently challenged Storer's illegal calling of all-white juries.[58] In addition, L. E. Oldham, the United States attorney for the Northern District of Mississippi, was cooperating with Storer "to humble, harass, and besmirch me with a worthless indictment" because Howard also had refused to recommend Oldham's reappointment. At the same time, Howard alerted his Mississippi followers of the charges, requesting them to report any irregularities to him so that he might purge the state party "of every semblance of crookedness" and asked the attorney general that the facts be "presented to a fair and impartial grand jury by a fair and impartial representative of the Department of Justice."[59]

To unravel the evidence, Attorney General Sargent asked three of his assistant attorneys general to review the facts and make recommendations to him. William J. Donovan, one of Hoover's close political friends, concluded that "there is no direct evidence" against Howard. He would not declare Howard guilty but added, "In frankness I must say that the circumstances are at least most suspicious." Therefore, he recommended that Howard be given the opportunity to defend himself before a grand jury.[60] H. S. Ridgeley disagreed with Donovan's recommendation. He too found no evidence against Howard, not even an "intimation" that he took or solicited money. He even conceded that Howard had a reputation for honesty and integrity, but he wanted him fired for other reasons. Ridgeley believed that the evidence revealed such "official impropriety" in Howard's handling of his political activities as to justify calling for his resignation.[61] The third assistant attorney general, J. M. Marshall, also agreed that direct evidence of patronage corruption was lacking, but unlike Donovan and Ridgeley he argued forcefully that Howard was innocent according to both the letter and the spirit of the law. Marshall maintained that Howard had been "entirely absolved" of the postmaster general's charges in 1921 and had a high standing in the Republican party.[62] All three assistant attorneys general had agreed with Holland's earlier conclusion that there was no direct evidence that Howard had accepted or solicited bribes for federal jobs, and on the basis of these four opinions the attorney general closed the case in August 1925.

However, by the end of 1926 the progressive and reformist *Independent* had resumed the attack. In an article entitled "Republicans for Revenue Only," Frederick Rush argued that the "existence of the Solid South today depends not so much on the perpetuation of any Democratic tradition as it does upon the thoroughgoing stupidity and self-seeking of the Southern Republicans." The South had long been "hoping for a strong second party," but instead it had become "more and more disgusted with sordid exhibitions of politics for revenue only." According to the *Independent*, "progressives" in Tennessee had also charged that Congressman J. Will Taylor, the white Republican boss of the Second Congressional District, was guilty of demanding political contributions from federal appointees. In this he had been assisted by a businessman, Claudius Huston, and another political lieutenant, Fred Arn. The progressives had brought their claims to William J. Butler, chairman of the Republican National Committee, to Postmaster General Harry S. New, and to President Coolidge himself, all of whom were unconvinced by the evidence. Nonetheless, the *Independent* concluded that in the hands of the Republicans the South had become "purely a plum tree for plundering politicians," that "the Southern G.O.P. has gone to the dogs," and that if "the Republican Party ever expects to be a factor in the South, it must rid itself of this type of political gangrene." Moreover, it called upon the Senate to launch an investigation that would "publicly probe the whole mess." Interestingly enough, the *Independent* made no mention of racism or of southern white Democratic practices.[63]

The *Independent*'s demand for reform was significant for another reason. One of its two editors, Christian A. Herter, later secretary of state under Eisenhower, had served Hoover as his private secretary from the middle of 1920 until March 1924, after which Herter kept the Chief fully informed of the progressive magazine's crusade for honest, efficient government. Hoover praised the journal as "honest, clean, fearless, well-written, and well-edited and specially distinguished by the fact that it lives up to its name, treating public questions with a fine impartiality." His close relationship with Herter ensured that he was aware of the "whole mess" in the South and gave special significance to his uncompromising stand that no patronage deals be made and his later efforts to reform the southern wing of his party.[64]

Sen. George Norris, chairman of the Senate Judiciary Committee, placed additional and continuing reformist pressure on the Coolidge administration. Twice in January 1927 he asked for the complete file of the Perry Howard investigation in 1924–25. At first Attorney General Sargent ignored the request, but on Norris's repeated demands he sent Assistant Attorney General J. M. Marshall to explain Mississippi politics and the department's findings. These assurances did not pacify the irate senator, who insisted on seeing the raw reports from all agents who had conducted the investigation. Norris also threatened to obtain a resolution establishing a Senate probe into southern Republican corruption unless the reports were forthcoming.[65]

Norris received advice and vigorous support from Henry F. Hunt, chairman of the National Civic Service Reform League's Special Committee on the Sale of Federal Office. Working closely with Norris, Hunt also demanded release of the investigation. He displayed intimate knowledge of the Howard case and demanded to know why the attorney general had refused to explain the results of the Howard investigation and other postal investigations in the South.[66] Assistant Attorney General Marshall revealed his department's exasperation at the repeated insinuations when he explained curtly that there was no wish or effort to conceal evidence, that they could not release reports by other departments of the government, and that the charges had been thoroughly investigated.[67] But Hunt was no more satisfied than Norris.

Moreover, in February 1927 Samuel Taylor Moore, writing for the *Independent*, attributed a statement of strong criticism to Director J. Edgar Hoover of the FBI. According to L. E. Oldham, a former United States attorney and one of Howard's principal political enemies, the director had attacked the alleged effort to conceal the investigation of southern patronage sales. It was, he said, "bigger than Tea Pot Dome. It could wreck this Administration."[68]

Thus by early 1928 the Republican party in general and Howard in particular were under heavy attack by strange allies—lily-white Republicans in Mississippi and powerful reform organizations and leaders in the capital. While Norris worked throughout 1927 at gathering Senate approval for an investigation of southern Republicans,[69] Howard was cautiously trying to determine which candidate would win the Republican nomination at the forthcoming national convention, for he knew that any mistake might mean political disaster for him and his political organization in Mississippi. He was not enthusiastic about Hoover. In August 1927, during the Mississippi flood, he had protested to Hoover that the Red Cross was conscripting black labor and that a black man had been killed in Greenville, Mississippi, for refusing to accept conscription. Hoover had not replied to the protest.[70] Eugene Booze, however, had been very favorably impressed by Hoover's work during the flood and by Hoover's interest in Mound Bayou. In mid-January 1928 Booze warned Work that Howard might not support Hoover, so Holland's help was needed. Grateful for the advice, Akerson assured him that "Mr. Hoover was interested" in his report and that he would take up the matter with Work that afternoon.[71]

The matter was somewhat more complicated than Akerson had suggested to Booze. By this time Hoover knew that L. O. Crosby, the director of the Mississippi State Flood Commission, with whom he had worked closely, had been in contact with George L. Sheldon and Charles U. Gordon, two of the leaders in the lily-white Southern Republican League established in 1926 to capture control of all state Republican parties throughout the South. At first Crosby reported that powerful white Republican federal appointees loyal to Hoover wanted to eliminate the "corrupt" Perry Howard so that a respectable party could be built in the state. He added that they were willing "to take the other negroes in." But the Sheldon-and-Gordon faction preferred to send an uninstructed delegation to the convention because, in fact, they favored Lowden and wanted to be in a position to vote for the winner in any case. Thus the lily-whites were united in their determination to eliminate Howard and his black allies but were disunited over which candidate to support. Akerson assured Crosby that Hoover appreciated his support but that they also understood that Howard would support Hoover. In this they were soon proved correct.[72]

The Howard-dominated state Republican convention did endorse Hoover, but Crosby remained unconvinced. He argued that as neither Howard nor "Boozer" could be trusted, it was important to work out a compromise between the Howard faction and the white-Hoover faction. Even though Hoover and Akerson were also apparently not yet certain of Howard's loyalty, they objected to Crosby's continual meddling, so they decided to accept Howard's endorsement and support the black-and-tan faction. Akerson carefully explained to Crosby that the Sheldon-Gordon "crowd" was in fact "for Lowden first and Dawes second." Because "Howard and Booze have come out for us," he said, "I believe that we ought to go along with them at least on the surface." Akerson did not want to antagonize Crosby or his lily-white friends needlessly, and his use of the phrase "on the surface" was certainly an attempt to encourage the wealthy lumber dealer. Nonetheless, Akerson made it clear to Crosby that nothing "should be done to antagonize either Howard or Booze."[73]

Crosby stubbornly refused to heed Akerson's warning. On the one hand, he advised the Sheldon-Gordon faction that it was poor strategy to talk openly of eliminating "the negroes in Mississippi from the Republican Party because some Negro delegates would be needed to gain recognition at the national convention." It was far wiser "to carry a few negroes but endeavor to have the leadership placed in the hands of whites, leaving the negroes for representatives."[74] On the other hand, Crosby also warned Akerson that support of Howard would ruin Hoover's chances in Mississippi and in "other Southern states that are friendly toward the Chief."[75] He believed that a compromise between the lily-white Sheldon-Gordon faction and the Howard regulars would result in a delegation "composed of both white and colored." Such a compromise would help to build the party in Mississippi and other southern states.[76] Disturbed by Crosby's persistence, Akerson informed Assistant Secretary of Commerce Walter Brown of Crosby's plans, and Brown, in turn, tipped off Howard.[77] It was obvious that Crosby was primarily interested in eliminating Howard and thereby creating a lily-white organization, a fact Howard soon established in a personal meeting with Crosby.

In their meeting Crosby offered to provide financial support for the new coalition on condition that Howard resign as leader of the state party and as national committeeman. Howard rejected the offer, telling Crosby that he and his allies were "not for sale," and he immediately took steps to fight the lily-white takeover.[78] To embarrass Crosby and inform Hoover of his suspicions, Howard described Crosby's efforts to Fred Sullens, managing editor of the Jackson *Evening News*, and demanded that Hoover disavow both Crosby and the lily-white movement in the South. To the delight of the Democrats, Sullens reported the internal squabble in full. He included Howard's warning that Hoover was in danger of losing the Mississippi state delegation and that should Howard's delegation be refused recognition at the national convention, Hoover would lose the black delegates from Louisiana, Tennessee, and Texas as well.[79]

Embarrassed by the public furor, Crosby denounced Howard as an untrustworthy "nigger." He told Akerson that the lily-whites' strategy was to include "very shrewd niggers" who would convince the national convention that they spoke for the colored people of Mississippi and that the lily-white takeover would help build the party in other southern states.[80] Moreover, the Sheldon-Gordon faction, soon to be headed by Crosby's wealthy business partner, Lamont Rowlands, had secured a court injunction against the election of the

Howard Republicans and had called for their own county and state conventions to elect trustworthy pro-Hoover lily-white delegates to the national convention.[81]

In Mississippi Hoover seemed "damned if he did and damned if he didn't," as the lily-whites and the Howard faction each threatened to withdraw support unless he repudiated the other. Actually Hoover strategists knew that Crosby misread or misrepresented lily-white sentiments and through Akerson Hoover informed Crosby that the Mississippi fight was "very disturbing." Once again he informed Crosby that "no one up here trusts the Gordon-Sheldon crowd," which "is for Lowden and Dawes." Moreover, as it was still possible to "keep the Howard group in line for Hoover," Akerson politely hinted that it would be best if Crosby removed himself from this political intrigue. The embarrassed Crosby himself had suggested this earlier, and he did, in fact, drop from view, but not before causing a considerable amount of suspicion, mistrust, and political damage.[82]

Even before the furor over Crosby's meddling, Brown and Holland had personally reassured Howard of support from Hoover's headquarters. Yet Howard needed more than reassurance. He explained to Brown that the costs of the county and state conventions, traditionally borne by the leader of the party, had already amounted to a considerable sum of money, not to mention added costs incurred in a lengthy legal battle to defeat the lily-white injunction before the state supreme court. Undoubtedly further legal action would be necessary at the credentials committee of the national convention, where lily-whites did indeed attempt again to unseat him. The total costs might be as high as $15,000. Brown admitted that Howard needed funds, but he explained that Hoover had ruled out any substantial financial help to state organizations. Howard reminded him that it was no easy task to solicit political contributions in Mississippi, where there were few wealthy Republicans. Brown had to agree, and before long Holland began supporting Howard with funds that eventually totaled $4,000. With some of this money Howard established a Washington, D.C., headquarters, partly to help the chairman of the Republican National Committee attract black support for the party, but primarily to direct the political battle in Mississippi from a safer distance.[83]

Despite Brown's and Holland's obvious respect for his political power, Howard remained suspicious of them. With challenges on many sides, he could ill afford to trust any group completely. Howard was aware of Hoover's regard for Crosby and for his business partner, Lamont Rowlands, who had also worked closely with Hoover during the flood. He no doubt reasoned that Crosby would not have demanded his resignation unless Crosby had been given some encouragement from Hoover.

Howard certainly could not be criticized for his suspicion concerning Crosby's activities. And although the Hoover organization had supplied $4,000 to Howard, they were not certain that they could rely on him, after ignoring his demand that Hoover repudiate the lily-white opposition in Mississippi.[84] Indeed, Akerson kept in close contact with the new lily-white leader, Lamont Rowlands. By 10 May Rowlands had succeeded in solidifying the newly elected lily-white delegation for Hoover. Meanwhile, however, Howard had convinced the state supreme court to lift the injunction against his delegation.[85] Thus, the Hoover leaders had played each side against the other to ensure that one of the two delegations would vote for Hoover at the national convention.

Hoover could avoid primary elections in the South because his managers did not care whether the necessary votes came from black-and-tan or lily-white delegations. In Arkansas they had broken the lily-white hold on the state party by engineering the election of blacks who provided the strength to ensure pro-Hoover control of the entire vote. In Florida they helped the pro-Hoover lily-whites to capture control of the state party from the anti-Hoover black and tans. For the same purpose they furnished money to the lily-white Oliver D. Street of Alabama and to the black and tan Benjamin Davis in Georgia. The national Hoover organization courted both sides and welcomed all delegates for their candidate, whether black or white. The principal criterion was whether the faction could deliver votes at Kansas City. With their thirty percent of the votes needed to elect the Republican nominee in June, the southern delegations were not to be alienated, not even the lily-white challengers in Mississippi, who might conceivably have unseated Perry Howard through court injunctions. Despite some challenges still to be decided by the credentials committee, Hoover's managers had brought the previously doubtful southern delegations into line and they intended to see that the entire southern vote remained secure.

4. The Nomination

On 10 April 1928, in the midst of the presidential primary contests, the oil magnate Harry F. Sinclair went on trial to face charges that he had conspired with a former secretary of the interior, Albert E. Fall, to defraud the government by illegally leasing the federal Teapot Dome naval oil reserves.[1] Teapot Dome was the scandal of the decade; new revelations continued to surface for several years to remind voters that cabinet members and other high officials in the Harding administration had been corrupt. Despite Coolidge's honesty and popularity, Republican leaders agreed with Democrats that by 1928 the best efforts of the Republican party had been insufficient to remove the taint of scandal. The issue of political corruption, they thought, would be among the most important in the forthcoming presidential contest. During the June keynote speech at the Democratic convention in Houston, Claude Bowers, as expected, opened the campaign with a blistering attack on corrupt Republican politicos.[2]

Fortunately for Hoover, most others viewed him as a "nonpolitician." In most respects they were correct. Yet because he was the obvious front-runner among many contestants for the Republican nomination, his rivals were naturally less charitable, and their supporters did their best to discredit him.[3] One of their favorite tactics was to accuse Hoover of involvement in the Teapot Dome scandal, through participation in the illegal oil leasing activities of the Interior Department. The lack of evidence did not prevent the allegations of corruption. In March 1928 the *Independent*, edited by Hoover's former private secretary, Christian Herter, attacked the unceasing Republican efforts to uncover a Hoover scandal because their only foundation was an assumption that if his opponents dug deeply enough, some sort of scandal could be unearthed. Where evidence was lacking, rumor might suffice. Hoover refuted each of the unfounded charges, but the *Independent* complained that the "gossip still goes on; and as soon as one deep dark deal has been exposed the scandalmongers get their wits busy and think up another."[4]

Although vigorously defending Hoover, the *Independent* admitted that a good deal of Republican corruption did exist and needed to be exposed.[5] Southern Republicans were among the journal's favorite targets, especially a white congressman, J. Will Taylor of Tennessee, and the black special assistant attorney general, Perry Howard of Mississippi.[6] The *Independent*, of course, was not alone in its beliefs. Southern Democratic leaders were also

50

convinced of widespread Republican wrongdoing in their region. In February 1928 W. B. Bankhead spoke for many Democrats when he urged his fellow senator George Norris to focus the attention of the Senate Judiciary Committee on "the manipulation of handpicked delegations to the Republican National Convention by a few men who are interested solely in Government patronage." Bankhead argued that "very high class" southerners were "deeply interested in restoring decency to the Republican organization in Alabama and other Southern states."[7]

Well before 1928 Norris had become convinced of Republican corruption in the South. As early as 1926 he confided to one southern Republican that "in a general way I have known for several years that what appeared to be well founded charges were made regarding the disgraceful actions of Republican organizations in various Southern States." Yet in 1926 Norris was not optimistic about exposing these "disgraceful actions." Whether he really believed that Republicans alone were guilty, Norris understood the difficulty of correcting the abuses. He concluded that as there "are many Republicans, prominent in National councils of the party, who are opposed to this investigation," and because "they are influential," it appeared quite possible they would "succeed in defeating an investigation."[8]

As chairman of the powerful Senate Judiciary Committee, Norris worked hard between 1926 and 1928 to win approval for an investigation of Republican patronage corruption in the South. He was convinced that the Republican attorney general and the postmaster general were deliberately covering up southern scandals within their departments. To expose the suspected corruption, he worked closely with Henry T. Hunt, chairman of the Special Committee on the Sale of Federal Offices of the National Civic Service Reform League.[9] Among those who complained most about the sale of federal offices in the South were Republican lily-whites, who were actively engaged in attempting to unseat the incumbent black-and-tan factions.[10] Moreover, when Republicans from the South insisted that their white counterparts in the Democratic state parties might be equally guilty of wrongdoing, Norris seemed uninterested, perhaps because he needed Democratic votes to gain Senate approval of any investigation.[11] This same reason may also have been the basis for his rejection of demands by blacks that he investigate disenfranchisement. Nowhere were southern fraud, corruption, and injustice more blatant, they argued, than in the illegal methods and enforcement of disenfranchisement.[12] Still Norris refused either to concede that he would not help blacks or to investigate the Democratic party's denial that it violated black people's constitutional rights.[13] He argued instead that there were "some indications that those who are asking for an investigation of one of these subjects [Democratic racism] are doing so in order to suppress any investigation of the other [Republican patronage sale] subject."[14]

Whatever his reasons or their validity, Norris lost his resolution for an investigation during an unrelated filibuster at the end of the congressional session. In 1928 he began the effort anew,[15] insisting, "I have sufficient evidence that I have gathered preparatory to the investigation that I thought would take place [in 1927] to convince anyone, I think, that the conditions are indescribable. Offices are sold and bartered like merchandise." More important, he told Lowell Mellett of the influential Scripps-Howard Newspaper Alliance that the "Administration was, of course, opposed to this investigation, ostensibly because it would have seriously interfered with the selection of [southern] delegates to the next Republican National Convention."[16]

Congress finally approved Norris's investigation in 1928, but not before the southern delegations had been chosen. Indeed, in this presidential election year the Senate suddenly became so concerned with corruption in American politics that it sponsored two investigations, one into the campaign expenditures of presidential candidates, most of whom were favorite son senators, and another into the sale of postmaster positions and other federal offices. The latter did not get under way until the summer of 1928, but the investigation of presidential campaign expenditures produced sensational charges well before the Republican National Convention, which was scheduled to be held in Kansas City in June.

On 5 May, taking his turn along with all of the numerous presidential hopefuls of both parties, Herbert Hoover informed the Special Senate Committee Investigating Presidential Campaign Expenditures that he had "no comprehensive knowledge either regarding the personnel, sources, contributions or the character or amount of the expenditures" of either the Hoover-for-President Club in Washington, D.C., or of the state Hoover clubs that had arisen spontaneously throughout the nation.[17] As Hoover and his principal advisers testified before the committee, the disjointed, loosely constructed nature of the early primary campaign quickly became apparent.[18] Asked if he had used the promise of patronage or incurred expenses in defeating possible contested delegations to the convention, Hoover replied, "No; I have not heard of anything of that kind." He denied authorizing "any fees or campaign expenditures" and stated, "I would be astonished at that suggestion." Sen. Alben W. Barkley of Kentucky was more persistent than the other five senators on the committee. He quizzed Hoover about Rush Holland's trips to the South, asking if Holland, a close personal friend of Hoover's, had been given money to dispense or if he had offered money to pay the campaign expenses of state delegations to the national convention. Hoover repeatedly denied knowledge of such activity. "Certainly that could not be done with any approval of mine," he insisted, "and against my distinct disapproval."[19]

Each of Hoover's major campaign managers appeared before the committee and denied knowing of Rush Holland's activities in the South. James Good of Iowa, whom Hoover referred to as the most knowledgeable of his campaign lieutenants, stated that he knew nothing of Holland's actions or expenses and dismissed him as "a free lancer" in the South.[20] Ferry K. Heath, the Hoover club treasurer, and George B. Lockwood, the chairman of the club, made similar denials.[21] The only person who admitted knowing of Holland's work was Claudius Huston, who acknowledged that he had given Holland $10,000 but did not know what he had done with the money.[22] By the time Huston testified, however, the committee had already gained that information from Holland himself.

Holland was a cooperative, candid witness. Senator Barkley appeared to have been well briefed on his activities, and the former assistant attorney general made no effort to withhold information. He told the committee of various disbursements: $500 to Glenn Skipper, $2,500 to the Protective Tariff League of Florida, $1,000 to Oliver D. Street of Alabama, $2,200 to Ben Davis of Georgia, and $4,000 to Perry W. Howard of Mississippi.[23] He directly contradicted Lockwood's testimony by revealing that he had spoken to Lockwood about Howard "a little prior to the time I made the arrangement with Mr. Howard."[24] He steadfastly denied that Hoover had either known or approved of his efforts to win the southern delegations. Still, he recalled, "it is altogether probable and likely that in my general talks with the Secretary, Perry Howard's name has been mentioned." This was a potentially damaging statement, yet the committee appeared unwilling to press Holland on that point or to pursue the apparent inconsistencies between Lockwood's denials and Holland's testimony.[25] Perhaps the senators believed that they had already significantly embarrassed Hoover and his campaign managers. Barkley was also interested in highlighting Hoover's desegregation order, but that line of questioning was also quickly dropped.[26]

When Holland's activities became known, southern lily-white Republicans expressed their anger over his financial support of black politicians. E. H. Bradshaw, president of the Jackson, Mississippi, chamber of commerce, reminded Akerson that he had specifically warned Hoover that his "cause could not get results down South, if the ones who headed up the movement receive any compensation for the effort."[27] Further embarrassment soon followed. On 29 May Benjamin Davis, the black Republican national committeeman from Georgia, made a very unfavorable impression on the committee. Awestruck by the senators, the proud political leader and newspaper editor became nervous and confused by the barrage of questions. Described by the *New York Times* as one "who still looks and talks like an old time Southern darky," Davis denied that the $2,200 he had received was intended to buy his delegation to the national convention. He was, he claimed, a Coolidge supporter, with Hoover a distant second choice.[28] When questioned further, Davis could not specifically recall how he had spent the money, other than for general party expenses. He had kept no records and had no receipts.[29] At one point the senators burst into open laughter at his testimony. Unskilled at this type of cross-examination,

Davis created the incriminating impression that he had been bribed. He recounted how rival black Republicans had circulated rumors that Holland had given him "a whole lot of money," but he also conceded that these rivals were angry because they felt that he had not shared the money equitably with the delegates.[30]

In contrast to the fumbling, inept testimony of Ben Davis was the articulate, urbane presentation made by Perry Howard.[31] He quickly and skillfully corrected senators who insinuated that Holland had "paid" him to pledge his delegation to Hoover. "The public might read that in the paper," he rejoined, "as though I was hired by some one in the campaign, and I think that puts it in a bad light."[32] Howard furnished detailed financial records of exactly how the $4,000 had been used for legitimate party business.[33] Like Davis, he had become suspicious of the Hoover organization, and he freely expressed his suspicions during the investigation. He told in great detail of the maneuvering by L. O. Crosby and the lily-whites to force him and his supporters out of the Republican party in Mississippi, of the injunction to prevent him from selecting delegates, and of the close relationship between Crosby and Hoover. Howard had enlisted the aid of "the Democrats [who] realized it would be setting a bad precedent to allow a few interlopers to enjoin the regular organization and set up an organization that would endanger their own party and they came to our rescue by getting the state supreme court to disallow the injunction."[34] At the conclusion of his testimony, Howard warned that his delegation would not support Hoover at the convention "should it develop that I have been played with, or there has been any double-crossing."[35]

Howard's testimony again focused national attention on the Republican southern question. Ben Davis himself had admitted that it was not possible to elect Republicans to office in the South, and northern black leaders and scholars were also well aware that Negro Republican leaders in the South could not translate their political prominence into concrete gains for black people. Except for the designation of federal patronage appointments, Negroes had very little political power indeed, and even that power was largely a "hollow pretense." Nonetheless, even black critics of southern Republican organizations could agree that control of the Republican party by black-and-tan groups was preferable to control by lily-whites, who would rob blacks of the small protection and influence that party leadership could mean in some parts of the South.[36] Clearly, blacks would not concede that white leadership was the "solution to the problem."

Black observers thought it significant that white Republicans had not been called before the Senate investigating committee.[37] Rush Holland had admitted that Glenn Skipper, the Florida victor over the black-and-tan George Bean faction, and Oliver D. Street, the head of the lily-white Alabama Republicans, had both received campaign money, yet only black politicians had been called to testify. This seeming harassment of two of the most successful black leaders from the deep South increased their followers' suspicion.

Black skepticism in the North was a persistent problem for the Hoover managers. Early in the search for delegates Ernest T. Attwell, former director of Negro affairs for Hoover during the Food Administration and a widely traveled field director of the Playground and Recreation Association of America, had warned that he would need to work hard at winning the increasingly independent black vote in the North.[38] Hoover's managers were aware that since 1916, because of the great migration, the number of Negro delegates to the Republican National Convention had steadily increased, and they were eager to secure support from these delegates.[39] To win that backing, Claude Barnett and Albon Holsey vigorously engaged in writing editorials, visiting prominent black leaders, defending Hoover's flood record, and securing the endorsement of the National Negro Press Association.[40]

One of the reasons why Barnett and Holsey succeeded in winning early endorsements was Hoover's dramatic desegregation of the Commerce Department. The NAACP congratulated Hoover for this, while southern senators added to his popularity among blacks by their vicious public attacks. Moreover, Hoover refused to bend to southern pressure, for when Sen. Hubert D. Stephens of Mississippi protested, Hoover simply replied, "If such action as was taken is against the interests of either white or colored employees, they have a full right to present the matter to me. I have received no complaint from either group."[41]

Unfortunately the belief of thousands of black voters that Hoover had not protected black rights during the flood far outweighed the positive effects of his desegregation order.[42] To counter the persistent flood criticism, Hoover solicited the speaking skills of C. C. Neal, the black president of Haygood College, whom he had met at Pine Bluff, Arkansas, during the ceremony honoring him for flood relief to Negroes.[43] Neal was also interracial secretary of the Negro Methodist Church. Alan Fox, the chief Hoover-for-president agent in New York State, had wanted Perry Howard to address a large Harlem rally, but Hoover had rejected the idea. Aware of the charges made against Howard in the *Independent*, and no doubt concerned over Howard's suspicions about Hoover's friendship with rival lily-white Mississippians, Akerson had suggested Neal and assured Fox that he was "one of the ablest colored orators in the entire South." Indeed, Neal was a good choice, for he could bear witness to Hoover's efforts during the flood, and he had the added advantage of not being a politician.[44] In this capacity of layman enthusiast, Neal did an excellent job of campaigning in New York State, Ohio, Indiana, Kansas, and Missouri. Praise of his oratorical skills and demands for his service flooded Akerson's office.[45]

Success in combating some of the distrust also came from other sources.

Motion pictures of Hoover's aid to black people during the flood were effectively utilized, but Hoover inexplicably refused to allow the use of the films in
the important Ohio primary, which he lost.[46] Moton also helped by personally
contacting influential northern black leaders, and Barnett never tired of pros-
elytizing or of stressing to white campaign leaders the need to present the
Chief to black people "from a racial viewpoint," a categorization that they had
difficulty understanding.[47] Although Hoover had his faults and may not have
handled the flood as well as he should have, no other Republican candidate had
acted openly against segregation.

At the same time that Neal, Moton, Barnett, and Holsey were reassuring
skeptical northern blacks, Akerson was working hard to reassure angry southern lily-whites. Hoover's desegregation order and the sensational national
attention given to it in the press were the first in a series of hard jolts to the lily-
whites in the South. Oliver D. Street had been especially perturbed, and to
mollify him Akerson characterized the furor over desegregation as a "fake
issue." Only sixteen colored employees, all working at the Census Bureau, had
been involved; and in addition President Coolidge himself had asked all of his
cabinet officers to enforce his desegregation instructions. Hoover had merely
followed orders. "Some of the negro press immediately played the story up"
and "some of the rabid Democrats from the South made a lot of it in an effort to
create prejudice." There was little to worry about, he insisted: "I cannot see
how it can have any political effect, but it is one of those things that our
enemies talk a lot about."[48]

As was often the case, Akerson was wrong. The desegregation order had, in
fact, given some influential anti-Hoover Republicans in the South and border
states an increasingly effective weapon to use against him at the convention.
Patrick J. Hurley, one of Hoover's staunchest supporters in Oklahoma and
later his secretary of war, warned Hoover and his top managers that enemies
were making damaging use of the claim that "[he] issued an order abolishing
negro segregation in [his] Department, thereby establishing social equality
between the white and black races." To prove the accuracy of his information,
Hurley sent an editorial from the Houston *Post-Dispatch* that attacked Hoover
for appealing to "negro political bosses in the South" and, in a reference to
Perry Howard, chided Hoover for importing "a Southern negro political boss
to open a Hoover office in the National Capitol itself." The *Post Dispatch*
continued that he had also expressed his "wide human sympathies" by championing "negro social equality."[49]

To white critics Akerson again played down the significance of the desegregation order. He had insisted to lily-white leaders in Alabama and in Maryland
that it was a "greatly exaggerated" issue, and he reiterated that line of defense
to Hurley.[50] Antiblack Republicans were to be reassured, but he warned
Hurley that this explanation "*should not be given publicity except by word of
mouth.*"[51]

Akerson's explicit instructions to Hurley revealed the persistent worry among Hoover's managers about a possible revolt among black supporters at the convention. Alerted by Howard, northern black leaders had become skeptical about the repeated courting of pro-Hoover lily-white delegations from the South. Albon Holsey, Robert R. Moton's private secretary, campaigned vigorously for Hoover in the North, but he too soon became anxious. He told Akerson that during his campaigning he had picked up some information in Louisville about the Texas primary that "requires determined action on your part in order to utilize to best advantage the prevailing sentiment for the Secretary among colored people."[52] Holsey referred to a complex battle within the Texas state party between R. B. Creager's pro-Hoover lily-whites, who controlled the state party and twenty-two delegate votes for Hoover, and the anti-Hoover black and tans led by William M. ("Gooseneck Bill") McDonald.[53] He may also have been alluding to the fact that in 1927, in the *Nixon vs. Herndon* case, the NAACP had won a ruling from the United States Supreme Court outlawing the white primary in Texas, thus opening the way for a significant increase in black votes.[54] Republican political pressure and support were obviously needed both to unseat the lily-whites and to exploit the new ruling, but to Holsey's bitter disappointment Akerson would not intervene.[55] To have done so would have lost the secretary twenty-two delegate votes.

Although Akerson refused to help blacks fight for their political rights in Texas and professed ignorance about the leaders of the NAACP, he worked diligently to reassure northern black convention leaders of Hoover's concern for black people. Among those who received his special attention were Oscar De Priest, a Chicago politician, and J. C. Mitchell, editor of the Saint Louis *Argus*. As the convention began, both men were still skeptical about Hoover, and both were exceedingly influential within their delegations.[56] To others who complained that Hoover was not doing enough to reassure black voters, Akerson argued that the exact opposite was true. Far from neglecting the Negro vote, he stated, "we are accused of being too fair to the negro."[57] To Akerson, it was a simple case of political expediency. All sides were courted because every pro-Hoover vote was needed.

Hoover's first-ballot victory at the convention and his landslide electoral victory over Al Smith understandably have overshadowed the battle that took place in the credentials committee prior to the opening of the Republican convention. In early June, as opposing delegations journeyed to Kansas City, more than the usual attention was focused on the credentials committee. Black leaders in the North and South, Progressive reformers led by Norris, lily-white southern Republicans, and rivals for the nomination were all intensely interested in the contest for the southern delegations. This interest was highlighted by the fact that Hoover had secured only 400 of the 545 delegate votes needed to win on the first ballot. His opponents, especially Governor Frank O.

Lowden of Illinois, believed as early as April that if Hoover could be stopped from a first-ballot victory, Lowden could pick up sufficient strength to win on later ballots.[58]

Hoover's managers were deeply worried about a first-ballot failure, which they believed would cause steady erosion of support on subsequent ballots. This might lead to a *brokered convention*, in which the nomination would be determined by a last-minute agreement among party leaders. A number of forces might deny Hoover nomination on the first ballot: favorite son senatorial delegations, unpledged delegations ready to switch to a likely winner in return for patronage, Old Guard enemies, and draft-Coolidge enthusiasts.[59] Thus, fear of the stop-Hoover forces was by no means unfounded.[60]

The strategy of the Lowden backers, aided by the supporters of Vice-President Dawes, was to solidify the draft-Coolidge and senatorial favorite son forces into a unified voting bloc. They planned that thousands of angry farm leaders would converge on the convention to protest Hoover's nomination. With a combined effort they also hoped to control the credentials committee, which would rule on the contested seats from the South. After Hoover had been deprived of these votes, the next step would be an alliance with his eastern banking opponents, who would spread the word that Hoover could not beat Smith in the east and would lose the midwestern farm vote. Anti-Hoover forces hoped that this combination would stop the secretary "until the fifth ballot when the Hoover forces will disintegrate."[61]

Hoover's need to gain 187 additional delegates galvanized the stop-Hoover forces. Dubbed the Allies, the coalition was unified only by the desire to prevent a first-ballot sweep. At the center of the coalition was a phalanx of midwestern Lowden supporters, most prominently a former Illinois senator, Clarence F. Buck, and the tall, stately Ruth Hanna McCormick, who was a progressive candidate for Congress, widow of Sen. Medill McCormick, and daughter of the legendary Mark Hanna. Joining them were delegates from the Dawes and favorite son camps and such eastern opponents as the chairman of the Republican national committee, William Butler of Massachusetts, and the equally influential vice-chairman of the Republican National Committee, Charles H. Hilles of New York State.[62]

At first glance the anti-Hoover forces seemed formidable, but Work had anticipated their strategy and had taken steps to thwart them. In early April 1928 he began to emphasize to undeclared leaders that the pledges of the southern delegations had given great momentum to Hoover's candidacy. He also warned loyal state chairmen darkly that while a first- or second-ballot victory was expected, he wanted only those delegates "who can be depended upon for a long and positive fight." Victory was certain, but they could "afford to take no risks in view of the very definite political cabal which has been organized from New York City and its ramifications."[63] By early May, one month before the convention, he was more explicit. To ten state chairmen he emphasized "the importance of the men selected to represent your state on the Committee on Contests and Credentials at this convention. The usual number of contesting delegations may be expected and we want to know that stable men compose this committee, so that we will not be traded out of what belongs to us."[64]

As Work had correctly anticipated, the immediate object of the Allies was to capture control of the credentials committee so that the seventy-three contested delegate seats would go to anti-Hoover candidates, thus breaking Hoover's "momentum." But Work had already ensured the election of a Hoover majority to the credentials committee.[65] His selection for chairwoman of the credentials committee was Assistant Attorney General Mabel Walker Willebrandt who could be trusted to keep tight control of the committee. At times as many as six top Hoover managers sat on the committee casting proxy ballots, thus guaranteeing a solid majority throughout all of the challenges.[66]

From the outset the strategy of the Hoover-dominated credentials committee was to seat only delegations that were loyal to Hoover. Some observers believed that the first challenge, involving anti-Hoover black and tans from Florida, would be the crucial test. Before a closed executive session of the committee, Willebrandt made a passionate appeal against seating the black-and-tan Florida faction led by George Bean. She threatened that if the committee did not seat the newly elected pro-Hoover lily-white delegation headed by Glenn Skipper, she would reveal to the public a liquor scandal implicating the leaders of the Bean faction and thus embarrass the entire party.[67] Willebrandt's strategy succeeded. Of course she was not the only person to level charges of corruption. In virtually every case involving a disputed delegation, either the challengers or those who were unseated loudly protested that their opponents were notorious, unsavory characters who sold federal offices and manipulated the selection of delegates.[68] Race made no difference. The delegations of black regulars headed by Ben Davis and Perry Howard declared their fealty to Hoover, and despite outcries of patronage corruption by their lily-white challengers, the committee duly seated them.[69] Also recognized was Robert R. Church, Jr., the wealthy, knowledgeable, and effective black Republican leader of Memphis, Tennessee, whose close political alliance with the white congressman J. Will Taylor had made him a special target of lily-white Tennessee opponents. Church's enemies claimed to have proof that he was guilty of selling offices, but nothing came of the allegations, and the Tennessee black and tans prevailed.[70]

Following the seating of the Florida, Mississippi, and Georgia delegations, the two most important remaining contests involved Louisiana and Texas. Walter Cohen, the respected leader of the Louisiana black and tans, raised the issue of greatest concern to all black Republican leaders. He argued that even though his delegation did not support Hoover, it must be seated because the lily-white challengers, led by Kuntz and Loisel, were determined to drive out black leadership from the party in Louisiana. In effect, Cohen was insisting that there was a bigger issue at stake than Hoover, that the committee and the party must defend and protect the black-and-tan loyalists without regard to their support of any single candidate. If not, he warned, the party would risk losing black voters in the northern states. Both Tieless Joe Tolbert, the white leader of the South Carolina black and tans and Ben Davis of Georgia steadfastly supported Cohen's position.[71] After decades of leadership Cohen was well known and respected as a spirited and determined leader of his people in New Orleans. Black sentiment for him was so strong that Hoover personally intervened to ensure that he would be seated.[72] But his anti-Hoover delegation was disallowed. In a split vote revealing the deepening divisions within the committee and the party over the lily-white resurgence in the South, the committee seated the pro-Hoover, lily-white Kuntz-Loisel faction by a vote of fifty-five to forty-one. Hoover's gesture of respect for Cohen did little to hide or salve the growing sense of bitterness and alienation felt by the ousted black-and-tan delegates.[73]

The Texas contest was even more dispiriting. Amidst the din of charges and countercharges of corruption, the lily-white, pro-Hoover faction, led by the suave R. B. Creager, squared off against the anti-Hoover black-and-tan regulars, headed by William M. ("Gooseneck Bill") McDonald. In the course of the debate, Congressman Henry W. Wurzbach angrily castigated the committee for allowing Ben Davis and Perry Howard, both national committeemen, to represent their states and vote on the committee. Everyone knew, he charged, that both men and their delegations had been bought and paid for by the Hoover forces prior to the convention.[74] As expected, the committee seated Creager's lily-white delegation, but not before some black-and-tan leaders on the committee, notably Ben Davis and Tieless Joe Tolbert, joined forces with the defeated anti-Hoover black and tans.[75]

As the same pattern held true for virtually all of the challenges, black leaders and their white allies became more and more frustrated and angry at the committee's rigid insistence on loyalty to Hoover as the criterion for recognition. From their perspective, the party owed its support to the black-and-tan party loyalists, not to any new group of lily-white former Democrats who would opportunistically favor the candidate supported by a majority of the credentials committee. There was also at stake the historic if long-neglected commitment of the party to protect and defend the black people of the South. For decades black-and-tan leaders had fought off lily-white challengers, but during the 1920s their enemies had gained more and more recognition at the national conventions and thereby increased legal control over the state organizations for the next four years. With lily-whites again triumphant in three states formerly controlled by black and tans, angry black leaders could not help believing that the Hoover majority cared little or nothing for black leaders in the South. Ben Davis, Robert Church, Walter Cohen, northern blacks, and white allies such as Tolbert were deeply upset. To them, the trend was evident and ominous. Once again events suggested that national leaders of the Republican party were attempting to "reform" the southern wing, to resolve the southern question by purging the black leaders and replacing them with whites. This time the instigator of the purge appeared to be Hoover.[76]

Besides black and tans, other Republicans such as the highly respected senator George Norris also became infuriated over the solid control of the credentials committee and the relentless seating of pro-Hoover delegations. Norris, who disliked Hoover, viewed him as a major spokesman for the private water power interests, which had defeated his efforts to develop federal water power resources, most notably at Muscle Shoals, Alabama.[77] In a statement to the press he implied that the forces responsible for Hoover's victory were the worst elements in the party—apologists for the Teapot Dome scandal; dishonest city bosses such as William S. Vare of Philadelphia; and the "illegal, corrupt, and disgraceful" southern patronage machines. He was convinced that Hoover had bought the nomination, a charge repeated by Drew Pearson and by *Look* magazine in 1939. Norris promised that his Senate Judiciary Committee would probe further into the cesspool of southern Republican politics. The New York *Evening Post* was equally disgusted by the contest for the "rotten Republican boroughs of Dixie," which "was a reproach to the Republican Party."[78]

Most convention delegates were more favorably impressed by the efficient Hoover machine than were Norris or the disappointed ousted delegates. The poorly organized Allies had failed to stop the secretary, and his managers had demonstrated relentless toughness and a tightly disciplined organization. Secretary of the Treasury Andrew Mellon had been secretly working for months to swing the deadlocked Pennsylvania delegation to Hoover, but on 12 June after the stop-Hoover effort had largely failed, William S. Vare, the disreputable but astute boss of Philadelphia, created a sensation by declaring for Hoover before Mellon could complete his work. As Edgar Rickard, Hoover's personal financial manager, recorded, "it was all over and the tension is relaxed."[79] The decisive victory in the credentials contests and, immediately following Vare's endorsement, the declaration of the entire Pennsylvania delegation for Hoover shattered the hopes of the Allies.[80] The ensuing bandwagon effect ensured a first-ballot victory well before the voting began.

After a futile effort by the Texas black and tans to convince the entire convention to seat them, the Republicans settled down to nominate Hoover for president and Charles Curtis of Missouri for vice-president.[81] The platform reflected the widespread concern over corruption in government by promising that Republicans would vigorously promote honest public service and prosecute all wrongdoers, a plank that Hoover would take quite seriously as president.[82] Other promises included an antilynching law, which was a carryover from past years. But the platform made no other reference to the welfare of black people, and concern among Negro leaders deepened.[83] Albon Holsey, who had worked hard for Hoover's nomination at the convention, warned his friend and boss, R. R. Moton, that the entire "colored situation" had been "menaced by selfish factions,"[84] meaning those black leaders who were suspicious of Hoover's motives.

Some critics would suspect later that Hoover had initiated a well-planned southern strategy during the credentials fight. Emphasizing the activities of Rush Holland, George Norris linked Hoover to the "waterpower trust" and indirectly to the convicted cabinet officers and officials of the corrupt Harding administration. Norris again charged that the strategy was nothing less than "the buying and selling and trading and trafficking in delegates in the Solid South." He lamented that although there was no possibility in the South of the election of a single Republican presidential elector, the southern delegates nonetheless held "the balance of power" and nominated a president of the United States.[85] Some black-and-tan organizations and their leaders, who had been loyal to the party for many years, saw the Texas and Louisiana battles as evidence that the Hoover managers had sacrificed blacks for temporary political gain.[86] Rejected lily-white delegates undoubtedly felt the same.

Hoover's convention strategy was more limited than any of these critics believed. The need to line up southern delegations was a problem that Hoover had inherited rather than created. His operatives became involved in southern states after splits had already appeared between the black-and-tan and lily-white factions. Had he told black supporters that he was also aiding selected lily-white delegations, or had he advertised to lily-whites that he also aided black and tans, Hoover might have lost desperately needed southern delegates. His managers' intention was neither antiblack nor anti-lily-white. His forces supplied small amounts of money to cover expenses of lily-whites in Florida and Alabama and blacks in Georgia and Mississippi. One may argue, as did Norris at the time and Drew Pearson later, that donations of $4,000 to Howard, $2,200 to Davis, $1,000 to Street, and $3,000 to the Florida supporters proved that Hoover had "bought" the delegations. A defender of Hoover, however, may as reasonably reply that the amounts were too small to buy entire delegations and that the payments represented needed expense money to political allies. In Louisiana and in Texas, where no money was involved, the criterion was the same: loyalty to Hoover.

In the search for delegates Akerson and Work had encouraged both blacks and lily-whites. That strategy became most difficult in Mississippi, where an undecided legal battle led Hoover managers to court both of the opposing factions until Howard emerged the victor. Moreover, Hoover had not double-crossed Howard. In fact, his support of Howard brought strong criticism from both antiblacks and progressive reformers. Despite loud cries of corruption from lily-whites and earlier from the *Independent*, the committee had seated the black-and-tan delegations from Mississippi, Arkansas, Georgia, Tennessee, and South Carolina. The only black-and-tan leaders to be excluded were those who had refused to declare for Hoover. It was a simple strategy and a simple test based not on race but on power politics. The strategy worked well enough to ensure a first-ballot nomination. Nonetheless, events soon after the convention made that strategy appear much more cynical than it was.

5. Double Cross

Herbert Hoover is a first-rate black and tan—nothing lily-white about him," insisted Perry Howard. Respected by northern and southern black politicians as one of the shrewdest and most politically knowledgeable of black leaders, Howard was also one of the most critical and outspoken. His endorsement, following the convention battle in the credentials committee, helped to erase doubts about Hoover's attitude toward blacks. During the Senate investigation of campaign expenses in May, Howard had publicly revealed his fear of a Hoover "double-cross" that might result in seating the lily-white Mississippi challengers rather than his own black-and-tan delegation, but now he reassured other Negroes that Hoover "had kept the faith with me in every particular."[1]

Hoover supporters argued that the secretary had also "kept the faith" with other blacks. Gooseneck Bill McDonald of Texas had been deposed not because Hoover and his lieutenants sought to eliminate black and tans but because McDonald had not adhered to Texas law in electing his delegation and thus had given his opponents a crucial advantage. Other black leaders had been treated well. Howard cited Robert R. Church and Walter Cohen, who had faced serious challenges from lily-whites and still had been recognized. (Cohen's delegation had not been accepted, but Hoover's intervention had won seating for Cohen himself.) Indeed, the Louisiana contest particularly bore out Howard's trust. When Cohen's delegates supported Curtis and were therefore unseated in favor of the pro-Hoover lily-whites, Hoover "heard the cry of Cohen and regardless of regularity, his heart went out to him and a voice came from the nation's capital to Kansas City saying 'don't turn Cohen personally out of that convention.' " Thus, Howard argued, the facts supported his contention that the "Hoover people played the game fairly and squarely." This was not the voice of a lily-white but that of the man who had desegregated his department, and Howard enthusiastically promised, "I shall take the stump and defend Mr. Hoover, without equivocation, [against] the charges of lily whitism."[2]

Howard's ringing endorsement was calculated in part to infuriate the lily-white Mississippi Republicans whom he had bested at the convention, and he succeeded admirably. One outraged opponent warned that if Howard were not silenced, his continued pronouncements would "ruin things in Mississippi, Arkansas, and Tennessee, also part of Alabama and Missouri." Akerson confidently advised the worried lily-white that it was difficult to depose an elected national committeeman, but he was nonetheless "certain that the situation will work itself out in some way."[3] What he alluded to was in fact known only to a few top Hoover aides. Ironically, at the moment of Howard's triumph at the convention, events had combined to destroy his high standing in the Republican party and bring him to trial on federal charges of political corruption.

Until now the story of Howard's indictment has been clouded in speculation. The usual version involves the suspicion that Hoover had waited until he had secured Howard's Mississippi delegate votes and then cruelly repaid Howard's loyalty by ordering his indictment. It would seem, therefore, that Hoover had indeed justified Howard's premonition of a double cross. More important, the indictment was understood by lily-whites to mean that blacks were no longer welcome in the Republican party. Some believed at the time and have either reiterated or suggested since then that Howard's indictment was a masterstroke in Hoover's southern strategy. Such critics perceived the chief goal of Hoover's strategy to be the "reform" of the southern wing of the party, which meant eliminating black participants so as to crack the solid South and ensure Republican gains in the election of 1928.[4] Actually, Howard's indictment was neither part of a grand strategy nor Hoover's fault.

Mabel Walker Willebrandt, the outspoken chairwoman of the convention credentials committee, was also the assistant attorney general in charge of Prohibition enforcement and the chief figure in the indictment proceedings. Born in a Kansas sod dugout, she became a public-school principal, graduated from law school in 1916, and practiced law and progressive Republican politics in Los Angeles until securing her appointment to the Justice Department from Harding in 1921, the same year that Howard was named a special assistant attorney general.[5] Prior to the convention Willebrandt had had little to do with Howard, spending all of her time and energy in a zealous crusade against lax law enforcement and well-organized Prohibition violators. She was familiar with southern politics and patronage, especially in Florida where, she informed Attorney General John G. Sargent, "the political organization obtruded itself into prohibition enforcement activities of the Customs, Coast Guard, and this office."[6] As chairwoman of the credentials committee she helped to ensure that George Bean, head of the reputedly corrupt Republican black-and-tan organization in Florida, would be replaced by the "reformers," a pro-Hoover, lily-white Republican contingent led by Glenn Skipper.

During the credentials battle Willebrandt suddenly felt compelled to play some politics on her own. At first she had held herself aloof from the contest over the seating of the Mississippi delegation. Because both the Perry Howard and the anti–Perry Howard delegations were for Hoover, she explained to the attorney general, the Hoover majority on the credentials committee listened to the arguments patiently. During the fray she had been favorably impressed by

Howard, who "made a clear, concise, and clever legal argument, showing that his delegation had been chosen according to law." In contrast, Howard's opponents, led by Lamont Rowlands, appeared to be politically inexperienced and failed to make a convincing legal case. The result was that the committee—even after listening to Rowlands insinuate "that Howard was buying and selling patronage"—seated the Howard delegation by an almost unanimous vote.[7]

The ease of Howard's victory infuriated his lily-white challengers. After consulting with E. E. Hindman, the Republican United States attorney for the Southern District of Mississippi, they confronted Willebrandt with the claim that "they had new evidence of the buying and selling of patronage,"[8] which they were prepared to make public immediately. Willebrandt, of course, was well aware of the widely publicized charges that Hoover had "bought" the southern delegations, especially Howard's. Because he had been seated despite these charges, it was obvious that Willebrandt and the Hoover forces were vulnerable to more embarrassing publicity.

Judging from what the disgruntled challengers had told her, Willebrandt suspected that Sen. George Norris had demanded and obtained documents from "the files of this Department." Willebrandt was also sensitive to Norris's repeated charges that the Justice Department had for years covered up southern Republican patronage corruption and that this immunity from prosecution was directly related to the power of the southern delegations in selecting the party's 1928 presidential nominee. Willebrandt observed that, like Norris, the angry, rejected Mississippi delegation "was obsessed by the n[o]tion that Perry Howard and his organization were utterly corrupt in Mississippi; that evidence of that corruption had twice been placed before the Department; and that our department had suppressed the facts and protected Howard; and that the actions of this Department had been induced by the intervention of Senator Butler [chairman of the Republican National Committee] in Howard's behalf."[9]

Under the circumstances Willebrandt felt compelled to make a quick deal. Because she believed that it was imperative to prevent these men, who were "tremendously in earnest," from "announcing such conclusions in the Credentials Committee (at which the Press was present) or on the floor of the Convention," she promised them that in return for their silence and their gracious acceptance of defeat, she would personally guarantee that the Department of Justice would fully investigate the new evidence against Howard. To Attorney General Sargent she defended her independent decision by insisting that it was her duty to defend the Department of Justice, the party, and the law. After all, she concluded, "I could see no good to be served, either for law enforcement or the party by these men 'letting off steam.' "[10] Soon after she had made the deal with the Mississippi lily-whites, Willebrandt informed Hoover, and trusting her judgment, he agreed to endorse her decision. He had, in fact, "kept the faith" with Howard, but events had moved beyond his control. Because Hoover had already been embarrassed and vexed by the sensational publicity surrounding Rush Holland's cash payments to Howard and by efforts of Democrats and opposing Republicans to associate him with Teapot Dome or any other convenient scandal, he could not afford to be accused of sheltering Howard from criminal prosecution in return for his convention votes.

Hoover was "greatly disturbed" by the charges against Howard. To Claudius Huston he confided that while he did "not wish to assume wrong doing on the part of any man until he had been heard," he nonetheless could not "countenance such conduct." He therefore ordered Huston to "apprise him [Howard] that the charges have been made and unless he can satisfactorily meet them, then I do not care to have his support."[11] Soon after Huston informed him of the charges, Howard requested a personal interview with the candidate, but Hoover, wary of political repercussions, would not meet him.[12] Howard would have to save his own political skin as best he could.

At the same time that Willebrandt became intensely involved in marshaling the evidence against Howard, she also actively cooperated in providing allegations of patronage corruption to a special subcommittee of the Senate Committee on Post Offices and Post Roads.[13] William H. Harris and Walter F. George, the two Democratic senators from Georgia, pushed through the resolution authorizing the probe. Their target was Benjamin Davis, a black former Republican national committeeman who capitulated after admitting that he had accepted $2,200 from Rush Holland. However, Davis had retained the powerful position of secretary of the Georgia Republican State Central Committee. Although the two senators refused to admit any political motivation,[14] Georgia Republicans were waging a vigorous campaign, and worried Democrats foresaw a significant shift to the Republicans in November.[15] As Al Smith made blunder after blunder, southern Democrats became more eager than ever to discredit Republicans by reviving and emphasizing the old Reconstruction stereotype of the corrupt black Republican politician.

Headed by the conspiracy-oriented maverick Republican, Sen. Smith Brookhart of Iowa, the post office subcommittee traveled to Georgia where it allowed the two Democratic senators to interrogate Davis. Senator Harris was far less interested in post office corruption than in Hoover's intrusion into the South. The "most important thing we have to deal with," he emphasized, was Rush Holland's payments to Davis.[16] Both senators tried repeatedly to trap Davis into admitting that he had used the money from Holland for personal rather than party purposes and that he had accepted bribes from white appointees who wished to obtain or keep patronage jobs. Davis represented himself better than he had before the Senate committee investigations of presidential campaign expenditures. He made few errors, admitted nothing, and at one point even reminded Senator George that he had obtained a copy of the law governing political contributions from the senator himself and had read the law to all who might not have understood it fully.[17]

Unable to shake Davis's testimony but still eager to discredit Republicans, the senators next called on the politically sophisticated Republican postmaster general, Harry S. New. Unlike Davis, who could not afford to appear disrespectful, New promptly attacked his two Georgia inquisitors. He had thoroughly investigated every report of corruption, New said, and despite all of the accusations he had uncovered few indictable offenses. Since 1921 he had personally obtained the consent of Georgia senators for sixty-two percent of the political appointments in their state. One appointee recommended by Democrats had been accused of bribery, and "the highest Democratic authority in Georgia" had tried unsuccessfully to get the charges dropped. Even more significant, New continued, was evidence that he provided that indicated the Democratic National Committee had itself violated the law by soliciting political contributions from Georgia postmasters. In addition, southern congressmen had informed him that it was common practice for southern Democratic state committees to require "voluntary" political contributions from their political appointees. Thus, he concluded, violations were not limited to one party. Both Democrats and Republicans had routinely engaged in practices that were difficult to prove yet were illegal nonetheless.[18]

New's offensive silenced the investigators for the remainder of the campaign. But the editors of the *New York Times*, which had reported on the hearings in great detail, had become convinced that the allegations of corruption were valid and that patronage corruption among southern Republicans was nothing less than a national scandal. The editors sought to make patronage corruption an important issue of the campaign, and they refused to believe either that Davis had used the money from Rush Holland for party purposes or that contributions to the party by political appointees had been voluntary and thus legal. If one were to believe Davis's testimony, the editors sarcastically concluded, one could as convincingly watch "the twenty-six letters of the alphabet be tossed into the air on Peachtree Street and the heap in which they fall be pointed out as the works of Uncle Remus."[19]

Patronage dispensation by black politicians in the South was a peculiarly complex problem for which the editors of the *Times* had no understanding or sympathy. Because racism in the South prevented blacks from being appointed to any of the prestigious, better-paying patronage jobs, and because there were often too few eligible white Republicans to fill the available positions, black patronage referees were often forced to recommend white registered Democrats. In the deep South the Republicans had been unable to sustain active political opposition. They usually offered no state candidates or waged political contests for national offices. Thus, whenever a white Democrat alleged that he had been forced to pay five percent of his salary to obtain and to keep his patronage position, northern critics of the "rotten borough" system tended to grant the charges more than the usual degree of plausibility. After all, why should a white southern Democrat regularly and voluntarily contribute five percent of his salary to black Republicans unless required to do so in order to obtain and protect his patronage job?[20] But how were Republicans in the South to finance their party except by contributions from those who benefited from the party? Certainly the white Democrats were not coerced into taking the patronage jobs offered by black Republicans. Even though the law prohibited outright solicitation of federal officeholders, it was legal for party officials to suggest that they make a voluntary financial contribution, and they most likely took the jobs with the understanding that voluntary contributions to the party would be expected.

Nonetheless, an angry white officeholder who had not been recommended for reappointment by a black politician could not only charge corruption but could often enough rely on sensational press coverage of his charges. The disgruntled former appointee might even receive, in exchange for his testimony, the promise of immunity from criminal prosecution. Most likely there was some degree of corruption, but it was far easier to make the charge and thus embarrass the opposition than it was to prove the allegation in a court of law. In effect, the charge of bribery corruption had become a potent political weapon to use against successful black politicians.[21]

A good example of this political intimidation began in mid-July 1928, when the United States District Court in Biloxi, Mississippi, convened in special session for the grand jury investigation of Perry Howard. Mabel Walker Willebrandt, flanked by three assistant attorneys general and a number of Department of Justice agents, presented the evidence against Howard. He was indicted for selling the office of the United States marshal—a charge that his lily-white political opponents, of course, had pressed upon the federal government. The *New York Times* was delighted with the indictment. While blacks saw the case as further evidence of the intimidation of Negro officeholders, the *Times'* editors believed that Howard epitomized corruption in the South. They congratulated Willebrandt as the civil servant who was "instrumental" in obtaining the quick indictment against "the smartest Negro in politics" and three of his top political associates. According to the *Times*, the southern Republican organizations were full of this type of corruption. Praising both Willebrandt and the special Senate subcommittee of the Committee on Post Offices and Post Roads, which had decided to expand its probe to other southern states after the election in November, the editors confidently predicted that Republican patronage scandals in North Carolina, South Carolina, Tennessee, Alabama, and Texas "would bring very sensational developments which might lead to many indictments." Then the *Times* gave a solemn warning to Hoover. Unless southern Republicans stopped selling offices and offering themselves to the highest bidder at the Republican national convention, "Republican national nominees, selected by Southern votes, cannot expect the support of respectable white Democratic elements in the south," and thus by implication at least, could never hope to expand their influence or the principles of their party throughout the entire nation.[22] The *Times* therefore seemed to be saying that ending corruption in the southern Republican state parties was essential to solid democratic government, and thus incumbent upon honest Republican presidents.

Hoover was "greatly upset," but his concern stemmed in large part from fear for his own reputation. Determined to avoid even the hint of corruption, he immediately insisted on enlisting new black leaders of impeccable standing. As early as 23 June, well before the grand jury handed down the indictment and only days after the close of the Republican convention, Hoover and Work had agreed that Assistant Secretary of Commerce Walter F. Brown should create a Colored Voters Division led by new black leaders.[23] Yet Work was slow to put together either a well-coordinated national campaign or a Colored Voters Division, and three weeks later on 14 July, just after Benjamin Davis had again made the headlines, Hoover this time ordered Work to appoint Brown to the new position.[24] Four days later, when the Howard indictment became front-page news, Hoover became even more vehement. He immediately informed Work that the indictment made it "most imperative that [a] special campaign committee be established in Mississippi with *some colored representation and leadership* that cannot be questioned."[25]

The order to Work was significant. Hoover had known for several weeks about the charges against Howard. From his experiences during the 1927 Mississippi flood, he was well aware that lily-whites wanted no black leaders whatsoever in the party or, at most, only a token contingent in minor posts. He also knew that lily-whites loyal to him, especially Crosby, Sheldon, and Lamont Rowlands, were eager to depose Howard and all black leaders from the party in Mississippi.[26] However, he did not direct Work to turn over control of the party to the lily-whites. Although Hoover certainly encouraged the admission of prominent southern whites into important party positions, the evidence is equally clear that he had no policy of driving out black leadership as long as its character could not be impugned. Later, as allegations against white Republican leaders arose, he would insist on the same criterion for them as well.

Not all black leaders respected Howard. In 1922 the NAACP was sharply critical of Howard for his narrow Republican partisanship during the fight to secure the Dyer antilynching bill. Indeed, W. E. B. Du Bois privately considered him a "traitor" to his race and publicly rebuked him. A. Philip Randolph bitterly resented Howard's efforts on behalf of the Pullman Company in attempting to defeat his efforts to unionize black railroad employees.[27] In retrospect, Ralph Bunche, later to become a diplomat at the United Nations and a winner of the Nobel Peace Prize, characterized Howard as a political expert who lived in Washington, D.C., and who was known by black Mississippians "for 'staying-in with white folks'" and as "a better lily-white than a white Republican would be—a robust, all-out, Lincoln-freed-the-slaves, the Democrats-be-damned brand of Republican soap-boxing" politician.[28] Nonetheless, for his time, and despite his faults, Howard was looked upon by many black Republican leaders as an extraordinary man capable of success in a dangerous political environment and as an exceptionally smart, handsome, and outspoken orator who had gained the highest position held by a black in the administration.

The indictment deeply troubled and vexed most blacks, however.[29] It certainly appeared, as Howard charged before black audiences in the North, that he had indeed been "double-crossed" by the Hoover forces. Black people knew that the lily-white Republicans were behind the charges. Thus, in their eyes Howard's claim that he was a race martyr, sacrificed to help Hoover build a lily-white South, was at least plausible. Separate pieces of evidence appeared to be forming a pattern. Two of the most successful black politicians in the South, both Republican national committeemen who had supported Hoover, had been publicly humiliated. Moreover, at the Republican convention the black-and-tan delegations of Florida, Louisiana, and Texas had been deposed in favor of pro-Hoover, lily-white delegations. Equally significant was the fact that no white Republicans or Democrats had been targets of the Senate investigations or grand jury indictments. The proceedings against Howard would continue beyond the election, and recalling also the widespread antiblack allegations made against Hoover during the 1927 flood, it was little wonder then that blacks, already wary of a party that had long ago ceased to represent their needs, should now become increasingly and openly suspicious.[30]

6. Southern Revolution

Hoover's primary motivation for attempting to attract white voters and new white leadership to the party stemmed from desires other than the political opportunism of some of his campaign advisers. Despite appearances, he did not wish to force black leaders out of the party merely to crack the solid South.[1] Instead, his primary motivation had much more to do with his personal pride as a public servant who acted on the basis of high principles rather than mere politics. Thus before he could wholeheartedly embrace a strategy for southern reform he had to convince himself that it was consistent with his principles.

Hoover was a proud man who valued his own strong sense of personal integrity and who had built his public reputation on solid, honest accomplishment. He believed deeply in the ideal of disinterested public service and in the moral cliché that public office was a public trust. At the same time, despite the boomlet in 1920 and his eight years as secretary of commerce, Hoover had not taken to politics or to politicians with any relish. His close associates were well aware that he disliked the necessities imposed on him by politics. Although he was pragmatic enough to allow his managers to make the kinds of political decisions that were necessary to win the nomination, he was at times much chagrined by the results. In particular, Hoover was both deeply humiliated and greatly angered by charges that he had "bought" southern delegations and that this corruption had "bought" him the nomination. He might have expected that unscrupulous Democrats would try their best to implicate him in the infamous Teapot Dome scandals, but it was intolerable to have respected Republican leaders like Sen. George W. Norris reinforcing the charges of corruption.

Under these circumstances, Hoover had a deeply personal reason for his revulsion against southern Republican politics. His nomination victory had been tarnished by the need to deal with the inordinate power of the southern delegations at the national nominating convention. He now became utterly determined to prove that he owed nothing to any corrupt southerners and that he would totally reform the southern mess just as quickly as he possibly could. Indeed, he would especially welcome new, honest, respected leaders who were willing to replace the disreputable and allegedly corrupt politicians who had dishonored him. Work appreciated this sentiment, and when he refused to recruit new black leadership in Mississippi, as Hoover had first ordered, he easily convinced Hoover that such an action would seriously interfere with the

72

flow of "men in important positions" who were joining the Hoovercrat movement every day.[2]

Southern "men in important positions" would be a great asset in rebuilding a respectable party in the South, but to accomplish this reform Hoover had to come to grips first with a historical situation of great complexity and difficulty. Southern politics in 1928 offset the Democrats' commitment to white supremacy against the competing Republicans' commitment to uphold and defend the rights of black people. The triumph of white supremacy had often resulted in dilapidated, powerless Republican state parties that, in some cases, did not even bother to run candidates for state or congressional offices or raise issues challenging the policies of the Democratic party. No one denied that these state parties existed only to dispense federal patronage, that their leaders were totally ineffectual or worse, that this situation had encouraged corruption in both parties, and that neither blacks nor whites were fairly served by this type of situation. Yet how could Hoover eliminate the stereotype of the corrupt black Republican politico without driving out black leadership? How could he initiate the sweeping reforms that he hoped would revitalize the state parties without abandoning the party's historic commitment to blacks?

Hoover was well aware of the lily-white Republican lament. Black leaders, stereotyped since Reconstruction, must be eliminated before the party could attract the white leaders and voters necessary to challenge and eventually defeat the Democrats. He was also well aware that many blacks naturally believed that this "lily-white strategy" was the first step in the total abandonment and exclusion of blacks and would establish white supremacy as a Republican principle. Yet some southern white Republicans, whom Hoover respected, attempted to refute these fears with the argument that blacks would gain far more than they would lose under the leadership of reforming white leaders.

Such an argument prompted Hoover's consideration when it came from southern white Republicans like Col. Henry W. Anderson and Jennings C. Wise. Anderson, a prominent Virginia lawyer, had served as a member of the American Red Cross famine relief team following World War I. He had been a special assistant to the attorney general of the United States, and since 1921 had twice run, albeit unsuccessfully, for governor. A Republican who commanded the respect of southern businessmen and industrialists, he was also an important spokesman for the movement to industrialize and diversify the economy of the "new South." Moreover, he took relish in attacking the fraudulent and illegal methods of Democratic one-party rule and in highlighting the corrupt and debilitating effects of the factionalism in both parties.

Wise, his law partner, was inspired by Anderson's fight to transform the South, and he, too, had entered politics to take control of the political process away from the corrupt bosses. A graduate of Virginia Military Institute, Wise won distinction in World War I before bringing his fighting qualities to politics. Hoover was so impressed by these two men that he later appointed Anderson to his prestigious commission to investigate and recommend improvements in law enforcement, popularly known as the Wickersham commission. Unlike Anderson, who limited his services to the Wickersham commission, Wise accepted Hoover's appointment as special assistant to the attorney general of the United States.[3]

Anderson and Wise first came to Hoover's attention at the Republican National Convention. Based on his own observations, Wise was convinced that if Hoover selected a southerner as vice-president, the Republicans could crack the solid South in a dramatic and lasting realignment of American national politics. Moreover, Virginia had the perfect candidate in Col. Henry W. Anderson. He was a handsome, distinguished-looking gentleman with wavy gray hair and a courtly manner who had won the respect of many opponents in two unsuccessful gubernatorial campaigns. Anderson, he believed, represented the best class of the South. A highly successful and prosperous lawyer, he had attempted since 1920 to revive and revitalize the Republican party into an effective, honest instrument of government in Virginia. But he had had no more success against the narrowminded, patronage-oriented Republican politicians led by white national committeeman Bascom Slemp than he had against the white supremacist Democrats.

Without consulting Slemp, who distrusted Wise because of his loyalty to Anderson and feared Anderson's potential rivalry for control of the state party, Wise scurried about the convention contacting the leaders of the southern delegations. To his delight they agreed with his analysis of a southern victory and were almost all willing to back Anderson's candidacy. Within a short time Wise had put together an influential coalition of southerners who could command a respectful hearing. Equally, if not more important, perhaps, was strong support from several influential Hoover advisers. Among those who generated enthusiasm for Anderson were Patrick J. Hurley, the exuberant Oklahoman who would become secretary of war; Claudius Huston, an expert on southern politics, who would soon become chairman of the Republican National Committee; and Lewis Strauss, a native of Richmond who had been Hoover's private secretary during World War I and who was currently a vice-president in the investment firm of Kuhn-Loeb.

Hoover responded to the boomlet for Anderson by inviting the dark horse to his suite for a personal talk. He was very favorably impressed by him and by his ideas for a "revolution" in southern political life. Eventually, however, Anderson withdrew his candidacy and national leaders selected the front-running senator from Kansas, Charles Curtis.[4] Nonetheless, Hoover remained interested in Anderson and in his thoughts about the future of the Republican party in the South. Soon after the convention, therefore, Hoover invited

Anderson and Wise to Washington, D.C., where they could explore the possibilities of a southern "revolution" at greater length.

On 17 June 1928 Anderson elaborated on his political vision for the Republican nominee. He had based his two gubernatorial campaigns on the issue of corruption. The corruption of southern politics, Anderson believed, was the source of the South's underdeveloped economy and its lack of social progress. The politicians of both parties were interested only in winning and retaining power in order to control federal patronage and thereby advance their own personal interests. This was especially true of the totally ineffectual southern Republican state parties, which were most often controlled by corrupt black and tans who could neither promote the public interest nor protect black people. The only solution lay in an entirely new class of leaders, a new white leadership that would gain control of the state central committee; throw the corrupt, patronage-soaked politicians out of office; and begin the long, hard task of reforming the Republican party in the South.[5]

Anderson's message was not new to black people in Virginia. To many blacks there appeared to be little real difference between the lily-white leadership of the "old order" of Republican patronage politicians controlled by national committeeman Bascom Slemp and the weaker, less well organized lily-white reform faction led by Anderson. Because both Slemp and Anderson insisted on exclusive white control of the party leadership, both of them appeared to be catering to white supremacist voters who, blacks feared, would steadily expand that exclusion until no blacks were welcome in the state party. To register their protest against the lily-white policy of both factions, an increasing number of blacks had begun voting for Democratic candidates.[6]

Anderson and Wise privately refuted this black perspective. They explained that the substitution of high quality white leaders for corrupt black-and-tan ones was only the first step in the reform process. White leadership was crucial to crack the white supremacist Democratic party's power, but white leadership was not sufficient in itself. There were significant differences between the lily-white Republican politicians and the white elite leadership that Anderson and Wise wanted to attract. When it came to using politics for their own personal aggrandizement, there was little difference between patronage-bloated politicos, whether they were black and tans or lily-whites. Reformers, therefore, had to be men of accomplishment, high idealism, and political vision who were willing to put their talents to work in the public interest of all citizens. They would transform the ineffective, corrupt state Republican parties into honest, reputable, efficient instruments of government, thereby overthrowing the blighted one-party rule of the Democrats and liberating the political process in the South.[7]

Returning the South to a state of healthy two-party competition required an even more drastic change in the identity of the two parties. Since Reconstruction days, Anderson explained, the Republicans had been fatally stereotyped as the party of corrupt black politicos. Race and racial fears had poisoned southern politics. He insisted that this racial basis of politics had to be eliminated. Once the association of racial ties to each party was no longer the determining factor in the thinking of voters; once the Republican party had achieved a new, more economically oriented identity; and once it had led the way by convincing southern whites that it no longer was the party of corrupt black patronage, it would then attract the outstanding leaders and white adherents who would realign southern political life.

Anderson and Wise anticipated the adverse reaction such charges would prompt among black voters in the South as well as in the North. Many of them would assume that the Republicans were abandoning the Negro in favor of white supremacy. But, they argued, this perception was false, and in time blacks would come to recognize this fact. Unlike the Democrats, for example, the reform Republicans would not restrict black voting nor seek to interfere with their rights under the Constitution. Little of real substance would be lost by blacks, and that only temporarily. What would change almost immediately were two historic practices that had failed to help black people since the end of Reconstruction. Black leaders would no longer hold prominent state party positions, and the Republican state parties would no longer appeal to blacks to vote for the party as a unified racial group. In fact, the state parties would no longer promote the misguided notion that blacks ought to vote for the Republican party because the party would protect and promote their racial interests. Anderson and Wise felt that blacks, as well as whites, had to be encouraged to think about the two parties in terms of their differing political policies and thus develop the practice of voting in terms of their individual interests rather than racial fears.

To encourage black voters in Virginia to begin thinking about politics in terms of individual self-interest rather than as a minority race dependent upon the Republican party, Anderson and Wise would have the new reform leaders adopt a policy of benign neglect. They would simply ignore race or racial issues in formulating party policies and refrain from making any appeal to voters based on race. All voters would be addressed in terms of the reform and economic issues dividing the Republican party from the Democratic party. Any deemphasis of race, they believed, was bound to lower the level of race hatred in campaigns and raise the level of politics generally. They assumed, of course, that the Democrats, as the party of white supremacy, would be unable to appeal to the black vote and thus black voters would have no choice but to cast their ballots in terms of the party that best represented their individual self-interest. The same would hold true for the whites. Because white voters would no longer perceive the Republican party as the party of the black and tans, they, too, would gradually shift their thinking away from the racial basis of politics. For the first time since 1865 southerners would have a real choice between two parties with clearly defined issues and goals.

In time, as the economic policies of the Republican party won over more and more whites, the numerical strength of each party would nearly equalize, and an intense competition would develop. With race no longer an issue, the Republicans would begin winning elections, and this would force the Democrats to throw out their corrupt leaders and to campaign on real issues rather than racial fears and stereotypes. The result would be closely fought elections in which the votes of individual black citizens, only five percent of whom could vote in Virginia in 1928, would be needed and welcomed by both parties. This in turn would revitalize and expand the democratic process and revolutionize the southern way of life. Because the elections would be hotly contested yet devoid of racial politics, both parties would presumably have to offer services and programs that would benefit blacks, who would thereby gain from this "revolution" far more than they had under the current corrupt and totally ineffective system.[8]

Southern Democrats were genuinely fearful of such a reformed, white-led Republican party. According to one scholar of southern politics, Democratic leaders had realistically assessed the effect of such a party and had concluded that white supremacy, the basis of Democratic dominance, could not survive in a two-party South.[9] Anderson and Wise perceived this and predicted that whites would flock to the type of reformed party that they had outlined because they were disgusted by the corrupt, self-serving Democrats who offered the voters little or nothing yet remained in power merely by their adroit use of the stereotype of the Negro-dominated Republican party. They might also have cited the already substantial success of the lily-white movement within the Republican state parties in the South. Indeed, Anderson was popularly identified with this lily-white movement. However, as lily-white politicians did not measure up to their standards of leadership, Anderson and Wise made no effort to associate their vision of the reform party with many lily-white politicians.[10] This was an important distinction that Hoover but few, if any, blacks recognized.

Southern whites who were dissatisfied with both the Republican and the Democratic parties in the South in the late 1920s might have seen some virtue in the "revolution" championed by Anderson and Wise, but there were obvious and serious problems with it. Because blacks would be excluded from all party leadership and thus effectively prevented from being either elected or appointed to public office, they would naturally interpret their exclusion both as a violation of their constitutional rights and as an abandonment of the historic protection of black people by the Republican party. This exclusion would naturally lead them to see the reformers as nothing more than racist lily-white politicians.[11] They would question the motives of the reformers and call for explanations. But, as Anderson and Wise had stressed, the reformers could not publicly reveal their good intentions toward blacks or identify the eventual benefits that their "revolution" would bring to black people. This silence was a necessity, argued Anderson and Wise, imposed by the current racial nature of southern politics, but it posed a fateful dilemma. On the one hand, if reformers explained how blacks would benefit, the Democrats would quickly distort their explanations and thereby have little difficulty in convincing fearful white voters that the "revolution" would elevate blacks more than whites and was thus merely a rhetorical ploy to hide the continuing black-and-tan nature of the Republican party. On the other hand, if the reformers did not clarify their intentions and differentiate themselves from the lily-whites, blacks would conclude that the rhetoric of "reform" was a flimsy disguise for antiblack lily-whites who were actually attempting to force the black people out of politics entirely.

Anderson and Wise obviously expected too much from black people. Blacks were being asked to relinquish all leadership positions within the southern state parties and to wait for an indefinite period of years before they would realize any of the vague, alleged benefits. They were supposed to make these sacrifices without any assurances or explanations. Black disappointment and anger were therefore inevitable. Yet Anderson and Wise felt that their plan was so much better than the current situation that they were confident that it would work well. They based their confidence on the assumptions that the Democrats could not and would not welcome the disaffected blacks as a racial bloc into their white supremacist party, and that blacks would be forced to vote as individuals in terms of the issues separating the parties because neither of the two parties would initially court the black vote. In this way, whether or not they agreed with the methods employed by the reformers, they would nonetheless be forced to participate in and eventually realize the advantages of the revolution.

Hoover was ripe for Anderson and Wise's utopian vision of a southern "revolution." Appalled by peonage and other injustices, Hoover agreed that a new political order was necessary before anything substantial could be accomplished for blacks in the South. Moreover, references that Anderson and Wise made to corrupt, patronage-bloated black-and-tan politicians spoke directly to Hoover's humiliating experience only days earlier at the national convention. Prior to the convention he had been forced to testify before a Senate committee investigating campaign expenditures that he had not authorized and, indeed, knew nothing about payments to southern black-and-tan politicians in return for their delegation support. The *New York Times* was not convinced of his innocence, and progressive reformers repeated their demands for an end to the long-standing practice of buying the southern delegations. Following the convention, Sen. George Norris had publicly accused Hoover of having "bought" the nomination from southern black and tans. Thus while the Democrats had largely failed to implicate him in the scandals of the Harding administration, members of his own party had succeeded in casting doubt on his integrity. Corruption therefore entered Hoover's thinking at this time in a very personal and threatening manner. Word from Mabel Walker Willebrandt of the investigation and likely indictment of Perry Howard and the sensational allegations of southern Republican corruption put forth during Sen. Smith Brookhart's investigations also served to predispose him to the arguments of Anderson and Wise about the need to rid the party of corruption in the South, establish an impeccable elite group of new leaders and bring about a revolution that would serve blacks and the party better than the present system.

The Virginia reformers' opposition to lily-white Bascom Slemp also made good sense to Hoover. As national committeeman and former secretary to Calvin Coolidge, Slemp controlled the Republican organization in Virginia and had opposed Anderson both as a leader in the state and as a candidate for the vice-presidential nomination.[12] Slemp was a good example of the lily-white patronage boss who blocked reform and whose chief interest was control of federal jobs to strengthen his inconsequential political machine. To Hoover's thinking, all of the rascals had to be ousted—the corrupt as well as the narrowminded, provincial patronage politicians of both races. However, because Slemp was a smart politician who controlled the Virginia party as well as a close personal friend of President Coolidge, whose support was still important to the campaign, Hoover did not want to endanger the excellent prospects for carrying the state in November by irritating Slemp before the election. Instead, Hoover maintained a cordial, even close relationship with the suspicious Virginia boss until after his unprecedented victory, whereupon he quickly and unceremoniously dumped him and began promoting the efforts of Anderson and Wise to "reform" the state.[13]

Anderson and Wise were ecstatic over Hoover's receptiveness to their plan for a political, economic, and eventual racial transformation of the South. In fact, at the conclusion of their meeting Wise was also convinced that "the Republican leadership in the South had definitely passed to Henry W. Anderson."[14] Yet Hoover's grim determination to make a clean sweep of southern politics also worried them. They feared that the inexperienced candidate would say too much and thus lose rather than gain southern adherents. More specifically, they feared that clever Democrats, long suspicious of Anderson's loyalty to the principles of white supremacy, would try to provoke Hoover into a public defense of Negroes with the taunt that he opposed segregation.[15] This fear also suggested that Anderson and Wise had reason to be concerned about Hoover's personal attitude toward black people and how that could be damaging if it was exposed to southern whites. In any case, if he wanted to see the southern "revolution" become a reality, they warned him, he must not respond to racial questions or charges but must instead allow his local supporters, who knew best the varying local attitudes toward race, to handle all questions dealing with black people. Hoover must say nothing about race or about their hopes for a southern "revolution." The success of the "revolution" depended upon his enthusiastic support and upon their ability to fool the Democrats.[16]

Hoover heeded their advice and believed that they were exactly the type of "important" leaders who he hoped would be attracted to the party and who must be recruited vigorously in the future. With such men he could build a new business-and-industrial Republican elite that could successfully challenge the old Democratic planter class and their followers. Moreover, it would be an elite of accomplished leaders who had risen to the top on the basis of merit rather than politics and patronage. Like Hoover, the new elite would believe that public servants must be well qualified, respected, and dedicated to honest, efficient service in the public interest. Men who had first proven their leadership in the professions or in business and who looked forward to the new challenges and the new responsibilities of public service, just as he had done, were exactly the type of leaders who could rout the tenacious, corrupt political bosses of both parties and of both races.

Hoover was willing to go to great lengths to attract spirited leaders of proven ability and moral worth who would offer their talents despite the personal hazards and financial loss of public service.[17] If he could attract the best class of southern whites—men of idealism and goodwill who were not antiblack and whose leadership would be helpful to Negroes—then Hoover believed that blacks themselves might well agree that they would have far less to fear and, in time, far more to gain from the transfer of leadership from corrupt, ineffectual black and tans, who only ensured Democratic victory, to a dynamic Republican lily-white, but not racist, elite.[18] Given his limited knowledge of southern politics in 1928, it seemed an appealing thought. If the southern "revolution," about which Anderson and Wise dreamed, became a reality, Hoover could see real benefits from the change. So too could his black southern advisers. Even if Anderson and Wise were less concerned with helping Negroes than they suggested, Hoover heartily agreed with the logic that everyone would benefit from clean, vigorous political competition in a progressive, transforming society where democracy was a vital force and where clean government and economic issues rather than race decided elections. "No one," Hoover told Anderson, "will be more anxious to join you in this program you suggest than will I."[19]

Even though Hoover was enthusiastic about the southern "revolution," he did not think that it was appropriate for every southern state. Not all Republican parties in the South were either corrupt or ineffectual. Some progress had already been made in a number of states by honest and impressive leaders, such as those in North Carolina. Moreover, he did not intend to force out honest black leaders or, as some critics feared, abandon the Negro people to the mercies of a new white supremacy, Republican style.[20]

Hoover desperately wanted to believe that the "revolution" led by his own new elite would transform the South while it eventually improved the life of Negroes and even incorporated them into both political parties. Today our understanding of the multifaceted and deep-seated nature of racism reveals that Hoover did not have a clear understanding either of racism or of southern society. The obstacles to a southern transformation in 1928 were simply too great. Yet given his hazy awareness of complex racial realities, the notion of a southern reformation beginning in several states and eventually spreading throughout the South appealed to his idealistic, even utopian faith in the ability of the United States to overcome its problems.

7. Southern Campaign

The chief architect of the southern campaign was Hubert Work. From the outset, well prior to the beginning of the primaries, Work had pressured lily-white southern state delegations, especially those from Alabama, Virginia, Texas, Louisiana, and Florida, for early endorsements.[1] He had also kept in close contact with the leading white Republican politicians of the South.[2] When southerners needed funds and advice, he sent Rush Holland, a close friend who lived in the same hotel and who often shared long evening conversations with Work.[3] After Holland had been exposed by the Senate committee investigating presidential campaign expenditures, Work turned to Horace A. Mann as his principal southern operative. Moreover, it was Work who gently yet categorically rejected Hoover's order. He certainly did not consider it "most imperative" that new black leaders replace the discredited ones in Mississippi.

This soft-spoken sixty-eight-year-old former physician had been first postmaster general and then secretary of the interior during the Harding-Coolidge years.[4] Although he was considered to be well versed in political campaigning and organization, the pundits of the capital did not regard Work's political expertise highly, and as the campaign progressed, Hoover became increasingly distressed by the frictions Work generated and by the haphazard, decentralized manner in which he conducted the campaign.[5] He was also known for his "testy manner" toward blacks, and as early as April, the Washington (D.C.) *Eagle* warned Hoover that should Work be appointed to a top campaign position, he would do Hoover "irreparable harm" among black people.[6] Still, Hoover could find no one better qualified to conduct the campaign; he valued Work's loyalty, admired him personally, and generally accepted his judgment.[7]

In handling the South, Work advised doing nothing in the open that would alienate white voters. He opposed Hoover's call for new black leaders and overt activity even in the regular Republican organizations. As he told Charles A. Jonas of North Carolina on 25 June, "If we make no mistakes nor say any unfortunate things, this campaign will turn the biggest Republican majority in history."[8]

Work's plan instead emphasized the encouragement of "independent Hoover organizations" of anti-Smith Democrats who supported Hoover and who had to be allowed to select their own local leaders and vote for their own local officials. He assured Hoover that these "supporters coming to us daily are men in important positions" who had been forming their opposition to the leaders of the Democratic party over a four-year span. Work obviously believed that any attempt to intervene in the bitter, complicated internal state struggles at this late date, especially if Hoover were to appoint "some colored representatives and leadership," might well unify the warring Democrats behind their time-tested banner of white supremacy. The immediate object was to keep the Democrats divided while welcoming "men in important positions." The political situation in the South, he advised Hoover, was "almost perfect," and he insisted upon keeping it that way.[9]

Work's optimism arose from his knowledge of the organization that he had already created for the South. Republicans were, in fact, operating covertly, and just as Rush Holland had taken the brunt of the publicity during the primary stage of the campaign, Horace Mann became the target in the opposition press during the postconvention contest. Work was careful to remain in the background. He did not want a repetition of the Holland exposé. To avoid publicity, he established Mann in a separate office in the Munsey Building and allowed him to develop a virtually independent southern operation, to keep his own records, to make political arrangements and confidential promises in the South, and to expend campaign funds without apparent supervision or accountability. As there had already been entirely too many editorials and headlines about the South, Work's chief goals were secrecy and Hoover votes, and the Mystery Man, as Horace Mann was soon dubbed by a puzzled press corps, knew how to secure those votes.[10]

Mann's sudden rise to a position of influence within the Republican ranks, coupled with his mysterious activities in the South, naturally encouraged a good deal of speculation in the press. Actually, Mann was not quite as mysterious as some believed. A large person with a pleasant, reassuring voice and direct manner, he had been recruited for the campaign by Claudius Huston, the wealthy Tennessee businessman and former assistant secretary of commerce under Hoover.[11] Huston concentrated his considerable political talents during the campaign in the East, where Hoover faced serious internal opposition from party leaders. He had worked with Mann for a Harding victory in Tennessee, and both had migrated to the capital in 1921, Huston as an assistant secretary of commerce and Mann as a lawyer specializing in tax cases before the Internal Revenue Service.[12] Robert R. Church, Jr., the millionaire black Republican leader in Tennessee, distrusted both Mann and Huston as lily-white opportunists, while northern Democratic critics, especially Charles Michelson, argued that Mann was under Hoover's direct orders to eliminate black leaders from the party in the South. Michelson insisted that Hoover was the architect of a new lily-white strategy that Mann was executing covertly. Nonetheless, however plausible they seemed at the time, Michelson's speculations were exaggerated and misleading.[13]

The covert strategy that Mann employed was essentially the same one that Work, Huston, and Holland had begun implementing prior to the convention and that Davis may well have cleverly identified in complaints at an early date in Georgia.[14] Basically, those on Hoover's campaign staff who were most knowledgeable about southern politics, namely, Work, Huston, Mann, and Holland, had decided to take full advantage of the intense anti-Smith feeling in the South by creating and nurturing independent pro-Hoover political organizations staffed by angry white Democrats who would not otherwise associate themselves with the despised regular Republican organizations. Their objective was simply to encourage white Democrats for Hoover or *Hoovercrats* to break from the regular Democratic state parties. National leaders hoped that following the election they could recruit the mavericks for the party. As Work explained it to Hoover, it was the "men in important positions," meaning prominent, highly respectable, often wealthy businessmen and influential white Democrats who would win the South for Hoover, not the discredited black-and-tan organizations.[15]

Moreover, black leaders had been consulted. Robert R. Moton, Albon Holsey, and Claude Barnett did not consider Mann to be a serious threat to southern black leadership. Both Holsey and Barnett worked closely with Mann during the campaign. The evidence strongly suggests that these black leaders knew of the strategy of attracting dissident Democratic voters and leaders to the Republican party in the South and approved of that strategy.[16] Indeed, Barnett explicitly admitted that they knew and approved of attracting new white leaders and voters.[17] Black and tans had cooperated with Democrats for years, and Hoover's black campaign managers believed that the new white Republican leaders would respect and be cooperative with the established black leaders.[18]

As the campaign progressed, Kelly Miller, a black sociologist at Howard University, became aware of Hoover's plan to "set up a new leadership, white and black, who come with clean hands," and offered him some advice. "I am willing to concede," he stated, "that in the present state of racial prejudice it is difficult to the point of impossibility to build up an effective competitive Republican party in the South under exclusive Negro leadership." He conceded still further that "to carry out your evident purpose to split the solid South it may have been necessary to remove Negroes from chief places in state organizations." But, at the same time, he continued, Hoover must be careful not to "stamp upon the Negro's forehead a brand of political unworthiness." Only by candor and courage could Hoover hope to succeed. Above all, Hoover must explain to blacks how they would benefit from the new white leadership, and he must once again exhibit the courage he had shown in desegregating the Department of Commerce by openly denouncing the lily-whites and "Ku Kluxers."[19] Hoover ignored Miller's advice, and his refusal to explain his intentions gave blacks little choice but to assume that his actions were those of a candidate pursuing an antiblack strategy.

At first knowledgeable observers did not believe that the Republicans could actually win many electoral votes in the solid South. In early October the editors of the *New York Times* confidently predicted that the only state that the Republicans might win was Kentucky.[20] Southerners knew better. As the campaign progressed increasingly large numbers joined the Hoovercrat movement and Republican campaign fund raisers were hard pressed to supply the ever-expanding needs of the new southern organizations.[21] Al Smith helped, of course. David Burner's excellent analysis of Smith contrasts Hoover's attractiveness with political provincialism and the intense prejudices about religion and Prohibition that characterized the campaign.[22]

By contrast to Smith, Hoover was the more progressive candidate, yet he carefully couched his appeal to the South in economic terms.[23] He was well aware of the growing sentiment for tariff protection, industrial development, farm relief, and flood control. While he was secretary of commerce, Hoover had become familiar with southern needs, and he had developed a genuine interest in and even an enthusiasm for promoting the economic development of the South. To Hoover the South was an immensely rich but underdeveloped region with great industrial and agricultural potential that the politicians in Washington had neglected for too long. His campaign therefore emphasized promises of federal policies that would promote economic development.[24]

More important to Hoover's pragmatic managers was the opportunity to establish a solid foothold for the party as an alternative to the Democrats. Republicans had already made some gains in parts of West Virginia, Virginia, North Carolina, Tennessee, and Florida; and there was good reason to believe that this process could be strengthened and expanded.[25] Al Smith's Roman Catholic faith, his open contempt for Prohibition, and his urban and Tammany Hall affiliations all presented opportunities for further Republican inroads.[26] Just as important, Hoover himself appealed to many southern interests. He was a dry, Protestant, small-town-born, self-made millionaire with a distinguished reputation as an international humanitarian, an extraordinary secretary of commerce, and the hero of the Mississippi Valley flood of 1927, who had repeatedly advocated federal assistance for the rapid economic development of the South.

Against these almost invulnerable qualifications the Democrats fell back upon their traditional white supremacy and hatred of the Negro to fend off the aggressive Hoovercrats.[27] The traditional association of the Negro with the Republican party was a prominent if not the predominant theme for Democrats.[28] Often Democrats simultaneously argued conflicting beliefs—that the Republicans were attempting "to hide the fact that they wish to make the negroes equal to whites" and at the same time steal the banner of white supremacy as well.[29] To refresh and reinforce the Reconstruction stereotype of the alliance between Republicans and blacks, Democrats urged blacks to declare openly their Republican loyalty and, among other things, falsely charged that Hoover had refused to speak to a white audience in Mississippi during the 1927 flood because he preferred to address Negroes at Mound Bayou.[30] Hoover's desegregation of the Census Bureau was perhaps the favorite target. Sen. Cole Blease, for example, sent his denunciation of the order, which had been published in the *Congressional Record*, in franked envelopes to his constituents.[31]

Most irritating to Democrats and blacks generally were the efforts of some Republican lily-whites and Hoovercrats to steal the mantle of white supremacy while trying to deny it to supporters of Al Smith. For example, lily-whites widely circulated a pamphlet that featured a photograph of a large Negro male, allegedly a Tammany-appointed civil service commissioner of New York City, towering over an attractive white female stenographer. The implication was that a Democratic victory would result in a flood of black political appointees who would control white employees. Another tactic of Republican lily-whites was their use of the "white man in the woodpile" theme, a transparent stratagem through which blacks were urged to voice their open support of Al Smith to white Democrats. Where the Negro vote was less feared, as in Alabama, anti-Catholic propaganda was emphasized and circulated, especially by Republican national committeeman Oliver D. Street. Democratic national leaders also alleged that similar materials originated in Horace Mann's office in Washington, D.C. Many of these and other charges are well known to scholars.[32]

What is less well known was the manner in which Hoover's top campaign managers allowed their thirst for an unprecedented victory to prompt them, on occasion, to utter lies and even racial slurs. Coming from the campaign leaders, these statements helped to lower the level of campaigning in the South. One of the worst precedents was set by Work himself. In response to allegations that Hoover's desegregation order proved that he favored the social equality of the races, Work flatly denied that Hoover had ever issued any such desegregation order. Work's desire for southern white votes was never more blatant. "Changes in the location of these people was [*sic*] an administrative necessity," he lied, "and was [*sic*] done by some of his people, rather than by himself."[33] Other top aides offered differing versions of the false denial: that the desegregation had been only a temporary arrangement, or that whites working near the Negroes had complained of their proximity and brought about their dispersion in preference to integration. Twice Hoover himself succumbed to political expedience, when in response to a southern inquiry he denied that he favored desegregation. The desire to crack and "revolutionize" the solid South at times took precedence over immediate racial progress.[34]

In October, as the campaign swung into its most heated phase, Gov. Theodore G. Bilbo of Mississippi did his part to provoke Hoover's supporters into blunders. When Bilbo proclaimed that Hoover had danced with a Negro woman, George Akerson, Hoover's political secretary, rose to the bait. Akerson had cultivated the support of the lily-whites in Mississippi prior to the convention, and in reaction to Bilbo's charge he lost his self-control and revealed the depth of his disrespect for blacks.[35]

The woman to whom Bilbo referred was Mary Booze, a national Republican committeewoman from Mississippi and wife of Eugene P. Booze, leader of the economically independent Negro farming community of Mound Bayou, the settlement that Hoover had addressed in 1927. Hoover genuinely respected both Mary and Eugene Booze, and it is possible that he had them in mind when he informed Work of the need to replace Howard with reputable black leaders.[36] In any case, as the claim was false, Mary Booze immediately issued a public denial, but her denial was virtually lost in the furor over Akerson's response.[37] Bilbo's claim that Hoover had danced with a Negro woman, Akerson retorted, was "the most indecent and unworthy statement in the whole of a bitter campaign." It was, furthermore, the most "untruthful and ignoble assertion ever made by a public man in the United States."[38]

Bilbo was delighted to have struck a nerve, but Eugene and Mary Booze and other black leaders were dismayed and angered.[39] Eugene Booze chided Akerson for having made a political fool of himself. Bilbo "drew you out in such a way as to bring about a division among Colored Republicans in the doubtful States," Booze informed him, and judging from the deluge of telegrams and letters to Booze and from the reaction of the black press, Bilbo had succeeded admirably. Akerson halfheartedly apologized but insisted that Booze and apparently everyone else had "taken an entirely wrong interpretation" of his response.[40]

Hoover was much disturbed by the intense racial hatred generated as the campaign progressed. On the one hand, he found racial politics repugnant and confessed that he did not know how to deal with it. On the other hand, he was not above political expedience when he believed it would serve his cause. He confided to Ruth Hanna McCormick, who had warned him of the Ku Klux Klan's bigotry in Illinois, "Like you I am anxious about the character of the stuff that is being put out by certain extremists." Still, he doubted that he could do much to stop them. As these racial extremists were "not subject to any restraint," he found it difficult to decide on the most effective "method of strong denunciation that will separate us from them." What Hoover seemed to be telling McCormick was that he and his advisers had not been able to find a political method that would "separate us from them" without jeopardizing the booming Hoovercrat movement in the South.[41]

On 6 October 1928 Hoover finally agreed to make a direct appeal for southern votes. His southern advisers attached great significance to the "Southern speech," as Rush Holland called it; he thought it "the most important speech you will deliver in the campaign." Horace Mann and other south-ern experts agreed, and they gave it their careful scrutiny.[42] Hoover's address in Elizabethton, Tennessee, recapitulated many themes about southern prog-ress that he had developed in previous years while he was secretary of com-merce.[43] He emphasized the end of sectionalism and the ways in which the Republican party would further the great economic revival of the South. It was a long speech covering many topics, but in it was a one-line sentence, which critics at the time and since have identified as a signal of encouragement to insurgent lily-whites. "I believe in the merit system of the Civil Service," he stated, "and I believe further that appointive offices must be filled by those who deserve the confidence and respect of the communities they serve." To some, this was a veiled promise to eliminate all blacks from federal patronage jobs and from leadership positions in the party.[44]

Whether this one sentence constitutes sufficient evidence to hold Hoover responsible for an appeal to anti-Negro voters is debatable. Certainly Robert R. Church, Jr., one of the most knowledgeable and militant southern black politicians of his day, did not think so. Church congratulated Hoover on his "wonderful speech." Moreover, in his official acceptance speech given at Stanford University on 11 August, Hoover had used almost the same words: "Appointive office, both North, South, East, and West, must be based solely on merit, character, and reputation in the community in which the appointee is to serve; as it is essential for the proper performance of their duties that officials shall enjoy the confidence and respect of the people whom they serve." Official corruption, which he felt too many Americans had come to view with indifference during the Prohibition era, was a "double wrong" that was "treason to the state. It is destructive of self-government." At that point no one took issue with this goal. These words were more than mere campaign rhetoric. Hoover meant it when he thundered that "moral incompetency by those entrusted with government is a blightening [*sic*] wind upon private integrity." He promised to root out corruption at any cost. These were deeply held beliefs, which he would act upon as soon as he attained power.[45]

Having already made the point forcefully in his acceptance speech, Hoover could have deleted it from his southern speech. Because he did not, his opponents argued that the statement was deliberately included to reassure southerners who were anxious about the appointment of blacks to prominent federal and state party positions.[46] Indeed, recently available evidence estab-lishes that he did try to appeal to white southerners, yet not for the reasons many of his critics assumed. As early as August, Anderson and Wise had traveled to San Francisco to advise Hoover on his official acceptance speech, and during their discussions Hoover not only reiterated his approval of the southern "revolution" plan but, according to Wise, also "pledged himself" to adopt Anderson's "negro policy." On the basis of this evidence, one must conclude that both the sentence in the acceptance speech and the almost identical one in the Elizabethton address in October were at least partially designed to appeal to southern white voters.[47] In fairness to Hoover, it must also be said that his object was the promotion of the "revolution" and that the appeal to white voters was not a cynical appeal to racism. But because he would not publicly explain his intentions this could not have been known at the time, and the activities of Horace Mann and other southern lily-whites certainly did not suggest noble motives.

In fact, noble motives were no more evident in Virginia, the home state of Anderson and Wise, than they were elsewhere in the South. Blacks in Virginia, for example, could not understand what the Republicans intended and quickly became confused. On the one hand, the reform Republicans were actively discouraging black support, while on the other the white supremacist Democrats were making determined efforts to attract the entire black voting bloc to their own party. Anderson and Wise had assumed that the Democrats would not be able to make an open appeal to blacks without relinquishing white supremacy and thus lose substantial numbers of their white constituents. But they were proved wrong by the Democrats, who pragmatically and cynically appealed to blacks to join them while at the same time they continued to promote their usual campaign of racial hatred against Republicans and Negroes. This flurry of sudden, unexpected tactics by both Republicans and Democrats created a strange, confusing, almost surrealistic political atmosphere.[48]

Wise was furious over the callous duplicity of his Democratic opponents. As the campaign hatred increased, he warned blacks of the Democrats' tactic, yet despite black appeals for an explanation of the reformers' attitude toward them, Wise would address them only in vague generalities. He advised them, for example, to vote as individuals and in terms of the issues dividing the two parties rather than allowing "yourselves to be exploited as a race." He pointedly refused to solicit the black vote and repeatedly insisted that they must not vote "collectively" or "as a separate racial group" or "under the orders of any racial organization." Race must no longer be a political issue, not even to black people. When blacks asked him if Hoover and Anderson had agreed to exclude blacks from federal patronage, despite their support of the Republican party, he admitted that this was true. But in excluding them from patronage, he argued, "there may be a more real regard for the Negro race than a sudden appeal for their vote by the Smithites." How this exclusion demonstrated "more real regard" was not explained.[49]

Wise assumed that blacks would misconstrue his hints of goodwill and he was more correct in this assumption than he or Anderson were on the many others they made about racial politics in the South. Although Wise and Anderson might well have been sincere in attempting to telegraph their goodwill to blacks without, at the same time, alarming whites, it is difficult to imagine how blacks could accept their claim of "real regard for the Negro race" while reform Republicans refused to accept black leaders in the party, denied them federal patronage, and refused to solicit the black vote. Albeit reluctantly blacks protested their exclusion by increasingly giving their votes to the audacious, hypocritical, yet clever Virginia Democrats.

Confused and irritated by the convolutions of racial politics in the campaign, Hoover erroneously predicted to Anderson, "The campaign [in Virginia] will be decided on color prejudice as much as anything else."[50] Yet he would not speak out forcefully in defense of the Negro.[51] Hoover was caught in a trap of his own making. On the one hand, he had no intention of either abandoning honest black southern leaders or his party's historic commitment to the Negro people. He also claimed he wished that he could devise a "method of strong denunciation" that would separate his supporters from the racial and religious "extremists." Yet, on the other hand, he was determined to drive out the corrupt Republicans throughout the South while taking full advantage of the unique splintering of the Democrats to attract an elite white leadership that would transform the South. Of the two, the latter desire proved to be more immediate; at any rate, it was the one that Work, Mann, Holland, and even his vice-presidential candidate, Charles Curtis, urged upon him, though for less idealistic reasons. They also agreed with Anderson and Wise on the need for silence on all racial matters. Any public explanation of his intentions or hopes, they argued, would allow the Democrats to close ranks behind white supremacy and doom Republican hopes.[52]

In the last analysis Hoover accepted these urgings of his campaign advisers. He did not explain to blacks why he believed that white Republican reformers would ultimately be more beneficial to black people than would the black and tans. Rather than devise, as Hoover called it, a "method of strong denunciation" of racists, he settled for twice repudiating bigotry in broad, sweeping terms, emphasizing religious prejudice, and then tried to ignore these issues.[53]

It was not so much what Hoover and Al Smith said about black issues as what they failed to say and do that gave blacks the greatest cause for concern. In the cities of the South, especially in Richmond, Portsmouth, Norfolk, Roanoke, Augusta, Savannah, Raleigh, Nashville, Memphis, and Atlanta, an "undercover" campaign for Negro votes by Democrats, Republicans, and Hoovercrats had deliberately and steadily intensified hatreds directed against Negroes. Members of each of these competing groups denounced blacks and championed white supremacy and racism while at the same time making covert efforts to capture the black vote.[54] Responsible white southerners were appalled by the extreme racial hatred unleashed by the contest, and some began making forceful public appeals to halt the vitriolic and "dangerous" charges and countercharges.[55]

On 25 October thirty-four prominent black leaders in both the North and the South put aside their political differences to band together in an "Appeal to America" for an end to the race baiting in the South. United in the "solemn conviction that the Presidential campaign of 1928, more than in previous campaigns since the Civil War" had treated the Negro unfairly, they accused the leaders of both parties of having permitted "without protest, public and repeated assertions on the platform, in the press, and by word of mouth, that color and race constitute in themselves an inputation of guilt and crime." The constant emphasis upon "racial contempt and hatred," they pointed out, was "an appeal to the lowest and most primitive of human motives and as long as that appeal can successfully be made, there is for this land no real peace, no sincere religion, no national unity, no social progress, even in matters far removed from race."[56]

Responding directly to the stereotype of the corrupt black politician and the sensational indictment of Perry Howard, the Negro leaders reassured the South that they had "absolutely no quarrel with standards of ability and character which will bring to public life the very highest type of public servant." Although they were "more troubled over political dishonesty among black folks than you are among white," it was "too late for us to submit to political slavery and we must earnestly protest against the unchallenged assumptions that every American Negro is dishonest and incompetent and that color itself is a crime. Will white America make no protest? Will the candidates continue to remain silent?"[57]

Yet neither candidate took convincing action to halt the outpouring of racial bigotry. Each ignored the appeal while he blamed the other side. Smith's campaign manager John J. Raskob twice complained bitterly to Work over the religious and other forms of prejudice generated by Republican speakers and circulated in scandalous campaign literature.[58] Work responded to Raskob in a letter that had actually been written by Hoover denouncing the Democrats' use of "cowardly innuendo" and character assassination.[59] In the final analysis, however, prejudice against Al Smith in the South was obviously stronger and more widespread than were the unprincipled attacks on Hoover. Whatever the merits and intensity of these charges, neither candidate can escape responsibility for not repeatedly and more forcefully denouncing the racial and other bigotry that grew alarmingly during their contest for the presidency.

The hatreds generated by the campaign bigotry tainted the great victory that Hoover achieved in 1928. He would have won without help from bigots in any section of the country. Although he correctly presented himself as an honest public servant, his failure to discipline free-wheeling subordinates immediately and to disavow bigoted "extremists" convincingly were great mistakes that would generate still more damaging hatred against him in the future. Immediately following Hoover's victory, John J. Raskob, aided by his skillful propagandist Charles Michelson, began still another campaign aimed at portraying the winner as a bigot to the American people.[60] Hoover would serve only one term, and throughout its four years vicious political attacks on him spawned by the hatreds generated during the campaign would continue until, defeated by the depression and suffering from self-inflicted wounds, he would leave the White House one of the most widely hated presidents in recent American history.

When the votes were counted, Hoover had carried West Virginia, Kentucky, Tennessee, Virginia, North Carolina, Florida, and Texas, a total of seven southern states. It was a stunning southern victory. Surprisingly, perhaps, the overwhelming majority of black voters in the North were also Hoover supporters. Many blacks who were disillusioned by his evasiveness on racial issues and his appeal to southerners voted for him reluctantly. Not privy to his utopian faith in a southern "revolution," they worried about what appeared to be the still shadowy outlines of a potentially repressive southern strategy. Yet despite their growing doubts, black people generally clung to the hope that Hoover and the Republicans were neither as overtly racist nor as dangerous to them as were the Democrats generally. The credit for this last glimmer of faith belongs to those black Republican supporters whose trust in Hoover during the campaign resulted from close personal contact.

8. Hoover's Doctors

At the same time that Hoover secretly adopted the utopian but fatally flawed reform strategy for the South, he also began to reorient his attitude toward black politicians in the North as well. This change originated at the national nominating convention when black politicians charged that his candidacy menaced racial interests. Indeed, these politicians began accusing him of being antiblack and of pursuing a "lily-white strategy" even before Hoover had in fact decided upon any particular presidential policy toward either the South or blacks. The charges had erupted during the credentials contests in which the pro-Hoover lily-white delegations from Florida, Louisiana, and Texas won recognition. Some, like Perry Howard, had correctly interpreted the lily-white victories as nothing more than the need to thwart the stop-Hoover movement.

By demonstrating iron discipline and control before the balloting commenced, the credentials committee had gathered enough votes to put Hoover within reach of a first-ballot victory. Other blacks believed that Negro rights and prestige had been damaged by the pro-Hoover strategy of the credentials committee, and on 14 June these more militant Negroes had presented a resolution to the platform committee demanding that the party leadership reaffirm its loyalty to black people by adopting planks to enforce the Fourteenth and Fifteenth amendments, to ensure that government employees were hired in strict compliance with the civil service laws, to enact federal antilynching legislation, and to disavow those lily-whites in the party who sought "to eliminate the colored citizen by discrimination, intimidation, and chicanery."[1]

The platform committee refused, agreeing only to repeat the party's earlier pledge to work toward antilynching legislation. Black disillusionment and the split between black leaders had deepened during the Texas contest. When the credentials committee had seated R. B. Creager's pro-Hoover lily-white faction rather than the anti-Hoover black and tans led by Gooseneck Bill McDonald, some black leaders objected that blacks should not be forced to support the candidate favored by a majority of the credentials committee as the requirement for their recognition by the convention. Loyal black Republicans should be seated regardless of which candidate the state delegation might favor. Equally obnoxious was the Texas law under which state party managers could call state conventions to select the entire delegation to the national convention. By honoring the Texas law, the credentials committee had accepted "a race-destroying precedent." Because blacks were excluded from participation in state conventions in the South, the only fair and just method was the established one of selecting some delegates by district vote and others at large. To impress the convention with the seriousness of their complaint, they brought their protest directly to the floor of the national convention for debate, whereupon Mabel Walker Willebrandt, the head of the credentials committee, won an easy victory. Further angered by the rebuff, these militants, including J. Finley Wilson, leader of the Colored Elks, and W. C. Hueston, a skillful lawyer and politician, immediately created the National Negro Voters League.

Ostensibly the purpose of the league was to expose and to bring into line those blacks who had refused to challenge the Texas case. But it had another, more significant purpose as well. Its founders argued that the league was necessary "to ascertain where the Negro stands in the Republican party" and "to play with pitiless publicity upon those of our race who vote in political conventions and elsewhere against race interest and then seek prominence and priority as the price thereof."[2]

Not all blacks welcomed the new league, however. Albon Holsey feared that the "entire colored situation" had been "menaced by selfish factions." His worry illustrated the foreboding that overcame black Hoover enthusiasts at the convention.[3] All were disappointed by the party's refusal to expand its platform on black rights beyond its previous promise to pass legislation against lynching. What they differed over was whether party policy under Hoover was, indeed, taking a new, less supportive turn and whether black militancy would help or hurt the quest for Negro progress. Some angry black Republicans warned that in the future both the candidate and his black supporters would be judged on the basis of "race interest" rather than by party loyalty or faith in Herbert Hoover. In rebuttal, Perry Howard, who at that point was still loyal to Hoover, had insisted that faith in Hoover was justified, for he was "a first rate black and tan" who had "kept the faith." An important problem in the black leadership split was that blacks themselves could not agree on the direction of Hoover's leadership. From the conflicting evidence available to black leaders at the convention, both pro-Hoover and anti-Hoover positions could be and were vigorously argued.

Thus, the creation of the National Negro Voters League was a dramatic signal of the serious division among black Republican leaders over the meaning of Hoover's nomination. Soon afterward the quick indictment of Perry Howard stunned and angered virtually all black Republicans. For some it was conclusive evidence that Hoover had been double-crossing all black leaders and imposing a lily-white strategy on the credentials committee.[4] In retrospect this seems a plausible conclusion. Black Hoover enthusiasts were perhaps the most dismayed and certainly the most damaged politically. They had argued forcefully that Hoover was a friend to black people and had defended the selection of pro-Hoover delegations, even lily-white ones, as an unfortunate but necessary political accommodation. The Howard indictment now cast grave doubts on their common sense.

As soon as he heard the news of the indictment, Holsey warned Moton that it was "sure to alienate a large bloc of negro votes which represent those who think he is a victim of racial prejudice *only*." Holsey was correct. Outraged black leaders such as Walter White already had reservations about Howard's politics, but like many others, he concluded that the indictment and Howard's suspension as assistant attorney general were "due to his race and not so much because of what he may or may not have done." In White's opinion, Republican leaders had begun a calculated attack on black political leadership in the South. Well aware of this possibility, black Republicans vigorously protested the action.[5]

According to Barnett, Moton immediately appealed to the "highest in the land," presumably meaning Hoover, but to no avail. Acting in his capacity as editor of the Associated Negro Press, Barnett went directly to Willebrandt with a series of relentless, carefully formulated questions. In his report to Moton, Barnett vividly recalled the encounter: "She squirmed, got angry, pounded her desk, said I could not force her to say what she did not want to say, denied there was anything political in her prosecution of Perry, that he deserved to be prosecuted, that he had been convicted by his own files, and showed an intense personal dislike of Howard which she said the department shared."[6]

Barnett emerged from the stormy interview convinced that the assistant attorney general "wanted to get Perry." In an Associated Negro Press release he used Willebrandt's display of temper to demonstrate her personal distaste for Howard and to throw the onus of the prosecution on her.[7] Highlighting her anti-Catholicism and the use of her Prohibition enforcement duties to call attention to Al Smith's wetness, the editors of the *Nation* also condemned her prosecution of Howard as "cheap political blatherskiting."[8]

The conviction that Howard was an innocent victim of Hoover's lily-white strategy was overwhelming among black people. Howard later privately passed word to friends exonerating Hoover "from any blame" for the prosecution.[9] Much of the intense criticism was then directed at Willebrandt, but she was not as insensitive as some charged. To her credit, she did accept Howard's confidential argument that a trial in Mississippi during the campaign would be unfair and even dangerous to him and his codefendants and therefore agreed to a postponement, although she recognized that a delay would open her to plausible and damaging attacks from black people. "I am getting word from colored organizations themselves," she complained to Howard, "who have been stirred up on your behalf, to this effect: 'Well, if it weren't for political purposes, why didn't you try the case right away and give him a chance to prove he was innocent in time to work for this campaign.' "[10]

Howard disagreed with his black defenders who believed that a speedy trial would free him to resume active campaigning. Fearing for his personal safety, he pleaded for a delay until after the campaign. A trial now, he insisted, would amount to "turning me over to the mob" in Mississippi during an election in which the central issue was race-hatred, a hatred directed most especially at black Republicans. Should Willebrandt force him to trial during the campaign, Howard assured her that he had "no idea of escaping without violence."[11] Finally, on 25 October following a second lengthy conference, Willebrandt reluctantly agreed to a postponement until December.[12] Ironically, as Willebrandt had complained, this delay appeared to critics to be a deliberate political ploy to prevent Howard's possible acquittal from detracting from the stereotype of the corrupt black politician during the drive for southern white votes.[13]

Hoover also had been "greatly disturbed" by the charges against Howard.[14] He was doubtlessly disturbed too by the northern black politicians who had severely criticized him during the convention. Consequently he decided to replace the "politicians" with black Republicans more to his liking. Traditionally, the Black Cabinet had evolved over the years as an informal yet influential political organization composed of the capital's leading federal office-holders and the most powerful black politicians residing in Washington, D.C.[15] By creating a Colored Voters Division and handpicking its leaders, Hoover sought to guarantee that he would no longer be linked to any black "politicians" who might cause him further embarrassment. Moreover, the new CVD would give him the opportunity to elevate men with attributes that corresponded more closely to his own conception of leadership. He therefore suggested to Assistant Secretary of Commerce Walter F. Brown that he "take over the management of the colored people during the campaign."[16] Brown was an old Bull Moose Progressive with lengthy experience in Ohio and national politics who later became Hoover's postmaster general. Because this assignment was obviously going to be a difficult one, Brown apparently was none too anxious to assume it and Work showed no interest in the black vote at all. Finally, after considerable delay, on 14 July Hoover told Work he was "convinced that the question of [a Colored Voters Division for] northern negroes should be put up to Brown with full responsibility to organize it."[17]

What Brown faced was a number of highly diverse groups of disunited and feuding black leaders, each trying to control the new Colored Voters Division. Few doubted that Hoover would defeat Smith, and still fewer that the victor would serve two terms as president. Hoover's black supporters were eager for him to reverse the long-term trend of appointing fewer and fewer blacks to prestigious positions in the federal government. All could agree that respect and protection for black people would improve with the appointment of prominent black leaders to positions of responsibility within the federal government. Presumably, the faction that controlled the new Colored Voters Division would later also dominate Hoover's Black Cabinet and thereby have the greatest voice in securing the coveted federal posts and winning recognition as the undisputed leaders of blacks within the new administration and the Republican party.

Those most confident of success were the loyal supporters of Robert R. Moton. Holsey and Barnett were determined to elevate Moton to the political heights once occupied by his predecessor, Booker T. Washington. The three men had worked closely with Hoover during the Mississippi flood and had campaigned effectively for him both during the primaries and at the convention, where Barnett and Holsey were Hoover's official entertainment hosts for black delegates. They believed in Hoover, and they freely communicated that belief to all who would listen. They were delighted with Hoover's still-secret plan to attack peonage, his enthusiasm for the practical-oriented education offered at Tuskegee Institute, and by his constant emphasis upon strengthening black professional and business leadership through his support of the National Negro Business League and the National Urban League. Moton remained in the background at Tuskegee, but he had been of invaluable assistance in privately reassuring black doubters of Hoover's desire to advance Negro interests and of his confidence in Hoover's potential as a president.[18]

Politically most active of the Tuskegee or Moton faction was Claude Barnett. As owner of the Associated Negro Press, Barnett had come to know virtually all of the important black newspaper editors and politicians in the North and South.[19] He was also well known and respected by powerful Republican leaders such as William M. Butler, chairman of the Republican National Committee, and by Akerson, who uncharacteristically lavished praise on Barnett, assuring him that he was "counted as one of the closest friends of this organization."[20] Hoover himself thought highly of him after their 1926 confrontation over the need for a black business specialist in the Commerce Department.[21] Hoover admired Barnett's outspoken, direct approach to problems, whether in assessing deficiencies within the Commerce Department or in recommending changes in the flood relief program, and had responded most favorably to his criticism. The secretary also appreciated him as his most ardent public defender, who used his national news service to promote Hoover's candidacy.[22]

In their campaigning for Hoover, Barnett and Moton's private secretary, Albon Holsey, relied upon several good lawyer friends who shared their enthusiasm for Moton and Hoover. Among these were Clarence Vena from Toledo, Ohio, who worked closely with Walter Brown;[23] Melvin J. Chisum, a well-known Chicago conservative, who, however, opposed black unions and would one day bitterly oppose Hoover;[24] Homer G. Phillips of Saint Louis, head of the National Negro Bar Association;[25] and Cornelius Richardson, an active campaign organizer from Indianapolis.[26] At the appropriate time Moton would use all of his influence with Hoover to secure appointments for these men. During the campaign, however, the Tuskegee principal left most of the election details to Barnett and Holsey, while he focused most of his own attention on securing control of the Colored Voters Division.[27]

Throughout the lengthy, internal, and mostly silent struggle for preferment, Moton felt confident that he would win. This confidence received a big boost on 29 June when he spoke personally with Hoover.[28] For almost a month following that meeting he remained convinced that he would be the most influential Negro in the Hoover administration. Friends who had spoken with those close to Hoover constantly reinforced that impression. To his private secretary, Holsey, Moton confided that "Hoover said that anything that I said would be approved."[29]

Moton's chief rival was Dr. John R. Hawkins, a distinguished-looking, prosperous physician and owner of the Prudential Bank of Washington, D.C. Hawkins was a man of national influence and prestige. For many years, including those of Hoover's presidency, Hawkins was also financial secretary of the African Methodist Episcopal Church.[30] He was further known as a leader in promoting Negro rights. In 1919 he was executive secretary of the National Race Congress, which had attempted to use political pressure on President Wilson to safeguard Negro lives and rights during the infamous race riots of that year.[31] And as a member of the executive committee of the National Negro Business League, Hawkins had an exceptionally wide acquaintance among black business leaders. At the Kansas City convention he had seconded Hoover's nomination. Successful as a physician, church leader, banker, and political leader, Hawkins greatly appealed to Hoover.[32] Indeed, he was probably the best single example of the type of elite black leadership that Hoover most admired and wished to promote.

Another influential black Washingtonian and very close friend of Hawkins, Emmett J. Scott, had long been prominent in Republican politics. College educated and a onetime journalist, he had served for many years as private secretary to Booker T. Washington. From 1900 to 1920 he was secretary of the National Negro Business League, which Washington had founded and headed until Moton succeeded him.[33] Over the years Scott's leadership had been both widely admired and sharply criticized. During the First World War, for example, when Scott served as special assistant to Secretary of War Newton D. Baker, the younger, more militant W. E. B. Du Bois ridiculed Scott for allegedly failing to correct and to publicize deplorable conditions suffered by black soldiers.[34] Du Bois also leveled the same charge at Moton, who had worked with and had come to dislike Scott.[35] Unlike Moton, who refused to respond in kind, Scott bitterly resented Du Bois's attack, offered a spirited defense, and challenged Du Bois to a list of particulars. After the war the furor died, but Scott never forgave the editor of the *Crisis*.[36]

In 1919 Scott accepted the position of secretary-treasurer and business manager of the federally funded all-black Howard University in Washington,

D.C. Throughout the 1920s he remained active in Republican politics and in the National Negro Business League.[37] In 1928 he worked hard to popularize the need for a Negro legislative bureau in the capital that would scrutinize proposed federal legislation and sound the alarm whenever bills harmful to blacks were introduced in Congress. Scott publicized his concern by chastising Sen. George Norris, chairman of the Senate Judiciary Committee, for his insensitivity to bills that would hinder federal prosecution of peonage and for a bill that Norris had introduced without a public hearing, which Scott believed would have forced blacks to fight for their constitutional rights in state rather than federal courts.[38]

Also connected with Howard University was James A. Cobb, judge of the Municipal Court of Washington, D.C. Graduated from Howard Law School in 1919 and vice-dean of its law faculty from 1923 until 1929, Cobb rose rapidly in Republican circles. Only a few years out of law school he won appointment as a special assistant attorney general of the United States and was soon consulting with Booker T. Washington and other prominent black leaders on patronage appointments. In 1926 President Coolidge appointed him to succeed Robert H. Terrell as judge of the Municipal Court, an appointment that, in theory, should have taken him out of the more active political arena but that actually increased his influence on black Republican politics.[39] Highly regarded as an excellent speaker and advocate of black rights, Cobb would also serve on the board of directors of the NAACP, which he kept informed of the administration's policies and on likely Hoover patronage appointees so that the organization could check on their backgrounds before the appointments were confirmed.[40] Like Coolidge, Hoover was also very favorably impressed by Cobb. He reappointed him to another term as judge in 1930 and gave careful attention to Cobb's recommendations for federal appointments.[41]

Moton, Holsey, Barnett, Hawkins, Scott, and Cobb were all college educated, professionally oriented university administrators or businessmen who had built their careers and attained their success outside of the political arena. They operated from no political power base of their own, and although they were politically oriented and ambitious, they were not experienced, practical politicians who ran for office and got out the vote, which was an attribute that appealed to Hoover. Moreover they tended to share many of Hoover's social and political ideas. All except Hawkins had either been associated with or worked closely with Booker T. Washington. All agreed with the basic elements of Washington's emphasis upon advancement through education and business enterprise. Most were officers who were actively involved in the National Negro Business League. Collectively they represented an older generation of black leaders who believed that blacks could best advance by working within established institutions and through the Republican party. Seldom as yet had they offered public criticisms of American society or championed the bolder, newer methods advocated by W. E. B. Du Bois. Nonetheless, while more conservative in their thinking and especially in their methods than Du Bois or the NAACP, each of them was conscious of his obligation to help black people attain full citizenship and equal rights. To Hoover they were representatives of the black elite. In his opinion they, rather than the patronage politicians, were the natural leaders of their people and should hold the dominant black positions within the Republican party.

The differences that divided these men were at least as important as their similarities. Scott, Hawkins, and Cobb lived in Washington, D.C., where they had long been close to northern politics and politicians and associated with Howard University. By contrast, the Moton faction was decidedly oriented toward the political elevation of Moton, the educational philosophy and advancement of Tuskegee Institute, and the development of federal programs to help southern blacks. Moton's followers were keenly interested in federal agricultural agencies to help southern black farmers in expanding federal vocational and home economics programs, in new rural education extension programs, in federal flood control, and in Hoover's plan to attack southern peonage through the creation of the private land development corporation. These interests and goals naturally meant less to the more northern-oriented Scott, Hawkins, and Cobb. Although they were certainly not provincial in their programs or outlook, the two groups of pro-Hoover leaders had different priorities and different nominees for federal positions, and, as a result, separate political identities.

There was one other powerful black faction within the party—the professional politicians. They were a highly diverse, unorganized lot with numerous regional differences and included Oscar De Priest, who was running for Congress as a member of the Chicago organization controlled by Big Bill Thompson; Harlem leaders who were in the process of actively shifting their allegiance to the Democratic party; Perry Howard of Mississippi and Benjamin Davis of Georgia, who have already been described; and Robert R. Church, Jr., of Tennessee. The handsome and distinguished-looking Church was the most widely respected of the professionals. Son of the Memphis real estate tycoon and skilled political chief Robert R. Church, Sr., the younger Church earned his college degree from Oberlin, spent five years in the banking business on Wall Street, and when his father died in 1912, returned home to take charge of the political organization that he had built.

Young Church was a bold and unusual leader in the South. He controlled black politics in Memphis, where blacks could vote in municipal elections and even in the Democratic primary. As an especially skillful politician he had consolidated his black political forces into a unified power bloc that often held the balance of power in closely contested municipal elections. To safeguard his position he established strong alliances with the Republican congressman J. Will Taylor and with the state Democratic machine controlled by Edward H. Crump. Avoiding both local publicity and public office, he worked quietly and before long had established his reputation for dignity, honesty, and the promo- tion of black rights.[42] In 1919, a year of great racial violence, he displayed his courage by organizing the first southern branch of the NAACP, and he served on the national board of directors as well as the executive committee of the National Urban League.[43]

Church had more influence in national politics than he did in state politics. He was most widely recognized as head of the Lincoln League, established in 1916 as a local political club and expanded in 1919 into a national organiza- tion. The league's purpose was to register black voters, arrange to pay their poll tax, ensure that they arrived at the polls, and thereby advance race interests through unified political power, which white politicians would have to respect. Southern and northern politicians enthusiastically swelled the mem- bership of the Lincoln League. In 1919 Walter Cohen of New Orleans was its treasurer, while Robert S. Abbott, editor of the Chicago *Defender* and James Weldon Johnson, director of the NAACP, sat on its executive committee. State officers included Perry Howard of Mississippi, Benjamin Davis of Georgia, Gooseneck Bill McDonald of Texas, and Mrs. Ida B. Wells Barnett of Illinois. Other active supporters included James A. Cobb, J. Finley Wilson, W. C. Hueston, and Scipio Jones. In February 1920 at its first national meeting, 400 delegates from thirty-three states heard Will Hays, the chairman of the Repub- lican National Committee, endorse its purpose and applaud its efforts.[44]

Church was a loyal Republican and Hoover supporter, but unlike Moton and Hawkins he represented the views of the practical politicians who had grown wise from successfully meeting the special tests and surviving the special dangers of black political leadership in the South. Church was much closer in his thinking about politics to Perry Howard, Walter Cohen, and Ben Davis than he was to Moton, Holsey, Barnett, Scott, Hawkins, or Cobb. Church, too, had repeatedly defeated his lily-white Republican opponents and had been repeat- edly accused by them of patronage corruption, but his reputation for honesty and his political alliance with Republican congressman J. Will Taylor com- bined to convince the credentials committee at the 1928 Kansas City conven- tion that the charges were politically motivated.[45] At the convention Church had witnessed the debates among black leaders and the victories of the lily- whites from Florida, Louisiana, and Texas. Those developments dismayed him, but he was even more disturbed by the later indictment of Perry W. Howard and by Hoover's selection of the leaders for the new Colored Voters Division.[46]

Moton and Scott fought an intense, protracted battle over the leadership of the Colored Voters Division. Until Perry Howard's indictment, Scott had favored a position for Howard, whom he considered a "liberal" on black matters. He also wanted two black national committeemen appointed, but apparently because virtually every black national committeeman had either been accused of patronage corruption or led an anti-Hoover delegation, none was chosen.[47] To head off Scott, Moton saw Hoover on 29 July, but Scott wisely countered by supporting Hawkins for the top post.

Hawkins was just as unacceptable to Moton as Scott himself. Moton argued against Hawkins and indirectly against the emerging Scott-Cobb-Hawkins alliance on the grounds that Hawkins lived in the District of Columbia and that, according to his understanding, Republican leaders had agreed that nobody should be appointed from "a non-voting state, that is, from Washington or from a southern state where the Negro vote does not count." He had cloaked his opposition to Hawkins in these general terms, he told Holsey, because he did not wish "to make Dr. Hawkins think I had any unusual authority."[48]

Despite Moton's confidence in his "unusual authority," the Tuskegee faction ran into intense opposition from black Republicans who remembered and resented the long dominance of Booker T. Washington in the party and who were determined to prevent Moton from recapturing that dominance for the "Tuskegee machine."[49] Southern black politicians argued that because only Robert R. Church, Jr., could harmonize the various factions, he should be appointed chairman of the new organization. In the end, Walter Brown worked out something of a compromise. After Hawkins spoke with Hoover on 13 July, the secretary immediately informed Work that Brown was to have "full responsibility" for organizing the "northern negroes."[50] Hoover wanted a Colored Voters Division of elite Negroes, and Brown quickly sought to mitigate the rivalries among these men by naming a black selection committee to choose the new leaders. He therefore appointed Scott, Hawkins, and Cobb of the Washington, D.C., faction and Barnett, Holsey, and Clarence Vena of the Moton faction to select the officers and appoint members to all of the various committees. Church believed that Cobb actually dominated the selection, was Brown's "chief aide and adviser," and, hiding behind his judgeship, manipulated events to Brown's liking.

On 26 July, after two more weeks of wrangling, the selection committee reported its slate to Brown, who, in turn, accepted the appointments without modification. No doubt with the blessings of Hoover and Brown, Dr. John R. Hawkins emerged as chairman of the executive committee and director of the CVD. His appointment was a clear defeat for both the professional politicians and the Moton faction. However, Albon Holsey, Moton's private secretary, was named second in command as secretary of the CVD, and Barnett secured a lesser post on the publicity committee, which was headed by a Scott appointee, Robert Vann, owner and editor of the Pittsburgh *Courier*. Scott and Church were appointed to the executive committee, while Judge Cobb, whose position as municipal judge precluded appointment, nonetheless remained exceedingly influential in the new Hoover Black Cabinet. As for the national campaign committee, a separate midwestern headquarters was established in Chicago, where the local black Republicans were well organized.[51]

From the outset internal strife severely hampered the CVD. As director,

Hawkins drew most fire from critics. His lack of experience in conducting a national campaign infuriated the excluded politicians and prompted harsh comment from the Moton faction. Charges circulated during the midst of the campaign accusing Hawkins of taking a lengthy trip to California, ostensibly, Scott insisted, to visit his sick wife, but, in reality, Holsey told Moton, because "he found that this job was much more than he expected." The constant internecine warfare was too distressing for the embattled physician and banker. According to Holsey, Hawkins from the beginning had "been torn from one decision to another so rapidly that, in desperation," he had retreated to California to escape from "the front ranks of battle."[52]

Holsey was not the only one who believed that Hawkins had "not waded into his job." Chicago politicians were distressed by both Hawkins and the entire clique of "educators" that Hoover and Brown had installed at the top levels of the CVD. Pointing to Hawkins as a onetime schoolteacher, Scott as secretary-treasurer of Howard University, and Holsey as secretary of Tuskegee Institute, they openly questioned their competence in politics and wondered why experienced politicians, who had worked hard for many years to win their positions of leadership within the black community and who knew how to deliver the vote, had not been appointed to direct the campaign. Hoover had not only selected educators; these amateurs were, in fact, either from the District of Columbia or from states where blacks could not vote in national elections.[53] To them, the implication was obvious. The candidate and his managers apparently looked with as much suspicion on northern black politicians as they did on their southern counterparts.

The attacks on Dr. Hawkins, Dr. Scott, Dr. Holsey, and Dr. Moton emphasized the increasing disdain with which black politicians viewed the Hoover Doctors, both during and following the campaign.[54] Foremost among those politicians leveling the negative assessment of the educators' leadership was Church. In his denunciation of Hawkins he was even more emphatic than Holsey. He told Work that Hawkins, Scott, and the other elite leaders knew nothing of politics and did not represent voting Negroes. They were men without political standing in the black community, and he was concerned that their selection would drag into the political arena the Negro religious and educational institutions that they represented. Yet in late August 1928, when Church asked Hoover to restructure the CVD leadership, Hoover rejected his advice.[55] From Hoover's perspective Hawkins's position as financial secretary of the African Methodist Episcopal Church and the academic positions held by the leaders of Howard University and Tuskegee Institute were the very credentials entitling them to lead the new elite. More important, Church suspected that their inexperience in politics might have allowed a significant, growing threat to black southerners to go unchallenged.

By August Church felt that he fully comprehended the extent of Mann's increasingly strenuous and perhaps bigoted efforts to win Hoovercrat votes in the South and in Tennessee. Understandably Church recognized the Hoover-crats as a future threat to his own organization in Memphis, and as a southern politician he also resented the lily-white strategy that Mann was obviously pursuing in the South against fellow black politicians whom he knew and respected. Hawkins and the new leaders of the CVD did not challenge Mann's activities in the South, and this fact added to Church's anger. In any case, by mid-September Church became so disgusted that he would no longer be associated with the CVD. Moreover, his public announcement of this fact made front-page news and alerted black leaders throughout the United States to the internal struggle. Walter Brown immediately recognized the significance of Church's defiance. Worried and upset over the failure of his compromise, he no doubt communicated the reasons to Hoover and began the process of mending the breach.[56]

Meanwhile, jealousies and hatreds continued to grow and fester. By late August, as Scott, Cobb, and Hawkins steadily increased their hold on the CVD, the Moton coterie became more and more perturbed. Barnett was especially upset with Scott's attempts to give him orders and by Hawkins's increasing ineffectiveness.[57] Holsey complained to Moton that Scott and Hawkins refused to consult with either Barnett or himself and that the lack of trust and cooperation among them was all too evident. He believed that Barnett had been especially abused. Angered that Robert Vann had been named publicity chief rather than Barnett, whom Hoover had apparently favored, Holsey complained to Barnett that he was "thoroughly convinced that Vann does not know what it is all about" when it came to campaign publicity.[58] This growing bitterness finally prompted Moton to confront Hawkins directly about Hawkins's and Scott's alleged lack of goodwill toward and cooperation with Holsey and Barnett, but there was no improvement. If anything, relations between them deteriorated even more.[59]

As it turned out, Robert Vann was not a good choice as publicity director. As owner and publisher of the Pittsburgh *Courier*, Vann was influential, but he was also a combative, caustic individual who had embroiled himself over the years in numerous public battles with other, often more prominent black leaders.[60] He had grown accustomed to attacking his opponents in the *Courier*, and when Church openly criticized Hawkins and Scott, Vann, in turn, attacked Church in his newspaper.[61] Church erroneously believed that the instigator of the *Courier* article was Scott himself, for it was Scott who had secured Vann's appointment as publicity director. Replying in the Washington (D.C.) *Eagle*, Church ridiculed the author by stating that the article was "of a kind familiar to all who know the fine African hand of its industrious but elusive author." Referring to Scott's position as private secretary to Booker T. Washington, he charged that Scott had for thirty years hurled his brickbats "from behind the coat-tails of protectors." Nonetheless, "whether Dr. Scott continues to operate Howard University or run good Dr. Hawkins" was less important, Church insisted, than his assessment of the leaders of the Colored Voters Division as "political parasites and pretenders." Forcing his readers' attention to events in the South, Church observed that the leaders of the CVD could not gain the respect and trust of blacks because they had not fought "against the crime of disenfranchisement." They had not won their positions in the bear pit of politics. He further taunted them for remaining in the North where it was safe, while the real battle was waged in the South. He pointed out that all three had been born in the South but that "neither Dr. Hawkins has returned to North Carolina, Dr. Scott to Texas nor Dr. Holsey to the Court House in either Georgia or Alabama to register his citizenship and play the full man." Church concluded that "there is not a colored apologist I would follow, not even at the request of Mr. Hoover, unless he is leading a procession to the public square there to receive the condemnation of an outraged people."[62] Hoover's new elite, he told black people, were not the courageous leaders they so desperately needed.

9. Reformer or Racist?

Church's public denunciation of the Hoover Doctors revealed the alarming extent and seriousness of black disillusionment with Hoover and his new Colored Voters Division. Even more important, the Church revolt highlighted the rapidly widening split between race interests and party harmony that had led to the creation of the National Negro Voters League at the convention in June. Church was highly respected among diverse black leaders as a Republican whose first loyalty was to the advancement of his race, and his political judgments therefore carried great weight. Years of leadership in southern politics, in the NAACP, and as head of the Lincoln League had earned him a national reputation as a courageous, honest, and skillful politician. Scott and Hawkins were well aware of Church's national prominence. Yet rather than try to heal the breach, they unwisely attempted to read Church out of the Republican party.

In protesting his own innocence, Scott took the opportunity to heap more ridicule on Church. He denied having written the *Courier* article criticizing Church for his "acrobatic activities during the campaign years 1920, 1924, and 1928"; its author, he said, was Robert L. Vann, the publicity director of the CVD and editor and publisher of the Pittsburgh *Courier*. Scott denounced Church for wrongfully attacking him as the author when Church allegedly knew through mutual friends that Vann had actually written the article. Because Church had acted out of personal pique, he was not a loyal Republican working for the party and Herbert Hoover, as he claimed. Instead, declared Scott, he labored "under hallucinations of super personal grandeur and self-exaltation in his all-too-apparent attempt to destroy party harmony" and the new black leadership.[1]

Scott's counterattack on Church was hardly adequate, for Church was criticizing much more than internal feuding among black leaders in the CVD. Even without publicly identifying the issues it was obvious to informed blacks that Church could no longer remain silent while the CVD ignored both Mann's increasingly aggressive and obvious tactics in the South and Hoover's unwillingness to respond to the "Appeal" issued by the nation's collective black leadership against the racial hatred generated by the campaign. Moreover, within several weeks, by early October, it was apparent that Church's warnings and criticisms were based on an accurate reading of black perceptions in the North as well as in the South.

At the insistence of Mann and Work, Claude Barnett, the hardworking editor of the Associated Negro Press, had undertaken an extensive survey to determine black political sentiment in the North. His findings revealed that the political damage from Hoover's effort to attract southern whites and from the disunity within the CVD was compounded by the gains of the Democratic party among urban blacks. In his personal canvass of twenty-four northern cities, Barnett discovered three principal reasons for black disaffection. The most important was the widespread belief that despite its repeated promises, the party had neglected the needs of blacks for many years. Another serious cause of discontent was the growing belief that the party had betrayed southern black political leaders to a racist strategy. Many black politicians no longer held to the notion that the Republican party was "the ship and all else the sea." Southern blacks were "being thrown overboard" and any Negro influence within the party ranks was being displaced by lily-whites. Finally, Democrats in the North had financed extensive state organizations that "played very cleverly upon [black] neglect and fears."[2]

The lack of enthusiasm for Hoover, even among black businessmen, was evident everywhere Barnett traveled. R. H. Rutherford, president of the National Benefit Life Insurance Company, for example, failed to see why blacks should flock to Hoover's banner. He agreed with the editors of the Baltimore *Afro-American* who asked, "Why the Rush?" Before endorsing Hoover, why not first determine from the candidate where he stood on the enforcement of the Fourteenth and Fifteenth amendments, recall of the Marines from the black Republic of Haiti, segregation, lynching, and the full implementation of Negro rights?[3] Scott had earlier tried to convince Hoover to reassure blacks on these points in his acceptance speech, but Hoover had refused. He told Scott, "I have always thought that the treatment of the negro as a separate entity either by candidates or the party is neither good psychology nor service to the colored folks. We do not act that way towards any other group in the United States, and I had always made up my mind to consider them part of our loyal citizenship, interested in every problem and not distinguishable from the rest."[4]

In light of what Hoover had learned during the Mississippi flood, his insistence that the rights and needs of black Americans should not be given special attention was ludicrous. In part his response was a campaign hedge that Anderson and Wise had insisted was essential to win southern votes, but it also revealed his own belief that he must remain above "racial politics." He may also have been influenced by the advice of some Negro supporters who felt strongly that blacks should not be singled out during political campaigns.[5] Unfortunately, Hoover's lofty remarks about his policy of Negro indistinguishability actually produced an impression of racial insensitivity. He had held this position earlier as secretary of commerce, yet his sponsorship of a

Colored Business Division and his desegregation order suggested a realization that blacks did, in fact, have special problems and needs. His reversion to the "principle" of indistinguishability led many blacks to question if he had learned anything at all. It is little wonder that black Republican leaders were discouraged. Even Barnett, who was intensely loyal to Hoover, privately lamented that because Hoover had "no program for Negroes," the leaders of the CVD confronted a "very muddled situation" with the consequence that they were "not doing much of anything."[6] To his black supporters Hoover seemed to be a man of good intentions. In his acceptance speech he did call for equality of opportunity "regardless of faith or color," and he also pledged that such equality would "tolerate no privileged castes or groups," but both he and his campaigners refused to go beyond these few vague generalities. Hoover offered no special program for blacks and no real inspiration to the CVD.[7]

Thoughtful black leaders and critics realized that Hoover was neglecting black voters during the campaign. So, too, did knowledgeable white observers. Former president William Howard Taft, who was now chief justice of the Supreme Court, spoke directly with Hoover over his worry that unless corrective actions were taken, the Democrats would win the black vote in Ohio, Illinois, Indiana, and Kentucky. To Taft's surprise, Hoover unburdened his deep sense of outrage over the sensational headlines and charges that he had bought corrupt southern delegations to win the nomination. He angrily denounced the southern Republican delegations, which used their inordinate strength at the national nominating conventions to "blackmail" every Republican administration into giving them federal offices to sell and even predicted to Taft that he could win the election without the black vote, if necessary. Perhaps because of his own unsuccessful attempt at a lily-white southern strategy, or because Hoover did not explain his position clearly, Taft misread Hoover's intent. Temporarily pushing aside his grave doubts about the candidate, the chief justice felt a sudden sense of exhilaration at Hoover's righteous insistence upon reform of the party. "Hoover is one of the strongest men I have known in public life," he recorded. "He will be a great find." Yet just as Taft overstated his approval, he also overstated Hoover's intention. Taft believed that Hoover's willingness to lose the northern black vote, if necessary, in order to end patronage "corruption" in the southern wing of the party meant that Hoover wanted "to break up the solid South and to drive the negroes out of Republican politics."[8]

This was clearly wrong. Hoover's action in selecting new leadership for the CVD establishes that he had no intention of losing the northern black vote or of driving all Negroes out of the party. Without a doubt, Hoover believed that he could make significant political gains in the South, and while he was willing to risk alienating some northern blacks in eliminating reputedly corrupt black-and-tan southern politicians and expanding the white basis of the party in the

South, there is no evidence to support Taft's impression that he intended to drive all Negroes out of the party. In fact, Hoover's explanation of his purpose to Col. Robert R. McCormick, the strongly opinionated publisher of the Chicago *Tribune*, specifically refuted such an interpretation.

Unlike Taft, McCormick was not even temporarily won over to the conclusion that Hoover was a "great find." McCormick supported Hoover against Smith and was pleased with Hoover's determination to rid Chicago of the criminal gangs protected by Mayor Thompson's Republican machine. Still, McCormick used his newspaper to blast Hoover's appeals to southerners and his simultaneous neglect of black sensibilities and needs.[9] Hoover explained to McCormick that his policy was not intended to be antithetical to blacks, only to public or party officials, whether black or white, who violated their public trust. The prosecution of Perry Howard, Hoover argued, should not be interpreted as antiblack. He stated to McCormick in October 1928 and again in March 1929 that neither whites nor blacks wished to be represented by politicians "who trade in public office." To Hoover the issue was reform and honesty in government, not race. He wished to win over prominent white southerners to the party to help reform and strengthen it, but he refused to believe that this would harm black interests. In his view the colored community could only benefit from new leadership, both white and black.[10]

Once again Hoover's public silence hurt rather than helped him, for it allowed northern Democrats to play on the suspicions of prominent black leaders that he wanted to drive them out of the Republican party.[11] Through his friend William Pickens, an active organizer for the NAACP, Barnett learned that Walter White had applied for a leave of absence to campaign for Smith but that the board of directors had turned down his request on the grounds that the NAACP must not allow itself to be dragged into the political thickets.[12] Nonetheless, both White and Du Bois were eager for a general repudiation of Hoover and his party, believing him either indifferent or hostile to black people. White actively although unofficially campaigned for a Smith victory to prove to the Republicans that blacks were no longer "unconsidered chattel," for he believed that Smith would appeal directly to Negro voters, as he had promised White.[13] Du Bois also favored a switch of black votes to the Democrats because he hoped to see the development of an independent black power bloc in the North, which could then use its vote to gain concessions from white politicians in both parties.[14] Du Bois suspected that Hoover's insistence on reform and honesty in government was a facade for covert antiblack attitudes. While he offered no defense of corrupt black politicians, Du Bois believed that white racism had created the one-party South and that black political corruption, placed in its proper context, would be revealed as "the thin cover of a white cesspool." More important, continued Du Bois ironically, when Hoover and his cohorts accused southern black politicians, they had not called on "the better class of colored leaders" to take their places but had turned instead to lily-whites. Indeed, both Hoover and Senator Brookhart had acted as if political corruption and Negro were "synonymous terms."[15]

In sharp contrast to the other campaign managers, who expected an unprecedented electoral victory, Walter Brown had become increasingly worried as the campaign progressed. Internal feuding in the CVD, Church's public denunciation, and the Democrats' gains with northern blacks added weight to Barnett's repeated warning that unless there was a "well organized plan of securing registration and bringing the issues, including the fine character of Mr. Hoover, home to the Negro, many Negroes will become easy prey for Democratic propaganda and there will be a heavy defection in the Negro vote."[16] By September Brown finally agreed to Barnett's plan, which pulled together several objectives into a coordinated publicity strategy.[17] To counter the widespread ignorance about Hoover and refute Democratic charges of neglect, Barnett wrote and distributed pamphlets explaining Hoover's efforts to help blacks during the Mississippi flood, his assistance to Negro businessmen, his hopes for the black farmer, the advantages of Prohibition to black people, and a treatise on desegregation in the Commerce Department that featured "Extracts From Speeches by Heflin, Blease and Caraway on the Floor of the United States Senate."[18] More effective still was a concerted effort to circulate "to every Negro newspaper North and South" the "chicken wire enclosure" photograph showing the high fence that separated Negroes from white spectators at the Democratic national convention in Houston, Texas, where Smith had been nominated.[19]

The most ambitious part of Barnett's plan was to win the support of black newspaper editors through a well-financed advertising campaign.[20] Black leaders, including Scott, were aware that the Democrats had attracted black voters in large part by first winning over the owners and editors of the black press.[21] This was a significant shift of potentially great political importance. Among those newspapers that had abandoned the Republican party for Al Smith were the Chicago *Defender*, the Baltimore *Afro-American*, the Boston *Guardian*, the Washington (D.C.) *Eagle*, the Harlem *Star*, the Kansas City *American*, and the New Jersey *Lance*.[22] Barnett believed that because the principal blacks in the churches, the schools, and the fraternal organizations had failed to provide political leadership, the only significant group on whom to depend were the black newspaper editors. Indeed, he insisted that the "future of the race" depended upon their ability to mobilize the black people.[23] He knew that all the editors were financially hard-pressed and, whatever their most recent political bent, eager to sell political advertising space. To some editors such sales were looked upon as a sign of respect and even friendship.[24]

With a budget of $32,000 approved by Walter Brown, the owner of the Associated Negro Press traveled throughout the North and into the border states signing contracts for advertising space in forty-four newspapers for as little as $200 and as much as $2,500. To spread the good word and mobilize editors behind Hoover, Barnett bought space from friends and foes alike, and at first the plan promised to be the party's most effective effort to reach the Negro editors and through them, Negro voters. However, Work soon cut all campaign budgets, and despite Barnett's repeated insistence that the contracts must be honored, Work forced him to cancel at least one-third of the space he had purchased. Moreover he compounded this injury by insinuating that Barnett had attempted to "buy" the support of the black press.[25]

The result of Work's insensitivity was probably more damaging than if no advertising campaign had ever been undertaken. To save approximately $10,000, Work destroyed the goodwill effort to win over or to retain the allegiance of one of the most politically influential groups in the Negro community. The editors interpreted the cancellations as insulting and illegal, and they protested vigorously to Barnett. C. A. Franklin of the Kansas City *Call*, William Monroe Trotter of the Boston *Guardian*, William H. Davis of the Amsterdam (N.Y.) *News*, N. B. Young of the Saint Louis *American*, Harry C. Smith of the Cleveland *Gazette*, and others demanded that the Republican party honor its contracts with them, but Work cared nothing for Barnett's plan and refused to listen to his pleas to restore the funds.[26] Indeed, the earlier prediction of the Washington (D.C.) *Eagle* seemed especially appropriate. In the spring when Hoover had desegregated the Commerce Department, the editors had warned him not to appoint Work to an important campaign post. They had predicted that his "testy manner" toward black people would do Hoover incalculable harm.[27]

Work's curtness toward virtually all of Hoover's closest friends and supporters increasingly alienated the candidate from his campaign manager and would contribute to his dismissal soon after the victory.[28] In the last weeks before the election, possibly because of the strain in their relations, Hoover became more assertive and began to direct more of the campaign himself. Brown's reports of many black editors opposing him and a possible great shift in black sentiment reinforced the earlier warnings from Taft and Colonel McCormick. Extensive conversations with Brown and Church finally convinced Hoover that he faced a serious loss of support among Negro voters.

Once fully alert to the great danger of black repudiation, Hoover acted quickly. He appointed Raymond Benjamin, a prominent California leader and close personal friend to take charge of the CVD. Benjamin, in turn, enlisted Church and arranged a meeting between Church and Hoover. To help counteract the impression that he was indifferent to black people and that his effort to win prominent southern whites to the party was an antiblack stratagem, Hoover gave personal assurances to Church sufficient to convince him that Horace Mann had misled southerners, that white leaders who would work with black leaders could be found in the South, and that his administration would respect black political leadership and the needs of black people.[29]

Hoover could not have converted a more effective black Republican leader. Church commanded the respect of anti-Hoover critics such as Robert S. Abbott, editor of the Chicago *Defender*, and Abbott gave Church's conversion, along with his full-page advertisement, prominent coverage in the *Defender*. In his full-page boldface *Defender* ad entitled "Why I Am For Hoover," Church made no effort to hide Republican shortcomings. He frankly acknowledged the party's acceptance of segregation; its willingness to work with lily-whites in the South; its failure to bring prominent black politicians into leadership positions within the government; its exclusion of the black-and-tan delegations led by Cohen, Davis, and McDonald; and its indictment of Perry Howard. Nonetheless, he stressed that for blacks there was a significant difference between Hoover and Smith. Although Smith had attracted northern black leaders to his campaign, he had refused to follow their advice. "Although surrounded by choice men of our fears and hopes and blood, who cry [to] him to be a Man among Men," Smith had proven incapable of rising above the level of the Democratic party and had continued to rely on the enemies of black people for victory. The Republicans offered little, but the Democrats offered nothing. Most important was Hoover. "I have made my choice," Church told black voters, "because I have talked with Mr. Hoover," and because his "association, travel, training, experience, and background" made Hoover the better man of the two candidates. Moreover, he would not destroy black leadership. Significant too was Church's assurance that Hoover was above politics and thus, unlike Smith, above the party that had nominated him.[30]

Following Church's lead, other southern black leaders now joined in the dramatic turnabout and quickly became Hoover's greatest source of campaign strength among blacks. These southern leaders responded vigorously to the charges leveled against Hoover by his black opponents. Walter Cohen, for example, released a letter to Barnett explaining that his delegation had supported Charles Curtis for the nomination initially, not because they opposed Hoover but because years earlier, as a senator, Curtis had rendered Cohen invaluable aid in winning Senate confirmation as comptroller of customs at New Orleans. He told also of Hoover's personal intervention to ensure that he, although not his delegation, would be seated at the convention despite defeat in the credentials committee, and he assured blacks that Hoover had "evidenced good will toward our people." To be sure, the Republican party was imperfect, he concluded, but the Democratic party was "both imperfect and ridiculous." Democrats were waging an intense anti-Negro campaign in the South, and in every southern state controlled by the Democrats "a whole string of anti-Negro laws congest the state books."[31]

One of Hoover's harshest critics was Neville Thomas, head of the District of Columbia branch of the NAACP. In early 1928 Thomas had helped convince Hoover to desegregate the Commerce Department, but following the seating of the lily-white delegations at the convention, and especially after the indictment of Perry Howard, Thomas launched a campaign to convince black voters that Hoover had betrayed the race and that because Hoover was supported in the South by bigots, fanatics, and the KKK, Negroes must now vote Democratic.[32] Like Howard, Benjamin Davis of Georgia also had been repeatedly accused of patronage corruption, and he too had been seated at the convention; but unlike the Howard case, Davis's chief prosecutors, the two Democratic senators from Georgia, had been unable to gather sufficient evidence for an indictment. Davis had no love for Hoover, but he defended him. In answer to Thomas, he correctly pointed out that bigots, fanatics, and the KKK in the South were campaigning for Al Smith. By contrast to the Democrats, who had not elected any black delegates and who had penned Negro spectators behind a chicken-wire fence at their convention in Houston, the Republicans, despite some lily-white successes, "did not expel the Negro from the Party at Kansas City." If Thomas were concerned about race prejudice, Davis asked, why did he not counsel Negroes to join the Socialist party, which had no color line? Why advise them to join the party of white supremacy?[33]

The rhetorical questions raised by Davis were not easy ones for black Democrats to answer. It was widely believed among Negroes that the Democratic party was the party of racism. It had discouraged Negro delegates to its national conventions. It had supported intolerance, segregation, and disenfranchisement and had done nothing to promote Negro welfare or to stop the lynching. A significant part of their case against Hoover had been the belief that the lily-white strategy had forced Church, Cohen, and Davis, along with the indicted Howard, out of the Republican party. Now, suddenly Church, Cohen, and Davis all vigorously supported Hoover and attacked the Democrats where they were most vulnerable. *Time* magazine concluded that in the last week of the campaign Church's stirring personal endorsement had swung over all but six of the leading twenty-five black newspapers that had been supporting Smith.[34]

Another important factor in black support for Hoover was Al Smith's failure to appeal to black voters. His steadfast refusal to call for northern black support was proof enough for many that he and the Democrats also had a southern strategy, and this greatly disillusioned White and Du Bois. Indeed, Du Bois finally advised the readers of the *Crisis* that there was not "a jot or tittle of difference between these two men in their attitude toward fundamental matters, and we sincerely advise our readers to vote for neither of them."[35] The dismay and confusion among black leaders was further exemplified by the stand of the National Negro Voters League. This had been formed at the Republican convention by black leaders who resented the platform's neglect of Negro rights and suspected a lily-white strategy. The league could not stomach either Smith or Hoover. In the end, however, although Smith made significant inroads among northern black and ethnic voters, Hoover won the vast majority of the Negro vote.[36] The failure of northern Democratic leaders to capitalize on Hoover's insensitive and bungled campaign among blacks and the ringing eleventh-hour endorsements by southern black supporters finally convinced many that the Democrats still posed the greater threat to their race.

Seemingly less important on election day, but in the long run more significant, was the large degree of unnecessary black alienation that Hoover forces inspired. Hoover wanted to be helpful to Negroes, but time after time he raised their doubts by not publicly explaining his intentions, by deprecating patronage, by choosing a Black Cabinet of amateur rivals rather than professional politicians, by championing party reform, and by allowing advisers such as Horace Mann to gain new prominence and influence, which they interpreted to mean lily-whitism. Through his election Hoover had won an opportunity to correct the mistakes and misconceptions of the campaign, but black suspicions remained. There was still hope that he would prove to be a genuine reformer rather than a racist, and influential newspaper editors, leaders of the NAACP, northern black Democrats, and loyal black Republicans would be watching him closely for evidence of more skillful leadership and greater personal sensitivity to the needs and cares of black Americans.

10. Mixing Racial and Reform Politics

The lush Belle Isle, Florida, estate of the multimillionaire J. C. Penney provided an ideal retreat for the weary president-elect. Following his preinaugural journey to Latin America, Hoover now mixed the pleasure of deep-sea fishing with the agony of selecting his cabinet. Few guessed the surprise and deepening disappointment Hoover experienced as the men he most wanted in his cabinet refused to serve, and he was forced to appoint men whom he did not believe met his standards or with whom he had not previously worked. Added to his growing discontent were swarms of patronage seekers and reporters gathering only a short distance away at Miami Beach.[1]

Because he needed some rest and some uninterrupted time to select his cabinet, Hoover unwisely refused to meet with reporters, although intimates warned him of their anger. Thus began Hoover's unhappy alienation of the press, which increased steadily over the next four years.[2] Because Hoover would not supply them with news, the resentful journalists turned to those who would, especially to Horace A. Mann, the so-called Mystery Man of the campaign in the South. Having avoided the press during the campaign, Mann now relished the attention. He arrived in Miami Beach uninvited, established himself in one of the fashionable hotels, and began a series of well-publicized conferences with the campaign manager Hubert Work and southern patronage seekers who had flocked to Florida for jobs. Mann's sudden prominence suggested that Hoover had called him to Florida to help capitalize quickly on the unprecedented victories in the South. Before long, Horace Mann emerged in the newspapers as one of the most powerful political brokers in the new administration—the uncrowned czar of southern patronage.[3]

Beneath the froth of journalistic speculation a new political undertow seemed apparent. Hoover had won seven border and southern states and also the northern black vote, although he had virtually ignored it. Many observers at the time and scholars since then believed that Hoover would attempt to make still further inroads into the Democratic monopoly on white supremacy and thus expand his southern state victories in 1932.[4] However, a careful analysis of southern white voting patterns suggests that southerners worried about race had not voted for Hoover. The only exception to this voting pattern was the urban South, where whites had voted for Hoover despite high concentrations of blacks because they felt least threatened by blacks. V. O. Key, the distinguished scholar of southern voting behavior, succinctly summarized his exhaustive analysis of the 1928 election returns: "The whites of the black-belt counties were bound in loyalty to the Democracy by a common tradition and anxiety about the Negro," but outside of these black belts whites "could afford the luxury of voting their convictions on the religious and prohibition issues."[5]

Democratic fears of a carefully planned southern strategy were far greater than the facts warranted. Despite appearances, Mann's well-publicized attempt to become the czar of southern patronage was in reality a last desperate effort to bolster his greatly weakened position.[6] During the campaign Mann had made many influential enemies within the party. Lily-white Republicans who had established their dominance prior to the campaign resented both Mann's claims to control of patronage and the separate Hoover-for-president clubs that he had financed in their states. These clubs created a rival power base from which Mann could threaten their own state organizations. Moreover, these clubs consisted primarily of Hoovercrats—Democrats who had supported Hoover and whose loyalty to the Republican party was questionable.[7] Black-and-tan Republicans were even more vociferous in their denunciation of Mann's clubs. Robert R. Church, Jr., of Tennessee, for example, had insisted to Hoover that he force Mann out of Tennessee and promise to repudiate Mann's lily-white organizations.[8] To those already inside the Republican fold, Mann was a threat, not an ally.

Reporters were also misled by Mann's frequent meetings with Hubert Work, the campaign manager, who was believed to be close to the sources of power in the forthcoming administration.[9] Work had appointed Mann to run the southern campaign and had given him a free hand, but he himself had already lost Hoover's trust.[10] The exact reasons for the break are not entirely clear. Work's frequent clashes with Hoover's closest advisers and his encouragement or tolerance of Willebrandt's and Mann's campaign bigotry were the two most probable causes for his dismissal. Without consulting anyone, Work had destroyed virtually all of the 1928 campaign files of the Republican National Committee.[11] Mann too either destroyed or secreted his separate southern campaign files, which Work had allowed him to maintain. Perhaps they sought to hide evidence that they had encouraged bigoted propaganda. Certainly this seems likely, for although surprisingly little direct evidence of Mann's undercover activities remains, there is enough to confirm the charges that he distributed misleading, even vicious, propaganda against Al Smith and promised white southerners that blacks would be eliminated from Republican politics. He supplied Gilchrist Stockton, head of the Hoovercrat movement in Florida, for example, with pamphlets emphasizing Smith's close ties to the notoriously corrupt Tammany Hall machine in New York City and represented to Stockton that when Republicans used the term "respectable party," they meant a party free of all blacks. "We are going to have a respectable party in every southern state," he insisted, "and that means the elimination of the negro in so far as political activities and office holding is concerned, and I think when you eliminate these two features, you practically eliminate the negro."[12]

Democrats continued their charges of campaign bigotry long after the election. Usually they directed their charges against Mann and through him took aim at Hoover. Charles Michelson, an experienced newsman and political propagandist contracted by Raskob to write stories that were critical of Hoover, made especially good use of Mann.[13] Taking advantage of Mann's sudden newspaper prominence, Michelson suggested to his readers in the New York *World* that Hoover had personally issued orders to Mann, whom he characterized as the "director general" of the "mobilization of bigotry." Ignoring, of course, any Democratic use of racial hatred (at least as frequent as that by Republicans), Michelson charged that Mann had enlisted the Ku Klux Klan to distribute hundreds of thousands of dollars worth of vicious anti-Catholic propaganda. "In some cases," he insisted, "hamlets awoke to find that there had been a snowstorm of this material in the night—airplanes had flown over and dropped them." The Republican National Committee had financed this "secret campaign" and Mann, who directed it, had "reported to Mr. Hoover only." Thus, Michelson concluded, because Mann had faithfully executed Hoover's personal orders, and because there was "no doubt that he did a wonderful job," he therefore had earned "whatever Hoover means to give him in recognition thereof."[14]

Michelson must have been surprised when, in the midst of the newspaper ballyhoo characterizing Mann as the czar of southern patronage, Hoover abruptly fired him.[15] Actually Mann seems to have had far less influence during the campaign than many have assumed. Soon after Hoover's victory, Stockton, who was eager to eliminate blacks, assured Mann that the election results had proven him to be "a political expert" on the South and hoped that now "the powers in Washington will be more ready to accept your advice on Southern political matters than they were before the election" and might even allow him to consolidate Republican gains throughout the South.[16] Instead Hoover had gradually become disgusted by the mounting evidence of widespread campaign bigotry in the South.[17] At the same time that he fired Work and Mann, he also dropped C. Bascom Slemp of Virginia, another adviser who had been accused of racial bigotry.[18] Equally significant was Hoover's renewed use of the press. As he dismissed these men, he told reporters that he had no intention of initiating a lily-white strategy. Racial hatreds, he insisted, must first be eliminated before the principles of the Republican party could flourish in the South.[19]

Hoover's swift action against Mann did not immediately end their relationship.[20] During a personal meeting Mann had assured Hoover that he did not wish to become a patronage czar and, indeed, would not accept any position in the administration. He wanted only to help Hoover as best he could with absolutely no reward.[21] Mann knew he could still be useful. He had worked with Hoovercrats throughout the South, and because Hoover wished to attract these people to the party, he occasionally consulted with Mann and even invited him and his wife to dinner.[22] Using these signs of continued influence, Mann kept alive the impression that he had retained the president's confidence. Moreover in long, detailed interviews with newspaper reporters he encouraged the impression that a lily-white strategy was still under serious consideration. Although well aware that Mann was manipulating the press, George Akerson was characteristically insensitive to the racial implications of Mann's continued visibility. When questioned about Mann's publicity tactics, the sanguine Akerson could "not see much harm" in Mann's futile efforts to create the illusion of influence, and he therefore took no action to counteract the damaging impression.[23]

Mann's indeterminate status combined with reports and rumors of Hoover's intention to reform the "southern mess" created a sense of uncertainty and anxiety among southern Republicans. Few knew precisely what he intended to do. Black Republicans were already deeply suspicious; so were lily-whites. Oliver D. Street, the race-baiting leader of Alabama Republicans, cautioned Hoover against acting too quickly on southern matters. He reminded him of the party's great opportunity in the South and twice warned him of "some puzzling aspects which need discreet handling" and of the need to develop this "most interesting situation" in such a way as to ensure "the best results not only for the Republican party but for the South itself."[24]

Obviously Street worried that Hoover's desire for reform would affect whites as well as blacks. Street, like others, had observed the close relationship that had developed between Hoover and Sen. Smith Brookhart, chairman of the Senate subcommittee investigating patronage corruption. Brookhart had campaigned for Hoover, and Hoover had enthusiastically supported his investigation of corruption of the southern Republican organizations. After the election the senator was heartened by Hoover's approval of his plans to broaden the investigation.[25] He had spoken three times with Hoover before his inaugural and twice immediately afterward. Reporters learned that at each of those five meetings they had discussed the "southern mess."[26]

Southern Republicans had cause to be alarmed over Brookhart's "expanded" investigations. Under threat of still further harassment from Brookhart's committee, Benjamin J. Davis earlier capitulated as national committeeman from Georgia. Davis's humiliation greatly angered northern blacks, who believed that he had been driven from his position of leadership primarily because he was black. They also suspected that Hoover might well be encouraging Brookhart in order to eliminate other southern black Republicans.[27] White leaders of black-and-tan organizations, notably J. Will Taylor, Republican national committeeman from Tennessee, and Tieless Joe Tolbert, Republican national committeeman from South Carolina, were also consistently being accused of corruption by lily-white rivals who were eager to take control of their state parties, and Brookhart apparently encouraged these detractors to testify before his committee.[28] Before long, however, lily-white Republican leaders were as angry as their black counterparts. They charged that as a Republican, Brookhart was incredibly naive, perhaps even antisouthern, because he accepted at face value charges of corruption hurled at Republicans by defeated Democrats or at the recognized leaders by rival factions within their own state parties.[29]

The stereotype of the corrupt southern Republican made it easy for northern whites to believe that Brookhart's committee was, in fact, uncovering widespread corruption. Indeed, to many northerners it was almost an article of faith that virtually all southern Republicans were corrupt. No one challenged this stereotype until much later in February 1929, when Brookhart encountered R. B. Creager, the lily-white leader from Texas, who offered a spirited rebuttal. Creager was furious at Brookhart for allowing "scandalous and malicious gossip" to be introduced before his committee by defeated political opponents without testing the accuracy of the charges. Any allegation of corruption against Republicans seemed sufficient to convince Brookhart, and furthermore, Creager complained, no southern Democrats or northern Republicans were called before his committee.[30] Creager was not alone in his anger.[31] Other southern Republicans feared that Democrats, eager to strike back after the 1928 defeat, would deliver a barrage of charges against all Republicans as crooks.[32]

Southern Republicans were further disheartened by Hoover's failure to appreciate the blighting effect of the sensational corruption stories upon his southern supporters. On 4 March 1929 when he was inaugurated, as earlier when accepting nomination, Hoover revealed that he was as zealous and as naive a reformer as Brookhart. On both occasions he sought to reassure his listeners of his own integrity, perhaps to throw off the campaign charges of his alleged corruption. He sincerely revered the principles of honest government, and in both his acceptance and his inaugural addresses he emphasized the necessity of sweeping reforms and placed the need for political and judicial honesty at the head of his list of problems facing the nation.[33] The breakdown of law and justice, he told his inaugural audience, was the "most malign of the dangers to self-government." It was "reform, reorganization, and strengthening our whole judicial and enforcement system" that remained "the most sore necessity of our times."[34] Several days later he announced the creation of a blue-ribbon national law enforcement commission to investigate and make recommendations for sweeping reforms. This became the famous Wickersham commission, headed by George W. Wickersham, Taft's attorney general.[35]

Another theme of Hoover's inaugural address was the obligation of the two-party system to offer the people real political alternatives. In fulfilling this obligation, he insisted, Republicans must avoid "intolerant partisanship."[36] His intention to build new southern state parties was evident, but the meaning of "intolerant partisanship" did not become clear until 8 March at his first news conference. Mere partisanship, he explained, was not a sufficient criterion for federal employment. The spoils system would not characterize his administration. Indeed, he saw no necessity for replacing Democrats with Republicans merely to enhance his own party and vowed that there would be "comparatively few changes" among federal personnel who were performing their public duties efficiently. To southerners who had bolted the Democratic party, and to Republicans who expected to be rewarded for their labors, Hoover's unexpected patronage policy was a "severe shock." Within four days of his inauguration Hoover's failure to reward the South with a cabinet office, Brookhart's gleeful predictions of a southern patronage "shake-up," and this latest vow to retain Democrats in the federal service prompted southerners to wonder openly if Hoover intended any rewards for the South.[37] Allowing southerners to parade in Confederate uniforms at his inaugural had been unprecedented, but it was hardly the recognition they sought.[38] Without extensive federal patronage they saw little likelihood of building a real political alternative to the Democratic party.

Gloom among southern white Republicans deepened still further on 11 March. At a special meeting of the Republican National Committee, called to discuss the rebuilding of the party in the South, Hoover finally laid to rest any lingering hopes that Horace Mann would play a part. Mann had clung to the belief that the separate campaign organization he had built in the South would be considered so important to rebuilding the party that his services, perhaps even his leadership, would be retained. His seemingly friendly relations with Hoover and his reputed influence with members of the committee had added to his expectations. But there was to be no reward for the campaign he had directed. Newspapers reported that he had been forced out of the party's councils without so much as a word of thanks.[39]

Mann's political demise delighted black Republicans. Many gave the credit to Robert R. Church, Jr., but Church generously passed it on to Hoover. Since the last days of the campaign Church and Hoover had been on excellent terms. In early March he had again met with the new president to discuss his plans for the reorganization of the southern parties, and Hoover had fulfilled his promises to Church. He had forced the Mann organization out of Tennessee and repeated his pledge not to grant patronage to any of Church's lily-white opponents. Equally satisfying were his assurances that he would not abandon honest black leaders in the South. Church emerged from the meeting with a renewed confidence in Hoover and with a sense of joy that he had not felt when he had rallied black voters to Hoover's banner late in the campaign. All of his doubts were now erased. The president, he exuberantly told black people, was a great leader who had "come from under the malevolent conspiracy of our political history as a strong, determined man who wipes down plagues and finds pleasure in the silence of his conquest."[40]

Church was convinced that blacks need no longer fear that this enlightened president had made any commitments to the hated lily-whites. The effort to eliminate black leadership, he assured them, had been the work of Horace Mann, whose unauthorized promises had been repudiated. "In my opinion," Church prophesied, "Mr. Hoover will prove to be a shocking disappointment to both the small but important element of colored Republicans who fear that his silence gives consent to their persecutors and to the close-knit band of 'famished lillies' and 'suit-case Democrats' who expect him to put colored people back into slavery."[41]

As Mann may also have understood, his ouster meant that Hoover had no intention of ordering a wholesale purge of southern black leaders and, in time, Mann would issue his own appeal to southern Republicans for an anti-Hoover lily-white crusade to take control of their state parties.[42] Other observers could not bring themselves to believe that Hoover had acted against Mann out of any genuine concern for blacks. According to their reasoning, Walter Brown, the reputedly astute postmaster general, must have convinced the president that a purge of southern blacks would mean the defection of the entire northern black vote to the Democratic party. Hoover's sudden change of heart, therefore, was based on cold, political calculation, and Mann's ouster was merely a change in tactics, not in strategy.[43] Yet this interpretation is unconvincing. Hoover had deliberately refrained from making any promises or even appeals to northern black voters during the campaign. He had told former president Taft that he would reform the southern parties regardless of the effect on northern black voters, and he had meant what he said. Moreover, he had no intention of changing his views on the desirability of attracting outstanding white leaders and white voters to the southern parties. Nonetheless, Church had clearly understood Hoover's determination to protect honest black leaders, and he had articulated that determination to black people even more forcefully than Moton or the other Negro leaders who had faith in the new president.

Unfortunately for Hoover, his rush to launch an immediate crusade to reform the southern wing of the party resulted in one of the most damaging utterances of his public career, the reform proclamation of 26 March 1929. This highly publicized yet deliberately vague statement confused virtually everyone while convincing most blacks that Hoover had, in fact, been lying to them. Central to the numerous, varied, and long-enduring misconceptions that it spawned was Hoover's belief that he could not—indeed, must not—explain all of the reasons for the reform strategy or all of the results he hoped to achieve. In this he fully agreed with the dubious advice offered by Anderson and Wise. According to them, the racial progress that Hoover expected from the revitalization of the democratic process in the South could not be mentioned lest the Democrats rally voters around the banner of white supremacy and defeat his reform objectives.

Hoover was personally convinced that racial progress was not possible without first attracting a new white elite that could defeat the Democratic oligarchies. This political revitalization required avoiding any mention of racial progress or of the party's historic commitment to blacks even though this new leadership would bring forth new political conditions and eventually help blacks far more than present circumstances permitted. He would not repudiate the historic commitment, but neither would he support it in public. Thus, by blaming the peculiar racial nature of southern politics, he convinced himself that he had no choice but to push vigorously for reforms within his own party, where he could effect change and hope that the fruits of this intraparty trans-formation would eventually create a new South in which leaders of high moral character and ability could realize genuine progress in human relationships. In time, he seemed to believe, his actions would prove his good intentions and the wisdom of his reliance on the new elite. The flaws in his thinking would soon become apparent—especially his inability to attract like-minded white southerners to that elite.

At first, in working drafts of the proclamation, Hoover could not resist indicting the Democrats. He blamed them for destroying the two-party system and thereby reducing the Republicans to "nothing but mere skeleton organiza-tions," which existed "for the sole purpose of fostering factionalism and controlling patronage." In retrospect, it is obvious that Hoover would have done well to retain this criticism. By implication it highlighted the Democrats' use of white supremacy and disenfranchisement as the principal cause for Republican decay. Certainly the degeneration of the state parties into mere patronage cliques had at least as much to do with one-party racist control as it did with the venality of Republican politicians. But in the final draft he dropped all mention of the Democrats.[44] Perhaps he felt the implication was apparent enough. Certainly he did not wish to anger southern Democrats in the House and Senate, for he needed their votes to pass important programs which he would recommend to the Congress. Also a denunciation of the Democrats might drive away the thousands of Hoovercrats who otherwise might eventu-ally join the Republican party. Instead of criticizing the Democrats, therefore, he contented himself with an appeal for "strong two-party representation" that would destroy "sectionalism in politics," generate new respect for govern-ment, and revitalize the democratic process.[45]

Not all of the southern states needed to be reformed. Hoover congratulated Republican leaders in Virginia, North Carolina, and the border states, which had created vigorous parties that sent Republicans to Congress. Most others required only limited improvements. Election gains in Alabama, Arkansas, Louisiana, Florida, and Texas, where "wholesome organizations" had won the increasing confidence of the voters, encouraged him to expect much greater progress in the future. To expand their appeal to the voters Hoover ordered these state parties to establish "advisory committees of the highest type of citizenship" that would bring new ideas, new talents, and a new respectability. They would further enable Republicans to enlist "independent democrats" while making important recommendations that would significantly upgrade the selection of appointees to federal offices. By thus ensuring the "strength, permanence, and constant improvement in public service," this elite group of civic-minded leaders would build state parties respected by the people for their devotion to honest, effective government. To Hoover's thinking, this was the most desirable kind of politics, democracy at its best. Clean government nurtured by the "highest type" of citizen would induce great numbers to join the Republicans in the important task of revitalizing the South.

Much more drastic measures were necessary in Mississippi, Georgia, and South Carolina, where Willebrandt, Brookhart, the *New York Times*, and others had generated shocking news of patronage corruption. Hoover scolded Republican leaders in these three states. They had conducted themselves in ways that were "intolerable to public service . . . repugnant to the ideals and purposes of the Republican party . . . unjust to the people of the South and must be ended." He would no longer recognize these discredited politicians as party leaders. A new "leadership of men who will command confidence and protect the public service" must be recruited immediately to replace them. Indeed, should these state parties refuse to appoint patronage advisory committees composed of the "highest type" of local citizens, Hoover vowed to find other methods for selecting federal officials in these states.[46]

A great weakness in Hoover's presidential leadership was his timid, guarded manner of explaining his motives and his failure to recognize the harmful political effects of this caution. Although frequently motivated by the best of intentions, he often created a wholly different impression by either neglecting or refusing to disclose his thinking and objectives fully.[47] In this instance he felt that he could not reveal his intention to protect honest southern black leaders, or the long-term beneficial results that he was convinced the reform would bring to blacks, without also alienating the vast majority of southern white voters. Thus he left too much unsaid, and the reform proclamation raised many more questions than it answered. It was only natural, therefore, that his listeners should draw their own conclusions.

Southern lily-white Republicans were simultaneously encouraged and embarrassed. Because Hoover had made no mention of race while insisting on leadership from the "highest type" of citizen, they assumed that he favored a lily-white reform movement. Yet his equally great emphasis upon the necessity of creating elite advisory committees in most of the states was an apparent indication that he neither trusted the judgment nor valued the quality of the current leaders. Some complained bitterly of the emerging Hoover "dictatorship." Other southern lily-whites worried that his appeal to "independent democrats" and his call for patronage advisory committees would complicate the distribution of federal offices to the party faithful, thereby depressing their morale and discouraging them from building stronger party organizations. Moreover, experienced party regulars considered it insulting to be monitored, if not controlled, by committees of nonpoliticians who knew little if anything of the imperatives and complexities of party building.[48]

Northern whites also had difficulty understanding the proclamation and divided sharply over its intent. To government crusaders such as Senator Brookhart, the president's address was laudable, a forthright demand for honest public service whose restoration would transcend short-term party advantage to the noble goal of restoring political competition essential to democratic self-government.[49] But to those better aware of the historic position of blacks in the southern Republican parties, Hoover's words smacked of blatant antiblack lily-whitism. This suspicion hardened into conviction on the following day, when Postmaster General Brown clarified Hoover's intention not to recognize the national committeemen from Mississippi, Georgia, and South Carolina as the legitimate leaders of their state parties. Republicans who had lost the confidence of or had no standing in their communities, he explained, would no longer be tolerated by the party.[50] Because black leaders had no standing in southern states and did not command political confidence, and because the three deposed national committeemen were black-and-tan leaders, Hoover's objective appeared obvious. The blunder brought immediate response as the editors of the *New York Times* and the Chicago *Tribune* quickly reached the same conclusion. According to them, what Hoover obviously meant by reform was the exclusion of black-and-tan leadership, whether those leaders were black, such as Perry Howard of Mississippi and Benjamin Davis of Georgia, or white, such as Tieless Joe Tolbert of South Carolina.[51] The *Times* bluntly charged that Hoover's reform "foreshadows a Republican Party in the South almost as pure a white man's party as is the Democratic Party there."[52] Through a spokesman Hoover immediately rejected the *Times*' interpretation, but no one seemed to take his denial seriously.[53]

Northerners and southerners, blacks and whites alike, seemed to agree that Hoover's real intent was a lily-white party.[54] Southern Democrats understood the threat but would say little for publication, while northern blacks were vociferous in their denunciation. They pointed out that the corruption charges on which Hoover based his expulsion of Howard, Davis, and Tolbert had not yet been proven. Besides, the president did not have the legal authority to depose them, for they had been duly elected by the legitimate state organizations and recognized by the Republican National Convention, which retained sole power to decide questions of leadership. Hoover's crusading moral fervor had been misplaced, and his political amateurism seldom seemed more evident.

But to blacks Hoover's words and actions seemed to reflect much more than excessive moral fervor or amateurish blundering. Perhaps Church was the most disillusioned. Howard, Davis, and Tolbert were his political allies, whom he respected for their ability to survive over the years in an intensely hostile, dangerous environment. But what hurt Church most was his recollection of

Hoover's recent personal assurances—assurances on which he had based his public tribute to Hoover and his public prophecy of the new president's great friendship for black people. Instead of becoming their great friend, Hoover had used his power to betray Negro leaders. "Where their hopes had been fondest," Church lamented, "their sorrow is keenest now and where they had been led to expect the bread of encouragement they have received the stones of contempt."[55]

W. E. B. Du Bois was neither surprised nor saddened. He gladly seized the opportunity to reemphasize the correctness of his earlier criticisms. He had argued since the 1927 Mississippi flood that Hoover was antiblack, and the reform proclamation strengthened his conviction. What angered Du Bois was not that a few black leaders had been accused of corruption, but that Hoover had held up only blacks and their black-and-tan allies for special ridicule and censure. He had not condemned corruption in the Democratic party and had refused to identify white supremacy as the principal source of the entire southern political "cesspool." Virtually all other black leaders and scholars since 1929 have agreed that Hoover's reform proclamation was an inept facade for his strategy to create a lily-white party in the South.[56]

Perhaps the most vigorous and certainly the most telling criticism came from Col. Robert R. McCormick, the white owner of the Chicago *Tribune*. McCormick's editorial not only charged that Hoover had "betrayed" the Republican party and its loyal Negro friends by attempting to "drive the Negroes from it," but that he was, in fact, creating a party that would be "more anti-Negro than the Democratic."[57] This was not the first time that McCormick had criticized Hoover's attitude toward blacks. During the campaign he had complained to Hoover directly about his neglect of black voters, and Hoover had met with him at some length to explain his views on the need for reforms in the South and presumably about his refusal to intervene in or even to criticize the federal prosecution of Perry Howard. Thus McCormick had been privy to Hoover's thoughts. But McCormick had not waited to speak with Hoover about the meaning of the reform proclamation; its meaning appeared all too evident, and he lost no time in denouncing it.

Hoover was as much dismayed by his critics' reaction as they had been by his reform proclamation. For McCormick he wrote a long personal letter. The *Tribune* editorial, he complained, "grossly misrepresents my position to the colored community" and "totally misrepresents both my intent and the action I have taken." It was not "a question of negroes or whites" but of "clean public service. Investigation shows," he insisted, "that scarcely a colored man has been given office in the states which I condemned" and that "the white men affected far outnumber the colored men in the organizations condemned and in some cases where encouragement was given there are colored as well as whites in their organizations." He again insisted that regardless of appearances, political reform was essential. "It is my emphatic view that neither the white nor the colored people of the United States wish to be represented by men who trade in public office and it is equally my view that as President I cannot tolerate abuse of public service. All I say is that I will not have any relations with those who maintain these abuses."[58]

Hoover also tried to convince McCormick of his high regard for black leadership. He informed the publisher that prior to issuing his proclamation he had first "discussed these questions with a number of the colored leaders in the country and they have given their unqualified support to the action which they, as well as I, know is not directed against any colored person except one who may be, equally with white men engaged in practices which debauch public service, and they are equally emphatic with me that it is unfair to the colored people that they should rest under the stigma which they have borne so many years from this kind of political activity."[59]

Hoover's defense of his motives had no public impact. Despite damaging criticism from allies as well as critics, the president kept his response to McCormick confidential.[60] Now more than ever Hoover must have understood how important it was to reassure blacks as well as their influential white allies. Perhaps he hoped that black leaders loyal to him would dispel the misperception, but he nonetheless remained steadfast in his conviction that he could not publicize his real intentions without destroying the more important objective of southern reform. Perhaps too he hoped that following a personal talk with McCormick the publisher himself would retract his harsh words or at least refrain from further denunciation. If so, Hoover was disappointed. McCormick accepted the invitation to the White House, but despite Hoover's best efforts the Chicago *Tribune* continued to condemn his southern strategy.[61]

Hoover's faith in the goodness and ultimate practicality of his intentions contributed to his increasingly tragic relations with black Americans. Trapped by a plan that did not allow him to explain his intentions publicly, he tried to do so privately and this too contributed to the tragedy. It was naive of him to expect political allies to accept private assurances from a man who must lead by public persuasion. Although he had consulted privately about the reform plan with members of his own black elite,[62] these men were not politicians. Moreover, their silence and inaction during the election campaign erroneously suggested that they were either indifferent or hostile to the fate of the southern black and tans. Certainly Hoover should have talked to Church, the politician who had done so much to convince blacks to vote for him, rather than Smith, during the last days of the campaign. He had met with Church only eleven days before the proclamation became public, and Church had left that meeting to express his joy in Hoover's friendship for black people. If Hoover had fully explained his southern reform ideas to Church at that time, the Memphis politician would no doubt have vigorously argued against them but, even so, at least he would not have later felt that he had been deliberately misled by the

Mann ouster, or that Hoover had betrayed him into making public statements that now humiliated him in the eyes of his black colleagues.

Indeed, Hoover's unwillingness to solicit views and exchange ideas with black politicians eventually cut him off from black leaders generally. Southern black politicians seemed to be especially distasteful to him. To be sure, he disliked politicians of any color, but he had suffered personal wounds from claims that he had won the nomination by bribing southern delegations, and he believed wholeheartedly in the charges of corruption emanating from the Brookhart investigation. Nor was this the only instance of Hoover's willingness to cut himself off from an influential group of blacks. In 1927, although his relief efforts during the Mississippi flood brought him into contact with the leaders of the NAACP, he made no determined attempt to open a dialogue. The same insensitivity characterized his relations with black politicians. Although Hoover yet hoped to prove by his actions that honest black southern leaders were still welcome in the party, his self-imposed inability to explain the good intentions behind the reform proclamation, coupled with his elitist view of political leadership, had by now made understanding and cooperation between Hoover and black leaders more difficult, if not virtually impossible. The gulf was clearly one of his own making. Rather than a reformer, he appeared instead to be playing politics with race.

11. Howard and De Priest: Incongruous Symbols

McCormick's public denunciation and his subsequent unwillingness to accept Hoover's private reassurances emphasized the untenable position into which Hoover's conflicting goals had forced him. Earlier, in March 1929, as he took the oath of office, it had seemed possible for him to establish better relations with black leaders. He had driven Horace Mann out of the party councils; Perry Howard had been acquitted of the sensationalized corruption charges; and Robert R. Church, Jr., had publicly proclaimed that despite all of the suspicious impressions and misunderstandings, Hoover was actually going to be a good friend to black people. Then, within only ten days, two events shattered hopes for improvement. First, Mabel Walker Willebrandt announced on 16 March 1929 that she had obtained another indictment against Perry Howard. Then, on 26 March the president's own reform proclamation convinced Church and other black leaders that Hoover had deliberately and callously misled them.[1] The second indictment of Howard immediately rekindled suspicions of a lily-white southern strategy, and the reform proclamation confirmed those suspicions.

Hoover understood that his competing objectives were alienating northern and southern blacks as well as southern whites, but he was convinced of their correctness. In time, he seemed to think, he would be able to demonstrate his good intentions, his good faith, and his good judgment to all parties; but meanwhile, confusion and frustration intensified. Repeated federal prosecutions of Perry Howard convinced blacks that the trials were politically motivated and indicated the relentless racist lily-white strategy of the Hoover administration. At the same time, visits to the White House by politically influential blacks infuriated white southerners and convinced them that Hoover was totally unreliable on the race question. Hoover's policy became an enigma to both sides and for historians long afterward. Only in retrospect can we understand his seemingly incongruous treatment of the nation's two most newsworthy black politicians: Perry W. Howard and Congressman Oscar De Priest.

In July 1928, soon after Hoover had won the nomination, the news that Perry W. Howard had been indicted by a federal grand jury in Mississippi for patronage corruption prompted immediate expressions of outrage by black leaders. The timing of the indictment contributed to the anger. It had followed quickly after the purge of anti-Hoover southern black and tans by the Hoover-controlled credentials committee, a purge that Howard himself had denied was part of a lily-white strategy. But appearances had now been altered significantly. Adding to this charge was the fact that the assistant attorney general who sought the indictment was Mabel Walker Willebrandt, who had presided over the credentials committee's alleged purge. At the very outset of the 1928 campaign, therefore, the evidence pointed to a well-planned, albeit clandestine lily-white southern strategy initiated by the Hoover forces during fights in the convention credentials committee.

The indictment made Howard an instant national celebrity among blacks. The tall, handsome, urbane orator had been too skillful a politician and too strong a fighter for his lily-white enemies in Mississippi to bring him down without help from powerful allies in Washington, D.C. Now more than ever, he was the symbolic representative of black resistance to the increasingly influential antiblack Republicans. It was an image that Howard expertly cultivated during campaign speeches in northern cities. Blacks who were eager to counter the revived stereotype of the corrupt black Republican politician demanded a speedy trial, but Howard objected. He explained that the campaign in the South had generated such intense racial hatred that a trial in Mississippi would result in mob violence against him.

Willebrandt could not deny the basis for Howard's concern; yet she was reluctant to agree to a postponement. As she had anticipated, some blacks charged erroneously that the delay of justice was motivated by the desire to attract southern white votes. These critics believed that the indicted Republican national committeeman was exceptionally useful to the lily-white campaign in the South as evidence of Hoover's dramatic purge of black leaders from the party. If Howard were tried quickly and acquitted, the Hoover forces would lose their symbol of the corrupt black politician under indictment by the new lily-white leadership of the Republican party. The trial must be delayed to keep this dramatic image of the purge before the voters. Indeed, the critics' suspicion was reinforced by the candidate's refusal to speak out against the racism of the southern campaign, his employment of Horace Mann, and his neglect of the northern black vote. Consequently it appeared that justice would be delayed until after Hoover had cracked the solid South.[2]

In December 1928, after Hoover had carried seven border and southern states, the Howard trial finally began. Willebrandt had had six months to amass evidence against Howard, and she had used that time well. The Federal Bureau of Investigation, cooperating fully, had completed an exhaustive investigation of all of the charges against Howard and several of his top political lieutenants who had been indicted with him. Most of the FBI's attention had been directed to the charge for which Howard had been indicted, the sale of the office of United States marshal to Anselm Prentiss Russell for $1,500. At first detailed examination of Howard's bank records encouraged Willebrandt, but the evidence proved to be much weaker than she had anticipated. Her entire case ultimately depended upon Russell's testimony against Howard. Realizing this, she warned the United States attorneys working with her that "proof of this whole incident rests fundamentally upon the way the jury takes the testimony of [Anselm] Prentiss Russell." She claimed to be satisfied with the "salient facts" but later instructed her colleagues that the testimony needed "a good deal more corroboration," and she detailed a long list of weak points in Russell's story.[3]

The all-white Mississippi jury agreed with Willebrandt's pretrial assessment of Russell's testimony, but as an experienced attorney, Howard had also detected the weaknesses and had moved, although unsuccessfully, for a dismissal of the charges for lack of evidence. The prosecutors hoped to incriminate Howard before the jury by shooting a barrage of questions at him. Throughout the cross-examination, however, a government attorney recorded, Howard "was well poised, frank, straightforward, and good humored."[4]

E. E. Hindman, the United States attorney who lost the case, blamed his failure on Howard's accuser, Russell. Hindman lamented to Attorney General William D. Mitchell that he had made "a bad witness" whose credibility the jury had "somewhat questioned." Howard had introduced evidence that at the time the $1,500 was exchanged, Russell had signed "two sworn affidavits . . . that he had not paid anyone any money for the appointment of Marshal, and when confronted with these affidavits he said well, this money paid to Howard was in the nature of a loan." In addition, Howard also established that the loan was between good friends for he showed that he and his black codefendants had frequently traveled, dined, and drunk with Russell. These facts, Hindman concluded, had "destroyed" Russell's testimony. On 14 December 1928 the all-white jury quickly and unanimously voted for acquittal.[5]

Willebrandt, Hindman, and the team of federal prosecutors were bitterly disappointed with the verdict. They refused to credit Howard's evidence or Russell's sudden recollection of a loan, or even the impartiality of the jury. To explain their defeat they turned from the legal evidence to another convoluted reading of partisan politics in the South. According to these prosecutors, Mississippi Democrats wanted Howard acquitted because it would ensure that Howard and his black codefendants would continue to control the Republican state party. And with this symbol of black corruption as the national committeeman and head of the state party, the Hoovercrats and lily-white Republicans would be hard-pressed to convince white voters anywhere in the South that the Republican party had been "reformed." White Democrats, Hindman told the attorney general, had even raised $4,000 to help defray Howard's legal costs. Moreover, in his conversations with Mississippi Democrats, Hindman discovered a general belief that the trial was simply a Republican plot "to make a goat of negro politicians" for partisan purposes. They had bluntly told him that if he wanted to uncover real corruption, he ought to investigate those high officials, presumably including Hoover, who had never been brought to trial for their involvement in the infamous Teapot Dome scandal. He concluded that there was, among white Mississippians, "a general opinion of great satisfaction that the defendants were turned loose."[6]

However plausible Hindman's interpretation may seem, given the intensity of racial politics in Mississippi, historians should require some proof before accepting the claim that white Mississippians, including the jurors, would turn loose blacks whom they believed guilty merely to embarrass the Republicans. It is more consistent with the evidence to believe what the facts had established, and what Willebrandt before the trial and Hindman afterward had both admitted: that the case against Howard was not strong enough to prove his guilt beyond a reasonable doubt. Although Russell's sudden recollection of a loan may, indeed, seem suspicious, one must conclude that the jury had little choice but to exonerate Howard and his codefendants.

Blacks were overjoyed at Howard's acquittal. He had once again foiled his lily-white enemies.[7] The unanimous, quick acquittal on the first ballot by an all-white jury in Mississippi was for them a convincing, triumphant vindication both for Howard, and, in a larger sense, for all black Republican leaders. Naturally they now expected that Howard would be reinstated as a special assistant attorney general. This was a position of great importance, for influence at the highest levels of the Justice Department was generally considered invaluable to any oppressed minority. For example, Moton had earlier requested Howard to initiate an investigation by the Justice Department of lily-whites in Arkansas for harassing black leaders who had served as delegates to the state Republican convention.[8]

Hopes for Howard's reinstatement proceeded logically from the acquittal, but his troubles were hardly over. Willebrandt was utterly convinced that Howard was guilty and a disgrace to the Department of Justice, and she wanted one more chance to convict him. Like Hindman, she was confident that Howard's acquittal was politically motivated, that the jury, in effect, had joined together in a political conspiracy to stop the reform of the southern state parties. Unable to prove conspiracy, she insisted that according to Howard's bank records he had deposited sums far in excess of his federal salary and that these sums corresponded exactly to the amounts given to him by men who had bought federal appointments for themselves or their relatives.[9] Howard, in turn, maintained that these sums were, in fact, loans that he had raised from his political friends to purchase property on Pennsylvania Avenue in anticipation of federal condemnation proceedings. He argued that these investments would net him and his partners a goodly profit. By now Hindman had admitted to the attorney general that in the first trial "the general opinion is that a conviction could not be had, especially on the evidence and the witnesses which the Government has."[10] Nonetheless Willebrandt argued that she had uncovered new, irrefutable evidence and demanded a second trial on new charges.

For all of her faults, which would soon drive her out of the administration, Willebrandt enjoyed a reputation as an incorruptible zealot in her pursuit of lawbreakers. Hoover trusted her and he needed little convincing of Howard's guilt. He told the philanthropist Julius Rosenwald that the entire party in Mississippi was a "perfect slough of corruption." Moreover, Willebrandt worked closely with Sen. Smith Brookhart, sending him detailed FBI investigations containing new allegations that Howard had sold post office jobs. Brookhart, in turn, publicized these unproven allegations, but FBI investigations failed to uncover any evidence to substantiate them. Despite intense opposition from the attorney general, postmaster general, and other leading Republicans of the outgoing Coolidge administration, Willebrandt secured a second grand jury indictment against Howard for selling the appointment of United States marshal in the Southern District of Mississippi to James G. Buchanan.[11]

Willebrandt again supervised the government's case against Howard. Fearing that a jury of partisan Democrats would free him a second time, she secured a change of venue from Jackson to Meridian, Mississippi.[12] The prosecutor, Lester G. Fant, the United States attorney for the Northern District of Mississippi, increased Willebrandt's confidence. One of Howard's lily-white political enemies, Fant was as eager as she to convict him. The Democratic politicians, he predicted, "will have a harder time handling a jury in Meridian than they would have in Jackson."[13] Nonetheless, all of their careful work to secure a favorable verdict ended in failure. On 26 April 1929 another all-white jury returned a verdict of not guilty. The Justice Department was stunned. After reviewing still more allegations against Howard, Attorney General William D. Mitchell concluded that a third trial would be a "waste of effort."[14] The showcase trials, which the administration by now desperately needed to win in order to justify its demand for sweeping reforms, had ended in total frustration.

By the time of Howard's second acquittal in late April 1929, the controversial Willebrandt had already decided to resign as assistant attorney general. Earlier during the campaign she had come under a barrage of intense criticism for her zealous campaign speeches that, her critics charged, inflamed religious prejudice by fusing the issues of Prohibition enforcement and religion in her attacks on Al Smith.[15] Characteristically, she fought back against her critics, most especially against campaign chairman Work, who sought to deflect the intense criticism of her speeches, dismissing them to the press as those of an independent "free lance."[16] Massing her evidence in a scathing counterattack, Willebrandt sought to put the onus on Work. She argued that all of her speeches had been scheduled by and had been submitted in advance to the Speakers' Bureau of the Republican National Committee in Chicago and that

J. Francis Burke, counsel of the RNC and a Roman Catholic, had personally approved one of the most controversial of them. She assumed that the others had also been read and approved.[17] But, she charged, when Al Smith had adroitly employed criticisms calculated to tempt the RNC "to disclaim responsibility" for her speeches, Work had taken the bait.[18] Rather than "showing up the fallacy of his attack," Work had instead fallen into Smith's trap and thereby greatly damaged the campaign by revealing its "disorganization and lack of solidarity."[19]

Willebrandt took her case directly to Hoover, who apparently agreed that Work was responsible and, apparently bowing to Willebrandt's demands, he forced Work to issue an embarrassing public retraction acknowledging the party's responsibility for her speeches.[20] At the same time her version of the story leaked to the press.[21] To her dry supporters Willebrandt was a courageous heroine, and following the election they clamored for her appointment as attorney general and later as solicitor general or at least as head of the president's new, prestigious Commission on Law Enforcement.[22] But to Work and other party leaders she was, as she admitted, a political "storm center" that critics skillfully exploited in their continuing attacks on Hoover.[23] Following the election, criticism of her zealous enforcement of Prohibition soon replaced her speeches as the source of controversy, and whatever the merits of her defense, even she reluctantly recognized that she had become an embarrassing political liability.[24]

Buffeted by intense criticism on the one hand and exaggerated praise on the other, Willebrandt was particularly anxious about her future in the new administration. Thus, when Hoover telephoned her in late February to tell her that William D. Mitchell, whom she had recommended, had accepted the post of attorney general, Willebrandt was alert to the implications for her own future. According to her, Hoover said: "I just wanted to tell you the new attorney general is a friend of yours. I say that because maybe when you see him you might not think so but he is and we want you to stay on." When Willebrandt inexplicably refused to respond, there was an awkward pause, after which he added, "at least for awhile." He then offered her reasons why he felt she ought to stay, but these only fueled her anger. She was convinced that his real intention was to suggest her resignation, and she interpreted "at least for awhile" as evidence of that desire.[25]

Willebrandt's interpretation of Hoover's intent may have been correct. Despite her uncomfortable pause, he offered her none of the prestigious positions mentioned in the press, only the assurance that she could remain as assistant attorney general.[26] Apparently that was not enough. In her momentary hurt and anger, perhaps because she was not appointed to a loftier position, she raised a very serious charge against Hoover. Immediately following the telephone conversation, she insisted to her parents that Hoover's way of suggesting that she resign was "part and parcel of the many back stairs methods he adopted of dealing with me and the drys during the campaign."[27] Willebrandt never elaborated on the charge and offered no proof to substantiate it, but before long she found another reason for her resignation.

Within a few weeks of the beginning of the new administration, it became clear that neither the new attorney general nor the president was very friendly to her repeated insistence on a controversial plan to reorganize Prohibition enforcement. Despite Hoover's explanations that he could not get congressional approval for her plan and his restated hopes that she remain to implement his less controversial alternative, Willebrandt could not be placated. She insisted on resigning.[28] Nonetheless, when she left her post in June 1929, Hoover gave her a well-publicized farewell dinner at the White House, an honor he had not offered Work when he had been forced to resign earlier.[29] Both at the convention and afterward Hoover respected her loyalty to him, solicited her advice and recommendations on patronage, and regarded her as a dedicated public servant. He continued to invite her to his weekend retreat on the Rapidian River, where she impressed his intimates as a more interesting and modest woman than the newspapers had led them to expect. Despite some momentary bitterness, Willebrandt acknowledged his goodwill and personal kindness by admitting that Hoover "said he'd do anything to make my private practice a success and he'd create the impression as well as hope it would remain the fact that I'd be a 'part of the family.' "[30]

Willebrandt's spirited independence was less obvious but just as vigorous in her decision to prosecute Perry Howard. Yet although she had twice failed to convict him, the president nonetheless accepted her evaluation of him and acted on her recommendation to force Howard's immediate resignation.[31] This act, Hoover believed, would demonstrate that regardless of his guilt or innocence, his conduct in office was not trustworthy enough for him to remain as a special assistant attorney general of the United States. However, to black leaders it suggested something quite different: that Howard's greatest crime was his race. No one defended his practice of raising investment capital from political appointees, but two acquittals by all-white juries in Mississippi convinced many blacks that Willebrandt had gone forward with two weak cases, and that, although the legal system had twice established his innocence, he had been summarily dismissed simply because he was a black politician in the most powerful and conspicuous appointive position held by a black in the Hoover administration. Coming as it did soon after the reform proclamation, Hoover's action seemed a clear indication to blacks and southern lily-whites that black politicians would be forced out regardless of their innocence.[32]

Howard's departure on 7 May dramatically eliminated the most skillful and the best-known black politician in the Hoover administration. Southern lily-whites had reason to be pleased, for Hoover seemed to have translated the fuzzy rhetoric of his reform proclamation into clear, forceful, and convincing action. The president had struck at two of their worst enemies: the corrupt black politician and the equally corrupt Democratic politicians, whose sinister influence in the South could be seen in the two "fixed" juries.

But Hoover did not remain a hero of the southern lily-whites for long. To retain his new status, he had still another important test to pass. In November 1928 Oscar De Priest, the black Republican politician from Chicago, had won election to Congress, the first black to do so since 1901. Tarnished somewhat by his membership in the infamous Chicago Republican machine, De Priest was nonetheless an outspoken advocate of black rights and assertiveness.[33] As early as February 1929, Charles Michelson informed his readers of the "dilemma" that De Priest's election had supposedly created. If the First Lady invited Mrs. De Priest to her traditional tea for congressional wives, political repercussions in the South would damage the administration's southern strategy. If Mrs. De Priest was excluded, northern blacks would be alienated. Hoover stood to lose either way. Under these circumstances, Michelson concluded, the president's decision would be a major test of his southern strategy.[34]

If Hoover had been pursuing the lily-white strategy, which virtually every knowledgeable observer had good reason to assume, he could simply have told his wife not to invite Mrs. De Priest to any of her tea parties for congressional wives. Given his unconcern with the northern black vote during the 1928 election, the hostile black reaction to his 26 March reform proclamation, and the even more damaging repercussions from his recent decision to fire Howard, he had little or nothing to lose by excluding Mrs. De Priest. By confirming appearances, and angering blacks again, it would further bolster Hoover's standing among southern lily-whites. But again current appearances were deceptive. After giving the question some careful consideration, Hoover may well have decided that the invitation to tea might serve a different purpose, as a symbolic public demonstration of what he had already privately argued to Chicago *Tribune* owner, Robert McCormick: that honest black politicians were welcome in the Republican party.

Whatever one may think of Hoover's awkwardly implemented reform of the southern state parties, it is abundantly clear from the historical evidence that both the president and his wife were much more sympathetic to blacks than they felt they could reveal publicly. Occasionally the enthusiastic public responses of Moton, Barnett, or Church, after they had spoken privately with Hoover, suggested the president's personal desires. During the 1927 flood, in his plan to combat peonage, in his sudden desegregation of the Census Bureau, and in his assurances to Church immediately before and after the election, Hoover revealed his inner thoughts to selected black leaders and won their warm public praise. David Burner's perceptive biography brings together several other widely scattered instances of genuine regard for blacks. When the Hoovers purchased their home in the District of Columbia, for example, they refused to sign an exclusive agreement that would prevent them from renting to Jews and Negroes. By later standards, these small episodes of goodwill would not seem especially noteworthy, but at the time when racism was taken for granted, such decisions constituted moral statements.

At the core of their thinking, the Hoovers believed that a well-educated, inspired group of progressive black leaders was essential to black progress. The president had already taken action by insisting on a new, elite leadership for the Colored Voters Division. At the same time he was equally determined to combat black leaders who he believed were abusing their positions of trust. For her part, Lou Henry Hoover privately stressed the importance of black women leaders. Noting that one of her maids was a potential leader, she offered to pay for her college education.[35] But her most dramatic and courageous effort came with her invitation to Mrs. Oscar De Priest.

The Hoovers were well aware of the problems that an invitation to Mrs. De Priest would present. After discussing these problems with her husband, Mrs. Hoover next sought the advice of friends on how best to arrange the tea. To minimize the expected criticism, the press was not notified; and to avoid refusals or even a boycott from congressional wives, she carefully selected a small group of friends and associates who would be willing to welcome Mrs. De Priest at the last scheduled tea.[36] On 12 June 1929 the president's wife, supported by her sister and the specially picked group, including the wives of the attorney general and the secretary of war, sat down to tea with a calm, dignified Mrs. De Priest in the Green Room of the White House.[37]

The rage and hatred that erupted at the news of this simple tea party is difficult to exaggerate. Southerners took the lead in condemning the Hoovers. Three southern legislatures quickly passed resolutions deploring the "affront," the "insult," and the "humiliation" to all white Americans.[38] The resolution of the Texas legislature caught the spirit of much of the reaction. Accusing Hoover of attempting to promote "social equality," the Texans proclaimed that "the only way that this beloved South land of ours can expect to maintain its dignity and Anglo-Saxon supremacy is to stand as a whole for the eternal principles of Democracy and Anglo-Saxon superiority."[39]

Individual southerners were given to less lofty expressions of prejudice and disdain. One furious citizen warned Hoover that "folks down this way wouldn't vote for you again, even in the capacity of city dog catcher." Some Democrats could not restrain their sense of relief; others their outright sense of joy. Overnight, it seemed, the formidable threat had vanished, as Hoover's southern strategy now lay in ruins. Recalling the popular slur during the 1928 campaign, one anonymous United States senator gloated, "I am constrained to believe that if Hoover didn't dance with that negro woman in Mississippi, as was charged, it was solely because he didn't know how to dance."[40]

Southern lily-white Republicans were exasperated. Most wanted to believe that Hoover had simply made a bad mistake. Few saw any hope of regaining the favorable political momentum that Hoover's reform proclamation and his firing of Howard had generated.[41] Their cries of anguish and halfhearted efforts to find excuses confirmed the widely held conviction that in one act Hoover had healed the wounds inflicted on the Democrats by the 1928 split over Al Smith.[42] Gov. Huey Long and his cohorts in Louisiana effectively utilized the De Priest invitation to defeat a promising Republican challenge in a closely contested special election.[43] Desperate to deflect some of the criticism, Col. Henry W. Anderson circulated the rumor that Gov. Franklin D. Roosevelt of New York State had extended similar invitations to Negroes. Already hard at work nurturing his own southern strategy for 1932, Roosevelt quickly demanded and received a retraction.[44]

Shocked by the outpouring of hatred, Hoover both retreated and attacked. Through Walter Newton, his political secretary, he insisted that the invitation had been an official duty and repeatedly denied the southerners' claim that it was an effort to promote social equality.[45] At the same time he looked quickly for a way to demonstrate that the invitation had not been an inadvertent blunder, that he had fully approved of the tea, and that he both welcomed and sought the support of black leaders. To this end, he decided to invite his own black guest to the White House. His call to Robert R. Moton was a bold political decision, one designed to clarify his policies. In one stroke, he hoped to defy Democratic bigots, demonstrate to blacks that his state reforms were not intentionally anti-Negro, and indicate to southern lily-whites that black leaders and black people were still welcome in the Republican party.[46]

Not since President Theodore Roosevelt's unprecedented invitation to Booker T. Washington had a prominent black leader been ushered into the White House. As Washington's successor at Tuskegee Institute in Alabama, Moton was well known to southerners as a quiet yet active Republican who had long been considered a leader of his race. Indeed, race and politics were the subjects of the well-publicized White House meeting. Hoover wished to display his respect for southern elite blacks for all white southerners to see and also to reassure northern blacks that his southern reform program had the approval of prominent southern black leaders and was not intended to drive their southern brethren from the party. Seeking clarification that his own words might no longer convey, Hoover arranged to have Moton meet the Washington press corps.[47]

Before Moton's news conference, he and Hoover discussed the president's intentions. After their talk, Moton's assurances to the press were all that Hoover could have wished. He was more convinced than ever, he told reporters, that the president was determined "to be fair and square" to Negroes. Under Hoover's administration, he emphasized, blacks would "receive greater recognition and be given fuller opportunity to serve our country's affairs in more responsible places than hitherto has ever been true."[48] Moton did not explain what this fuller opportunity might be, but in their private talk Hoover may well have included promises of expanded federal patronage for blacks.

Nor was this new hope inconsistent with the president's reform of the southern state parties. Moton saw no danger to blacks from the type of white leadership that Hoover was seeking for the special patronage advisory committees. "I am not worried about the so-called lily-white situation in the South," he declared. The reforms could be accomplished without injury to blacks, especially, he added, if black representatives were also included on the patronage advisory committees.[49]

Some whites and blacks might have been surprised at Moton's willingness to give his public support to a reform program that threatened the elimination of other prominent southern black politicians. Influential leaders such as Du Bois and Church had nothing but scorn for such a policy. Yet Moton was not a mere tool of the whites. A proud race leader who would win a coveted award from the NAACP acknowledging his courage, he was willing to risk the new white leadership because of his trust in Hoover and his disdain for black patronage dispensers who did not use their political influence to help black people. Moton was not alone in his judgment. Years later, Ralph Bunche, the Nobel Prize-winning diplomat and black scholar, expressed much of what Moton had left unsaid to the Washington reporters. Although he referred specifically to Georgia, his words underscored the ineffectiveness of Republican patronage politics throughout the South. According to Bunche, "The fact that Georgia had two Negro Republican National Committeemen meant nothing to Georgia Negroes except [to] that pitiful handful who grovelled and slobbered at the patronage trough." Under this system the Republican party's promise to protect and promote black rights in the South was a "hollow pretense," and Bunche concluded that southern blacks were "well rid of the patronage bloated black lackeys of the black and tan days."[50]

Nonetheless, Moton's dramatic White House meeting and press conference failed to impress the president's black critics. Ironically, their reaction— influenced by black political splits—focused more on Moton than on Hoover's dramatic gesture. Remembering that Theodore Roosevelt had given Booker T. Washington virtual control over federal patronage among Negroes, some black leaders believed that Moton's politically conservative Tuskegee machine hungered for a return of power. They may also have suspected that Hoover had made patronage promises to Moton, as seems likely, and that Moton had hopes of dominating black patronage in the Hoover administration.[51] Neither were they much impressed by the Hoovers' courage in inviting Mrs. De Priest to the White House or by the consequent anguish it caused Republican lily-whites. Indeed, the president's immediate staff, and especially Anderson, had attacked the Democrats' misrepresentations with such zealous denials that they helped to create the lasting impression that Hoover's wife had acted without thinking or consulting with the president, and that the entire affair was simply an official duty without racial or political significance.[52] Invitations to the White House and private presidential assurances of good intentions were no longer sufficient to mollify the increasingly sophisticated and politically militant black critics. Still fresh in their memory were the two trials and the final expulsion of Perry Howard. Thus, virtually none applauded Hoover's efforts or accepted Moton's assurances at face value.[53] Some scholars also have accepted the notion that neither the president nor Mrs. Hoover fully realized the political significance of the invitation to Mrs. De Priest—indeed, that they had given the matter little thought. This line of reasoning, advanced by understandably suspicious blacks at the time and by historians afterward, ignores the facts that Hoover was well acquainted with southern white bigotry and that he and Mrs. Hoover, fully expecting an adverse reaction, carefully planned the unprecedented gathering to ensure optimum receptiveness for Mrs. De Priest.[54]

In retrospect Hoover's dismissal of Howard and his invitations to Mrs. De Priest and to Moton were not as baffling as his rapidly expanding number of critics seemed to think. Hoover could no more think of excluding Mrs. De Priest merely on the basis of color than he could of retaining Howard merely because he was black. He could have made a clear and convincing argument against Howard by emphasizing that the assistant attorney general, although not guilty of a criminal offense, had compromised his high office by repeatedly securing "loans" from men whom he then recommended as federal marshals. He could also have made clear his intention to elevate an elite class of blacks to leadership within the black community. Both Moton and the wife of Congressman Oscar De Priest were important examples of the new black leadership that he and his wife were anxious to encourage. It was inconceivable to him that southerners expected him to shun all black leaders from every section of the United States. He had consulted with his black elite during the campaign, and he had every intention of continuing to do so as president.[55] But as was all too often the case during his four years in the White House, he had acted without publicly explaining his reasons. By sticking to his hopes for a southern revolution and to his policy of silence on race, he confused almost everyone.

Because few interested observers had any knowledge of his hopes for racial progress and knew only of his dismissal of Howard and of his alleged purge of southern black Republicans, they naturally interpreted these latest events in terms of self-serving politics. Thus most analysts could agree on only one conclusion: the president's actions made no political sense. And because Hoover held fast to Anderson's advice not to discuss race, these observers had little choice but to continue to guess at the possible meanings. This continued speculation, fueled by his seemingly contradictory relations with prominent black leaders, turned once-enthusiastic supporters, both black and white, into either contemptuous critics or bewildered doubters who would increasingly question Hoover's political talents and even his personal integrity.

His decisions on Howard and the invitation to Mrs. De Priest infuriated both blacks and southern whites, each group concluding an opposite intent. Few perceived the distinctions in his views or credited him for his attempts, not even after Moton's White House press conference. Each group emphasized the evidence that best supported its own conclusion and tended either to discredit or to ignore other evidence that would complicate or confuse that view. One of those who did credit Hoover was Robert R. McCormick, but he, too, overstated or misread Hoover's intentions. The hitherto angry owner of the Chicago *Tribune* and critic of the president's "purge" of southern black leaders now seemed to be as reassured as the southern lily-white Republicans were dismayed. If the De Priest invitation had driven the "southern fanatics" out of the party, he informed his readers, "it has been the best use of tea since the night it was thrown into Boston harbor."[56]

Herbert Hoover, 1928 (courtesy of Henry Miller, New York Herald Tribune*)*

Robert R. Moton (courtesy of the Chicago Historical Society)

The Moton commission met 6 December 1927 at Tuskegee Institute to reconsider problems of relief. They are, left to right lower row: Miss Mary E. Williams, public health nurse, Tuskegee Institute; Claude A. Barnett of the Associated Negro Press, Chicago; Mrs. John Hope of Atlanta; Bishop Robert E. Jones of New Orleans; Dr. Robert R. Moton, Chairman of the Commission and Principal of Tuskegee Institute; Dr. J. S. Clark, President of Southern University, Baton Rouge, La.; R. R. Taylor, Vice-Principal of Tuskegee Institute. Upper row: H. C. Ray, state agricultural agent, Arkansas; M. M. Hubert, state agricultural agent, Mississippi; L. M. McCoy, president of Rust College, Holly Spring, Miss.; A. L. Holsey, Secretary of the Commission, Tuskegee Institute; J. C. Thomas, National Urban League, Atlanta; Dr. J. B. Martin of Memphis; and T. M. Campbell of Tuskegee Institute, field agent, U.S. Agricultural Extension Service. Not shown: Eva D. Bowles, Roscoe C. Brown, Eugene K. Jones, S. D. Redmond, Bert M. Roody, and Jesse O. Thomas (courtesy of The Tuskegee Institute Archives)

Hubert Work and Herbert Hoover greeting supporters from North Carolina and Virginia, 1928 (courtesy of Henry Miller, New York Herald Tribune*)*

Presidential secretaries, left to right, George Akerson, Lawrence Richey, Walter Newton (courtesy of Herbert Hoover Presidential Library)

Mabel Walker Willebrandt (courtesy of the Library of Congress)

Perry W. Howard (courtesy of the Chicago Historical Society)

Jennings C. Wise (courtesy of the Virginia Historical Society)

Henry W. Anderson (courtesy of the Virginia Historical Society)

Claudius H. Huston (courtesy of United Press Syndicate Mushkin Studio, New York, Hubert Work Papers, Hoover Institution, Palo Alto, California)

Hoover greets black Republican leaders at White House, October 1932. Background, left to right, Roscoe Conkling Simmons (finger pointing), Herbert Hoover, Postmaster General Walter Brown (behind Hoover) (courtesy of the Herbert Hoover Presidential Library)

*John J. Parker as a student at the University of North Carolina at Chapel Hill
(courtesy of the North Carolina Collection, Wilson Library, University of North
Carolina, at Chapel Hill)*

Robert R. Church, Jr. (courtesy of the Robert R. Church, Jr., Papers and the Mississippi Valley Collection, Memphis State University)

James A. Cobb (courtesy of the Chicago Historical Society)

Emmett J. Scott (courtesy of the Chicago Historical Society)

Oscar De Priest (photo by R. D. Jones, courtesy of the Chicago Historical Society)

Claude A. Barnett (courtesy of the Chicago Historical Society)

Albon Holsey (courtesy of the Chicago Historical Society)

12. Reiterating Principles

In attempting to make sense out of the many conflicting signals from the White House, few observers saw any evidence of the national and the state patronage advisory committees that the president had mentioned in his reform proclamation of 26 March 1929. Many assumed that Hoover's elite groups of nonpoliticians, his so-called high-minded business and professional volunteer reformers, were simply parts of a skillful public-relations facade, designed to hide the removal of the old black and tans while the new state parties were renovated by instituting white supremacy. Actually Hoover was in earnest about reforming politics and politicians through these elite committees of nonpoliticians. He believed that they would raise the quality of patronage appointments, and he hoped that eventually they would take charge of the entire state apparatus. Yet few southern politicians could accept this reform scheme enthusiastically. Patronage and party building in the one-party South were intertwined in a complex process not easily rearranged by nonpolitical outsiders. The result was continued confusion, a second presidential reform proclamation, and the threat by lily-whites to form their own anti-Hoover faction within the party.

The national patronage advisory committee was Hoover's personal watchdog over southern state politics. Two of his closest advisers constituted the national committee. One was Postmaster General Walter F. Brown, an aloof Ohio Bull Moose Progressive who had long served in sensitive party posts and had acquired a reputation as one who said little but knew much.[1] Equally colorless and private was Walter Newton, a former congressman from Minnesota who replaced George Akerson as Hoover's political secretary[2] and served as the chief contact between the committee and southern leaders. Neither man had any special knowledge or understanding of southern politics, and both were already heavily burdened with other duties. Often they manipulated the reform effort behind the scenes, a practice made necessary by the complicated internal circumstances within each state but one that fostered confusion and suspicion. Rapid turnover of other influential personnel compounded the problem.

For brief periods several other members of the administration also influenced southern reform policy. At first James F. Burke, general counsel for the Republican National Committee, served with Brown and Newton, but he soon returned to his private law practice in Philadelphia.[3] Until June 1929, when

Hoover finally forced the resignation of Hubert Work as Republican national chairman, Work had figured in some of the discussions, but he, and his own handpicked southern strategist, Horace A. Mann, were quickly discarded.[4] Assistant Attorney General Mabel Walker Willebrandt influenced policy through her insistence on twice prosecuting and repeatedly recommending the firing of Perry W. Howard. Claudius Huston also became prominent, but like Willebrandt and Work, after a brief time he, too, was forced to resign. Because Huston was considered an expert on southern politics, his elevation to chairman of the Republican National Committee was correctly understood as an effort to underscore the president's strong desire to attract elite white southerners to the state advisory committees.[5]

Hoover's insistence on appointing only well-qualified candidates at the state level (citizens who had the respect of their local communities) might have seemed hackneyed rhetoric to disguise lily-white intentions, but as close advisers understood, Hoover did not care whether these principles had racial implications. In his opinion, local people knew far more about a potential appointee's qualifications than did state party professionals bent upon enlarging their own influence. Hoover would have no Ohio gang in his administration, as there had been in Harding's, no scandals to embarrass him or to foster public cynicism about the democratic process. Such cynicism had long been endemic in the South, while the inability to enforce Prohibition, coupled with the continuing Teapot Dome scandals, had lowered the morale of public servants throughout the country. The incompetent, the immoral, and the indifferent had no place in the federal service.

Hoover's high standards for public service showed unfamiliarity with the important political duties of federal public servants in the South. Honesty, efficiency, dedication, the esteem of the community, and respect for democratic procedures were not enough. Selecting a candidate for United States marshal or district attorney also required careful attention to local politics, especially when attempting to rebuild Republican organizations in the hostile South. Without loyal marshals and district attorneys, local party leaders could not expect to challenge an entrenched and often corrupt one-party rule. Because marshals and district attorneys could investigate, prefer, or drop charges and enforce or not enforce the law, the state party leaders felt that they had to have politically loyal men appointed to these sensitive and prestigious posts. Whether their nominees met all of Hoover's criteria was less important to them than their commitment to help Republican candidates and to keep Democratic officials from intimidating and harassing them.

If reform was based upon the building of a rival political party that could field slates of candidates against the Democrats and thereby give the voters a choice between competing philosophies of government, as Hoover had promised, then obviously the practical politics of party building had to be taken seriously. Unfortunately Hoover had little or no real sympathy for politics or politicians. He insisted that parties were built on principles by principled men who put public service and community welfare above sordid partisanship. To that end the new state patronage advisory committees were specifically intended to enable the nonpolitical local elite to stop state party leaders from nominating mediocre men out of political expediency. Under these circumstances repeated clashes between Hoover's high standards for public service and the imperatives of local southern politics strained or destroyed party unity.

The southern reform apparatus was supposed to be simple. In each of the states designated by the reform proclamation, the Republican central committee would recommend an independent state patronage advisory committee approved by Newton and Brown. The members of the new state advisory committees were to be selected from the state's most distinguished "nonpolitical" leaders, who could attest to the honesty, competence, and local reputation of those nominees. Hoover and his advisers seemed to expect that the nominees recommended by the elite advisory committees would also have the approval of the state central committee. However, if disagreements arose, the new elite could independently reject nominees favored by the state central committees, insist upon its own nominees, and forward their recommendations directly to the president. In theory, therefore, Hoover's elite "nonpolitical" advisory groups would have more patronage power than the states' Republican political leaders.[6]

Hoover soon learned that it was easier to promise reform than it was to force it upon state political parties. Within a relatively short time Newton and Brown were finding it difficult or impossible to quiet patronage disputes that the president's standards often encouraged or exacerbated. As outsiders, the elite advisory committees often had great difficulty appreciating the many complexities that state leaders faced. Moreover, as factional disputes multiplied, it became virtually impossible to determine which of the warring state factions they should trust. Charges and countercharges soon abounded in fast-moving patronage battles and contests for control of the various state organizations. Hoover's elite were the first to become discouraged. Unaccustomed to incessant, vicious infighting, and often disagreeing with the state leaders, they despaired of reform and fled the arena, nursing their bruises. Within a relatively short time, the president and his advisers discovered, only the politicians remained to carry on the work.

The disruptive effect of factional politics on Hoover's reform efforts first became evident in Florida. In June 1928, at the National Republican Convention, the credentials committee recognized Glenn A. Skipper, a wealthy cattleman and leader of the lily-white pro-Hoover challengers, as head of the reorganized Republican state party in place of George W. Bean, who for twelve years was national committeeman and chief of the disorganized and lethargic black-and-tan faction.[7] The deposed Bean protested to Sen. George Norris that his opponents were a small group of "disgruntled politicians . . .

who are no more than character assassins."[8] Moreover, Skipper was a cracker with no social standing, little political experience, and even poorer advisers. As a result, during the 1928 campaign, the Florida Republicans split into warring factions. The most important of the anti-Skipper factions was one put together by William J. Howey, a wealthy citrus grower who insisted that Skipper's failure to help had resulted in his defeat for the governorship. Hoover himself was, of course, more successful. With enthusiastic aid from prominent Democrats, he won easily.

Among the nonpolitical elite whom Hoover sought to attract to the party were northern Republican businessmen who had retired to or lived part of the year in Florida. These men had the time, the means, the organizational ability and the interest in Republican principles to give the reform effort the respectability and guidance it needed to succeed. He also wanted to win over their counterparts among Florida Democrats. Hoover's appointment of Gilchrist Stockton, a prestigious Democratic leader, to the American embassy in Austria was an effort to assure Democrats that their "best elements" were welcome and would be rewarded.[9] But intense rivalry among competing Republican groups threatened to drive off the new elite whom Hoover hoped to attract. Rival Republican leaders warned Hoover that should the Skipper faction's crude efforts to consolidate its power by monopolizing federal patronage succeed, this power play would be interpreted as a victory for Horace Mann, with whom Skipper had worked closely, and control of the party would pass into the hands of the less reputable, even corrupt and incompetent politicos whom the Skipper faction had attracted.[10]

Skipper's own patronage recommendations and evidence from an unexpected source lent weight to his rivals' allegations. According to special investigations by the United States Coast Guard, federal marshals and district attorneys in Florida were cooperating with criminals violating the Prohibition and drug laws. The Coast Guard's chief of intelligence reported to the president that "alien smuggling, liquor and narcotic running, and violations of the quarantine laws" were rife in the state, especially in Tampa.[11] Skipper had exerted himself to be appointed collector of customs at Tampa.[12] He had not selected a cross-section of the pro-Hoover elite to serve on the new patronage advisory committee but had packed it with his cronies, who then divided up the major federal patronage posts. Even more damaging were reports on his nominees for United States marshal and district attorney. After careful investigation Attorney General William D. Mitchell twice rejected entire slates of candidates for these top positions as incompetent or unqualified.[13]

The Justice Department's repeated refusal to appoint the most influential members of the Skipper faction convinced them that Hoover was secretly cooperating with their party opponents to destroy their organization.[14] In retaliation Skipper's new chairman of the state central committee, E. E. Callaway, one of the rejected nominees, publicly accused the Hoover Democrats of conspiring with dissident Republicans to capture control of the party for their own selfish ends.[15]

Hoover reacted quickly. He was disgusted by the absence of Florida's elite from the state patronage advisory committee, the wretched quality of Skipper's nominees for federal appointments, and the public squabble over control of the party—everything he abhorred about politics. Acting under Hoover's orders Postmaster General Brown humiliated Skipper by forcing him to remove loyal supporters from the state patronage advisory committee in favor of an elite group acceptable to the administration.[16] Then, without consulting with Skipper or Callaway, Hoover appointed William P. Hughes to be United States district attorney for the Southern District.[17] In this he relied principally on the recommendation of Assistant Attorney General Mabel Walker Willebrandt, who had extensively investigated Prohibition violations in Florida and assured him that Hughes was honest and vigilant.[18]

The president's show of disapproval further complicated the internal struggle within the Florida party. None of the major Republican factions supported Hughes, and he was associated with the discredited black-and-tan faction that Willebrandt, as head of the pro-Hoover credentials committee, had helped to unseat at the last Republican National Convention on grounds of corruption.[19] Furthermore, Hughes's appointment suggested that Hoover had secretly reestablished connections with the black and tans, and this infuriated the suspicious state central committee.[20]

The new rebuff seemed too much for Skipper to bear. On 21 September Fred E. Britten, secretary of the state central committee, sent Hoover an irate letter. Britten accused the president of violating his own reform guidelines and of attempting to destroy the state party. By appointing their enemies to powerful federal positions, Hoover had callously refused to recognize the state party leaders who had supported his nomination and helped him to carry the state. But the party leaders would not accept his dictates. If necessary, they would carry their fight directly to George Norris, the chairman of the Senate Judiciary Committee, who had publicly charged Hoover with buying the convention votes of the Florida delegation.[21]

In turn Britten's threat exasperated Hoover. The Skipper crowd reinforced his conviction of the need for reform in the southern state parties, especially when both respected Republicans and prominent Florida Hoovercrats encouraged him to denounce Skipper's leadership and thereby set an example for reform throughout the South. Hoover needed little encouragement. Almost immediately he lashed out against the state central committee in a well-publicized counterattack that stressed the great need for honest, respected Republican leadership in Dixie.[22]

Hoover's public letter to Britten was emotional and deeply personal. The "most sacred" responsibility of the presidency, he lectured Britten, required "that he shall, to his utmost capacity, appoint men to public office who will execute the laws of the United States with integrity and without fear, favor or political collusion." For seven months the Justice Department had investigated nominee after nominee recommended by the state central committee, but it could not "conscientiously recommend to me any one of the names presented" because the nominees did not "measure up to my requirements of public service." One principle must guide all Republicans. The success of the Florida party and all other Republican parties "rests upon good government, not on patronage." His reforms were based upon the public pledge that "no longer shall the laws of the United States be flaunted by federal officials: no longer shall public office be regarded as mere political patronage." Nor would he be intimidated by appeals "to the opponents of the Administration to attack me." The political principles articulated in the 26 March statement were the basis for renewal of the southern state parties. And that statement, he concluded, was "no idle gesture."[23]

Many Republicans throughout the United States welcomed the brave words, but most of those in the South were angry or dismayed.[24] Without rejecting Hoover's principles, they understood patronage as the rightful expression of the administration's appreciation and confidence in their leadership and judgment.[25] In denouncing the entire Florida central committee, Hoover seemed insensitive to the difficulties of party building in the South. E. E. Callaway went further. Because the Skipper faction had worked closely with Horace Mann in building the pro-Hoover lily-white state party, Callaway felt that by appointing an ally of the black and tans and repudiating the Skipper leadership Hoover had proved that he was not seriously interested in building a lily-white party. Southern newspapers took up this interpretation and predicted that Hoover's "purge" of the Florida leaders would result in an open revolt of lily-whites throughout the South. Watchful Democrats were even more intrigued by Callaway's threat to organize all lily-white Republicans into an anti-Hoover bloc that would send 260 delegates to the next Republican National Convention to create "a new order."[26]

The Florida "purge" and the threat of a lily-white revolt added to the confusion over the administration's southern strategy.[27] Since March Hoover's repeated scoldings had clearly implied that most southern Republican politicians were tainted by patronage abuse or incompetence or self-serving politics of one kind or another. Because lily-white politicians did not appear to be any higher in his esteem than black-and-tan politicians, some lily-whites felt unjustly stigmatized.[28] Party leaders were also baffled. Apparently reform now meant appointing not only honest but superior public servants, and patronage was divorced from party building. If Hoover really believed that strong parties arose from good government and good government was therefore good politics, southern Republicans concluded, he must not understand the first essentials of competing with the entrenched Democrats.

As Republican morale plunged, that of the Democrats soared. From New

York State Franklin D. Roosevelt asked Claude Pepper, a prominent Florida Democrat, to assess the effects of Hoover's action. Pepper, amazed at Hoover's blundering reform tactics, assured Roosevelt that they would materially enhance the revival of the Democratic party in 1932. The president's tight control of patronage and his stern intervention in local party squabbles would so unsettle the state's Republican party that it could not hope to mount a serious challenge in 1932.[29] To experienced southern politicians of both parties it was all too clear that Hoover cared more about reform principles than he did about successful politics.

13. Southern Strategies

Having thoroughly confused political observers by his obviously contradictory treatments of Perry Howard and Mrs. De Priest, Hoover busied himself with a host of other reforms. The task of implementing southern reform fell almost solely upon the president's national patronage committee consisting of Newton, Brown, and for a short time Claudius Huston, the new chairman of the Republican National Committee. But, as the Florida feud suggests, their efforts were hamstrung before they had even begun. Bitter factionalism and accompanying patronage squabbles plagued them incessantly. Only in retrospect, after a detailed examination of the historical records of each state, is it possible to comprehend how compelling, often unique political circumstances within those states designated for reform forced these men to adopt increasingly pragmatic and, at times, contradictory policies. Rather than one southern strategy, they were in fact pursuing several strategies at the same time. Rather than strictly adhering to the reform principles articulated by the president, they found themselves embroiled in confusing political entanglements to which reform principles eventually had to be adjusted or abandoned entirely.

An examination of the internecine struggles in all of the southern states eventually becomes so convoluted that it ultimately confuses rather than clarifies. Therefore, it is necessary to limit detailed analysis to those states which best illustrate the different strategies that finally emerged. At the time no one but Newton, Brown, and possibly Hoover could make much sense out of the crazy-quilt pattern of southern "reform." Neither the southern lily-whites nor the northern black critics fully understood the administration's efforts, partly because there was more than one strategy and partly because much of the evidence lay in private communications and was inaccessible to them. Unable to interpret events in the several states with any degree of clarity or consistency, they selected the available evidence that buttressed their shared belief that Hoover's reform was merely a facade for a single-minded scheme to eliminate black leaders in the South. Inconsistencies in the strategy and its great political cost to the administration only indicated to them that Hoover was a clumsy politician opposed by skilled opponents. Indeed, more often than not appearances seemed to support those assumptions.

Although Hoover was convinced in his own mind that the reform of the southern state parties was directed toward laudable goals, he soon discovered that he could not work with lily-whites and hope to escape from political problems involving racial decisions. Louisiana, for example, offered him the best opportunity to create the "model, exhibit A" reform showcase for the entire South.[1] Because of the importance of this precedent-setting model, Hoover worked closely with Claudius Huston for a brief time to win over the state leaders to the reform plan. Success in Louisiana, they believed, would create reform momentum and help them convince other southern state parties to adopt similar reorganization.

At first the model reform appeared certain to be adopted by the Louisiana Republicans. The man responsible for negotiating the new plan was Claudius Huston, a lily-white Tennessee entrepreneur who had been recently appointed by Hoover to succeed Work as chairman of the Republican National Committee. Huston was one of Hoover's most trusted and valued political advisers. Long familiar with southern politics, he had spent most of his time during the 1928 campaign troubleshooting in the East, but his selection was interpreted to mean that the president placed great importance on southern reform, an interpretation that Huston quickly confirmed.[2] Lily-whites were delighted with the appointment, but blacks divided sharply over him. R. R. Moton approved of Hoover's choice, regarding Huston as the type of white leader who would respect and work with southern black Republicans. Robert R. Church, Jr., however, did not trust Huston, for he knew him as a Tennessee lily-white who would not hesitate to purge black politicians.[3] Because he was acceptable to Moton, the president concluded that Huston could work with both lily-whites and blacks, but the Tennessean was not as sympathetic to black leadership nor as committed to black progress as he had led Moton to believe.

Although Huston appeared to be something of a pragmatic expert on southern politics generally, he was most knowledgeable about the intense factionalism within the Louisiana state party. He had twice earlier attempted and had twice failed to unify the state party for President Harding. Now his third attempt seemed much more fruitful. As the new Republican National Chairman, he quickly convinced Emile Kuntz and Victor Loisel, leaders of two of the competing lily-white factions, to agree to unify under a "model, exhibit A set-up, which would be helpful to their own state and of value in other places in the South." At the top of the state party hierarchy Kuntz and Loisel would establish an elite patronage advisory committee "made of outstanding men and women," the best of Louisiana Republicans and Hoovercrats. This committee would replace the current patronage advisory group, which had been hurriedly put together in response to Hoover's reform proclamation but was staffed with cronies and fellow officeholders. The new patronage committee, Huston told the president, would have real independence and political power. It would make patronage recommendations to the state central committee and directly to the president, if necessary, and it would also have the right to bring issues of importance directly before the state central committee. The new elite would therefore become a vital force in the deliberations of the party's inner councils.[4]

Hoover was overjoyed with Huston's swift and skillful work. As an example of the elite corps he hoped to attract to the reformed party, Hoover had appointed the prominent Louisiana shipbuilder Ernest Lee Jahncke as first assistant secretary of the navy, and he now looked forward to attracting many more prominent Louisianans.[5] With distinguished men at the top of the state party wielding real patronage and policy influence, Hoover dreamed of other southern states adopting this model and of a Republican elite throughout the South that would soon be competing with the old Democratic planter elite. But Kuntz and Loisel had their price. In addition to a complicated series of patronage arrangements that would divide the federal appointments between their two factions, they insisted that the president purge Walter Cohen, the highly respected black collector of customs at New Orleans and head of the state's black-and-tan faction.

Cohen had lost control of the state party at the 1928 Republican National Convention where his faction had supported Charles Curtis rather than Hoover. Incensed that the credentials committee should transfer power to the lily-whites, black leaders had complained directly to Hoover, who sought to mollify them by instructing his people on the committee to recognize Cohen but none of his followers.[6] As a result the lily-whites were legally in command of the state party. But they had argued to Hoover that it was not possible to attract elite whites or to build a strong political opposition as long as blacks retained prominent positions. Kuntz proposed therefore that Cohen be appointed to the most prestigious diplomatic position available to a black, that of minister to Liberia. This promotion would effectively eliminate him, presumably without embarrassing him or humiliating blacks generally, while allowing Kuntz to fill the customs position with an important white member of his own faction.

Quite possibly reassured by Huston that Cohen would be receptive, Hoover decided that the Kuntz proposal was not too high a price to pay for this model for southern state party reform, and accordingly, he personally offered the diplomatic position to Cohen. As anticipated, Cohen was willing to accept this new honor, but he, too, had his price. He unexpectedly stipulated that he would need an annual salary of $10,000, a sum that Hoover soon discovered was considerably higher than either the State Department or Congress would authorize. Moreover, a further complication quickly arose. Upon hearing of the impending appointment, Moton vigorously protested to Hoover that it was a transparent lily-white stratagem, which Hoover must avoid. Shortly thereafter, the physically ailing Cohen had second thoughts about living in Liberia and the matter ended with him still in the New Orleans Custom House.[7]

Despite the repeated urgings of Louisiana lily-whites, Hoover refused to make any further effort to remove Cohen. This started a series of complex internal repercussions between the two lily-white factions. Basically, the unity that Huston had managed to achieve between the Kuntz and Loisel factions depended first on the elimination of Cohen as collector of customs and second on a succession of carefully balanced patronage appointments that were now made too difficult, if not impossible, to effect. Moreover, some Louisiana lily-white leaders interpreted Hoover's refusal to oust Cohen as proof of his sympathies for blacks. Before long the internal feuding became so complex and bitter that Huston was powerless to quiet it.[8] If Hoover had moved Cohen out of the Customs House promptly, either by appointment to another federal post or simply by replacing him, and then had acted on the patronage arrangements that Huston had negotiated with Kuntz and Loisel, the president might well have succeeded in creating his model. But the price was too high, and to his credit, he refused to force Cohen's retirement.

Hoover's decision won him no credits from either blacks or lily-whites. Yet if he had been pursuing a southern strategy designed to eliminate all black leaders, he knew that Louisiana would have been an excellent place to promote it. Why did Hoover protect Cohen? Cohen himself apparently believed that the president could not eliminate him without losing black votes in the North.[9] Although this is certainly a plausible argument, the evidence to support it is nonexistent. Hoover had done little to court the northern black vote during the 1928 campaign, and there is no evidence that his decision to retain Cohen stemmed from such a pragmatic political calculation. In fact the evidence clearly establishes that Hoover was almost totally unconcerned with the storm of black protest and criticism generated by black politicians during the campaign and afterward. A Republican elite in the southern state parties was clearly of much greater importance to him than courting the northern black vote, especially if those votes meant compromising the southern reform.

Much more plausible and in accordance with the evidence is Hoover's own privately expressed concern. He would not create the impression that he favored purging all black leaders, that his reform effort was merely a lily-white stratagem. Earlier he had insisted to the Chicago *Tribune* owner, Robert R. McCormick, that the purpose of southern reform was to eliminate corrupt politicians, both white and black. Although he was sincere when he assured McCormick that honest black southern leaders had nothing to fear from him, this pledge did not mean refusal to cooperate with lily-white leaders willing to effect genuine party reform. The actions of the credentials committee during the 1928 nominating convention had already established his willingness to work with lily-whites. Still, there were limits to what he would do to realize his reform goals, and Louisiana is an early and significant example of those limits. Even when sorely tempted as he was in Louisiana, Hoover would not do what lily-white leaders insisted must be done to attract a new southern elite and build strong state parties, which was to systematically purge honest, reputable black leaders. As the lily-white Louisianans had predicted, the result was disastrous.

Hoover's refusal to remove Cohen not only generated internal party chaos but opened the way for Huey Long and other Democrats to exploit the decision. Long skillfully linked Hoover's protection of Cohen with the much-publicized De Priest tea. In turn, angry lily-white Republican factionalists soon accused Kuntz of secretly supporting black political participation. Cohen died in December 1930, but his death did nothing to end the intense squabbling.[10] Democratic senators and congressmen added to the complications by continually intervening through friends on the Senate Judiciary Committee and by threatening to invoke senatorial courtesy to prevent or delay important Republican patronage appointments.[11] Under these circumstances, not even Jahncke could gather together an elite or prevail upon the Louisiana Republicans to unite.[12]

While Louisiana illustrated both Hoover's willingness to promote an elite lily-white party and his unwillingness to sacrifice honest black leaders, not every southern state proved to be such a difficult challenge. Hoover enjoyed harmonious relations with a number of southern organizations. Where there was no question in the president's mind about the honesty of the Republican leaders, Newton and Brown followed a pragmatic policy of honoring their patronage recommendations and promoting goodwill. If the lily-whites had captured control of the party and had been officially recognized by the 1928 Republican National Convention, Hoover cooperated fully with them as he did in North Carolina, where Charles A. Jonas led a vigorous, growing party that offered consistent, statewide opposition to the Democrats and often succeeded in electing its candidates to state and even congressional offices.[13]

Less rewarding was Hoover's cooperation with R. B. Creager, the lily-white Texan who had engineered the defeat of the anti-Hoover black and tans at the 1928 national convention.[14] Election disputes and charges of corruption tarnished Creager's victory over Gooseneck Bill McDonald, and shortly after the election Sen. Smith Brookhart's investigating subcommittee began looking into the charges. Brookhart accepted the testimony of Creager's political opponents at face value while he seemingly dismissed Creager's lengthy explanations and denials. This angered Creager who in turn began to criticize Brookhart for investigating only Republican southern parties while avoiding Democrats and for insisting to the press that he had uncovered corruption when, in fact, he had only heard the oft-repeated charges of political opponents who offered no evidence to substantiate them.

Unaccustomed to feisty witnesses, Brookhart became entangled in a lengthy personal feud with Creager and publicly demanded that Hoover honor his pledge to reform the South by taking disciplinary action against the Texas Republican. Gooseneck Bill McDonald's black and tans and black leaders throughout the United States were especially interested in the president's reaction when a lily-white like Creager was charged with corruption. Hoover had repeatedly given Brookhart his enthusiastic public support, and his actions in Florida had already demonstrated that he would not protect incompetent or corrupt lily-whites. Yet, bolstered by his own investigation that cleared Creager, Hoover had reason to reject Brookhart's uncritical acceptance of these charges as either "evidence" or as conclusive proof of Creager's guilt.

The president's steadfast refusal to discipline Creager in the face of Brookhart's repeated public demands reinforced the impression that Hoover acted against only blacks who were accused of corruption. In reality Hoover had ordered a secret FBI investigation that failed to uncover evidence to substantiate the sensational corruption charges. The president's disappointment in Brookhart's investigative methods and his education in southern factional infighting convinced him that Creager was telling the truth. Brookhart was furious. He now began criticizing Hoover, but despite the senator's repeated public denunciations the president continued to honor Creager's patronage recommendations.[15] To the best of Hoover's knowledge Creager was an honest politician, and he had no intention of purging any such party leader.

The Creager-Brookhart feud created the impression that Hoover "reformed" only black and tans and thus reinforced the belief in an antiblack southern strategy. At the same time the public paid little attention to the president's harmonious relations with black-and-tan leaders in Arkansas, Missouri, and West Virginia. In Missouri, for example, Hoover made available to E. B. Clements, the national Republican committeeman, United States marshals to help blacks register and vote in the southern part of the state, where white opposition was strongest.[16] Black-and-tan leaders in Arkansas led by Scipio Jones also worked well with the administration.[17] West Virginia congressmen, who relied heavily on black votes for the margin of victory, received special patronage considerations to help them retain the allegiance of black voters.[18] In these states the administration made no effort to encourage lily-whites to challenge the black and tans. As with the lily-whites in North Carolina and Texas, the administration was content to work harmoniously with those state leaders whose honesty and competence it trusted.

Another category of reform that received little or no public attention involved lily-white state leaders who had not been charged with corruption but who were, nonetheless, regarded as patronage spoilsmen. Instead of working to build political opposition to Democrats, these leaders manipulated the state party for their own selfish purposes. In such cases, as in virtually all relations with southern leaders, Hoover relied upon his political secretary Walter Newton, who quickly became the dominant figure in Hoover's national patronage advisory committee. Although often inept and humorless, Newton did his unimaginative best to encourage new leadership to challenge the older, parochial, patronage politicos in control of the party.

The most prominent of the disreputable state leaders was Bascom Slemp, national committeeman and lily-white boss of the Virginia state party. As congressman for many years and then as Calvin Coolidge's private secretary, Slemp had built a considerable political organization in the Ninth Congressional District, where he distributed federal patronage liberally while allowing the party in the rest of the state to remain weak and undeveloped. Because Hoover had eagerly sought Coolidge's endorsement in his race for the nomination and during the election campaign, he had courted the onetime private secretary at every opportunity. Slemp was a frequent visitor during the campaign, and before long he felt secure enough with Hoover to push for appointment as postmaster general. Following the campaign, however, on the advice of reform-minded Virginians Col. Henry W. Anderson and Jennings C. Wise, Hoover abruptly drew away from Slemp.[19]

Perhaps because Slemp was known to be a skillful and tenacious politician, the president and his advisers were unwilling to risk an open break with the Virginia boss. Instead Hoover publicized his high regard for Anderson and imagined that this recognition would rally the "best elements" to Anderson's reform faction. He hoped that Anderson would take control of the party away from Slemp at the next party convention, which would select the party's candidates for the special November 1929 statewide election. But Anderson and Wise proved as weak and ineffective as politicians as they were ignorant and naive as advisers on race and reform. Lacking their own political organization, they had neither the time nor the talent to build one. If they expected their sudden prominence to attract the state's "best elements" to their reform standard, they were quickly disillusioned.

Faced with this discouraging lack of enthusiasm and tired of the incessant demands of politics, the aging Anderson refused to run for the gubernatorial nomination, with the result that the reformers had no outstanding candidate to lead them or to attract the "best elements" to their crusade. Finally, after a long and damaging delay, during which Hoover was busy launching reform efforts in other areas, and the outgoing chairman of the Republican National Committee, Hubert Work, revealed his lack of interest by ignoring pleas for financial help, Anderson and Wise decided on a more limited objective. They recommended to Hoover that the only way to begin reforming the state party was to organize a new coalition consisting of Democrats who had bolted their party in favor of Hoover, Slemp's regular Republican organization, and the elite, which they still hoped to attract.[20]

The coalition strategy was as disastrous as it was desperate. When Hoover ordered Slemp to support the coalition, the angry boss lent his outward allegiance, but worked covertly to ensure its eventual defeat. He had no intention of sharing power with "reformers" or of helping to build a rival organization within the state party. Ironically, this feuding among the rival Republican factions allowed the Hoover Democrats to dictate the slate of Republican candidates for the November 1929 election. Anderson, Wise, Hoover, and other hopeful northern Republicans assumed that these Hoover Democrats were the upright, intelligent, and informed citizenry of the South who had embraced Republican principles and economic policies and would welcome this opportunity to restore democracy and clean government to their state and communities. It was these people, led by the reform elite, who would constitute the vanguard of the Republican crusade. Convinced of this vision, Anderson and Wise closed their eyes to the type of Hoover Democrats they had attracted and to the lackluster candidates whom these Democrats selected to lead the fight in the November state election.[21]

The Virginia Democratic party won an easy, indeed, overwhelming victory. Many reasons have been offered to explain the Republicans' humiliation, but the most pointed analysis was offered by Wise's own brother, Henry A. Wise, a New York City lawyer who was actively engaged in Republican politics and a keen observer of the party in his home state. Rather than representing the "better elements" in the state, the Hoover Democrats who joined the coalition, he insisted, were instead a motley collection of Klansmen and religious fanatics, "a miserable lot of narrow-minded, small-souled people" who would have been a liability to any political party, including the Democrats. But these "blind bigots" were not the principal cause of the fiasco. More important than any other factor was Hoover's ineptness. His failure to appoint a southerner to his cabinet in recognition of his historic victories in the South had deeply offended the sensibilities of the numerous independents and disaffected Democrats who had voted for him a year earlier. As a result they had not trooped to the colors even though Hoover was blowing the horn. The invitation to Mrs. De Priest had further disillusioned them and had, in fact, created the opportunity for her husband, Congressman Oscar De Priest, to berate the South in an angry speech in Norfolk that "antagonized thousands and opened up the old race prejudice issue." Then, too, Hoover had done nothing to "unhorse" Slemp, and this made it virtually impossible to convince already skeptical Virginians that Hoover fully supported Anderson's vision of a southern revolution. It was obvious to Wise that "Hoover knew or could have known all of this and he did nothing." Besides, he told his brother, "the people are absolutely right in calling you an idealist." In failing "to see the practical side" of politics, Jennings Wise had not understood that "the promise of reforms to come is a promise of something too remote."[22]

Wise respected his brother's analysis, but he refused to place the blame on the president. Race, not Hoover, he insisted, was the chief cause of the defeat. Soon after the special election Wise had a long, private conversation with the troubled president. Wise reassured him that even without the invitation to Mrs. De Priest, the Democrats would have found other excuses to exploit racial hatred. At Hoover's urging, Wise undertook his own investigation of the debacle, and in his two subsequent reports he emphasized the cynical yet skillful manner in which the Democrats had used racial hatred against Republicans while covertly organizing and winning the eligible black vote for them-selves. Even after his two reports, however, Wise did not concede that his findings demolished the theory that he and Anderson had sold to Hoover: that by eliminating black leadership and ignoring racial politics, southern white Republicans could rebuild their party, revitalize democracy, and eventually benefit black people by forcing two evenly matched parties to compete for the black vote. Their flawed theory had collapsed when the Democrats refused to play their game, and the "better elements" did not flock to the crusade.

The totally demoralized reformers never recovered from the debacle. An-derson retired from politics. Wise eventually accepted a position as a special assistant attorney general in Washington, D.C.[23] Slemp, of course, remained in control. For all of their efforts and good intentions, the Hoover reformers in Virginia accomplished little or nothing. Racial politics remained more power-ful than their visionary goals. The "revolution" in Virginia had failed, and the likelihood of failure throughout the South was becoming more and more of a worrisome probability.

Oliver D. Street was even more objectionable than Slemp, but this lily-white patronage boss of Alabama proved much craftier and more resilient. Well known among Alabama blacks as intensely hostile to them, Street none-theless always kept one token black on the state central committee, which he controlled.[24] Roman Catholics such as Al Smith were equally anathema to Street, and during the campaign he distributed vicious anti-Catholic propa-ganda, for which Charlie Michelson blamed Hoover. Perhaps aware of the administration's disfavor, Street wisely professed a willingness to cooperate and quickly established a state patronage advisory committee. At the same time, however, he did everything within his power to undo the new patronage scheme, complaining that Alabama Hoovercrats had refused to associate with Republicans.[25]

Hoover and Newton were not fooled by Street. Nonetheless, alternative Republican leaders were harder to find in Alabama than in Virginia. Street's only rival was Joseph O. Thompson, vice-president of the American Cotton Association. Moton enthusiastically endorsed Thompson, who had worked actively with Horace Mann in promoting Hoover during the 1928 campaign, but Thompson was unable to prove that Street was corrupt, and Huston, the new chairman of the Republican National Committee, who was now, for a brief time, directing the southern reform effort, unaccountably considered Thompson to be too "garrulous" to be the new leader of the state party.[26] Undaunted, Moton continued his efforts to unseat Street. He presented evi-dence of his racial and religious bigotry, and eventually Moton succeeded in preventing Street from securing for himself an appointment to the federal bench. Moton also convinced the administration to investigate and to delay Street's patronage appointments, but Street managed to survive until Newton and Brown needed his delegate support for the 1932 national convention, and this ended any chance of dislodging the skillful bigot or stopping his patronage appointments.[27] It was a bitter defeat for Moton, who had hoped to prove that Hoover's reform effort could eliminate white racists as well as disreputable black politicians.

Bigoted lily-whites, even such an odious character as Street, survived the reform campaign because no corruption charges against them could be substantiated, but they were frustrated and angered by the confusion over the meaning of southern reform. One of these was John W. Farley, an Anglo-Saxon purist and executive director of the Southern States Republican League, a rather loosely organized, weak lily-white regional organization formed in 1926 to win over all the state parties from the black and tans. Farley demanded that Hoover "reform" Tennessee by removing Robert R. Church, Jr., from the party. Farley, and no doubt others among his Ku Klux Klan–affiliated followers, were well aware that Church had become an outspoken critic of the president's "reform," and they apparently assumed that Hoover would be happy to get rid of him. But again appearances belied realities in the tangled thickets of "reform" politics.

Following Hoover's 26 March reform proclamation, Church suddenly switched from one of the president's most enthusiastic black supporters back to one of his most caustic and influential critics. Hoover had allayed his earlier misgivings over the credentials committee "purge" of anti-Hoover black and tans, the appointment of the Hoover Doctors to the new Colored Voter Division, and race hatred generated in the South by Horace Mann. After considerable persuasion, Church had accepted that Hoover was not antiblack and that, as president, he would correct the excesses and clarify the misunderstandings that had developed. Because of these assurances, Church had thrown his support to Hoover in the last days of the campaign.[28] Hoover had then ousted both Work and Mann and these actions had further boosted Church's confidence in him. But after the 26 March proclamation and the appointment of Claudius Huston, his old lily-white enemy from Tennessee, as chairman of the Republican National Committee and director of southern state reform, Church interpreted Hoover's reform efforts as little more than a mask for a lily-white offensive against southern black leadership. He remembered that after delivering convention delegates to Hoover, Perry Howard had been "double-crossed" and was being prosecuted on corruption charges brought by his defeated lily-white opponents. Now Church too felt double-crossed and concluded that Hoover had deliberately misled him.

Hoover understood Church's suspicions but he did nothing further to reassure him either publicly or privately. Hoover knew Church better than he did other southern black politicians. He knew him as an honest, courageous leader who had long fought for black rights and participation in political life. He knew therefore that Church would never acquiesce to the administration's utopian strategy for reforming the South. Nonetheless, despite their politically significant differences, Hoover was determined to protect Church against those who assumed that all black leaders were to be purged from the party. Privately but unmistakably Hoover frustrated every effort of the lily-whites to force him out of his prominent positions as one of the two national committeemen from Tennessee and as a member of the Republican State Executive Committee.[29]

Church's chief political ally in Tennessee was the other Republican national committeeman, Congressman J. Will Taylor, a white politician who also served as the chief dispenser of federal patronage in the state. To remove Taylor and his black-and-tan allies, the lily-white Republicans accused him of corruption. These charges were prominently featured in the influential progressive magazine *Independent*, but by this time Hoover was less impressed by them. After repeated conversations with Taylor, the president brushed aside the accusations as mere partisan politics. Hoover's approval and support allowed Church and Taylor to continue their political alliance. In Memphis Church was the head of the largest number of blacks voting in general elections in the South, and Taylor respected his leadership by recommending all of Church's nominees for federal patronage in Memphis to the administration. Another alliance with Ed Crump, boss of the state Democratic organization, enabled Church to wield considerable political influence.[30]

The lily-whites had worked hard in helping Hoover win Tennessee in 1928, and, like Church, they had interpreted the 26 March statement to mean the end of black leaders, particularly Church. To lessen the friction, Hoover relied on Claudius Huston to arrange some sort of compromise. But Huston's efforts were in vain. Church understandably did not trust Huston, and the lily-whites would not tolerate Church.[31] Nonetheless, Hoover would not act against the black leader.[32] By this time Hoover had begun to realize that charges of corruption often contained more political motivation than substance, and he believed that Church, although a politician, was the kind of honest, dedicated official he wanted to encourage in his "black elite." Unfortunately, his ties with Church were broken, and he did not communicate these views. To embarrass Hoover for his continued support of Church, Farley arranged a congressional investigation into charges against Church, but Taylor effectively defended Church, and the lily-whites suffered still another defeat.[33] But in a way so also did Hoover's reform program. This time it appeared to lily-whites that the president was defending a white boss and his corrupt black lackeys. Once again it seemed to some that Hoover's reforms were subject to political expediency.

Church retained his positions on the state executive committee and as national committeeman, and Hoover regularly approved his patronage nominees. But the president got no thanks from Church or from the lily-whites either for his support of Creager in Texas against Senator Brookhart's incessant onslaughts. Relatively few seemed to know about the choices involved in protecting Cohen in Louisiana, and when they did, frustrated lily-whites criticized Hoover for not removing Cohen, and suspicious blacks were angered by the evidence of his willingness to cooperate, though not fully, with the lilies. Because these observers assumed that there was only one southern strategy, they were baffled by Hoover's strange twists and turns and by his inconsistencies. Above all, they were understandably unable to make sense out of his reform efforts. Refusing to oust Creager, despite Brookhart's anguished public remonstrances, created the impression that charges of corruption impressed Hoover only when they were directed against blacks. Congressman Taylor, rather than Hoover, garnered the credit from blacks for protecting Church, while lily-whites called Hoover a hypocrite for refusing to act against the "corrupt" black and tans in Tennessee and against Cohen in Louisiana. Concentrating on their own disappointments, both lily-whites and blacks failed to recognize the variety and complexity of Hoover's southern strategies. To those who tried to understand Hoover's "southern strategy" the president seemed inept and either naive or callous. Despite prodigious efforts by Newton, Huston, Brown, and other assistants, Hoover's attempt to reform the South failed. It was naive, ambitious, and complex—probably too ambitious and certainly more utopian and complex than any of his critics realized.

14. Frustrating Purges

Mississippi, South Carolina, and Georgia were supposed to be the administration's foremost showcase reform states. It was in these three states that the allegedly corrupt black-and-tan parties had been repeatedly investigated. Newspaper publicity had convinced virtually everyone that the charges against the Republican leaders were true, indeed, that the evidence against them was overwhelming.

Charges of a deliberate Hoover purge of black and tans and the institution of a lily-white strategy were appropriate in all three states. In Mississippi and South Carolina Newton and Brown replaced the black-and-tan leaders with lily-whites of their own choosing and bent every effort to help them retain control and reconstitute the power structure of the state organization. However, in Georgia a somewhat different pattern eventually emerged. Instead of an all-white leadership, Newton and Brown secretly experimented with a coalition of black and tans and lily-whites that would allow black leaders real influence and recognition within the party councils.

In each instance the purge failed to reform the party along the lines desired by the president. Of course, neither the deposed leaders nor the white Democrats wished to see Hoover succeed. Aided by Democratic senators, the black and tans fought a skillful, tedious rearguard battle, which soon demonstrated how difficult it would be for the distant White House to impose its will on the state parties. At the local level partisan politics and personal relationships were often more important and enduring than Hoover's lofty principles.

Virtually everyone in the administration believed that Perry Howard and his political lieutenants would be convicted. From July 1928, when Howard was first indicted, until May 1929, when he won a second acquittal, the presumption of their guilt had dominated the thoughts of the president and his top advisers. Willebrandt and the district attorneys who prosecuted Howard had convinced Attorney General Mitchell and Hoover of his guilt long before he was exonerated. Accordingly, before Howard finally emerged triumphant, the president had already designated Howard's most vehement critic, the lily-white Lamont Rowlands, as the new leader of the Mississippi state party.[1]

If Hoover had turned instead to other black-and-tan Republicans whom he knew and respected, such as Eugene P. Booze and his wife Mary, the national committeewoman with whom he had been accused of dancing, Negro public opinion might not have turned so sharply against him. At one point, indeed, it had seemed that Hoover might seek new black leaders to replace Howard. In July 1928, when Howard was indicted, Hoover had suggested that Work find other respectable black leaders to replace Howard, but Work had refused. The campaign chairman had argued that as the best elements in Mississippi and other southern states were rallying to the Hoover standard, any intervention at this stage was undesirable. This fateful acquiescence signaled the shift in Hoover's thinking toward the desirability of attracting a white southern elite.

The appeal of the civic leader who was not a "politician" can hardly be exaggerated in any assessment of Hoover's concept of political reform. Because Eugene and Mary Booze were members of the Howard organization, and because the entire state party had been tainted by the indictment of its top leaders, Hoover convinced himself that an entirely new set of leaders was necessary. Even more important was Hoover's belief that Rowlands was not a "politician." He was instead a dedicated civic leader who had volunteered his services during the 1927 Mississippi flood and a high-minded reformer who had courageously entered the political arena to fight corruption in government. This was the type of leader who would attract the best elements in the state to the party and its principles.[2]

Hoover's simplistic evangelical faith in principled, nonpolitical reformers who would cleanse state government and restore democracy rendered him incapable of dealing with the complexities of southern politics. By forcing Howard's resignation without encouraging other Mississippi black and tans, and by selecting Rowlands as the new state leader, Hoover put his own personal stamp of approval upon the lily-white movement in Mississippi. Ironically, his approval had less to do with race than appearance suggested. To his way of thinking, reform principles championed by civic leaders, rather than by politicians, transcended traditional Republican politics in the South. Whether the reformers were lily-white or black and tan, or a combination of the two, made less difference to him than their dedication to good government.

In the complex world of political realities, and especially in southern factional politics, reform was often in the eyes of the beholder. To blacks the president's support of the lily-whites who had engineered Willebrandt's abortive crusade against Howard was certainly not their idea of reform but crass, dirty politics, a view that was shared by some white Mississippians. Following the first trial, their sympathy turned toward Howard, the racial scapegoat, rather than to Rowlands and Hoover, the champions of southern reform. To their way of thinking, the prosecution had been based on such dubious evidence that the trials seemed an effort to advertise the administration's lily-white strategy rather than to reform the party.

More outrageous still were the allegations that the all-white jury had subverted justice for partisan political purposes. This popular explanation for the first acquittal surfaced again in March 1929 during Howard's second trial, when Frederick Sullens, editor of the Jackson (Mississippi) *Daily News*, suggested it in an editorial. The real question, Sullens had insisted, was not Howard's guilt or innocence, "but whether a jury will be willing to encourage the establishment of a white Republican Party in Mississippi." Sullens's alleged attempt to influence the jury resulted in five years' probation for contempt of court from the federal judge presiding over the trial.[3] Mississippians were well aware that there were better ways to defeat the lily-white Republicans than by subverting juries and obstructing justice.

Howard was skilled in those ways, as were the Democrats. Whether he was convicted or not, the Mississippi Democrats had no intention of allowing Hoover to create a lily-white party to challenge them. Keeping blacks in the top councils of the Republican party was the easiest way to hinder the lily-whites, and if the leader was not Howard, there were other black politicians who could carry on the fight.[4] Nonetheless, Howard was probably best able to direct the battle. Since 1921, when he was appointed a special assistant attorney general, Howard had lived in Washington, D.C., where he established good working relationships with a wide spectrum of politicians, including the two Democratic senators from Mississippi. He was an experienced, pragmatic politician who had long controlled federal patronage and who was well aware that important appointments were often subject to congressional review and always to senatorial courtesy. Quite naturally, during the long period of Republican control of the federal patronage, Howard had frequently consulted with the white Democratic senators before making recommendations, and he had cooperated with them concerning their own patronage needs. He was still the legal leader of the black-and-tan organization in Mississippi, and regardless of being stripped of his federal job and patronage powers, he was still a Republican national committeeman, a position that could be revoked only by the Republican National Convention in 1932. Moreover, there was nothing to prevent one of the Mississippi senators, Hubert Stephens, from continuing his political relationship with Howard. In fact, there was a very good reason why that relationship became stronger, for neither Howard nor Stephens wished to see Lamont Rowlands and his lily-white Republican challengers succeed in establishing a successful opposition.

Before long Rowlands was beside himself with rage and frustration. He was convinced that his most important patronage nominations, especially those involving United States marshals, district attorneys, and judges, were being delayed by the Senate Judiciary Committee because of the clandestine opposition of both Democratic senators.[5] Rowlands had no proof that Howard was involved, and, in any case, the administration felt that it could not afford a confrontation with the two Mississippi Democratic senators, whose votes were needed on a variety of issues. Rowlands's fears and assumptions were probably correct. He knew that the long delays were seriously hampering his party-building efforts. He could not attract Hoovercrats or other dissident Democrats until he could prove that his organization had replaced Howard's, and the best proof of that was appointment of Rowlands's nominees for United States judges, district attorneys, and marshals. Meantime, Howard was regrouping his forces within the state and rallying his northern black allies to help him maintain his legal control of the official state party at the Republican National Convention to be held in 1932. With that control, he could refuse to seat the Hoover-sponsored yet unofficial Rowlands party while reaffirming the legal status of his own black-and-tan organization.[6]

Each state posed its own problems, but sometimes similar strange alliances formed elsewhere in response to Hoover's reform. The unlikely coalition of anti-Hoover black Republicans and white Democrats was as strong in South Carolina as it was in Mississippi. Like Howard, Tieless Joe Tolbert, the white head of the South Carolina black and tans, retained his position as national committeeman despite Hoover's designation of the lumber merchant J. Carl Hambright as the unofficial new leader of the state party. Senatorial investigations notwithstanding, the evidence against Tolbert was not sufficient to warrant indictment. Tolbert had earlier protested the unproven charges of corruption to Work, who in turn had advised Newton that Tolbert was "not altogether bad, and will be more helpful to us if given some recognition inside than if left entirely on the outside."[7] Yet Tolbert's case was one of the early cases for Hoover to judge, and, not yet educated by Creager about the pitfalls of accepting Brookhart's charges without question, Hoover brushed aside Tolbert's protests. Newton and Brown duly recognized the new business-oriented state patronage advisory committee created by Hambright, instructing him to go about building a new leadership.[8]

Initial confusion over Hambright's authority further complicated the already complex factional divisions. After weeks of useless wrangling, Hambright finally succeeded in establishing himself as the leader who would engineer the overthrow of Tieless Joe at the state convention in the spring of 1930. Tolbert was no southern gentleman, and as one scholar has concluded, his leadership may have made a "joke" out of Republican politics in South Carolina, but whatever he was, he was no political amateur as Hambright was.[9] He quickly and skillfully countered Hambright's efforts and, like his Mississippi counterpart, enlisted the help of the two Democratic senators, most especially the Hoover-hating Cole Blease, to delay Hambright's recommendations for United States marshals and district attorneys.[10]

Tolbert understood the crucial importance of political momentum. Hambright needed an immediate demonstration of his ability to secure major federal posts, especially the United States marshals. Without them, he lacked security and the proof of leadership needed to build a new state party.[11] To harass him, Tolbert employed the same tactic used against himself by his own political enemies; he accused the Hambright nominees of corruption. Under Hoover's strict guidelines on appointments, such charges required lengthy investigations and, thus, long delays. They also made it easier for senators and congressmen to request that their colleagues on the Senate Judiciary Committee withhold confirmation. In one instance, Senator Norris sought to expedite an appointment by holding a special hearing on Hambright's nominee for United States marshal of the Western District. The Senate eventually confirmed the man, but not before his reputation had been publicly tarnished.[12]

Hambright was understandably angered by the personal damage inflicted on his nominees by public charges, investigations, and confirmation hearings. Few people would relish this type of public ordeal, and few would consider the appointment worth the suffering and damage to their reputation. Hambright complained also that he was forced to consult with the Democratic senators and congressmen before making recommendations for even minor post office jobs. And when he put forth well-qualified candidates, he still faced unreasoning opposition. Senatorial courtesy, he lamented, was "playing havoc with the little progress we might be able to make under more favorable circumstances."[13]

Newton and Brown's choice of Hambright as chairman of the state patronage advisory committee proved to be a poor decision, and the lumber merchant made his job even more difficult by attempting to remove Samuel J. Leapheart, the respected white incumbent marshal for the Eastern District of South Carolina who had a reputation for protecting blacks. Hambright's decision was a lily-white decision that was not based on genuine reform. To make matters worse, he attempted to appoint his own brother as collector of internal revenue, thus seeming guilty of both racism and nepotism. To frustrate his attempts, Tolbert and Blease shrewdly backed the popular Leapheart.[14] This clever strategy brought Tolbert the assistance of valuable northern allies, notably the NAACP, which now joined in the effort to retain the marshal who protected black people.

The incessant patronage squabbles and charges of corruption took a heavy toll on the Hambright organization. Members of his elite advisory committee became discouraged and gradually withdrew from the internecine warfare. He was himself often discouraged, and Newton repeatedly sought to revitalize his spirits. Yet Hambright had done poorly. Although he had temporarily driven out the black and tans, they had won powerful allies in the Senate and in the NAACP. Thus Hambright was actually losing political momentum while Tieless Joe steadily mended his fences and rebuilt his forces for a major counterattack at the 1932 national convention.[15]

As Howard and Tieless Joe Tolbert fought their battles against Hoover's lily-white appointees in a silent war behind the scenes, Benjamin Davis, owner of the Atlanta *Independent*, was much more vocal. Under intense pressure from two separate Senate investigating committees and the *New York Times*, Davis had lost out as national committeeman from Georgia, yet the widely heralded evidence against him proved to be too weak to sustain indictments. Championing his own innocence, Davis made good use of his newspaper to castigate Hoover. The president, he insisted, was not fooling black people with all his lofty talk of reform. The 26 March reform proclamation "admits of many interpretations," but the one that made the most sense to Davis was "a surrender to lily-whitism and a denial of the Negroes' constitutional rights within the party councils." He warned that previous presidents who had tried to build southern lily-white parties had only "made a mess of it." He concluded that " 'God is not mocked, and He does not love ugly.' "[16]

In the hope that they could somehow avoid an administration purge of their top leaders, the Georgia central committee instituted its own realignment. George F. Flanders, a highly respected white United States marshal, became the newly designated national committeeman and chairman of the state central committee. Josiah T. Rose, a white collector of internal revenue, became vice-chairman; and Ben Davis took the less prominent but still important post of secretary.[17] Flanders immediately sought conciliation. He explained to Newton that although the Georgia party would not associate with the Horace Mann faction, it would select white leaders who commanded the respect of both whites and blacks. "The Negro is willing to follow white leadership," Flanders advised, "but not white leadership which disregards the negro's rights and privileges as a citizen."[18]

If Newton and Brown had been skilled, sensitive politicians, they would have responded to Flanders's overture more positively, for he was trusted and respected by the state party leaders and by the citizens of both races. After Davis had stepped down to a less prominent post, Flanders had promised to cooperate with the administration's reform. But Hoover had demanded a clean sweep in Georgia, and Newton and Brown apparently concluded that they wanted their own choice to head the party. Accordingly, they selected Rose, which was hardly a "clean sweep," because Rose had been Flanders's vice-chairman in the black-and-tan coalition's own reform effort. Moreover, Newton and Brown did not inform any of the other state leaders of their choice. Rose was to act as their undercover, secret party reorganizer and patronage adviser.[19] He was instructed to select a group of new leaders secretly from among the various factions within the state party. Then at the proper time, after all of the selections had been made, the administration would suddenly recognize Rose's group as the legitimate party organization.

The Georgia reform plan was inept, amateurish, and almost certain to fail. Newton and Brown expected much more than Rose could deliver. He already had a demanding job as collector of internal revenue, and although he was trustworthy and sincere, his political skills were understandably more limited than the task required. The Democrats were naturally uncooperative, and, worse yet, within a short time Rose reduced his chances for quick confirmation of his patronage nominees by angering several influential Democratic senators and congressmen.[20] Winning over the legally recognized black-and-tan leaders to the new leadership would have been a feat in itself, but he was also expected to gain the cooperation of the lily-white faction and to create a united harmonious coalition party. Rose's task was made even more difficult by an ambitious rival, United States Marshal Lewis H. Crawford, a political trickster who had the enthusiastic backing of Congressman John Q. Tilson, the House majority leader. Thinking himself to be the most likely new leader of the party in Georgia, Crawford sought to take advantage of the confusing leadership tangle to gain personal control.

At first it appeared that Rose might be able to bring the rival factions together. Sensing that Rose had the administration's tacit support, Flanders agreed to back him as head of the party on condition that Rose reappoint him as United States marshal.[21] Rose was delighted and eager to please Flanders. Because Ben Davis and Flanders were close allies, the reappointment could well lead to a smooth relationship with the important black-and-tan faction, which trusted Flanders. Unfortunately for Rose, the appointment soon ran into unexpected difficulties. In checking on Flanders, the FBI uncovered charges that he had once sought medical treatment for excessive drinking. The Justice Department consequently refused to agree to his reappointment, and Newton fully supported this decision.[22] Rose protested, arguing that Flanders no longer had a drinking problem and that unless he was reappointed, the black and tans would not cooperate. Rose added that unless he himself could demonstrate his ability to secure his major patronage recommendations, no one would acknowledge his leadership, and he would have little chance of harmonizing the party.[23]

Perhaps aware of Rose's difficulties, Crawford now made his own move to gain control. The lily-white faction was angered by the administration's effort to create a coalition of black and tans and lily-whites, and Crawford therefore sought to join his influence over the House majority leader, Tilson, to that of the discontented lily-whites in a bid for leadership.[24] But apparently none of the factions, not even the lily-whites, trusted Crawford.[25] His unsuccessful coup only brought still more factional infighting. To demonstrate his leadership, Rose now demanded that Newton deny Crawford reappointment as United States marshal.[26]

The administration's response was disappointing. Newton sympathized with Rose's problems but insisted he could do little to help him, for Crawford's close ties to Tilson made his ouster impossible. According to Newton, the White House simply could not afford to alienate the House majority leader.[27] At the same time, the Justice Department refused to reconsider its opposition to Flanders's reappointment. In effect, Newton could offer Rose nothing but personal encouragement. Yet Rose was supposed to continue working toward a unifying solution and trying to make the best out of an apparently impenetrable political tangle.[28] Newton seemed to think that somehow, in time, factional realignments would enable Rose to recommend well-qualified candidates who

commanded the respect of their communities. Until such a time when politics
and principles meshed, the Georgia Republicans would have to struggle along
as best they could.

By the spring of 1930 Hoover's much-heralded purge of the allegedly
corrupt trio, Howard, Davis, and Tolbert, had bogged down in factionalism.
The reputedly overwhelming evidence against these leaders had proven to be
insufficient, and this insufficiency cast doubt on the validity of the whole
reform program. Certainly the need for reform appeared less real than had
once been assumed. Moreover, the strength and tenacity of the Democrats was
surprising. After splitting apart over Al Smith, they seemed now to have
relatively little difficulty in closing ranks to obstruct Republican "reform."
These developments made little difference to Hoover. Until the southern state
parties measured up to his standards, they were unworthy of the Republican
party, and he would not recognize them.

None of the three states designated as showcases for reform fulfilled Hoover's high expectations. In Mississippi Howard remained unconvicted, a shock
to administration preconceptions; and Rowlands, the prototype of the nonpolitical civic leader, was no match for Howard's clever alliance with the Democratic senators. In South Carolina Tolbert, the white leader of the black and
tans, could not be indicted, while his lily-white successor, Hambright, appeared particularly headstrong, bigoted, and inept, first by refusing to support
a protector of blacks who was respected by both races, and then by attempting
to place his own brother in office. The situation in Georgia had looked much
more promising, but it, too, ended in a shambles. Like Tolbert, Davis escaped
indictment because of insufficient evidence against him. For awhile it appeared that the administration's appointment of Rose, a white member of
Davis's black-and-tan coalition, might actually unite the various Republican
factions. However, a prominent black and tan unexpectedly failed to achieve
reappointment because of an alleged prior drinking problem, and at the same
time a discredited lily-white trickster could not be ousted because his chief ally
was the House majority leader. To many who had no knowledge of and
therefore could not understand the complex factional battles, the appointment
process in all three states seemed to reveal a callous strategy on the part of
Hoover to purge blacks simply because of their race.

Hoover's attempt to weed out corruption in the South failed partly because it
was poorly conceived in the first place. He attempted a clean sweep in showcase states before there was sufficient evidence to convict the deposed leaders.
The failure to convict or even indict clearly surprised Hoover. The copious
reports and charges of corruption in state governments, particularly in the
South, as well as the numerous congressional investigations and the still-fresh
memories of Harding had placed considerable pressure on the president to
keep his administration free of taint. Despite the unjust allegations that Hoover
would not press charges against southern lily-whites, charges now hammered

home by his former close ally Senator Brookhart, Hoover had in fact thoroughly investigated every charge he encountered against accused politicians, whether black or lily-white.

Too late he learned how unreliable were accusations of corruption and how cynically public investigations were used to damage opponents in the constant wars fought among southern factions. He had also vastly underestimated the resilience of the deposed national committeemen who joined forces with the Democrats to defeat his new elite at every turn while loudly proclaiming that the president had no legal right to depose them and that they were still the legitimate state leaders despite their lack of patronage.

15. Federal Assistance

Perhaps unavoidably some scholars and nonscholars alike have tended to regard Hoover's alleged purge of southern blacks as revealing his innermost thoughts about race.[1] His behind-the-scenes, convoluted, and varied efforts to "revolutionize" the South were so difficult to understand, both at the time and later, that they have obscured or distorted Hoover's thinking about racial progress. It is important, therefore, to emphasize another important reason why race-conscious black leaders at the time and scholars since then came to distrust him. This was his little understood but persistent belief that problems of black-white relationships were primarily aspects of broader social problems rather than unique and specifically racial in nature. Clearly he had a shallow understanding of racism and its central importance in American society because he was convinced that the practical solutions to racial antipathies could not be discovered outside of the broader social problems that generated the racial hatreds. Racial progress in the South, he thought, must begin with democratic reform and revitalization. Moreover, to identify racial problems anywhere in the United States as somehow special, or as unique political problems, would lead to special interest rather than public interest thinking. Thus Hoover often agreed to appoint knowledgeable black leaders to study black problems, but, almost invariably, these were subcommittees of larger, more comprehensive groups analyzing national social problems.

Important in Hoover's thinking, which created misunderstanding, was the odd fact that, although he was a political leader, Hoover had relatively little faith in political or legislatively devised solutions to basic social problems. This does not mean that he would not use the federal government as an instrument to promote progress. Nevertheless, he had inordinate faith in private voluntary associations and local solutions to social problems instead of those imposed by the government. This faith was a key factor in Hoover's plan for a unique American society that could continually improve upon the quality of life. With active participation and assistance from the federal government, he believed, the voluntary self-help institutions could become the most significant agencies in solving many of the nation's social problems. Unfortunately, as we have seen with the example of the Red Cross during the Mississippi flood of 1927, this concept made it all but impossible to combat racism in the South.[2]

Hoover further revealed his superficial understanding of racism through his belief in the almost limitless ability of an *elite*—local leaders of high moral character and selfless devotion to the public good—to discover and solve social problems, including those of race. This reliance on the morally responsible individual as the principal agent of social progress was part of his Quaker heritage and reflected his own experience. The aborted scheme to combat peonage, for example, was to have been a fitting illustration of the morally and socially responsible leaders, both white and black, working together to redress a social evil in a specific, pragmatic manner. If such leaders, both white and black, could be brought to respond in a similar manner to the social and racial evils in their communities, these problems would be solved. In Hoover's estimation the creation of this type of leadership was one of the foremost obligations of the president, and he welcomed all those who would join him, even those leaders whom blacks had reason to suspect.

Scholars have been highly doubtful about Hoover's racial views both because his southern reform efforts created misleading appearances and because he incorporated the notion, almost universally accepted at that time, of the biological inferiority of Asians and Negroes.[3] A few references make clear that he did indeed share these conventional racist ideas. Yet, there is little evidence to prove that he allowed these seldom-expressed ideas to direct his thinking about the need to overcome racial hatred in the United States. In fact, once appearances are carefully separated from realities, the bulk of the evidence clearly indicates that Hoover was much more optimistic about the prospects for great advances in black progress and in race relations than his few expressions about biological inferiority would suggest.

What is crucial to understanding his conception of racial progress is his insistence that by developing its own elite leadership, every racial group could rise to successively higher levels of achievement. However, this type of progress would not be possible without help from elite white leaders, who influenced the vast majority of the population and controlled its resources. For the blacks, therefore, the best racial politics would provide black people with an elite leadership, both black and white, that would combat racial hatred and promote racial progress by carrying out broad social reforms. Thereby black people would have the opportunity to prove to the larger community of the nation that their talents and virtues were equal to those of any other race. Hoover believed that black people had already demonstrated their great capabilities and talents and that they were capable of making far greater progress and at a much faster rate than most white Americans would believe. As a leader he felt a moral obligation to help them.[4]

In a national radio address of April 1931 celebrating the fiftieth anniversary of the founding of Tuskegee Institute and again the following year in his commencement address at Howard University, Hoover stressed two themes that characterized much of his thinking about black progress. The first theme was the great advances that blacks had made since their release from slavery in 1865. "No group of people in history ever started from a more complete economic and cultural destitution," he observed, and yet, within only sixty-six years they had multiplied their wealth more than 130 times, reduced their illiteracy rate from ninety-five to twenty percent, cut their death rate in half, owned more than 750,000 homes and accumulated billions of dollars in property. One of the most important reasons why blacks had made this progress was the subject of the second theme, black leadership, which had "developed a far reaching internal network of social, religious and economic organization." From this base Hoover expected blacks to make greater and more rapid progress in the future. Because blacks had created these social agencies through their own initiative, Hoover believed that, now, more than before, their future progress depended upon the work of talented men and women graduates of black universities and professional schools.[5]

Perhaps too indirectly the words of praise in Hoover's addresses to blacks sent them another message. By constantly stressing their talents, abilities, and progress, he seemed to be saying that the pessimistic advocates of biological inferiority and naturalistic Social Darwinism might well be wrong. If blacks and whites worked together as a cooperative group, there seemed no limit to the progress that they could make. He used historical facts to prove that through their own efforts blacks had within the short span of sixty-six years overcome great obstacles to reach a stage from which they were ready for swifter and greater progress in the future. Significantly, however, he never mentioned any black political organizations.[6]

When one compared Hoover's message to the realities that Negroes faced, the disparities were so great that one might well have dismissed his words as worthless political rhetoric. His faith was easy to criticize, but the president wrote his own addresses, which expressed his own beliefs and hopes, and he obviously enjoyed sending these messages of encouragement. He seldom missed an opportunity to inspire the black elite in whom he placed such great faith and responsibility. Unfortunately, the NAACP did not impress Hoover as progressive, elite black leadership but as merely a political organization, probably financed by his Democratic enemies.[7] This serious blind spot cut him off from a basically nonpartisan organization that generally used nonpolitical legal methods of which Hoover would have approved.[8]

One of Hoover's favorite self-help social agencies was the National Urban League, an organization that sought to promote economic opportunity for blacks living in cities. Hoover had worked with its director, Eugene Kinckle Jones, during the 1927 flood, and when Jones asked him for a personal endorsement of the league, the president was happy to comply. In a public message he praised the league and its members, emphasizing their vital role in promoting black progress through economic advancement. Hoover believed that economic independence, through both steady employment and the ownership of one's own business, was "the soil in which self-respect takes root and from which may then grow all the moral and spiritual enrichments of life." Its importance in breaking down racial barriers could hardly be overemphasized. It was in fact "fundamental to the progress of the race." Hoover sent Jones a secret personal contribution of $500 and later, at Jones's urging, he allowed him to cite his donation in private efforts to raise additional funds from wealthy contributors.[9]

Perhaps the greatest self-help institution in Hoover's estimation was the school and, not surprisingly, teachers were among Hoover's most respected leaders. The president delighted in sending uplifting messages to them and in expounding on the unlimited benefits that good education would bring black people. Teaching, he told the members of the National Association of Teachers in Colored Schools, was both great "social service" and "practical patriotism of [a] high order." In the schools he found the ideal combination of self-help and public responsibility, the institution that best served the society and the individual. Education developed the individual's talents, and this, in turn, promoted racial progress. It was, he believed, "not only the foundation of personal efficiency, but the solvent of many of the problems which confront the nation."[10]

Yet economic independence and a good education were insufficient in the struggle against racial hatred without the active support and participation of white leaders. Hoover considered politicians to be more sensitive to the prejudices of their constituents than to the advancement of human rights. Instead he looked to the Interracial Commission as a model for the South where it had originated and "where the problems of interracial adjustment are presented on a large scale." This institution, he stressed, "has been represented in its leadership and direction by the best element of both races working in effective cooperation for the good of each and rendering valuable service to the whole country." The Interracial Commission further exemplified Hoover's strong Quaker conviction that "the solution of all conflict is that men and women of good will shall search and find areas where they can cooperate, and thus minimize differences." By using the commission as their model, black and white leaders throughout the nation would discover the "proper spirit," the "sympathetic understanding," and sense of "absolute justice" that were essential to racial problem solving.[11]

Hoover was not merely a booster of familiar methods. Although he was obviously in almost complete accord with the philosophy of racial progress articulated by Booker T. Washington, he also differed from Washington. By 1929 Hoover had moved beyond Booker T. Washington's philosophy of racial advancement and beyond the ideas that he himself had expressed in *American Individualism* seven years earlier. He now more forcefully advocated active federal assistance to promote black self-help, and, even more important, scholarly research into the root causes of major social problems, including the racial aspects that he believed formed an integral part of these larger social problems. Like many other progressive leaders, Hoover believed that intelligent social problem solving first required the collection and dispassionate analysis of the facts. To ensure this, he insisted on establishing his own federal study commissions. After investigating a national social problem, the experts, as "social engineers," would make recommendations to the president, who would then consider the appropriate executive or legislative action. In setting forth this deliberate process, he assumed that he had at least eight years to formulate and implement reforms. To critics who complained that he was proliferating special reform commissions at the rate of one per day, Hoover replied that he ought instead to be establishing two per day.[12] His procedure was necessarily a slow one, too slow for activist critics who became increasingly discontent as the depression increasingly absorbed the president's attention and thereby doomed many of his promising reform initiatives.[13]

Not all of Hoover's efforts to help blacks required lengthy investigations. Often he designated cabinet officers to help carry them out. Most sympathetic to blacks was Secretary of the Interior Ray Lyman Wilbur, the former president of Stanford University and Hoover's close personal friend.[14] He shared Hoover's enthusiastic assessment of black progress. He believed that the Negroes' "advancement in our civilization has been phenomenal."[15] Wilbur quickly initiated an extensive national effort to improve the health of black people and significantly expanded the number of black educational programs sponsored by the interior department. He appointed a specialist in Negro education to analyze curricula in secondary education and recommend improvements.[16] Later the secretary expanded this analysis by creating the National Advisory Committee on National Illiteracy.[17] At the same time he fully supported Hoover's increased federal appropriations for Howard University, which enabled an expansion of the faculty, the national accreditation for the law school, and the strengthening of the college of medicine. Mordecai W. Johnson, president of Howard University, characterized the federal increase in funds as "the most comprehensively helpful appropriation ever received" by the university, and he added, the "colored people throughout the United States will rejoice with us because of your helpful attitude in these matters."[18] From these beginnings Negro educators had reason to hope that more vigorous and extensive federal assistance would follow.

Federal promotion of new economic opportunity was an important part of Hoover's desire to help blacks. In addition to the black specialist he had appointed to his department while still secretary of commerce, the president encouraged and paid close attention to the Conference on the Economic Status of the Negro, financed privately by his friend, the philanthropist Julius Rosenwald.[19] The work of the National Urban League was aided by his appointment of a black employment adviser for the Department of Labor. This specialist was added to analyze Negro job needs and to offer suggestions for improved federal employment services.[20] The National Negro Business League, led by Robert R. Moton, Jr., also continued to benefit from Hoover's enthusiastic support. He ordered federal surveys conducted for the league by the Department of Commerce to improve black life insurance practice and to make recommendations for more effective general business practices.[21]

Moton's hopes for federal aid to southern Negro farmers had a special appeal. As we have seen, Hoover wanted to encourage the widespread development of the independent black farmer as the eventual solution to the peonage system. Northern as well as southern blacks gave high priority to such federal assistance. Kelly Miller, a highly respected northern black leader and educator, observed that although he understood that politics made it advisable "to lay comparatively little stress on the race problem," Hoover could fulfill his objective of improving black economic status by selecting a black representative to the Federal Farm Board. Such an appointment, Miller believed, "would go further to stimulate the mind of the race in the direction of its greatest usefulness to itself and to the nation than the appointment of a dozen candidates as register for something, recorder of something else, assistant to somebody or minister to somewhere."[22] Hoover agreed. His newly created Federal Farm Board appeared to be an ideal vehicle for the promotion of southern farm reforms, and Hoover immediately put Moton in contact with Alexander Legge, the head of the Board.[23]

Moton was delighted with his initial progress. Legge was sympathetic to his proposal for special educational courses for Negro farmers and expressed his support for a national conference at Tuskegee Institute to coordinate the educational programs of the land-grant colleges with those of the federal Agricultural Extension Service and the federal Board of Vocational Education.[24] A national Negro farmers' cooperative and a Negro farm journal were among Moton's fondest hopes, and they too appeared to be distinct possibilities. Arthur M. Hyde, the secretary of agriculture, also seemed willing to help.[25] At Moton's request he ordered an investigation of the "improper activities" of the federal Extension Service in the South and appointed black inspectors to check on discrimination against black farmers by regional crop production loan officers.[26]

Unfortunately, black efforts to secure the appointment of either Moton or Eugene P. Booze of Mound Bayou, Mississippi, to the Federal Farm Board ended in failure. Because the law required that members of the board represent commodities rather than geographic areas, a fierce battle among the powerful farm organizations over seats on the eight-member board greatly complicated the appointment process. In this sort of contention black applicants lacked the political power to prevail, as Hoover finally explained to Moton. He felt that in order to give his new board a chance to succeed, he had to select only those who represented powerful farm organizations. He did not add that neither Hyde nor Legge was inclined to support a black representative or brave the political storm that a black appointment would have created. It must have been a hard blow for Moton and other southern black farmers. Ultimately no one accomplished much for the increasingly desperate black farmer because the depression soon left Hoover's ambitious agricultural experiment in a shambles,[27] and under the New Deal's Agricultural Adjustments Administration, the plight of the poor farmer worsened.[28]

Several other federal initiatives characterized Hoover's early efforts to help blacks to help themselves. He doubled the federal appropriations for the Negro veterans hospital at Tuskegee, Alabama; encouraged Negro representation on the new federal parole board; and intervened to improve the combat status of black soldiers at Fort Benning, Georgia, where previously they had been restricted to menial labor.[29] Perhaps the most valuable of his study commissions, the President's Committee on Recent Social Trends, sought to enhance understanding of race relations by including among its many important investigations a special analysis of national racial patterns and developments.[30] A favorite project of Hoover's was better housing and home ownership to further individual well-being. He had been interested in Negro housing conditions since 1925, and in August 1930, when he selected participants for his prestigious White House Conference on Home Building and Home Ownership, he included a committee of prominent Negro educators and social workers to study and make recommendations for increasing and improving black housing.[31] Excellent studies on the appalling neglect of black education, the need for public and private agencies to assist handicapped black children, and a comprehensive analysis of black health needs suggested that the information on which to base a program to help blacks had been gathered by the end of his term. Finally, he fulfilled the intent of the previous Congress by appointing a Negro Memorial Commission to plan a building honoring Negro contributions to American life.[32]

Because the Great Depression soon forced Hoover into massive deficit spending and increasingly absorbed almost all of his time and energy, one cannot determine how much further he would have gone with federal projects to provide help for blacks. Clearly he felt he had made a promising beginning in bringing the resources of the federal government to bear on important racial problems and in creating a new alliance between the federal government and the nation's voluntary institutions before the full impact of the economic collapse. Yet for all the promise, there were also obvious deficiencies and disappointments. As early as the 1928 campaign, for example, Claude Barnett had complained that Hoover had no clearly defined goals or a clearly identifiable program for blacks.[33] Moreover, he never designated anyone to initiate such a program or to facilitate communication between black leaders and the administration.[34] Blacks tried to reach him through his secretaries George Akerson or Walter Newton or through Postmaster General Brown with little success. Other cabinet members were no more responsive and, as we shall see, when Hoover sent them recommendations for black patronage appointments, they often felt free to reject or oppose them.[35] Hoover instead responded to black suggestions with unsystematic improvisations, so his assistance was often unplanned, widely scattered, usually unpublicized, and almost always nonpolitical.

This lack of coordination and a purposeful program reflected, in part, his inability to bring into focus the fact that racism was one of the most important problems facing the nation. He never could decide exactly how he ought to respond to black requests because he was often torn between the conviction that they needed and deserved special federal help and the suspicion that they might become an undesirable, "special interest" group more interested in "politics" than progress. Hoover's responses were therefore often baffling and irritatingly inconsistent.

A good example of this confused reasoning appeared very early in Hoover's administration. The first reform commission designated by the new president was the National Commission on Law Observance and Enforcement, more popularly known as the Wickersham commission after its chairman, former Attorney General George W. Wickersham. When the names of the appointees became known, a host of prominent black leaders, including James Weldon Johnson and W. E. B. Du Bois of the NAACP, William Monroe Trotter of the National Equal Rights League and Race Congress, the more conservative Claude Barnett, and several college presidents asked Hoover to include a black representative. In justification they argued that the failure to enforce the nation's laws, especially the Fourteenth and Fifteenth amendments to the Constitution, resulted in more suffering for blacks than for any other single group in the nation.[36] But Hoover refused, apparently on the same grounds as those for his reply to William Green, head of the American Federation of Labor, who had also complained about the lack of a labor representative. Hoover disposed of these complaints by explaining that because the national law enforcement commission would discuss only questions of a "legal charac-ter," he would not appoint representatives of "any special group." This rejec-tion the leaders of the NAACP and the AF of L would long remember.[37] Hoover insisted on the "administrative principle" that appointees must have the "public interest" as their sole priority. But it was easier for blacks and union men to believe that his "principle" was merely a lame excuse for either a racist or an antilabor bias. More likely, Hoover sought simply to avoid favor-ing any special group and thereby stimulating "political" resentment and demands from other groups wanting appointment. If this was the case, he did not enlighten anyone.

Added to the confusion, inconsistency, and lack of a black program was another aspect of Hoover's thinking about racial problems that diminished its effectiveness. His many encouraging messages to blacks also seemed to be telling them that there were limits to what he could do for them. He was well aware of the intense antiblack sentiments in both the North as well as the South, and he was no doubt equally aware of the fact that the Republican party had long ceased to concern itself significantly with black welfare. Despite his willingness and desire to help, Hoover had come to the conclusion that the public consensus against black rights effectively prevented any political or legislative recourse. Indeed, Congress had continuously refused to pass a federal antilynching bill,[38] and Hoover was not prepared to brave the political firestorm that any legislative effort would doubtlessly provoke. After the furor over the De Priest tea, the president shrank from further public controversy.

In effect, by avoiding any mention of black requests, which he considered politically impossible, Hoover was saying to black people that they themselves must provide the principal leadership for overcoming the numerous and immense obstacles that blocked their future progress. With assistance from a white elite in the South they must destroy the barriers of hatred by sheer force of their repeatedly demonstrated courage, virtues, and abilities. He seemed to assume that blacks faced problems that were only slightly more difficult than those confronted by white immigrants. They must and could empirically prove that they were, in fact, worthy to be treated as equals, just as so many other disadvantaged people had done. Because he was unable to recognize the special nature of racism, his well-meant efforts to act on the basis of "reform principles" inevitably appeared to blacks as little more than a shallow facade raised to hide his truly racist beliefs and intents. Although he wished to encourage racial progress, Hoover found that his efforts failed and his intentions were misunderstood.

Like most others of his generation he could not appreciate the depth, the complexity, and the centrality of racism to American life and society. Years later racial and social solutions imposed by the federal government would prove to be more necessary and more practical than Hoover perceived, for racism was much more than merely one aspect of broader social problems to be solved by "nonpolitical" elites. Without an understanding of the unique and central character of racism and a willingness to combat it as a distinct evil, Hoover was tragically incapable of transforming his desire to help into effective leadership.

16. Patronage Delayed

 One of Hoover's most unusual characteristics as a political leader was his open disdain for the traditional practice of rewarding political support with federal patronage. Partially responsible for this attitude were his intimate knowledge of the betrayals and disgrace visited upon Harding by his patronage appointees, his own lack of experience and respect for elective politics, and his determination to avoid a repetition of Harding's mistakes. But, as we have seen, there was another reason as well. Hoover believed strongly that the democratic character of the republic could be materially strengthened, even revitalized, by a patronage policy that rewarded ability and virtue, a policy that would build a corps of dedicated, efficient civil servants and leaders. His public refusal to remove incumbent Democratic appointees of proven competence and his public attack upon the Florida Republicans over unfit nominees testified to the importance of this belief in the thinking of the president.[1]

This belief was especially significant in his thinking about black patronage. Hoover was convinced that the patronage policies of past Republican administrations had hindered racial progress. To him Perry Howard was the fitting symbol of the corrupt, ineffectual politician who had dominated black Republican patronage politics for too long. Rather than use his federal position as a means to protect and enhance the public interest, Howard, like most politicians, relied upon patronage for his own personal aggrandizement. The tendency to appoint this type of politician thus accounted for the absence of a black elite leadership in responsible federal positions. Unfortunately at first Hoover divorced this process of finding and appointing leaders of the black elite from "politics." He understood the importance of patronage in the traditional party-building process, but he had little personal regard for this usage and, as a result, even less understanding of why his own black elite sought federal patronage as earnestly as any politician of either race.[2]

According to Hoover and many other like-minded progressives, patronage had all too often produced corruption that undermined good government and brought democracy into low esteem, especially in the South, where the Republican state parties had become symbols of this national decay.[3] To an extent, blacks could agree with Hoover. They understood that patronage politics had seldom benefited black people directly. Even in the North, where they enjoyed greater political freedom, politics, like everything else, was dominated by whites. To gain the blacks' votes white politicians regularly professed friendship and concern for them. Yet, as blacks were well aware, after the polls closed their participation in the democratic process had rarely been translated into political efforts to improve their lot. This indifference had steadily increased since Reconstruction, and by 1928 it had become an increasingly significant source of disaffection, even among those blacks who still voted Republican to repay Lincoln and his party for the Thirteenth, Fourteenth, and Fifteenth amendments to the Constitution.[4]

Because racism ensured that they could rarely be elected to public office, blacks often viewed patronage differently from white progressive reformers. Unlike white reformers, who often denounced the spoils system, knowledgeable black leaders usually considered patronage as vital to their interests and the only avenue by which they could participate in government. With black spokesmen in office who would listen to them and would use their influence to promote or at least try to safeguard their rights and interests, black people could feel somewhat more secure in their own communities. The more influential the position, the more likely the tangible benefits for black people. Black leaders believed that as the black appointees gained personal status and political power, the black community consequently commanded greater respect in the eyes of whites.[5] Thus a patronage appointee as a special assistant to the attorney general, the secretary of labor, or the secretary of agriculture (special assistants did not require Senate approval) might have enough influence to correct abuses; initiate long-overdue reforms; work toward immediate, tangible benefits; or, at the very least, try to dissipate the fog of indifference that surrounded blacks within his own department. Working together with sympathetic white leaders, especially with a sympathetic president, he might even bypass the Congress and make good use of the executive branch to bring direct benefits to black people. Certainly the potential for much progress was evident and exciting to black Hoover loyalists.

The black elite were understandably eager for the president to demonstrate his good faith by quickly appointing blacks to highly visible and influential patronage posts. By June 1928 almost 52,000 blacks worked for the federal government, but the number of prestigious positions they held, such as special assistant to one of the cabinet officers, had not increased since 1909, when Theodore Roosevelt had made a number of relatively high-level black appointments.[6] Indeed, for several administrations it had steadily fallen.[7] Should Hoover reverse this trend, as his supporters fully expected, it would have a dramatic effect on black people. Perhaps even more important was the need to demonstrate convincingly the erroneous nature of the impressions created by the reform proclamation of 26 March and the charges by black critics concerning a southern lily-white strategy and its alleged purge of black leadership. Granting prestigious federal positions to his loyal black elite was the best proof, indeed now virtually the only proof, that could effectively counteract the growing suspicion that he was antiblack.

At first the Tuskegee faction hoped that Hoover would designate Moton as the unofficial successor to Booker T. Washington. For over a decade the founder of Tuskegee had been the powerful black patronage adviser to the Republican party, and his dominance had generated bitter resentment among many other black politicians.[8] The editor of the Associated Negro Press, Claude Barnett, was well aware of the suspicions created by the close relationship that had developed between Hoover and Moton during the 1927 Mississippi flood and the 1928 campaign, but he was confident that Moton would triumph over his black rivals in the struggle for black patronage dominance within the Hoover administration. Barnett's personal survey of administration leaders convinced him, he told Moton, that "we are 'sitting pretty' and that beyond cavil you will be able to say the last word on any action affecting blacks." Such an exalted position would, in Barnett's judgment, mean that Moton would have "the responsibility of developing some sort of program which will strike popular approval as effectively as big appointments."[9]

Moton shared Barnett's optimism. His discussions with the new president, especially when Hoover called him to the White House in the wake of the De Priest incident, had convinced him that Hoover intended to follow all of his patronage recommendations[10] and expand the number of important black positions. Moton was heartened by Hoover's intention to fill Perry Howard's post as a special assistant attorney general with a black who "would demonstrate the ability of the race" and who had the "character to reflect credit upon the post and his people."[11] Hoover's refusal to solidify the Louisiana lily-whites by forcing Walter Cohen out of his post as collector of customs at New Orleans was yet another source of encouragement. Hoover had repeatedly insisted that honest black leaders had nothing to fear from his reform of the southern state parties, and when Moton heard of the Louisiana lily-whites' demand, he advised Hoover of the effect such a dismissal would have on black leaders. The president kept his word and heeded Moton's counsel.[12] Someday, Barnett predicted, "when we dare give it publicity," this protection of the highly respected Cohen would clearly establish Moton as the most influential political leader in the Hoover administration.[13]

At the same time that Moton was making the patronage recommendations for the Tuskegee faction, John R. Hawkins consulted with his allies Emmett J. Scott and Judge James A. Cobb about a plan to cut the Tuskegee machine down to size and establish the dominance of his own faction. As director of the Colored Voters Division and chairman of its executive committee, Hawkins had discovered, to his own delight and to the disgust of the Moton faction, that his clique could control the activities of the CVD. He now proposed the creation of a permanent Colored Voters Division, which, he argued, would enable black leaders to keep together a national political network capable of supporting the administration more effectively in the forthcoming 1930 off-year campaign and two years later in the president's own reelection. He assured Hoover that it would also serve as a "clearinghouse of expression" and as a "medium of interpretation" of the hopes and ambitions of the black people.[14]

In thus proposing a permanent Colored Voters Division, Hawkins exemplified the growing political activism and pride of race among black leaders in the 1920s, even among the more conservative blacks. Recalling that Hoover's acceptance speech had emphasized the right to equality of opportunity for all people and all races, Hawkins reminded him that "the principle of equality has not been applied to all . . . citizens alike." The Republican party, he told Hoover, had to renew its commitment to ensure the right to vote to all Negroes in all parts of the country, and, in a thinly veiled reference to the much-publicized southern strategy, guard against any "attempt to eliminate negroes from party councils." Moreover, he pointed out that blacks had also experienced widespread discrimination in federal employment. They had been denied federal jobs even after passing Civil Service examinations and still had to suffer under "regulations and practices enforced against colored employees that subject them to inconveniences and indignities purely because of their racial identity." To realize equality of opportunity required executive action, and the establishment of a permanent CVD within the Republican National Committee would help Hoover toward that goal.[15]

Hoover rejected Hawkins's request for several reasons. Well aware of the intense, bitter rivalries among his black supporters, he obviously wanted to avoid the wrangling that had earlier characterized the CVD. Moreover, as Hawkins had hinted, a permanent, more activist CVD might have created difficulties with some of his newly enlisted but already disgruntled southern supporters. Important, too, was Hoover's failure to understand why blacks should desire a recognized political organization within the administration. To him, this request was simply politics as usual and thus easy to dismiss.

While he could avoid the factional problems arising from a permanent CVD, he could not escape the pressure to select black patronage appointees. On this question both the Moton and the Hawkins-Scott-Cobb factions called for the expansion of important federal patronage, and each faction urged the appointment of its own nominees. In addition to the twenty-three significant posts already reserved for blacks, each one independently recommended from twelve to fourteen new important positions.[16] These were, most often, special assistant or assistant attorney positions in the Departments of Justice, Labor, Agriculture, and the Post Office, and in the newly created Veterans Bureau. They also submitted nominees for appointment to a Latin American diplomatic post, to the Haiti Commission, and for specialists assigned to the Department of Education, Children's Bureau, and Federal Board of Vocational Education. In addition, the Hawkins group wanted a black register of the treasury and a special assistant secretary of war, while Moton requested an appointment to the Federal Farm Board.[17]

As none of these new posts required Senate confirmation, it would seem that Hoover could have made the appointments easily and swiftly from among the nominees submitted to him by both factions. Eventually, he did fill most of these posts with exceptionally well-qualified black appointees. But a number of problems prevented quick appointments and increased black discontent, which persisted despite Hoover's notable appointments record. An important reason for delay was the intense rivalry between the two major black Republican factions, neither of which would even discuss the qualifications of the other's nominees. Barnett would choose only men who had exhibited "fealty of the purest type" to Moton; others resented any such favoritism.[18] Ernest T. Attwell, a black social worker and recreational expert whom Hoover respected, complained directly to Hoover and warned him against these "professional fixers."[19] To Hoover this rivalry smacked too much of the old "politics."

Postmaster General Walter Brown agreed with Attwell. As the nominal head of the Colored Voters Division, he was aware of the rivalries and of the resentment against the Tuskegee machine among northern blacks. He saw no advantage to the administration in elevating Moton.[20] As a political pragmatist he understood the necessity of pleasing northern black politicians as well as the influential northern white senators who were sensitive to the large numbers of voting blacks in their states and who would later become increasingly important in dictating black patronage appointees. These senators wished to reward their own black supporters, who often had no connection with either of the two elite factions that Hoover had created. Moreover, Brown wished to work in harmony with all of the competing patronage interests. For example, he appointed as assistant solicitor in the Post Office Department W. C. Hueston, a black politician who had spoken out against the neglect of race interests and had helped organize the National Negro Voters League to protect those interests at the 1928 national convention. This revealed Brown's own preference for rewarding black political leaders from northern or border states where blacks were politically powerful. Barnett soon caught the drift of Brown's thinking, reporting to Moton that the postmaster general was his "usual cool blooded self."[21]

Another impediment to quick appointments was Hoover's unbending determination to select only the best-qualified candidates and thereby prevent mere "politicians" from gaining responsible federal positions because of their political support. The depth and pervasiveness of his determination is shown by the case of Alan Fox, not a black but an important Hoover Republican in New York State and a close personal friend whom the president was eager to please. Fox had worked hard in both the primaries and in the general election and in a state where powerful Republican leaders were intensely hostile to Hoover.

During one of his visits to the White House Fox confided to Hoover that only an appointment as United States district attorney would effectively demonstrate his standing with the administration and establish his leadership of the New York State Republicans. The investigating power of the district attorney was a potent political weapon that opponents were bound to respect. Hoover forwarded the recommendation to Attorney General Mitchell, who repeatedly advised that Fox was not qualified for the post. As an intimate commented, Hoover had never had "such a disagreeable job" as turning him down; but turn him down he did, and Fox refused alternative posts.[22] Not even close, valued friends of great political influence could break Hoover's resolve to prevent cronies, incompetents, or even good men who lacked adequate qualifications from infiltrating his administration, as they had Harding's.

Hoover's refusal to appoint a man whom he liked and respected was not well known among Republican office seekers, but it is part of a clear pattern. Time and time again, as in Florida, Hoover refused to grant politically advantageous appointments when he considered the nominee to be unfit or unqualified.[23] All potential judges, federal marshals, and district attorneys had to undergo thorough investigation by the Justice Department.[24] The effects of this scrupulosity were devastating, in part because it was not well understood. As more and more frustrated applicants were either encouraged to withdraw their applications or forced to wait for long, embarrassing investigations, their anger mounted. Enthusiastic loyalists turned into sour critics, and the president discovered that he had fewer and fewer friends either in the Congress or the state parties.[25]

The insensitivity of Hoover's political secretaries complicated the cumbersome appointment process. As already noted, Akerson had revealed his insensitivity toward blacks during the 1928 campaign in his outrageous reply to Governor Bilbo of Mississippi.[26] Apparently Walter Newton had little if any sympathy for blacks and spent much of his time attempting to soothe irate southern lily-white leaders.[27] Another close political aide, French Strother, was hostile to the NAACP. In May 1929 James Weldon Johnson wrote Akerson requesting a message from the president to commemorate the twentieth-anniversary celebration of the NAACP. Considering the strained relationship that had developed during the 1927 flood and the 1928 campaign, this was a good opportunity to mend political fences, but instead of consulting the president, Akerson turned for advice to Strother, who directed that not even a reply be given.[28] Walter White later guessed correctly that Hoover's secretaries were short-circuiting attempts by the NAACP to reach the president.[29] Moton also came to believe that they were mishandling relations with blacks, while Melvin J. Chisum, one of Moton's close associates, who had been rejected for a federal appointment, publicly attacked these advisers in 1932 as Negro haters and race baiters.[30] As frustrations mounted, the quiet indiscretions of Hoover's secretaries would increasingly be interpreted as evidence of his own personal disrespect for important black leaders and organizations.[31]

By 1 January 1930 Moton's patience with the interminable delays came to an end. Coming to Washington, he spoke with Hoover about the unfortunate political effects that the delays were having among black leaders and urged him to act swiftly on at least six of the most important recommendations he had made. Moton wanted immediate appointments of a special assistant attorney general, an assistant attorney in the Post Office Department, a special assistant secretary of labor, a special assistant secretary of agriculture, a specialist in black education, and a well-qualified woman for the Children's Bureau.[32] Moton's directness, coupled with his sense of urgency, impressed Hoover, and he did fulfill his promise to forward Moton's nominees directly to his cabinet officers. Moton naturally thought this meant immediate appointment. Unfortunately he was unfamiliar with the lengthy investigations; the likelihood of adverse responses from at least some investigating officials; and Hoover's practice of consulting with Brown, with cabinet officers, with senators, and with other interested parties or groups before acting. As a result, nothing happened for some time, and the president, who was increasingly preoccupied with the depression, did not follow through to determine the cause of the delays.[33]

Continued inaction had an increasingly demoralizing effect on Hoover's black loyalists. Virtually everyone seemed to be more aware than the president of the importance of moving quickly to demonstrate good faith and to solidify political loyalties. Moton and Barnett were particularly discouraged. Once again Moton felt compelled to warn the president that his "widely scattered sources" had collected convincing evidence that the high hopes of black people in him had already been replaced by the growing realization that he was not considering their needs.[34] Still later, he bluntly told Hoover that the continuing patronage delays were seriously damaging his reputation among black leaders.[35]

Moton had good reason to be concerned. More than any other black leader he had steadfastly defended Hoover against the charges of indifference, hostility, and a purge of black leadership. By March 1930 it appeared to many that there might have been more to those charges than the mere political self-interest of disgruntled Democrats. Finally, Barnett, thoroughly disgusted by the inaction, could wait no longer. Journeying to Washington, he sought out George Akerson, who was reputed to be knowledgeable about black affairs, and bluntly informed him of "the definite bitterness which was growing in the minds and hearts of colored people." This bitterness stemmed directly from "the absence of any outstanding [patronage] recognition" and contributed to the belief among black people that "they had been neglected and that their welfare was a matter of indifference to the president." Akerson reassured him that Moton's nominees were "now being worked out with the departments" and erroneously denied that "political considerations" were delaying the appointments. Indeed, Akerson insisted, Moton's "word on them was sufficient."[36]

This last untruth created a totally unrealistic sense of confidence in Moton, who continued to act as if his special relationship with Hoover would enable his nominees to triumph over the others. This attitude angered rival black leaders, who were determined to prevent Moton from becoming another Booker T. Washington. However, by maneuvering against him behind the scenes they seriously undermined the influence of all black leaders. Hawkins, in fact, openly acknowledged this source of weakness, assuming responsibility for it and professing to be deeply disappointed that Moton had not confided in him about black appointments. Yet Hawkins and his allies were certainly as much to blame for the harmful infighting as the Moton faction. The Hawkins group had made no attempt to consult with Moton before unsuccessfully seeking Hoover's approval of a permanent Colored Voters Division or before submitting their own rival slate of nominees.[37]

One month later, in early February 1930, Emmett J. Scott also spoke with Hoover about the interminable delays in black patronage. The encounter left him dispirited. Because almost all of Scott's correspondence during the Hoover period is missing from his collection of private papers, it is not possible to know exactly what was discussed, but he reportedly told Barnett that his conversation with Hoover had convinced him that "little would be done" to make the necessary number or ensure the quality of black appointments.[38] Scott may have been discouraged by his lack of success in gaining appointments for his own nominees, and he may also have reflected Hoover's own dissatisfaction with the problems created by the patronage infighting between the two rival factions. In any case, Hoover was well aware of the interminable delays. The burst of unqualified nominees from the lily-white southerners, for example, had thoroughly clogged the patronage investigation machinery. In desperation, Hoover demanded that Postmaster General Brown speed up the process by using local southern post office employees to conduct background checks on southern nominees.[39] But it was already too late to dim the impression of indifference, and when Hoover finally did make the appointments, his black loyalists were often disappointed that their own nominees had not been selected.

Hoover was not quite as oblivious to black appointments as the laments of Moton, Barnett, or Scott suggested. Soon after assuming office, he had asked Scott to serve on a commission to investigate the slave trade in Liberia, but Scott had refused on grounds of health, family, and his duties as secretary-treasurer of Howard University. Yet rather than turn to another prominent black political leader Hoover chose Charles S. Johnson, chairman of the Department of Sociology at Fisk University. Like Bess Gordy Koontz, professor of elementary education at the University of Pittsburgh, whom he selected as assistant commissioner of education, Johnson was a fitting representative of the black elite, which Hoover was actively seeking out. His appointment won praise for its recognition of a black scholar, but it did nothing to raise Hoover's standing among black politicians.[40]

For minister to Liberia, one of the most prestigious posts, Hoover delayed appointing his own nominee because Scott recommended retaining the incumbent. In July 1929, when the latter died, Hoover sought to promote his Louisiana model reform plan by interesting Walter Cohen in the position.[41] Following Cohen's rejection, the president again avoided a prominent black political leader. Instead, he again selected a black professor, Charles E. Mitchell of West Virginia, a Hawkins intimate who had the support of Sen. Henry D. Hatfield.[42] Little wonder that Church and other black politicians continued to complain loudly of Hoover's Doctors and the disregard of prominent black politicians.

As late as 4 April 1930 Barnett still puzzled over the president's delays and intentions regarding Moton's slate of candidates. Suspicion centered increasingly on Postmaster General Brown, who remained noncommittal.[43] By contrast, Akerson continued to be confident, apparently reassuring Barnett again that "the doctor's word is final" and that no further political support for the Moton slate was necessary. But Moton wanted more than words, for he was being constantly reminded by the "exceedingly restive" Negro press, which kept the delays before the attention of black people.[44] Finally, in desperation Moton advised Newton that if the president "should find other men who are more acceptable than those I have suggested it would be all right so far as I am concerned." The important point, he stressed, was to "appoint some Negroes to some outstanding positions" immediately.[45]

As much as Hoover respected Moton, he stubbornly refused to hurry, being no more disposed to gain political advantage by appointing blacks quickly than to meet the political needs of his trusted yet unqualified friend Alan Fox. Good appointments, he seemed to be saying—those which met his qualifications and which would advance the goals and values he shared with blacks—simply could not be rushed, regardless of the political consequences. Yet political appearances and their consequences were crucial to his presidential leadership. Not only were the delays discouraging, but they fed the growing belief in an antiblack conspiracy. By early April 1930, with Hoover's nomination of Judge John J. Parker to the United States Supreme Court, his failure to act swiftly in making prestigious appointments convinced even those black leaders, who earlier had quietly approved of his plan to reform the southern state parties, that the president's southern effort was not merely a somewhat worrisome regional experiment, but a potentially dangerous national policy. The Parker nomination made it possible for them to suspect that Hoover never intended to make these black appointments at all and that he and his secretaries had all along, as Barnett bitterly put it, been "playing politics pure and simple."[46]

17. Lily-White Symbol

The president's "southern strategy" met its greatest challenge in the spring of 1930 when Hoover nominated John J. Parker of North Carolina to the United States Supreme Court. Since 1912 the North Carolina Republicans had been building a strong lily-white party, and its leaders had been in the forefront of those southerners championing Hoover's nomination and election. In April 1928, early in the hunt for convention delegates, Charles A. Jonas, a congressman and national committeeman from that state, succeeded in defeating the Lowden forces and delivering the state's entire convention vote to Hoover. Campaign manager Hubert Work was overjoyed. North Carolina had appeared lost until Jonas had "energetically and intelligently" broken the opposition.[1] Even more impressive was the electoral victory in November. Wracked by the nomination of Al Smith, the North Carolina Democrats divided into two warring factions as United States senator Furnifold M. Simmons led a group of anti-Smith bolters out of the party. This split helped the increasingly powerful and well-organized Republicans to elect two congressmen, to capture seven seats in the state legislature, and to give Hoover a 63,000-vote margin of victory.[2]

With the Democrats in bitter disarray, Republican state leaders talked confidently of building an even stronger state party. Hoover naturally felt indebted. For a brief time he heartened his North Carolina allies by seriously considering Stuart W. Cramer, a wealthy member of the national Cotton Textile Institute and a graduate of the United States Naval Academy at Annapolis, for the position of secretary of the navy.[3] Cramer lost the post, however, to Charles Francis Adams. Disappointed, the North Carolinians next tried to ensure that the post held by retiring North Carolinian David H. Blair, United States commissioner of internal revenue, would be passed on to another North Carolina Republican. Already powerful in the western industrial part of the state, these Republican leaders were eager to expand their influence into the eastern sector. But to do this, they argued, they needed important federal patronage both in the state and nationally. Like other southerners who were eager to strengthen their organizations, the North Carolinians were unanimous in their conviction that prestigious federal patronage was essential to expand and strengthen their state party.[4] Yet other southern states had also voted for Hoover, and ultimately the commissioner's post went to the Kentucky Republicans, who had carried their state for Hoover and who had a more experienced candidate, Robert H. Lucas, the federal collector of internal revenue for Kentucky. To ease the loss, Hoover appointed a North Carolina Republican, Joseph M. Dixon, as first assistant secretary of the interior.[5]

Twice disappointed in securing top national posts, the North Carolinians concentrated on expanding their political base within the state through the appointment of influential United States marshals and district attorneys.[6] The Republican party in North Carolina, although exceptionally strong, had its difficulties. Bitter internal patronage squabbles soon complicated their efforts and revealed fully the importance of loyal federal marshals and district attorneys in the politics of party building. When Jonas attempted to reward and advance the career of a younger, exceptionally able leader with one of the two district attorney posts, the incumbent Republican, who had held the job for eight years, refused to agree to any rotation scheme. He would not resign and when pressured, he replied with an unwarranted and politically embarrassing investigation of the younger man selected by the state leaders to replace him.[7] Obviously the power to investigate or to indict could be of great political importance, especially in the hands of political opponents. Enticing able people to run for public office was not easy for Republicans in the South, and if the political opposition controlled the internal revenue office, the marshal, or the district attorney and could hint at an embarrassing public investigation, the task became almost impossible. An eager candidate might be willing to risk an impartial investigation, but not one conducted by opponents and promising only embarrassment and defeat. It was little wonder that patronage appointees often became so firmly entrenched.

On 8 March 1930, as the North Carolina Democrats reestablished party harmony in a determined effort to win the off-year election in November, the Republicans got an unexpected chance for greater national influence. An associate justice of the United States Supreme Court, Edward Terry Sanford, suddenly died, and the North Carolina Republicans were placed in an excellent position to influence the nomination of his successor. Sanford had been the only southerner on the Court, and Hoover was known to have an unusually high regard for a North Carolinian, John J. Parker, the forty-four-year-old judge of the Fourth Federal Circuit Court.

In early 1929, while searching for members of his cabinet, the president-elect had given serious thought to appointing Parker as attorney general of the United States. The liberal justice Harlan Stone of the Supreme Court, asked to assess Parker's qualifications, had rated him highly as a man of attractive personality, solid character, and a good legal scholar. "During the past three years," Stone reported, "I have read a good many of his opinions," which "have generally been vigorous, able documents of good literary quality."[8] Stone assessed Parker's legal talents accurately. In 1946, at the end of Parker's long career as a federal judge, the American Bar Association hailed him as "one of the most distinguished jurists on the Federal bench."[9]

Mabel Walker Willebrandt, whom Hoover respected, also had high praise for Parker. She told Hoover that Parker "represents the new South." According to Willebrandt, Parker had a fine mind, understood politics, and was respected and admired by politicians in both parties. He "possesses swift judgment," she continued, is "progressive, has great energy and turns out a prodigious amount of work." Ultimately Hoover selected Willebrandt's first choice, the Minnesota Democrat William D. Mitchell, for the position of attorney general. Nonetheless, he did not forget Parker, who was an excellent example of the elite whom Hoover hoped to attract to southern politics generally.[10]

The North Carolina judge had still other sources of strength. Before taking the bench he had been a highly successful lawyer and an energetic Republican office seeker who had earned the admiration of both parties by laboring against great odds. In 1910 he lost the race for the United States House of Representatives, in 1916 the contest for state attorney general, and in 1920 election for governor. Yet for all of his losses, Parker was an exceptionally attractive campaigner who polled 230,000 votes in 1920, more than any other Republican gubernatorial candidate in the state's history.[11] By 1920 Democrats were worried about this progressive Republican, and as so often happened in potentially close contests against Republicans, they used the race issue to frighten voters and discredit their opponent. This was true in 1920 and again in 1928.[12] Republicans were powerful in the western part of the state, especially in Durham, Raleigh, and Greensboro, where large black populations were ably led by well-developed professional and business classes. Some of these Negroes were allowed to vote, and Democrats liked to charge that if elected, Republicans would extend the franchise to all Negroes in the state.[13] In 1920, race baiting was a common method of diminishing an opponent, and they repeatedly accused Parker of favoring Negro suffrage and a return to Reconstruction—charges that Parker emphatically denied. The Democrats warded off the Parker challenge in part by racial fear tactics, but they could not deny him an impressive electoral showing, mostly from white voters.

From 1923 to 1925 Parker served for brief periods as a special assistant to the United States attorney general, and in 1925 Coolidge rewarded him with appointment to the Fourth Circuit Court.[14] By 1929 Congressman Jonas was determined to elevate him to the Supreme Court. "It is a Republican vacancy," he told Parker, "and also rightfully belongs to the South." More specifically, he thought, it belonged to North Carolina, which had not yet been awarded a national appointment for its role in the 1928 victory.[15]

To his credit, Jonas handled the politics of the nomination with great skill. Ably assisted by united statewide leadership, the Republicans carefully avoided any reference to a North Carolina appointment or to the impetus that the Parker appointment could give to the lily-white movement in the South. Only Dixon, the first assistant secretary of the interior privately argued in strictly partisan political terms and his indiscretion would later embarrass and hamper the Parker advocates.[16] Instead they secured endorsements from re-spected law firms, leading state and federal jurists, prominent state Demo-cratic leaders, and finally "our Southern and border-state Congressmen." These tactics soon made Parker the leading contender.[17] The former United States collector of internal revenue David H. Blair and the former United States circuit judge Elliot Northcott helped Jonas win the support of the state's two Democratic senators, Furnifold M. Simmons, to whom Hoover was in-debted for leading the anti-Smith forces in the 1928 election, and Lee S. Overman, the ranking Democrat on the Senate Judiciary Committee.[18] Added to this phalanx were several platoons of visiting southern delegations who had little difficulty convincing Hoover that the South deserved the honor of a nomination and that Parker's selection "would be more universally approved in the South than any other."[19]

Reassured by Stone; Willebrandt; southerners in both parties; Attorney General William D. Mitchell, who had carefully scrutinized Parker's circuit court decisions; and by the lack of opposition, Hoover sent the Parker nomina-tion to the Senate on 21 March 1930, only thirteen days after Judge Sanford's death.[20] The swiftness of the nomination surprised some observers; yet Hoo-ver had good reason for the quick decision. He wanted to dramatize Parker as the symbol of all he desired in the new elite leadership for the South. In this respect too Parker appeared to be the ideal candidate: a highly successful lawyer and popular Republican politician who had helped to build a strong, respected organization in North Carolina and who had earned and retained the admiration of both parties. He had served as a special assistant to the United States attorney general and had gained valuable experience for three years on the Fourth Federal Circuit Court. Moreover, because Parker would replace another eminently qualified southerner, Democrats could not charge Hoover with making the appointment merely to facilitate reform of the Republican state parties. His nomination thus appeared to be above partisan politics yet would obviously enhance the party's prestige and image in the southern states. Southern reaction to the nomination revealed a genuine, widespread satisfac-tion both in the man and in the special recognition that Hoover had finally granted the South.[21] Indeed, in their own private assessment of Parker some southern Democratic senators no doubt came to the conclusion that he was the perfect partisan Trojan horse for the president's "southern strategy."

The quick selection startled interested observers but none more than the NAACP, which since 1915 had won a series of important civil rights cases before the Supreme Court. Less than two years earlier, in 1927, in the cele-brated *Nixon vs. Herndon* case, the Court had outlawed the Texas white primary. This highly promising judicial trend boded well for other equally important cases pending in lower courts or being appealed to the Supreme Court.[22] The NAACP was thus especially interested in any new nominee and had taken pains to check on the background of likely prospects. Walter White, who had replaced James Weldon Johnson as executive secretary, had suspected that Hoover might name a lily-white southerner to bolster his sagging southern strategy, and he had made inquiries about leading lily-white possibilities. Advised erroneously that Parker was out of the running, however, he had not solicited information and judgments on his fitness.[23]

Now White placed long-distance telephone calls to allies in North Carolina for information about Parker's position on Negro rights.[24] Within several days he had an old yellowed newspaper clipping of the 19 April 1920 issue of the Greensboro *Daily News*, which quoted Parker's vehement denials of Democratic claims that he had been soliciting Negro votes and favored the return of the Negro to political power.[25] He had made his statements during his gubernatorial campaign at a time of intense racial hatred directed against blacks in both the North and the South. Only a year earlier, in 1919, infamous race riots in northern cities and in other parts of the nation had inflamed hatreds and swelled membership in the rapidly reemerging Ku Klux Klan.[26] In his zeal to throw off the charges that Republicans wanted to reinstitute Reconstruction, Parker felt compelled to use terms that would satisfy his Democratic critics. Thus, to the state convention in March 1920, Parker had reiterated his own and the state party's position.[27]

One of the issues was the state grandfather clause, an amendment to the state constitution that had been declared illegal by the United States Supreme Court in 1915. This clause had given permanent voting registration to male whites whose fathers and grandfathers had qualified to vote before 1867, the year in which Congress enfranchised male blacks by the Fifteenth Amendment to the United States Constitution.[28] These white males would therefore not have to pass literacy tests or meet other criteria commonly used to prevent blacks from voting. Yet five years after the United States Supreme Court declared it illegal, Parker soothed Democratic fears by insisting that the Republican party still accepted the grandfather clause "in the spirit in which it was passed and the Negro has so accepted it." Parker also pointed out, moreover, that during his political career Negroes had not attended any of the party's state conventions and had not been invited to do so. The Democrats knew this. They also knew, he continued, that the party had repeatedly asserted "the fact that he [the Negro] has not yet reached that state in his development when he can share in the burdens and the responsibilities of Government." Political participation by Negroes would be, therefore, "a source of evil and danger to both races and is not desired by the wise men of either race or by the Republican Party of North Carolina." Given these well-known facts "the attempt of certain petty Democratic politicians to inject the race issue into every campaign is most reprehensible." Parker concluded with an ironic declaration: "I say it deliberately, there is no more dangerous or contemptible enemy of the state than the man who for personal or political advantage will attempt to kindle the flame of racial prejudice or hatred."[29]

Considering the NAACP's long-held belief that Hoover was driving the Negro out of Republican politics in the South, Parker's 1920 statements appeared to fit into a familiar pattern. Still, before making a judgment, the leaders of the NAACP telegraphed the nominee to ascertain if the newspaper quotations were accurate, and if they reflected his current position on Negro rights. Parker received the telegram on 26 March 1930, but he refused to reply.[30] After waiting two days, the NAACP launched its spirited opposition in telegrams to thirty-five United States senators and to all of its own branches.[31] The burden of their message was simple: Hoover's southern strategy, with Parker as its exponent, must not be allowed to penetrate the thinking of the Supreme Court justices.

Having been injured by racial politics earlier, Parker feared the effects of the telegram and decided not to make any comment whatever.[32] From the beginning his first thought was to gain confirmation. Privately he defended himself with profuse rationalizations to Jonas, Blair, and Northcott, all sympathetic, understanding southern Republicans. He repeatedly denied that he had been "attacking the colored people." Within the context of that 1920 campaign he had only tried to undercut race-baiting Democrats who sought to enflame public opinion by claiming that if elected, the Republicans would give blacks the vote and bring back Reconstruction. "The colored people have taken no part in politics in North Carolina for many years," he told Northcott, "and I was merely stating what every well informed person knew for a fact, namely, that the colored people were not trying to obtain political power and that the Republican party was not trying to bring them back into power, and that it was wrong to them as well as to the state to stir up racial feelings."[33] Parker felt that his own remarks were mild compared to the racism of the Democrats. He was convinced that if the NAACP had "understood the real spirit in which the speech was made," it would not have criticized him.[34] He pledged that as a justice of the Supreme Court he would never deny blacks their constitutional rights and pointed to the Richmond case in which, as a judge of the Fourth Circuit Court, he had sustained an earlier Supreme Court decision outlawing residential segregation of the races.[35]

At least one North Carolina black leader who knew Parker believed that he was not prejudiced and would be fair to Negroes. James E. Shepard, president of North Carolina College for Negroes, was his most vocal defender. In response to an inquiry from Carl Murphy, president of the influential Baltimore *Afro-American*, Shepard argued that blacks should not take the "campaign utterances" of 1920 as "the true test of the man." From his personal knowledge of Parker's beliefs, Shepard predicted that "the Negro will have no fairer or truer friend."[36] But few other black leaders would defend Parker, and they were not as enthusiastic as Shepard.[37] The overwhelming majority of black people were outraged by Parker's 1920 statements. They viewed him as a lily-white Republican racist who even now when he was no longer running for public office refused to repudiate the views he had expressed ten years earlier. To them it was obvious that Parker's racial beliefs were contrary to the Constitution and the principles of the Republican party and that he would therefore render decisions denying blacks the respect and rights due them as American citizens.[38]

The debate began on 5 April 1930, when Senator Lee Overman of North Carolina convened a hearing by a Senate judiciary subcommittee on Parker's nomination. Walter White led the NAACP attack.[39] To establish the background for the NAACP's concern, White presented the subcommittee with a digest of eight important cases involving black rights on which the Supreme Court had ruled favorably between 1915 and 1929 and pointed out that many other equally important cases were in the process of appeal from lower courts.[40] Obviously, the racial attitude of any nominee was crucial to the Negroes' long battle to achieve justice under the Constitution. Yet, White emphasized, Parker had consistently refused to repudiate his 1920 campaign statements or even to respond to inquiries from the NAACP for clarification. Moreover, Parker had supported the grandfather clause five years after it had been declared illegal by the Supreme Court in 1915. The facts were clear. Both his statements and his actions demonstrated that Parker would disregard the law as political expediency dictated, that he lacked the impartiality necessary to uphold the Constitutional rights of black people, and that he would therefore be "most dangerous" to blacks as a justice of the United States Supreme Court.[41]

Senator Overman was surprised and upset at White's effectiveness. He sought to confuse and embarrass him, but White remained calm. He repeatedly reminded the senator that the only evidence furnished of Parker's attitude toward Negroes lay in the 1920 campaign statements that Parker had refused to repudiate. It was reasonable to assume, White concluded, that Parker still believed what he had declared publicly in 1920.[42]

Privately White was not certain that Parker's confirmation could be stopped, but he hoped nonetheless that the opposition from the NAACP would "make other Southerners who have national ambitions careful of what they say on the Negro question in the future."[43] In one respect Overman agreed with White. He had been upset by the testimony, but he did not think that the NAACP could defeat Parker. He was more worried about the American Federation of Labor.

William Green, president of the AF of L, had voiced objection soon after Parker's nomination became known. At the subcommittee hearings Green carefully avoided any contact with White or any identification with the arguments put forth by the NAACP. Both the NAACP and the AF of L spoke for still relatively weak minorities, and although both groups were considered to be liberal, the unions would not admit blacks and refused to support their rights, either in general or as workers. Green instead centered labor's objections on Parker's defense of the yellow dog contract.[44]

In 1927 Parker ruled in the *United Mine Workers vs. Red Jacket Coal and Coke Company* that a lower court injunction against the United Mine Workers was valid. The injunction prevented the union from recruiting miners who had previously signed yellow dog contracts (which forbade them to join a union or by a strike to force the company to recognize a union). The injunction in effect prevented any efforts by the union to organize the workers.[45]

Overman defended Parker by explaining that he had merely followed the Supreme Court's precedent in a prior case, *Hitchman Coal Company vs. Mitchell*, which had validated yellow dog contracts. This gave Green the opportunity to argue that much more than Parker's confirmation was at stake. The larger issue was the conservative majority on the Court. The same issue had induced the agrarian Progressive senators George W. Norris, William E. Borah, and Robert M. LaFollette, Jr., to undertake a futile effort only weeks earlier in February to defeat Hoover's first Supreme Court nominee, Charles Evans Hughes. In 1916 Hughes had resigned his position on the Supreme Court to run against Woodrow Wilson as the Republican presidential candidate. After his defeat Hughes had defended large corporations, and this had become an important issue in the Senate debate over his selection to replace retiring Chief Justice William Howard Taft. He too was accused of placing property rights over human rights, but the twenty-six senators who voted against him could not convince the others to deny the prestigious Hughes his seat as Chief Justice. Green now appealed to these twenty-six senators that the trend toward increasingly conservative justices must be reversed. In order eventually to "liberalize" the Court, Hoover's latest conservative nominee could not be allowed to join the reactionaries already dominating this crucial institution.[46]

Because Hoover had long supported the rights of organized labor, Green's objection seriously disturbed him.[47] He asked Attorney General Mitchell for another review of Parker's decisions, but especially of the *Red Jacket* decision, to which Green had objected. Mitchell assured the president that Parker had "had no freedom of judgment" and "was bound by the decision of the [Supreme] Court, which he could not refuse to follow." Moreover, Mitchell emphatically denied that Parker had expressed a personal opinion on yellow dog contracts. "There does not appear to be a point," he told Hoover, "decided in the Red Jacket case on which Judge Parker assumed any independent judgment or opinion." To deny him a seat on the Court, Mitchell insisted, "will amount to refusing to confirm him because he followed and gave binding effect to the decisions of the Supreme Court of the United States."[48] Parker too felt that he had had no choice.[49] "Had I done otherwise," he told Congressman Jonas, "I should not only have been reversed but rebuked by the Supreme Court."[50]

Reassured by his attorney general, Hoover sent Mitchell's digest of Parker's decisions to Green, seeking to convince him that he had been "entirely misled" and would do "a great injustice" in opposing Parker's confirmation.[51] But despite Hoover's apparent suggestion that Parker personally favored the rights of organized labor, Green remained unconvinced. The yellow dog contract, he informed the president, was extracted by force from hopelessly poor and defenseless miners to perpetuate "industrial servitude," and both Parker and the Court had upheld its constitutionality. Furthermore, Green's reading of the *Red Jacket* decision convinced him that Parker had failed to express any reservations whatever about the Supreme Court precedent. In Parker's written decision there was "not one single word, sentence or paragraph . . . that would justify the conclusion that he is not in sympathy and accord" with yellow dog contracts. What this nation needs, Green lectured Hoover, are men on the Court "who are human and socially-minded, who understand modern industry and human relations in modern industry and who place human rights at least upon an equal basis with property rights."[52]

While deeply offended by the charges of the NAACP and the AF of L, Parker was not especially worried about their opposition. He was confident that he would be confirmed with little opposition and that the best thing he could do was to keep quiet and let things take their course.[53]

On 14 April two members of the three-man Senate subcommittee, Overman and Felix Hebert of Rhode Island, voted to recommend confirmation. Sen. William E. Borah of Idaho, who had campaigned for Hoover in the South, was no more impressed by White's arguments than were the other two, but he supported legislation already pending in Congress to outlaw both the yellow dog contract and the labor injunction, and therefore he voted against the nominee.[54] Apparently the NAACP had made no impact whatever. Hoover had rejected White's argument that the real issue was not Parker as much as the need to refuse rewards to those guilty of "demagogic appeals to race prejudice."[55] The president would not withdraw the nomination, but he was not totally insensitive to black objections. High officials in the Justice Department secretly contacted Municipal Judge James A. Cobb, a member of the NAACP and one of Hoover's trusted black advisers. They asked Cobb to relay to White that Hoover "wants to do the right thing but that he has been terribly embarrassed" by the unanticipated opposition and hoped that the NAACP could consider withdrawing its objection. White told Cobb that he believed it was already too late for a mere denial of race prejudice, but he held out the hope that Parker's "unequivocal" public repudiation of the 1920 statements might change black opinion.[56] Although Hoover was no doubt "terribly embarrassed," he would not work with the NAACP because he did not trust the organization that had repeatedly leveled charges against him during the 1927 Mississippi valley flood. For assistance in arriving at an acceptable public repudiation of the 1920 campaign statements Hoover turned instead to another group well known for its promotion of racial justice.

As a Quaker, the president knew of the long and devoted support that the

Society of Friends had given to black rights, and as we have seen, Hoover sympathized with Quaker beliefs on race.[57] On 17 April 1930, Robert Gray Taylor, secretary of the Committee on Race Relations of the Society of Friends, told Hoover and Parker that the society could not accept Parker's refusal to answer the NAACP's inquiries.[58] On 19 April, five days after the subcommittee's split vote, Parker suddenly invited Taylor to his office, where the two would work out a public statement acceptable to the liberal Society of Friends and to blacks. Although there is no direct proof that Hoover actually arranged this meeting, the evidence suggests that he at least approved it. Taylor, for example, kept the president informed of his progress. Moreover, it is highly unlikely that Parker would have consented either to the meeting or "to make any comment whatever on a thing as delicate as the race issue" without Hoover's approval.[59]

The meeting was obviously of great importance. A dramatic shift from opposition to support by the liberal Society of Friends would significantly offset the opposition of the liberal NAACP and perhaps disarm those concerned with black rights. After consulting with Taylor on the contents and wording of the public letter, Parker agreed to address it to Sen. Henry D. Hatfield of West Virginia, who was under intense pressure from voting blacks within his state to vote against confirmation and who had complained loudly to Hoover. In the letter Parker denied charges of racial prejudice, expressed the hope that the 1920 statements would be understood as an honest effort to reduce racial tensions during the campaign, and promised to uphold the Constitution impartially.[60] Like so many others who knew him, Taylor took an immediate liking to Parker and before long became totally convinced of his sincerity. He was not completely satisfied with the contents of the letter that Parker agreed to write, but he seemed to understand and even to sympathize with the political difficulties Parker would encounter from southern Democrats if the letter were more strongly or specifically worded. Immediately after the meeting Taylor informed Hoover that although differences over wording and emphasis still existed, he was nonetheless persuaded that if a southerner had to be appointed, Parker would be satisfactory and that the protest lodged by the Society of Friends would be withdrawn.[61] What he did not tell the president was that Walter White had already summarily rejected the letter as totally inadequate.

While Taylor was still in Parker's office, Taylor had read Parker's letter to White over the telephone and informed him that on the basis of this letter he would recommend withdrawal of the Society of Friends' protest. White was upset by Taylor's conversion. He warned Taylor that "withdrawal of any of Parker's opponents at this critical juncture might defeat and nullify all of the work which had been done and which has had such a notable effect."[62] Later that same day White showed the letter to the staff of the NAACP and reported to Taylor that they had vehemently rejected it. This time White explicitly raised the political purposes that the NAACP believed had motivated the nomination. The letter, he stated, neither repudiated lily-whitism nor gave any reason to believe that as a member of the Supreme Court Parker would oppose the underlying social and political philosophy of lily-whitism. Instead "his entire background" supported their belief that his decisions would be "harmful to the best interest of race relations."[63] In response to his objections the Society of Friends Executive Committee of the Committee on Race Relations immediately invited White to attend its meeting in Washington, D.C., on the following day.

Upon his arrival White recalled that all but one of the eight members of the committee "had made up their minds to accept Judge Parker's statement at face value." For three hours White argued the NAACP's case. The letter had not repudiated the 1920 racist beliefs that Negroes had not yet reached the stage in their development that enabled them to share in the burdens and responsibilities of government. Neither did it specifically retract Parker's statement that Negro participation in politics was a source of evil and danger to both races and had been rightly prohibited by the "spirit" of the state's grandfather clause. At least as important was the fact that it could not be considered an "unequivocal" retraction because there was "no direct repudiation of lily-whitism." The political philosophy of lily-whitism was the issue.[64]

In making his appeal to the Society of Friends, White outlined the belief of the NAACP that Hoover had deliberately selected a man he knew to be a lily-white racist in order to strengthen and advance a southern strategy based on racism.[65] Herbert J. Seligmann, publicity director of the NAACP, had summarized the reaction of the NAACP leadership to the Parker letter: "Regardless of what he says now, he was for years a leader of lily-whitism in North Carolina . . . and represented what I feel to be a part of a vicious policy to conciliate the worst elements in Southern public opinion."[66] At the conclusion of the meeting all eight members of the committee, swayed by White's effective appeal, agreed to continue to fight the nomination.[67] To both white and black liberals concerned with advancing black rights, Parker now seemed the lily-white symbol of a southern strategy that they attributed to Hoover.

18. The Parker Defeat

The decision of the Society of Friends to continue its opposition to Parker was a bitter blow to Hoover.[1] His own reputation was at stake at least as much as Parker's, and the help of respected and influential liberals now seemed beyond his reach. Significantly, however, although Taylor may have accepted the argument of the NAACP, he still clung to the personal conviction that Parker was being made to suffer for the historic and political wrongs of his region rather than for his personal beliefs, and he felt compelled to apologize to Parker for having led him to believe that the public letter to Senator Hatfield would be satisfactory to the Society of Friends.[2] Hoover shared the liberal Taylor's assessment, and he consequently refused to withdraw the nomination. Still, with an increasing number of influential liberals aligning against Parker as a symbol of Hoover's "lily-whitism," the president more than ever needed the steadfast support of conservatives, especially influential black conservatives.

As the opposition grew stronger, Senator Overman warned Parker that White was "a pretty smart negro," and he advised Parker to seek the endorsement of Robert R. Moton, Jr., the Tuskegee principal, who he believed would be more understanding of the demands that southern politics had put upon white Republicans and would be of great value in countering Walter White and the NAACP in the "pretty big fight" that lay ahead.[3] Parker agreed and so did Hoover. Moton was not only a staunch friend and ally who knew the president's innermost thoughts on racial progress, but in this fight he might well become the key figure in minimizing the attack by the NAACP and its allies. Moton was the one black leader whom Hoover felt he could rely upon to dispel the odious charge that Parker was a lily-white racist and therefore the fitting symbol of Hoover's white supremacist, antiblack southern strategy. Accordingly the president ordered his political secretary Walter Newton to speak with Moton personally.[4]

If Moton had issued a ringing endorsement of Parker, he might well have become as influential within the Hoover administration as Booker T. Washington had been during that of Theodore Roosevelt. Moreover, there appeared to be an excellent likelihood that Moton would support the president. During the 1928 campaign Moton had argued forcefully that black people would have a good friend in Hoover, whose personal views and efforts on their behalf would satisfy the "most radical." Immediately following the furor over the De Priest tea, Hoover had invited Moton to the White House, and at that time he had met the national news correspondents and told them that black people need have no fear of Hoover's reform of the southern state parties because it was not antithetical to black interests.[5] Yet Moton had not endorsed all aspects of Hoover's southern reform. In fact, he had gently warned that blacks must not be ignored during the reform process. He had told reporters that black interests would best be protected by the appointment of black representatives to the state patronage advisory committees, a recommendation that had not been adopted. As a personal friend Moton could not bring himself to believe that Hoover had foreknowledge of Parker's 1920 statements. To Newton he confided his belief that if Hoover "had known of the attitude of Judge Parker in this matter he would not have nominated him."[6] But that "attitude" was a fact that Moton refused to ignore.

Having thoroughly investigated the charges, Moton was satisfied that Parker had indeed made the anti-Negro statements, although not, as Moton and others had believed, the false claim that he would resign as governor if elected by one black vote. Nonetheless, Moton clearly saw the racism of Parker's statements. "Personally I can forgive a great many things that are the reflection of our common human weakness," he told Hoover, "but when a man sets himself up to publicly attack, revile or express his contempt for my people for no other reason than that they belong to another race, he places himself in a position where I can have nothing less than an uncompromising and everlasting hostility."[7] As he put it, the time had come when Hoover must join with black people to fight the ideas expressed by Parker openly.

Moton's carefully worded written response to the president's oral appeal marked a chilling break with past trusts. Moton no longer accepted Hoover's personal assurances at face value. The collapse of the attempts to find private financing for the antipeonage land scheme and Hoover's unwillingness to pursue other avenues may have helped to cool some of Moton's earlier ardor. The president's slowness to respond to his patronage requests may also have lessened his trust in Hoover's promises. Moreover Parker's "attitude" toward blacks disqualified him as a representative of the southern white elite who could help black people. Most important however was the blatant racism of Parker's statements. Negroes were "registering their protest" against these ideas, he warned, and he joined them in wondering about "the President's persistent support of Judge Parker." Should Hoover continue to ignore the black protest, he would certainly lose their political allegiance. "I know of nothing that would so effectively turn the tide of Negro support against the President and the party, that could perpetuate such an outrage against the Negro's political rights as deliberately to place on the Supreme Court a man who has openly declared his contempt for them."[8]

Moton understood what he was sacrificing in his refusal to support the nomination. Newton had made the political stakes clear to him, even to the point of emphasizing the patronage influence he would lose. This especially offended Moton. There is no doubt that Moton had worked for and fully expected to receive recognition as the most powerful black patronage broker in the Hoover administration. But Newton's use of patronage to pressure Moton on a matter of principle and racial pride so galled him that he chided both Newton and Hoover. "To have our friends," he told them, "ask us to palliate such hostility and to connive at a sacrifice of principle for political advantage is more than our self-respect can swallow."[9]

Hoover was so deeply disappointed at Moton's firm response that he failed to acknowledge the forthright advice of his loyal booster. Moton had acted honorably and courageously by giving him the perspective he sorely lacked, but Hoover, as Moton may have suspected, had already made up his mind. He was stubbornly convinced that Parker's political opponents had victimized him by introducing his 1920 campaign statements into the discussion out of their proper context and thus deliberately misrepresented his real beliefs. Parker had understandable reasons for what he had done. As the attorney general had emphasized, he had no choice in the matter of the yellow dog contract. Moreover, he had upheld the Supreme Court's earlier ruling outlawing racial residential segregation, and he had demonstrated his personal sincerity to Taylor, who was satisfied with the public letter explaining his decisions and pledging that he would uphold the principles of the Constitution impartially.

Moton's response to Hoover highlighted the racial and political sensitivity that Hoover lacked. Moton did not mention what each of them knew to be the "special context" in which the nomination had been made, namely the widespread perception of a lily-white southern strategy. Parker's refusal to repudiate the 1920 statements was sufficient in Moton's judgment to rule out any further consideration and to cast serious doubt on the president's reform of the southern state parties. The NAACP had already highlighted the nomination as a crucial feature of the administration's alleged southern strategy, a strategy that the NAACP believed was dominated by the political thinking that Parker had expressed in 1920 and that, unless decisively rejected, would gain strength in the southern state parties, in the Republican party, and in the Supreme Court. Hoover was incensed by this line of attack. The NAACP, the Society of Friends, and now Moton seemed to be insisting on personal guarantees that Parker would interpret the Constitution to their political satisfaction rather than according to the dictates of his own best judgment. Moreover, Hoover felt personally insulted at their charge that he would support an anti-Negro nominee in order to promote an anti-Negro southern strategy.

In his frustration and anger Hoover reverted to a way of thinking about Negroes that he had displayed before. In 1921, for example, he had rejected requests that Negroes be represented at the special unemployment conference that he had organized, and again in 1925 he had reacted defensively to Claude

Barnett's criticism of the Department of Commerce for failing to help black business leaders. In the early 1920s Hoover tended to view requests for black representation as pressure to recognize a special interest. He had insisted that his decisions and those of special commissions must be based on the principle of the public interest, on what was beneficial to all Americans rather than only to a few.[10] Later, his education during the Mississippi flood of 1927 alerted him to the need for special studies and special actions to help blacks, but in the spring of 1930, as black leaders almost unanimously urged him to withdraw Parker's nomination, Hoover returned to his earlier view of special black interests. To counter the NAACP, the Society of Friends, Moton, and the AF of L, he began to insist that the overriding issue was the principle of an independent judiciary, which could render its judgments free from the pressure of political special-interest groups. To allow special-interest minorities to determine the selection of Supreme Court justices would inevitably lead to judicial chaos. It was not Parker's fitness for the position but the erroneous perception of his alleged politics that motivated the opposition, and that opposition stemmed from two politically active minorities: the blacks and union labor.

Although Hoover no doubt convinced himself of his sincerity in emphasizing the principle of an independent judiciary, he was inconsistent or even disingenuous in his identification of blacks and organized labor as mere special-interest groups that did not seek to advance the best interests of all Americans. Certainly in promoting the trade association movement, a subject that is lucidly explained by Ellis Hawley, Hoover suggested that by helping special interests he could in fact promote the economic prosperity of all Americans. He himself had repeatedly recognized that pressure from special-interest minorities sometimes served the public interest as well. Moreover, he was already sufficiently well informed about the special problems created for blacks by white racism to recognize that this minority could hardly be viewed in the same category with other special-interest lobbies. But in his anger Hoover could not bring himself to understand how his good intentions and high-minded motives might well promote or seem to promote the forces of racism and the repression of labor that he wished to combat. He had selected a good candidate in good faith. He believed in that candidate's desire to be fair to both blacks and labor. He would therefore stand by him, and in later years Parker's record would justify Hoover's faith.[11]

Having lost the arguments with labor, with black people, and with liberals generally, the beleaguered president turned for support to a number of conservative United States senators. The most eminent of these, in Hoover's judgment, was Arthur Vandenburg of Michigan.[12] Hoover desperately wanted to convince Vandenburg of the righteousness of his position. His unusually high regard for Vandenburg stemmed in part from Vandenburg's vigorous defense of Charles Evans Hughes, Hoover's first nominee to the Supreme Court, against the criticisms of liberal senators. In replying to such critics as

Brookhart and Norris, who opposed Hughes because of his staunch legal defenses of big corporations, Vandenburg had stressed the importance of the principle of separate branches of government, which, he told his fellow senators, dictated that they must not use their current political beliefs as the criteria for approving Supreme Court nominees.[13]

Of course, Hughes was a highly respected leader with admirers even among those who disagreed with his politics, so Vandenburg found it much easier to defend Hughes than Parker.[14] Vandenburg questioned Hoover about Parker's support of the grandfather clause and literacy test, and the president immediately ordered Attorney General Mitchell to find convincing evidence exonerating Parker. Vandenburg had "probably touched on the worst phase of this misrepresentation," Hoover told Mitchell, and "it would be most desirable to have it cleared up as I believe Senator Vandenburg is a man whose sincerity is such that he would respond quickly on such a point, if it could be done."[15]

On 19 April 1930, following Mitchell's advice, Hoover confidently informed Vandenburg that Parker had "never favored" the literacy test or "anything of the kind." Nor could he have supported the grandfather clause, which had expired in 1908. This new evidence, Hoover reassured Vandenburg, proved beyond question that it was "utterly impossible" for Parker to have "given any support to such proposals."[16] But Mitchell's summation was narrowly focused. It did not address Parker's support of the "spirit" of the grandfather clause, of an "attitude," as Moton had put it, that was hostile to black rights; and in this sense Mitchell's report served the president poorly.

Privately Hoover expressed his conviction that the opposition to Parker was based on partisan politics, not principles, and he would not allow his administration to bow to such pressures. He erroneously believed that the NAACP was being financed either by John J. Raskob, chairman of the Democratic National Committee, or by Tammany Hall.[17]

Hoover justified his refusal to withdraw the nomination on several grounds. Most important was his belief that Parker would be an excellent justice who would uphold the rights of labor and the rights of black people. Constant reassurances from Parker, Parker's close associates, and the president's own advisers bolstered this conviction. In addition, Hoover felt a personal sense of outrage at the frequent charge that he had deliberately nominated a man who would violate the rights of his fellow citizens. Neither Moton nor Vandenburg thought that the president would have nominated Parker if he had known about the 1920 statements and the yellow dog contract decision.[18] Yet Attorney General Mitchell had led Hoover to believe that Parker's political opponents had deliberately misrepresented and distorted Parker's record, and Hoover had pressed this line of reasoning. In this, however, he was no more successful with Vandenburg than he had been with Moton.[19]

Hoover's case for Parker was much weaker than he was willing to admit. The fact that Parker had not supported the state constitutional amendment establishing the grandfather clause or the state literacy test did not prove that he really opposed either. Through its Michigan branches the NAACP made certain that Vandenburg understood that Parker had persistently rejected appeals to make a public repudiation of the anti-Negro racist campaign statements of 1920.[20] Significantly, although Parker knew of Vandenburg's concerns, he did nothing to reassure the senator. He did not repudiate his 1920 statements or deny that these statements represented the administration's lily-white southern strategy. He merely expressed the hope that he would get Vandenburg's vote.[21]

Because both the black and the labor votes were of obvious importance in Michigan, Vandenburg was probably as much concerned about his own political survival as he was about the principle of the separation of powers. However, to his credit, he did understand that more was at stake than the independence of the judiciary. A competing principle, which he ultimately found more compelling, was the constitutional rights of minorities. Both labor and blacks had excellent arguments, and both pressed their cases on Vandenburg. Labor believed that its freedoms of speech and assembly had been unconstitutionally abridged by yellow dog contracts, and blacks argued that their rights under the Fourteenth and Fifteenth amendments had been repeatedly violated by politicians. Each found recourse only in appeal to the Supreme Court. Should the Court be composed of men out of sympathy with the constitutional rights of these minorities, injustices would be continued and even strengthened. How the Constitution was interpreted was, therefore, crucial, and the NAACP and the AF of L made much of this point.[22] White was especially pleased when Felix Frankfurter, professor of law at Harvard University and later himself a Supreme Court justice, supplied him with Charles Evans Hughes's statement that the Constitution was what the Supreme Court judges said it was.[23]

Hoover's inability to convince Vandenburg to vote for Parker indicated both the weakness of his own position and the increasing effectiveness of his opponents. Labor organizations and liberal white organizations such as the American Civil Liberties Union added to the swell of black rage.[24] Because newspaper publicity was a key element in combating apathy and in winning converts, White welcomed the "magnificent editorials" in the Scripps-Howard newspaper chain. To Ludwell Denny, a close friend on the New York *Telegram*, he confided, "I don't know any factor which has helped more in what seemed at first to be an almost hopeless fight than these editorials in the Scripps-Howard papers."[25] White, of course, exaggerated. He knew better than anyone that the greatest source of strength was the "steady and unyielding pressure" from black newspapers, black politicians, black pastors, black fraternal lodges, women's clubs, civic organizations, and branches of the NAACP.[26] Conservative blacks such as Moton united with liberals in a determined effort that greatly worried northern and border-state senators, especially those up for reelection in six months.[27] As they well knew, a united black vote in a close election during the depression could well provide the margin between victory and defeat. Yet despite anguished appeals from these senators, Hoover steadfastly refused to withdraw the nomination.[28]

Careful attention to political details was another source of strength. On 16 April White discovered that the full Senate Judiciary Committee was tied eight to eight on whether to recommend confirmation.[29] To swing the vote in its favor, the NAACP marshaled all of its influence in Illinois and Massachusetts to bear on two senators running for reelection, Charles S. Deneen of Illinois and Frederick H. Gillette of Massachusetts.[30] Oscar De Priest and the Chicago black organization eventually ensured Deneen's vote.[31] White and Green also courted George Norris, who opposed Parker because of the yellow dog contract rather than concern for black rights, and who, as chairman of the powerful Senate Judiciary Committee, proved an influential ally.[32] Indeed, any senator thought to be on the fence or opposed, was bombarded with petitions and letters from organizations and individuals within their states.[33] Even southern Democratic senators were not overlooked. White allies of the NAACP took special pains to remind them of Hoover's "southern strategy" and of the political prestige and momentum that Republican opponents in the South would gain as a result of a Parker victory.[34]

By contrast to the effective crusade waged by the NAACP and the increasing efforts of the AF of L, the administration at first did relatively little to win Senate approval. As late as 18 April, only three days before the vote of the full Senate Judiciary Committee, Attorney General Mitchell informed Newton that "we have no written endorsements from any Senator except Overman."[35] According to a count by the NAACP on that day, only thirty-eight Senators favored Parker, with thirty-one opposed and twelve on the fence.[36] The attorney general apparently had done nothing to promote Parker's nomination, while Newton's most vigorous action appeared to be an inconsequential FBI investigation of the NAACP and the gathering of faulty unreliable information on its leaders.[37]

In the early stages the fight for Parker was carried less by the administration than by the nominee and his North Carolina political allies Blair, Northcott, Jonas, and Thomas W. Davis. They concentrated their efforts on winning endorsements from state bar associations and, like the NAACP, on pressuring senators by galvanizing support from groups within each senator's state.[38] Congressman Jonas personally pressed the case with Senate Republicans. To Sen. Arthur Robinson of Indiana he argued that if Parker had not reassured the Democrats in 1920, race riots would have erupted.[39] To the Republican senator from Colorado, Charles W. Waterman, Jonas voiced the great fear of southern Republicans. If Parker were not confirmed, he lamented, it would "sound the death knell of Republican hopes in North Carolina and the states bordering."[40] Nor was Jonas alone in this partisan fear. Willebrandt, who was actively working for Parker, believed that southern Democratic senators were deliberately plotting to defeat Parker in order to destroy the party in the South.[41] Opposition from southern senators was, in fact, a source of great irritation. The two Georgia senators who had taken turns grilling Ben Davis during the 1928 election and were surely aware of the administration's efforts to build a new, stronger coalition in their state, flatly refused to support Parker.[42] Other Senate Democrats were also reported to be suspicious of the administration's motives and tactics. Their willingness to place partisan political advantage ahead of southern pride and solidarity greatly disappointed and angered the Republican North Carolinians.[43]

The administration's failure to win over the support of conservative blacks and many northern senators, both Democratic and Republican, finally became clear to Hoover on 21 April. With the full Senate Judiciary Committee close to a vote and reportedly tied eight to eight, Overman convinced Hoover to allow Parker to make a personal appearance before the committee. But it was already too late.[44] As Hoover listened to the Tuskegee Choir on the south lawn of the White House, Norris convened the Judiciary Committee, which unexpectedly rejected the request to hear Parker and abruptly recorded its opposition to his confirmation by a vote of ten to six.[45] It was an embarrassing, indeed, a stunning setback that seriously endangered the nomination.

The rejection by the Senate Judiciary Committee, interpreted as a victory for the NAACP, convinced Hoover that Parker must answer the charges against him more fully. At once he began to consult with Parker by telephone and telegram about answering them. The result was an open letter to Senator Overman in which Parker made no effort to change the minds of his liberal, labor-oriented opponents but reiterated that Supreme Court precedent had left him no choice or freedom of judgment in the ruling on the yellow dog contract.[46] He also introduced a new and more combative justification for his decision: that the case had involved union efforts to use "violence and intimidation, to induce employees, in violation of their contracts, to join the union and go on a strike."[47]

Judging from the available evidence, Parker's letter to Overman had originally been aimed at convincing northern and border-state senators that he was not anti-Negro, thus easing the burden on them and winning their vote. In what Hoover believed to be the final draft of the letter, which reflected the president's urging, Parker specifically addressed himself to Vandenburg's concerns. He argued that as he was only fourteen years old when the grandfather clause had been adopted, it was "absurd" to charge him with political support of such a device. He also specifically denied that he had rebuffed Negro votes, thus creating the impression that he favored Negro participation in the Republican party. On 24 April Parker read the letter to Newton over the telephone and probably received Hoover's blessing. Shortly afterward, however, Parker and Northcott had second thoughts about answering Vandenburg's concerns, and apparently without consulting Hoover, they decided to delete the references to the grandfather clause and the implication that the nominee favored Negro participation in politics.[48]

At this stage of the contest, despite the adverse recommendation from the Senate Judiciary Committee, the Parker forces believed that the chances for confirmation were still good.[49] In their judgment the key to success was the nearly solid vote of the southern senators. Therefore, Parker and Northcott rejected Hoover's instructions. They agreed instead that Parker's denial of supporting the grandfather clause might lead the southern senators to think that he was hostile to the amendment. "I am afraid that some of them might not like it," he remarked. For the same reason, he also deleted the implication that he favored Negro participation in politics. Instead, he substituted a bland, non-committal statement: "While I made it clear that my party was not seeking to organize the Colored People of the state *as a class* I at no time advocated denying them the right to participate in the election in cases where they were qualified to do so."[50] In making these changes, Parker had decided on his own southern strategy, one that counted on southern racial solidarity to tip the Senate balance in his favor.[51]

Hoover's reaction to the revised letter is not known, but upon its release one of Parker's liberal supporters changed his mind about the nominee. William Gray Taylor, who had so recently defended Parker before the Committee on Race of the Society of Friends, told him that his letter showed that he still believed the 1920 campaign statements. Unknown to Hoover, Taylor immediately communicated this same message to Vandenburg, who was considered to be among the undecided senators. Despite the embarrassment, there was still time for Hoover to withdraw the nomination on the grounds that Parker's revised letter placed Hoover in an intolerable position (which Moton had so clearly foreseen). The NAACP quickly rejected Parker's letter as a "disingenuous piece of sophistry."[52] Indeed it made Hoover appear to be steadfast in his support of a lily-white who had repeatedly and defiantly refused to recant his racist beliefs and who now, apparently with Hoover's permission, was courting anti-Negro votes to win confirmation.

Parker had concluded that politics was ultimately more important than principles and that if he were going to be confirmed he must take the initiative in the final stage of the battle.[53] Apparently he and his North Carolina advisers did not believe that Hoover was doing enough to ensure victory. Unlike Hoover, who still clung to the belief that the battle could be won if the deliberate misrepresentations were dispelled, Parker did not believe it was possible to placate either the prolabor or the problack senators without alienating the other southern senators who were more important and reliable. He viewed the contest as a simple test of strength between those who valued the independence of the judiciary and the "organized minorities." He did not believe that the time had come when organized minorities like the AF of L or the NAACP could dictate judicial appointments.[54] Rather than attempt to win over either prolabor or problack senators, as Hoover wished, Parker had decided that "any attempt to please all parties would probably result in pleasing nobody."[55]

Parker was not wholly wrong if he thought Hoover was not fighting as hard as he might. The president's military aide, Col. Campbell B. Hodges, spoke for several of Hoover's intimates when he declared in frustration that Hoover "ought to whip some of the 'outlaw' Senators into line by letting them know they would have no part whatever in patronage for their states unless they got into line." But Akerson and French Strother, two staff members close to the president, disagreed with Hodges. Strother reflected Hoover's belief that it would be very poor politics to try the patronage whip. Apparently, having made the contest one of principle, Hoover was determined to win or lose on that basis. Besides, Strother added, the president "was handicapped because he didn't understand playing the political game well enough—trading and swapping one thing for support on another later."[56]

Hoover's reluctance to use patronage did not prevent opponents from charging him with patronage abuse. As the Senate debate neared, attacks by both sides became increasingly open and vicious. The most sensational was the claim that the president was offering federal judgeships in return for favorable votes. But senators were knowledgeable about the use of patronage, and none of them, not even his bitter enemy Senator Norris, believed the claim.[57] Some patronage promises were probably made, though not for federal judgeships. As he must have indicated, Hoover would not forget those border-state and northern Republican senators who had large numbers of black voters in their states and feared black retaliation at the polls. Patronage to these senators, especially black patronage, would help repair the political damage they would suffer for supporting him. But there is no evidence that he attempted to wield patronage as an important means of influencing any others than those who already supported him in principle but feared the political costs. He dismissed the suggestion of patronage pressure as merely another "misrepresentation" in this later, "dirty stage" of the debate.[58]

While Hoover remained above the mudslinging and vicious attacks, some of the Parker advocates could not contain their tempers or their tactics. Walter White noted that the North Carolinians were attempting to frighten prominent blacks into signing endorsements of Parker. Blacks complained to him about "being assailed as Communists, liars, political tricksters and everything else by Parker's friends and supporters."[59] A good example of what White meant was an editorial in the Washington (D.C.) *Post* charging that all of the anti-Parker activists were in fact subversives. "The purpose of the radicals who call themselves 'liberals,' " the *Post* claimed, "is to terrorize all Federal judges" so that "the Supreme Court and all inferior courts shall shape their decisions to suit the political aims of the demagogues in the Senate."[60]

On 22 April, six days before the full Senate debate began, White once again asked Hoover to withdraw Parker's nomination, but the president did not even acknowledge the request.[61] This was a serious but typical mistake on Hoover's part. As often happened, he became stubborn when he believed he was the victim of "misrepresentations" or "dirty politics." This blind spot often prevented him from reassessing controversial situations and developing more flexible responses to them. As a result he damaged his capacity to lead.[62]

White was incensed by Hoover's rebuff. To him, the president was "going out of his way to insult Negroes." Hoover had not only "stood by Parker despite Parker's anti-Negro utterances," but, he noted, his "whole attitude seems to me to be nothing but that of disregard and contempt for Negroes."[63] In striking back White effectively cultivated nationally prominent newspaper columnists.[64] He succeeded, for example, in convincing Heywood Broun that Parker was a "reactionary of reactionaries" and that Hoover hoped to get Parker confirmed by appealing to the "race prejudice of Southern Democratic senators" who might vote in favor "simply because Negroes oppose Parker." Hoover's plan, he told Broun, was "to line up Southern Democrats on the race issue, and their vote added to those of the Administration's Republican or Northern Senators who are not up for reelection this year, will put Parker through, by the skin of his teeth."[65]

These perceptions illustrate how misleading appearances could be and how insensitive Hoover was to these appearances. White, of course, did not know that the "southern strategy" he had described to Broun was Parker's own invention and at odds with the explanation he had worked out with Hoover. But because the president did not contradict Parker, White and virtually everyone else naturally assumed that the open courting of the anti-Negro senators was Hoover's plan. Certainly Hoover should have corrected the misapprehension, for his silence not only lent support to Parker's tactic but also opened him to most if not all of the blame. Ironically, White's plausible theory about how southern senators would vote also contained a serious flaw. As we have already seen in Mississippi and South Carolina, southern Democrats and Republican blacks sometimes made strange bedfellows. Indeed, when southern Democrats felt threatened by lily-white Republican incursions, their fear of Republican gains sometimes overcame their revulsion toward blacks.

White did not rely solely on publicity, pressure tactics, and argumentation. He was well aware of southern Democratic fears. Believing that the southern Democratic votes were crucial to the administration's hopes, White decided to play on those fears. To do so he contacted Robert R. Church, Jr., of Memphis. Church's own sense of Hoover's betrayal was still fresh. Ever since the reform proclamation of 26 March 1929 he had become one of the leading black critics of Hoover's "lily-white Southern strategy." White knew Church as a member of the executive committee of the NAACP. He was well aware of Church's political skills, and he sought to enlist those skills in the fight against Parker. Although he was a black Republican, Church had a close working relationship in Tennessee with the state's prominent Democrats. His friendship with Sen. Kenneth McKellar was an asset that White hoped Church could turn to good advantage. White informed Church that Parker appeared to have a margin of safety between two and five votes, and he asked Church to use all of his influence with McKellar to expose the administration's southern strategy and thereby lessen the chance that southern Democrats would support the nomination.[66] Exactly what Church was able to accomplish is not clear, but within a few days McKellar produced the evidence that would make it easier for southern Democrats to vote against Parker.[67]

The Senate debate was hardly the dramatic event that many had anticipated. Beginning on 28 April, it dragged on until 7 May, but few Republican senators would defend the nomination or the president. The "strange indifference" of the Republicans was in keeping with the "silent verdict" that characterized the dispirited mood of the entire Senate toward the nomination.[68] A few flurries did occur and those who spoke often displayed strong conviction. Sen. Robert Wagner of New York State coupled labor rights and black rights together in an attack on Parker's indifference to those seeking to better their condition in life.[69] But the senators generally avoided any mention of race, preferring instead to emphasize Parker's support of the yellow dog contract. A few Republicans defended the nomination while Simeon D. Fess of Ohio attacked the NAACP as an organization infested with radicals and socialists. Sen. Henry F. Ashurst created a sensation with his unfounded charge that Hoover had attempted to bribe Senator Dill of Washington with a federal judgeship, but few, if any, credited the claim, including Senator Dill. More influential was Senator McKellar's dramatic revelation of a letter written to Newton only five days after Judge Sanford's death by the North Carolinian Joseph M. Dixon, first assistant secretary of the interior. Dixon had argued that Parker's nomination would be "a master political stroke" because it would solidify Republican gains in the South.[70]

Much has been suggested about the impact of the Dixon letter on the extremely close vote against Parker. Although the letter undoubtedly proved a convenient excuse to southern Democratic senators, there is no evidence to suggest that it resulted in any last-minute switch of votes against Parker. Southern surprise and outrage notwithstanding, these senators could hardly have failed to understand the politics of the confirmation. The NAACP and its allies had bombarded them with the lily-white southern strategy, and as the battle developed even Jonas had dropped the initial emphasis upon a nonpartisan southern as opposed to Republican nomination. As early as 19 April Jonas and other Parker supporters were informing wavering Republican senators, "I need not say if Judge Parker should fail in this confirmation it will sound the death knell of Republican hopes in North Carolina and the states bordering."[71] Indeed, administration officials investigating the impact of the letter discounted its effect on the forthcoming vote. Mabel Walker Willebrandt con-

cluded, for example, that those southern senators who cited the Dixon letter
were doing so "as just a miserable excuse," for they never had any intention of
voting for Parker. Sen. Daniel F. Steck of Iowa would have agreed. On 24
April, a week before the Dixon letter surfaced, Steck justified his reluctance to
support Parker on the grounds that both regular Republican and southern
Democratic senators saw the Parker nomination as "essentially a political
appointment" designed merely to strengthen the party in North Carolina and
the South. Nonetheless, the letter made as convenient a political excuse as
these senators could have wished, and White and Church deserve some recognition for encouraging the Democratic senator from Tennessee to introduce it
into the battle.[72]

Although the Dixon letter has most probably been overemphasized, it nonetheless became clear to both sides during the last days of the Senate debate that
the vote would be exceedingly close. Accordingly both sides redoubled their
efforts. Interestingly both the NAACP and Hoover identified the same three
senators as crucial to their causes. White organized mass rallies in Michigan to
pressure Arthur Vandenburg and in Illinois to hold Charles S. Deneen and Otis
F. Glenn. Senator Deneen had opposed the seating of lily-white rather than
black-and-tan delegations at the 1928 national convention, but the powerful
black Republican organization in Chicago was taking no chances with either
senator. At the same time White sent out dozens of appeals to black leaders
throughout the United States, warning of the close vote and admonishing them
not to relax the pressure.[73]

Hoover also galvanized his forces. In a last-minute drive to stave off defeat
he directed a well-coordinated campaign in which he personally assigned his
top aides to speak with senators and kept his own daily tally of each senator's
apparent inclination.[74] When he realized he was one vote short of confirmation, he called to the White House the three conservatives who had given him
loyal support. Hoover pleaded with Vandenburg, Deneen, and Glenn but to no
avail. They declined to support him, Hoover recalled, "on the ground that to
vote for him [Parker] would raise opposition to their reelection."[75] On 7 May
the Senate cast forty-one votes against and thirty-nine votes in favor of confirmation, with the remaining sixteen evenly paired. One vote would have
allowed Vice-President Charles Curtis to break a tie in Parker's favor.[76]

Hoover was bitter in defeat. Publicly he warned against the political effect
of organized minorities and the danger of such pressure groups "fundamen-
tally altering the balance of our institutions."[77] Privately he was more specific.
Both Quaker leaders and Republican senators were responsible for failing to
stand against the false charges and "misrepresentations" that had defeated
Parker. "I am constrained to say," he later told Robert Gray Taylor, "that your
opposition, due to misrepresentation, to men of such high character as Judge
Parker . . . does not reflect credit upon the Society of Friends."[78] The Republican senators were equally guilty. They had run "like white mice."[79] Vanden-

burg escaped his immediate wrath. Soon after the vote Hoover called him to the White House to reassure him that he respected his decision, one which, Vandenburg privately recorded, was based on the principle of the protection of the rights of black people.[80] Nonetheless, after so many personal appeals the vote of the Republican senators had deeply wounded the president. The "failure of my party to support me," he recalled, "greatly lowered the prestige of my administration."[81]

Hoover seemed to place most of the blame on the NAACP. He not only suspected that it was financed by Democratic enemies, but he even had the Justice Department investigate it for radical or illegal activities. In his *Memoirs* he erroneously and unfairly claimed that Parker had been denounced "by a Negro association upon the wholly fictitious statement that, when twenty-one years old, he had made some remark bearing on white supremacy in the South."[82]

Throughout his life Hoover continued to believe that Parker was neither antilabor nor antiblack. In this judgment he was ultimately proven correct. Parker retained his seat on the Fourth Circuit Court and years later no less an enemy than Walter White concluded that since Parker's rejection "his decisions on both Negro and labor cases which have come before him have been above reproach in their strict adherence not only to the law but to the spirit of the Constitution."[83]

Others who analyzed the defeat differed widely. Senator Fess advanced two reasons: the success of the "socialist" assault on the judiciary and the desire to attack Hoover and "embarrass him for political reasons."[84] Although there was a considerable amount of truth in Fess's assessment of the anti-Hoover trend in the Senate, his first reason was no more credible than Walter Lippmann's claim that Parker was defeated because he was a judicial mediocrity.[85] Equally unconvincing to the *New York Times* was the argument that the Senate had been motivated by high principles. Would these same Republican senators who had voted against Parker because they allegedly championed black rights, the editors asked rhetorically, vote for measures to enforce the Fourteenth and Fifteenth amendments to the Constitution? The editors did not think so. "It is not a case of conviction or sincerity on the part of these demoralized Republican Senators," they concluded, "but solely of political scheming."[86]

Blacks fully recognized the mixture of motives. They knew that some senators, both northern and southern, had voted against Parker not because they believed in the constitutional rights of black people but for a variety of other, more selfish reasons. William Pickens, for example, felt that when Sen. Hiram Johnson of California voted against Parker, he had acted out of personal animosity toward Hoover, and that he remained "a very dangerous enemy to colored people because of his anti-oriental complex."[87] Walter White and W. E. B. Du Bois naturally credited the NAACP with the victory and rejoiced in the belief that the Parker fight had made it a powerful national force.[88]

Another black leader reminded White that when the 100,000 NAACP membership was compared to the over 3,500,000 union members, it became obvious that the AF of L had also been important.[89] Both White and Du Bois agreed. The AF of L, Senate liberals who wanted a more liberal Supreme Court, and worried southern Democrats had all contributed to the victory. Nonetheless in their judgment it had been the NAACP that had added the voting element crucial to the defeat of Parker: the border-state and northern Republicans who would have normally voted with the president but who were fearful of a united, aroused black electorate.[90]

Disappointed southerners offered still another explanation. Jonas spoke for many when he told Parker that southern senators were to blame. They had sold out, he insisted, "to unholy and unnatural allies." These southern Democrats had "traded the representation of our section on the highest court for supposed brief partisan advantages."[91] One-half of the southern senators had voted against Parker. The border states of Kentucky and Tennessee and the deep-South states of Georgia and Alabama had joined with the two senators from Texas and one from Florida in opposing Parker. The black vote in Kentucky was significant, but it is less likely that the senators from Tennessee, Georgia, Alabama, and Texas had much to fear from the NAACP or from the AF of L.[92] What they probably feared more was the impetus that a Parker victory might give to southern lily-white Republicans in the November state and congressional elections.

Because the vote was so close, it is not possible to determine conclusively which of the several explanations was the most important one in Parker's defeat.[93] Nonetheless, the evidence does suggest that still another explanation may be more significant than those already mentioned. The unexpected convergence of "unnatural allies" can only be understood in terms of the shared conviction that Parker's nomination was a crucial element, indeed the key indicator of what appeared to be Hoover's carefully planned lily-white southern strategy. Hoover perceived Parker as the epitome of a new and dynamic southern elite leadership, but Hoover's opponents interpreted the nomination differently.

The perception of traditional lily-whitism caused the more conservative black leaders, such as Moton, to join the more liberal leaders of the NAACP and form a united black front against the nomination throughout the United States. These black leaders in turn convinced conservative northern senators—such as Deneen and Glenn of Illinois, Robinson of Indiana, and Vandenburg of Michigan as well as border-state senators such as Arthur Capper of Kansas who normally voted with the president but who valued the black vote—to vote against Parker.[94] Southern Democratic senators, who were bombarded with the NAACP's emphasis upon lily-whitism, agreed with that view, and fearing that the southern Republicans might steal their lily-white mantle and capture the white vote, they combined with the northern and border-state senators and blacks to form the "unholy and unnatural" alliance.[95] Without this new belief that Parker epitomized Hoover's "southern strategy" and the resulting determination to align against it, the liberal bloc, which had voted against Hughes, and those senators who championed organized labor could not have mustered enough votes by themselves to stop Parker's confirmation. In the final analysis, Hoover failed to see that it was not merely the Parker fight that had greatly lowered the prestige of his administration but the perception of his "southern strategy" itself, of which Parker had become the preeminent symbol.

19. "Pretty Much Disgusted"

The president and his intimate advisers felt "very gloomy" over the Parker defeat. It was a major blow to the president, one which he later admitted had greatly diminished the prestige of his administration. Partly as a result Hoover, who always found it difficult to relax, became more tense than ever.[1] Rickard and George Barr Baker blamed the Parker defeat on his political secretaries Walter Newton and George Akerson, whom they considered to be bunglers.[2] They were right as far as they went, but they should have included the president himself in that judgment. In one respect Rickard did blame Hoover. After conducting his own survey of the president's White House advisers, Rickard concluded that Hoover had refused to consult with them as a group. He preferred instead to consult with only one individual about a problem. The result, Rickard concluded, was that Hoover had "no close advisers" and "at no time since he has been in public life has he been so completely alone."[3]

Unfortunately in an unguarded outburst of anger Hoover soon revealed his "great disappointment . . . in finding political contacts so uncertain and political individuals so untrustworthy."[4] The recipient of this indiscretion was Robert N. Hardy, a delegate to the American Bankers Association convention and close friend of Hoover's military aide, Col. Campbell B. Hodges, who had requested a brief, private interview. While shaking hands with the president, Hardy offered the remark that the American Bankers Association had supported him in the Parker fight, and Hoover shot back, "Judge Parker's rejection is an outrage. I don't know what the country is coming to if things are to be run by demagogues and Negro politicians."[5]

Although this outburst was offered in the privacy of his office, Hardy saw no reason to respect its confidentiality. Returning home to Yakima, Washington, he soon told local newspaper reporters of his meeting with the president. Judging from Hodges's own immediate record of the incident, Hardy quoted Hoover accurately. Apparently Hardy saw Hoover for only a brief handshake and a few quick words, yet he created the impression of a more extensive conversation. The president, he added, "could talk of nothing but the Parker case and the part Negroes had played in having him defeated."[6]

Before long the black press had picked up the story, and the Chicago *Defender*, a consistently vehement critic of Hoover's "Southern strategy," gave the quotation front-page exposure.[7] The editors were understandably upset. By lumping Negro politicians and demagogues together Hoover helped to confirm their fear that he was bent upon driving all black leaders out of the Republican party. The president's recent actions, namely the confusion and misunderstanding he had created in reforming the southern state parties, his steadfast defense of Parker, and the long delay in appointing blacks to prominent positions within his administration, seemed to fit this foreboding pattern. Hoover's "indifference to dark citizens," was well known, they noted, but until now "it was thought that he had at least the decency not to insult the entire race."[8] Barnett, like other black Hoover loyalists, was also shocked. He pleaded with Hoover for an immediate official denial, but the president ignored him and allowed Hardy's account to go unchallenged.[9]

Hoover's defeat in the Parker battle marked a significant but unrecognized change in his attitude toward the black elite whom he had selected to replace the black politicians. As his retort to William Howard Taft during the 1928 campaign had indicated, Hoover had no more respect for black politicians, especially corrupt ones, than for white.[10] That had not changed. Yet he had placed great hope in those new black leaders who, he believed, did not use politics for personal gain or advancement but instead put their abilities in the service of their race and their faith in him as a trustworthy leader who would help them to advance. This faith meant more to Hoover than Moton or other loyalists realized, and they little understood how personally he responded to opposition or criticism from friends on whom he relied. Rickard knew this reaction from Hoover's days as secretary of commerce. "Individual gross betrayal of his trust," wrote Rickard, "disturbs his sense of fairness and loyalty."[11]

Moton had repeatedly told Hoover that he was "no politician," and Hoover undoubtedly had the same general impression of Judge Cobb, Dr. Scott, Dr. Hawkins, Barnett, and others of his black elite.[12] As Hoover understood the term, these men were true leaders. They had achieved their status as leaders outside of politics in respected professions in which they were still engaged. They had seemed to share the same values, the same goals, the same dreams of a better future, and he was pleased therefore to have them serve as his unofficial national black patronage advisory committee. Yet when the "Negro politicians" of the NAACP had attacked him for nominating Judge Parker, Hoover had asked for the help of his black elite; had asked for their "nonpolitical" support at a time when he desperately needed it, and they had refused. Moton had not only rebuked Parker, but in chastising Newton for linking federal patronage to his support of Parker, he had also rebuked the president, who had obviously authorized Newton to make such a connection.

Despite his great efforts to separate principles and politics, Hoover sometimes failed, and the unfortunate disaffection that developed between him and his black elite, who were also men of high principle, is a good example of the president's confusion. Because he placed so much emphasis on principle over politics, and because he was an exceptionally conscientious man, Hoover tended to assume that his goals and actions were based on noble principles, and that, therefore, his followers should loyally support him. What he failed to realize fully was that he was calling for acts of political loyalty even when that loyalty ran counter to other principles that were at least as important to his followers. When his handpicked black elite placed their own principles above loyalty to him, he felt betrayed and angry.

In Hoover's narrow, stubborn opinion, the Parker fight was dirty politics at its worst. He refused to believe that Parker was either an antilabor reactionary or a racist, and he was deeply hurt that once-enthusiastic black supporters believed he would nominate such a man, much less continue to defend him. Probably, too, he was angry at the extraordinarily effective manner in which black critics had tied the allegedly racist nominee to his alleged purge of black leaders from the party. Small wonder, if so, that Hoover "could talk of nothing but . . . the part Negroes had played."[13]

Evidence of the sudden chill between Hoover and his black elite had become apparent immediately after Moton rejected the president's call for help. Earlier, when the battle lines over the Parker nomination were forming, Hoover had already set in motion actions that he hoped would strengthen his conciliatory policy toward Latin America. As evidence of his good intentions, he wanted to withdraw United States Marines from Haiti, a policy fervently supported by all black American leaders, including the NAACP. But in appointing a commission to arrange the details with the Haitians, he had discovered that Haitian leaders did not want any black Americans assigned to this commission because they regarded them as inferiors; they would deal only with white officials.[14]

Although Hoover was aware that the exclusion of American blacks from a process for which they had deep feelings would be insulting to them, he had not wished to jeopardize the diplomatic mission. Therefore he decided to create another separate all-black American commission headed and selected by Robert Moton to investigate and make recommendations for improvements in the classics-oriented Haitian educational system.[15] Moton had warned the president of the certain criticism he would receive for separating the more important white commission from the obviously less important black one, but he had agreed, nonetheless, to accept the president's assignment. Moton had insisted upon only one condition: that the black educational commission be transported on the same navy cruiser that carried the white commission.[16] It was a small enough condition, yet despite the agreement it was not granted. Moton discovered this shortly after he rejected Newton's telephone call for support in the Parker furor and he protested directly to Newton.[17]

Newton was deliberately and unnecessarily rude. He denied any knowledge of such an agreement, summarily dismissed Moton's protest, and refused to arrange for transportation aboard the cruiser.[18] Moton was furious. He knew that the NAACP had taken a particular interest in the independence of Haiti, and he had no intention of allowing himself and the commission, which he had personally selected, to be treated as second-class citizens. Because Newton would not help, he appealed directly to Hoover, explaining that the failure to provide the cruiser might subject both his commission and the president to severe criticism from American blacks. Because this was a minor issue known to only a few officials, Hoover could certainly have intervened without any political risk to himself. His assistance would have reassured Moton of his sensitivity to black pride in the midst of the Parker battle, a reassurance that the loyal Moton had every right to expect. Unfortunately, Hoover refused to become involved.[19] Eventually Moton and his educational commission quietly accepted passage on a commercial ship, virtually without notice.[20] Although it is not clear why Hoover rejected Moton's personal appeal, the timing strongly suggests pique at Moton's refusal to support the Parker nomination.

The emergence at the same time of a much more controversial issue, the "Jim Crowing" of black Gold Star mothers, was an extra reason for Moton's insistence on the navy cruiser. As the Parker battle grew in intensity, blacks discovered that the mothers of black soldiers who had been killed in World War I would not be allowed to travel to Europe in the navy ships that were carrying white mothers but must take passage on commercial steamers. This decision had not originated with Hoover. On 2 March 1929, before he was inaugurated as president, Congress had voted funds to send the mothers to Europe and had authorized the secretary of war to make arrangements. The responsibility thus fell to Patrick J. Hurley of Oklahoma.

Hoover had never thought well of the idea, but inasmuch as Congress had already acted before he became president, he had not voiced any public opposition and had allowed Hurley to go ahead with his plans. To dramatize the pilgrimage Hurley had prevailed upon the president's wife, Lou Henry Hoover, to draw lots that would determine in what order and when the thousands of Gold Star mothers would travel to Europe. It was a well-publicized ceremony that had created the impression of direct White House approval and involvement.[21] Hurley was no friend of Negroes but an avowed segregationist and lily-white.[22] If he had segregated whites from blacks aboard the same ships or had arranged for separate warships, black leaders might not have raised as great a public outcry. But the use of commercial steamers—"cattle boats," the black critics called them—was carrying discrimination further than they could stand. They thought it a deliberate, calculated attempt to humiliate all black people.

Here was another opportunity for Hoover to demonstrate some sensitivity to black pride, perhaps by ordering that all Gold Star mothers be transported on navy ships, even if they were segregated. But protests and appeals from prominent blacks, both friends and opponents, and from the liberal press had even less effect on Hoover than did the swelling chorus against Parker.[23] He refused all public comment, ignored the vehement black protest, and argued feebly in private that Congress had given the War Department "sole authority" so he could not intervene in any way. William Monroe Trotter, leader of the National Equal Rights League and Race Congress, warned Hoover that blacks interpreted the use of separate ships as part of his "deference to the prejudice of Southern white women."[24] Because women could now vote in national elections, Trotter was thus associating this prominent display of discrimination with the belief in Hoover's southern strategy. The Republican congressman, Oscar De Priest, publicly voiced the general black opinion that Negro mothers were being transported on commercial vessels because the president of the United States had ordered them so segregated.[25] Again there was no denial from the White House, and Hoover's silence appeared to confirm the charge.

To some more conservative blacks the issue was not so much segregation, although they opposed it, but the humiliating refusal to transport Negro mothers aboard the ships of the United States Navy. These blacks were not asking Hoover to end segregation or even to strike a blow against it, for they realized the political danger in such an act. Providing navy vessels for all mothers, however, would have risked little white reaction while it appeased blacks. Tom Canty, a Negro who was friendly to George Akerson, believed that the incident of the Gold Star mothers was Hoover's "worst boner" to date, worse apparently than the nomination of Parker, who, after all, upheld the Supreme Court's decision against residential segregation. "You may rest assured George," he concluded, "that it will take some hokus pokus raised to the Nth power, to repopularize Mr. Hoover with our people in the Middle West."[26] The same could be said for blacks in other parts of the United States. What was even worse, the process of transporting thousands of mothers to Europe—and the constant goading of blacks—lasted well into 1932, the all-important election year.[27]

Hoover seemed to give further evidence of anger at blacks by continuing to delay key patronage appointments for the nominees put forth by his own black elite. Despite appearances, the real reason lay mainly in his need to shore up crumbling relations with Congress and, in particular, to fulfill patronage promises to border-state senators who had voted for Parker. Even before the Parker battle, Hoover had found it necessary to be responsive to congressmen who supported his legislative program and had large numbers of voting Negro constituents. For this reason, for example, when congressman John H. Robison of Kentucky learned of the new post for a black education specialist, he requested and was granted it for one of his own black supporters.[28] Senatorial courtesy was yet another important consideration, which the Moton faction would later find especially frustrating.[29] Before Secretary of the Interior Ray Lyman Wilbur appointed a black woman, Bess Gordy Koontz, professor of elementary education at the University of Pittsburgh, as assistant commissioner of education, he first secured the approval of Pennsylvania senator David A. Reed.[30] Thus patronage was complicated by more influence than Moton's hopeful and frequently reassured supporters may have realized.

The influence of the border-state Republican senators on black patronage did not emerge as a complicating factor until after the Parker defeat. Hoover's desperate last-minute efforts to stem the anti-Parker tide had forced him to offer assurances of black patronage to those border-state senators who stood for reelection in November 1930 and who feared that angry black voters might tip the scales against them, especially in the midst of a worsening depression. Even if Hoover had withdrawn the Parker nomination, these senators still would have exercised considerable influence on black patronage, but probably with less influence on the president. In any case, the maneuvering over the post of recorder of deeds for the District of Columbia, the "favorite position" as Hoover sarcastically dubbed it, is an excellent illustration of the complexities of black patronage both before and after the Parker battle.[31]

From the time of his election Hoover had faced a host of critics in the Congress, including a number of Republicans, and immediately upon his inauguration he was eager to cultivate as many congressmen and senators as he could.[32] Advised that Henry D. Hatfield, the new Republican senator from West Virginia, was a strong supporter and would be of great help in the Senate, the president took pains to woo him.[33] As it happened, the incumbent recorder of deeds, Arthur G. Froe, was a highly popular black politician from West Virginia, where the black vote was crucial to Republican victory in both state and national contests. Hatfield naturally urged Hoover to retain Froe as recorder of deeds.[34] He was supported by all five of the West Virginia Republican congressmen, by the Republican governor, and by the Republican national committeemen.[35] Having recently defeated the Democrats in a close, bitter contest, they warned that their foes would certainly launch "a determined and aggressive campaign to alienate the negro vote from the Republican ticket" in 1930 and that the black vote represented "the balance of power" in the election.[36]

Unfortunately for the West Virginians, Daniel J. Donovan, the United States auditor for the District of Columbia, reported that Froe was unequipped to carry out his duties effectively, so in September 1930, only two months before the crucial off-year election, Hoover summarily demanded and received Froe's resignation.[37] Thereupon the two Kansas senators, Arthur Capper and Henry J. Allen, who also had a large and important black constituency to please, and who had voted for Parker, immediately began lobbying for the post. They had earlier gathered the signatures of sixty-four congressmen and senators in support of their nominee, but Hoover twice rejected their requests.[38] He had first rejected the Kansas senators when retaining Froe, but this time he did so because he had decided that Sen. Daniel O. Hastings of Delaware, who had also voted for Parker, needed the political help more than they did. Hastings had a large, growing black electorate that he had to placate, and he had also been a consistently loyal Hoover booster in the Senate.[39] By appointing Jefferson Coage as recorder of deeds, Hoover pleased Hastings but angered loyal senators in both West Virginia and Kansas. In his exasperation Hatfield even threatened to protest Coage's nomination on the Senate floor unless he was given other federal positions for his black supporters. The result was an extraordinarily complicated arrangement for deputy recorder, which ultimately pleased the senators from West Virginia.[40] To placate the two Kansas senators, Hoover allowed them to name their black choice, David E. Henderson, as special assistant attorney general, the highly prestigious position formerly held by Perry Howard.[41] Thus, some of the most coveted black appointments were withheld from nominees of both the Moton and Hawkins factions and, indeed, of any other nationally prominent black Republican leaders. Instead Hoover appointed little-known black supporters of white border-state Republican senators with large black voting populations who had voted for Hoover's nominee to the Supreme Court and who were still needed to support Hoover's legislative program through the Congress.

News of Coage's impending appointment as recorder of deeds created widespread consternation among leading black Republicans. Among those complaining were Judge James Cobb and Perry Howard, who was still influential among black leaders. They insisted that the recorder of deeds should have been reserved for the nominee of a prominent national black leader who had worked actively for Hoover's election.[42] Moton and Barnett had pressed hard for the appointment of Clarence R. Vena, while rival leaders had nominated their own candidates.[43] Howard's criticisms were the most pointed. He informed Newton that for several good reasons the appointment of Coage would be a political joke. In the first place, because Coage already had a desirable federal job, he was "compelled to stay with us" in elections, and there was "no use throwing away [another] good job on him." More important, he had not been "active politically in Negro politics," was not a national figure, and was not even known to the black people of Delaware.[44] Howard may have exaggerated somewhat, but the sense of betrayal felt by the black Hoover loyalists was nonetheless significant. To Judge Cobb, Newton explained that he had talked with Hastings about the objections to Coage's appointment but that Hastings had insisted that the appointment would be "very helpful," and the president had no choice but to honor his wishes.[45]

At the same time that Hoover sorted out black patronage squabbles among border-state senators, he imposed new criteria for all black appointments that virtually eliminated the influence of the southern-oriented Moton faction. No doubt at Postmaster Brown's strong urging, the president informed black Republican leaders that their nominees must be not only well qualified but also politically helpful to the administration and to the senators of their state. Senatorial approval had always been an important consideration, but the explicit emphasis upon political value suggested the president's changing attitude toward the black elite and in particular toward Moton's nominees, who generally had few political connections. Before the Parker fight a nominee's political value either to the administration or to the individual's senators had been noticeably less important. Indeed, Akerson had repeatedly told Barnett that political influence was not a criterion, that Moton's recommendation alone was sufficient. Moreover, an obscure professor was apparently no longer thought to be a suitable nominee, even if he had an outstanding reputation and the support of the black community. Under the new appointment criteria, Judge Cobb happily explained, a nominee with endorsements from "the outstanding colored people of his own state as well as from the country at large," must also be able "to back up his Senators and the administration as well as circumvent justified criticism from colored people" who demanded the appointment of prominent blacks to federal office.[46] All of this meant further delays as nominees sought state, national, and senatorial endorsements.

Northern Democrats were quick to exploit the widening rift between Hoover and the black community. They had not forgotten the significant increase in urban black support in 1928, and as the depression worsened and more and more blacks lost their jobs, northern Democrats prepared for the 1930 elections by emphasizing Hoover's alleged hostility as well as his obvious political neglect.[47] In New York City, for example, where the Democrats were running two black candidates for municipal judgeships, they had put out a particularly effective brochure attacking his administration. With a photograph of Governor Franklin D. Roosevelt prominently displayed between the photographs of the two Negro candidates, the Democrats argued to blacks that the "present day New York Democracy stands for exactly the same principles and policies toward the Negro that the Republican Party of Abraham Lincoln represented." They claimed also to have appointed hundreds of qualified blacks to civil service jobs and to the police and health departments where they could help other black people. The Democrats further insisted that by contrast to their fine record of appointments the actions of the Republican party had made it obvious to all blacks that it "assumes that the Negro has neither manhood nor intelligence, that he does not know where his best interests lie, and that no insult can drive him out of the Republican Party—not even an insult to the womanhood of his race."[48]

Parker, insults, humiliation of Gold Star mothers, a mere trickle of major political appointments, and neglect in general were northern Democratic campaign themes with enough truth in them to unsettle black Republicans. Scott told Hoover that, although distorted, these charges were credible to black voters. To counter the Democrats, Scott urged Hoover to create a permanent black political arm of the Republican party, which he called the National Negro Republican League.[49] Naturally, Scott and Hawkins believed that as northern black leaders they ought to head this new organization. To this end they held a meeting in Hawkins's office to devise strategy and organization.[50] Already outmaneuvered by the new appointments criteria, the Moton faction, which also included a few northern black political leaders in Illinois, Indiana, and Pennsylvania, helped stymie the Hawkins-Scott scheme with the result that the league was not organized until after the 1930 elections.[51]

No doubt sensing that they had lost their high standing with the president, Moton and Barnett became increasingly critical of his neglect. In desperation Moton turned to Robert Lucas, the new executive director of the Republican National Committee, who was personally friendly but totally unfamiliar with black needs.[52] Moton suggested to Lucas that the lack of any interest in black welfare was made evident by the absence of any definite program to promote black progress. Negro leaders who could articulate and help carry out such a program had not been appointed to the new prestigious patronage posts that Hoover had promised. There was no Black Cabinet or anyone interested in creating one. Neither was there anyone in the administration with specific responsibility for black affairs. Unfortunately Lucas ignored Moton's complaints, being apparently too much absorbed in a vain effort to defeat a fellow Republican, Sen. George Norris. The November election was a disaster for the party, for the loss of eight Senate and thirty-seven House seats reduced the Republicans to rough equality with the Democrats.[53]

Virtually nothing was done to hold blacks to the Republican party in 1930, and in Harlem, New York, where the Democrats worked hardest, over twenty-five percent of black voters switched their allegiance.[54] Administration officials were critical, with one reportedly complaining that "the more we do for the Negro, the more they help the Democrats." Disgusted at this public criticism, Barnett blamed the blacks' disaffection on the administration's failure to initiate constructive programs for them.[55] The responsibility for that failure, he told Akerson, "lies in the lack of understanding of the Negro psychology on the part of those who interpret to the chief." These advisers, notably Newton and Akerson, had not given Negro matters "intelligent, deft treatment."[56] For example, although a number of political appointments had already been made, "they have not been sold to the public, nor have the people ever had the feeling of being let in on them."[57]

Barnett had accurately identified a major cause of Hoover's rapidly worsening relations with blacks, but because few Negroes were aware of the inner councils of the administration, they naturally blamed Hoover himself.[58] This was not unreasonable, for in any administration the president must assume final responsibility for coups and blunders alike. As Holsey pointed out to Barnett, all of the black Hoover elite, including Hawkins, Scott, and Cobb, felt neglected, almost abandoned by the president.[59] They rarely saw him, and except for Secretary of the Interior Ray Lyman Wilbur, no one appeared interested in their proposals or sought their advice. Wilbur urged Hoover to make some appeal to blacks before the November election, but Hoover ignored this suggestion also. It was little wonder that blacks throughout the nation were "pretty much disgusted" with the president.[60]

Paradoxically, southern lily-whites shared the same attitude toward Hoover. After ousting Horace Mann and making his sweeping yet vague reform pronouncements, Hoover had turned over the entire southern reform program to Claudius Huston, whom he named to replace Hubert Work as chairman of the Republican National Committee. Within six months of his appointment Huston had become a serious liability. As a Tennessee businessman he had long fought alongside Hoover against George Norris's plan for federal development of hydroelectric resources at Muscle Shoals, Alabama, on the Tennessee River. Among other things, including conservation efforts, Norris wanted federal operation of the Muscle Shoals dam as a "yardstick" by which to judge the fairness of utility rates charged by private utility monopolies. As secretary of commerce Hoover had fought tenaciously against the concept of federal ownership and control, and in the long, bitter fight with Norris he had earned the senator's undying enmity.[61] Huston had assisted Hoover in his capacity as president of the Tennessee River Improvement Association, a political lobby seeking congressional support for private development.

Early in 1930 Huston's usefulness was seriously impaired by scandal. In March congressional investigators discovered that as president of the Tennessee River Improvement Association, Huston had taken $36,000 that had been contributed by Union Carbide for his personal use in stock market deals. He had repaid the entire amount within a few months, and although he had done nothing for which he could be indicted, Republican leaders, weary of the Teapot Dome notoriety, demanded his immediate resignation. Huston refused to resign under fire, insisting that he had done nothing illegal, and Hoover could not bring himself to add to his loyal friend's humiliation by forcing him out.[62] As a result the Huston scandal dragged on throughout the spring and summer of 1930, tarnishing Hoover's reputation for integrity in government and weakening the party's responses to the Democratic counterattack in the off-year campaign of 1930. Finally in August Hoover reluctantly agreed to force Huston's resignation, naming Sen. Simeon D. Fess of Ohio as chairman of the Republican National Committee and reassigning Norris's opponent, Robert H. Lucas, from his post as commissioner of internal revenue to that of RNC executive director.[63]

Like his fellow Tennessean Horace Mann, Huston was bitter at being ousted.[64] Having had enough of party wars, he retired from politics. Both of these men had worked hard to create a lily-white Republican party in the South, yet both had failed. Repelled by Mann's scurrilous campaign tactics, Hoover had also scuttled Huston's lily-white reform in Louisiana, the "model" for all other southern states, by refusing to remove Walter Cohen. With Huston's ouster, Mann finally became convinced that Hoover had betrayed the southern lily-whites and that he never intended to create the white Republican party that Mann and the vast majority of southern white Republicans desperately wanted. Both to punish the president and to rescue the failing lily-white movement, Mann generated national publicity with the creation of the Southern States Republican League, a political organization aimed at fostering a wholesale revolt of southern lily-white Republicans. His strategy called for capturing the 232 votes of the southern delegates to the 1932 national convention in order to replace Hoover with a presidential nominee who would vigorously support the lily-whites. Ultimately the Southern States Republican League came to nothing, but its meeting in Savannah, Georgia, in August 1930 forced administration strategists to take its potential force seriously and advertised the developing resentment against Hoover by lily-whites throughout the South.[65]

Mann had good reason for concluding that Hoover's conception of southern reform was politically inadequate to the building of a viable lily-white Republican party. The De Priest tea was still a live, damaging issue in the South. To this were added the well-publicized cries of betrayal from the Louisiana lily-whites, who were outraged by Hoover's refusal to oust Walter Cohen and from the inept Florida lily-whites, who openly and erroneously accused the president of secretly dealing with their black-and-tan opponents. In Georgia the administration was hard at work trying to build a coalition consisting of black-and-tans and lily-whites, in which Ben Davis would play a prominent public role.[66] And the lily-white politicians—in much the same manner as Hoover's onetime black supporters—were disheartened or antagonized by the long, damaging delays resulting from his insistence on well-qualified patronage nominees and the ineffectual yet humiliating "elite" patronage advisory committees.

Not all of the problems were attributable directly to Hoover. Southern senators played a skillful game of political delay and disruption, which the president could not afford to counter. Senator Stephens of Mississippi, for example, who had voted for Parker and who sat on the powerful Senate Judiciary Committee, continually frustrated his lily-white Republican opponents by delaying crucial patronage appointments while at the same time encouraging Perry Howard's state organization to remain active and visible. Hoover needed Stephens's legislative support, and with George Norris as chairman of the judiciary committee, he could not afford another enemy on the committee that reviewed all of the administration's nominees for federal judgeships, district attorneys, and marshals. To the anguished appeals from the Mississippi lily-whites for any sort of help, Walter Newton could think of nothing better than to blame the failures on the already discredited Claudius Huston.[67]

There were still other important factors about which Hoover could do little or nothing. With the onslaught of the depression, and a disastrous drought in Arkansas and the southwest, the great promise of "Hoover prosperity" for a revitalized South became an ironic weapon in the hands of his skillful Democratic opponents. As expected, the Democrats charged that Hoover's mistaken economic policies and inept leadership were responsible for the disaster. Moreover, the Democratic party was once again united. Gone were the emotional, divisive issues of 1928. Without Al Smith, Tammany Hall, the Pope, Prohibition, and prosperity to divide them, the Democrats had joined to drive the anti-Smith bolters from the party, and in the 1930 primaries they were almost uniformly successful.[68] They were now ready to take on the Republican upstarts who had gained office in the 1928 debacle.

Perhaps even more distasteful to Hoover was the intense, hateful factionalism that soon characterized almost all of the southern state parties. The president and his advisers had hoped that the state party conventions in the spring of 1930 would enable their own handpicked state leaders to win undisputed legal control of their organizations and thus put an end to the continuous, debilitating internecine warfare. But either the failure to win Senate approval or the administration's refusal to appoint unqualified yet key leaders to important patronage posts added to the factional squabbling, so that the result was more often chaos than unity. In some states the pattern was unrelenting struggle and backroom intrigue between the lily-whites and the black and tans; in others between the pro- and anti-Hoover lily-white factions.[69] On the one hand in Florida Hoover was accurately advised that there were "two factions everywhere, each trying to control or get control of the machine and the patronage."[70] On the other, the Virginia lily-whites ensured their own defeat in a gubernatorial election because the regulars led by disgruntled Bascom Slemp refused to cooperate with the "reform coalition" headed by Hoover's good friend Col. Henry W. Anderson.[71]

In states where the lily-whites were not busy fighting one another, the discredited black and tans skillfully sabotaged their efforts by shrewd legal maneuvers. Although Hoover had refused to grant patronage either to Tieless Joe Tolbert of South Carolina or to Perry Howard of Mississippi, these men and the state parties that they controlled nonetheless remained as the legitimate state organizations that the 1928 Republican National Convention had legally recognized. Hoover had no legal authority either to depose these men or to create, as he did, rival state parties to replace them. Therefore both Tolbert and Howard held their own state conventions in the spring of 1930, elected their own officers, declared the rival lily-white party to be illegal, and waited to challenge these rivals before the credentials committee at the 1932 Republican National Convention. At times it appeared to be a strategy of desperation, but time and changed circumstances would eventually prove it to be more effective than anyone had expected, and meanwhile it also served to keep the impression of active black leadership in the party before the southern voters.[72]

The collapse of a "secret" effort to build a genuine coalition of black and tans and lily-whites in Georgia added to the disillusionment. Hoover had hoped that the elite whites whom he wanted to attract to the party would cooperate with black leaders in the state organizations and eventually include some of them in the party leadership. Georgia offered an opportunity to effect such a coalition quickly, and Newton and Brown had therefore devised an elaborate strategy to unite the three competing factions. Among its many features, the plan required that blacks who controlled Republican county organizations where the whites were predominant should voluntarily relinquish their leadership posts. This would allow the election of white leaders who could then attract white voters to the party.[73] At first Ben Davis, leader of the black politicians, agreed to cooperate.[74] But when one prominent black county chairman, S. S. Muncy, refused to step aside, he was dragged from his home by hooded men who beat him to death in the brutal style of the KKK. Davis immediately placed the responsibility for the sensational murder upon the administration's "lily-white" strategy, but southerners were not so easily convinced, and, to them, the "secret" Georgia coalition strategy became one more reason for lily-whites to distrust Hoover.[75]

Even where the lily-whites were united Hoover supporters, as in North Carolina, the president sorely disappointed them. The Parker fight had earned him a good deal of sympathy in the judge's home state, and an enthusiastic state party was challenging the Democrats for both state and federal offices.[76] In October 1930 Hoover finally agreed to make a "nonpolitical" address at King's Mountain, South Carolina, to celebrate the 150th anniversary of the famous revolutionary war battle. Despite the awkward location, the North Carolinian Republicans were highly enthusiastic. The site was near enough to the North Carolina border for party leaders to rally their followers in a festive gathering that they hoped would help the Republican faithful get out the vote in November. But despite the large crowd, Hoover refused to talk southern politics or southern strategy.[77] He delivered instead a long, boring, vague, and at times highly idealistic speech, which left party leaders depressed and worried.[78] Probably nothing he could have said would have affected the election greatly; not surprisingly the North Carolinians went down to defeat in November.[79] Indeed, following the 1930 midterm election, only ten of the twenty-four southern Republicans remained in Congress.[80]

The sudden, devastating depression coupled with the successful reunion of southern Democrats would almost certainly have sharply reduced Hoover's popularity and cut deeply into Republican strength in Congress. Yet more than mere political losses were evident by November 1930. Beginning in April with the Parker controversy and climaxing in May with his insulting reference to "demagogues and Negro politicians," Hoover's personal reputation plummeted. This loss of respect for the president affected not only blacks. Liberals in both parties became more convinced than ever that he was a reactionary, a bigot, or both. Black loyalists who had only recently defended him against criticism fell silent as they witnessed a sudden, dramatic change in his attitude toward them. His anger over the Parker defeat; his petulant attitude toward Moton; his refusal to intervene in the Jim Crow treatment of black Gold Star mothers; his continued slow, unpublicized patronage appointments of very worthy yet politically obscure blacks; his refusal to establish a Negro political organization to formulate a program and to represent his administration in the election of 1930; and his rejection of Secretary of the Interior Wilbur's suggestion to make some appeal to black voters all served to reinforce the NAACP's oft-repeated claim that he was antiblack.

Remembering the Hoover he knew from personal experience, Claude Barnett could not bring himself to believe that the president had suddenly become antiblack. Like Edgar Rickard and George Barr Baker, he too, albeit for different reasons, placed the blame for Hoover's repeated bungling and ineptness on his political secretaries. Yet regardless of the justice of such a claim, the president himself can hardly escape the major burden of responsibility for the disastrous series of mistakes. His personal regard for Claudius Huston had resulted in a long, debilitating internal battle that damaged his standing in the party and left precious little time for the new executive director, who was trying to defeat George Norris, to prepare for the vigorous Democratic counterattack in November. Moreover, after insulting blacks and convincing even his black loyalists that he would do nothing for them, he went on to complete the alienation of southern lily-whites by steadfastly refusing to promote an avowed lily-white strategy in the South. The murder of S. S. Muncy in Georgia exposed the confusing, convoluted maneuverings of the administration's Georgia coalition and no doubt further convinced Hoover of the difficulty of realizing his hopes for a new South. To be sure he had attracted a few of the southern elite, but for only a short time. What he usually got were lilywhites who did not share his lofty goals and principles and became angry when they were not immediately rewarded for services rendered. The chief beneficiaries were the Democrats, who easily recouped most of their losses in the South and cut still more deeply into Republican Harlem and other cities in the North. To lily-white and black Republicans alike the chief problem had become the president himself. Indeed, by November 1930 they were all "pretty much disgusted" with Herbert Hoover.[81]

20. Black Expectations and Designs of Oppression

By the end of 1930 Hoover was as much disgusted with black "politicians" and with the incessantly squabbling southern lily-whites as both of these groups were with him. It was clear to him by now that the vast majority of the new southern Republicans he had attracted to his cause were far more interested in factional politics and federal patronage than they were in his idealistic reform goals. He made no more efforts to encourage these southern "politicians." Politically his best course would have been to appeal more openly and directly to northern black voters, but he would not do that either. In nominating his two additional choices to the Supreme Court, for example, he made no attempt whatever to recoup political losses among blacks. Owen J. Roberts, who replaced Parker, was a trustee of all-black Lincoln University, but no special point was made of this. Benjamin Cardozo was already recognized as an exceptionally distinguished liberal jurist, and the NAACP, which had carefully investigated both Roberts and Cardozo, was overjoyed with them, but its reaction was not mentioned either. Congress quickly approved the two men, yet few thought to give Hoover much credit, and the president refused to use these nominations as a means to mend his political fences.[1] Thus, the Parker nomination continued to predominate in the memories of black people while Hoover busied himself in the White House, where he nursed his wounded pride.

During 1931, as the economic collapse worsened, Hoover spent long hours each day trying his best to combat its ravages. But despite his earlier progressive, innovative programs the disaster was so overwhelming that he soon lost sight of many persistent problems that he had hoped to solve before the Great Depression. A good example was the conditions retarding black economic progress. Because Hoover was convinced that blacks faced special handicaps in employment and business ownership, and because, in his view, economic progress was absolutely essential to any social progress, he had appointed a special commission to study the economic needs of black Americans and to make recommendations for correcting abuses and encouraging new programs. This was no ordinary commission. Because it was privately financed, it was not subject to pressures from southern congressmen. He had appointed his secretary of commerce, his secretary of agriculture, and such knowledgeable leaders as Moton; William Green, the head of the AF of L; and Julius Rosenwald, the respected Chicago philanthropist with whom the president had consulted about his land scheme to combat peonage and who offered to meet the expenses of this extensive investigation. Moreover, these were leaders whom he knew and trusted and whose judgments he respected; and the evidence suggests that had the economic collapse not suddenly occurred, he would almost certainly have taken action to implement at least some, if not all, of their recommendations calling for federal assistance to blacks.

Hoover received the report of this special commission, "The Economic Status of the Negro," in October 1930. It established that even before the depression, in a period of unprecedented industrial prosperity, American blacks had suffered from shocking discrimination and disadvantages that could be overcome only by vigorous federal programs. With the depression their plight had worsened rapidly, and the commission urged immediate federal action. Included in its recommendations were the establishment of black employment bureaus by the Department of Labor, a variety of job-related measures to be undertaken by the Federal Board of Vocational Education, sponsorship of a wide variety of agricultural projects and market cooperatives by the Department of Agriculture, as well as a host of state and private proposals.[2] The president now had the scientifically collected facts and the carefully considered recommendations for a constructive black program prepared by his own experts, indeed by the very leaders who were already in positions to act on them quickly. Such a program followed the scientific, social-engineering approach to problem solving in which Hoover placed so much faith and that black leaders like Moton had believed would be given high priority in his administration.

Even under normal economic circumstances Hoover would have had to exert himself to ensure that these recommendations were translated into executive action by an understaffed and racially prejudiced federal bureaucracy. Yet with numerous, unprecedented problems arising daily from the mysterious steadily worsening collapse, Hoover apparently believed that he did not have the time, the energy, the human resources, or the money to implement the recommendations until after the crisis abated. If Hoover had not already become angry at Moton and black "politicians," one might be able to make a more defensible case for his inaction, but the context suggested more than delay that was due to overwork; it also suggested a loss of interest in black welfare, even, perhaps, a deliberate snub. Moton waited patiently for six months, and finally in March 1931 he startled the president by informing him that black people no longer trusted him or his concern for their well-being. They "question not only the faith of the party of which you are the leader," he reminded him, "but also your personal concern for the welfare and progress of this one-tenth of the citizens of the United States."[3]

Hoover was shocked and "deeply affected" by Moton's candid outburst, and he resolved to "strengthen the situation" immediately.[4] At first he asked Secretary of the Interior Ray Lyman Wilbur to represent him at the fiftieth anniversary of Tuskegee Institute, but Wilbur could not attend and suggested instead that the president arrange a radio network speech to commemorate it.[5] In his speech Hoover reaffirmed his personal faith in the great abilities of the Negro race. Emphasizing statistical evidence of great progress and the even greater, swifter progress that higher education would promote, he concluded, "I am convinced that there are within the Negro race, as a result of these institutions of which Tuskegee stands in the front rank, a body of men whose leadership and unselfishness can be depended upon to accomplish advancement and adjustment." It was this black elite, the graduates of institutions of higher learning, who would "make a higher contribution to the adjustment of interracial problems which must awaken the gratitude of the nation." Working together, the "best element" of both races would achieve "the absolute justice" on which continued progress depended.[6]

Hoover sincerely believed his own rhetoric. When he told Moton of the joy he felt in assisting him in "the beautiful work you are carrying out," he was speaking from his heart.[7] Moreover, he gave the impression that he would encourage federal programs helpful to black people. Among these, immediate relief was perhaps the most urgent.[8] The Southern Regional Office of the National Urban League, for example, reported that in Georgia blacks had been forced out of menial jobs by whites who had once scorned such work. Even more serious was the fact that they had been "excluded entirely from relief measures."[9] In response Hoover appointed to the President's Organization on Unemployment Relief John W. Davis, a member of the National Urban League's executive committee, and another black, T. Arnold Hill, who could serve as liaison with the black community.[10] The action was much less significant than it seemed. Although this was Hoover's principal relief committee, it was, like its predecessor, almost totally ineffectual.[11] Moreover, the appointment of blacks had come only after many protests and long delays, which Newton unconvincingly blamed on the lack of agreement among black leaders over who was to be appointed. Finally, no executive officer undertook any sustained, determined action to implement the recommendations put forth by Hoover's commission on black economic progress.

Two months later in May 1931, as members of his black elite attempted to soften the impression of presidential neglect, the NAACP gave Hoover the opportunity to improve relations between them. In March Walter White had received word from "an individual who is rather closely connected with the Republican Party," asking what the NAACP thought Hoover could do during the next two years "which would cause the Negro to feel more kindly towards the administration." White had asked for time to consult with other NAACP officials. By May he had not yet replied to this inquiry, but, possibly encouraged by it, he asked the president for a message to the forthcoming convention of the NAACP. White may have hoped that Hoover had himself initiated the inquiry or that his praise of black people in his Tuskegee address indicated a more positive attitude toward all black leaders. If so, he was mistaken.[12] Hoover was unalterably convinced that the NAACP was composed of black "politicians" who were probably financed by his Democratic enemies.[13] Moreover, he held an entirely different opinion of Moton's leadership at Tuskegee from the one that he held of White's in the NAACP. Only recently he had offered glowing praise of Moton and Tuskegee, and he had also sent warm messages of encouragement to other black organizations, but he had few good words for either White or the NAACP. He might have taken this opportunity to answer his critics, outline his efforts to help blacks, and reassure the NAACP of his future goodwill and good intentions, but he saw no necessity to explain or defend himself, and he could not repress his anger at the NAACP over its attacks against him during the Parker fight. Doubtless too he recalled the criticism of him by both White and Du Bois during the 1927 Mississippi flood and the 1928 election.

Instead of conciliation, Hoover was in a mood to strike back at the NAACP, and he unwisely used this official message to reveal publicly the low esteem in which he held the organization. The original draft of the message, like the earlier secret inquiry asking how he might help black people during the remaining two years of his administration, was probably written by a member of his black elite. The final draft shows Hoover's extreme resentment, for in it he crossed out the words "cordial," "good-wishes" and "warm greetings" and a whole line reading "the association stands for the qualities of good citizenship which contribute to justice, obedience to law, and the devotion to the common good."[14] The result was a curt message that offered little more than the recognition of the need to protect blacks against lawlessness "of the gross type [lynching?]" and admonished the NAACP to view the problems created by the depression with "a breadth of vision and a willingness to cooperate."[15]

White responded with more anger and eloquence. In his address to the convention he sought to incite a black political crusade against Hoover and the Republican party, just as he had earlier against Parker. Some of his charges were highly questionable, especially one that Hoover had failed to appoint blacks to diplomatic posts in Haiti and to the Haitian commission or that his new secretary of labor, William Doak, was antiblack (which White admitted privately would be difficult to prove but which he and Du Bois were convinced was accurate).[16] Nonetheless, most of his other accusations, although distorted or only half-true, were much more damaging to Hoover both politically and personally. They summarized succinctly what any outsider was likely to believe and seemed accurate to black critics, even Hoover's own black elite. Indeed, some later scholars have accepted them as fair and truthful.[17]

In essence White argued to the NAACP that Hoover's actions fell into an unmistakably antiblack pattern. Recalling abuses during the 1927 Mississippi flood, he accused Hoover of defending the Red Cross against charges of discrimination by suppressing the facts that his own black investigating committee had uncovered. To win the presidential nomination, he had encouraged the purchase and manipulation of the southern state delegations to the national convention, where he had initiated the purge of black Republican leaders. To disguise the purge, he had then prosecuted dishonest black politicians while at the same time encouraging dishonest white politicians to take control of the southern state parties and dictate patronage. The capstone of this racist strategy was Hoover's determined fight to put a lily-white Republican judge on the United States Supreme Court. Along the way he had insulted black people, humiliated the Gold Star mothers, refused to support antilynching efforts, and avoided appointing blacks to important federal positions. No black could afford to ignore this record of hostility, White insisted; all blacks must offer united, unyielding opposition to Hoover's continued leadership.[18]

If Hoover had been half as sensitive to White's charges as he had been to Moton's, he would have recognized that these criticisms came from liberal and conservative blacks alike, and he might have understood the depths to which he had sunk in the eyes of the black community. He did not seem to notice that none of his own black elite volunteered to refute White. Perhaps if he had fully realized the extent and intensity of black feeling, he might have utilized still another opportunity to disprove the widespread impression that he was indifferent or actively hostile to blacks.[19]

In August 1931 a highly emotional controversy erupted in which Hoover could have intervened to his own personal credit and political benefit. In order to expand the size of the emerging air force while complying with congressional dictates on budget and manpower limits, the army chief of staff, Gen. Douglas MacArthur, had begun a sweeping reduction in the size of infantry and cavalry units. As part of this program he had ordered a drastic cut in the Tenth Cavalry, the famous black combat unit that had fought in every conflict since the Civil War. Naturally this aroused heated protests from black leaders throughout the United States. Many feared that the prestigious Tenth Cavalry would be dissolved and its men scattered in various camps where they would be assigned menial, noncombat roles as stable orderlies or servants, as black soldiers had been treated during World War I.

"I do not know of any thing that has happened recently that has so inflamed the Negro all over the country," Hawkins told Hoover.[20] He and many other black leaders urged Hoover to rescind the order.[21] As a former commander of black troops and a special assistant to the secretary of war during World War I, Moton had investigated the army's abuse of black soldiers, and he confidently assured Hoover that the cuts were yet another example of the persistent discrimination that was both "un-American and calculated to arouse the resentment of Negro voters in all parts of the country."[22] Congressman James G. Strong of Kansas agreed with Moton's political assessment. Unless the cuts were reduced or rescinded, he advised, the party would lose thousands of black voters in Missouri, Kansas, and other border states in 1932.[23]

MacArthur was well known to the president. Hoover had personally selected him over thirty senior officers to reorganize the army. MacArthur had reason to be grateful to the president, but any such feelings were dampened by Hoover's refusal to fight congressional cuts in the army's size and budget, his support of the Geneva Disarmament Conference, and MacArthur's overweening self-esteem. As Hoover no doubt expected, MacArthur refused to consider any changes whatever. All white units, he insisted, had been reduced in size for the same purpose, and as white and black soldiers were treated "absolutely alike," it was obvious to the chief of staff that a conspiracy was "now being made to establish the principle that the negro soldier shall receive preferential treatment over the white soldier."[24]

News of MacArthur's obstinacy traveled quickly. Walter White pointed out that as the proportion of black to white troops was very low to begin with, to ask the Tenth Cavalry to give up 556 enlisted men, especially when blacks were prohibited from joining the air force, was "manifestly unfair."[25] Again the army denied any discrimination.[26] White concluded that the real problem lay not so much in the army or Congress as in Hoover, who had the power to save the black combat battalion but simply did not care enough for black people to do so.[27] Moton agreed with White on the president's authority, and he, too, kept up the pressure on him. He refused to accept Hoover's reiteration of the army's insistence that the cut was a "vital part" of its reorganization or that it was essential to the national defense.[28] As a result of the order the total number of black combat regulars would be reduced by seventy-five percent; after a time the famous combat unit would be dissolved; and black combat troops would become mere servants for white officers, an outcome, Moton insisted, that was "repugnant to all self-respecting Negroes." Despite the army's denials, he was certain that blacks were being "absolutely excluded from the Air Corps" and that its explanations amounted to "falsification" and "mockery."[29]

In an effort to get "the thing quiet," Hoover finally turned to his secretary of war, Patrick J. Hurley of Oklahoma, but Hurley would no more protect the honor and dignity of black combat troops than that of the Gold Star mothers.[30] At this point Hoover should have ordered Hurley and MacArthur to reduce the cuts and ensure that the Tenth Cavalry would remain a viable combat unit, but he did nothing at all. The missed opportunity was all the more regrettable because Hoover could have acted without fear of significant adverse political repercussions. Indeed, if he had taken a tough stand with MacArthur at this time, the chief of staff might not have cavalierly disobeyed his orders a year later concerning the dispersal of the Bonus Army. In July 1932 he brushed aside Hoover's repeated orders and drove the unarmed and penniless men, women, and children out of their encampment in the capital, thereby burdening the hapless president with the intense and lasting hatred of millions of Americans.[31]

The lack of any evidence that Hoover cared enough about either black dignity or black welfare to defend them was as obvious to his worried white advisers as it was to his disgusted black ones. Mere messages of encouragement to black organizations without some action to back them up could never convince anyone of his good intentions.[32] His repeated unwillingness to respond positively to legitimate black complaints and the chorus of denunciation from outraged blacks alarmed an inner circle of his political intimates. This was, in itself, a significant change. In the past these men had more often fretted lest Hoover's responsiveness to blacks set off harmful repercussions among white voters. They had made misleading excuses or offered outright lies to white critics upset over the desegregation of the Census Bureau and the invitation to Mrs. De Priest. But now they began to worry about the northern black vote.

The most interesting convert among his close advisers was his political secretary Walter Newton, who supervised the day-to-day implementation of the president's effort to reform the southern state parties. More than anyone else, Newton knew how disastrous the southern experiment had been. Almost daily he read the letters of outrage and lament from frustrated lily-whites, few of whom were the "best element" that Hoover had hoped to attract into the party to reform and revitalize southern society. Like Postmaster General Brown, he knew also that there was no chance that Hoover could win southern electoral votes in 1932 and he had heard the private warnings from the president's most trusted and respected supporters about the rising anger of black groups. Edgar Rickard and Theodore Roosevelt, Jr., who had contacts among black leaders in the East, were especially concerned.[33] And William C. Hueston, the black solicitor in the Post Office Department, informed him of the prevalent belief that Hoover had consistently refused to have his photograph taken with any black group. James J. Jackson, the black small-business specialist, and Julius Klein, a top official of the Commerce Department, argued that personal meetings with professional, business, and fraternal organizations were essential to dispel the sense of distrust and neglect among these formerly enthusiastic supporters.[34] Prompt action was vital to begin winning back the loyalty of black voters before the 1932 election.

During a long relaxed weekend in early September 1931 at the president's secluded vacation camp in the mountains of Virginia, Newton made a carefully planned effort to convince Hoover that the northern black vote was important to his reelection and that he needed to mend political fences with black leaders. Newton suggested to him the wisdom of increasing the number of prestigious black patronage appointments, especially in the Department of Justice. Hoover had already appointed a special assistant attorney general to replace Perry Howard, three special United States attorneys, and four assistant

United States attorneys, but Newton wanted more appointments. Newton may have raised the issue of Moton's claim that Hoover had promised him to appoint three, rather than one, special assistant attorneys general. Newton had even gone to the extent of trying to convince top Justice Department officials to agree in advance to accept additional black appointees, but he was no more successful with the president than in his prior efforts with the Justice Department. Hoover flatly refused to consider more black patronage appointments. Moreover, he made it clear to Newton, Rickard, and his other intimates that he did not share their concern over the possible loss of the black vote in 1932. More than a year after the Parker defeat, he still smarted from the wounds inflicted by "Negro politicians" and he was, as Rickard noted, still "adverse to making any unusual effort to pacify the belligerent negro leaders." Try as he might, Newton could not make any headway with Hoover, and neither could anyone else.[35]

During the remaining months of 1931 the president did little publicly to revise the damaging impressions he had created. Only after persistent prodding, and as a personal favor to his friend, Secretary of the Treasury Ogden Mills, would he meet briefly with the National Negro Technicians Association.[36] Hoover had made certain that his $500 personal contribution to the National Urban League remained private knowledge, and although he continued to send warm messages of encouragement to black teacher and professional organizations that requested them, he did not invite these groups to the White House or initiate any of his own efforts to win black votes.[37]

Because Hoover would not move closer to black leaders, they decided to carry their messages of complaint directly to him by a well-coordinated strategy that would rivet attention on "The Man in the Lily-White House." William Monroe Trotter, editor of the Boston *Guardian* and leader of the National Equal Rights League and Race Congress, and Congressman Oscar De Priest, the organizer of the National Non-Partisan League, agreed to hold simultaneous national conventions during December in Washington, D.C., to pressure Hoover into reacting to their proposals. Trotter was bent upon getting the president to respond to the recommendations of the Anti-Lynching Congress, which had petitioned Hoover in 1930 without results. De Priest's purpose was frankly political. Unlike the Lincoln League, which Robert R. Church, Jr., had earlier created to support the Republican party, the National Non-Partisan League was designed to win black voters away from their traditional allegiance so that blacks could educate and mobilize themselves in terms of race interests and thus operate as an independent political force that could extract political concessions from both political parties. With these two groups meeting in the capital at the same time, black attention would be once again riveted on the president.[38]

Both Postmaster General Brown and Secretary of the Interior Wilbur, the two administration officials most respected by black leaders, understood the strategy as a potentially serious threat that required decisive political action.[39] For some time Brown had been quietly promoting the influence of the northern black faction headed by Hawkins, Scott, and Cobb over that of the southern-oriented Moton faction, and by October 1931 Brown had earned their loyalty.[40] When White asked Judge Cobb to investigate a complaint that Brown had advocated white leadership for the black and tans, Cobb forcefully denied the allegation.[41] At Hawkins's urging, Brown now used his influence with Hoover to create the National Negro Republican League. This was to be the official black political organization that would further black concerns and needs within the administration. More immediately, it was supposed to blunt the impact of the critics who would be assembling in December.

Unfortunately the National Negro Republican League further weakened Hoover's standing among black leaders. Moton, Barnett, and the members of this once-enthusiastic faction were totally excluded, apparently by Brown, and they made this known to a wide variety of their influential friends. Black leaders such as Robert R. Church, Jr., refused to serve in any Hoover organization. Despite his best efforts to attract Church and other black politicians into the administration's fold, Brown discovered that black politicians did not wish to be bossed by either faction of Hoover's elite. Besides, the reason for the league's sudden creation was transparently obvious, and its chances for success appeared miniscule.[42]

Because the number of patronage jobs and federal employees had often been used in the past as perhaps the single most important measure of a president's attitude toward black people, Hoover's advisers were optimistic about the new league's chances of surprising and confounding the opposition at the forthcoming conventions in December.[43] Hoover was, in fact, secretly proud of his black patronage efforts. He was convinced that his administration employed more black federal employees than any previous one and that his high standards, especially for the most important posts, had ensured that all of his appointees were a "credit to their offices."[44] In this assessment Hoover was correct, and eventually Monroe Work, an associate of Moton's at Tuskegee Institute, informed blacks of Hoover's outstanding black patronage record—but, alas, only after Hoover's defeat in 1932.[45]

Not all Republicans were pleased with Hoover's patronage policies. His steadfast refusal to fire thousands of competent Democrats in non–civil service jobs continued to infuriate House Majority Leader John Q. Tilson, whose repeated pleas were consistently ignored.[46] Democratic opponents were also critical. They claimed to have hired more blacks than the Republicans, and despite the lack of any proof for that assertion, black leaders were giving disturbing credence to the Democrats' claim. To set the record straight, the president's personal troubleshooter, Lawrence Richey, asked all cabinet officers to compile a complete listing of blacks serving in their departments.[47]

The lists were impressive. They revealed that the number of blacks employed by the federal government had increased from 52,000 in June 1928 to 58,000 in 1932 and depending on one's definition of prestigious or important, that Hoover had made at least as many prestigious appointments as any recent presidents.[48] If one were to expand the list beyond strictly patronage appointments to include prominent black leaders appointed to important reform commissions or conferences, his record could be considered superior even to that of Theodore Roosevelt, whose black appointments had become the generally acknowledged yardstick for all subsequent administrations. Whatever criteria are used, it is clear that Hoover had no reason to fear embarrassment in this matter. Although unwisely rejecting Newton's advice to increase the number of the more impressive and influential patronage appointments, he had, nonetheless, a creditable and defendable record.[49]

Black expectations, however, were probably a more important political factor in measuring Hoover's black patronage than Theodore Roosevelt's record. On several different occasions Hoover had created the impression that he would do more to benefit black people and make more prestigious black appointments than any other previous president. The evidence strongly suggests that in moments of enthusiasm (most likely in his meetings with Church before the election of 1928 and his inauguration and with Moton at the White House following the De Priest tea) Hoover had privately reassured these leaders that their fears over Howard's indictment and his southern reform were groundless and that he would prove his good faith in making numerous and outstanding political appointments. Both of these men had emerged from these meetings brimming with renewed confidence, extravagant in their praises, and communicating high expectations to black people. But the long series of bitter, frustrating disappointments had dashed their bright hopes and destroyed their confidence in him. Moton had not received any patronage for his nominees, and in his disgust with the exaggerated importance of patronage among "politicians," Hoover had neither expanded the number of posts considered most prestigious nor publicized his politically obscure but very well qualified appointments.[50] It is not surprising, therefore, that few black leaders were willing to praise or defend his record or, indeed, even knew about it.

Many nationally influential black leaders were among the 179 delegates from twenty-five states who gathered in Washington for the first convention of the National Non-Partisan League. Many also were former Republicans who had come to deliver a message to Hoover. Among the resolutions passed by the league were some that attacked the Republican party, but one in particular stood out—the one that stated that the difference between the two major parties was quickly "dwindling to the point of indistinction."[51] Hawkins and the members of the National Negro Republican League sought to allay this and the other familiar criticisms by distributing the highly detailed patronage lists.[52] But the delegates were unimpressed. As an official arm of the administration, and a factional one at that, the Hawkins group's credibility was suspect, and the delegates either did not believe the information or were beyond the point of caring about Hoover's patronage or both. In any case they questioned the value of patronage in the hands of those who were not national leaders and in an administration that they believed was purging black leaders from politics.

As members of the National Negro Republican League tried vainly to defend the administration, Hoover also worked at taking the edge off black anger by talking with a delegation from Trotter's second Anti-Lynching Congress. Over a year earlier, in November 1930, Hoover had listened to Trotter and the delegates from the first Anti-Lynching Congress. Earlier still, in August 1930, Hoover had condemned lynching as "undermining the very essence of justice and democracy"; although his statement had been reported in the press, it had gone almost unnoticed.[53] Walter White demanded a stronger, better publicized declaration. In October 1930 he had told Hoover that during the past ten months twenty-five blacks had been lynched, which was eleven more than in 1929, and that that number appeared to be rising. White had urged the president to call a conference of all southern governors to marshal public opinion against lynching, but Hoover, not trusting White, had not acted.[54] Shortly thereafter, in November 1930, Trotter notified the president that the National Equal Rights League and Race Congress was sponsoring the national Colored Anti-Lynching Congress to be held in Washington, D.C., and Hoover had agreed to meet with Trotter and a delegation from the Congress. But to Trotter's dismay, after the meeting the president had refused even to issue another public statement.[55]

This time Hoover prepared himself in advance. Before meeting with Trotter, he contacted the Southern Commission for the Study of Lynching, headed by George Foote Milton, which included black leaders and scholars such as John Hope, Monroe Work, and Moton. The commission's report impressed him with the shocking truth and the South's seeming inability or unwillingness to put an end to this terrorism. Then after talking again with Trotter and the delegation from the second Anti-Lynching Congress, Hoover was ready to initiate the dramatic presidential action that blacks had been urging since the Republicans had abandoned them in the 1870s.[56]

Several weeks later, on 31 December 1931, Hoover sent the draft of his proposed message on law enforcement to Attorney General William D. Mitchell for his commentary. In this draft Hoover condemned lynching as "the negation of the Republican form of government guaranteed to our citizens by the Constitution." To combat it, he proposed a combined force of mobile army troops and air force, which would bring the lynchers to swift justice. He was convinced that with "the modern expedition through aerial and motor forces of federal troops located at all important centers throughout the country, it is possible to bring them almost instantly to the assistance of local authorities if a system were authorized by Congress that would make such action swift and possible."[57] Yet as Hoover understood, there was little likelihood that Congress would authorize the additional funds, but he would at least have publicized the need and located the moral responsibility for inaction.

The attorney general argued forcefully against the mobile deployment force. Congress would surely deny the necessary funds, he declared, and even if these were forthcoming, local juries would not convict anyone accused by federal authorities. Worst of all, the use of federal forces to prosecute lynchers for murder or state officials for failing to uphold the Constitution would stimulate an even greater breakdown of law enforcement. "Federal interference" would create "bitter local antagonism and develop angry passions which would stimulate lynchings."[58] Thus instead of stopping the terrorism, Hoover's plan would put blacks in still greater jeopardy.

As Mitchell agreed that Congress would refuse to expand the army's miniscule budget for such a purpose, most of his objections were moot. He did not comment on the educational benefit of the proposal or the moral obligation of a leader to expose evils in need of reforming. Apparently, however, his incomplete reply was convincing, for nothing more was heard of the antilynching bill or, indeed, of lynching in general. Hoover and his advisers may have decided to drop the subject for a related yet different reason. As they were well aware, the depression had made Hoover an increasingly unpopular leader within the Republican party and his old political foes were actively looking for allies to build a coalition against him. His advisers might have been impressed by Mitchell's fear of a furious southern reaction and reasoned that if the president supported such a plan, especially without any hope of carrying it out, the already disgruntled southern lily-whites would accuse him of betrayal and blatant pandering to the northern black votes. The result might well be a sudden revival of Horace Mann's abortive lily-white revolt, which might still deny Hoover enough of the 236 southern delegates at the forthcoming Republican national convention in June to prevent Hoover's renomination.

Whatever Hoover's reasons may have been, he had once again encouraged black leaders to expect some sort of favorable action, and once again he had disappointed them. He made no mention of a mobile deployment force or even of lynching. Instead, the party's long-standing promise to work toward the elimination of the evil silently disappeared from the 1932 national platform.[59] Hoover acted without any effort to explain his reasons to Trotter or other black leaders. Later during the 1932 campaign, when Walter White criticized his silence on the subject, he could only point lamely to the unnoticed letter of 1930 in which he had briefly expressed his disapproval of lynching.[60]

Perhaps some advisers argued that it was more honest to drop the antilynching pledge than to retain a dishonest, cruel mockery that the party had no intention of fulfilling. Although such a self-serving argument might have been advanced, Hoover's action in dropping the pledge and without consulting anyone or at least explaining his reasons, repeated a familiar pattern that Robert R. Church, Jr., had wisely counseled him to avoid. In November 1929,

after waiting patiently since March for news about the appointment of prominent blacks to important patronage posts, Church had written to Hoover urging
him to speak out against the charge that he was not appointing blacks because
of his southern strategy. This failure to speak, to explain his policies to black
people, would hurt him severely. Blacks could "stand the indifference and
neglect," Church advised, "of even so good a man as you are," but the
combination of silence and neglect was an "invitation to the designs of oppression."[61]

Church had put his finger on a major cause of the steadily worsening
relations between Hoover and black leaders. Any man of sensitivity would
have understood that silence was bound to infuriate black leaders. Occasionally Hoover would send them warm personal greetings and uplifting and
inspiring messages, but mostly he avoided the important questions. He repeatedly declined to respond when they asked him to explain his southern policy or
reassure them that he did not intend to drive black leaders out of the party. He
gave no reasons for not carrying out the recommendations of his commission
on the economic status of the Negro. He would not challenge the familiar
charges voiced by Walter White or designate someone else to do so. The nature
and number of black patronage appointments went unpublicized until blacks
were too angry or suspicious to be impressed by them. Pleas to protect the
Tenth Cavalry or to attack the barbarism of lynching went unanswered. Failure
to speak out on those issues was part of a pattern that had become evident
during the 1928 campaign and that convinced many blacks that Hoover was
hiding "designs of oppression" behind his lofty silence.

21. Difficult Choices

As Hoover worked feverishly in the early months of 1932 to maneuver innovative legislation through a troublesome Congress, black anger against him continued to increase. Small businessmen were especially upset by the lack of black representation on the Reconstruction Finance Corporation; the Federal Farm Board; and on the newer federal agencies, such as the Federal Home Loan Bank Board, which Congress finally created before adjourning in July.[1] Complaints from other influential conservative Republican-oriented blacks reinforced those of the businessmen. The bishops of the African Methodist Episcopal Church criticized the president by admonishing its adherents "to support for political office only those who stand for the social, civil, and political rights of our race, as well as for our right to have places in the administrative affairs of the government."[2] Black Democrats reinforced these complaints. They repeatedly pointed out that the Reconstruction Finance Corporation made huge loans to powerful corporations and banks while the millions of destitute blacks in need of jobs and federal relief and the small businessmen about to go broke were conveniently forgotten.[3]

Black Republican loyalists despaired of Hoover's reelection chances. They felt that they had played a crucial role in helping Hoover win the nomination in 1928, but by 1932 they no longer felt they could defend him. They now began a blunt attack on his southern strategy. Unless he took actions that would enable his defenders to "mitigate this feeling that the Administration in its general political attitude is pro-Lily-White," Scott told Hoover, there was little possibility that black people would continue to support him.[4] Claude Barnett was even more blunt. He admitted that black leaders close to Hoover during the 1928 campaign had agreed to the reform of the Republican party in the South "through new white leadership," but, he reminded Hoover, they feared and opposed white leaders who would exclude blacks from the party councils. He believed that Hoover had never "intended to pursue a policy as bold" as appearances suggested, yet by repeatedly refusing to explain the intention of his administration, the president had "jockeyed it into the position of seeming to condone" a lily-white strategy.[5]

By early 1932 Hoover had begun to understand how vulnerable he had become. To an extent, perhaps, he felt guilty about suppressing his call for a mobile deployment force against lynching and also about dropping the pledge to support antilynching efforts from the 1932 platform. These decisions may have forced him to understand the degree to which his abortive southern reform efforts had made him a captive to the southern lily-white politicians with their 236 votes at the Republican National Convention. He may even have recognized that his innermost convictions were held hostage to election politics, only this time, in 1932, by southern lily-whites rather than by reputedly corrupt blacks, as at the 1928 convention. Or he may simply have come to the reluctant realization that he needed northern black votes to win in November and must therefore make concessions to "belligerent" black politicians.

Although the most likely explanation for Hoover's sudden appeal to blacks was political necessity, there was a certain amount of personal conviction in his action. Hoover had never been comfortable with the southern experiment and especially with the consequent belief that he was antiblack. Now he felt the need to express his personal racial convictions. On 7 March 1932, according to Alonzo V. Fields, a black butler at the White House, Hoover entertained three prominent black politicians, Oscar De Priest, Roscoe Conkling Simmons, and Bishop Carey. As Fields served the guests, Hoover expressed his conviction that a black man was his "Colored Brother" who had the "right" to live in a racially integrated society. Unfortunately, Hoover continued, although society "should be" integrated and although blacks should have the same rights as whites, the time had not yet arrived when integration would be acceptable. To hasten that day Hoover wanted to involve the federal government more actively in building an elite corps of federal administrators who presumably would be able to help black people by providing them a wide range of services in all federal agencies. Fields recalled the president's plan to create a division of black civil servants at "every level of the government," which would train other blacks for positions in the various federal services provided by that "level of government." This sketchy but intriguing proposal was never developed further. De Priest liked the idea, but both Simmons and Carey argued against it on the ground that it would increase rather than decrease segregation, and Hoover consequently dropped it.[6]

More significant than his proposal for a black federal elite was his expressed belief in racial integration, a belief that was consistent with his strong support of the Interracial Commission, and his decision to seek out and win over important northern leaders such as De Priest and Simmons.[7] Previously these men had been excluded from the Hoover inner circle, and De Priest in particular had been openly critical of his policies. The private White House meeting did not change the Hoover administration's acceptance of segregation, and it produced no new policies, yet Hoover's willingness to invite these black politicians to the White House for an exchange of ideas suggested that Newton and Brown had finally begun to prevail.[8] In keeping with this shift in technique, Newton had begun urging southern lily-white leaders to include some black members in their delegations to the forthcoming Republican National

Convention in June. Exasperated by their undisguised hostility to the suggestion, he bluntly informed them that the northern black vote was "a very substantial factor" in a number of states where the result would be close, and it was imperative, therefore, that some blacks be included to dispel the impression of a lily-white policy.[9]

By contrast to the 1928 campaign, in which Hoover had done almost nothing to win northern black support, the administration embarked in 1932 upon a well-coordinated, carefully planned appeal to black voters. On 18 May Hoover sent Secretary of the Interior Ray Lyman Wilbur to convey his personal message to the national convention of the NAACP. Again his language was guarded, but his tone was more cordial, and he characterized black efforts to improve their condition as "an amazing story of courage and enterprise in which the colored people take a proper pride and which their neighbors of other races view with satisfaction and admiration." His praise did nothing to prevent Walter White from again cataloging for the convention the familiar charges against him. Hoover continued to ignore White.[10] Several weeks later the president expanded on this theme of courage and pride in his commencement address to the black graduates of Howard University. He defined the university's mission as one of training the "natural leaders" who would guide black people to the full realization of their "natural rights." His emphasis upon the great importance of nurturing a black elite and his praise of black determination to continue progress against any and all obstacles were not new, but his presence before this large black audience was, and it also suggested that he was quietly working, albeit unsuccessfully, to restore the drastic reduction in the university's budget resulting from congressional cuts in appropriations to the Department of the Interior.[11]

At the same time that Hoover was speaking to the black graduates in Washington, the Republican national committeemen were gathering in Chicago for the important committee work that preceded the adoption of the platform and the nomination of candidates by the fully assembled convention. Greeting these national committeemen as they arrived, Robert R. Church, Jr., Perry Howard, and Oscar De Priest had little trouble in convincing a solid majority of them that the president's reform of the southern state parties was a very serious challenge to the autonomy and authority of the national committee itself. They correctly pointed out that the sole authority to recognize and depose national committeemen resided with the Republican National Convention. Thus, they argued, only those national committeemen who had been duly recognized by the preceding convention could issue the call to the state party to elect delegates to the next national convention. This meant that the delegations from Mississippi and South Carolina, where Hoover in effect had created his own national committeemen and his own state parties, were illegally elected and not entitled to be seated. Only the organizations headed by Perry Howard of Mississippi and Tieless Joe Tolbert of South Carolina, the national committeemen who had been legally recognized by the 1928 convention, had the right to elect state delegations to the 1932 national convention, and only those delegations should be seated.[12]

The Republican National Committee agreed with Church, Howard, and De Priest. To create a precedent that allowed a president to replace national committeemen who might displease him for any reason might have harmful results in case of a national defeat. A lame-duck president, such as Hoover was likely soon to become, could pack the next convention with his own rump national committeemen and their factions, thereby dictating the selection of his successor and destroying the democratic process within the party.[13] This sudden powerful opposition by the national committee to Hoover's reform of Mississippi and South Carolina took the president and his top aides completely by surprise.[14] Suspecting a secret plot by Republican opponents to rob the unpopular Hoover of renomination, Brown and Newton rushed to Chicago to defend him.[15]

On 10 June in an all-day session of the national committee, Brown and Newton listened to a barrage of accusations against the president. Some charged Hoover with masking his purge of black leaders under the guise of reform. Others extended this to include an attempt to gain control of the party machinery so that he could dictate the nomination in 1936 as well as in 1932. Brown denied these accusations. Again and again he tried to convince the national committee that the administration had not purged honest black leaders; that the sole objective of the reform was to replace disreputable and corrupt patronage bosses with respectable leaders who would win the confidence of the voters and revitalize democracy in the South.[16]

Try as he might, Brown made little headway. Accusations of corruption against black leaders by disgruntled lily-white opponents made little impression on Republicans who were worried about the devastating impact of the depression. The Democrats were no longer pushing the issues of Teapot Dome and Republican political corruption. Besides, Hoover's opponents argued tellingly, neither Howard nor Tolbert had been convicted of any crimes. Both had been accused and extensively investigated, yet Howard had twice been exonerated. Neither of them had any charges currently pending against him. Moreover, each of them had been legally recognized as a national committeeman by the Republican National Convention in 1928, and unlike Ben Davis of Georgia they had not yielded their posts. With the prospect that a long, divisive convention battle between Al Smith and Franklin Delano Roosevelt would split the Democrats and force them to turn to a weaker compromise candidate, the national committeemen hoped that a unified Republican party might still emerge victorious, providing they could keep the allegiance of their traditionally loyal constituencies, including the large black vote in the North.[17]

Facing almost certain repudiation, Newton sought desperately, nonetheless, to prevent the recognition of Perry Howard. Like Hoover, he still believed

Howard to be corrupt. Perhaps, too, some sort of dramatic fight had to be made to convince the other southern lily-white delegates that Hoover had not simply abandoned his devotion to good government at the first sign of black opposition. Acting for the president, Newton instructed William G. Skelly, the wealthy oil tycoon from Oklahoma, to offer a compromise. Because the lily-white Mississippi reform delegation, headed by Lamont Rowlands, did not include any token black delegates (contrary to Newton's explicit advice), Skelly proposed that the national committee recognize both Rowlands and Howard, thus giving half a vote to Rowlands's lily-white faction and half a vote to Howard's black-and-tan delegation.[18] Newton later claimed that Howard had agreed to the compromise, but Church angrily denounced the deal, and the national committee quickly rejected it. To have accepted it would have weakened the principle of the autonomy of the national committee and risked needlessly angering northern black voters. The national committee thereupon recognized Tieless Joe Tolbert of South Carolina and Perry Howard of Mississippi as the legitimate leaders of their respective delegations.[19]

Howard was jubilant. Having been twice tried and exonerated by all-white juries, he and his followers had finally been reinstated by the predominantly white Republican National Committee. The battle for "the eternal principles of justice and the regularity of the Republican organization," he exulted, had been won.[20] In talking to the press Church placed a different interpretation on the outcome. Race had been the dominant issue, he pointed out, and the national committee had recognized the importance of black leadership and black votes in the tough battle for reelection. But the war was not yet over. If the credentials committee, which was controlled by the Hoover forces, should refuse to seat the Howard or Tolbert delegations, Church vowed to carry his fight to the floor of the national convention and to the black electorate in November.[21]

Church and Howard were in a strong position. The Republican National Committee had accepted their argument, and a floor fight over black exclusion, in the opinion of most delegates, would be both foolish and costly.[22] Indirectly Lamont Rowlands had added to their strength by his repeated demands for the appointment as United States marshal of a valued political lieutenant who was considered antiblack and who had been accused of insulting Negro women.[23] In the months preceding the convention, Mary Booze, the national committeewoman from Mississippi with whom Hoover had been accused of dancing in 1928, had convinced the NAACP and powerful northern black politicians such as Oscar De Priest, whose own wife had been repeatedly insulted, that the nomination of such a man was an affront to all blacks as well as a threat to the exercise of their constitutional rights.[24] Booze may have understood that such an accusation was almost certain to draw the attention of the president. Hoover had great respect for her and for her husband Eugene Booze. Indeed, he had made repeated efforts to help them secure federal funds to keep Mound Bayou, the highly successful independent black farming community where Hoover had spoken in 1927, from being destroyed by the depression.[25]

As a result of the lengthy furor and his obstinate insistence on the appointment, Rowlands no longer appeared to be quite the representative of the best class of whites that Hoover had once believed him to be, and a spirited coalition of southern and northern black leaders succeeded in stopping the appointment of the obnoxious nominee.[26] Rowlands further damaged his credibility before the credentials committee by introducing "new evidence" to prove Howard guilty of patronage corruption. This evidence appeared no better than that which had been twice rejected by all-white juries.[27] Moreover, Howard remained calm and poised, skillfully rebutting Rowlands and adding a stern warning to the Republicans that seating Rowlands's lily-whites would "rise to plague you in your big states" on election day. As Barnett put it, these were arguments that "the politicians understood."[28]

In his despair and disbelief Rowlands falsely accused Hoover of having betrayed him. The only reason he had been defeated, he insisted, was that Brown had made a secret deal with De Priest and other black leaders to drop the administration's opposition to Howard in exchange for black acquiescence in blocking the seating of Tolbert's corrupt South Carolinians.[29] But the Hoover-controlled credentials committee paid no more attention to Rowlands in 1932 than it had in 1928. Now there was no Mabel Walker Willebrandt with whom to make a deal or arrange another federal indictment or a touchy Hoover under fire by Sen. George Norris for buying the nomination by bribing the southern delegates.

If Brown had struck a deal with black politicians, Rowlands exaggerated its significance. For years Tolbert had talked of black rights and included blacks in his state party, but members of the South Carolina black community had grown tired of his protestations and had alerted the NAACP to the fact that Tolbert had rarely used his position as party leader to help black people. He included blacks, they believed, merely to perpetuate his own power at the national conventions of the party, where token black delegations made good politics.[30] Tolbert was weakened still further by new charges of corruption leveled by respected leaders such as Charles Jonas of North Carolina and Robert A. Taft of Ohio. At the same time Carl Hambright, the administration's reform leader in South Carolina, loudly denied that he was a lily-white, and he could lend plausibility to this claim by pointing to the four well-educated, articulate token black delegates whom he had selected on Newton's advice, and who had made an exceptionally favorable impression on influential northern black delegates from Pennsylvania and Ohio.[31]

All these factors enabled Brown and Newton to convince black leaders and the members of the credentials committee that Tolbert and his delegation should not be seated, so the administration managed, with black help, to save some face for its largely discredited southern reform program. No one seemed to care that Tolbert had been rejected, but he was tenacious, and four years later, when the Hoover forces no longer controlled the credentials committee, he too returned in triumph.[32]

The Georgia contest added a new twist to the charge of a lily-white strategy and illustrated once more how confusing and ultimately how politically destructive Hoover's refusal to explain his reform ideas had become. For three years Newton and Brown had expended a considerable amount of time and energy quietly trying to build a genuine coalition of black-and-tans and lily-whites in Georgia. By August 1930 their efforts appeared doomed after S. S. Muncy, the black county chairman, was murdered by lily-whites dressed as members of the KKK, and Benjamin Davis blamed the administration, which he accused of encouraging lily-white violence.[33] For a time it appeared that the coalition had been destroyed, but in early 1931 Newton and Brown had again convinced Davis to join with Josiah T. Rose, the administration's designated reform party chairman, in a new attempt to build a coalition state party. Working together, Rose and Davis had elected a new state central committee, and the administration had honored their patronage nominees, including Fred Flanders, a reformed alcoholic who was sympathetic to black rights, as United States marshal.[34]

The new coalition quickly broke apart. Some of the Georgia lily-whites had apparently hoped that the Muncy murder would end the administration's interference, and they now sought ways to destroy this second coalition as well. Among the tactics they employed was the surreptitious introduction of a bill in the Georgia State Legislature that would have prevented blacks from holding office in any state political party.[35] Failing to get their bill enacted, they were aided nonetheless by the rebellion of most of the state party's black county Republican chairmen. Long suspicious of the feasibility of a coalition with lily-whites and dismayed by the growing number of lily-whites who had displaced them in elections to county leadership posts, they sought to discredit the administration by charging that rather than a coalition, Newton and Brown had agreed to a lily-white strategy. Newton and Brown denied the charge, but it was too late to prevent Georgia's black county Republican chairmen, who no longer trusted Ben Davis, from leaving the second coalition. The dissident county chairmen decided instead to establish their own black-and-tan party and to challenge the administration's coalition before the national convention's credentials committee as nothing more than a lily-white charade.[36]

Claude Barnett was fascinated by the Georgia contest. Four years earlier he had been among those black leaders who had defended Hoover against charges of a lily-white strategy, but as a bitterly disappointed member of the abused and neglected Moton faction, he no longer believed in the good intentions of Brown or Newton, as he had in 1928. Ironically, despite his suspicion, Barnett's detailed notes of the debate in the credentials committee, used in conjunction with other independent sources of evidence, establish that the administration had in fact been striving, albeit unsuccessfully, to create a genuine coalition of black-and-tans and lily-whites in Georgia. Ben Davis was well known as a vocal critic of Hoover, but he now defended the administration, explaining to the committee that the challenging black county chairmen had at first joined the second coalition and had bolted only after they had not been given enough influence to satisfy "their own selfish interests." Like Barnett, the credentials committee concluded that Davis had presented the facts "in a way that they stuck."[37] Still, Barnett had been misled too often in the past, and he could not resist the understandable suspicion that the county chairmen might be telling the truth and that Davis might have thrown in with the "white crowd" that now dominated the state delegation.[38]

At the conclusion of the credentials committee battles only Brown and Newton, who had directed the administration's twists and turns in the South, could fully assess the results. Knowledgeable observers at the convention such as Barnett remained suspicious, while those less informed probably did not know quite what to believe. Nonetheless, some of the consequences were clear enough. Virtually everyone had repudiated Hoover's attempts to reform the South, including many lily-whites. Few Republicans had bothered to defend or credit his efforts. Those who spoke did so to criticize the results of his meddling. Brown and Newton managed to get the Georgia delegation seated, but only after the black county chairmen had cast doubt on their motives and intentions. The administration had kept Tolbert from being seated, but only because the NAACP had convinced northern black politicians that Tolbert was not worth saving. More sensational was the triumphant return of Perry Howard and Ben Davis, the two nationally known southern black Republican politicians whose alleged corruption had ignited Hoover's movement to clean up the southern state parties. They had been welcomed back as leaders of the party and by the Hoover-controlled credentials committee. It was a humbling, and, as some must have thought, a humiliating defeat for the president.

Although at first the fights within the Republican National Committee and the credentials committee seemed to have produced a great victory for black political leaders, the furor masked several more important revelations and prompted some black observers to wonder whether the victory was more apparent than real. Brown and Newton had employed several strategies in the South. They had protected black and tans in some states and cooperated with lily-whites in others, and in Georgia they had repeatedly tried to coax blacks and whites into forming a "reform" coalition. Yet these revelations at the 1932 convention came so late, and the surrounding opportunism and double-dealing were so confusing that their backstage stratagems could not possibly be understood. On the one hand, lily-whites had long known that Hoover would not condone either the purges of honest black leaders or the party-building patronage appointments that they deemed essential to success, and this realization became even more obvious to them at the convention. On the other hand, blacks were aware that lily-whites were still far stronger in the South than the recent black-and-tan victories had suggested. Northern black politicians had no basis to challenge the unified lily-white delegations from Florida, Texas, Virginia, and North Carolina, or those posing as black and tans from Louisiana, Alabama, and South Carolina.[39] They knew, too, that the administration would continue to cooperate with these particular lily-whites.

On top of these complications came the startling news that the party's long-standing promise to combat lynching had disappeared from the 1932 platform. This may have pleased the lily-whites—and, indeed, it may well have been meant to pacify their anger—but no explanations were offered.[40] By the end of the convention many blacks felt a sense of betrayal or quiet disgust or outrage. Church refused to campaign for Hoover or associate with his lieutenants, while Barnett's suspicion was transformed into open distrust. Indeed, the once-faithful editor of the Associated Negro Press was almost ready to join the Democratic party. Should the Democrats, he wrote Walter White, insert "a real [anti-lynching] plank it would be a most strategic thing to do."[41]

Although Barnett's anger was understandable, his hope that the Democrats might help blacks was not. In fact, there was even less chance that the Democrats might appeal to black voters in 1932 than there had been in 1928. Since Al Smith's crushing defeat Franklin D. Roosevelt, the newly elected governor of New York State, had been skillfully executing his own southern strategy. Roosevelt's close ties to the southern Democratic state parties are already well known to scholars.[42] The southern-state files at the Roosevelt Library in Hyde Park reveal his early and continuing efforts to unify the South behind his candidacy.[43] To head off Al Smith's determined bid for a second nomination in 1932, Roosevelt needed to win as many delegate votes as possible, and in this pursuit he wisely allowed southern politicians, who feared the consequences of another Smith candidacy, to organize their states for him without interference. He was also careful to avoid association with black Democrats in the border states.[44] Directed largely by two of his most astute political advisers, Louis Howe and Big Jim Farley, the Roosevelt southern strategy had proceeded smoothly, with only one exception.

In 1931, after Roosevelt had won his second term as governor of New York State and was more actively pursuing the presidential nomination, Farley authorized F. B. Summers and C. W. Jones to establish Roosevelt clubs in Georgia. This was out of keeping with Roosevelt's usual practice of working through the regular Democratic leadership in each state and soon led to trouble when state leaders complained that Summers and Jones were competing with the party's regular organizations. By February 1932 Summers and Jones were pressing Farley to reimburse them for the money they claimed to have spent in establishing the independent Roosevelt clubs. Unable to control them, Farley informed Roosevelt about the two men and their attempted "holdup." More important than the money, however, was the fact that in organizing the Roosevelt clubs, Summers and Jones had relied for assistance upon members of the state Ku Klux Klan and that on the advice of these two men, Farley had written encouraging letters to these Klan members without realizing their connection. When Farley and Roosevelt discovered this and refused reimbursement, Summers and Jones filed suit in court to recover their expenses and apparently supplied to FDR's political enemies copies of the correspondence, apparently establishing the connection between the Roosevelt clubs and the Klan.[45]

As the Democrats gathered in Chicago to decide whether Roosevelt or Al Smith, who was a famous opponent of the Klan, should receive the nomination, John M. Callahan, a delegate from Wisconsin, circulated an open letter to all delegates, complete with copies of Farley's letters to the Klan members, and called on the party to repudiate FDR and his Klan allies.[46] Roosevelt immediately denounced the letters as "deliberate forgeries" and disavowed any Klan support.[47] Yet despite his disavowal, black Democrats were deeply disturbed. Walter White correctly judged that the correspondence was authentic. This called in question FDR's insistence on "deliberate forgeries," and White refused to accept his repudiation of the Klan at face value.[48] In his view these letters had "eliminated" Roosevelt. If the Democrats were to nominate him after this exposé, he lamented, "it will mean absolute delivery of the Negro vote to Hoover."[49]

Roosevelt's nomination and the absence of any statement on black rights or needs in the Democratic platform greatly disappointed blacks who had hoped for an attractive alternative to Hoover, and the selection of John Nance Garner as vice-presidential candidate added to their worries.[50] Hailing from Uvalde, Texas, a town that reputedly banned even the presence of Negroes, Garner was undeniable proof for many blacks of Roosevelt's total dependence on the white South. Roosevelt had had to make a deal with Garner to win the presidential nomination and this had added to the impression of Garner's influence in shaping Roosevelt's attitudes toward blacks. Rumors that the crippled nominee was already in poor health convinced others that Garner and his Negro-hating cohorts would soon control the White House.[51] This fear was a potent weapon for black Republicans, and they made the most of it.

Mary Church Terrell, campaign director of the Colored Voters Division of the Republican eastern campaign headquarters, fashioned her campaign speeches around "the horrible possibility of having Garner the Texan in the White House." To fix the alliance between Roosevelt and the South, which Garner's antiblack racial views supposedly personified, she reiterated the message "that the laws which have been designed to impede the progress of the colored people, wound their sensibilities, crush their pride and destroy the manhood and womanhood of the race had been enacted by the Democratic party."[52] Failure to reelect Hoover, she prophesied, would be a tragedy for the Negro race.[53]

Black Democrats as well as Republicans feared the inordinate power of the

South in a Roosevelt administration. Earl B. Dickerson, a regional director for the Democratic party's national campaign in 1928 and chief spokesman for the Democratic Resolutions Committee in 1932, ultimately felt compelled to decline Du Bois's request that he write an article for the *Crisis* explaining why blacks should vote for Roosevelt.[54] At first Dickerson had agreed to write it, but after several unsuccessful attempts he confessed to Du Bois that such an article would be unfair to the Negro people. He personally favored Roosevelt over Hoover because of the former's progressive record, but he told Du Bois, "I doubt if Roosevelt . . . will be able to carry through any of his progressive views, largely because of the fact that the reactionary, bourbon South would be in control of both the Senate and the House of Representatives—and we could expect certainly no more, if as much, under Roosevelt in such circumstances, than under Hoover."[55]

Disillusioned members of the Moton faction, who questioned the degree of Hoover's concern for black people and who no longer trusted his top aides, had to agree with Dickerson.[56] Barnett finally consented to campaign for Hoover only because he had come to the conclusion that Roosevelt's election would be "fatal" to the Negro race.[57] Moton refused to endorse Hoover, and he complained openly of Hoover's failure to keep his promise to appoint three black special assistant attorneys general. Still, he felt on balance that Hoover was "as good a man and as capable and efficient as we can get now."[58] Having visited Haiti as a member of Hoover's educational reform commission, Moton had only contempt for Roosevelt. He told Barnett, "Nothing could have condemned Mr. Roosevelt more in my mind in spite of his personal charm, than his constitution—the treaty set-up for Haiti—which he wrote himself, he says when he was assistant secretary of the navy, and I don't see how any people could be treated worse than the Haitians were treated in their own territory." Besides, he added, if Roosevelt "has done anything for Negroes as Governor of New York, I have not heard of it."[59]

Other former black Hooverites were not even that charitable to the president. Melvin J. Chisum, one of Moton's valued adherents, who had campaigned diligently for Hoover in 1928 and who had been passed over repeatedly for important patronage posts by the president's top advisers, openly attacked the administration. In a sensational article for the Baltimore *Afro-American*, Chisum vented the anger and frustration felt by many in the Moton faction. He also characterized Brown, Newton, and Everett Saunders, the new chairman of the Republican National Committee, as "confirmed Negro haters and political Negro baiters."[60] Barnett warned Moton that his close ties with Chisum had "shocked" the White House. Moton did not agree with Chisum's charges, and he denied that Chisum spoke for him, yet he refused to intervene to stop Chisum's attacks.[61]

Robert Vann, editor of the Pittsburgh *Courier*, joined Chisum in propagating the charge of Hoover's racial hatred. Vann had been director of publicity in the Colored Voters Division during the 1928 campaign, and according to his enemy, Robert R. Church, Jr., a double agent for the Democrats at the same time.[62] Vann also had been repeatedly passed over for a prestigious patronage post. For that and other reasons he turned his newspaper against Hoover, and for this the Roosevelt administration later rewarded him with an appointment as a special assistant attorney general. Reiterating the theme of racial hatred, Vann falsely portrayed Hoover as a Negro hater who had made his fortune by cruelly exploiting nonwhite laborers in China and South Africa.[63] Du Bois shared the same view. He had long believed Hoover to be a sinister enemy of the black race.[64] In the November issue of *Crisis* he wrote the editorial that Dickerson had earlier refused, claiming, "No one in our day has helped disenfranchisement and race hatred more than Herbert Hoover by his 'Lily-White' policy, his appointments to office, and his failure to recognize and appreciate the plight of the Forgotten Black Man."[65]

Du Bois's obvious exaggeration went unchallenged, perhaps in part because of still another source of intense frustration and anger: the administration's prolonged delay in taking action against private firms under federal contract who abused black workers. Both the National Urban League and the NAACP had complained that contractors working under the supervision of the Army Corps of Engineers at Boulder Dam and on the massive Mississippi River flood control project had either refused to hire blacks, or when they did, subjected them to numerous abuses.[66] In July 1932, after months of White House inaction, the NAACP contacted an experienced independent investigator who confirmed the validity of the complaints.[67]

Walter White was furious. He informed United States senators that "Negroes are being held in virtual slavery by men operating under government contracts," and he succeeded in convincing Sen. Robert Wagner of New York State to threaten the administration with a Senate investigation.[68] To Secretary of War Patrick J. Hurley and Attorney General William D. Mitchell he charged that black workers were being subjected to physical violence, excessive hours of labor, unsanitary living conditions, and low wages.[69] Once again, as in the controversy over the Tenth Cavalry, Hoover ordered the army to investigate, and once again the army steadfastly denied the validity of the allegations. Maj. Gen. Lytle Brown, the commander of the Army Corps of Engineers, told White that his claims were based on "unwarranted distrust and suspicion."[70]

Because the army took its time looking into the allegations, White was able to keep the controversy before the public in the hope too that it would help swing the black vote against Hoover in November.[71] Hurley and General Brown inadvertently aided White, who guessed correctly that they were "doing nothing but trying to cover up the whole situation and to whitewash the affair."[72] Eventually Hoover became exasperated. As the same sensational charges continued to make news into late October, he asked Moton to gather together an independent investigating commission; but as Hoover soon had to admit that he had no funds to pay its expenses, the commission never materialized and the unfavorable publicity continued.[73] Eventually, in February 1933, Will Alexander, head of the Interracial Commission, completed an investigation that the army found "useful" in correcting some of the abuses, but it continued the whitewash in its own reports to Hoover.[74]

As the Democrats made steady progress in converting black voters in Harlem, Pittsburgh, Indianapolis, Saint Louis, and Kansas City, Brown and Newton ended months of confusion and indecision over the fate of the Colored Voters Division by suddenly sweeping out the remainder of the "Doctors" who had dominated the CVD during the 1928 campaign. Scott, Cobb, and Hawkins were pushed into the background just as Moton, Barnett, and Holsey had been.[75] The Colored National Planning Board replaced both the National Negro Republican League and the CVD. The new board was split into an eastern division headed by Francis E. Rivers, a prominent New York City attorney and confidant of Edgar Rickard, and a western division directed by Ray Benjamin, the skilled political operative who had converted Church to the Hoover cause in the last days of the 1928 campaign, and whom the disillusioned Church characterized as the "White House Ringmaster for Hoover's Negro Side Show."[76] Big-city practical politicians, the very black men with whom Hoover had refused to deal in 1928, were now in command. During September Roscoe Conkling Simmons and L. K. Williams, both of Chicago; John Marquess of Philadelphia; Charles Mitchell of New York; and other black politicians experienced at getting out the northern black vote planned a dramatic, well-publicized White House ceremony to begin their campaign.

On 1 October 1932 Hoover greeted almost two hundred black Republicans whom he had invited to the White House for a carefully staged photo session. Surrounded by the two hundred politicians, the president sought to dispel any lingering doubts about his southern reform and allay the charge that he would not have his picture taken with black leaders.[77] Then, when Simmons implored him to repudiate the charge of "unkind men" who had claimed "that you, our great leader, the soldier and savior in the storm and shock of our country's heaviest hour, are no believer in the equality of men," Hoover responded by pledging that the Republican party would "not abandon or depart from its traditional duty toward the American Negro" and that the "right of liberty, justice, and equal opportunity is yours." Although they politely applauded, some of those present must have felt emotions ranging from anger to cynicism and laughter, but as this was the official, joyful celebration of the black politicians' return to preeminence, everyone at least seemed pleased. Following the ceremony the two hundred guests gathered together for a gala banquet in a nearby Masonic temple, where the most famous politician of them all, Perry Howard, appropriately served as toastmaster, and rousing political speeches lasted well into the early morning hours.[78]

Hoover had offered them little, and he would steadfastly refuse, like Roosevelt, to respond to a detailed questionnaire from the NAACP,[79] but this did not interfere with the campaign strategy of his new black allies. Rather than worry and fret over what Hoover had not yet done, said, or might do in the future, or become discouraged and fall silent as the Hoover Doctors had, they concentrated on black fears of what the white supremacists in the Democratic party might do if they won control of the Congress and the White House. Black Democrats, they loudly insisted, were "race traitors" whose appeal for a "protest vote" against Hoover was in reality asking the race to commit "deliberate suicide." A Democratic victory would usher in a "reign of terror" and "lynch law." In 1917, for example, as assistant secretary of the navy, Roosevelt had "enslaved and crushed down Black Haiti with a devilishly conceived constitution and brutal marines." Garner was perhaps even worse. When he was Speaker of the House, they continued, he had fired thirty-three black employees, voted against appropriations for Howard University three times, and against antilynching legislation seven times. He had also introduced a bill to abolish the army's proud black cavalry. The Parker nomination and the Gold Star mothers incident, they conceded, were blots upon the Republican record. Nonetheless, these were only temporary departures from traditional Republican policy, whereas the Democrats had cooped up blacks in a wire cage during the 1928 convention in Houston, and they would translate the black "protest vote" against Hoover into a license to pass more legislation expanding and enforcing discrimination and segregation.[80]

As nearly everyone had anticipated, the election was a Republican rout. Roosevelt easily defeated Hoover; the Republicans suffered serious congressional losses; and the South returned en masse to the Democratic fold. Local black Democratic organizations scored notable victories in Harlem, Pittsburgh, and Kansas City; and New Deal relief policies and the absence of the predicted "reign of terror" would enable them to expand these victories into a massive shift in the 1936 election.[81] But the majority of blacks in 1932 were not yet ready to trust the Democrats, even if they were inclined, as Vann had admonished them, to turn Lincoln's portrait to the wall.[82]

Considering the spreading anger directed against Hoover by most black newspapers and many black leaders since the 1928 Republican convention, the fact that most black voters supported Hoover in 1932 seemed surprising. Yet black Republican victories in Chicago, Cleveland, Columbus, Cincinnati, Philadelphia, and Baltimore were not difficult to understand.[83] Black voters simply did not agree with Du Bois's claim that "no one in our day has helped disenfranchisement and race hatred more than Herbert Hoover." It appeared evident to them that his description fit a number of powerful Democrats better than it fit the president. To be sure, Hoover was not popular or even respected by them. Four years of constant criticism from trusted black leaders, his own silence, and the ravaging effects of the depression had ensured black disaffection. Still, the alternative to Hoover appeared more threatening. They had the dismal choice of voting against the president and his neglect or against Roosevelt and his racist southern cohorts.

By inviting 200 Republican politicians to the White House and responding positively to Simmons's question concerning equality, Hoover had largely dispelled long-standing fears of an antiblack southern strategy and thereby opened the way for a choice that not even the Chicago *Defender*, long a hostile critic, was willing to oppose.[84] In addition, Hoover had courted the most influential black Republican politicians; he had sent Secretary Wilbur and a personal message to the NAACP convention; he had delivered the commencement address at Howard University; he had accepted Benjamin Davis and Perry Howard back into the fold; he had assigned two blacks to make seconding speeches at the convention; and he had revamped his black electoral organization with pragmatic politicians and tough campaigners. He did these things without regard to the possible disaffection of the once-important southern white voter. It was not an admirable effort, but it was much more than he had done in 1928, and it was far more than Roosevelt had felt he could do. As a result, in November 1932 black voters concluded that the Democrats were still more lily-white and antiblack than Hoover and the Republicans.

22. Shattered Hopes

On 12 January 1933 following Hoover's reelection defeat, Moton once again reminded him of their earlier land scheme to combat peonage in the South. Hoover still favored the plan. "I have not dismissed from my mind," he responded, "the ideal toward which we have both been striving, at least in thought, during these past years." But if Moton had hoped that Hoover might act on that ideal now that he no longer needed to worry about reelection or political retaliation, he was disappointed. "The intervention of the terrific world depression has, of course, paralyzed" whatever might have been possible to help blacks, Hoover explained. However, after his term of office expired and he had had a good rest, he promised that he would be glad "to hear from you and to join with you in a renewed effort toward these ends."[1]

Moton never again approached Hoover for help. He was disappointed over Hoover's repeated failures to fulfill his promises to him. But four years later, on 14 January 1937, Moton told the ex-president about the New Deal Resettlement Administration's program to help black tenant farmers, a program that was "exactly along the lines of our plans." Moton hinted that they ought to publicize their own prior efforts, but he got no response.[2] Hoover's silence must have again disappointed Moton, yet Hoover retained an exceptionally high regard for the Tuskegee principal. When Moton died in 1940 he hailed him as a "great force in American life" and a "great leader" who was "my constant friend."[3] Later, in 1951, Hoover remembered him as a "welcome visitor at the White House," as "a great gentleman and inspiring soul . . . one of the great educators and leaders of his time," and, he added, "I did what I could to help him."[4]

What exactly Hoover had done to help Moton remained unclear. Indeed, in 1949 Barnett warned him that the vast majority of blacks thought of him as "cold" and "impassive." He urged him to reveal his personal attitude toward black people, and especially his efforts on their behalf while president.[5] But Hoover was unwilling to do so. "At this time of my life," he told Barnett, "I do not want to take up any more battles."[6] Perhaps he feared that Drew Pearson or some other critic would respond by again reviving the charge, as Pearson had in 1939, that he had "bought" his presidential nomination by bribing the southern delegations.[7] Still, he regretted the "smears as to my attitude toward Negroes" and wistfully reassured Barnett that the interpretations advanced by his critics were "far from my thoughts and [from] a long series of [my] actions."[8]

By continuing his silence Hoover did himself a great disservice. Today Hoover's claim that he had done what he could to help Moton and black people appears hardly credible. Certainly he knew the "long series of actions" better than any other single individual. Equally certain was his great concern for his place in American history. At the time that Barnett had warned him about speaking up in 1949, Hoover was writing his *Memoirs*, yet he did not discuss his efforts to help black Americans. One year earlier in 1948, President Harry S Truman had openly bid for black votes by championing a civil rights plank in the Democratic platform. Perhaps he thought little of Truman's black "politics." Even more likely, however, his silence may well have masked an embarrassed confusion as well as a sense of failure.

Hoover's silence helped perpetuate the confusion surrounding his southern strategy. Without carefully analyzing the contradictory evidence, the easiest conclusion was the still widely held view that his southern strategy was aimed at driving blacks out of the party and turning over control of southern Republican politics to white racists. Because he maintained his silence, Hoover must bear considerable responsibility for the persistence of this harsh view. But it adds little to our understanding of Hoover or of racism to dismiss him as a bigot who sought to purge black leaders from the Republican party. To be sure, he was no champion of black rights; he neither issued executive orders nor sponsored legislation to challenge racial bigotry. Yet his encounter with racism was much more complex, more human, and thus more interesting and instructive than previous accounts have recognized.

Any balanced assessment of Hoover's failure to reform the southern state parties and his disastrous relations with black Americans must place some of the blame on both the poor advice and the unauthorized actions of loyal yet politically second-rate aides. Some of the more important examples would include Work's use of money to win the nomination and his use of Horace Mann to win the biggest popular vote in American history; Mann's misrepresentations of Hoover's intentions and his undercover use of racism; Willebrandt's deal with the lily-white enemies of Perry Howard and her zealous determination to convict him; the well-intentioned yet confused and compromising dream of Anderson and Wise of a southern revolution; Huston's thinly disguised lily-white model reform scheme; MacArthur's insistence on drastic reductions in the Tenth Cavalry; Hurley's insensitivity to the Gold Star mothers; and Mitchell's opposition to combatting lynching. Yet, important as these may be, the sources of his failures did not lie solely in the poor advice or the unauthorized actions of his aides. They were also within him and within the society that he tried to lead.

Rather than the skillful politician that his 1928 triumph suggested to his admirers and critics alike, Hoover was, in fact, woefully unprepared, and, in time, would prove himself inept in the politics of democratic leadership. Some of the earliest evidence of this political blundering could be found in his dealings with the South and with blacks. His determined attempt to promote a southern "revolution" was so utopian, ambitious, and misguided that sophisticated political opponents could not imagine such thinking, and Hoover's silence allowed them, indeed encouraged them, to depict his campaign and reform efforts in the worst possible light. To Hoover, the cleansing and revitalization of the southern state parties was akin to a moral crusade. It was not just another in a long series of Republican schemes to crack the solid South for mere political advantage or a plan motivated by cynical vote-getting racism. Yet this is exactly how it appeared to all but a few of those with whom he had talked privately.

Hoover was almost as uninformed about southern politics as he was about racism. Unable to understand that racism was at the core of corrupt southern politics, he focused his reforming energies instead on the more narrow and familiar issue of traditional patronage corruption, a malady to which he knew both white and black politicians of both parties were equally susceptible. This focus was narrowed further by the assumption that although he could do nothing about the internal corruption of the entrenched white supremacist Democrats, he could at least force southern Republicans to cleanse their own state parties. He would help in this reform by insistence on highly qualified, honest patronage appointees and by the creation of a new elite leadership. His reform program was the most practical approach, he believed, to the rebirth of his party, the defeat of the Democrats, and the revival of democracy. Despite appearances, he did not pursue a single lily-white strategy in the South but rather several different strategies simultaneously, strategies that Newton and Brown tailored to the varying conditions in the individual states. But because he refused to explain his views or goals publicly, disgruntled and confused state party members were left to their own perceptions and complained loudly about his constant meddling in their affairs or in the affairs of like-minded allies in other states. Instead of revitalizing Republicanism in the South, Hoover's efforts succeeded only in creating a host of enemies: blacks and whites in both the North and the South.

Ironically, Hoover was confident that he understood how race had been used by southern politicians. It was so disarmingly simple and obvious to him. Republicans had allowed unprincipled Democrats to play on racial fears, and this tactic had enabled them to destroy the two-party system and reduce the Republicans to mere patronage spoilsmen. But he would outwit the Democrats by rising above racial politics. He believed that he could force a return to political competition by attracting the "better white elements" and by cutting himself and his party off from both racial condemnations and appeals, thereby removing race as an issue. Thus during the 1928 campaign he steadfastly withstood the urgings of former president William Howard Taft and the owner of the Chicago *Tribune*, Robert R. McCormick, that he appeal to the traditionally Republican black electorate. In his most publicized effort, the attempt to attract a new southern white elite to the Republican party, he agreed to Work's pragmatic vote-gathering scheme, which was to be independently directed by Horace Mann, and he even made a campaign speech at Elizabethton, Tennessee, to assure white southerners that they were now an important part of his thinking. Without being aware of it, Hoover had ensnarled himself in a net of responsibility from which he would find it increasingly difficult to escape.

Thus, by compromising with racism, Hoover became its captive. In order to rise above racial politics he assumed that he had little choice but to follow the advice of Anderson and Wise: he must remain silent on race. If he were to explain his hope that his reform program would eventually promote racial harmony and progress, he believed that he would play into the hands of the white supremacist Democrats and strengthen the enemies of racial progress. Only by remaining silent, by refusing either to appeal to race or respond to bigotry could he succeed. But given the centrality of race to southern politics and the Republican party's historic, if not actual, protection of black rights, his silence appeared to convey a distinctly different message. Moreover, to attract southern white votes he denied that he had desegregated the Commerce Department, dodged Ruth Hanna McCormick's appeal to renounce the Ku Klux Klan, avoided the black electorate in the North, ignored the nefarious and bigoted tactics employed by lily-white Republicans or by Horace Mann's new recruits, and rejected the united black "Appeal to America" to end the race baiting and hatred that dominated the southern campaign. For all of his idealism and good intentions Hoover must bear a large share of responsibility for the moral and political evasions that encouraged racists and other undesirable elements to join the 1928 Hoovercrat movement. Although he could not have stopped the excesses, he could at least have spoken out forcefully against them. By muzzling himself, he poisoned his own certain victory, seriously diminished his moral stature, damaged his ability to lead the nation, and increasingly alienated black Americans and their allies. Thus his attempt to rise above racial politics only convinced many that he himself was a bigot. This sad misconception clung to Hoover long after he died.

Hoover's black "Doctors" also paid a high price for their silence. Because of his distrust of politicians, Hoover staffed the Colored Voters Division with professional men, his new black elite who shared his social and economic ideas and idealism. To them he explained his plan to revolutionize the South with a new white elite leadership and won their agreement, if not their enthusiastic approval. He assured them that honest black leaders would be protected and that both blacks and whites would benefit from a strong Republican and correspondingly weakened Democratic party in the South. But they too must remain silent.

Black politicians frozen out of the Colored Voters Division and not privy to Hoover's misguided vision complained loudly about the new black elite. As representatives of a candidate who avoided black audiences, who offered no program of any kind, and who refused to quiet fears of a sinister racist southern strategy, they appeared to these critics as neither an elite nor real leaders. Black Republican politicians scorned private assurances from the Doctors by increasing their attacks on Hoover for his apparent capitulation to racism. As their faith in Hoover decreased, the black elite themselves became disgruntled and then demoralized. Factionalism intensified, and the competition to control patronage accentuated the very attributes that would undermine their influence with Hoover and thereby further weaken the already slim chances for a well-defined, coordinated approach to black needs.

Hoover's silence about race also failed to satisfy lily-whites for long. The prosecution of Perry Howard and Horace Mann's assurances encouraged them, but they were eager for more concrete evidence. At first the reform proclamation of 26 March 1929 appeared to be aimed at the black-and-tan leaders in Mississippi, Georgia, and South Carolina. However, after closer examination lily-whites soon realized that the simultaneous creation of patronage advisory committees in Alabama, Arkansas, Louisiana, Florida, and Texas was also an expression of the president's distrust of them as well. Obviously, in Hoover's view, they were not leaders of the "highest quality."

Moreover, his subsequent directives and actions quickly disillusioned them. Instead of helping to capitalize on Democratic disarray by dispensing patronage as a means to unify and strengthen their state parties, the president persistently rejected many of their most important patronage recommendations, meddled in the selection of the patronage advisory committees, precipitated a destructive battle with loyal Florida lily-whites, refused to force Walter Cohen from his prestigious position as collector of customs at New Orleans, and protected Robert R. Church, Jr., in Tennessee. But it was the invitation to Mrs. Oscar De Priest that dashed the hopes of most lily-whites. Within a year of his inauguration most of them had concluded that Hoover was both untrustworthy on the race issue and too inept a politician to defeat the Democrats. Increasingly he appeared to be his own worst political enemy.

The prolonged, bitter battle over the nomination of John J. Parker to the Supreme Court epitomized the widespread misunderstanding that Hoover's silence continued to generate. Instead of viewing Parker as an outstanding example of the South's new Republican white elite, as Hoover saw him, the majority of senators chose to believe he was an undistinguished, perhaps reactionary candidate selected to further Hoover's lily-white Republican party in the South. Rather than a battle for the independence of the judiciary, as Hoover insisted, most senators disagreed. They refused to believe either Hoover or his pitifully few spokesmen, at least in part, because the president had failed to establish credibility for his southern reform. It was the perception of a racist lily-white southern strategy that created the "unholy and unnatural" alliance that defeated the Parker nomination and "greatly lowered" the prestige of Hoover's administration. If the president had carefully and fully explained his intentions and hopes for the southern reform program or if Parker had repudiated his 1920 campaign rhetoric instead of attempting a southern strategy of his own, the results might have been different. Certainly they could hardly have been worse.

Indeed, the evidence suggests that candor would have been more beneficial both to Hoover and to Parker, at least in the long run, if not in the final vote. Instead, Hoover emerged from the battle with a growing reputation as a devious, reactionary bigot who had sought to use the nomination to the highest court in a sordid effort to steal the mantle of white supremacy from the Democrats.

Yet this impression of hostility to black people, however much he deserved responsibility for it, was not an accurate one. Certainly Hoover wanted to promote black progress, and, for his time, he offered several promising approaches for achieving it. The most notable was in line with his strong conviction that social progress depended upon careful study into the root causes of problems. He delighted in appointing commissions of experts who would use the scientific methods and new knowledge of the still emerging social sciences to devise solutions or make recommendations for solving specific social problems. He brought together private self-help organizations and federal agencies, as in the case of the report on the economic status of the Negro, to combine their talents and resources in providing new avenues for cooperation and coordination in prompting racial progress. A combination of federal and private methods was clearly discernible and gave promise of both expansion and future results. He was also receptive to appointing well-qualified blacks to appropriate federal agencies where they could utilize federal resources in helping black people make headway against more immediate problems. As the 1932 campaign approached, he even suggested the creation of a special black patronage elite at every level of the federal government. By present standards these efforts may not seem substantial, but at that time, considering the general acceptance of racism, they represented fresh presidential initiative.

Unfortunately Hoover failed to achieve any significant progress for blacks. To an extent Hoover was doubtless correct in arguing that the depression had paralyzed his efforts. With continued prosperity his record most likely would have been far more impressive, especially in expanding use of the federal bureaucracy. Yet there were significant flaws in his thinking that would have imposed serious limitations even if prosperity had continued. In initiating investigations of specific national problems, Hoover usually assigned black study groups as a part of larger national study commissions on the assumption that the solution leading to racial progress could only emerge within the context of new understanding of larger national problems. These solutions would not therefore touch upon the nature of racism or how racism created or complicated these problems. When T. J. Woofter's study of race for the President's Research Committee on Social Trends pointed out the need not just to seek one source of prejudice but to examine the multiple forms of discrimination and exclusion, this significant conclusion was inexplicably dropped from the brief published report.[9]

Blacks were expected to progress within a society that was barely aware of its racism, except perhaps as a general fear and hatred of blacks that erupted periodically when they failed to keep their "proper place" in society. But Hoover was not alone in his imperfect understanding of racism. It was shared by his associates; indeed it was part of the intellectual failure of the whole era.

Raising up a broadly based black elite that would provide the leadership needed to help other blacks make greater progress was Hoover's constant theme. Educational institutions, teachers, professional and economic associations, and private self-help organizations such as the National Urban League, the National Negro Business League, and the Interracial Commission were central to his thinking. These educational and self-help institutions loomed so large to him that he could not imagine the great political and legal efforts that would be necessary to make progress against racism. Hoover saw enough evidence of black leadership, black initiative, and black self-help to convince him that blacks themselves could overcome the obstacles confronting them, especially if they were assisted by the federal bureaucracy. Such a notion is yet another example of his ignorance about the nature and pervasiveness of racism.

In one important respect Hoover understood the limits of black leadership and initiative. He stressed the need for an elite white leadership as well—one that would rise above the hatreds of race and strive toward the ideals that he believed were powerful, shaping forces in American society. Apparently Hoover saw some evidence of this type of white leadership in the North, and he was eager to cultivate it in the South. Anderson and Wise convinced him that it did exist but needed the dynamic encouragement and sustenance that only the president of the United States could provide. Working together with black leaders, the white elite would create the political, economic, and social conditions in which racial progress and harmony could be realized. Unfortunately, the hatred that the 1928 campaign had generated in the South encouraged more bigots than elitists to join the Republican party.

Another major impediment to Hoover's success with black leaders was his distrust of traditional politics and politicians. To him, the politician's lust for patronage was one of the worst features of politics, and in his determination to end its abuse and to ensure high standards of honesty and competency, he resisted the use of patronage merely to build a strong, unified following among either lily-whites or blacks. By contrast, black Republicans had a much better understanding of the benefits that politics, patronage, and the federal government could bring to black people. In some areas of the South, for example, their ability to influence the selection of United States attorneys, marshals, and judges was an important means of defense. They also recognized the need to act quickly to avoid prolonged internal quarrels and the appearance of neglect. Moreover, they had a much more realistic assessment of the limits and weaknesses of private voluntary associations in overcoming racism.

For his part, Hoover was convinced that patronage politics corrupted blacks at least as much as it corrupted whites, especially in the South. Squabbles for appointments between the two factions of the new black elite reinforced Hoover's disdain and widened the gap in communication between them. Hoover's failure to appoint a high-level official for liaison with black leaders who could pull together their diverse ideas into a unified program intensified the factionalism. Competition for control of a new black organization approved by the administration complicated and delayed a decision until both Hawkins and Moton eventually realized that the failure of their two factions to present a united front had seriously hurt black interests. Nonetheless, the principal responsibility was Hoover's.

Hoover also demanded far more personal loyalty and trust from his black elite than he had any right to expect. He repeatedly required that they trust in his moral character and good judgment while disregarding the ugly realities and damaging impressions that he or his reform efforts created. They responded with surprising tolerance, steadfastly maintaining their faith in his good intentions despite the increasingly hostile criticism they received from other respected and influential black critics. But when they could not support Parker without specific public disavowals of his 1920 racist campaign statements, Hoover reacted as if he, not they, had been insulted, as if their refusal was somehow a repudiation of his good character and judgment. All too often during his years in Washington, Hoover had lost supporters because he had difficulty in distinguishing between political disagreement and personal repudiation, and this was no exception. Moreover, this personal pique reinforced his insensitivity to the important correlation between political appearances and the perception of political realities and led increasingly to misunderstanding, suspicion, and mistrust even among his most loyal black supporters. As a result, these men of high principles grew further and further apart.

Ironically, Hoover had wanted to be helpful to black Americans. Although the evidence establishes that he accepted conventional assumptions about white superiority, he nonetheless believed that black Americans could make great progress, that racial harmony and goodwill could and should be achieved, and that he had the obligation to work toward these goals. His landreform program to combat peonage and his desegregation of the Commerce Department, one a goal for private initiative and the other an expression of public responsibility, represented his best thinking.

He expected most progress to result from the combined efforts of black and white self-help organizations, and accordingly he placed great faith in the National Negro Business League, the National Urban League, Tuskegee Institute, and the Interracial Commission. But he also believed that the federal government had an important responsibility to promote and sustain racial progress. This was evident in a number of his actions: his support of black business by the Commerce Department, his assignment of blacks to commissions studying national problems, his increased financing for Howard University, his recommendations to cabinet officers, and several patronage appointments. It was also evident in the cooperation he fostered between private institutions and the federal government in dealing with racial problems. Clearly, Hoover had begun to break new and highly promising paths toward future racial progress. Unfortunately, during that quest he failed to understand the obstacles of racism that blocked the way. His distrust of politics and of political solutions to social problems and inordinate faith in self-help organizations, voluntarism, and the goodwill and high principles of an elusive white elite left him substantially unprepared for the task before him.

In retrospect, it is clear that Hoover was more an unwitting victim of racism and of his own peculiar failings as a political leader than he was an enemy of black people. His encounter with racism is not the story of a bigot who sought to drive black people and their leaders out of the Republican party and thereby capture the once-solid South in order to promote lily-whitism and to expand his political power. It is rather the tragic yet instructive tale of a good man who insisted that he was color-blind but could not even see and understand the racism that engulfed him and his society. It is the story of a leader whose misguided compromise with racism stunted his developing understanding and desire to resist racial injustice and eventually reduced him to baffled capitulation. For all his good motives and idealistic goals, he could never penetrate the fog of racism that confused, humiliated, enraged, and ultimately stifled him. Thus, Hoover's venture into southern politics proved a sad encounter both for him and for black Americans.

Notes

Abbreviations

ARC	Records of American National Red Cross, Record Group 200, National Archives, Washington, D.C.
CAB Papers	Claude A. Barnett Papers, Chicago Historical Society, Chicago, Illinois
C & T	Campaign of 1928 and Transition, Presidential Papers, Herbert Hoover Presidential Library, West Branch, Iowa
CQ	Colored Question, Presidential Papers, Hoover Presidential Library
EJS Papers	Emmett J. Scott Papers, Morgan State University, Baltimore, Maryland
ER Papers	Edgar Rickard Papers, Hoover Presidential Library
FDRL	Franklin D. Roosevelt Library, Hyde Park, New York
GA Papers	George Akerson Papers, Hoover Presidential Library
GBS Papers	Gilchrist B. Stockton Papers, Hoover Institution on War, Revolution, and Peace, Stanford University, Palo Alto, California
GN Papers	George Norris Papers, Library of Congress, Washington, D.C.
HH	Herbert Hoover
HHPL	Herbert Hoover Presidential Library
HW Papers	Hubert Work Papers, Division of State Archives and Public Records, Denver, Colorado
JAC Papers	James A. Cobb Papers, Howard University, Washington, D.C.
JCW Papers	Jennings C. Wise Papers, Virginia Historical Society, Richmond
JJP Papers	John J. Parker Papers, University of North Carolina, Chapel Hill
JSCP	Judiciary, Supreme Court, Parker, Hoover Presidential Library
LC	Library of Congress
LS Papers	Lewis Strauss Papers, Hoover Presidential Library
MFC File	Mississippi Flood Control File, NAACP Papers
MVFR File	Mississippi Valley Flood Relief Work File, Commerce Papers, Hoover Presidential Library
NAACP Papers	National Association for the Advancement of Colored People Papers, Library of Congress
NCS File	North Carolina State File, Presidential Papers, Hoover Presidential Library

Pres. Papers	Presidential Papers, Hoover Presidential Library
PP File	President's Personal File, Presidential Papers, Hoover Presidential Library
PWH File	Perry W. Howard File, Department of Justice, Record Group 60, National Archives
RNC Papers	Republican National Committee Papers, Presidential Papers, Herbert Hoover Presidential Library
RRC Papers	Robert R. Church, Jr., Papers, Memphis State University, Memphis, Tennessee
RRM Papers	Robert R. Moton Papers, Tuskegee Institute, Tuskegee, Alabama
WDP Papers	War Department Presidential Papers, Hoover Presidential Library

1. The Mississippi Flood

1. Herbert Hoover, *The Memoirs of Herbert Hoover*, 3 vols. (New York: Macmillan Co., 1951–52), 2:190–91; George Akerson to Walter Newton, 2 August and 3 September 1926, GA Papers; Edgar Rickard diary, 2 December 1926, 27 January 1927, ER Papers; Joan Hoff Wilson, *Herbert Hoover: Forgotten Progressive* (Boston: Little, Brown and Co., 1975), p. 123.

2. Hoover's popularity is well described by Richard Hofstadter, *The American Political Tradition* (New York: Alfred A. Knopf, 1948), pp. 283–85; but more recent scholarly assessments can be found in the excellent brief account of Hoover's public leadership by Joan Hoff Wilson and the best one-volume biography of Hoover by David Burner, *Herbert Hoover: A Public Life* (New York: Alfred A. Knopf, 1979).

3. For the best book on the Hoover presidential boom of 1920 see Gary Dean Best, *The Politics of American Individualism: Herbert Hoover in Transition, 1918–1921* (Westport, Conn.: Greenwood Press, 1975). See also Burner, *Hoover*, pp. 138–58.

4. A brilliant analysis of Hoover as secretary of commerce is Ellis W. Hawley, "Herbert Hoover, the Commerce Secretariat, and the Vision of an Associative State, 1921–1928," *Journal of American History* 61 (June 1974): 116–40; and Ellis W. Hawley, *The Great War and the Search for a Modern Order* (New York: St. Martin's Press, 1979), especially pp. 100–117.

5. Frederick Simpich, "The Great Mississippi Flood of 1927," *National Geographic* 52 (September 1927): 243–89; Bruce Alan Lohof, "Hoover and the Mississippi Flood of 1927: A Case Study of the Political Thought of Herbert Hoover" (Ph.D. dissertation, Syracuse University, 1968); Wilson, *Hoover*, pp. 114–16; Pete Daniel, *Deep'n As It Come: The 1927 Mississippi River Flood* (New York: Oxford University Press, 1976); and Pete Daniel, *The Shadow of Slavery: Peonage in the South, 1901–1969* (Urbana: University of Illinois Press, 1972), pp. 150–54.

6. Hoover, *Memoirs*, 2:123–31; Wilson, *Hoover*, pp. 114–16; Daniel, *Deep'n As It Come*, p. 11.

7. Hoover, *Memoirs*, 2:126, 130.

8. Quoted in Wilson, *Hoover*, p. 115. A fascinating analysis of Hoover's devotion to voluntarism is Robert D. Cuff, "Herbert Hoover, the Ideology of Voluntarism, and War Organization during the Great War," *Journal of American History* 64 (September 1977): 358–72; David E. Hamilton, "Herbert Hoover and the Great Drought of 1930," *Journal of American History* 68 (March 1982): 850–75.

9. Arkansas *Gazette*, 27 June 1927. Also see Public Statements, 27 June 1927, HHPL.

10. Claude A. Barnett to HH, 4 May 1927, MVFR File.

11. Chicago *Defender*, 7 May 1927.

12. Arthur Capper to HH, 10 May 1927, MVFR File.

13. Harold M. Kingsley to John M. Parker, 2 May 1927; Assistant Secretary to Kingsley, 6 May 1927, MFC File.

14. James Weldon Johnson to Robert R. Church and George W. Lucas, 10 May 1927, MFC File; Robert R. Moton to Church, 6 June 1927, RRC Papers.

15. Walter White to Kingsley, 12 May 1927, MFC File.

16. White to Johnson, memorandum, 24 May 1927; and "The Negro and the Flood," 12 pp.; White to Church, 14 May 1927, MFC File. White and Church would later become estranged (see Church to White, 6 February 1932; White to Editor, Chicago *Defender*, 2 February 1932, Walter White Papers, Yale University).

17. HH to Capper, 13 May 1927; Capper to HH, 14 May 1927; Lawrence Richey to Akerson, 12 May 1927, MVFR File. Criticism from other white sources also angered Hoover (see Rickard diary, 31 May 1927, ER Papers).

18. Margaret Butler to James L. Fieser, 14 May 1927; J. W. Richardson to Fieser, 18 May 1927; Henry W. Baker to Fieser, 14 May 1927, MVFR File.

19. HH to Baker, 13 May 1927, ibid. Hoover ordered Baker to send the telegrams to all Red Cross representatives.

20. Minutes of meeting, Hoover and Fieser, 6 June 1927; memorandum, 13 June 1927, General Plans and Policies Folder; Memorandum on principles of organization and published version, Herbert Hoover and James L. Fieser, *The Principles of Organization and Procedure for Relief and Reconstruction in the Mississippi Valley Flood Relief, Memoranda of May 12, 19, and 25, 1927* (New Orleans: American Red Cross, 1927), ARC.

21. Moton to Robert E. Bondy, 18 June 1927; Bondy to Walter Wesselius, 20 June 1927, ARC. Bondy was the Red Cross assistant director for flood relief.

22. Moton to HH, 26 May 1928; HH to Moton, 28 May 1928, MVFR File; Daniel, *Shadow of Slavery*, pp. 132, 148–49; Lohof, "Hoover and the Mississippi Flood," pp. 154–58; "Negroes Held in Peonage in Mississippi Flood Area," press release, 27 May 1927, MFC File.

23. For extensive analyses of the growing split within the Negro leadership see August Meier, *Negro Thought in America, 1800–1915: Racial Ideologies in the Age of Booker T. Washington* (Ann Arbor: University of Michigan Press, 1963), pp. 161–206; Charles Flint Kellogg, *NAACP: A History of the National Association for the Advancement of Colored People* (Baltimore: The Johns Hopkins Press, 1967), pp. 40–88; Francis L. Broderick, *W. E. B. Du Bois, A Negro Leader in a Time of Crisis* (Stanford: Stanford University Press, 1959), pp. 55–122; John Hope Franklin, *From Slavery to Freedom: A History of American Negroes* (New York: Alfred A. Knopf, 1967), pp. 444–51, 486–88 and passim; Elliot M. Rudwick, *W. E. B. Du Bois: A Study in Minority Group Leadership* (Philadelphia: University of Pennsylvania Press, 1960), pp. 63–71, 150–51.

24. Kellogg, *NAACP*, p. 87; Broderick, *Du Bois*, pp. 119–20 and n. 76; Meier, *Negro Thought*, p. 184.

25. Jervis Anderson, *A. Philip Randolph: A Biographical Portrait* (New York: Harcourt Brace Jovanovich, 1972), pp. 98–99. Randolph categorized Moton as among those "Old Crowd Negroes" or "hand-picked, me-too-boss, hat-in-hand, sycophant, lick-spittling Negroes" (pp. 98–99). See also Langston Hughes, *Fight For Freedom: The Story of the NAACP* (New York: W. W. Norton and Co., 1962), p. 79. Hughes characterized Moton as "conservative," p. 79.

26. Robert R. Moton, *What the Negro Thinks* (New York: Garden City Publishing Co., 1929), pp. 238–39, 13, 99, 55, 69–70, 93–94. See also Walter White, *How Far the Promised Land?* (New York: Viking Press, 1955), p. 164.

27. Kellogg, *NAACP*, pp. 142, 234; Rudwick, *Du Bois*, p. 187; Broderick, *Du Bois*, p. 110.

28. Broderick, *Du Bois*, p. 175.

29. For more information on Moton see William H. Hughes and Frederick D. Patterson, eds., *Robert Russa Moton of Hampton and Tuskegee* (Chapel Hill: University of North Carolina Press,

1956); Robert Russa Moton, *Finding a Way Out: An Autobiography* (New York: Doubleday, Page and Co., 1920). See also August Meier, "Booker T. Washington and the Rise of the NAACP," *Crisis* 61 (February 1954): 118–22.

30. E. Franklin Frazier, "The American Negro's New Leaders," *Current History* 28 (April 1928): 56–59; Meier, *Negro Thought*, pp. 256–76.

31. Meier, *Negro Thought*, pp. 256–76; Daniel, *Shadow of Slavery*, p. 164; Pete Daniel, "Black Power in the 1920's: The Case of Tuskegee Veteran's Hospital," *Journal of Southern History* 36 (August 1970): 368–88; Broderick, *Du Bois*, p. 163.

32. Meier, *Negro Thought*, p. 124; Franklin, *From Slavery to Freedom*, p. 449; Nancy J. Weiss, *The National Urban League, 1910–1940* (New York: Oxford University Press, 1974), pp. 248–49; David Gordon Nielson, *Black Ethos: Northern Urban Negro Life and Thought, 1890–1930* (Westport, Conn.: Greenwood Press, 1977), pp. 70, 141, 91, 99.

33. Moton, *What the Negro Thinks*, pp. 257, 260, 265–66. See also Henry Lee Moon, *Balance of Power: The Negro Vote* (Garden City, N.Y.: Doubleday and Co., 1948), pp. 104–5.

34. Rudwick, *Du Bois*, pp. 65, 71.

35. W. E. B. Du Bois, "Peonage," *Crisis* (September 1927): 311. See also Richard B. Sherman, *The Republican Party and Black America: From McKinley to Hoover, 1896–1933* (Charlottesville: University Press of Virginia, 1973), p. 227.

36. See n. 27.

37. Rudwick, *Du Bois*, pp. 306, 22–23, 152, 165, 261.

38. Hughes, *Fight for Freedom*, p. 79. Moton selected Claude A. Barnett; Eva D. Bowles; Dr. Roscoe C. Brown, assistant secretary of the National Medical Association; Thomas M. Campbell, U. S. Department of Agriculture; Dr. J. S. Clark, president of Southern University; Albon L. Holsey; Mrs. John Hope, director of the Atlanta Neighborhood Union; Bishop Robert E. Jones; Eugene K. Jones; Dr. J. B. Martin, regional director, National Negro Business League; Dr. L. M. McCoy, president of Rust College; Dr. S. D. Redmond, Mississippi physician and Republican party official; Bert M. Roody, vice-president of the National Negro Business League; Robert R. Taylor, vice-principal of Tuskegee Institute; Jesse O. Thomas, southern secretary for the National Urban League; Mary E. Williams, American Red Cross, Tuskegee, Alabama. See HH to White, 21 June 1927; and "Final Report of the Colored Advisory Commission," MVFR File.

39. Richey to Akerson, telegram, 9 June 1927, MVFR File.

40. HH to Irwin, 10 June 1927, MVFR File.

41. Secretary of Labor John J. Davis to HH, 10 June 1927; press release for week of 6 June 1927, "Daily Worker Propagandists," MVFR File.

42. Irwin to White, 11 June 1927, MFC File.

43. Ibid., 16 June 1927.

44. White to HH, 14 June 1927; HH to White, 21 June 1927, MVFR File.

45. Walter White, "The Negro and the Flood," *Nation* 124 (24 June 1927): 688–89; White to Ida Roberts, 3 June 1927, NAACP Papers.

46. White to Helen Boardman, 10 June 1928, MFC File; Walter White, *A Man Called White* (New York: Viking Press, 1948), pp. 80–81.

47. White to HH, 14 June 1927; HH to White, 21 June 1927, MVFR File.

48. Compare White's article in *Nation* and 14 June letter to HH with Moton to HH, 13 June 1927, HH to Fieser, 20 June 1927, HH to Moton, 17 June 1927, MVFR File; Barnett report, "Conditions As We Observed Them," Barnett to Hoover, 14 June 1927, CAB Papers. In 1922 Perry Howard, the black Republican national committeeman from Mississippi, accused the NAACP of being the "Negro Democratic Organization" (see Eugene Levy, *James Weldon Johnson* [Chicago and London: The University of Chicago Press, 1973], p. 263).

49. The most complete and candid account is Claude Barnett's report "Conditions As We Observed Them," Barnett to HH, 14 June 1927; and his numerous reports on specific locations and drafts of reports to HH in 1927 Flood File, CAB Papers. Moton was less critical in presenting

the commission's recommendations. See Moton to HH, 13 June 1927, and Associated Negro press release, "Hoover Meets Colored Advisory Flood Commission," 14 June 1927, MVFR File.

50. HH to Moton, 17 June 1927, MVFR File; Rickard diary, 10 July 1927, ER Papers.

51. Quoted in Sherman, *Republican Party and Black America*, p. 228. HH and Fieser to T. J. McCarty, 8 July 1927; HH to E. T. Clark, 15 June 1927; McCarty to HH and Fieser, 14 July 1927, MVFR File.

52. See, for example, drafts and final letter, HH to Ida B. Wells, 17 June 1927, MVFR File. Hoover deleted "that the people in the camps are in a state of servitude or refused access to relief is absolutely untrue" and instead emphasized the implementation of the Moton commission's recommendations.

53. HH to Eugene P. Booze, 11 July 1927; HH and Fieser to McCarty, 8 July 1927, MVFR File; Moton, *What the Negro Thinks*, pp. 257, 260, 265–66; "Memorandum of Conference, 8 July 1927," MVFR File.

54. HH to R. E. Malone, 5 July 1928, MVFR File.

55. Barnett to HH, 10, 14 June 1927, MVFR File.

56. Baltimore *Afro-American*, 18 June 1927; New York *Age*, 25 June 1927; and Pittsburgh *Courier*, 4 June 1927; Barnett to HH, 14, 16 June 1927 and newspaper clippings and press releases, CAB Papers.

57. Arkansas *Gazette*, 27 June 1927; "Public Statements," 755A, HHPL.

58. One of Hoover's secretaries drafted the president's remarks for public release, but Hoover refused to reveal his innermost thoughts. See draft of release, "Public Statements," 6 February 1931, HHPL.

59. HH to William Townsend, 7 July 1927; Walter Wesselius to Bondy, 29 June 1927; Booze to HH, 6, 9 July 1927; HH to Booze, 11 July 1927; HH to Shaeffer, 11 July 1927, MVFR File. Also see Booze to Newton, 9 February 1933; Booze to Director, Reconstruction Finance Corporation, 19 January 1933; Newton, file memo, 30 January 1933, Reconstruction Finance Corporation, HHPL. Hoover later attempted to help Booze to gain eligibility for a federal loan.

60. See Bruce A. Lohof, "Herbert Hoover's Mississippi Valley Land Reform Memorandum: A Document," *Arkansas Historical Quarterly* 24 (Summer 1970): 112; Daniel, *Shadow of Slavery*, p. 163. See also Bruce A. Lohof, "Herbert Hoover, Spokesman for Human Efficiency: The Mississippi Flood of 1927," *American Quarterly* 22 (Fall 1970): 697; and George F. Garcia, "Herbert Hoover and the Issue of Race," *The Annals of Iowa* 44 (Winter 1979): 507–15.

61. Jones to Moton, 29 June 1927, RRM Papers.

62. Daniel is highly critical of Moton for not insisting upon the release of the report (*Shadow of Slavery*, pp. 165–66, 150; and Daniel, *Deep'n As It Come*, pp. 139–40).

63. White to HH, 14 June 1927, MFC File; HH to White, 22 June 1927, MVFR File. (Copies of both letters are in MVFR File.)

64. White to Fieser, 12 July 1927; Fieser to HH, 15 July 1927, MVFR File. Fieser refused to respond to White's letter.

65. Wilson Record, *Race and Radicalism: The NAACP and the Communist Party in Conflict* (Ithaca: Cornell University Press, 1964), pp. 44–45, 31–32, 50–51; Franklin, *Slavery to Freedom*, p. 416; Rudwick, *Du Bois*, pp. 112–13, 266, 268–69; Francis L. Broderick and August Meier, eds., *Negro Protest and Thought in the Twentieth Century* (New York: Bobbs-Merrill Co.), pp. 67–107; I. A. Newby, *Jim Crow's Defense: Anti-Negro Thought in America* (Baton Rouge: Louisiana State University Press, 1965), p. 140.

66. HH to Couch, 8 July 1927; HH to Crosby, 8 July 1927, MVFR File.

67. HH to Couch, 12 July 1927; HH to Crosby, 12 July 1927, ibid.

68. Fieser to HH, 27 August 1927, ibid.

69. Redmond to HH, 5 January 1928, ibid.; Redmond to HH, 10 June 1927, copy in CAB Papers; Daniel, *Shadow of Slavery*, p. 158. Redmond was later unofficially dropped from the committee.

70. Crosby to HH, 15 July, 29 July, 22 October 1927; Redmond to HH, 5 January 1928, MVFR File. Crosby later agreed to a black representative.

71. Fieser to HH, 27 August 1927, MVFR File.

72. Ibid.

73. Moton to HH, 6 September 1927; HH to W. M. Kennedy, 14 July 1927; Sen. Charles S. Deneen to HH, 11 July 1928; Ella R. Hutson to Fieser, 15 August 1927, MVFR File. On the immediate need for black rehabilitation agents and funds for extension service experts to help rural black sufferers, see Holsey to Moton, 19 July 1927, RRM Papers.

74. HH to Moton, 7 September 1927; HH to Moton, 29 September 1927, MVFR File.

75. Moton to HH and confidential report, 1 October 1927; HH to Fieser, 6 October 1927; De Witt Smith to HH, 13 October 1927; HH to Moton, 17 October 1927, MVFR File. See also Moton to Fieser, 1 October 1927, ARC, NA.

76. HH to Moton, 17 October 1927; HH to De Witt Smith, 3 November 1927; Smith to HH, 7 November 1927, MVFR File. Smith was the assistant national director. See also Chicago *Defender*, 15 October 1927; E. B. Redman to Douglas Griesemer, 25 October 1927, ARC.

77. See Moton commission, *The Final Report of the Moton Commission, Mississippi Valley Flood Disaster, 1927* (Washington, D.C.: American Red Cross, October, 1929), pp. 1–29, but especially pp. 20–25. This is the official censored report. Copies in HHPL and ARC. The best sources are Moton to HH, 16 December 1927 with unpublished, uncensored flood report, MVFR File; and Barnett to J. S. Clark, 19 December 1927, RRM Papers. For the official Red Cross report on the entire flood operation, see *The Mississippi Valley Flood Disaster: Official Report of the Relief Operations* (Washington, D.C.: American Red Cross, 1929), pp. 1–152.

78. Barnett to Clark, 19 December 1927, CAB Papers; Moton to Bishop Jones, 16 December 1927, RRM Papers.

79. Fieser to Smith, 19 December 1927, ARC. Also quoted in Daniel, *Deep'n As It Come*, pp. 140–41. See also Burner, *Hoover*, p. 195.

80. John D. Cremer, Jr., to Smith, 23 October 1928, ARC. Cremer was the Red Cross associate director of the disaster relief. There is no evidence to indicate that Hoover knew about or approved of the Red Cross action, yet the thrust of his comments suggests that he would have supported the revision. See also Barnett to Fieser, 20 June 1928, CAB Papers.

81. HH to Fieser, 14 December 1927; HH to Moton, draft letter, 16 December 1927; HH to Moton, 22 December 1927, MVFR File. More black advisers were appointed (see Wesselius to Bondy, 10 January 1928, ARC).

82. Crosby to Committee Chairman, 30 November 1927, ARC. Crosby's chief of staff was Lamont Rowlands, one of the men Hoover respected in Mississippi.

83. W.E.B.D. [W. E. B. Du Bois], memorandum to Mr. Johnson on Miss Boardman's report, 14 November 1927, MFC File. See also "Postscript," *Crisis* (November 1927): 311. Helen Boardman conducted the study. It was not leaked to the NAACP by a member of the Moton commission, as Fieser suspected. See also [Helen Boardman] "The Flood, the Red Cross and the National Guard," *Crisis* (January 1928): 5–7; *Crisis* (February 1928): 41–43; and *Crisis* (March 1928): 80–81.

84. Moton, press release, "To the Negroes of America," 17 November 1927, ARC; HH to Moton, 16 December 1927, MVFR File; HH to Moton, 18 January 1928, RRM Papers; HH to Barnett, 10 January 1928, Barnett File, Commerce, HHPL. See also Daniel, *Deep'n As It Come*, p. 87 and Daniel, *Shadow of Slavery*, p. 167; Lohof, "Hoover, Spokesman for Human Efficiency," p. 697; Burner, *Hoover*, pp. 193–94; Hawley, *Great War*, p. 174. Daniel is nonetheless highly critical of both Hoover and Moton for not revealing the ravages of peonage to the American public. His view is well taken. The same criticism is made by Sherman, *Republican Party and Black America*, p. 228. Additional correspondence and documents on the flood are in MVF, Hoover Papers, Hoover Institution, Stanford University. Hoover's praise of the Red Cross as "that

great moral and spiritual force" is in "Testimonial at Little Rock, A Symposium on Hoover's Work as Secretary of Commerce," unpublished commentaries, MVF, Hoover Papers, Hoover Institution, Stanford University, Palo Alto, Calif.

85. Moton to HH, 31 December 1927; Moton to HH, 4 January 1928, MVFR File; Albon L. Holsey, "Hoover Discovers South," Pittsburgh *Courier*, 21 January 1928. See also numerous press releases by Claude A. Barnett praising Hoover in both MVFR File, HHPL and CAB Papers.

86. Many black leaders were bitter toward Hoover. See Sherman, *Republican Party and Black America*, p. 229; and Record, *Race and Radicalism*, p. 50.

87. See the extensive correspondence in Commerce Papers, "Plan to Make Farm Land Available," Survey of Land Situation File, and Moton File, HHPL, but especially HH to Moton, 9 January 1928; HH to William J. Schiefflelin, 12 January, 8 February 1928; Edwin R. Embree to HH, 1 March 1928; and HH to Moton, 3 March 1928, HHPL. See also Hoover File, RRM Papers. A well-researched master's thesis that also deals in part with the flood is George F. Garcia, "Herbert Hoover's Southern Strategy and the Black Reaction," (University of Iowa, 1972). On p. 48 Garcia points out that Will Alexander, one of Moton's close friends, was instrumental in convincing the New Deal to inaugurate the farm program. For a summary of his views on Hoover, see Garcia, "Hoover and the Issue of Race," pp. 507–15. See also Garcia, "Black Disaffection from the Republican Party during the Presidency of Herbert Hoover, 1928–1932," *The Annals of Iowa* 45 (Fall 1980): 462–77. Another assessment of the 1927 flood and of Hoover's racial views is in Burner, *Hoover*, pp. 194–97. One should see also a paper by Larry H. Grothaus, "The Hoover Administration and Blacks," August 1979, HHPL.

88. Turner Catledge, oral history, p. 3, HHPL. Catledge was a top newspaper reporter who was later hired by the *New York Times* and assigned to its Washington bureau. He recalled that Hoover refused to take political advantages during the flood situation.

2. Racial Education

1. W. E. B. Du Bois, "Postscript," *Crisis* 35 (May 1928): 168.

2. Johnson to Sidney B. Thompson, 13 March 1928, Politics File, NAACP.

3. Moton to HH, 4 January 1928, Commerce, HHPL; Moton to C. C. Goines, 1 October 1928, RRM Papers.

4. Pittsburgh *Courier*, 21 January 1928, copy in GA Papers.

5. For examples of enthusiastic support see James H. Howard, "An Estimate of Herbert Hoover," Associated Negro press release in GA Papers; "Hoover Revealed as Square Shooter," *America's New Magazine* (10 March 1928): 12–13, Reprint File, HHPL.

6. Among the best of the scholarly accounts are I. A. Newby, *Jim Crow's Defense: Anti-Negro Thought in America 1900–1930* (Baton Rouge: Louisiana State University Press, 1965); and his essay "Segregationist Thought Since 1890," in *The Development of Segregationist Thought*, ed. I. A. Newby (Homewood, Ill.: Dorsey Press, 1968); C. Vann Woodward, *The Strange Career of Jim Crow*, 2d ed. rev. (New York: Oxford University Press, 1966), and *The Origins of the New South, 1877–1913* (Baton Rouge: Louisiana State University Press, 1951); David W. Southern, *The Malignant Heritage: Yankee Progressives and the Negro Question 1901–1914* (Chicago: Loyola University Press, 1968); John W. Cell, *The Highest Stage of White Supremacy: The Origins of Segregation in South Africa and the American South* (Cambridge: Cambridge University Press, 1982); Wilson Jeremiah Moses, *The Golden Age of Black Nationalism, 1850–1925* (Hamden, Conn.: The Shoe String Press, 1978); August Meier, *Negro Thought in America, 1900–1915: Racial Ideologies in the Age of Booker T. Washington* (Ann Arbor: University of Michigan Press, 1963); Thomas F. Gossett, *Race: The History of an Idea in America* (Dallas: Southern Methodist University Press, 1963); Milton M. Gordon, *Assimilation in American Life: The Role of Race,*

Religion, and National Origins (New York: Oxford University Press, 1964); S. P. Fullinwider, *The Mind and Mood of Black America: Twentieth-Century Thought* (Homewood, Ill.: Dorsey Press, 1969); and the scholars cited in nn. 7 and 8.

7. The best examinations of racism in the 1920s are Thomas Gossett, *Race*, pp. 370–409; June Sochen, *The Unbridgeable Gap: Blacks and Their Quest for the American Dream, 1900–1930* (Chicago: Rand McNally, 1972), pp. 27–63, and passim; and Fullinwider, *Black America*, pp. 47–171 and passim.

8. I am indebted to a number of scholars for their reflections on the nature of racism. On 9 April 1976 at the Organization of American Historians convention in Saint Louis, Missouri, James M. McPherson, Robert B. Toplin, and George M. Fredrickson exchanged ideas in a stimulating session, "Racism in Concept and Theory." These scholars explored racism as an ideology, an attitude, and as a cultural way of thinking that may be indeterminate as well as determinative. Although differing in their concepts of racism, they agreed that the term *racism* has been used almost indiscriminately by scholars and nonscholars alike. Pierre L. van den Berghe, in *Race and Racism: A Comparative Perspective* (New York: John Wiley and Sons, 1967), agrees with McPherson, Toplin, and Fredrickson that no one definition is satisfactory. He stresses a comparative and "holistic approach" that evaluates "the total institutional and cultural context of the society" (see especially pp. 6–7 and 148–49). In the introduction to the second edition (1978) of his important study van den Berghe provides an excellent summary of the many changes in definition and emphasis that have become current since the late 1960s. He succinctly divides scholars into major schools of thought and offers an evaluation of the impact of sociological thinking upon our understanding of racism. A definition that is similar to the one offered in this study and that reflects several of the concepts examined during the previously mentioned session, "Racism in Concept and Theory," is in George M. Fredrickson, *White Supremacy: A Comparative Study in American and South African History* (New York: Oxford University Press, 1981), pp. xi–xiii. In his earlier study, *The Black Image in the White Mind: The Debate on Afro-American Character and Destiny, 1817–1914* (New York: Harper and Row, 1971), Fredrickson focuses attention on the "interplay of basic racial conceptions with social or political ideologies" (p. xii). Also, see his article "Toward a Social Interpretation of the Development of American Racism" in Nathan I. Huggins, et al., *Key Issues in the Afro-American Experience*, 2 vols. (New York: Harcourt, Brace, Jovanovich, 1971), 1:240–45. Two studies that make important distinctions among different degrees of racism and racists are Newby, *Jim Crow's Defense* and Fredrickson, *Black Image in the White Mind*. One must also consult Cell, *The Highest Stage of White Supremacy*, pp. 3–4, 14, 18–19, 174–76, 191.

9. Newby, *Jim Crow's Defense*, pp. 19–109; Gossett, *Race*, pp. 144–309, 339–69; Fredrickson, *Black Image in the White Mind*, pp. 198–319; Woodward, *Strange Career of Jim Crow*, pp. 60–118; John Hope Franklin, *From Slavery to Freedom: A History of Negro Americans*, 3d ed. (New York: Alfred A. Knopf, 1967), pp. 433–98; Robert L. Zangrando, *The NAACP Crusade against Lynching, 1909–1950* (Philadelphia: Temple University Press, 1980), pp. 22–97; David W. Southern, *The Malignant Heritage: Yankee Progressives and the Negro Question, 1901–1914* (Chicago: Loyola University Press, 1968), pp. 4–5, 33, 43, 47, 53–54, 68–69, 72, 83; George E. Mowry, "The South and the Progressive Lily White Party of 1912," *Journal of Southern History* 6 (February 1940): 237–47; and Jack Temple Kirby, *Darkness at the Dawning: Race and Reform in the Progressive South* (Philadelphia: Lippincott, 1972), pp. 1–5, passim.

10. HH to Mark Requa, 21 April 1924, Requa File, Commerce, HHPL. Herbert Hoover, *Principles of Mining* (London: Hill Publishing Company, 1909), pp. 163–64; Herbert Hoover, *The Memoirs of Herbert Hoover*, 3 vols. (New York: Macmillan Co., 1951–52), 1:70; "Discussion of Papers: 'Stabilization of the Bituminous Coal Industry,'" *Mining and Metallurgy* (March 1920): 3–4; Sacramento *Union*, 19 August 1920. His remarks in the "Discussion of Papers" and the *Union* are in the HHPL.

11. For another account of Hoover's racial views see George F. Garcia, "Herbert Hoover's

Southern Strategy and the Black Reaction" (M.A. thesis, University of Iowa, 1972), pp. 39–43; and "Herbert Hoover and the Issue of Race," *The Annals of Iowa* 44 (Winter 1979): 507–15. See also Richard B. Sherman, *The Republican Party and Black America: From McKinley to Hoover, 1896–1933* (Charlottesville: University Press of Virginia, 1973), p. 225. Although I differ with some aspects of Garcia's and Sherman's interpretations of Hoover's racial views, I have found little to add to the specific racial references first cited by them.

12. Herbert Hoover, *Memoirs*, 2:44–46.

13. A. L. Jackson to HH, 2 September 1921, Commerce, Unemployment, HHPL.

14. Eugene K. Jones to Edward E. Hunt, 31 August and 10 September 1921; Emmett J. Scott to HH, 19 September 1921, Commerce, Unemployment, HHPL.

15. Hunt to Jones, 3 September 1921; Blaine to Hunt, 19 September 1921; Hunt to Blaine, 21, 29 September 1921, Commerce, Unemployment, HHPL.

16. For the quotation by Harding and his policies toward blacks, see Robert K. Murray, *The Harding Era: Warren G. Harding and His Administration* (Minneapolis: University of Minnesota Press, 1969), pp. 397–403. For a more critical assessment of Harding see Sherman, *Republican Party and Black America*.

17. Baker to HH, 5 November 1925, Commerce, Barnett File, HHPL.

18. For background on Barnett see Summary in CAB Papers; Richard L. Beard and Cyril E. Zoerner, "Associated Negro Press: Its Founding, Ascendency, and Demise," *Journalism Quarterly* 46 (Spring 1969): 47–52; *New York Times*, 3 August 1967.

19. Claude A. Barnett, "Autobiography," pp. 16–18, CAB Papers. On the National Negro Business League see Wilson Jeremiah Moses, *The Golden Age of Black Nationalism*, p. 218.

20. Barnett, "Autobiography," p. 18.

21. Moton to HH, 10 January 1925; HH to Moton, 23 January 1925; Akerson to Moton, 21 September 1926, Commerce, Moton File, HHPL. Also seee HH to Moton, 10 August 1926, Negroes, Hoover Papers, Hoover Institution, Stanford University, Palo Alto, Calif.

22. James J. Davis to HH, 11 February 1925, Commerce, Negroes, HHPL.

23. HH to H. O. Stickney, 9 June and 5 August 1926; W. L. Sledge to HH, 7 July 1926; HH to Sen. Woodbridge W. Ferris, 10 June 1926, Commerce, Sesquecentennial Exposition File, HHPL; Harold Keats to HH, 4 August 1926, Commerce, Colored, HHPL.

24. Memorandum, n.d., Hoover File, RRM Papers; HH to Gentlemen, 20 March 1925, message for meeting at Carnegie Hall, March 23, 1925, in campaign for Hampton-Tuskegee endowment fund, Hampton-Tuskegee Endowment Fund, Commerce, HHPL. For a fascinating study of the positive effect of educational environment upon significant increases in measured I.Q. among blacks, see Lowry C. Fredrickson, "Measured Intelligence: Species Specific? Perhaps; Race Specific? Perhaps Not," *Journal of Genetic Psychology* 130 (1977): 95–104.

25. HH, commencement address, University of Alabama, 24 May 1926, Major Speeches File, HHPL; Fredrickson, "Measured Intelligence," pp. 102–3.

26. HH to Alfred Williams Anthony, 19 April 1926, Alfred Williams Anthony Collection, New York Public Library, New York City, N.Y.

27. HH to M. Grant Lucas, 28 July 1931, Major Speeches File, HHPL; David Burner, *Herbert Hoover: A Public Life* (New York: Alfred A. Knopf, 1979), p. 216 and n. 10, chapter 13; Mordecai W. Johnson to Ray Lyman Wilbur, 7 June 1930; Julius Rosenwald to Wilbur, 26 December 1929, Howard University File, Wilbur Papers, Hoover Institution, Stanford University, Palo Alto, California. Johnson was president of Howard University. Federal appropriations for Howard originated with the secretary of the interior.

28. Nashville *Tennesseean*, 26 April 1930; HH to Augustus T. Murray, 23 April 1930, Augustus T. Murray Collection, HHPL.

29. See chapter 1, nn. 53 and 54 for sources of quotes in preceding paragraph.

30. HH to Will H. Hayes, 25 November 1927; C. C. Spaulding to HH, 25 November 1927, Commerce, Colored Industries File, HHPL.

31. J. Finley Wilson to HH, 1 February 1928; Akerson to Wilson, 1 March 1928; Finley to Akerson, 3 April 1928; Akerson to Finley, 9 April 1928, Commerce, Census, HHPL. See also press release, 14 March 1928, Commerce, Negroes, HHPL.

32. Memorandum to Dr. Hill, 13 March 1928; B. D. Nash, memorandum to the secretary, 13 March 1928; HH to Thomas, 16 March 1928; memorandum, 31 March 1928; Thomas to HH, 6 April 1928, Commerce, Negroes, HHPL.

33. See, for example, Washington (D.C.) *Eagle*, 6 April 1928; Washington (D.C.) *Sentinel*, 21 April 1928; Houston *Informer*, 14 April 1928; Los Angeles *New Age Dispatch*, 14 April 1928; and Johnson to HH, 20 April 1928, Misrepresentations File, Commerce, Campaign 1928, HHPL.

34. Lewis A. Pick to Akerson, 15 November 1927, GA Papers. (Pick quoted from Caraway's speech.)

35. *New York Times*, 20 May 1928. See also Sen. Hubert D. Stephens to HH, 2 April 1928 and correspondence in Misrepresentations File, HHPL. See also *New York Times*, 11, 12 April; 4, 5, 20, 22 May 1928.

36. *Congressional Record*, 70th Cong. 1st sess., 1928, pp. 6739–41; Washington (D.C.) *Post*, 31 March 1928.

37. Washington (D.C.) *Sentinel*, 21 April 1928. The editors believed that Hoover had acted out of conviction rather than political expediency. However, during the 1928 presidential campaign Hoover assured one southern supporter that the "colored situation" in the Department of Commerce was the same as it had been during the administration of Woodrow Wilson. This was a disingenuous attempt to win southern votes and a misrepresentation of his original intent. See L. M. Osborne to HH, 28 August 1928 and HH to Osborne, 31 August 1928, C & T, HHPL. At least one scholar has used evidence such as this to argue that Hoover was a racist trying to reorganize "southern Republicanism under the leadership of white racists" (see Allan J. Lichtman, *Prejudice and the Old Politics: The Presidential Election of 1928* [Chapel Hill: University of North Carolina Press, 1979], pp. 154, 151 and 144–59). Because many of Lichtman's conclusions about Hoover's southern campaign are based on inadequate research, they are both exaggerated and inaccurate.

38. John D. English, "Herbert Hoover's Americanism in Retrospect: A Survey of the Years from Versailles to the New Deal," unpublished ms., HHPL. For Hoover's high praise of Jews, see HH to Max Abelman, 17 October 1928; Mordecai Israel, "Some Jews Who Helped 'Make' Hoover," *The Jewish Tribune* [1929?], in Hoover Papers, Box 13, Hoover Institution, Stanford University, Palo Alto, Calif.

39. See, for example, Larry H. Grothaus, "The Hoover Administration and Blacks," unpublished paper, 8 August 1979, p. 35, HHPL. A brief but excellent analysis of Booker T. Washington's social philosophy is August Meier, *Negro Thought in America, 1880–1915* (Ann Arbor: University of Michigan Press, 1963), pp. 103–18. The best lengthy account of Washington is Louis R. Harlan, *Booker T. Washington: The Making of a Black Leader, 1865–1901* (New York: Oxford University Press, 1972).

40. On Hoover's changing ideas see the commentary on "American Individualism," in *Herbert Hoover as Secretary of Commerce: Studies in New Era Thought and Practice*, ed. Ellis W. Hawley (Iowa City: University of Iowa Press, 1981), pp. 252–54. Hoover shares many but not all of the characteristics of what I. A. Newby calls the "reform group of racists" (see *Jim Crow's Defense*, pp. ix–x, 186–87). He also indirectly suggests that actions that were taken by Hoover were among the first signs of significant change. See especially his references to the De Priest tea on pp. 128 and 140 and to integration in federal employment on p. 161. Hoover also shared some ideas that were, in part at least, similar to what Fredrickson identifies as "accommodationist racism" (see Fredrickson, *Black Image in the White Mind*, pp. 292–319). Hoover's ideas on racial progress come closest to those which June Sochen argues were held by the major black leaders of the 1920s (see Sochen, *Unbridgeable Gap*, pp. 27–63, and especially pp. 55–59).

41. Hoover did not continue to combat segregation within the federal government. See also

August Meier and Elliot Rudwick, "The Rise of Segregation in the Federal Bureaucracy, 1900–1930," *Phylon* 28 (1967): 183.

3. Preconvention Infighting

1. Joan Hoff Wilson, *Herbert Hoover: Forgotten Progressive* (Boston: Little, Brown and Co., 1975), pp. 79–80, 118–21, 123–26. See also Gerald D. Nash's untitled essay in *Herbert Hoover and American Capitalism*, ed. J. Joseph Huthmacher and Warren I. Sussman (Cambridge, Mass.: Schenkman Publishing Co., 1973), pp. 102–11.

2. Wilson, *Hoover*, pp. 123, 117–18. For the best analysis of Hoover's promotional efforts see Craig Lloyd, *Aggressive Introvert: A Study of Herbert Hoover and Public Relations Management, 1912–1932* (Columbus: Ohio State University Press, 1972).

3. Edgar Rickard diary, 27 August, 19 September, 3, 15, 16 October 1927, ER Papers.

4. Donald R. McCoy, "To the White House: Herbert Hoover, August 1927–March 1929," in *The Hoover Presidency: A Re-appraisal*, ed. Martin L. Fausold and George T. Mazuzan (Albany: State University of New York Press, 1974), pp. 32–34. See also Kent Schofield, "The Public Image of Herbert Hoover in the 1928 Campaign," *Mid-America* 51 (1969): 284–85, 291.

5. Herbert Hoover, *The Memoirs of Herbert Hoover*, 3 vols. (New York: Macmillan Co., 1951–52), 2:191. Also see his testimony in U.S. Congress, Senate Special Committee Investigating Presidential Campaign Expenditures, *Hearings on Presidential Campaign Expenditures*, 70 Cong., 1st sess., 5 May 1928, pp. 45–48.

6. Rickard diary, 28 August 1927, ER Papers.

7. Special Committee Investigating Presidential Campaign Expenditures, *Hearings*, pp. 46–48, 112–20, 181, 237, 632–47.

8. Ibid., p. 54; Hoover, *Memoirs*, 2:191.

9. I am indebted for information on the statistical importance of the southern delegation to David J. Ginzl, "Herbert Hoover and Republican Patronage Politics in the South, 1928–1932," (Ph.D. dissertation, Syracuse University, 1977), pp. 14–15.

10. C. C. Couch to Akerson, 7 November 1927; and 8 September 1927 issue of *Manufacturer's Record*, GA Papers.

11. Paul Lewinson, *Race, Class, and Party: A History of Negro Suffrage and White Politics in the South* (New York: Russell and Russell, 1973), p. 167. See also Donald S. Strong, *Urban Republicanism in the South* (University, Ala.: University of Alabama Press, 1960), pp. 52–57.

12. Couch to Akerson, 7 November 1927, GA Papers.

13. Akerson to Col. William Henry Sullivan, 17 September 1927; Sullivan to Akerson, 26 September 1927; Akerson to Sullivan, 29 September 1927, ibid.

14. For background on Akerson see Newspaper Clipping File, ibid.

15. Lewinson, *Race, Class, and Party*, p. 171; Richard B. Sherman, *The Republican Party and Black America: From McKinley to Hoover, 1896–1933* (Charlottesville: University Press of Virginia, 1973), pp. 102, 47–49, 78; C. Vann Woodward, *Origins of the New South* (Baton Rouge: Louisiana State University Press, 1951), p. 467.

16. Rickard Diary, 31 December 1927, ER Papers.

17. Among the best sources on the relationship between Negroes and the Republican party after Reconstruction are C. Vann Woodward, *Origins of the New South, 1877–1913* (Baton Rouge: Louisiana State University Press, 1951); C. Vann Woodward, *The Strange Career of Jim Crow* (New York: Oxford University Press, 1955); Paul Lewinson, *Race, Class, and Party*; V.O. Key, *Southern Politics in State and Nation* (New York: Alfred A. Knopf, 1949); Vincent P. DeSantis, *Republicans Face the Southern Question* (Baltimore: The Johns Hopkins Press, 1959); and Sherman, *The Republican Party and Black America*.

18. Hanes Walton, Jr., *Black Republicans: The Politics of the Black and Tans* (Metuchen, N.J.:

Scarecrow Press, 1975), pp. 14–46, 137–41; Lewinson, *Race, Class, and Party*, pp. 127–70; Monroe Lee Billington, *The Political South in the Twentieth Century* (New York: Charles Scribner's Sons, 1957), pp. 51–55; Alexander Heard, *A Two Party South?* (Chapel Hill: The University of North Carolina Press, 1952), pp. 223–26.

19. Ralph J. Bunche, "The Political Status of the Negro," unpublished research paper, pp. 82–83, Schomberg Collection, New York Public Library; Monroe N. Work, ed., *Negro Year Book: An Annual Encyclopedia of the Negro 1931–1932* (Tuskegee Institute, Ala.: Negro Year Book Publishing Company, 1931), p. 97. Work cites an editorial opinion from the Baltimore *Herald-Commonwealth*. Also see references in nn. 20 and 21.

20. Scholars differ in their assessment of the origins and intentions of the lily-white movement. See Walton, *Black Republicans*, pp. 45–47, 39, 63–64, 138, 140; Heard, *Two Party South?* pp. 223–26; Lewinson, *Race, Class, and Party*, pp. 110–11, 129–31, 184; George F. Garcia, "Herbert Hoover's Southern Strategy and the Black Reaction" (M.A. thesis, University of Iowa, 1972), pp. 5, 12–13; Ginzl, "Hoover," pp. 17–19; Henry Lee Moon, *Balance of Power: The Negro Vote* (Garden City, N.Y.: Doubleday and Co., 1948), pp. 79–80, 108; John G. Van Duesen, *The Black Man in White America* (Washington, D.C.: Associated Publishers, 1938), p. 99; Paul D. Casdorph, *Republicans, Negroes, and Progressives in the South, 1912–1916* (University, Ala.: University of Alabama Press, 1981), pp. 11–12; Gunnar Myrdal, *An American Dilemma* (New York: Harper and Brothers, 1944), p. 478; V. O. Key, *Southern Politics in State and Nation* (New York: Alfred A. Knopf, 1949), pp. 289, 478–79. For an interesting identification of racist "reformers" whose thinking was similar to some lily-whites, see I. A. Newby, *Jim Crow's Defense: Anti-Negro Thought in America, 1900–1930* (Baton Rouge: Louisiana State University Press, 1965), pp. ix–x. Also see references in n. 21 and Kelly Miller to HH, 4 October 1928, C & T.

21. Sherman, *The Republican Party and Black America*, pp. 48, 154; Stanley P. Hirshson, *Farewell to the Bloody Shirt: Northern Republican and the Southern Negro, 1877–1893* (Bloomington: Indiana University Press, 1962), pp. 169–214; Vincent P. DeSantis, "Republican Efforts to 'Crack' the Democratic South," *Review of Politics* 14 (April 1952): 259–61, and *Republicans Face the Southern Question—The New Departure Years, 1877–1897* (Baltimore: The Johns Hopkins Press, 1959). See also the briefer account in George Brown Tindall, *The Disruption of the Solid South* (Athens, Ga.: University of Georgia Press, 1972), pp. 9–28. For the years 1912 to 1916 see the excellent analysis by Casdorph, *Republicans, Negroes, and Progressives*, pp. 1–16, 208–9, and passim.

22. Walton, *Black Republicans*, p. 159; Bunche, "Political Status of the Negro," p. 36; Heard, *Two Party South?* p. 224; "A New Deal for the Solid South," *Literary Digest* (17 September 1929): 14.

23. Work to Hayes, 16 August 1927, HW Papers.

24. Work to H. L. Rummel, 23 August 1927; Work to George Bean, 29 August 1927; Work to Joe Tolbert, 29 August 1927; Work to Emile Kuntz, 28 August 1927; Work to E. B. Clement, 29 August 1927, HW Papers.

25. Memorandum, 16 September 1927, HW Papers. Work thought only Tennessee and Kentucky would vote for Hoover.

26. See numerous letters in Secretary's Political File, 19 August 1927 to 31 December 1927, HW Papers.

27. Work to Brownlow Jackson, 17 December 1927, ibid.

28. Work to R. B. Creager, 5 October 1929; see also report of Dinner, at Willard Hotel, 24 March 1928, HW Papers.

29. Work to Street, 19 December 1927, 24 January 1928; see also letters emphasizing momentum in correspondence for March, April, May 1928, ibid.

30. Work to Kuntz, 17 December 1927; see also Work to C. E. Pitts, 26 October 1927; Work to G. L. Mallory, 17 December 1927, ibid.

31. Work to John G. White, 15 February 1928; Work to Robert E. Noble, 16 January 1928; Work to Walter E. Edge, 3 April 1928, ibid.; Special Committee Investigating Campaign Expenditures, *Hearings*, pp. 722, 297; *New York Times*, 30 May 1928.

32. Special Committee Investigating Campaign Expenditures, *Hearings*, pp. 52–53, 65, 120, 134, 258, 178, 180–81.

33. Work to White, 15 February 1928, HW Papers; Special Committee Investigating Campaign Expenditures, *Hearings*, pp. 632, 636–45; Sherman, *Black Republicans*, p. 154.

34. Couch to Mallory, 2 January 1928; Couch to Akerson, 21 September 1927, GA Papers.

35. Couch to HH, 26 September 1927; Akerson to Fletcher Chenault, 16 January 1928; Chenault to Akerson, 18 February 1928, GA Papers. Hoover was adamantly against any promise of patronage in return for delegate support. See also Rickard diary, 30 November, 31 December 1927, HHPL. Alan Fox, who led the Hoover forces in New York City, had insisted on patronage deals, but Hoover steadfastly refused. On justice to Negroes, see Chenault to Akerson, 18 January 1928 and also 20 March 1928, GA Papers.

36. Akerson to Chenault, 23 March 1928 and also undated memorandum, Political File, GA Papers.

37. See chap. 1, n. 53. See also Akerson to Holsey, 18 January 1928–27 March 1928, and 25 April 1928; Jones to Moton, 24 March 1928, GA Papers; see also Lewinson, *Race, Class, and Party*, p. 175.

38. Sherman, *The Republican Party and Black America*, pp. 153–54, 167.

39. Kuntz to Akerson, 2 February 1928, GA Papers.

40. Lewinson, *Race, Class, and Party*, p. 129; Sherman, *Republican Party and Black America*, pp. 9, 34, 47–48, 136, 153–54. Quotations in the preceding paragraph are in Willebrandt to her parents, 14 February 1928, Mabel Walker Willebrandt Papers, LC.

41. Kuntz to Akerson, 27 December 1927; Akerson to Kuntz, 8 February 1928, GA Papers; Work to Loisel, 1 February 1928, HW Papers.

42. Kuntz to Akerson, 18, 20 February 1928, GA Papers.

43. Loisel to Holland, 30 April 1928; Akerson to Loisel, 4 May 1928, ibid.

44. Special Committee Investigating Presidential Election Expenditures, *Hearings*, pp. 287–88, 295, 298–300; Work to Walter E. Edge, 3 April 1928; Work to C. E. Pitts, 26 October, 2 September 1927, HW Papers.

45. Ibid., p. 287.

46. Ibid., pp. 696–98; Work to Mr. Mellon, memorandum, January 1928; Work to Mellon, 26 January 1928, ibid. For quotations in this and in the preceding paragraph see Willebrandt to her parents, 14 February 1928, Mabel Walker Willebrandt Papers, LC.

47. Lewinson, *Race, Class, and Party*, pp. 129n., 144, 161–62.

48. Special Committee Investigating Presidential Campaign Expenditures, *Hearings*, pp. 698–718. Davis told the committee that if a draft-Coolidge effort had been made, he would have supported Coolidge over Hoover.

49. Hanes Walton, Jr., *Black Political Parties: An Historical and Political Analysis* (New York: Free Press, 1972), p. 68; Sherman, *Republican Party and Black America*, pp. 104–5, 150, 167, 204. See also Jervis Anderson, *A. Philip Randolph: A Biographical Portrait* (New York: Harcourt Brace Jovanovich, 1972), p. 172. Howard opposed Randolph's efforts to unionize black railroad porters. He referred to the union as "an agent of communism and its leaders as 'starving Bolshevists.'" Another critical appraisal appears in Ralph J. Bunche, *The Political Status of the Negro in the Age of FDR*, ed. Dewey W. Grantham (Chicago and London: University of Chicago Press, 1973), p. 81.

50. Samuel Taylor Moore, "Mississippi Auction Block—New Style," *Independent* (26 February 1927): 231–34. For the correspondence and documents relating to the changes, see PWH File. To avoid duplication specific references will be cited in the following notes.

51. There are numerous affidavits and exhibits concerning the 1921 case, but the most impor-

tant are Benjamin G. Diess and V. V. Sugg to Chief Post Office Inspector, 16 September 1921; Howard to Jesse F. Bulloch, 27 June 1921, PWH File.

52. Moore, "Mississippi Auction Block," p. 231.

53. A. M. Storer to William G. Butler, 5 June 1925, PWH File. He sent copies of the letter to President Coolidge and to Attorney General John G. Sargent.

54. Storer to Coolidge, 3 June 1925, ibid.

55. Holland to Storer, 13 February 1925, ibid.

56. E. T. Clark to Attorney General, 24 February 1925; Holland to Clark, 25 February 1925, ibid. Clark was acting secretary to President Coolidge.

57. Storer to Coolidge, 3 March 1925, ibid. See also numerous letters from Storer to Coolidge, Butler, William Howard Taft, and Harry New.

58. Howard to Attorney General, memorandum, 5 October 1925; L. E. Oldham to Howard, 11 October 1924, ibid. Oldham complained to Howard about Howard's decision not to recommend him for reappointment as United States attorney for the Northern District of Mississippi.

59. Howard to Attorney General, memorandum, 5 October 1925; Howard to William J. Donovan, 20, 25 May 1925; Howard to the Republicans of Mississippi, 16 September 1925, ibid.

60. Donovan to Attorney General, memorandum ("In the Matter of Charges against Perry W. Howard"), 14 July 1925, ibid.

61. Ridgeley to Attorney General, memorandum, 5 August 1925, ibid.

62. J. M. Marshall to Attorney General, memorandum, 4 August 1925, ibid.

63. Frederick Rush, "Republicans for Revenue Only," *Independent* (4 December 1926): 635, 638–39.

64. See Christian A. Herter file, Commerce, HHPL. See especially HH to Herter, 16 April 1925; HH to Herter, 12 August 1926; and HH to Herter, 8 November 1928.

65. Norris to Sargent, 19, 31 January 1927; Sargent to Norris, 5 February 1927; Norris to Sargent, 13 February 1927, PWH File. See also Norris to Hunt, 15 April 1927, GN Papers.

66. Hunt to Sargent, 6 May 1927, PWH File. By other investigations in the South, Hunt apparently had in mind the 1921 Post Office investigation of Howard and of Congressman Will J. Taylor of Tennessee.

67. Marshall to Hunt, 14 May 1927, PWH File.

68. Moore, "Mississippi Auction Block," p. 231.

69. Norris to Henry T. Hunt, 15 April 1927; Norris to Lowell Mellett, 8 August 1927, GN Papers. Norris explained to Mellett that a filibuster over an unrelated matter had made it impossible to get consideration of the resolution on southern Republican corruption before the full Senate.

70. Howard to Hoover, 1 August 1927, Commerce, HHPL.

71. Booze to Hubert Work, 16 January 1928; Booze to Akerson, 16 January 1928; Akerson to Booze, 19 January 1928, GA Papers.

72. L. O. Crosby to Akerson, 1, 9 February 1928; Akerson to Crosby, 4 February 1928; Crosby to Akerson, 6 February 1928; Akerson to Booze, 9 February 1928, ibid.

73. Akerson to Crosby, 13 February 1928, ibid.

74. Crosby to E. E. Hindman, 14 February 1928, ibid. Hindman was U.S. district attorney for southern Mississippi.

75. Crosby to Akerson, 21 February 1928, ibid.

76. Ibid., and Crosby to Akerson, 10 April 1928, ibid.

77. Special Committee Investigating Presidential Campaign Expenditures, *Hearings*, pp. 722–23. Howard testified that Brown told him that Crosby "was going to back us in Mississippi, and I went to Mr. Crosby" (pp. 722–23).

78. Ibid., p. 720.

79. Ibid., p. 733; Crosby to Akerson, 10 April 1928, GA Papers. Crosby enclosed a copy of the report in the Jackson (Miss.) *Daily News*, 2 April 1928, "Hoover May Lose Votes From State."

80. Ibid.

81. Lamont Rowlands to Akerson, 10, 16 May 1928; Special Committee Investigating Presidential Campaign Expenditures, *Hearings*, p. 733.

82. Crosby to Akerson, 10 April 1928; Akerson to Crosby, 16 April 1928, GA Papers.

83. Special Committee Investigating Presidential Campaign Expenditures, *Hearings*, pp. 721–22, 729–35. See also David J. Ginzl, "Lily-Whites Versus Black-and-Tans: Mississippi Republicans During the Hoover Administration," *Journal of Mississippi History* (August 1980), p. 196. Lack of sources limits the value of this article.

84. Rush Holland to Secretary Hoover, memorandum, 3 May 1928, GA Papers.

85. Rowlands to Akerson, 10 May 1928, ibid.; Special Committee Investigating Presidential Campaign Expenditures, *Hearings*, pp. 733–34.

4. The Nomination

1. Francis Russell, *The Shadow of Blooming Grove: Warren G. Harding and His Times* (New York: McGraw-Hill, 1968), p. xiv. See also Burl Noggle, *Tea Pot Dome: Oil and Politics in the 1920's* (New York: W. W. Norton, 1965), pp. 200, 205–6; and Robert K. Murray, *The Harding Era: Warren G. Harding and His Administration* (Minneapolis: University of Minnesota Press, 1969), pp. 472, 491–92.

2. *New York Times*, 1, 5, 10, 16, 29 April and 15, 17, 24, 28 June 1928; Herbert Hoover, *The Memoirs of Herbert Hoover*, 3 vols. (New York: Macmillan Co., 1951–52), 2:53–55, 206–7; Noggle, *Tea Pot Dome*, pp. 204–10.

3. Kent Schofield, "The Public Image of Herbert Hoover in the 1928 Campaign," *Mid-America* 51 (1969): 284-85, 291.

4. "Back Stage in Washington," *Independent* (24 March 1928): 279; New York *Evening Post*, 15 April 1928; Hoover, *Memoirs*, 2:192.

5. See Christian A. Herter File, GA Papers.

6. See chapter 3, nn. 42 and 55.

7. W. B. Bankhead to George Norris, 9 February 1928, Southern Patronage File, GN Papers.

8. Norris to A. F. Knotts, 28 December 1926, GN Papers.

9. See chapter 3, nn. 56, 57, and 58.

10. Norris to A. F. Knotts, 28 December 1926; Glenn B. Skipper to Norris, 18, 28 December 1926; Norris to Skipper, 19 December 1926; Norris to H. E. Balzhisen, 15 January 1927; O. B. Burtness to Norris, 11 January 1927, GN Papers.

11. J. R. Shanault to Norris, 23 December 1926, ibid.

12. Louis R. Lautier to Norris, 23 December 1926; Norris to Lautier, 28 December 1926; Norris to L. C. Coles, 29 December 1926, ibid.

13. Ibid.; W. E. B. Du Bois, *The Correspondence of W. E. B. Du Bois*, ed. Herbert Aptheker (Amherst: University of Massachusetts Press, 1973), 1:440–41.

14. Norris to L. C. Coles, 29 December 1926, GN Papers.

15. Norris to Henry T. Hunt, 15 April 1927, ibid.

16. Norris to Lowell Mellett, 8 August 1927, ibid.

17. U.S. Congress, Senate Special Committee Investigating Presidential Campaign Expenditures, *Hearings on Presidential Campaign Expenditures*, 70 Cong., 1st sess., 5 May 1928, pp. 45–46.

18. Ibid., pp. 112–13, 236–37, 181, 645, 292.

19. Ibid., pp. 49–65. From August 1925 until April 1926 Hoover made extensive efforts to sponsor Holland for membership in the Metropolitan Club. See the correspondence in Clubs,

Rush Holland File, Commerce Papers, HHPL. At that time Holland was assistant attorney general in charge of political appointments.

20. Special Committee Investigating Presidential Campaign Expenditures, *Hearings*, pp. 133–34.

21. Ibid., pp. 170, 258.

22. Ibid., pp. 636, 647–48.

23. Ibid., pp. 285–304.

24. Ibid., p. 296.

25. Ibid. Hoover's lieutenants were preparing a counterattack against the senators that would apparently allege that the senators were themselves guilty of excessive campaign expenditures. See correspondence and documents in Campaign 1928, Contribution and Finance, Senate Committee, LS Papers. Strauss was actively involved in raising campaign funds in the South.

26. Ibid., pp. 307–8.

27. E. H. Bradshaw to Akerson, 16 May 1928, GA Papers.

28. *New York Times*, 30 May 1928; Special Committee Investigating Presidential Campaign Expenditures, *Hearings*, pp. 711, 717–18.

29. Ibid., pp. 702–3.

30. Ibid., p. 718; *New York Times*, 30 May 1928.

31. *New York Times*, 30 May 1928.

32. Special Committee Investigating Presidential Campaign Expenditures, *Hearings*, pp. 702, 729.

33. Ibid., pp. 731–32.

34. Ibid., pp. 720–22, 733–34.

35. Ibid., p. 733; *New York Times*, 30 May 1928.

36. Ralph J. Bunche, "The Political Status of the Negro" (Schomberg Collection, New York Public Library; Carnegie-Myrdal Study of the Negro in America, 1940): 1210; W. E. B. Du Bois, "The Negro Politician," *Crisis* (May 1928): 168; James Weldon Johnson, "A Negro Looks At Politics," *American Mercury* 18 (September 1929): 88–93; Thomas L. Dabney, "Southern Negroes and Politics," *Opportunity: Journal of Negro Life* (September 1930): 273; Paul Lewinson, *Race, Class, and Party: A History of Negro Suffrage and White Politics in the South* (New York: Russell and Russell, 1963), pp. 88–94, 129–31; Alexander Heard, *A Two Party South?* (Chapel Hill: University of North Carolina Press, 1952), pp. 223–24.

37. Charles S. Johnson, *The Negro in American Civilization* (New York: Henry Holt and Co., 1930), p. 468.

38. Ernest T. Attwell to Akerson, 11 February 1928, GA Papers. For more information on Attwell see John Hope Franklin, *From Slavery to Freedom* (New York: Alfred A. Knopf, 1967), p. 471. See also Attwell to Edgar Rickard, 5 January 1928, GA Papers.

39. Elbert Lee Tatum, *The Changed Political Thought of the Negro* (New York: Exposition Press, 1951), p. 85; Grosvenor Clarkson to HH, 2 December 1927; Akerson to Clarkson, 5 December 1927, GA Papers.

40. Holsey to Akerson, 16 March 1928; Barnett to HH, 17 January 1928; Akerson to Barnett, 3 February 1928; Holsey to Akerson, 8 May 1928; Akerson to Holsey, 15 May 1928; "Annual Statement of the National Negro Press Association, April, 1928"; Holsey to Akerson, 16 April 1928, GA Papers.

41. James Weldon Johnson to HH, 20 April 1928, Misrepresentations File, 1928 Campaign, HHPL; *Congressional Record*, 70th Cong., 1st sess., 1928, 69, pp. 6740–41; *New York Times*, 4 May 1928; Stephens to HH, 2 April 1928; HH to Stephens, 2 April 1928, Prepresidential, HHPL; *New York Times*, 11, 12 April 1928; 5, 20, 22 May 1928.

42. Baker to Akerson, 12 April 1928, GA Papers.

43. Akerson to William J. Donovan, 20 March 1928, ibid.

44. Alan Fox to Donovan, 13 March 1928; Akerson to Fox, 23, 30 March 1928, ibid.

45. Couch to Akerson, 25 February 1928; Akerson to Couch, 5 April 1928; Couch to Akerson, 23 April 1928; Akerson to R. E. Ritchey, 28 April 1928; Cleveland A. Newton to Akerson, 16 April 1928, ibid.

46. Rickard diary, 6 April 1928, ER Papers. Walter Brown was upset by Hoover's decision. The motion picture was used elsewhere. See Ritchey to Akerson, 22 May 1928, GA Papers.

47. George B. Lockwood to Akerson, 24 March 1928 and Barnett File, GA Papers.

48. Akerson to Street, 15, 24 April 1928; Street to Akerson, 21 April 1928, GA Papers. Also see Akerson to Elmer Shaffer, 20 April 1928, Commerce, HHPL.

49. Hurley to HH, 3 June 1928; Houston *Post-Dispatch*, 19 May 1928; Ray Bell to Hurley, 29 May 1928, GA Papers.

50. Akerson to Dr. Klein, memorandum, 16 April 1928, GA Papers.

51. Akerson to Hurley, 5 June 1928, ibid.

52. Holsey to Akerson, 16 April 1928, ibid.

53. The best source for the 1928 Republican Texas fight is Paul Casdorph, *A History of the Republican Party in Texas, 1865–1965* (Austin: Pemberton Press, 1965), pp. 118–37.

54. Wilson Record, *Race and Radicalism: The NAACP and the Communist Party in Conflict* (Ithaca: Cornell University Press, 1964), p. 48; James Weldon Johnson, "A Negro Looks at Politics," *American Mercury* 18 (September 1929): 91–94.

55. Holsey to Akerson, 14 May 1928, GA Papers. Holsey enclosed a confidential letter on Negro attitudes that he had received from C. F. Richardson, editor of the Houston *Informer*.

56. Lockwood to HH, 2 June 1928; Akerson to Holsey, 5 June 1928; Holsey to Akerson, 6 June 1928; Akerson to Moton, 1 May 1928, ibid.

57. Akerson to George Barr Baker, 12 April 1928, ibid.

58. Joan Hoff Wilson, *Herbert Hoover: Forgotten Progressive* (Boston: Little, Brown and Co., 1975), p. 126. See also confidential campaign materials in Frank O. Lowden File, GA Papers.

59. See Frank O. Lowden File, GA Papers; "How the Ring Operates," Portland (Oregon) *Evening News*, 31 January 1928, in GA Papers.

60. Edgar Rickard diary, 8 June 1928, ER Papers. See also Donald R. McCoy, "To the White House: Herbert Hoover, August 1927–March 1929," in *The Hoover Presidency: A Re-appraisal*, eds. Martin L. Fausold and George T. Mazuzan (Albany: State University of New York Press, 1974), p. 31.

61. See the excellent three-page report "The Lowden Dawes Strategy," in Lowden File, GA Papers. On the number of contested seats see David J. Ginzl, "Herbert Hoover and Republican Patronage Politics in the South, 1928–1932" (Ph.D. dissertation, Syracuse University, 1977), p. 40. On the seriousness of the Lowden threat also see William T. Hutchinson, *Lowden of Illinois: The Life of Frank O. Lowden*, 2 vols. (Chicago: University of Chicago Press, 1957), 2:594–96, 583, 587, 591–92.

62. "Lowden Dawes Strategy," GA Papers. See also *New York Times*, 8, 9 June 1932; New York *World*, 8 June 1932.

63. Work to Charles Hebbard, 23 March 1928; Work to Fred E. Kiddle, 23 March 1928; Work to William P. Jackson, David W. Malone, O. M. Lanstrum, and James E. Davidson, 6 April 1928, HW Papers. See also the same message in numerous letters of other state leaders.

64. Work to William P. Jackson, 5 May 1928, ibid. See also the same message to J. Matt Chilton of Wyoming, Oliver D. Street of Alabama, Emile Kuntz of Louisiana, R. B. Creager of Texas, Robert W. Shingles of Hawaii, James E. Davidson of Michigan, John T. Thomas of Idaho, O. M. Lanstrum of Montana, and George Wingfield of Nevada, 5 May 1928, ibid.

65. New York *Herald Tribune*, 9 June 1929.

66. Edgar Rickard diary, 10 June 1928, ER Papers; *New York Times*, 5 June 1928; New York *Evening Post*, 6 June 1928; Dorothy M. Brown, *Mabel Walker Willebrandt, A Study of Power, Loyalty, and Law* (Knoxville, Tn.: University of Tennessee Press, 1984), pp. 153, 189.

67. New York *Herald Tribune*, 5 June 1928. Willebrandt was apparently knowledgeable about

the gathering of preconvention votes in Alabama, Georgia, Mississippi, and Florida (see Brown, *Mabel Walker Willebrandt*, p. 154).

68. *New York Times*, 9, 13 June 1928.

69. Ibid., 7 June 1928.

70. Ibid.

71. Ibid., 6, 13 June 1928; Cohen to Barnett, 7 June 1928, CAB Papers.

72. Cohen to Akerson, 17 June 1928; Akerson to Cohen, 2 July 1928, GA Papers. See also Lewinson, *Race, Class, and Party*, pp. 129, 172.

73. *New York Times*, 6, 7, 13 June 1932.

74. Ibid., 7 June 1928.

75. Ibid., New York *Evening Post*, 7 June 1928.

76. *New York Times*, 14 June 1928; Harold F. Gosnell, *Negro Politicians: The Rise of Negro Politics in Chicago* (Chicago: University of Chicago Press, 1935), pp. 29–30; Lewinson, *Race, Class, and Party*, pp. 172–73; Monroe N. Work, ed., *Negro Year Book: An Annual Encyclopedia of the Negro* (Tuskegee Institute, Alabama: Negro Year Book Publishing Company, 1931), pp. 90–98.

77. Norris to Phil La Follette, n.d., National Politics, Campaign for Progressives, 1928 File, GN Papers; *New York Times*, 8 June 1928.

78. *New York Times*, 8, 17 June 1928; New York *Evening Post*, 8 June 1928.

79. Edgar Rickard diary, 12 June 1928, ER Papers; Work to Mellon, 18 February, 14 May 1928; Work to Frank H. Howbart, 14 May 1928, HW Papers; Norris to Phil F. La Follette, n.d., National Campaign for Progressives File, GN Papers.

80. For the story of Vare's alleged influence, see Lawrence L. Murray, "The Mellons, Their Money, and The Mythical Machine: Organizational Politics in the Republican Twenties," *Pennsylvanian History* 42 (July 1975): 236–37. See also press statement, 16 June 1928, Hoover 1928 Campaign File, GN Papers; HH to Arch W. Shaw, 31 July 1939; HH to Robert M. Hutchins, 30 July 1939; NBC transcript of broadcast, 30 July 1939; *Look*, 15 August 1939; HH to J. Yozell Guinter, 6 August 1939, in Colleges and Universities, University of Chicago, 1939 file, HHPL. Hoover told Guinter, "We have a surplus of professional libelers, slanderers, and smearers" (HH to Guinter, 6 August 1939, ibid.).

81. For the details on the Texas convention floor fight see official report of the *Proceedings of the Nineteenth Republican National Convention, Kansas City, Missouri, 12–15 June 1928* (New York: Tenny Press, 1928), pp. 51–69.

82. Hoover, *Memoirs*, 2:206–7, 269–70, 277–78. For the importance of the corruption issue in the preconvention campaign, see *New York Times*, 1, 5, 10, 16, 29 April and 15, 16, 24, 27 June 1928.

83. Richard B. Sherman, *The Republican Party and Black America: From McKinley to Hoover, 1896–1933* (Charlottesville: University Press of Virginia, 1973), pp. 229–30; Rickard diary, 31 July 1928, ER Papers.

84. A. L. Holsey to R. R. Moton, 14 June 1928, RRM Papers; J. M. to Strauss, 30 June 1928; Cleveland *Gazette*, 30 June 1928 and Chattanooga *Times*, 20 August 1928 in 1928 campaign, Negroes, LS Papers.

85. *New York Times*, 8, 17 June 1928; New York *World*, 8 January 1928.

86. Tatum, *The Changed Political Thought of the Negro*, pp. 131–32; Lewinson, *Race, Class, and Party*, pp. 171–74, 274; Ginzl, "Hoover and Republican Patronage Politics," pp. 40–41; George F. Garcia, "Herbert Hoover's Southern Strategy and the Black Reaction" (M.A. thesis, University of Iowa, 1972), p. 85; Allan J. Lichtman, *Prejudice and the Old Politics: The Presidential Election of 1928* (Chapel Hill: University of North Carolina Press, 1979), pp. 151–52. Ginzl recognizes that the contests were not decided on the basis of race (see Ginzl, "Hoover and Republican Patronage Politics," p. 41).

5. Double Cross

1. For Howard's statements see newspaper clipping in correspondence of E. H. Bradshaw to Akerson, 28 June 1928, GA Papers.

2. Ibid.

3. Ibid.; Akerson to Bradshaw, 2 July 1928, GA Papers.

4. W. E. B. Du Bois, "Is Al Smith Afraid of the South?" *Nation* 127 (17 October 1928): 392–93; "The Roots of Corruption," *Nation* 127 (19 September 1928): 258; Hanes Walton, Jr., *Black Republicans: The Politics of the Black and Tans* (Metuchen, N.J.: Scarecrow Press, 1975), pp. 134–35, 161; Richard B. Sherman, *The Republican Party and Black America: From McKinley to Hoover, 1896–1933* (Charlottesville: University Press of Virginia, 1973), pp. 230–31; Allan J. Lichtman, *Prejudice and the Old Politics: The Presidential Election of 1928* (Chapel Hill: University of North Carolina Press, 1979), pp. 151–52; Louis M. Jiggitts, "Post Offices and Politics," *Independent* 121 (11 August 1928): 135–36.

5. For background information on Willebrandt see the useful biography by Dorothy Brown, *Mabel Walker Willebrandt: A Study of Power, Loyalty, and Law* (Knoxville, Tn.: University of Tennessee Press, 1984), pp. 25–55. See also the Willebrandt File, Prepresidential Papers, HHPL.

6. Willebrandt to Sargent, 29 June 1928 in PWH File.

7. Ibid.

8. Ibid.

9. Ibid.

10. Ibid. Brown mentions the first Howard trial but does not examine this aspect of her career. Brown did not utilize the papers in the PWH File. See Brown, *Willebrandt*, pp. 153, 158–78.

11. Copies of Hoover's communications to Huston and Willebrandt can be found in Dale McMullin to HH, 3 August 1939, Postpresidential, College and Universities, University of Chicago Round Table, HHPL. See also Claudius Huston File, C&T, HHPL.

12. Howard to Akerson, 19 June 1928, Commerce, HHPL.

13. Willebrandt to Sargent, 29 June 1928, PWH File.

14. U.S. Congress, Senate Subcommittee of the Committee on Post Offices and Post Roads, *Hearings on Influencing Appointments to Postmasterships*, 70th Cong., 2d sess., 9 July 1928, pp. 1–3.

15. W. C. Lyle to Work, 27 June 1928; J. T. Rose to Work, 26 June 1928; Work to J. G. Standifer, 25 June 1928, HW Papers. See also Lewis A. Pick to Akerson, 15 November 1927, GA Papers.

16. *Hearings on Influencing Appointments to Postmasterships*, p. 20.

17. Ibid., pp. 18–19, 21, 81–82, 166–67.

18. Ibid., pp. 177–98.

19. *New York Times*, 11 July 1928. See also reports on 10, 12, 13, 14 July.

20. *New York Times*, 10 July 1928; Walton, *Black Republicans*, p. 135.

21. For example, see ibid. See also n. 17 and especially Jiggitts, "Post Office and Politics," pp. 135–36.

22. *New York Times*, 18 July 1928. The *New York Times* is a good example of the attention given to and the importance placed upon Republican "reform" in the South during the election of 1928.

23. Work to Brown, 23 June 1928, HW Papers.

24. Edgar Rickard diary, 1 August 1928, ER Papers; HH, memorandum to Dr. Work, 14 July 1928, PP File.

25. HH to Work, 18 July 1928, Work File, HHPL (emphasis mine).

26. See chapter 3, nn. 71–76.

27. Eugene Levy, *James Weldon Johnson* (Chicago and London: The University of Chicago

Press, 1973), pp. 245–46, 263–64; Robert L. Zangrando, *The NAACP Crusade Against Lynching, 1909–1950* (Philadelphia: Temple University Press, 1980), pp. 75, 62 (for evidence of the income that Howard received from the Pullman Company, see his federal tax returns for 1925, PWH File); Jervis Anderson, *A. Philip Randolph: A Biographical Portrait* (New York: Harcourt Brace Jovanovich, 1972), p. 172. See also memorandum re Perry Howard Meeting, 15 December 1931 [?], James Weldon Johnson Papers, Yale University.

28. Ralph J. Bunche, *The Political Status of the Negro in the Age of FDR*, ed. Dewey W. Grantham (Chicago: University of Chicago Press, 1973), p. 81.

29. Neville H. Thomas to Willebrandt, 21 July 1928, PWH File; Holsey to Moton, 18 July 1928, RRM Papers; Barnett, memo, n.d., "Perry Howard Case," CAB Papers; George F. Garcia, "Herbert Hoover's Southern Strategy and the Black Reaction" (M.A. thesis, University of Iowa, 1972), pp. 60–62; Andrew Buni, *The Negro in Virginia Politics, 1902–1965* (Charlottesville: University Press of Virginia, 1967), p. 97; Elbert Lee Tatum, *The Changed Political Thought of the Negro, 1915–1940* (New York: Exposition Press, 1951), pp. 99, 103; Lichtman, *Prejudice and the Old Politics*, p. 152.

30. See all sources in n. 29. Neville Thomas, head of the NAACP in Washington, D.C., who had convinced Hoover to desegregate the Census Bureau, was especially explicit in his charge of "outrage" to black people. See also Walter White to Hester Greene, 19 September 1928, NAACP. White told Greene that the indictment of Howard was solely "due to his race."

6. Southern Revolution

1. Ralph J. Bunche, "The Political Status of the Negro," research memorandum, Carnegie-Myrdal Study of the Negro in America, Schomberg Collection, New York Public Library, New York City, p. 1177; Henry Lee Moon, *The Balance of Power: The Negro Vote* (Garden City, N.Y.: Doubleday and Co., 1948), pp. 107–8; George F. Garcia, "Herbert Hoover's Southern Strategy and the Black Reaction" (M.A. thesis, University of Iowa, 1972), pp. 66–68; David J. Ginzl, "Herbert Hoover and Republican Patronage in the South, 1928–1932" (Ph.D. dissertation, Syracuse University, 1977); Robert H. Brisbane, *The Black Vanguard: Origins of the Negro Social Revolution, 1900–1960* (Valley Forge, Pa.: Judson Press, 1970), p. 124; Hanes Walton, Jr., *Black Republicans: The Politics of the Black and Tans* (Metuchen, N.J.: Scarecrow Press, 1975), pp. 135, 163; Harold F. Gosnell, *Negro Politicians: The Rise of Negro Politics in Chicago* (Chicago: University of Chicago Press, 1935), p. 30; Walter White, *How Far the Promised Land?* (New York: Viking Press, 1955), pp. 76–77; Richard B. Sherman, *The Republican Party and Black America: From McKinley to Hoover, 1896–1933* (Charlottesville: University Press of Virginia, 1973), pp. 230–33; Andrew Buni, *Robert L. Vann of the Pittsburgh Courier: Politics and Black Journalism* (Pittsburgh: University of Pittsburgh Press, 1974), p. 181; Alexander Heard, *A Two-Party South?* (Chapel Hill: University of North Carolina Press, 1952), pp. 224–25; Oscar Handlin, *Al Smith and His America* (Boston: Little, Brown and Co., 1958), p. 134. See also nn. 32, 34, and 40 in chapter 7.

2. For the importance of the corruption charges see chapter 4, nn. 23–30. On Hoover's dislike of politics and politicians, see Joan Hoff Wilson, *Herbert Hoover: Forgotten Progressive* (Boston: Little, Brown and Co., 1975), pp. 125–26, 134, 147–65.

3. Anderson to HH, 29 August, 25 September, and 8, 11 October 1928; HH to Anderson, 30 August and 13 October 1928, Pres. Papers. See also his file in Cabinet Appointments and Paul Lewinson, *Race, Class, and Party: A History of Negro Suffrage and White Politics in the South* (New York: Russell and Russell, 1963), pp. 176–78. Lewis Strauss also kept Hoover informed on southern politics. See his report of interviews with southern leaders, 5 September 1928, Campaign 1928, LS Papers.

4. Letterbook, 30 January–6 November 1928, pp. 70–93, 122, JCW Papers. See also the

Wise manuscript entitled "Henry Watkins Anderson of Virginia: A Political Interpretation and A Potential Vice-President," pp. 1–20, in ibid.

5. Letterbook, 1928, pp. 120–22, and Wise, "Henry Watkins Anderson," JCW Papers; Anderson to Strauss, 17 August 1928, LS Papers.

6. Andrew Buni, *The Negro in Virginia Politics, 1902–1965* (Charlottesville: University of Virginia Press, 1967), pp. 103, 181. However, Ralph J. Bunche concludes that Negroes were not allowed to vote in the Democratic primary until 1930 (see Bunche, *Political Status of the Negro*, p. 518); Kelly Miller to HH, 4 October 1928, C & T, HHPL.

7. See, for example, Wise, "The Necessity of the Bi-Party System," Letterbook, December 1928–April 1930, pp. 124–26, and Wise to HH, 30 June 1928, JCW Papers.

8. See especially Wise, "Henry W. Anderson," pp. 11–12; Letterbook, 1928, pp. 70–122; and Wise to J. D. Eggleston, 13 October 1928; Wise to editor, "The Planet," 22 October 1928, Campaign Correspondence, JCW Papers. See also numerous other letters in which Wise explains parts of the Anderson-Wise reform program. Fear expressed by Democrats is in Paul Lewinson, *Race, Class, and Party: A History of Negro Suffrage and White Politics in the South* (New York: Russell and Russell, 1963), pp. 176–78, 180–81 and Anderson to HH, 25 September 1928, 11 October 1928, and 6, 9, November 1928; HH to Anderson, 13 November 1928, 26 January 1929, Pres. Papers; Wise to HH, 11 August 1928 and Wise campaign pamphlet, "Why Virginia Should Support Hoover," 14 July 1928, especially pp. 10–11, in General Correspondence, C & T; Wise to HH, 25 October 1928, PP File, HHPL. See also *New York Times*, 4 February 1929 and New York *World*, 4 February 1929. The *World* reported that Anderson had twice run for governor of Virginia on a reform platform that included the vote for all Negroes. On black voting in Virginia see Lewinson, *Race, Class, and Party*, p. 162, and V. O. Key, *Southern Politics in State and Nation* (New York: Alfred A. Knopf, 1949), p. 323.

9. Lewinson, *Race, Class, and Party*, pp. 180–81, 184.

10. On the importance of the class issue, see ibid., pp. 188–91.

11. See n. 6.

12. Wise, Letterbook, 1928–1930, p. 93, JCW Papers. See also "A New Deal for the Solid South," *Literary Digest* 64 (17 September 1927): 14; New York *World*, 4 February 1929; Garcia, "Hoover's Southern Strategy," pp. 6, 49, 57–58, 129; and Ginzl, "Hoover and Republican Patronage Politics," pp. 88–89.

13. See correspondence in Bascom Slemp File in Pres. Papers, in Cabinet Appointments File, and especially Akerson "Memo to Chief," 4 February 1928, GA Papers. See also President's Appointments Calendar 19, 29 June, 2,5 July, 28 August, 1, 6, 13, 21 September, and 2, 5 October 1928, HHPL, and Rickard diary, 7–14 July, 4 August, and 31 December 1930, ER Papers.

14. Wise, Letterbook, 1928, p. 120, JCW Papers.

15. On Democratic suspicions of Anderson see Lewinson, *Race, Class, and Party*, p. 180, and *New York Times*, 4 February 1929; New York *World*, 4 February 1929.

16. Anderson to HH, 25 September 1928, Pres. Papers. Also in this file are other Anderson letters giving Hoover advice and commenting on southern politics.

17. See, for example, HH to Col. Robert R. McCormick, 30 March 1929, HHPL.

18. Ibid. See also George F. Garcia, "Herbert Hoover and the Issue of Race," *The Annals of Iowa* 44 (Winter 1979): 513–15. Garcia is puzzled by Hoover's apparent inconsistency but ultimately insists that his support of lily-whites stemmed from his "theory of white supremacy."

19. HH to Anderson, 14 November 1928, PP File. Evidence that his black advisers were aware of and generally approved of his goals is in Barnett, "Memorandum for Mr. Saunders: The Attitude of the Negro Voters," n.d. [1932], CAB Papers. See also important evidence cited in chapter 11, nn. 29, 30, and 31, but especially Moton to HH, 19 April 1929, Moton File, HHPL.

20. See chapter 17; HH to Col. Robert R. McCormick, 30 March 1929, HHPL.

7. Southern Campaign

1. Oliver D. Street to Work, 21 January 1928, 10 March 1928; Street to George B. Lockwood, 9 March 1928; Work to Street, 3 January 1928, 24 January 1928, 1 February 1928; Work to Emile Kuntz, 12 December 1927; Work To Victor Loisel, 1 February 1928; Work to C. E. Pitts, 26 October 1927, 2 September 1927; Work to William P. Jackson, 6 April 1928 and copies to other leaders; Bascom Slemp to Work, 3 March 1928, HW Papers.

2. The correspondence is too numerous to cite but see, for example, sources in n. 1.

3. Work to Gen. Robert E. Noble, 16 January 1928; Work to John G. White, 15 February 1928; Work to Sen. Walter E. Edge, 3 April 1928, HW Papers. See also U.S. Congress, Senate Special Committee Investigating Presidential Campaign Expenditures, *Hearings on Presidential Campaign Expenditures*, 70 Cong., 1st sess., 16 May 1928, p. 291. Rush Holland obviously lied to the committee when he denied close political contacts with Work. He was no doubt protecting his good friend Work from publicity.

4. For background on Work see "Hubert Work: Word Portrait of the Man" and other materials in Work File, C & T.

5. *New York Times*, 8 July 1928. For Hoover's increasing dissatisfaction see HH to Work, 7 February 1929; Edgar Rickard, diary, 1, 17, 22, 25 August 1928, ER Papers.

6. Washington (D.C.) *Eagle*, 6 April 1928.

7. Edgar Rickard diary, 25 August 1928, ER Papers; HH to Work, 4 June 1929, Republican National Committee Papers, HHPL. During the campaign Hoover specifically denied that he had taken charge of the campaign from Work. See HH to W. F. Durant, 11 September 1928, Work File, HHPL. For the view that Hoover took charge, see David J. Ginzl, "Herbert Hoover and Republican Patronage Politics in the South, 1928–1932" (Ph.D. dissertation, Syracuse University, May 1977), pp. 69–70, 72–73. See also Allan J. Lichtman, *Prejudice and the Old Politics: The Presidential Election of 1928* (Chapel Hill: University of North Carolina Press, 1979), p. 153.

8. Work to Jonas, 25 June 1928, HW Papers.

9. Work to HH, 21 July 1928, Pres. Papers, Work File, HHPL.

10. W. J. Donald to Newton, 31 January 1930, South Carolina State File; Newton to J. C. Hambright, 28 December 1929, Secretary's File; Newton to postmaster general, 31 January 1931; White House File Memo, 13 August 1930, PP File, Mann File, HHPL. See also *New York Times*, 30 August, 1 September, and 3, 13 October 1928; Atlanta *Constitution*, 26 December 1930, and New York *World*, 29 January 1929.

11. New York *Herald Tribune*, 29 January 1929; *Hearings on Presidential Campaign Expenditures*, p. 645.

12. Frederich Rush, "Republicans For Revenue Only: Unmasking a Tennessee Patronage Scandal," *Independent* 117 (4 December 1926): 635; New York *Herald Tribune*, 29 January 1929; New York *World*, 29 January 1929.

13. New York *World*, 28, 29 January 1929; clippings in W. E. Evans file, Prepresidential, HHPL; New York *World*, 25 January 1929. For scholars who have accepted this interpretation see Ginzl, "Hoover and Republican Patronage Politics," pp. 70, 72–73; Lichtman, *Prejudice and the Old Politics*, p. 153; Harold F. Gosnell, *Negro Politicians: The Rise of Negro Politics in Chicago* (Chicago: University of Chicago Press, 1935), p. 30. See also nn. 51 and 52 and chapter 9, nn. 29 and 30.

14. *Hearings on Presidential Campaign Expenditures*, pp. 697–98.

15. New York *World*, 4 February 1929; *New York Times*, 4 February 1929; New York *Evening Post*, 9 February 1929. See the correspondence in the Slemp, Anderson, and Cramer Files, C & T.

16. Before his indictment Howard praised Mann in the informative newspaper clipping sent to Akerson by E. H. Bradshaw, 28 June 1928, GA Papers. See also Holsey to Moton, 18 July 1928; Holsey to Mann, 3 July 1928; Barnett, "Report on Survey of Sentiment Among Negro Voters," copies in CAB Papers and RRM Papers; Eugene P. Booze to Mann, 10, 29 August 1928, Pres.

Papers. Emmett J. Scott was also aware of Mann's activities: see Scott to HH, 13 July 1928, Prepresidential, General Correspondence, Scott File, HHPL. For another view that does not utilize the Moton or Barnett papers see Ginzl, "Hoover and Republican Patronage Politics," p. 112, and George F. Garcia, "Herbert Hoover's Southern Strategy and the Black Reaction" (M.A. thesis, University of Iowa, 1972), pp. 60–61; Kelly Miller to HH, 4 October 1928, C & T.

17. Akerson to Henry M. Robinson, 25 June 1928, GA Papers and especially Barnett, memorandum to Mr. Saunders, "The Attitude of the Negro Voters," n.d., CAB Papers. Mann's tactics would soon disappoint these black leaders.

18. When J. Leonard Replogle asked Hoover with whom he should discuss "important matters" in the Florida campaign, Hoover directed him to Horace Mann. See Replogle to HH, 14 August 1928; HH to Replogle, 14 August 1928, Pres. Papers. Hoover's desire for cooperation between white and black leaders was made clear during the campaign in his 18 July order to Work and following the campaign in his interviews with newspaper reporters. See also New York *Evening Post*, 1 February 1929, and *New York Times*, 2 February 1929.

19. Kelly Miller to HH, 4 October 1928, C & T, General Correspondence, HHPL.

20. *New York Times*, 7, 13 October 1928.

21. Edgar Rickard diary, 17, 22, 25 October 1928, ER Papers.

22. David Burner, *The Politics of Provincialism: The Democratic Party in Transition, 1918–1932* (New York: Alfred A. Knopf, 1967), pp. 179–216.

23. On the contrast between Hoover's and Smith's progressivism during the campaign see ibid., pp. 196–98.

24. See, for example, Herbert Hoover, "The South's Development," *Manufacturer's Record* 17 (11 December 1924) and Pittsburgh *Press*, 9 July 1926. Also see Major Addresses, HHPL. The Republicans also stressed the South's future economic development in their political fund-raising efforts in the South. See, for example, Lewis Strauss to Mr. Boyce, 23 October 1928, Anti-Smith Democrats File, LS Papers.

25. Paul Lewinson, *Race, Class, and Party: A History of Negro Suffrage and White Politics in the South* (New York: Russell and Russell, 1963), pp. 124, 152–62; Ginzl, "Hoover and Republican Patronage Politics," pp. 12–13.

26. Burner, *Politics of Provincialism*, pp. 202–16; Edmund A. Moore, *A Catholic Runs for President: The Campaign of 1928* (New York: Roland Press, 1956), pp. 148, 155, 172.

27. Moore, *Catholic Runs for President*, p. 157; I. A. Newby, *Jim Crow's Defense: Anti-Negro Thought in America, 1900–1930* (Baton Rouge: Louisiana State University Press, 1965), pp. 164–65.

28. Newby, *Jim Crow's Defense*, p. 166.

29. Alston Cockrell to Congressman Park Trammerall, 10 October 1928, Trammerall Papers, University of Florida, Gainesville.

30. Akerson to Charles Kuhn, 19 October 1928; Charles Ulysses Gordon to Akerson, 24 September 1928; Akerson to Gordon, 1 October 1928, Pres. Papers; Ralph J. Bunche, "The Political Status of the Negro," research memorandum, Carnegie-Myrdal Study of the Negro in America, Schomberg Collection, New York Public Library, pp. 1153–60.

31. R. S. Regar to Work, 10 October 1928, HW Papers. Regar was acting postmaster general. Blease's use of franked envelopes was legal. See also Jennings C. Wise memorandum to Lewis Strauss, n.d. [November, 1928?]; his enclosed radio address of 23 October 1928, "The Political Conspiracy of 1928"; and his pamphlet, "The Smithite Negro Policy: A Betrayal of the Democratic Party and Virginia," Campaign of 1928, LS Papers.

32. Bunche, "Political Status of the Negro," pp. 1153–76; Lewinson, *Race, Class, and Party*, p. 110; Moore, *Catholic Runs for President*, pp. 149–57; Henry Lee Moon, *Balance of Power: The Negro Vote* (Garden City, N.Y.: Doubleday and Co., 1948), pp. 106–8; Garcia, "Hoover's Southern Strategy," pp. 65–68. For a copy of the anti-Catholic pamphlet distributed by the Republican national committeeman Oliver D. Street, "Governor Smith's Membership in the

Roman Catholic Church," see Street File, Prepresidential Papers. Hoover would later attempt to discipline Street. See RNC Papers, Alabama State File, HHPL. In Virginia Republicans circulated pamphlets claiming that Tammany Hall Democrats had appointed 276 Negroes to public office and favored social equality between blacks and whites. See "Why Va. Voters Are For Hoover," in Sam to Strauss, 10 October 1928, Campaign 1928, Negroes, LS Papers.

33. Work to J. M. Schreiber, 29 June 1928, HW Papers.

34. See numerous letters and campaign statements, but especially Lawrence Richey to J. W. Sumner, 13 October 1928 and "Alleged Charge that Mr. Hoover Made Order Compelling the White People to Work with the Colored People in the Department of Commerce," Misrepresentations File, Campaign 1928, HHPL. Lichtman claims that Hoover directed "appeals to religious bigotry, prohibitionism, and racism" (see Lichtman, *Prejudice and the Old Politics*, pp. 154 and 147).

35. Jackson *Daily News*, 11 October 1928; Akerson to Bilbo, 19 October 1928; Bilbo to Akerson, 24 October 1928, Misrepresentations File, Campaign 1928, Mississippi Flood, HHPL.

36. Akerson to Booze, 1 September 1928, Prepresidential Papers.

37. Mary C. Booze to Rev. T. J. Bailey, 17 October 1928; *Jackson Daily News*, 11 October 1928, HHPL.

38. Akerson to Bilbo, 19 October 1928, Misrepresentations File, Campaign 1928, Mississippi Flood, HHPL.

39. See n. 36.

40. Booze to Akerson, 22, 25, 29 October 1928; Akerson to Booze, 27 October 1928, Prepresidential Papers.

41. McCormick to HH, n.d.; HH to McCormick, 6 September 1928, ibid. In fairness to Hoover, Edmund A. Moore points out that his opponents were quick to "misinterpret both his words and his silence" (see Moore, *Catholic Runs for President*, p. 149). Still, Moore concludes that Hoover could have done more to help reduce "the torrent of intolerant speech and writing" (p. 149).

42. Holland to HH, 18 September 1928; Slemp to HH, 30 August 1928, Pres. Papers.

43. See n. 24.

44. Herbert Hoover, *The New Day: Campaign Speeches of Herbert Hoover 1928*, ed. Ray Lyman Wilbur (Stanford: Stanford University Press, 1928), pp. 89–111, but especially p. 106; Richard B. Sherman, *Republican Party and Black Americans: From McKinley to Hoover, 1896–1933* (Charlottesville: University Press of Virginia, 1973), pp. 230–31 and Memphis *Triangle*, 20 October 1928 (James Good, his western campaign manager, did not consider it a southern speech [see Good to HH, 6 October 1928, Pres. Papers]); Gosnell, *Negro Politicians*, p. 30. Anderson told Hoover that his speech was "exactly suited" to the South (see Anderson to HH, 8 October 1928, Pres. Papers), and "Hoover's Attempt to Melt the Solid South," *Literary Digest* 99 (20 October 1928): 5–7.

45. Robert R. Church, Jr., to HH, 8 October 1928, Prepresidential General Correspondence, HHPL; Hoover, *New Day*, pp. 9–44, but especially pp. 36–37. See also Hoover, *The Memoirs of Herbert Hoover*, 3 vols. (New York: Macmillan Co., 1951–52), 2:206–7, 217; and HH to Wise, 18 October 1928, JCW Papers.

46. Lewinson, *Race, Class, and Party*, p. 158; Pat Watters and Reece Cleghorn, *Climbing Jacob's Ladder: The Arrival of Negroes in Southern Politics* (New York: Harcourt, Brace and World, 1967), p. 10; Walter White, *How Far the Promised Land?* (New York: Viking Press, 1955), pp. 76–77; Robert H. Brisbane, *The Black Vanguard: Origins of the Negro Social Revolution, 1900–1960* (Valley Forge, Pa.: Judson Press, 1970), p. 124; Ralph J. Bunche, "The Political Status of the Negro," research memorandum, Carnegie-Myrdal Study of the Negro in America, Schomberg Collection, New York Public Library, New York City, p. 1176; Moore, *Catholic Runs for President*, p. 158; Henry Lee Moon, *Balance of Power: The Negro Vote* (Garden City, N.Y.: Doubleday and Co., 1948), pp. 106–7; Lichtman, *Prejudice and the Old Politics*, pp.

147, 153; Wilma Dykeman and James Stokely, *Seeds of Southern Change: The Life of Will Alexander* (New York: W. W. Norton and Co.), p. 122.

47. Wise to HH, 30 June 1928; Wise to Joseph P. Brady, 10 October 1929, Letterbook, and "Memorandum prepared For Mr. Lewis Strauss," n.d., in Campaign Correspondence, last entry in Letterbook to November, 1928, JCW Papers; Anderson to Strauss, 17 August 1928, LS Papers.

48. Wise to Editor, Richmond *Times-Democrat*, 11 November 1929; Wise to John L. Williams, 2 November 1928, Letterbook, JCW Papers.

49. Wise to Editor, "The Planet," 22 October 1928, ibid. See also editorial from the Oklahoma *Bee*, 14 August 1928, which expresses views almost identical to those of Wise and Anderson. Other southern Republicans were also frustrated by Democratic efforts to capture the votes of both white supremacists and blacks (see George Fort Milton to Gilchrist B. Stockton, 3 August 1928, and Stockton to Milton, 1 August 1928, GBS Papers).

50. HH to Anderson, 13 October 1928, Pres. Papers. On the black vote in Virginia, see chapter 6, n. 6.

51. W. E. B. Du Bois, "Is Al Smith Afraid of the South?" *Nation* 127 (17 October 1928): 393; Sherman, *Republican Party and Black Americans*, pp. 229–30. Like Hoover, Al Smith failed to speak out forcefully.

52. Charles Curtis to HH, 24, 26 July 1928; HH to Curtis, 3 August 1928; Holland to HH, 18 September 1928; Slemp to HH, 30 August 1928, Pres. Papers. See also nn. 1, 3, 9, 13, 34, 35. Gilchrist Stockton, one of Hoover's trusted lieutenants in the feeding of Europe during and following World War I, and now his chief campaigner in winning over dissident Democrats in Florida, advised the candidate that he "could not possibly carry the state if any Republican appeal was made . . . to the negro vote." Despite the fact that the Democratic campaign "against [him] in Florida will be waged almost exclusively on the negro question," and the widespread fear that Hoover's election will be "dangerous to white supremacy in the South," Hoover must remain silent about racial politics (see Gilchrist Stockton to HH, 29 August 1928, GBS Papers).

53. Moore, *Catholic Runs for President*, p. 148. In his *Memoirs* Hoover does not discuss the race issue but does recall his repudiations of religious bigotry. "The worst plague in the campaign," he stated, "was the religious issue" (see Hoover, *Memoirs*, 2:207–8). See also "Statement to Washington *Post*," 21 September 1928, Misrepresentations File, 1928 Campaign; HH to Max Feldman, 2 October 1937, Misrepresentations, Post-Presidential, Ickes; and Misrepresentations File, Democratic National Publicity Bureau, 1929–1934, HHPL.

54. Lewinson, *Race, Class, and Party*, pp. 158, 161–62; *New York Times*, 21 October 1928; White, *How Far the Promised Land?* p. 77; Moon, *Balance of Power*, pp. 106–7; Pat Watters and Reese Cleghorn, *Climbing Jacob's Ladder: The Arrival of Negroes in Southern Politics* (New York: Harcourt, Brace and World, 1967), p. 10.

55. *New York Times*, 21 October 1928, and Dykeman and Stokely, *Seeds of Southern Change*, p. 122.

56. Monroe N. Work, *Negro Year Book: An Annual Encyclopedia of the Negro, 1931–1932* (Tuskegee Institute, Ala.: Negro Year Book Publishing Co., 1931), pp. 87–90.

57. For the entire texts and the names of the signers of both the southern white protest and the Negro "Appeal to America," see Work, *Negro Year Book*, pp. 87–90. See also Robert R. Moton, *What the Negro Thinks* (New York: Garden City Publishing Company, 1929), p. 251; NAACP, "Politicians Overwork Negro Equality as Issue in 1928 Campaign," press release, 31 August 1928, Politics, NAACP Papers; Moon, *Balance of Power*, p. 107.

58. John J. Raskob to Work, 6, 31 October 1928, JCW Papers.

59. Akerson to Work, 20 October 1928, Pres. Papers, Work File, HHPL.

60. Charles Michelson, *The Ghost Talks* (New York: G. P. Putnam, 1944), pp. 35, 14–35, 41–42. See also *New York Times*, 3 November 1928 and Washington (D.C.) *Post*, 3 November 1929.

8. Hoover's Doctors

1. Monroe N. Work, *Negro Year Book: An Annual Encyclopedia of the Negro, 1931–1932* (Tuskegee Institute: Negro Year Book Publishing Co., 1931), pp. 85–86.

2. Ibid.

3. Holsey to Moton, 14 July 1928, RRM Papers.

4. Neville Thomas to Mabel Walker Willebrandt, 21 July 1928, PWH File. For the source of the Perry Howard quote in the preceding paragraph see chap. 5, n. 1.

5. Holsey to Moton, 18 July 1928, RRM Papers; *New York Times*, 18 July 1928; Pittsburgh *Courier*, 21 July 1928; White to Hester Greene, 19 September 1928, NAACP Papers. See also George F. Garcia, "Herbert Hoover's Southern Strategy and the Black Reaction" (M.A. thesis, University of Iowa, 1972), pp. 61–62; Allan J. Lichtman, *Prejudice and the Old Politics: The Presidential Election of 1928* (Chapel Hill: University of North Carolina Press, 1979), pp. 151–52.

6. Barnett to Moton, n.d., "Perry Howard Case," RRM Papers.

7. Ibid.

8. "The Roots of Corruption," *Nation*, 28 September 1928, p. 258.

9. The best source is the eight-page single-spaced stenographic "Report of Conference Held in Mrs. Willebrandt's Office, 15 October 1928," p. 4, PWH File. Walter White was angered that Perry Howard and Ben Davis had been harassed but white Republican politicians had not been touched (see White to Hester Greene, 19 September 1928, NAACP Papers).

10. Ibid., p. 3.

11. Ibid., pp. 4, 5, 6.

12. "Second Conference with Perry Howard Held October 25, 1928 in Mr. Jones' Office," PWH File.

13. Ibid.

14. Hoover to Claudius Huston, 12 June 1928, in Dare McMullin to Hoover, 3 August 1939, Colleges and Universities, University of Chicago Round Table, Postpresidential Papers, HHPL.

15. James Weldon Johnson, *Along This Way: The Autobiography of James Weldon Johnson* (New York: Viking Press, 1933), p. 239. For a list of the members of the National Republican Executive Colored Committee, see W. L. Sledge to Samuel E. Shortridge, 13 March 1928, HHPL. Included were Perry W. Howard, Robert R. Church, and Walter H. Cohen.

16. Work to Brown, 23 June 1928, HW Papers.

17. HH to Dr. Work, memorandum, 14 July 1928, PP File.

18. For example, in October 1931 HH sent a confidential donation of $500 to the National Urban League; James Kinckle Jones to Lawrence Richey, 25 July 1932, Negro Matters, PP File. Moton was convinced that Hoover had taken "radical steps" to correct abuses during the flood and would continue to help black people as president (Moton to Joseph E. Bowman, 14 April 1928, and Moton to Thomas E. Campbell, 9 January 1928, RRM Papers). For Barnett's role at the convention, see Francis H. Omes to Alex Harris, 9 June 1928, CAB Papers. For additional information on Moton see Robert Russa Moton, *Finding A Way Out: An Autobiography* (New York: Doubleday, Page and Co., 1920) and Wilson Jeremiah Moses, *The Golden Age of Black Nationalism, 1850–1925* (Hamden, Conn.: Shoe String Press, 1978), pp. 242–44; Claude A. Barnett, "A Southern Statesman," in *Robert Russa Moton of Hampton and Tuskegee*, ed. William H. Hughes and Frederick D. Patterson (Chapel Hill: University of North Carolina Press, 1956), pp. 187–203.

19. See, for example, Barnett to Perry Howard, 21 February 1920; Barnett to Benjamin J. Davis, 4 May 1920, CAB Papers.

20. Barnett to William M. Butler, 13 April 1925, CAB Papers. Barnett told Butler that campaign promises to blacks two or three months before each national election had to be replaced with "some program of accomplishment" for black people. See also George Barr Baker to HH, 5

November 1925, Commerce Papers, HHPL; and Barnett, "Autobiography," pp. 16–18; J. E. Mitchell to Barnett, 8 June 1928, CAB Papers.

21. Akerson to Barnett, 15 May 1928, CAB Papers.

22. See chapter 1 and HH to Barnett, 16 June 1928, CAB Papers. James A. Jackson, the man Barnett recommended for the Commerce Department position, had performed his job very well (see Newton to Richey, 21 May 1931, Jackson File, HHPL).

23. Barnett, "Report on Ohio," March 1928, GA Papers; Vena to Barnett, 1 May 1928, CAB Papers.

24. Jervis Anderson, *A. Philip Randolph: A Biographical Portrait* (New York: Harcourt, Brace, Jovanovich, 1972), p. 183. See also numerous letters between Barnett and Vena in Politics File, CAB Papers.

25. Phillips to HH, 15 June 1928, HHPL; Phillips to Barnett, 30 June 1928, and other letters in CAB Papers. See also Barnett, "Memo on Flood Commission Report," Political, Colored People, GA Papers.

26. See extensive correspondence between Barnett and Richardson in CAB Papers.

27. Barnett and Holsey to HH, n.d., CAB Papers. Barnett and Holsey explicitly informed Hoover that their services to him during the campaign were as representatives of R. R. Moton.

28. Appointments Calendar, 29 June 1928, HHPL. Hoover spoke with Moton for thirty minutes, twice the amount of time usually given to the vast majority of important visitors.

29. Moton to Holsey, 6 July 1928; Holsey to Barnett, 22 January 1929; Barnett to Walter Brown, 13 July 1930, CAB Papers; Holsey to Moton, 13 September 1928, RRM Papers.

30. Charles Flint Kellogg, *NAACP: A History of the National Association for the Advancement of Colored People, 1909–1920* (Baltimore: The Johns Hopkins Press, 1967), p. 264.

31. Ibid., p. 278.

32. See news release, National Republicans League, box 41, EJS Papers.

33. See autobiographical materials in box 145, ibid.

34. The details of this bitter feud between Du Bois and Scott are in box 115, ibid. (see specifically Scott to Samuel A. Berger, 27 May 1932). Also see Boston *Chronicle*, 24 May 1919 and *Crisis*, May 1919; Andrew Buni, *Robert L. Vann of the Pittsburgh Courier: Politics and Black Journalism* (Pittsburgh: University of Pittsburgh Press, 1974), p. 157.

35. Alvin E. White to Barnett, n.d., William Pickens File, CAB Papers. For the Scott-Moton correspondence during this period see box 109, EJS Papers.

36. See n. 34 and Moses, *Golden Age of Black Nationalism*, pp. 243, 264, 269.

37. Walter Cohen to Scott, 14 October 1926, EJS Papers. The Scott-Cohen correspondence extends as far back as 1909. For Scott's activities in the National Negro Business League, see materials in box 92 and for Republican party activities see box 95, ibid.

38. George W. Harris to Scott, 5 April 1928; James H. Hubert to Scott, 1 May 1928; press release, "Federal Rights of Colored Americans Endangered," box 74, EJS Papers. See also *New York Times*, 22 April 1928; Philadelphia *Sunday Transcript*, 15 April 1928. Harris was editor of the New York *News*.

39. George E. C. Hayes, "Another Howard Alumnus Honored by the President of the United States," *Howard Alumnus* 4 (15 July 1926): 158–59. See also Booker T. Washington to Cobb, 16 June 1909 and resumé in JAC Papers. At one time Cobb was a senior partner in the law firm of Cobb, Perry W. Howard, and George E. C. Hayes. On Cobb's political activities while judge of the municipal court, see Robert R. Church, Jr., to the attorney general, 27 February 1934, RRC Papers.

40. Cobb to Walter White, 8, 16 August 1930; White to R. T. Andrews, 30 December 1930; White to Cobb, 17 December 1930, NAACP Papers. Theodore Roosevelt, Jr., to Cobb, 24 June 1926, JAC Papers. See also n. 56, chapter 17.

41. HH to Cobb, 18 June 1928, 30 June 1928, 24 March 1930, JAC Papers. For evidence of the coolness between Moton and Cobb, see Moton to Cobb, 26 March 1934, RRM Papers. Cobb's

continuing influence is evidenced in White to James Weldon Johnson, 26 April 1932, James Weldon Johnson Papers, Yale University.

42. Ralph J. Bunche, "The Political Status of the Negro," research memorandum, Carnegie-Myrdal Study of the Negro in America, 1940, Schomberg Collection, New York Public Library, New York City, pp. 1140–44; Paul Lewinson, *Race, Class, and Party: A History of Negro Suffrage and White Politics in the South* (New York: Russell and Russell, 1963), pp. 138–41.

43. Jesse O. Thomas to Barnett, 29 August 1929, CAB Papers; Annette E. Church and Roberta Church, *The Robert R. Churches of Memphis* (Ann Arbor, Mich.: Edwards Bros., 1974), pp. 67–72; "Robert R. Church," *Journal of Negro History* 38 (April 1953): 249–51.

44. See Lincoln League and NAACP Files in RRC Papers; Church and Church, *Robert R. Churches*, pp. 87–110. I am indebted to Roberta Church for special permission to research the Robert R. Church, Jr., Papers.

45. Church was not mentioned in the scathing article by Frederick Rush, "Republicans for Revenue Only: Unmasking A Tennessee Patronage Scandal," *Independent* 117 (4 December 1926): 635–39; nonetheless he was quizzed by the Brookhart Committee (see Church and Church, *Robert R. Churches*, pp. 127–30).

46. Church and Church, *Robert R. Churches*, p. 131. Church to HH, 25 May 1929, HHPL.

47. Scott to Work, 25 June 1928; Work to Scott, 27 June 1928, HW Papers.

48. Moton to Holsey, 6 July 1928, CAB Papers.

49. Homer Phillips to Barnett, July 1928 [no specific day]; Percival L. Prattis to Barnett, 18 July 1928, CAB Papers. Prattis was feature editor of the American Negro Press and a very good friend to Barnett. He remarked to Barnett, "You have seen, I am sure, that Tuskegee influence can hurt as well as help" (Prattis to Barnett, 18 July 1928, CAB Papers).

50. Appointments Calendar, 13 July 1928; HH to Dr. Work, memorandum, 14 July 1928, HHPL; Walter Cohen to Work, 26 July 1928, RRC Papers.

51. One of the most valuable documents for understanding the Colored Voters Division is the thirteen-page memorandum to Walter F. Brown, 26 July 1928, "Proposed Set-Up of Office of Negro Organization, Hoover-Curtis Headquarters of the Republican National Committee, 1928," CAB Papers. The memo is a who's who in black Republican politics in 1928. See also Church to the attorney general, 27 February 1934, RRC Papers.

52. Scott to Akerson, 17 September 1928, HHPL; Holsey to Barnett, 15 September 1928; Barnett to Prattis, 7 September 1928, CAB Papers.

53. See the editorials that R. R. Church sent to Hoover after the election (Church to HH, 25 May 1929, HHPL). The editorials revealed the disgust with the CVD leadership that had developed during the campaign (see especially Chicago *Whip*).

54. Ibid. See also Lichtman, *Prejudice and the Old Politics*, p. 157. Lichtman relies on black newspapers that were hostile to Hoover.

55. Holsey to Moton, 22 August 1928, RRM Papers; Chicago *Defender*, 25 August 1928. Church's public statement, carried by the Baltimore *Afro-American* on 25 August, is also in Church and Church, *Robert R. Churches*, p. 131. Church's appeal to Hoover was reported by the Baltimore *Afro-American*, 25 August 1928, and Church kept a copy of this report for his files (RRC Papers).

56. Church to Work, 15 August 1928, RRC Papers; Holsey to Barnett, 21 August 1928, CAB Papers; Church and Church, *Robert R. Churches*, pp. 131–34.

57. Barnett to Prattis, 7 September 1928; Scott to Barnett, 8 September 1928; Barnett to Scott, 8 September 1928; Scott to Barnett, 10 September 1928, CAB Papers. Scott denied that he was attempting to cause friction and controversy.

58. Holsey to Moton, 22 August 1928, RRM Papers; Holsey to Barnett, 21 August 1928, 15 September 1928, CAB Papers. Barnett told Brown that Akerson had informed him that "Hoover dictated a memo . . . directing that I handle publicity" (Barnett to Brown, memorandum, n.d., CAB Papers).

59. Moton to Hawkins, 20 August 1928, RRM Papers.

60. Buni, *Vann*, pp. 133, 138–40, 146, 156, 161, 180.

61. Pittsburgh *Courier*, 30 August 1928 and 1 September 1928; Baltimore *Afro-American*, 15 September 1928; Church and Church, *Robert R. Churches*, p. 132; Scott to Akerson, 17 September 1928, HHPL. See also copies in RRC Papers.

62. Scott to Akerson, 17 September 1928, HHPL. Scott enclosed his newspaper reply to Church. Later Church worked tenaciously to prevent Vann from being appointed as a special assistant attorney general (see T. A. Huntley to Lawrence Richey, 16 July 1929, Vann File and Richey to Mr. Attorney General, 7 June 1929, Church File, HHPL).

9. Reformer or Racist?

1. Scott to Akerson, 17 September 1928, HHPL.

2. Barnett to George Barr Baker, 8 October 1928; Barnett, "Report on Survey of Sentiment Among Negro Voters," n.d., CAB Papers. See also Claude Barnett, "Autobiography," unpublished ms., chapter 4, pp. 2–5, ibid. The survey is a highly detailed, excellent analysis. See also "Memo for Mr. Brown," n.d., CAB Papers, on the need for black instead of white leaders in Harlem.

3. R. H. Rutherford to Barnett, 28 March 1928, CAB Papers. Rutherford's attitude exemplified the hesitancy among black people that existed well into October and early November.

4. Scott to Hoover, 13 July 1928; HH to Scott, 21 July 1928, Prepresidential, Scott File, HHPL.

5. Grosvenor Clarkson had advised Hoover to talk with Emmett J. Scott as early as 2 December 1927. However, Clarkson did not believe that Hoover should use "political expediency" in his appeal to Negroes. Hoover was very interested in Clarkson's views and invited him to a private conference in Washington, D.C. (see Grosvenor Clarkson to HH, 2 December 1927; Akerson to Clarkson, 5 December 1927, GA Papers).

6. Barnett to Prattis, 7 September 1928; Holsey to Barnett, 15 September 1927; Homer Phillips to Barnett, 6 August 1928; Prattis to Dear Claude, 8 August 1928; Fred C. Williams to Barnett, 22 August 1928, CAB Papers. These letters are especially valuable in documenting the chaos, discouragement, and lack of any program for blacks. For discontent among Kentucky blacks, see W. T. Merchant to Phillips, 20 July 1928, ibid.

7. See all of the letters cited in n. 6. See also Barnett's campaign flyer attempting to highlight the few remarks applicable to blacks in Hoover's acceptance speech. The flyer, complete with photographs of Hoover, is entitled "Hoover Urges Equality for All" (CAB Papers).

8. Quoted in Alpheus Thomas Mason, *William Howard Taft: Chief Justice* (New York: Simon and Schuster, 1964), pp. 151–52; William Howard Taft to Robert Taft, 4 November 1928, William Howard Taft Papers, LC. Taft misunderstood Hoover's views on Negroes and Negro leaders in the Republican party. Hoover meant to eliminate black politicians whom he believed to be corrupt, such as Perry Howard, and therefore he would not act to save Howard from prosecution regardless of the political consequences. See also William H. Taft to H. D. Taft, 31 October 1928, Taft Papers, LC. Taft's recollection has been accepted at face value by scholars. See Richard B. Sherman, *The Republican Party and Black America: From McKinley to Hoover, 1896–1933* (Charlottesville: University Press of Virginia, 1973), p. 231. For Taft's southern strategy see Sherman, *Republican Party and Black America*, pp. 83–112, but especially pp. 88–89, 111–12; Elliot M. Rudwick, *W. E. B. Du Bois: A Study in Minority Group Leadership* (Philadelphia: University of Pennsylvania Press, 1960), p. 259; Paul D. Casdorph, *Republicans, Negroes, and Progressives in the South, 1912–1916* (University, Ala.: University of Alabama Press, 1981), pp. vii, 1–9 and passim; George Brown Tindall, *The Disruption of the Solid South* (Athens: University of Georgia Press, 1972), p. 19.

9. Hoover invited McCormick to lunch on 2 October 1928 and spoke with him at some length.

The following morning the Chicago *Tribune* reported that Hoover fully approved of the GOP's effort to break the solid South by offering political power and patronage to bolting Democrats (see Appointments Calendar, 3 October 1928, HHPL and Chicago *Tribune*, 3 October 1928). See also McCormick to HH, 13, 16 August 1928; HH to McCormick, 16 August 1928, HHPL.

10. See the citations in n. 9 and HH to McCormick, 30 March 1929, PP File, HHPL.

11. See, for example, J. L. Webb to Barnett, 28 October 1928, CAB Papers. Webb, supreme custodian of the Arkansas WOU, informed Barnett that Hoover's "leaders and managers are not bidding for the Negro vote nor have they offered anything tangible but they are making their strongest bid for the Klan and Lily Whites." He further warned Barnett that the Smith supporters were claiming 10,000 blacks on the Democratic payrolls in the North and would do well in Harlem. Actually Smith had not made any Negro appointments (see acting secretary to L. G. McMorris, 1 October 1928, NAACP Papers).

12. Prattis to Barnett, 18 July 1928, CAB Papers. Upon Pickens's request Prattis sent Barnett a copy of the letter he had received from Pickens. See also Pickens to Prattis, 16 July 1928; and "Report on Survey of Sentiment among Negro Voters," p. 2, CAB Papers.

13. White to Hester Greene, 19 September 1928; White to Baltimore *Afro-American*, working copy, not sent, August 3–22 File; White to Walter H. Lewis, 7 August 1928, NAACP Papers. Another good source is Walter White, *A Man Called White* (New York: Viking Press, 1948), pp. 99–101. See also evidence in n. 12.

14. W. E. B. Du Bois, "Is Al Smith Afraid of the South?" *Nation* 127 (17 October 1928): 392–94.

15. Ibid.; W. E. B. Du Bois, "Mr. Hoover and the South," *Crisis* 37 (April 1929): 131–32; W. E. B. Du Bois, "Postscript," *Crisis* 35 (December 1928): 418; George F. Garcia, "Herbert Hoover's Southern Strategy and the Black Reaction" (M.A. thesis, University of Iowa, 1972), p. 62.

16. Claude A. Barnett, "Report on Survey of Sentiment among Negro Voters," pp. 1–2, CAB Papers.

17. Barnett to Work, 10 December 1928, ibid.

18. Barnett to Brown, 6 September 1928; Barnett to Hawkins, 31 August 1928; Barnett to A. H. Kirchhofer, 5, 6 September 1928, ibid. Typewritten copies of the pamphlets are in a file marked "1928 undated," ibid. See also "Herbert Hoover and the Mississippi Flood," issued by the CVD in RRM Papers.

19. Barnett to A. H. Kirchhofer, 25 September 1928, CAB Papers. A copy of the photograph used by the *Herald Commonwealth* is in the Barnett scrapbook, ibid.

20. Barnett did not originate the practice. See John G. Van Deusen, *The Black Man in White America* (Washington, D.C.: Associated Publishers, 1938), p. 219.

21. Barnett to R. L. Vann, 16 September 1928, CAB Papers; Scott to Work, 26 June 1928; Work to Scott, 28 June 1928, HW Papers. Work was unimpressed by the success of the Smith forces in recruiting prominent black newspaper editors. See also Henry Lee Moon, *Balance of Power: The Negro Vote* (Garden City, N.Y.: Doubleday and Co., 1948), pp. 105–6; Andrew Buni, *Robert L. Vann of the Pittsburgh Courier: Politics and Black Journalism* (Pittsburgh: Pittsburgh University Press, 1974), p. 179.

22. Monroe N. Work, *Negro Year Book: An Annual Encyclopedia of the Negro, 1931–1932* (Tuskegee Institute, Ala.: Negro Year Book Publishing Co., 1931), p. 87. See also Allan J. Lichtman, *Prejudice and the Old Politics: The Presidential Election of 1928* (Chapel Hill: University of North Carolina Press, 1979), p. 158.

23. See Barnett's fascinating essay "Future of Race Depends on Control of Colored Press," September 1928, CAB Papers. Just as he had argued to RNC chairman William P. Butler on 13 April 1925 that the Republican party must offer programs rather than campaign promises, so too did he believe that the editors must offer "a definite program for racial progress."

24. Claude A. Barnett, "Memorandum on Publicity," 26 October 1928; Barnett to Vann, 27

October 1928; Barnett to Raymond Benjamin, 20 November 1928, CAB Papers. See also numerous letters from Barnett to the various newspaper editors, ibid.

25. Barnett to Raymond Benjamin, 20 November 1928; Barnett to Work, 10 December 1928; Claude A. Barnett, "Report on Activities of the Publishing Department," 15 October 1928, ibid. A complete list of the forty-four newspapers and the amount of money to each is in ibid.

26. See numerous letters from editors to Barnett in the October 1928 file, but especially C. A. Franklin to Barnett, 15 October 1928; William Monroe Trotter to Barnett, 17 October 1928; William A. Davis to Barnett, 31 October 1928; N. B. Young to Barnett, 1 November 1928; Harry C. Smith to Barnett, 12 October 1928; Work to C. A. Franklin, 15 January 1929, ibid. Barnett was justifiably angry at suggestions of his personal monetary gain or that the editors could be bought (see Barnett to Raymond Benjamin, 20 November 1928, ibid.). Benjamin was one of Work's chief assistants during the campaign and a close friend of Hoover's. Benjamin refused to allow advertising in Ben Davis's Atlanta *Independent* (see Barnett to Davis, 26 October 1928; Davis to Barnett, 2 November 1928, ibid.). Newspaper editors did not forget the cancellations and continued to criticize Hoover and the party leaders (see R. R. Church to HH, 25 May 1929, with enclosed editorials, in HHPL).

27. Washington (D.C.) *Eagle*, 6 April 1928.

28. Work to HH, January 1929, Work File, HHPL. See also chapter 10, nn. 10 and 11.

29. Appointments Calendar, 12, 25 August 1928, HHPL. Hoover granted Church a special Sunday interview at Palo Alto on 12 August 1928. He saw no other visitors that day. Back in Washington on 25 August, he spoke with Brown for one hour and again with Church later that afternoon. See also chapter 10, nn. 40 and 41. Also important are Akerson to Church, 30 June 1928; HH, memo to Mr. Brown, 28 September 1928, HHPL; Holsey to Barnett, 21 August 1928, CAB Papers. Further evidence of Hoover's concern, his restraints on Mann, and his respect for Church are in the New York *Herald Tribune*, 26 January 1929; New York *World*, 4 February 1929; Annette E. Church and Roberta Church, *The Robert R. Churches of Memphis* (Ann Arbor, Mich.: Edward Bros., 1974), pp. 133–35; Ray Benjamin to Mr. President, 3 May 1929, RRC Papers. For Hoover's assertiveness late in the campaign see *New York Times*, 5 June 1929; Brooklyn *Eagle*, 5 June 1929; Boston *Transcript*, 5 June 1929; and Philadelphia *Ledger*, 5 June 1929.

30. Chicago *Defender*, 3, 10 November 1928. See also Claude A. Barnett scrapbook, CAB Papers; Church and Church, *Robert R. Churches*, p. 133; and working copies of "Why I Am For Hoover" in RRC Papers.

31. Cohen to Barnett, 27 October 1928, CAB Papers.

32. Neville Thomas to Mabel Walker Willebrandt, 21 July 1928, PWH File.

33. Benjamin J. Davis to Barnett, 25 October 1928, CAB Papers.

34. "G.O.P. South," *Time*, 18 February 1929, p. 10; Baltimore *Afro-American*, 23 February 1929 in the RRC Papers; Chicago *Defender*, 10 November 1928 in CAB Papers. Raymond Benjamin, a prominent New York City Republican who was close to Hoover during the campaign, later told Hoover that Church deserved the credit for "a large part of the effective effort that was put forth to prevent a complete stampede of the colored vote to the Democratic party" (see Benjamin to Mr. President, 3 May 1929, RRC Papers). Lichtman accepts the view of critical black editors (see Allan J. Lichtman, *Prejudice and the Old Politics: The Presidential Election of 1928* [Chapel Hill: University of North Carolina Press, 1979], pp. 149, 158). On 4 February 1929 the New York *World* reported that "most" of the anti-Hoover black newspapers switched to support of Hoover. See also n. 22.

35. Elbert Lee Tatum, *The Changed Political Thought of the Negro* (New York: Exposition Press, 1951), pp. 77, 88; White, *A Man Called White*, pp. 100–101; W. E. B. Du Bois, "Postscript," *Crisis* 35 (November 1928): 381.

36. For a more detailed analysis see Robert H. Brisbane, *The Negro Vanguard: Origins of the Negro Social Revolution 1900–1960* (Valley Forge, Pa.: Judson Press, 1970), p. 125; David Burner, *The Politics of Provincialism: The Democratic Party in Transition, 1918–1932* (New

York: Alfred A. Knopf, 1967), pp. 224–25, 228, 237–42; V. O. Key, *Southern Politics in State and Nation* (New York: Alfred A. Knopf, 1949), pp. 318–29; Sherman, *Republican Party and Black America*, pp. 231–33; and Lichtman, *Prejudice and the Old Politics*, pp. 145–47, 237–38, 288–90.

10. Mixing Racial and Reform Politics

1. For Hoover's disappointments in the selection of cabinet officers, see Edgar Rickard diary, 19 February 1929, ER Papers, and *New York Times*, 22, 23 January 1929.

2. Franklin Fort to HH, 1 February 1929, Pres. Papers. Fort warned Hoover that these reporters would constitute the White House press corps and that their unhappiness was already well known to members of Congress, who had warned him of the danger. For the best analysis of Hoover's relations with the press, see Craig Lloyd, *Aggressive Introvert: A Study of Herbert Hoover and Public Relations Management, 1912–1932* (Columbus: Ohio State University Press, 1972).

3. *New York Times*, 23, 24, 25 January 1929; New York *Herald Tribune*, 24, 26, 27, 28, 29 January 1929; New York *Evening Post*, 24, 26, 27, 28, 29 January 1929; New York *World*, 24, 25, 28, 29 January 1929. See also the Washington *Post* clipping in the W. E. Evans file, Pres. Papers. Evans was a congressman from California who championed Mann's strategy.

4. Paul Lewinson, *Race, Class, and Party: A History of Negro Suffrage and White Politics in the South* (New York: Russell and Russell, 1963), p. 167.

5. V. O. Key, *Southern Politics in State and Nation* (New York: Alfred A. Knopf, 1949), pp. 318–23, 326–29; Lewinson, *Race, Class, and Party*, pp. 104–6, 136–62.

6. Immediately after the 1928 election Hoover and Mann were on friendly terms (HH to Mann, 18 November 1928, Mann File; Mann to HH, 12 November 1928, Stuart Cramer File, HHPL). Judging from his appointments calendar, Hoover only occasionally spoke with Mann or someone sent by him.

7. New York *Evening Post*, 26 January 1929; Claudius Huston to HH, 29 January 1929, C & T. See also Tennessee *Commercial Appeal*, 15 April 1929; Mann to Akerson, 11 March 1929; and J. W. Arnold to HH, 19 March 1929, Georgia State File, HHPL; Oliver D. Street to Horace Mann, 25 August 1928, in Campaign 1928, Alabama, LS Papers.

8. "GOP South," *Time*, 18 February 1929, p. 10; Annette E. Church and Roberta Church, *The Robert R. Churches of Memphis* (Ann Arbor, Mich.: Edwards Bros., 1974), pp. 133–35. See also New York *World*, 3 March 1929; Norfolk *Journal and Guide*, 16 March 1929; Baltimore *Afro-American*, 9, 16 March 1929; Washington (D.C.) *Tribune*, 15 March 1929; and nn. 29 and 30 in chapter 9.

9. New York *Herald Tribune*, 27, 28 January 1929; New York *World*, 28 January 1929.

10. Work to HH, January 1929, Work File, Pres. Papers, and correspondence and letters in this file. See especially HH to Work, 7 February 1929. Also see newspaper articles in Work scrapbook, Work Papers, Hoover Institution, Stanford University, Palo Alto, Calif.

11. Franklin Fort to HH, n.d. [January 1929?], Pres. Papers. Fort was second in command of the Republican National Committee. Work did not destroy financial records. Hoover had very high regard for Fort (see HH to Charles H. Martens, 25 October 1928, Pres. Papers).

12. W. J. Donald to Newton, 31 January 1930, State File, South Carolina, HHPL. Donald, the assistant to the chairman of the Republican National Committee, informed Newton, "During the campaign Mr. Mann maintained his own files, and unless he destroyed these after the campaign, they are still in his office." The Mann files have never been found. The best evidence on Mann is in the GBS Papers. The correspondence between Mann and Stockton is especially revealing. Mann's quotation on eliminating all blacks is in Mann to Stockton, 18 December 1928, but also see Mann to Stockton, 12, 15, 17 and 22 October 1928 and Stockton to Mann, 28 September and 3

December 1928, ibid. Stockton was one of Hoover's volunteer executives in the feeding of Europe during and following World War I. Hoover had great personal regard for Stockton and appointed him ambassador to Austria (see HH to Stockton, 28 January, 21 June 1929, and Stockton to George Fort Milton, 23 January 1930, ibid).

13. Charles Michelson, *The Ghost Talks* (New York: G. P. Putnam's Sons, 1944), pp. 35, 14–35, 41–42.

14. Charles Michelson, "Col. Mann at Hoover's Heels Waits Reward for Services," New York *World*, 29 January 1929. The latest scholar to accept the interpretation that Hoover personally orchestrated Mann's southern campaign is Allan J. Lichtman, *Prejudice and the Old Politics: The Presidential Election of 1928* (Chapel Hill: University of North Carolina Press, 1979), pp. 152–53. In an unpublished paper on file at the HHPL, Larry H. Grothaus concludes that the relationship between Hoover and Mann during the 1928 campaign "is not clear" (see Grothaus, "The Hoover Administration and Blacks," 8 August 1979, p. 20, HHPL).

15. Baltimore *Sun*, 28 January 1929; New York *Evening Post*, 28 January 1929; *New York Times*, 29 January, 2 February, and 11 March 1929.

16. New York *World*, 28 January 1929; Stockton to Mann, 3 December 1928, GBS Papers.

17. *New York Times*, 24, 25 January, 2 February 1929; New York *Evening Post*, 24 January, 1 February 1929; HH to Richard H. Edmonds, 7 November 1928 in Major Addresses File, HHPL; New York *World*, 25 January 1929. The *World* accused Hoover and his top Republican advisers of attempting to "soft-pedal intolerance" after they had won. See also George F. Garcia, "Herbert Hoover's Southern Strategy and the Black Reaction" (M.A. thesis, University of Iowa, 1972), p. 67, n. 28.

18. For the full story of the Slemp dismissal, see correspondence in Bascom Slemp File and in Cabinet Appointments File, Pres. Papers and especially Akerson "Memo to Chief," 4 February 1928, GA Papers. Also Henry W. Anderson to HH, 6 November 1928; and Anderson to Lewis L. Strauss, 17 January 1929, Pres. Papers. Hoover denounced the bigotry during the campaign in Virginia (see Herbert Hoover, *The Memoirs of Herbert Hoover*, 3 vols. [New York: Macmillan Co., 1951–52], 2:208).

19. See n. 17 and especially New York *Evening Post*, 1 February 1929, HHPL.

20. Huston to HH, memorandum, 29 January 1929, C & T, HHPL.

21. Mann categorically denied any desire for political power or reward (see Mann's message to HH in Mann File, Pres. Papers). See also his denials in the newspapers cited in nn. 15 and 16.

22. Appointments Calendar, 3 February, 24 March 1929, HHPL.

23. Akerson to Richey, 1 February 1929, Pres. Papers.

24. For speculation on Mann's continued influence, see editorial in the *New York Times*, 2 February 1929; Street to HH, 24 January, 9 February 1929, Pres. Papers. Another good example of Hoover's denunciation of the "southern mess" and his resolve to reform the party is Sen. William Borah's account of his conversation with Hoover in the *New York Times*, 13 December 1928. Even at this early date Hoover revealed his conviction that special patronage advisory committees would be necessary (see front-page story, *New York Times*, 4 February 1929).

25. In January 1929 the Senate expanded the scope of the Brookhart investigation to include any person appointed to federal office. See U.S. Congress, Senate Subcommittee of the Committee on Post Offices and Post Roads, *Hearings on Influencing Appointments to Postmasterships*, 70th Congress, 2d sess., part 2, p. 307. For Brookhart's support of Hoover during the campaign, see Brookhart to HH, 8 October 1928; HH to Brookhart, 12 October 1928, Pres. Papers.

26. Appointments Calendar, 9, 16 January, 23 February, 14, 28 March 1929, HHPL; *New York Times*, 24 February 1929; New York *Evening Post*, 31 January 1929.

27. *New York Times*, 18 November 1928.

28. U.S. Congress, *Hearings on Influencing Appointments*, pp. 260–62, 282–306.

29. New York *Evening Post*, 24 January 1929.

30. *Hearings on Influencing Appointments*, pp. 519–26, 1065–66. See also Creager to HH, 23

December, 24 February 1929, Creager File, HHPL; Houston *Post-Dispatch*, 6 December, 1929; New York *Evening Post*, 31 January 1929; Creager to Ray Lyman Wilbur, 17 June 1929, Wilbur Papers, Hoover Institution, Stanford University, Palo Alto, Calif.

31. New York *Evening Post*, 24 January 1929.

32. HH to attorney general, 7 April 1929; Attorney General William D. Mitchell to HH, 9 April 1929; Brookhart to HH, 12 April 1929; Richey to Attorney General, 15 April 1929; Creager to HH, 14 June 1929, Texas State File, HHPL; Brookhart to HH, 11 June 1930, with copy of his criticism of Hoover in the *Congressional Record* in Brookhart File, HHPL. On Hoover's pursuit of those charged with corruption, see HH to attorney general, 17 March 1930; William D. Mitchell to HH, 29 October 1930, Republican National Committee File, HHPL. See also Hoover's press conference statement, 18 March 1930, "Comment on the Report of the Senate Committee on Federal Patronage in the South" in Herbert Hoover, *The State Papers and Other Public Writings of Herbert Hoover*, ed. William Starr Myers, 2 vols. (New York: Doubleday, Doran and Co., 1934), 1:220–21.

33. Edgar Rickard diary, 15 April, 29–30 June, 25, 26 September 1926, ER Papers; Robert R. McCormick to HH, 13 August 1928; HH to McCormick, 16 August 1928, Pres. Papers. Other Republican leaders also worried about corruption in the party (see Gerald P. Nye to George Norris, n.d., National Politics File, GN Papers; Sacramento *Bee*, 11 October 1928; *New York Times*, 11 October 1928; New York *World*, 11 October 1928; Henry J. Allen to John J. Raskob, 10 October 1928 in Misrepresentations File; HH to Charles Evans Hughes, 24 September 1928, Pres. Papers). Work was also later accused of involvement in Teapot Dome. See *New York Times*, 14 December 1928; Hubert Work, "Statement to Senate Public Lands Committee," 13 December 1928 in Pres. Papers. See also Henry L. Doherty to Work, 20 November 1928; Albert B. Fall to Work, 10 December 1928; Work to Fall, 18 December 1928, in HW Papers. For his acceptance speech see Herbert Hoover, *The New Day: Campaign Speeches of Herbert Hoover, 1928* (Stanford, Calif.: Stanford University Press, 1928), pp. 29–30. His inaugural address is in Hoover, *State Papers*, 1:4–6.

34. Hoover, *State Papers*, 1:4–6.

35. Alpheus Thomas Mason, *William Howard Taft: Chief Justice* (New York: Simon and Schuster, 1964), pp. 152–55.

36. Hoover, *State Papers*, 1:10, 15.

37. *New York Times*, 11 March 1929. For Brookhart's predictions see *New York Times*, 24 February 1929.

38. New York *World*, 19 February 1929.

39. H. A. Mann to George E. Akerson, 11 March 1929, Georgia State File, HHPL. *New York Times*, 11 March 1929.

40. Robert R. Church, Jr., "The President and the Lily-White Movement," *Nation-Wide Review* 3 (March 1929): 5, RRC Papers.

41. Ibid. See also Church to HH, 27 December 1928, RRC Papers; n. 8; Atlanta *Constitution*, 17 March 1929; and especially Chicago *Defender's* front-page story "Bob Church Forces Colonel Horace A. Mann to Resign," 16 March 1929. Hoover's support of Church is also clearly stated in the complaints of Tennessee lily-whites. See Paul J. Kruesi to Lewis Strauss, n.d.; Kruesi to J. R. Nutt, 8 October 1928, Campaign 1928, Negroes, LS Papers. Useful, too, are reports in the New York *World*, 3, 10 March 1929; the Baltimore *Afro-American*, 16 March 1929; and Washington (D.C.) *Tribune*, 15 March 1929.

42. H. A. Mann to Joseph O. Thompson, 10 April 1930; Mann to HH, 26 April 1930, PP File; *New York Times*, 2, 3 May 1929; Memphis *Commercial Appeal*, 15 April 1929; Atlanta *Constitution*, 26 December 1930; Mann, press release, 25 December 1930 [?], PP File.

43. Lewinson, *Race, Class, and Party*, p. 174; Atlanta *Constitution*, 17 March 1929.

44. The working drafts are in Subject File, Pres. Papers, Appointments, Southern, HHPL.

45. Hoover, *State Papers*, 1:22–23.

46. Ibid.

47. See, for example, Donald J. Lisio, *The President and Protest: Hoover, Conspiracy, and the Bonus Riot* (Columbia: University of Missouri Press, 1974), pp. 71–75, 104–8.

48. See letters of protest in the Georgia State File, Florida State File, Alabama State File and other southern state files. See also Henry Lee Moon, *Balance of Power: The Negro Vote* (Garden City, N.Y.: Doubleday and Co., 1948), pp. 80, 108–9. The lily-whites in Mississippi interpreted the speech to mean the end of the Howard faction, and unlike other, established Republicans, they were delighted (see Lamont Rowlands to Richey, 27 March 1929; Charles Ulysses Gordon to Newton, 27 March 1929, Mississippi State File, HHPL). Hoover appointed Lamont Rowlands as his patronage referee in Mississippi.

49. *New York Times*, 27 March 1929.

50. Ibid.

51. *Hearings on Influencing Appointments*, pp. 282–306; *New York Times*, 27 March 1929; *Chicago Tribune*, 28 March 1929.

52. *New York Times*, 27 March 1929.

53. *New York Times*, 28 March 1929.

54. Mann to Newton, 10 April 1929; M. W. Wells to HH, 30 March 1929, Florida State File, HHPL; Lewinson, *Race, Class, and Party*, p. 173; Garcia, "Hoover's Southern Strategy," p. 76; Hanes Walton, Jr., *Black Republicans: The Politics of the Black and Tans* (Metuchen, N.J.: Scarecrow Press, 1975), p. 161; Lichtman, *Prejudice and the Old Politics*, p. 147.

55. For Church's quote see *Chicago Defender*, 30 March 1929; W. E. B. Du Bois, "Mr. Hoover and the South," *Crisis* 37 (April 1929): 131; Robert R. Church to HH, 25 May, 24 June 1929 with editorials; Harry M. Pace to HH, 27 April 1929; Herbert D. Myers to HH, 30 May 1929; Charles O'Neal to HH, 17 April 1929; Arthur M. Mitchell to HH, 30 March 1929, CQ. Pace was president of the National Negro Insurance Association, and Mitchell was president of Phi Beta Sigma fraternity. See also Cincinnati *Union*, 16, 23 May 1929; Sherman, *Republican Party and Black America*, pp. 234–37; and Andrew Buni, *The Negro in Virginia Politics, 1902–1965* (Charlottesville: University Press of Virginia, 1967), p. 107; Monroe N. Work, *Negro Year Book: An Annual Encyclopedia of the Negro, 1931–1932* (Tuskegee Institute, Ala.: Negro Year Book Publishing Co., 1931), pp. 93–98; John Hope Franklin, *From Slavery to Freedom: A History of Negro Americans* (New York: Alfred A. Knopf, 1967), pp. 524–25.

56. Sherman, *Republican Party and Black America*, p. 238; Lewinson, *Race, Class, and Party*, pp. 173, 110–11, 184; Moon, *Balance of Power*, pp. 79–80, 108; Garcia, "Hoover's Southern Strategy," pp. 13, 76–79; Walton, *Black Republicans*, pp. 134–35; Robert H. Brisbane, *The Black Vanguard: Origins of the Negro Revolution, 1900–1960* (Valley Forge, Pa.: Judson Press, 1970), p. 125–26; Vincent P. DeSantis, "Republican Efforts to 'Crack' the Democratic South," *Review of Politics* 14 (April 1952): 261. See also nn. 51, 52, 53, and 54.

57. *Chicago Tribune*, 28 March 1929; William T. Hutchinson, *Lowden of Illinois: The Life of Frank O. Lowden*, 2 vols. (Chicago: University of Chicago Press, 1957), 2:580–81.

58. HH to Col. Robert R. McCormick, 30 March 1929, HHPL.

59. Ibid. The original of this letter is in the Robert R. McCormick Papers at the Chicago *Tribune*, but the collection is closed to scholars, and I was denied access by the archivist. The Hoover Library has a copy of the letter sent by the archivist of the McCormick collection.

60. Ibid. Hoover wrote "Confidential" at the top of the letter. Hoover had consulted with Moton (see Moton to Brown, 21 March 1929; Moton to HH, 1, 19 April 1929, RRM Papers).

61. HH to McCormick, 8 April 1929; Akerson to McCormick, 8 April 1929, *Tribune* File, HHPL. See also Appointments Calendar, Pres. Papers, HHPL.

62. Claude A. Barnett, "Memorandum for Mr. Saunders: The Attitude of the Negro Voters," n.d., CAB Papers.

11. Howard and De Priest: Incongruous Symbols

1. Chicago *Defender*, 16 March 1929.

2. Willebrandt to director of FBI, 12, 26 July, 1 August 1928, PWH File.

3. See "General Suggestions with Reference to *Perry Howard et al. Indictment*," ibid. I obtained access to Howard's federal income tax returns for 1926, 1927, and 1928 under the Freedom of Information Act, and copies are in ibid.

4. E. E. Hindman to attorney general, 2 January 1929, ibid.

5. Ibid. The investigation of Howard by the FBI involved eight investigators who spent well over 355 days on the case (see E. E. Conway to director, FBI, 17 October 1928, ibid.).

6. E. E. Hindman to attorney general, 2 January 1929, ibid. Millar McGilchrist to Lester G. Fant, 28 December 1928. Much of the evidence and the basis for the government's case is in the file marked *U.S. vs. Perry W. Howard et al.*, No. 9579, in the District Court of the United States for the Southern District of Mississippi, Jackson Division. On Howard's hearing in court, see New York *World*, 15 December 1928.

7. Washington (D.C.) *Sentinel*, 15 December 1928; New York *World*, 15 December 1928. See also New York *World*, 3 December 1928.

8. J. W. Cassedy, Jed Franklin, and J. D. Thomas to attorney general, 14 December 1928, PWH File. The defendant's attorney informed the attorney general that Howard "was acquitted on the first ballot." All of the defendants were acquitted, but the jury apparently differed on one or more of them, and therefore additional balloting was necessary. For Moton's request to Howard, see Moton to Howard, 18 February, 6 June 1928, RRM Papers. On his acquittal, see *New York Times*, 15 December 1928.

9. Millar McGilchrist to Lamont Rowlands, 28 December 1928; Willebrandt to E. C. Hawkins, 27 March 1929; J. C. Tyler to Willebrandt, 20 March 1929; Ben F. Cameron to Attorney General, 6 November 1929; Willebrandt to Smith W. Brookhart, 11 March 1929, PWH File. See also Jackson (Miss.) *Daily News*, 20 March 1929 and New York *Evening Post*, 31 January 1929. For scholars who accept this explanation see Paul Lewinson, *Race, Class, and Party: A History of Negro Suffrage and White Politics in the South* (New York: Russell and Russell, 1963), pp. 181–84; Richard B. Sherman, *The Republican Party and Black America: From McKinley to Hoover, 1896–1933* (Charlottesville: University of Virginia Press, 1973), p. 238; George F. Garcia, "Hoover's Southern Strategy and the Black Reaction" (M.A. thesis, University of Iowa, 1972), p. 85; V. O. Key, *Southern Politics in State and Nation* (New York: Alfred A. Knopf, 1949), p. 287; Hanes Walton, Jr., *Black Republicans: The Politics of the Black and Tans* (Metuchen, N.J.: Scarecrow Press, 1975), p. 135.

10. Willebrandt to attorney general, 14 July 1928; Willebrandt to attorney general, memorandum, 16 March 1929, PWH File. See especially U.S. Congress, Senate Subcommittee of the Committee on Post Offices and Post Roads, *Hearings on Influencing Appointments to Postmasterships*, 70th Congress, 2d sess., part 2, pp. 1493–97 and 347–93. See numerous copies of "Deed of Property Owned Jointly with John R. Hawkins." The property was valued at $27,400. Howard's bank records are not available. See also nn. 2 and 7 and E. E. Conroy Report, "Perry W. Howard *et al.*, Purchase and Sale of Public Office," 26 September 1928, PWH File.

11. HH to Julius Rosenwald, 29 November 1929, PP File; Willebrandt to attorney general, memorandum, 22 November 1928; Willebrandt to E. E. Hindman, 29 January 1929; E. E. Conroy to director, FBI, 12, 17 October 1928 and 26 September 1928, PWH File. These three detailed reports are extraordinarily valuable. On the failure to uncover evidence of the sale of post office positions, see report sent by J. Edgar Hoover to Willebrandt, 13 March 1929, ibid. See also U.S. Congress, *Hearings on Influencing Appointments*, pp. 427–49; Chicago *Defender*, 16 March 1929. Willebrandt was convinced that Brookhart's investigation was a "miracle" that gave her the opportunity to seek a second indictment. See Willebrandt to parents, 22 January 1929, Mabel Walker Willebrandt Papers, LC.

12. Willebrandt to Mitchell, memorandum, 16 July 1928; Willebrandt to E. M. C. Hawkins, 27 March 1929, PWH File.

13. Lester G. Fant to Willebrandt, 11 March 1929; Willebrandt to attorney general, 11 March 1929, ibid. See also Chicago *Defender*, 16 March 1929.

14. *New York Times*, 27 April 1929; J. C. Tyler to Willebrandt, 3 March 1929; E. M. C. Hawkins to Willebrandt, 22 March 1929; Ben F. Cameron to attorney general, 6, 14 November 1929, PWH File. For the decision to drop further charges, see Howard T. Jones to attorney general, memorandum, "Patronage Indictments Pending in Mississippi," 8 October 1929, PWH File. Mitchell penned his response on the memo, noting, "This is good sense. I think it would be a waste of effort to go forward with these cases." See also Howard T. Jones to Ben F. Cameron, 10 October 1929, PWH File.

15. Dorothy M. Brown, *Mabel Walker Willebrandt: A Study of Power, Loyalty, and Law* (Knoxville, Tn.: University of Tennessee Press, 1984), pp. 153, 158–78, 164–65, 172–73. Brown argues that Willebrandt's controversial campaign speeches had Hoover's approval. She accepts Allan Lichtman's claim that Hoover was in complete control of the campaign and was willing to exploit social tensions. See especially pp. 164–65, 172–73.

16. Willebrandt to Work, 27 September 1928, Willebrandt File, C & T, HHPL. Willebrandt does not claim that Hoover either saw or approved of her speeches.

17. Ibid.

18. Ibid.

19. Ibid.

20. Willebrandt to Hoover, n.d., Willebrandt File, C & T, HHPL. Willebrandt sent Hoover a copy of her letter to Work. In the undated memorandum to Hoover Willebrandt stated: "This letter of yesterday to Dr. Work gets at the telegraph record I mentioned to you." Willebrandt had saved all of the telegrams from the Speakers' Bureau requesting that she make additional speeches and scheduling those she did make. See also Baltimore *Sun*, 3 October 1928 and coverage in other newspapers in Work scrapbook, HW Papers. Five days prior to the confrontation between Willebrandt and Work, Hoover told a reporter that he intended to issue "an absolute injunction to his subordinates to eliminate the religious issue and to subordinate the prohibition issue." He also warned that he would fire anyone guilty of the "dissemination of religious propaganda of any sort." See New York *Sun*, 22 September 1928, copy in Work scrapbook, HW Papers. Under these circumstances Willebrandt may have taken her case directly to Hoover because she feared that she might be fired.

21. Baltimore *Sun*, 3 October 1929 and Work scrapbook, HW Papers.

22. Robert Barry, "Washington Day to Day," New York *World*, 6 June 1929; Washington *Herald*, 2 January 1929.

23. Willebrandt's reference to herself as a "storm center" is in a letter to Work in which she stated: "I seem to be a sort of storm center. In the minds of many I guess I personify 'Prohibition.'" See Willebrandt to Work, 6 September 1929, Willebrandt File, C & T, HHPL. Later she also told her parents that she had come to "personify prohibition" and that the "anti-Hoover forces wish to break him [Hoover] on prohibition and to do that any pretext is seized to discredit me." See Willebrandt to her parents, 29 March 1929, Willebrandt Papers, LC. The reaction of party officials is in the Philadelphia *Ledger*, 5 June 1929 and Providence *Journal*, 5 June 1929.

24. See all of the references in n. 22.

25. Willebrandt to her parents, 22 February 1929, Willebrandt Papers, LC.

26. See correspondence relating to her possible higher appointment in Cabinet Appointments File, HHPL. See also n. 21.

27. Willebrandt to her parents, 22 February 1929, Willebrandt Papers, LC.

28. See especially Willebrandt to her parents, 29 March 1929, 21 April 1929 and 8 May 1929, Willebrandt Papers, LC. See also Brown, *Willebrandt*, pp. 175–78.

29. Willebrandt to her parents, 21 March 1929, Willebrandt Papers, LC. See also Chicago

Tribune, 2 June 1929; HH to Willebrandt, 7 February 1929; and letters in Willebrandt File, C & T, HHPL.

30. Willebrandt to her parents, 21 March 1929, Willebrandt Papers, LC. For her continuing influence see chapter 12, n. 18, chapter 17, n. 10, and chapter 18, n. 72.

31. See, for example, Willebrandt to attorney general, memorandum, 16 March 1929, and 12 September 1929, PWH File. See also *New York Times*, 7 May 1929; Chicago *Tribune*, 2 June 1929; Edgar Rickard diary, 1 August 1930, ER Papers. David Ginzl also accepts Howard's guilt but he did not utilize the materials in the PWH File. See David J. Ginzl, "Lily-Whites Versus Black-and-Tans: Mississippi Republicans During the Hoover Administration," *Journal of Mississippi History* (August 1980), pp. 200–202.

32. Ralph J. Bunche, *The Political Status of the Negro in the Age of FDR*, ed. Dewey W. Grantham (Chicago: University of Chicago Press, 1973), p. 81; Holsey to Moton, 18 July 1928, RRM Papers; Walton, *Black Republicans*, p. 135. Walton claims that Howard did sell offices and that the evidence against him was "massive." Other blacks believed him to be innocent. See especially the editorial from the Newark *Herald* and Houston *Informer* sent to Hoover by Robert R. Church (Church to HH, 25 May 1929, CQ). See also U.S. Congress, *Hearings on Influencing Federal Appointments*, pp. 498, 1493–1501. The FBI continued investigating Howard in 1931 (see Nugent Dodds to HH, memorandum, 17 April 1931, PWH File).

33. Harold F. Gosnell, *Negro Politicians: The Rise of Negro Politics in Chicago* (Chicago: University of Chicago Press, 1935), pp. 184, 195.

34. Charles Michelson, "Political Undertow," New York *World*, 7 February 1929.

35. Oral history, Carrie Butler Massenburg; oral history, Mrs. Leon Thompson, HHPL. Both were black maids, and both testify to her fairness toward blacks. Mrs. Hoover offered to pay for Carrie Butler's college expenses. See also David Burner, *Herbert Hoover: A Public Life* (New York: Alfred A. Knopf, 1979), pp. 214–17.

36. On 30 September 1978, at my request, Ruth Fesler Lipman, who was personal secretary to Mrs. Hoover, sent excerpts from her diary to the director of the Herbert Hoover Presidential Library (see excerpts from diary, 11, 12, 13 June 1929 but most especially the entry on 8 June). She also enclosed a signed statement in which she explicitly recalled that "the President asked Mrs. Hoover to ask Mrs. De Priest to tea." The Lipman diary is now open to scholars. See also Helen B. Pryor, *Lou Henry Hoover: Gallant First Lady* (New York: Dodd, Mead, 1969), pp. 179–218; Ruth Fesler Lipman, oral history, pp. 30–32, HHPL; and Herbert Hoover, *The Memoirs of Herbert Hoover*, 3 vols. (New York: Macmillan Co., 1952), 2:324. The fact that this particular tea, with the complete guest list, was recorded in the president's official appointments calendar is noteworthy because Mrs. Hoover's tea guest lists were not normally included in this source (see appointments calendar, 12 June 1929, HHPL). Because of the importance of this event, I requested special permission to examine the relevant portions of the Lou Henry Hoover Papers, which are closed to scholars. Mr. Allen Hoover informed me that he would not make any exceptions in the use of his mother's papers. The director of the Herbert Hoover Presidential Library at that time, Mr. Thomas Thalken, was most helpful to me in this matter. He also expressed his unofficial view that there was no helpful documentary evidence relating to the De Priest tea in the Lou Henry Hoover Papers.

37. Skeptics include W. E. B. Du Bois, Richard B. Sherman, and Monroe Work. See "Mrs. De Priest Drinks Tea," *Crisis* 36 (September 1929): 298; Sherman, *Republican Party and Black America*, pp. 235–37. Lewinson referred to the invitation as "pro forma" (see *Race, Class, and Party*, p. 180). David J. Ginzl called it "seemingly innocent" in "Herbert Hoover and Republican Patronage Politics in the South, 1928–1932" (Ph.D. dissertation, Syracuse University, 1977), p. 188. Some blacks did congratulate Hoover (see Thomas E. Jones to HH, 30 June 1929, CQ. Jones was president of Fisk University). Among the whites who praised and defended Hoover was Richard H. Edmunds, editor of the *Manufacturer's Record* (see "The White House and the Race

Issue," *Manufacturer's Record* 65 [27 June 1929]: 49–50). See also Mark K. Sullivan's defense in the New York *Herald*, 30 June 1929.

38. See, for example, Dallas *Morning News*, 21 June 1929; Tallahassee *Daily Democrat*, 16 June 1929; Tennessee *Tattler*, 22 June 1929; *New York Times*, 18 June 1929 and numerous examples of southern reaction in the De Priest File, HHPL. One scholar accounts for the intensity of the southern reaction by arguing that the invitation to tea was less important than the skillful manner in which Congressman De Priest then capitalized on the publicity to raise funds for the NAACP and thereby successfully demonstrated rising black political assertiveness (see David S. Day, "Herbert Hoover and Racial Politics: The De Priest Incident," *Journal of Negro History*, Winter, 1980, pp. 11–15).

39. Texas House *Journal* and Senate *Proceedings*, 41st Leg. 2d sess., 18 June 1929, pp. 326–27. Copy in De Priest File, HHPL.

40. Unidentified editorial dated 14 June 1929 in De Priest File. See also H. I. Crumpler to HH, 17 June 1929, De Priest File, HHPL.

41. See, for example, Emile Kuntz to Akerson, 20 June, 7 August 1929; Kuntz to Newton, 9 August 1929 and other evidence in Louisiana State File, HHPL. Kuntz was convinced that the vicious use of the De Priest tea by Democrats accounted for the loss of the 3,092 voters, which spelled defeat for the Republican candidate for Congress in the third district. There are numerous expressions of dismay from leading southern Republicans throughout the state files and in the De Priest File. See also *Crisis* 36 (September 1929): 298–99.

42. See n. 25. See copy of the Texas House *Journal* and Senate *Proceedings*, 41st Leg. 2d sess., 18 June 1929, pp. 326–27 and Dallas *Morning News*, 21 June 1929. See also R. B. Creager's protest to Gov. Dan Moody for signing the joint resolution; Creager to Moody, 19 June 1929, Texas State file, HHPL; Newton to Henry W. Anderson, 16 June 1929, HHPL. See also "A White House Tea-Party Tempest," *Literary Digest* 101 (29 June 1929): 10.

43. Emile Kuntz to Akerson, 7 August 1929, RNC Papers, Louisiana, HHPL.

44. FDR to Henry W. Anderson, 4 November 1929; FDR to Harry F. Byrd, 21 November 1929; Anderson to FDR, 7 November 1929, in private correspondence, 1928–1932, Group 12, box 4 FDRL. See also FDR's letters to southern Democratic state leaders asking how he might help rebuild the party after the 1928 debacle. These letters are in the various state files in FDRL.

45. See examples in Official Misrepresentations File and in De Priest File, HHPL; *New York Times*, 22 June 1929. The Robert R. McCormick Papers are still closed to scholars. See also "Social Equality Not Issue Says De Priest," Washington (D.C.) *Star*, 20 June 1929.

46. Hoover placed strong emphasis upon the Moton invitation as a counter to white criticism of the De Priest tea (see Hoover, *Memoirs* 2:324).

47. Moton to Walter Brown, 21 March 1929; Moton to HH, 1 April 1929, Hoover Folder, RRM Papers; Moton to HH, 19 April 1929, Moton File, HHPL.

48. Saint Louis *Argus* and Chicago *Whip* sent to Hoover by Robert R. Church. Both newspapers were critical of Moton's defense of Hoover's southern policy. R. R. Church to HH, 25 May 1929, CQ. See also nn. 8, 18, 37 in chapter 16.

49. See newspapers cited in n. 48. See also n. 47 and Garcia, "Hoover's Southern Strategy," pp. 128–29.

50. Ralph J. Bunche, "Political Status of the Negro," research memorandum, Carnegie-Myrdal Study of the Negro in America, 1940, p. 1210, Schomberg Collection, New York Public Library, New York City.

51. See n. 48. See also chapter 13, "The Tuskegee Machine," in Louis R. Harlan, *Booker T. Washington: The Making of a Black Leader* (New York: Oxford University Press, 1972), pp. 254–71.

52. See n. 37. See also material in Official Misrepresentations File, HHPL; and Larry H. Grothaus, "The Hoover Administration and Blacks," 8 August 1979, p. 25, HHPL.

53. W. E. B. Du Bois, "The Campaign of 1928," *Crisis* 35 (December 1928): 418; n. 48.

54. See n. 37.

55. See, for example, R. B. Creager to Richey, 14 December 1928; Glenn Skipper to Richey, 28 November 1928 in Pres. Papers. Richey had sent out a questionnaire on the results of the election in the southern states to the national committeemen. The first question asked how Negroes had voted (see questionnaire in the State Files, HHPL. See also numerous letters to Hoover insisting on a lily-white party in these same State Files).

56. The quotation from the Chicago *Tribune* editorial is in the excerpts from editorial reactions New York *World*, 21 June 1929. David S. Day argues that the results of the De Priest incident pushed the Hoover administration further toward a lily-white policy ("Herbert Hoover and Racial Politics," p. 15).

12. Reiterating Principles

1. The Walter F. Brown Papers are in the Ohio Historical Society. Unfortunately Brown's wife burned most of his papers, and there is virtually nothing of value to this study. A resumé of his career is included in the collection. There are also few Brown documents of value in the Hoover Papers (see personal file at HHPL and TRB, "Washington Notes," *New Republic* [10 September 1930]: 100–101).

2. To date efforts to uncover the private papers of Walter Newton have been unsuccessful. Most of the southern political correspondence intended for the president was addressed to Newton. It appears that he filed all of the correspondence in the appropriate state files, and thus the vast bulk if not all of the important documentation is in the HHPL.

3. Burke remained as general counsel to the Republican National Committee. For more information on Burke, see the appropriate personal files at the HHPL. For Burke's implication in campaign bigotry see chapter 5, n. 11.

4. For a good description of Work, Huston, and Lockwood, see Indianapolis *Star*, 27 January 1929; Appointments, Press Reaction, HHPL. For Work's dismissal see chapter 10, n. 10 and Brooklyn *Eagle*, 5 June 1929; Boston *Transcript*, 5 June 1929; New York *Evening News*, 6 June 1929 and other newspaper accounts in Work scrapbook, Work Papers, Hoover Institution, Stanford University, Palo Alto, Calif.

5. Materials on Huston are scattered throughout several collections. See personal file in C & T, and Pres. Papers; scattered references in General Correspondence, and in CQ, HHPL. See also Huston File in RRM Papers.

6. For Democratic recognition of his serious purpose in making excellent appointments, see Congressman Robert A. Green to J. L. Dozzett, 1 June 1930; Green to H. J. Dame, 1 July 1930, Robert Alexis Green Papers, University of Florida, Gainesville, Florida. Evidence of his patronage reforms in the U.S. Customs Service, Post Office Department, and Treasury Department is abundant in the early correspondence and directives in each of the appropriate files at the HHPL. For the importance of United States marshals in party building, see, for example, R. E. L. Pryor to Newton, 12, 18 January 1931, Appointments, Justice, U.S. Marshals, 1931–1932, HHPL. The "model plan" for the entire South is explained in C. H. Huston to the President, memorandum, 21 December 1929, Louisiana State File, Justice, HHPL.

7. Florida *Times-Union*, 2 October 1928; Tampa *Times*, 8 August 1928. The best source for a day-to-day explanation of the factional disputes in Florida are the political scrapbooks in the William J. Howey Papers, Florida State University, Tallahassee, Florida. Another indispensable source is the Florida State File, RNC Papers.

8. Tampa *Morning Tribune*, 6 September 1928. Bean denied the corruption charge. See George W. Bean to George Norris, 10 January 1927; H. H. Lindelie to Norris, 8 January 1927;

Norris to Lindelie, 1 January 1927, GN Papers. See also Howey Scrapbook, 1928, Howey Papers.

9. The most succinct and best summary is Emmet C. Choate to Patrick J. Hurley, 3 September 1929. After reading Choate's analysis Newton informed Hurley that Choate "has it sized up fairly well" (Newton to Hurley, 6 September 1929). See also Louis W. Fairfield to Newton, 17 May 1929, all in RNC Papers, Florida, HHPL. For a more detailed, but narrowly focused analysis, see David J. Ginzl, "Herbert Hoover and Republican Patronage Politics in the South 1928–1932" (Ph.D. dissertation, Syracuse University, 1977), pp. 270–95. See also David J. Ginzl, "The Politics of Patronage: Florida Republicans During the Hoover Administration," *Florida Historical Quarterly* (July 1982), pp. 1–19.

10. John F. Harris to Newton, 13 June 1929; Charles R. Pierce to Newton, 12 June 1929; E. Ross Bartley to Newton, 13 June 1929; Newton to Walter F. Brown, 19 June 1929; Albert R. Walsh to Brown, Newton, and Burke, 3 September 1929; John F. Harris to Robert P. Lamont, 3 June 1929; Akerson to Richey, 1 February 1929, Pres. Papers, Akerson File, HHPL.

11. Charles S. Root, "Secret and Confidential Report for Mr. Richey, 21 March 1929," Prohibition, Enforcement File, HHPL. Root was chief intelligence officer, United States Coast Guard. He believed Skipper to be honest.

12. A. W. Mellon to HH, 13 March 1929, Treasury, Florida, HHPL.

13. Skipper submitted several lists. See Skipper to HH, 8 March 1929; Newton to Brown, 16 April 1929; Newton Memo of Talk with Skipper, 6 April 1929; H. A. Mann to George E. Akerson, 13 April 1929; HH to Attorney General, 16 April 1929; Newton to Brown, 20 April 1929; Newton to Attorney General, 30 April 1929, RNC Papers, Florida, HHPL.

14. Fred E. Britten, resolution to HH, 1 May 1929, RNC Papers, Florida, HHPL. The state central committee reminded Hoover that under party rules only the national commiteeman Glenn Skipper could appoint a patronage committee.

15. L. G. Haugen to Newton, n.d.; E. E. Callaway to Brown, 17 August 1929; W. J. Sears to Newton, 23 August 1929, RNC Papers, Florida, HHPL.

16. Attorney general to Mr. President, 27 August 1929, Justice, Florida File, HHPL.

17. Mabel Walker Willebrandt to Senator William E. Borah, 28 September 1929, RNC Papers.

18. Ibid. Gilchrist B. Stockton to Newton, 25 September 1929; Newton to Stockton, 1 October 1929, RNC Papers, Florida, HHPL. See also HH pencil remarks denying that it was a political appointment, in Lawrence Richey to Albert E. Bennett, telegram, 19 September 1929, HHPL.

19. See n. 18. See also E. E. Callaway to H. G. Hastings; E. C. Davis and G. W. Bingham to Charles P. Sisson, 30 August 1929; Albert E. Bennett to HH, 19 September 1929, RNC Papers, Florida, HHPL.

20. Postmaster General Walter Brown told Lewis Strauss that Skipper had begun fighting with the state leaders because he insisted on being "absolute dictator on all appointments." Brown began his own investigation of Skipper. See Walter F. Brown to Lewis Strauss, 11 July 1929, LS Papers. See also Fred E. Britten to Lawrence Richey, 13 May 1929; Louis W. Fairfield to Newton, 17 May 1929; L. Y. Sherman to John F. Harris, 27 May 1929; Harris to Newton, 3 June 1929 and enclosed clippings Jacksonville *Times-Union*, 26, 29 May 1929, RNC Papers, Florida, HHPL. Callaway confirmed that northerners close to Hoover were attempting to take over the Florida party (see Callaway to H. G. Hastings, 30 August 1929, RNC Papers, Florida, HHPL).

21. Britten to Hoover, 21 September 1929, RNC Papers, Florida, HHPL.

22. Gilchrist B. Stockton to HH, 25 September 1929, ibid.

23. HH to Britten, 26 September 1929, ibid.

24. See *Manufacturer's Record*, 7 November 1929. See also numerous letters in RNC Papers, Florida, Justice, 23 September–31 December 1929 File.

25. Britten to HH, 30 September 1929; Lakeland (Fla.) *Evening Ledger and Star Telegram*, 22 October 1929; Tampa *Morning Tribune*, 28 November 1929, RNC Papers, Florida, HHPL. See also Callaway to H. G. Hastings, 30 August 1929, RNC Papers, Florida, HHPL.

26. Columbia (S.C.) *State*, 16 October 1929; Macon (Ga.) *Telegraph*, 17 October 1929; Atlanta *Constitution*, 16 October 1929; Lakeland *Evening Ledger and Star Tribune*, 22 October 1929.

27. Atlanta *Constitution*, 16 October 1929.

28. Hoover's open distaste was reflected earlier by Postmaster General Brown, who informed Lewis Strauss, "It was a joy to see your friend [Lamont] Rowlands, he is so different from the other southern leaders we have been seeing" (Brown to Strauss, 5 April 1929, Walter F. Brown File, LS Papers). Callaway claimed to have received many letters from southern white Republicans complaining of the disgraceful manner in which Hoover dictated to southerners (Callaway to H. G. Hastings, 30 August 1929, RNC Papers, Florida, HHPL).

29. Claude Pepper to Franklin D. Roosevelt, 22 December 1929, Democratic National Committee, Florida, FDRL. See also Fred P. Cone to FDR, 15 November 1929. Cone was convinced that the Republicans had now lost the entire South.

13. Southern Strategies

1. Claudius H. Huston, Memorandum For The President, 21 December 1929, RNC Papers, Louisiana State File, Justice, HHPL.

2. Herbert Hoover, *The Memoirs of Herbert Hoover*, 3 vols. (New York: Macmillan Co., 1951–52), 2:42, 191; *New York Times*, 9, 11 September 1929. See also n. 22 in chapter 4; n. 12 in chapter 5; and Edgar Rickard diary, 27 November 1927, 15 February 1929, ER Papers.

3. Robert R. Church, Jr., to HH, 7 September 1929; Church to Akerson, 3 October 1929, Church File, Secretary's File, HHPL; New York *Herald Tribune*, 29 January 1929; Memphis *Commercial Appeal*, 15 April 1929; Charleston (S.C.) *News and Courier*, 12 August 1929; Atlanta *Constitution*, 7 August 1929; Washington *Post*, 10 September 1929. See also newspaper clippings in Hambright, Secretary's File, HHPL. On congratulating Huston as the new chairman of the Republican National Committee, Moton told Huston, "I think the action is wise from every point of view. Your own knowledge of the situation, nationally, and particularly your knowledge of the South, makes your selection most happy. I was glad to say this to the President when I saw him a few days ago." (See Moton to Huston, 26 September 1929, C. H. Huston file, RRM Papers. This file also contains additional correspondence bearing on their relationship.)

4. C. H. Huston, memorandum, 21 December 1929, RNC Papers, Louisiana, HHPL; Huston to HH, memorandum, 25 April 1929, CQ; David J. Ginzl, "Hoover and Republican Patronage Politics in the South, 1928–1932" (Ph.D. dissertation, Syracuse University, 1977), pp. 181–88.

5. Kuntz to Akerson, 14 March 1929, Louisiana State File, HHPL.

6. See chapter 4, n. 72.

7. Walter Cohen to HH, 6 March 1929; HH to Cohen, 12 March 1929 and 8 June 1929; A. W. Mellon to the president, 27 March 1929; Kuntz to Newton, 1 October 1929; Moton to Newton, 21 August 1929; Kuntz to Akerson, 17 March 1929, and 23 April 1929; Moton to Newton, 6 December 1930; John R. Hawkins to Newton, 19 December 1930, Louisiana State File and Liberia File, HHPL. See also Moton to Cohen, 28 February 1929, RRM Papers; and Hanes Walton, Jr., *Black Republicans: The Politics of the Black and Tans* (Metuchen, N.J.: Scarecrow Press, 1975), pp. 67–69; Hanes Walton, Jr., *Black Political Parties: An Historical and Political Analysis* (New York: Free Press, 1972), pp. 66–67; Ralph J. Bunche, *Political Status of the Negro in the Age of FDR* (Chicago and London: University of Chicago Press, 1973), p. 540.

8. See n. 7 and correspondence in Louisiana State File, HHPL.

9. See Walter Cohen to Claude Barnett, 7 June 1928, CAB Papers.

10. New Orleans *Times-Picayune*, 14 January 1930; Emile Kuntz to Ernest Lee Jahncke, 14 January 1930, RNC Papers, Louisiana, HHPL. See also chapters 3 and 4 and Ginzl, "Hoover and Republican Patronage Politics," p. 185.

11. Hammond (La.) *Vindicator*, 24 May 1929; Louis P. Bryant to Horace A. Mann, 29 March 1929; W. C. Voelher to George Akerson, 28 March 1929; Kuntz to Newton, 17 October 1929; Newton to Kuntz, 27 October 1929, RNC Papers, Louisiana, HHPL.

12. Kuntz to Newton, 28 October 1929; John E. Jackson to Jahncke, 25 September 1931, RNC Papers, Louisiana, HHPL.

13. Charles A. Jonas to Huston, 29 November 1929; Jonas to Newton, 17 December 1929, RNC Papers, North Carolina, HHPL. See also numerous other letters that detail the close working relationship and mutual respect between the leaders in Washington and Jonas. For black political influence see Paul Lewinson, *Race, Class, and Party: A History of Negro Suffrage and White Politics in the South* (New York: Russell and Russell, 1963), pp. 141–43; and V. O. Key, *Southern Politics in State and Nation* (New York: Alfred A. Knopf, 1949), pp. 321–22.

14. R. B. Creager to HH, 6 March 1929, RNC Papers, Texas, HHPL; Key, *Southern Politics*, pp. 320–34; Walton, *Black Republicans*, pp. 66–67; Walton, *Black Political Parties*, p. 66. The best source on Creager is Roger M. Olien, *From Token to Triumph: The Texas Republicans Since 1920* (Dallas: Southern Methodist University Press, 1982), pp. 1–72. Creager destroyed all of his papers.

15. Creager to HH, 24 February 1929, Prepresidential, Creager File; appointments calendar, 1, 5 March 1929; HH to attorney general, 7 April 1929; attorney general to HH, 9 April 1929; Smith Brookhart to HH, 12 April 1929; Lawrence Richey to attorney general, 15 April 1929; HH to Creager, 5 June 1932, RNC Papers, Texas, HHPL; Brookhart to HH, 11 June 1930, Pres. Papers, Secretary's File, HHPL. See also Paul Casdorph, *A History of the Republican Party in Texas, 1865–1965* (Austin: The Pemberton Press, 1965), pp. 119–44; Lewinson, *Race, Class, and Party*, p. 176. For the conclusion of the Senate investigation see U.S. Congress, Senate Subcommittee of the Committee on Post Offices and Post Roads, Report No. 272, *Influencing Appointments to Postmasterships and Other Federal Offices*, 71st Cong., 2d sess., 6 January 1930, pp. 521–26, 1065–66, 1509–30. Hoover fully investigated all charges of corruption in the South. See attorney general to Hoover, 29 October 1930, RNC Papers, HHPL. See also press conference statement, 18 March 1930, "Comment on the Report of the Senate Committee on Federal Patronage in the South," Herbert Hoover, *The State Papers and Public Writings of Herbert Hoover*, ed. William Starr Myers, 2 vols. (New York: Doubleday, Doran and Co., 1934), 1:220–21. See also William G. Shepherd, "A Job for Jack," *Collier's* (15 June 1929): 8–9. Although Olien is critical of Creager's political methods, he concludes that "Creager probably never sold federal office for outright political gain" or coerced federal employees to make campaign contributions. However, he does not discuss the FBI investigation ordered by Hoover. See Olien, *From Token to Triumph*, pp. 15, 19–20, 14–21, and 53.

16. E. B. Clements to Newton 15 August 1930; Newton to Clements, 7 November 1932; Newton to the Attorney General, memorandum, 31 October 1932, RNC Papers, Missouri, HHPL; Lewinson, Race, Class, and Party, p. 104.

17. Scipio A. Jones to Lawrence Richey, 1 February 1932, RNC Papers, Arkansas, HHPL. Jones enclosed a resolution "adopted at a mass meeting of the colored citizens of Arkansas yesterday endorsing President Hoover's administration, and going on record in favor of his re-election." For letters of cordial relations with other state leaders, see the Arkansas State File. Additional evidence of black-and-tan harmony is in Lewinson, *Race, Class, and Party*, pp. 175, 104.

18. T. G. Nutter to Newton, 17 September 1932; Senator H. D. Hatfield to Newton, 15 July 1932; Carl G. Backmann to Newton, 10 September 1932, RNC Papers, West Virginia, HHPL; and Lewinson, *Race, Class, and Party*, pp. 153, 185, 104.

19. David Hinshaw to Newton, 8 [?] February 1930, and 24 June 1930; Jennings C. Wise to HH, 29 March 1929, RNC Papers, Virginia, HHPL. For background on the success of the lily-whites in gaining control of the state, see Bascom Slemp Appointment, NAACP Papers; Lewinson, *Race, Class, and Party*, pp. 178–79; and especially Andrew Buni, *The Negro in*

Virginia Politics, 1902–1965 (Charlottesville: University Press of Virginia, 1967). The most complete account is Ginzl, "Hoover and Republican Patronage Politics," pp. 315–27. See also Key, *Southern Politics*, p. 323; Bunche, *Political Status of the Negro*, p. 518. Unfortunately, Ginzl was not able to utilize the papers of Jennings C. Wise and of Lewis L. Strauss. Both collections are invaluable in understanding the Republican party in Virginia during the Hoover period.

20. *New York Times*, 3, 4 February 1929; New York *World*, 4 February 1929; Henry W. Anderson to HH, 6 November 1928, C & T, Anderson File; Anderson to HH, 14 April 1929, RNC Papers, Virginia, HHPL; Henry W. Anderson to Lewis Strauss, 19 December 1929, Anderson File, Campaign 1928, LS Papers; Jennings C. Wise to Curtis M. Dozier, 6 November 1929, Letterbook, Wise Papers; Wise to HH, 25 October 1929, PP File, HHPL; B. C. Slemp to Newton, 13, 14 May 1930; Slemp to Newton, 23 March 1932, RNC Papers, Virginia, HHPL. See also Hoover, *Memoirs*, 2:277; and "A New Deal For the Solid South," *Literary Digest*, (17 September 1927), p. 14; Ginzl, "Hoover and Republican Patronage Politics," pp. 315–27. Anderson's letter to Strauss is especially important.

21. Anderson to Strauss, 19 December 1929, LS Papers; Anderson to Newton, 18 December 1929, RNC Papers, Virginia; Wise to HH, 25 October 1929, PP File, HHPL. See also Washington (D.C.) *Post*, 25 October 1929 and Richmond *Times-Dispatch*, 25 October 1929; Ginzl, "Hoover and Republican Patronage Politics," pp. 316–21; and the excellent documents in Virginia Politics, 1929, LS Papers.

22. Henry A. Wise to Jennings Wise, 9 November 1929, Letterbook, JCW Papers.

23. Anderson blamed the defeat on "the De Priest incident." See Anderson to Strauss, 19 December 1929, LS Papers. For the sense of bitter disappointment, see Anderson to Wise, 8 November 1929; Wise to Anderson, 9 November 1929, Letterbook, JCW Papers; and Strauss to HH, draft letter, n.d., Virginia Politics, 1929, LS Papers. For the analysis offered by Wise, see Wise to Claudius Huston, 7 November 1929, with enclosure, "The Gubernatorial Election in Virginia, 1929: Influence of the Ku Klux Klan and the Race Issue," Letterbook, JCW Papers; and Wise to HH, 26 September 1930, with enclosure, "The Fetish of the Solid South," CQ. Wise claims to have sent Hoover a third analysis entitled "The Democratic Negro Policy," but no record of it has been found. See Wise to Anderson, 7 November 1929 and undated memorandum on p. 307, Letterbook, JCW Papers. Wise fully explained his understanding of how Democrats won the black vote while appealing to white fears of the Negro at the same time (see Wise to Editor, Richmond *Times-Dispatch*, 11 November 1929, Letterbook, JCW Papers). An excellent example of the efforts by Republican opponents to exploit the race issue is the pamphlet "The Poll Tax Requirement," in Virginia Politics, 1929, LS Papers. Wise also undertook a highly detailed analysis of the 1929 vote (see Wise to Anderson, 22 April 1930, Letterbook, JCW Papers). On his appointment as special assistant to the attorney general, see Wise to Patrick J. Hurley, 14 September 1932, Hurley Papers, University of Oklahoma, Norman, Oklahoma.

24. Emmett J. Scott to James A. Cobb, 10 May 1916, JAC Papers; Moton to Newton, 5 February 1930, RRM Papers; Lewinson, *Race, Class, and Party*, p. 175.

25. Newton to Bartow Strang, 30 March 1929; Oliver D. Street to HH, 23 March 1929; Street to Newton, 3 April 1929; Street to Newton, 12, 20 April 1929, RNC Papers, Alabama, HHPL.

26. C. P. Lunsford to Newton, 6 April 1929; J. O. Thompson to HH, 8 April 1929; Thompson to Newton, 25 April 1929; Moton to Newton, 17 December 1929; Huston to Lawrence Richey, 26 April 1929; J. O. Thompson to HH, 8 April 1929, RNC Papers, Alabama, HHPL. Moton to Newton, 5 February 1930; Moton to William D. Mitchell, 4 February 1930, W. H. Newton File, RRM Papers; Chattanooga *Times*, 20 April 1929.

27. Street to Huston, 30 December 1929; Street to Newton, 1, 3 January 1930; Newton Memo, 17 January 1930; HH to attorney general, 15 January 1930; Moton to Newton, 5 February 1930; Street to Newton, 5, 8, 14 February 1930; Street to Newton, 3 June 1930, RNC Papers, Alabama, HHPL (see also Ginzl, "Hoover and Republican Patronage Politics," pp. 297–300); Key, *Southern Politics* pp. 324–25; Walton, *Black Republicans*, p. 85; Buni, *Negro in Virginia Politics*, p. 536.

28. Farley's speech to the Southern State Republican League, reprinted in the *Louisiana Republican*, 20 March 1926, is in Tennessee State File. See also John W. Farley, *Statistics and Politics* (Memphis: Saxland Publishing Co., 1920), pp. 1–55; newspaper editorials sent to HH by Church, in Tennessee State File.

29. See chapters 9 and 10.

30. John F. Farley to George Akerson, 10 April 1929, 16 April 1929, 26 June 1929; Akerson to Farley, 3 July 1929, State File, Tennessee, HHPL; appointments calendar, 7 March 1929; Ginzl, "Hoover and Republican Patronage Politics," pp. 344–50; Walton, *Black Republicans*, pp. 120–22; Lewinson, *Race, Class, and Party*, p. 162.

31. Walter L. Wellford to Newton, 11 July 1929, State File, Tennessee, HHPL. Wellford, like Farley, was a member of the Memphis Hoover Club, which was known to contain former Klansmen. See also Paul J. Kruesi to Lewis Strauss, n.d., Campaign, 1928, Negroes; J. M. Johnson to Kruesi, 29 September 1928; and P. J. Kruesi to J. R. Nutt, 8 October 1928, Campaign, 1928, Negroes, LS Papers, HHPL. These men supported Wellford and opposed Hoover's cooperation with black and tans during the 1928 campaign.

32. W. M. Steuart to Newton, 12 July 1929; Huston to Newton, 30 July 1929; Newton to Farley, 9 September 1929; Huston to Newton, 25 November 1929; attorney general to president, 24 January 1930; Newton to Huston, 26 February 1930, State File, Tennessee, HHPL.

33. A copy of the investigation of the postmaster at Memphis, Tennessee is in State File, Tennessee, Commerce, HHPL.

14. Frustrating Purges

1. Rowlands's official title was chairman, Mississippi Finance Committee. For Hoover's favorable view of Rowlands, see HH to Julius Rosenwald, 29 November 1929, PP File. See also Aberdeen (Miss.) *Weekly*, 22 March 1929 and Newton, memorandum, 5 April 1929, RNC Papers, Mississippi, HHPL.

2. HH to Julius Rosenwald, 29 November 1929, PP File.

3. Jackson (Miss.) *Daily News*, 20 March 1929; Ben F. Cameron to attorney general, 6,14 November 1929; J. C. Tyler to Willebrandt, 20 March 1929; E. M. C. Hawkins to Willebrandt, 22 March 1929, PWH File.

4. Paul Lewinson, *Race, Class, and Party: A History of Negro Suffrage and White Politics in the South* (New York: Russell and Russell, 1963), p. 184.

5. Rowlands to Newton, 12 August, 17 October 1929; Hubert D. Stephens to HH, 24 September 1929, 15 March 1930, RNC Papers, Mississippi, HHPL. See also correspondence in Mississippi, Judiciary and Justice File, HHPL.

6. Rowlands to Newton, 21 March, 7 June 1930, 5 February 1931, RNC Papers, Mississippi, HHPL. See also David J. Ginzl, "Herbert Hoover and Republican Patronage Politics in the South, 1928–1932" (Ph.D. dissertation, Syracuse University, May 1977), pp. 246–56 and David J. Ginzl, "Lily-Whites Versus Black-And-Tans: Mississippi Republicans During the Hoover Administration,"*Journal of Mississippi History* (August 1980), pp. 194–211. Ginzl's analysis suffers from a lack of important sources and from a narrow state, rather than national, focus.

7. Joe Tolbert to Hubert Work, 29 July 1929; Work to Moton, 29 July 1929; Newton to Work, 8 August 1929; Edward Durant to Senator Frederic C. Walcott, 14 May 1929; Gordon B. Lockwood to Newton, 4 May 1929, RNC Papers, South Carolina, HHPL; Hanes Walton, Jr., *Black Republicans: The Politics of the Black and Tans* (Metuchen, N.J.: Scarecrow Press, 1975), pp. 114–15, 162; Ralph J. Bunche, *The Political Status of the Negro in the Age of FDR*, ed. Dewey W. Grantham (Chicago: University of Chicago Press, 1973), p. 519.

8. Newton to Work, 8 August 1929; J. C. Hambright to Newton, 31 May 1929, RNC Papers, South Carolina, HHPL.

9. V. O. Key, *Southern Politics in the State and Nation* (New York: Alfred A. Knopf, 1949), p. 288.

10. Hambright to Newton, 7 January, 21 February 1930, RNC Papers, South Carolina, HHPL.

11. Hambright to Newton, 15, 20 August 1929, RNC Papers, South Carolina, HHPL.

12. U.S. Congress, Senate Committee on the Judiciary, *Hearings, Confirmation of J. Duncan Adams*, 71st Cong., 2d sess., 10 January 1930, pp. 1–7. For more details see Ginzl, "Hoover and Republican Patronage Politics," pp. 230–46.

13. Hambright to Newton, 21 February 1930; Newton to Hambright, 23 February 1930; Hambright to Charles P. Sisson, RNC Papers, South Carolina, HHPL.

14. Sisson to Newton, 6 June 1930; Judge John J. Parker to Sisson, 23 June 1930; Simeon D. Fess to Newton, 31 January 1931; Hambright to Newton, 2 August 1930, RNC Papers, South Carolina, HHPL.

15. Lewinson, *Race, Class, and Party*, p. 175.

16. Atlanta *Independent*, 28 March 1929 in RNC Papers, Georgia, HHPL. The credentials committee had refused to recognize Davis, and the post of national committeeman was technically vacant.

17. Ben Davis to Messrs. Brown, Burke, Newton, 26 April 1929; George F. Flanders to Newton, 1 May 1929; Flanders to James W. Good, 3 April 1929, RNC Papers, Georgia, HHPL.

18. Flanders to Newton, 1 May 1929, RNC Papers, Georgia, HHPL.

19. Ibid. See also Josiah T. Rose to Newton, 7 September 1929; Edwin Shortess to Good, 28 June 1929, RNC Papers, Georgia, HHPL. There are numerous letters of recommendation supporting Flanders in this file.

20. Rose to Brown, 15 October 1947, Walter Brown Papers, Ohio Historical Society, Columbus, Ohio. See also W. M. Steuart to Newton, 24 October 1929; Sen. Walter F. George to Rose, 17 August 1929; Sen. Arthur H. Vandenburg to Newton, 12 September 1929, RNC Papers, Georgia, HHPL. Rose admitted to Brown that he had "given little thought and attention" to the politics of his job. See Rose to Brown, 15 October 1947, Walter Brown Papers, Ohio Historical Society, Columbus, Ohio.

21. Flanders to James W. Good, 3 April 1929; Flanders to HH, 13 April 1929; Rose to Newton, 16 September 1929, RNC Papers, Georgia, HHPL.

22. Rose to Newton, 16 September 1929; Newton to Rose, 23 September 1929; Newton [WHN] to Huston, memorandum, 20 September 1929, Georgia, Justice, HHPL.

23. Rose to Newton, 7 October 1929; Newton to Rose, 11 October 1929; Rose to Newton, 11 December 1930, ibid.

24. Huston, Memorandum for the President, 1 April 1929, RNC Papers, Georgia, HHPL.

25. Newton to Charles Adamson, 23 October 1929; Rose to Newton, 4 February 1930; Henry C. Davis to Newton, 26 August 1930; Sen. Frederic C. Walcott to Newton, 14 April 1930; Walter Akerman to Fred Walcott, 23 March 1930; Sisson to Newton, 11 March 1930, RNC Papers, Georgia, HHPL.

26. Rose to Newton, 12 February 1930, RNC Papers, Georgia, HHPL.

27. Huston to the president, memorandum, 1 April 1929; Rose to Newton, 19 March 1930; Rose to Newton, 25 March 1930, ibid.

28. Newton to Brown, 24 March 1930; Durelle Chaney to Brown, 11, 22 March 1930, RNC Papers, Georgia, HHPL. For a more extended and somewhat different interpretation see Ginzl, "Hoover and Republican Patronage Politics," pp. 195–210 and David J. Ginzl, "Patronage, Race, and Politics: Georgia Republicans During the Hoover Administration," *Georgia Historical Quarterly* (Fall 1980), pp. 280–91. See also Garcia, "Hoover's Southern Strategy," pp. 87–90; Walton, *Black Republicans*, pp. 61, 163–64; Bunche, *Political Status of the Negro*, p. 526.

15. Federal Assistance

1. See, for example, George F. Garcia, "Herbert Hoover and the Issue of Race," *The Annals of Iowa* 44 (Winter 1979): 507–15. Garcia's article is based upon his Master's thesis, "Herbert Hoover's Southern Strategy and the Black Reaction" (University of Iowa, 1972). See also Richard B. Sherman, *The Republican Party and Black America: From McKinley to Hoover, 1896–1933* (Charlottesville: University Press of Virginia, 1973); Paul Lewinson, *Race, Class, and Party: A History of Negro Suffrage and White Politics in the South* (New York: Russell and Russell, 1963); Hanes Walton, Jr., *Black Republicans: The Politics of the Black and Tans* (Metuchen, N.J.: Scarecrow Press, 1975); David J. Ginzl, "Herbert Hoover and Republican Patronage Politics in the South, 1928–1932" (Ph.D. dissertation, Syracuse University, 1977), pp. 170–73; Larry H. Grothaus, "The Hoover Administration and Blacks," unpublished paper, August 1979, HHPL; and Allan J. Lichtman, *Prejudice and the Old Politics: The Presidential Election of 1928* (Chapel Hill: University of North Carolina Press, 1979), pp. 144–59.

2. See chapter 1. An excellent analysis of his views on voluntarism is Robert D. Cuff, "Herbert Hoover, the Ideology of Voluntarism and War Organization during the Great War," *Journal of American History* 64 (September 1977): 358–72. Another excellent analysis is David E. Hamilton, "Herbert Hoover and the Great Drought of 1930," *Journal of American History* 68 (March 1982): 850–75.

3. See chapter 2. See also the citations in n. 1.

4. See n. 5.

5. "Address of President Hoover by Radio from the White House upon the Occasion of the Celebration of the Fiftieth Anniversary of the Founding of Tuskegee Institute at Tuskegee, Alabama, April 14, 1931," Major Speeches File, HHPL; "Importance of Training Leaders of the Negro Race," commencement address, Howard University, 10 June 1932 in Herbert Hoover, *The State Papers and Other Public Writings of Herbert Hoover*, ed. William Starr Myers (New York: Doubleday, Doran and Co., 1934), 2:207–8. See also Hoover to James A. Jackson, "Greetings to National Negro Bankers Association," 18 September 1930, PP File. See also HH to M. Grant Lucas, 28 July 1931, Major Speeches, Volume 53, No. 1620, HHPL. Similar ideas are expressed in HH to Alfred Williams Anthony, 19 April 1926, Commerce, Negroes; HH to James F. King, 12 May 1931, PP File, Negro Club, HHPL. For numerous other messages of encouragment to a variety of Negro organizations see Commerce, Negroes; Negro Club; and Negro Matters, PP File; National Negro Insurance Association, PP File; and National Negro Business League, PP File. Additional evidence is cited in chapter 2, nn. 24–32.

6. See "Address of President Hoover by Radio from the White House" and "Importance of Training Leaders of the Negro Race," cited in n. 5 above. On his refusal to send messages to black political organizations, see Richey to Robert H. Lucas, 1 March 1932, CQ.

7. See chapter 1, nn. 47 and 48. Hoover's ideas on racial progress were strikingly similar to those held by many leading blacks. For an excellent analysis of black hopes, see June Sochen, *The Unbridgeable Gap: Blacks and Their Quest for the American Dream, 1900–1930* (Chicago: Rand McNally and Co., 1972), pp. 1–63 and passim but especially pp. 1–10, 27–31, 34–37, 54–56.

8. In defending Judge John Parker, his nominee for the United States Supreme Court, he left no doubt of his approval of seeking justice for racial grievances through the courts. See chapter 17.

9. HH to Eugene Kinckle Jones, 1 April 1929; Jones to Richey, 25 July 1932; Richey to Jones, 26 July 1932, PP File, Negro Matters, HHPL.

10. HH to M. Grant Lucas, 28 July 1931 in Major Speeches File, Volume 53, No. 1620; HH to H. R. Butler, 28 July 1931, Major Speeches File, appendix; and HH to Alfred Williams Anthony, 26 April 1926, Commerce, Negroes, HHPL. See also n. 5 and Barnett to Moton, 19 November 1930, RRM Papers.

11. Newton to Moton, 23 November 1929; Moton to Newton, 17 December 1929; HH to

Moton, 3 December 1929, Moton File and Commission on Inter-Racial Cooperation File, HHPL.

12. See Barry Karl's excellent analysis, "Presidential Planning and Social Science Research: Mr. Hoover's Experts," *Perspectives in American History* 3 (1969): 347–409; and chapter 11 in his *Charles E. Merriam and the Study of Politics* (Chicago and London: University of Chicago Press, 1974), pp. 201–25. See also Ray Lyman Wilbur and Arthur M. Hyde, *The Hoover Policies* (New York: Charles Scribner's Sons, 1937), pp. 41–42 and Garcia, "Hoover's Southern Strategy," pp. 39–40. For excellent analyses of Booker T. Washington's ideas, see August Meier, *Negro Thought in America* (Ann Arbor: University of Michigan Press, 1963), pp. 103–18; and Louis R. Harlan, *Booker T. Washington: The Making of a Black Leader, 1856–1901* (New York: Oxford University Press, 1972), pp. 203–53.

13. David Burner, *Herbert Hoover: A Public Life* (New York: Alfred A. Knopf, 1979), pp. 211–16. Burner succinctly discusses a number of Hoover's early reform efforts. Claude Barnett was impatient with the studies (see Barnett to William Pickens, 10 December 1931, Pickens File, CAB Papers).

14. Barnett to Moton, 19 November 1930, RRM Papers. The Ray Lyman Wilbur Papers at the Hoover Institution provide ample evidence of Wilbur's desire to help blacks and Indians. For example, see Wilbur to Newton, 24 June 1930, Political; Wilbur to Louis C. Cornish, 21 November 1934, in HH-RLW File, 1933–1934; and Wilbur, memorandum of visit of Richard Bransten, 18 May 1945, Wilbur Papers, Hoover Institution, Stanford University, Palo Alto, Calif.

15. Wilbur to HH, 25 July 1929, Interior, Bureau of Education, HHPL.

16. Press releases, 11 February 1932; 30 June 1932, in ibid. Wilbur appointed the committee in December 1930. See also Interior, Accomplishments, HHPL; and Mordecai W. Johnson to Wilbur, 8 December 1931, Hoover Papers, Hoover Institution, Stanford University, Palo Alto, Calif.

17. W. E. B. Du Bois, *The Correspondence of W. E. B. Du Bois: Selections 1877–1934*, ed. Herbert Aptheker (Amherst: University of Massachusetts Press, 1973), 1:408–11. See also the four volumes of reports by the National Advisory Committee on Illiteracy in Ray Lyman Wilbur Papers, Hoover Institution, Stanford University, Palo Alto, Calif.

18. Mordecai W. Johnson to Wilbur, 7 June 1930; Julius Rosenwald to Wilbur, 26 December 1929; Wilbur to Abraham Flexner, 18 March 1932, Howard University File, Ray Lyman Wilbur Papers, Hoover Institution, Stanford University, Palo Alto, Calif.; Ray Lyman Wilbur, *The Memoirs of Ray Lyman Wilbur, 1875–1949* (Stanford, Calif.: Stanford University Press, 1960), pp. 477–78.

19. Both Garcia and Burner cite Hoover's attention to this conference. See George F. Garcia, "Hoover's Southern Strategy and the Black Reaction" (M.A. thesis, University of Iowa, 1972), p. 51; and Burner, *Hoover*, p. 216. A copy of the report on the conference is in CQ.

20. Garcia, "Hoover's Southern Strategy," p. 50. Evidence for this appointment is questionable.

21. Newton to Holsey, 5, 11, 12 October 1929; National Negro Business League File, HHPL. See also chapter 2.

22. See chapter 1. For the Kelly Miller quote see Townsend to Russell, 6 July n.d., and newspaper clipping in Kelly Miller File, Secretary's File, HHPL. See also Richey to Miller, 21 June 1929, Miller File; Perry Howard to Newton, 31 August 1931; Richey to Thomas B. Love, 10 July 1929; H. L. A. Clark to Newton, 3 August 1929; Legge to HH, 16 September 1929; HH to Legge, 8 October 1929, Federal Farm Board File, HHPL.

23. HH to Moton, 5 October 1929; HH to Legge, 5 October 1929, CQ.

24. Moton to HH, 14 November 1929, RRM Papers.

25. Barnett to Moton, 8 February 1930, ibid.; Newton to Hyde, 25 March 1930, CQ.

26. Hyde to Moton, 30 April 1930; Moton to Hyde, 16 November 1929; Moton to Hyde, 8 March 1932; Hyde to Moton, 27 February 1932; Moton to Hyde, 16 February 1932; Hyde to Moton, 14 January 1932, Hyde File, RRM Papers.

27. HH to Moton, 5 July 1929; Moton to HH, 18 April 1929, ibid.; James P. Davis to Akerson, 23 September 1929, CQ. See also Moton draft letter on failure to appoint blacks to federal farm agencies, n.d., Hoover File, and Moton to Barnett, 24 February 1930, RRM Papers.

28. Hyde to Newton, 29 May 1932, CQ; C. F. Marvin to Newton, 31 January 1931, CAB Papers; John G. Van Deusen, *The Black Man in White America* (Washington, D.C.: Associated Publishers, 1938), pp. 24–25; Ralph J. Bunche, *The Political Status of the Negro in the Age of FDR*, ed. Dewey W. Grantham (Chicago: University of Chicago Press, 1973), pp. 506, 610.

29. HH to attorney general, 14 May 1930, Prison's File, HHPL; Peter Daniel, "Black Power in the 1920's: The Case of Tuskegee Veterans Hospital," *Journal of Southern History* 36 (August 1970): 368–88; Burner, *Hoover*, p. 216.

30. HH to Wesley C. Mitchell, 20 December 1929, HHPL; report of the President's Research Committee on Social Trends, *Recent Social Trends in the United States*, 2 vols. (New York: McGraw-Hill Book Co., 1933), 2:553–601. Unfortunately the study's most promising findings were not released to the public. See n. 9 in chapter 22 for a complete explanation.

31. HH to Julius Rosenwald, 26 August 1925, Commerce, HHPL; Charles S. Johnson, *Negro Housing: Report of the Committee on Negro Housing* (National Capitol Press, 1932), pp. 1–282, but especially pp. 114–15.

32. Newton to Mary McLeod Bethune, 8 August 1929, Moton File, HHPL (Newton sent the same letter to other members of the commission); Ambrose Caliver, "Education of Negroes" in Katherine M. Cook, ed., *Biennial Survey of Education in the United States, 1928–1930* (Washington, D.C.: United States Department of Interior, 1931), pp. 37–56; Eugene Kinckle Jones, "The Negro Child," in *White House Conference on Child Health and Protection: Preliminary Committee Reports* (New York: The Century Co., 1930), pp. 512–13, 592; "The Negro in the United States," in *White House Conference on Child Health and Protection, Dependent and Neglected Children: Report of the Committee on Socially Handicapped—Dependency and Neglect* (New York: Appleton-Century Co., 1933), pp. 279–312; and detailed reports on a variety of black health problems and needs in Survey in Race Relations, Ray Lyman Wilbur Papers, Hoover Institution, Stanford University, Palo Alto, Calif.

33. See chapter 9, nn. 6 and 7. For Hoover's attempts to coordinate public and private institutions in solving social problems, see the excellent studies by Ellis W. Hawley, *The Great War and the Search for a Modern Order: A History of the American People and Their Institutions, 1917–1933* (New York: St. Martin's Press, 1979), pp. 175–80, 184–87; Ellis Hawley, et al., *Herbert Hoover and the Crisis of American Capitalism* (Cambridge, Mass.: Schenkman Publishing Company, 1973), pp. 2–33; Ellis Hawley, "Herbert Hoover, the Commerce Secretariat, and the Vision of an 'Associative State,' 1921–1928," *Journal of American History* 61 (June 1974): 116–40.

34. See, for example, Barnett to Moton, 19 November 1929, RRM Papers; Sherman, *The Republican Party and Black America*, p. 234.

35. See correspondence in files cited in nn. 23–28 and in chapter 16, nn. 23–33.

36. Johnson to HH, 29 March 1929; Ira W. Jayne to HH, 15 April 1929; John Hope to HH, 16 April 1929; J. E. Shepard to HH, 22 April 1929; William Monroe Trotter to HH, 29 April 1929; Mordecai W. Johnson, Claude Barnett, W. J. Wells, W. E. B. Du Bois, Charles E. Mitchell, and F. B. Ransom submitted a petition to HH. All in National Commission on Law Observance and Enforcement, HHPL.

37. HH to William Green, 7 March 1929, ibid.

38. For an excellent analysis see Robert L. Zangrando, *The NAACP Crusade Against Lynching, 1909–1950* (Philadelphia: Temple University Press, 1980), pp. 72–121.

16. Patronage Delayed

1. See chapter 10, nn. 36, 37, 45; and chapter 12, nn. 6 and 23.

2. See chapter 8; chapter 9, n. 10; chapter 10, nn. 43–44; chapter 11, n. 11.

3. See chapter 3, nn. 63–68; chapter 4, nn. 5–16, 28–36, 78; chapter 9, nn. 7–8, 15, 18, 20, 23–25.

4. I am indebted for this insight into the black perspective on patronage to William H. Chafe, "The Negro and Populism: A Kansas Case Study," *The Journal of Southern History* 34 (August 1968): 402–19. Although there were obvious differences between the black Kansas Populists of the 1890s and the black Republicans of the late 1920s, black leaders had not altered their views on the importance and significance of patronage. Indeed, because black Hoover loyalists expected to be appointed to influential federal posts, they had even more faith in the benefits that patronage would bring to blacks than did the black Kansas Populists.

5. Ibid.

6. James J. Davis to Richey, 22 March 1929, Negro Appointees, HHPL. Davis was secretary of labor.

7. See the excellent chart compiled by Emmett J. Scott in Negro Appointees, HHPL. Scott listed all the positions presently awarded and three that had been discontinued over the years.

8. See, for example, Elliot M. Rudwick, *W. E. B. Du Bois: A Study in Minority Group Leadership* (Philadelphia: University of Pennsylvania Press, 1960), p. 100.

9. Barnett to Moton, 28 January 1929, CAB Papers.

10. See especially Barnett to Moton, 1 July, 26 July 1929, Barnett to Moton, 3 June 1929, RRM Papers; Moton to HH, 15 January, 5 February 1930, HHPL.

11. Barnett to HH, 10 October 1949, PP File, Colored, HHPL.

12. See chapter 10, nn. 53, 59–60; and chapter 13, nn. 7–8.

13. Moton to Cohen, 28 February 1929, RRM Papers; Moton to Newton, 21 August 1929, Liberia, HHPL.

14. Hawkins to Hoover, 26 February 1929, CQ.

15. Ibid. See also Hawkins to Work, 22 January 1929, CQ.

16. See chart, "Principal Negro Officials," 22 March 1929, Negro Appointees, HHPL.

17. Scott to Richey, 25 June 1929, Negro Appointees, HHPL; memorandum to Dr. Moton, n.d.; Barnett to Moton, 6 December 1929, RRM Papers; Moton to HH, 15 January 1930; Moton to HH, 5 February 1930, CQ.

18. Barnett to Moton, 1 July, 3 June 1929, RRM Papers. For the quality of Hoover's black appointees see Monroe N. Work, ed., *Negro Year Book: An Annual Encyclopedia of the Negro, 1931–1932* (Tuskegee Institute, Ala.: Negro Year Book Publishing Company, 1931), pp. 82–83; and Monroe N. Work, ed., *Negro Year Book: An Annual Encyclopedia of the Negro, 1937–1938* (Tuskegee Institute: Negro Year Book Publishing Company, 1937), p. 112.

19. Attwell to Akerson, 26 July, 2 August 1929, CQ.

20. See chapter 8, nn. 49, 50 and 51.

21. One of the best political reports is simply designated "Memorandum: Dear Dr. Moton," n.d., from CAB [Barnett] in RRM Papers. Another excellent report is Barnett, "Political Memo for Dr. Moton," 22 September 1930, ibid. W. C. Hueston was from Gary, Indiana.

22. Edgar Rickard diary, 9, 19, 24, 26 November and 31 December 1930, HHPL. Rickard worried about the break between Hoover and Fox and gives excellent details.

23. See chapter 12, and especially nn. 13, 16 and 22–23.

24. See Justice Department Files at the HHPL. There are numerous examples scattered throughout the various appointment files. Assistant Attorney General Charles P. Sisson usually supervised the investigations for the Justice Department. See also William D. Mitchell to Mark Sullivan, 6 July 1935, Mitchell Papers, Minnesota Historical Society, Minneapolis, Minnesota. For Hoover's excellent record on appointments to the federal bench see Justin G. Green and John

R. Schmidhauser, "President Herbert Hoover and the Federal Judiciary," paper read at the Seminar on the Presidency of Herbert Hoover, August 1974, HHPL.

25. For the growing discontent see the state files of the Republican National Committee, especially the southern state files. For his worsening relations with Congress, see Jordan A. Schwarz, *The Interregnum of Despair: Hoover, Congress, and the Depression* (Urbana: University of Illinois Press, 1970), pp. 10–11, 18–22.

26. See chapter 7, nn. 35–39.

27. See the article by Melvin J. Chisum in the Baltimore *Afro-American*, 23 July 1932; and Newton's correspondence in the Southern State Files.

28. Johnson to HH, 24 May 1929; File memo, Akerson to Strother, 1 July 1929, NAACP File, HHPL.

29. Walter White, memo to office staff, 3 September 1931, White File, NAACP Papers. See also Barnett to Moton, 19 November 1930, RRM Papers.

30. Moton to Barnett, 20 September 1932, RRM Papers. See also the Baltimore *Afro-American*, 23 July 1932.

31. Richard B. Sherman, *The Republican Party and Black America: From McKinley to Hoover, 1896–1933* (Charlottesville: University Press of Virginia, 1973), p. 235.

32. Moton to Newton, 17 December 1929; Moton to HH, 15 January 1930; Moton to HH, 5 February 1930; Moton to HH, "Confidential Memorandum For President Herbert Hoover," 5 February 1930, CQ.

33. Newton to postmaster general, 25 March 1930, ibid.

34. Barnett to Moton, 3 June 1929; Barnett, "Political Memo for Dr. Moton," 22 September 1930; Moton draft letter to HH, n.d., RRM File.

35. Moton to Newton, 22 February 1930, ibid.

36. Barnett to Moton, 7 March 1930, ibid.

37. Ibid.; Barnett, "Political Memo for Dr. Moton," 22 September 1930; CAB [Barnett] memorandum, n.d., ibid.; Moton to Newton, 22 February 1930, HHPL.

38. See the references in n. 37.

39. HH to postmaster general, 20 March 1930, Post Office, HHPL.

40. On the Koontz appointment, see Wilbur to HH, 26 July 1927; LR [Larry Richey] memorandum, 29 July 1929 in Interior, Bureau of Education, HHPL; Henry L. Stimson to HH, 24 October 1929; HH to Stimson, 30 October 1929; Scott to Stimson, 15 November 1929; Stimson to HH, 21 November 1929; Stimson to HH, 29 November 1929, Liberia, HHPL; *Dunbar News* (New York, N.Y.), 15 January 1930. See also Eugene Levy, *James Weldon Johnson* (Chicago and London: University of Chicago Press, 1973), p. 309. Johnson was a leading interpreter of the black experience in America. See David Gordon Nielson, *Black Ethos: Northern Urban Negro Life and Thought, 1890–1930* (Westport, Conn.: Greenwood Press, 1977), p. 50 and passim.

41. William R. Castle to Akerson, 4 June 1929; Emile Kuntz to Akerson, 6 June 1929; Cohen to Akerson, 8 June 1929; HH to secretary of state, 24 July 1929; Moton to Newton, 21 August 1929; Akerson to Kuntz, 22 May 1929; Stimson to HH, 7 September 1929; Mrs. Walter Cohen to HH, 29 December 1930, Liberia, HHPL.

42. Hatfield to Newton, 8 September 1930; memorandum for the files, 15 August 1930; Castle to Newton, 27 September 1930; Newton to Felix Herbert, 31 August 1932, in Liberia, HHPL. See also Hatfield to HH, 16, 20 March, 6 April 1931; Newton to Hatfield, 8 May 1931; Hatfield to Newton, 12 May 1931, Henry D. Hatfield Papers, University of West Virginia, Morgantown, West Virginia. Hatfield nominated exceptionally well-qualified black candidates. See, for example, Hatfield to HH, 21 January 1930, Hatfield Papers.

43. Barnett, "Political Memo for Dr. Moton," 22 September 1930, RRM Papers; Andrew Buni, *Robert L. Vann of the Pittsburgh Courier: Politics and Black Journalism* (Pittsburgh: University of Pittsburgh Press, 1974), pp. 182, 233–34; Barnett to Hardin Hughes, 28 March 1951, CAB Papers; Barnett to Moton, memorandum, n.d., RRM Papers. Most of Postmaster Brown's papers

were destroyed by his wife. His remaining papers are in the Ohio Historical Society, Columbus, Ohio.

44. See especially Barnett to Moton, 7 March 1930; Moton draft letter to HH, n.d.; Barnett to Moton, 19 November 1930; Barnett to Moton, 18 March 1930; Moton to Newton, 22 February 1930, RRM Papers; Moton to HH, 15 January 1930, Moton File, HHPL.

45. Barnett to Moton, 18 March 1930, RRM Papers; Barnett to Cornelius Richardson, 4 April 1930, Indiana File, CAB Papers; Moton to Newton, 22 February 1930, CQ.

46. Barnett to Moton, 7 March 1930, RRM Papers; Barnett to Richardson, 4 April 1930, Indiana File; Barnett to Holsey, 20 July 1930, CAB Papers. Barnett was particularly disillusioned and became increasingly bitter over Hoover's broken patronage promises to Moton (see Barnett to Moton, 25 October 1932, RRM Papers; and Barnett to HH, 10, 12 October 1949, 24, 25 July 1935, 11 August 1943; HH to Barnett, 13 August 1943, 17 October 1949, PP File, Colored, HHPL).

17. Lily-White Symbol

1. Hanes Walton, Jr., *Black Republicans: The Politics of the Black and Tans* (Metuchen, N.J.: Scarecrow Press, 1975), p. 90; Paul D. Casdorph, *Republicans, Negroes, and Progressives in the South, 1912–1916* (University, Ala.: University of Alabama Press, 1981), pp. 171–73, 207–9; Work to Jonas, 16 April 1928; Jonas to Work, 21 June 1928, HW Papers.

2. Elmer L. Puryear, *Democratic Party Dissension in North Carolina 1928–1930* (Chapel Hill: University of North Carolina Press, 1962), pp. 19–21. For a detailed analysis see Richard L. Watson, Jr., "A Political Leader Bolts—F. M. Simmons in the Presidential Election of 1928," *North Carolina Historical Review* 37 (October 1960): 516–43.

3. HH to Cramer, 18, 19 October 1928, Pres. Papers; *New York Times*, 24 January 1929; New York *Evening Post*, 9 February 1928; New York *World*, 25 January 1929.

4. Cramer to Newton, 4 May 1929; Newton to the president, memorandum, 7 May and 20 May 1929; Richey to the president, memorandum, 6 May 1929, Treasury, HHPL.

5. Frederic M. Sachett to HH, 3 May 1929; John M. Robison to HH, 28 May 1929; A. W. Mellon to HH, 24 May 1929, Treasury, HHPL. See also Robert H. Lucas to L. P. Brewer, 29 April 1929, Robert H. Lucas Papers, HHPL. Lucas believed his appointment as commissioner of internal revenue would give him vast patronage power and thus greatly strengthen the Republican party in the South. Lucas was well liked in neighboring southern states (see Congressman J. Will Taylor to HH, 6 May 1929, Robert H. Lucas Papers, HHPL).

6. Jonas to Huston, 29 May 1929; Huston to Newton, 6 December 1929; Newton to Huston, 9 December 1929, NCS File.

7. Jonas to Huston, 29 November 1929; Jonas to Newton, 17 December 1929; Newton to Cramer, 30 December 1929; Mitchell to HH, 20 December 1929 and 28 February 1930, ibid.

8. Akerson to Richey, Message N. 58 to Chief, 15 February 1929, Pres. Papers, GA Papers; Akerson to Richey, 14 February 1929, Pres. Papers, Cabinet Appointments, HHPL. For Hoover's close relationship with Stone, see Alpheus Thomas Mason, *Harlan Fiske Stone: Pillar of the Law* (Hamden, Conn.: Archon Books, 1968 [1956]), pp. 262–89, 299–300.

9. For an excellent account of the Parker nomination fight, see Richard L. Watson, "The Defeat of Judge Parker: A Study of Pressure Groups and Politics," *Mississippi Valley Historical Review* 50 (September 1963): 213–34. See also David Burner, *Herbert Hoover: A Public Life* (New York: Alfred A. Knopf, 1979), pp. 235–36.

10. Willebrandt to HH, 8 February 1929, Pres. Papers, Cabinet Appointments, HHPL. Only a week after taking office Hoover recommended to his new attorney general that Parker be appointed solicitor general, but nothing came of it (see HH to attorney general, 12 March 1929;

Mitchell to HH, 14 March 1929, Justice, Solicitor General, HHPL).

11. Watson, "Defeat of Judge Parker," p. 213.

12. Ibid., p. 217; Puryear, *Democratic Party Dissension*, p. 18; William C. Burris, "John J. Parker and Supreme Court Policy: A Case Study in Judicial Control" (Ph.D. dissertation, University of North Carolina, 1965), pp. 60–62.

13. Paul Lewinson, *Race, Class, and Party: A History of Negro Suffrage and White Politics in the South* (New York: Russell and Russell, 1963), pp. 141–43.

14. Watson, "Defeat of Judge Parker," p. 213.

15. Jonas to Parker, 9 March 1930, JJP Papers.

16. Watson, "Defeat of Judge Parker," p. 228.

17. Brownlow Jackson to Parker, 11 March 1930; George M. Pritchard to Parker, 11 March 1930; Parker to Jonas, 12 March 1930, JJP Papers.

18. Parker to P. F. Henderson, 13 March 1930; Parker to Jonas, 13 March 1930, ibid. See also Watson, "Defeat of Judge Parker," pp. 214–15.

19. Jonas to Parker, 14 March 1930; Parker to Jonas, 17 March 1930, JJP Papers.

20. Parker to HH, 22 March 1930, ibid.

21. See letters from all parts of the South in folders dated 22–26 March 1930, ibid.

22. John Hope Franklin, *From Slavery to Freedom: A History of Negro Americans*, 3d ed. (New York: Alfred A. Knopf, 1967), pp. 447–48.

23. White to James A. Cobb, 13 March 1930; White to Elliot Thurston, 18 March 1930; and especially Elliot Thurston to White, 19 March 1930, Parker File, NAACP Papers.

24. Walter White, *A Man Called White* (New York: Viking Press, 1948), p. 104.

25. White to A. M. Riviera, 22 March 1930; Riviera to White, 24 March 1930; White to Riviera, 7 April 1930, Parker File, NAACP Papers. See also White, *A Man Called White*, pp. 104–5.

26. Franklin, *From Slavery to Freedom*, pp. 479–86. See also William M. Tuttle, Jr., *Race Riot: Chicago in the Red Summer of 1919* (New York: Atheneum, 1970); Robert Moats Miller, "The Ku Klux Klan," in John Braeman, et al., *Change and Continuity in Twentieth-Century America: The 1920's* (Columbus: Ohio University Press, 1968), pp. 215–55; and David Burner, "1919: Prelude to Normalcy," in Braeman, *Change and Continuity*, pp. 3–31.

27. See copy of Greensboro *Daily News*, 19 April 1920, in JSCP.

28. Franklin, *Slavery to Freedom*, p. 447.

29. See n. 27.

30. White to Parker, 26 March 1930; White to Arthur Capper, 2 April 1930, JJP Papers. See also White, *A Man Called White*, p. 105.

31. See letter to senator, 28 March 1930, with attached list, and White to branches, 28 March 1930, Parker File, NAACP Papers.

32. Parker to Jonas, 3 April 1930, JJP Papers.

33. Parker to Northcott, 26 March 1930 [?], ibid.

34. Parker to David H. Blair, 26 March 1930, ibid.

35. Parker to Jonas, 3 April 1930, ibid.

36. J. E. Shepard to Parker, 5 April 1930; Shepard to Carl Murphy, 5 April 1930; Parker to Morris A. Soper, 1 April 1930; Parker to Shepard, 26, 31 March 1930; Shepard to Parker, 21 April 1930, ibid.

37. H. L. McCrorey to White, 24 March 1930; Clara I. Cox to White, 25 April 1930, Parker File, NAACP Papers; White, *A Man Called White*, p. 108.

38. Sen. H. D. Hatfield to HH, 8 April 1930, JSCP. See also Walter White, "The Negro and the Supreme Court," *Harper's* 162 (January 1931): 240.

39. White to George W. Norris, 29 March 1930, Parker File, NAACP Papers.

40. See "Statement Read to the Sub-Committee of the Senate Judiciary Committee on Behalf of

the National Association for the Advancement of Colored People, April 5, 1930 by Walter White, Acting Secretary" and "To the Sub-Committee of Senate Committee on the Judiciary, April 2, 1930," Parker File, NAACP Papers.

41. U.S. Congress, Senate Subcommittee of the Committee on the Judiciary, *Hearings on the Confirmation of Hon. John J. Parker to be Associate Justice of the Supreme Court of the United States*, 71st Cong., 2d sess., 1930, pp. 74–79.

42. Ibid., p. 76; White, *A Man Called White*, p. 106.

43. White to George L. Johnson, 2 April 1930; White to Ernest Gruening, 7 April 1930, Parker File, NAACP Papers.

44. White, *A Man Called White*, p. 106.

45. Overman to Parker, 28 March 1930; Parker to Overman, 28 March 1930, JJP Papers.

46. U.S. Congress, *Hearings on Confirmation of John J. Parker*, pp. 23–60, but especially 52–56; Green to Norris, Borah, and Overman, 4 April 1930, JSCP; Merlo J. Pusey, *Charles Evans Hughes*, 2 vols. (New York: Macmillan Co., 1951),2:648–62, but especially pp. 659–61.

47. See Robert H. Zieger, *Republicans and Labor, 1919–1929* (Lexington: University Press of Kentucky, 1969); Robert H. Zieger, "Labor, Progressivism and Herbert Hoover in the 1920's," *Wisconsin Magazine of History* 67 (Spring 1975); and Robert H. Zieger, "Herbert Hoover, the Wage-Earner and the 'New Economic System,' 1919–1923," Business History Review 51 (Summer 1977). See also Burner, *Hoover*, pp. 143–46, 173–78.

48. Mitchell to HH, "Memorandum of the Opinion Circuit Judge John J. Parker in International Organization, United Mine Workers of America v. Red Jacket Consolidated Coal and Coke Co., 18 F (2d) 839," n.d., JSCP.

49. Parker to Jonas, 11 April 1930, JJP Papers.

50. Parker to H. H. Williams, 7 April 1930, ibid.

51. HH to Green, 14 April 1930, ibid.

52. Green to HH, 16 April 1930 and "Memorandum Concerning Opinion of Circuit Judge John J. Parker on the Case of United Mine Workers of America vs. Red Jacket Coal and Coke Co., et al.," 18 Fed. Rep. (2d) 839, JSCP. Although the author of this memorandum is not identified, it clearly expresses the view of the AF of L. It insists that Parker went beyond Supreme Court precedent by ruling that even peaceful persuasion was illegal.

53. Parker to Thomas S. Rollins, 1 April 1930; Parker to A. M. Stack, 5 April 1930, JJP Papers.

54. "Memorandum, Re: Judge John J. Parker," 3 April 1930, Parker File, NAACP Papers.

55. White to HH, 12 April 1930; Richey to White, 14 April 1930, ibid.

56. Cobb to White, 15 April 1930; White to Cobb, 16 April 1930; White to Harry E. David, 16 April 1930; White to Cobb, 27 March 1930; "Memoranndum From Mr. White, Re: Telephone Conversation With Judge Cobb," 21 April 1930, ibid.

57. See chapter 2.

58. Taylor to HH, 17 April 1930; Gray to Parker, 17 April 1930, JJP Papers; Taylor to White, 17 April 1930, Parker File, NAACP Papers.

59. "Memorandum from Mr. White, Re: Telephone Conversation with Robert Gray Taylor, Secretary of Interracial Committee, Society of Friends," 19 April 1930, Parker File, NAACP Papers. See working copies of draft letters written by Taylor and edited by Parker, 19 April 1930, JJP Papers.

60. Parker to Henry D. Hatfield, 19 April 1930, JJP Papers.

61. Taylor to HH, 19 April 1930; Taylor to Parker, 21 April 1930, ibid.

62. "Long Distance Telephone Message to Mr. White from Mr. Taylor, in Judge Parker's Office: 11:45 AM, April 19, 1930" and "Memorandum From Mr. White, Re: Telephone Conversation With Mr. Robert Gray Taylor, April 19, 1930," Parker File, NAACP Papers.

63. Ibid.; White to Gray, 19 April 1930, ibid.

64. "Memorandum from Mr. White, Re: Trip to Washington, D.C., April 21, 1930," ibid.; and references in n. 62.

65. White to Newspaper Editors, 14 April 1930, Parker File, NAACP Papers. See also Memorandum, Blair, n.d., JSCP.

66. "Memorandum to Mr. White from Mr. Seligman, April 19, 1930," and Robert W. Bagnall to White, 19 April 1930, Parker File, NAACP Papers.

67. "Memorandum from Mr. White, Re: Trip to Washington, D.C., April 21, 1930," ibid.; Taylor to Parker, 20 April 1930, JJP Papers.

18. The Parker Defeat

1. HH to Taylor, 18 February 1932, JSCP.
2. Taylor to Parker, 21 April 1930, JJP Papers.
3. Overman to Parker, 7 April 1930; James H. Winston to Parker, 17 April 1930, ibid.
4. Moton to Newton, 18 April 1930, JSCP.
5. See, for example, chapter 2, n. 3; chapter 8, nn. 14–27; and chapter 10, n. 62.
6. Moton to Newton, 18 April 1930, JSCP.
7. Ibid.
8. Ibid.
9. Ibid. Robert Vann, editor of the Pittsburgh *Courier*, actively fought the nomination. Vann had been publicity director of the Colored Voters Division in the 1928 campaign (see editorial, Pittsburgh *Courier*, 11 October 1930).
10. See chapter 2, n. 15.
11. See chapter 17, n. 9. See also n. 83 in this chapter.
12. See Hoover's working papers dealing with Parker's public letter to Senator Overman, 22 April 1930, JSCP. See also Herbert Hoover, *The Memoirs of Herbert Hoover*, 3 vols. (New York: Macmillan Co., 1951–52), 2:268–69.
13. *New York Times*, 14 February 1930; New York *Herald Tribune*, 14 February 1930; New York *World*, 14 February 1930, and Vandenburg personal scrapbook no. 2, Arthur H. Vandenburg Papers, Bentley Historical Library, University of Michigan, Ann Arbor, Michigan.
14. Vandenburg to W. B. Mershon, 12 May 1930, W. B. Mershon Papers, Bentley Historical Library, University of Michigan, Ann Arbor, Michigan.
15. HH to Attorney General, 18 April 1930, JSCP.
16. HH to Vandenburg, 19 April 1930, ibid.
17. White, memorandum to files, 20 October 1931, Parker File, NAACP Papers. White received this information from a strong Hoover supporter, Theodore Roosevelt, Jr. See also T. J. Nutter to White, 19 April 1930, Parker File, NAACP Papers. Administration officials made the charge openly.
18. Moton to Newton, 18 April 1930, JSCP; Vandenburg to Mershon, 12 May 1930, W. B. Mershon Papers, Bentley Historical Library, University of Michigan, Ann Arbor, Michigan.
19. Vandenburg to R. K. Smathers, 28 April 1930, JJP Papers.
20. White to R. E. Rudd, 23 April 1930, Parker File, NAACP Papers. See also C. David Tompkins, *Senator Arthur H. Vandenburg: The Evolution of a Modern Republican, 1884–1945* (Lansing, Michigan: State University Press, 1970).
21. Parker to Earl J. Davis, n.d. [?], JJP Papers.
22. Vandenburg to Mershon, 12 May 1930, Mershon Papers; Vandenburg memo, "The Parker Vote, May 7, 1930" pasted in scrapbook no. 2, Vandenburg Papers, Bentley Historical Library, University of Michigan, Ann Arbor, Michigan; Tompkins, *Vandenburg*, pp. 55–57.
23. White to Felix Frankfurter, 25 April 1930, Parker File, NAACP Papers.

24. For a complete list of the organizations, see Assistant Attorney General Charles P. Sisson to HH, 30 April 1930, and accompanying papers in JSCP.

25. White to Ludwell Denny, 15 April 1930; White to Roy Howard, 16 April 1930; White to Cecelia C. Saunders, 16 April 1930, Parker File, NAACP Papers.

26. White to Bruce T. Bowers, 17 April 1930; White, "To the Editors of the Colored Press," 8 May 1930; News Release, 9 May 1930, Parker File, NAACP Papers.

27. Barnett at first appeared to be supporting Parker (see news release, Associated Negro Press, in 1–5 May file, JSCP), but after White's appeal he ceased comment altogether (see White to Barnett, 21 April 1930, Parker File, NAACP Papers).

28. Vandenburg estimated that one-half of the senators who finally voted for Parker did so "under mental protest or with mental reservations" (Vandenburg to Mershon, 12 May 1930, Mershon Papers, Bentley Historical Library, University of Michigan, Ann Arbor, Michigan); Thomas W. Davis to Silas H. Strawn, 12 April 1930, JJP Papers. Davis claimed that Vice-President Curtis asked Hoover to withdraw the nomination because of intense pressure on senators, but Hoover refused. See also Washington (D.C.) *Post*, 18 April 1930.

29. White to Charles E. Russell, 16 April 1930; White to Oscar De Priest, 16 April 1930, Parker File, NAACP Papers.

30. See telegrams sent to key leaders in Illinois and Massachusetts on 16 April 1930, ibid.

31. Oscar De Priest to White, 18 April 1930, Parker File, NAACP Papers.

32. See numerous letters from leading union leaders and blacks in Parker Nomination File, GN Papers. See also Willebrandt telephone message to the White House, 18 April 1930, JSCP.

33. See especially "Memorandum from WW [Walter White] re Parker confirmation," 18 April 1930; and White to W. H. Hannum, 16 April 1930; White to Eleanor Alexander, 19 April 1930, Parker File, NAACP Papers.

34. Thomas Leaper Taylor to Senator, 5 May 1930, ibid. Taylor contacted eleven southern Democratic senators.

35. Attorney general to Mr. Newton, 18 April 1930, JSCP.

36. Telephone message from Ludlow Denny, 1 April 1930, Parker File, NAACP Papers. Denny was with the Washington bureau of the New York *Telegram* and supported White with invaluable political information.

37. J. Edgar Hoover to Assistant Attorney General Charles P. Sisson, 19 April 1930; Carl G. Buchmann to Newton, 21 August 1930, CQ; J. Edgar Hoover to Newton, 25 April 1930, JSCP. The administration believed that Joel Spingarn rather than White was the "chief figure back of objection" to Parker (see Edgar Rickard diary, 25 April 1930, ER Papers).

38. Davis to Blair, 15, 17, 23, 24 April 1930; Parker to Davis, 14 April 1930; Parker to Blair, 16 April 1930 and numerous other letters in JJP Papers.

39. Jonas to Arthur R. Robinson, n.d., [?]; Jonas to Parker, 19 April 1930, ibid. Jonas sent the same letter to all undecided senators. He argued that Parker had refused to play politics with the race issue in 1920.

40. Jonas to Charles W. Waterman, 19 April 1930, ibid.

41. Willebrandt, message, 17 April 1930, JSCP.

42. David H. Blair to Thomas W. Davis, 23 April 1930; Davis to Blair, 17, 23, 24 April 1930, JJP Papers. A close analysis of the political maneuvering of the Parker forces is in the folder marked "Letters to Thomas W. Davis."

43. Telephone message from Ludlow Denny, 18 April 1930, and memorandum from Mr. White, 26 April 1930, Parker File, NAACP Papers. Denny identified at least four southern Democrats who would certainly vote against Parker. He incorrectly placed one of the Georgia senators in the favor column. By 18 April 1930 five southern Democrats were identified either by Denny or the Parker forces as definitely against confirmation, long before the 7 May vote or the impact of the Dixon letter on 1 May 1930. On 26 April 1930 Denny reiterated the administration's inability to win over southern senators on the race issue. Richard L. Watson points out that the

Parker forces made a determined effort to use approval by the American Bar Association and by state bar associations as well as race as a means to convince southern Democrats ("The Defeat of Judge Parker: A Study of Pressure Groups and Politics," *Mississippi Valley Historical Review* 50 [September 1963]: 223).

44. Overman to Parker, 18 April 1930, JSCP.

45. President's calendar, 21 April 1930, HHPL; Watson, "Defeat of Judge Parker," p. 222.

46. See telegram and telephone messsages dated 24 April 1930 in JSCP, and drafts in JJP Papers and HHPL dated 22 April 1930. See also White to Fred R. Moore, 22 April 1930, Parker File, NAACP Papers.

47. Parker to Overman, 24 April 1930, JJP Papers.

48. Parker to Blair, 24 April 1930, and drafts of letter to Overman, JJP Papers; transcript of Parker letter dictated by him to Hoover over telephone, 24 March 1930, JSCP.

49. Jonas to Parker, 28 April 1930, JJP Papers.

50. Emphasis mine. Parker to Overman, 24 April 1930, ibid. See also Parker to Blair, 24 April 1930, ibid.

51. Watson recognized Parker's deliberate appeal to southern senators, but he does not discuss it in the context of Hoover's concerns (see "Defeat of Judge Parker," pp. 223–24).

52. Taylor to Parker, 30 April 1930, JJP Papers; Vandenburg memorandum, "The Parker Vote," 7 May 1930, pasted in scrapbook no. 2, Vandenburg Papers, Bentley Historical Library, University of Michigan, Ann Arbor, Michigan; Seligmann to Senator H. F. Kern, 6 May 1930, Parker File, NAACP Papers.

53. Parker to A. B. Andrews, 24 April 1930, JJP Papers. Parker was very discouraged by the adverse vote of the judiciary committee.

54. Parker to J. Elwood Cox, 26 April 1930, ibid.

55. Parker to Frank R. McNinch, 25 April 1930, ibid. See also Parker to Cameron Morrison, 26 April 1930, ibid.

56. Campbell B. Hodges diary, 9 May 1930, HHPL.

57. Norris, "Memorandum, 1 May 1930," GN Papers. Norris refused to believe that Hoover would make a corrupt deal in order to get Parker confirmed. See also Watson, "The Defeat of Judge Parker," pp. 228–29; and Parker to Overman, 6 May 1930; Parker to Henry F. Ashurst, 6 May 1930, JJP Papers.

58. Several of the most important black patronage posts eventually went to senators who voted for Parker. For example, Hoover later rewarded both Senator Hatfield of West Virginia and Senator Hastings of Delaware who had large black constituencies that they needed to placate after supporting Parker (see chapter 16).

59. White to Harry E. Davis, 21 April 1930; White to Heywood Broun, 23 April 1930; White to HH, 24 April 1930; L. E. Austin to White, 23, 28 April 1930 and copy of 13 April 1930 Greensboro *Daily News*, Parker File, NAACP Papers.

60. Washington *Post*, 20 April 1930.

61. White to HH, 22 April 1930, Parker File, NAACP Papers.

62. See Donald J. Lisio, *The President and Protest: Hoover, Conspiracy, and the Bonus Riot* (Columbia: University of Missouri Press, 1974).

63. White to Nannie H. Burroughs, 23 April 1930, Parker File, NAACP Papers.

64. White to David Lawrence, 23 April 1930; White to Walter Lippmann, 26 April 1930; White to Editor, Brooklyn *Daily Eagle*, 23 April 1930, ibid.

65. White to Heywood Broun, 23 April 1930, ibid. See also Heywood Broun's assessment in *Nation* 130 (21 May 1930): 591.

66. White to R. R. Church, 23 April 1930, Parker File, NAACP Papers.

67. The *New York Times* printed the letter and reported that it "had been contained in a file of all the recommendations in the Parker case sent by the Department of Justice to the Senate Judiciary Committee, and Senator McKellar obtained it in that file from Senator Norris" (1 May 1930).

68. For the debate see *Congressional Record*, 71st Cong., 2d sess., 1930, pp. 7930–8487. A good brief account is in Watson, "Defeat of Judge Parker," pp. 225–30. For the lack of support from Republican senators see New York Evening *Post*, 29 April 1930; *New York Times*, 21 April 1930; New York *World*, 30 April 1930, and especially Sen. Daniel F. Steck to Verne Marshall, 24 April 1930, Marshall Papers, HHPL. Steck reported that " a number of real regular Republicans are actively opposing the confirmation of this nomination and there is a disheartening lack of enthusiasm on the part of all the Republicans who ordinarily can be relied upon to support the administration."

69. Watson, "Defeat of Judge Parker," p. 227.

70. Ibid., p. 228; Parker to Henry F. Ashurst, 6 May 1930, JSCP.

71. See the evidence cited in nn. 41, 42, and 43, and Jonas to Sen. Charles W. Waterman, 19 April 1930; Jonas to Parker, 19 April 1930; Johnson J. Hayes to Senator Borah, 18 April 1930, JJP Papers. See also Walter White to Heywood Broun, 3 April 1930, Parker File, NAACP Papers; and Walter White, *A Man Called White* (New York: Viking Press, 1948), p. 108. For the impact of the Dixon letter see Watson, "The Defeat of Judge Parker," p. 127; and George F. Garcia, "Herbert Hoover's Southern Strategy and the Black Reaction," (M.A. thesis, University of Iowa, 1972), p. 135.

72. Ibid. Daniel F. Steck to Verne Marshall, 24 April 1930, Verne Marshall Papers, HHPL; and Josephus Daniels, *The Wilson Era: Years of War and After, 1917–1923*, 2 vols. (Chapel Hill: University of North Carolina Press, 1946), 1:326.

73. White to Herbert A. Turner, 22 April 1930; White to Herbert E. Millen, 23 April 1930; Seligmann to White, 2 May 1930; De Priest to White, 3 May 1930; Thomas Leeper Taylor telegram to eleven southern senators, 5 May 1930; White to Robert P. Jones, 23 April 1930, Parker File, NAACP Papers. See also Walter White, "The Negro and the Supreme Court," *Harper's* 162 (January 1931): 241–42 and *New York Times*, 14 June 1930.

74. White to HH, 5 May 1930, Parker File, NAACP Papers. See Hoover's lists of senators and other evidence in 1–5 May, 1930 file, JSCP.

75. Herbert Hoover, *The Memoirs of Herbert Hoover*, 3 vols. (New York: Macmillan Co., 1951–52), 2:269; New York *Herald Tribune*, 5 May 1930.

76. *Congressional Record*, 71st Cong., 2d sess., 1930, p. 8487; *New York Times*, 8 May 1930.

77. See copy of public statement corrected and added to by Hoover, 7 May 1930, JSCP.

78. HH to Taylor, 18 February 1932, JSCP.

79. Hoover, *Memoirs*, 2:269.

80. See n. 22. Vandenburg refused to reveal his motives. He told White that he had "several reasons" for voting against Parker (see Vandenburg to White, 7 May 1930, Parker File, NAACP Papers). Some in Michigan believed that the negative votes of both Michigan senators were based on political pressure (see Hiram T. Johnson to HH, 15 May 1930, JSCP).

81. Hoover, *Memoirs*, 2:269.

82. Ibid.

83. White, *A Man Called White*, p. 114; William C. Burris, "John J. Parker and Supreme Court Policy: A Case Study in Judicial Control" (Ph.D. dissertation, University of North Carolina, 1965), pp. 130, 211–12. Ten years later Newton was still angry over the rejection (see Newton to HH, 8 May 1940, HHPL).

84. Fess to Parker, 1 May 1930, JJP Papers.

85. White to Lippmann, 26 April 1930, Parker File, NAACP Papers.

86. *New York Times*, 21 April 1930.

87. William Pickens to Claude Barnett, 6 September 1932, CAB Papers.

88. White, "Negro and Supreme Court," pp. 244–46; W. E. B. Du Bois, "The Defeat of Judge Parker," *Crisis* 37 (July 1930): 225; NAACP press release, 23 May 1930; White to Harry E. Davis, 16 April 1930, Parker File, NAACP Papers. See also Henry Lee Moon, *Balance of Power: The Negro Vote* (Garden City, N.Y.: Doubleday and Co., 1948), pp. 111–12.

89. Charles Edward Russell to White, 17 April 1930, Parker File, NAACP Papers. See also Bureau of the Census, *Historical Statistics of the United States 1789–1945* (Washington, D.C.: U.S. Government Printing Office, 1949), p. 72.

90. See n. 88 and William Starr Myers and Walter H. Newton, *The Hoover Administration: A Documented Narrative* (New York: Charles Scribner's Sons, 1936), p. 428.

91. Jonas to Parker, 8 May 1930 [?], JJP Papers. See also Houston *Southern Advance*, 9 May 1930; Tampa *Morning Tribune*, 9 May 1930, and examples in 8 May folder, JSCP.

92. White to F. G. Haling, 4 September 1930, Parker File, NAACP Papers; Du Bois, "Defeat of Judge Parker," pp. 225–28.

93. Richard L. Watson, Jr., concluded that the liberal vote was "probably" most important. Richard B. Sherman is also tentative. He stressed the liberal vote but included both labor and racial issues in his determination of liberal. Jordan A. Schwarz argues that the "major opposition" came from Negroes, but he deals only briefly with the Parker nomination. Roger W. Corley believes that "it was probably the organized labor pressure that was most telling." George F. Garcia tends to emphasize the southern Democratic vote as does David James Ginzl, who defends Parker. All recognize that a combination of factions contributed to the defeat. None of them attempts to argue for one as against the others. See Watson, "Defeat of Judge Parker," pp. 231–34; Richard B. Sherman, *The Republican Party and Black America: From McKinley to Hoover 1896–1933* (Charlottesville: University Press of Virginia, 1973), pp. 239–46, but especially p. 244; Roger W. Corley, "Hoover's Judicial Appointments," paper read at the Missouri Valley History Conference, 1980, p. 9; George F. Garcia, "Herbert Hoover's Southern Strategy and the Black Reaction" (M.A. thesis, University of Iowa, 1972): 99–107, but especially p. 105; David James Ginzl, "Herbert Hoover and Republican Patronage Politics in the South, 1928–1932" (Ph.D. dissertation, Syracuse University, 1977), pp. 331–39, but especially p. 337; Jordan A. Schwarz, *The Interregnum of Despair: Hoover, Congress, and the Depression* (Urbana: University of Illinois Press, 1970), p. 9.

94. Senator Capper had long been a supporter of the NAACP. See chapter 1, n. 17, and Capper to White, 11 May 1930, Parker File, NAACP Papers. See also *New York Times*, 21 April 1930, Chicago *Evening Post*, 8 May 1930, and of course Hoover's own explanation cited in n. 75. Heywood Broun drew attention to "the consensus that it was the disaffection of conservative Middle Western Republicans" that accounted for Parker's defeat (see Heywood Broun's column in *The Nation* 130 [21 May 1930]: 591).

95. Du Bois, "Defeat of Judge Parker," p. 226; White, *A Man Called White*, p. 108. A Brief conclusion similar to mine is in Ellis W. Hawley, *The Great War and the Search for a Modern Order: A History of the American People and Their Institutions, 1917–1933* (New York: St. Martin's Press, 1979), p. 188. I should like to acknowledge several excellent papers written by my undergraduate seminar students at Coe College: Kent Kraus, "The Rejection of Judge Parker's Nomination to the Supreme Court: A Case Study of Political Force," March 1975; Denice M. Petska, "The American Federation of Labor's Opposition to Judge John J. Parker's Nomination to the Supreme Court," December 1978; Kelley Rice, "Conflict and Consensus: President Hoover's Nominations to the Supreme Court," honors paper, 1979.

19. "Pretty Much Disgusted"

1. Edgar Rickard diary, 14, 15 May 1930, ER Papers.

2. Ibid., 7 May 1930; 31 December 1930; 7 November 1932.

3. Edgar Rickard to Hugh Gibson, 20 May 1930, Hugh Gibson Papers, Rickard File, Hoover Institution, Stanford University, Palo Alto, California. See also Donald J. Lisio, *The President and Protest: Hoover, Conspiracy, and the Bonus Riot* (Columbia: University of Missouri Press, 1974), pp. 139–65.

4. Rickard diary, 12 February 1925, 31 December 1930, ER Papers.

5. Col. Campbell B. Hodges diary, 9 May 1930, HHPL. Handy was a personal friend of Lt. Col. C. B. Hodges, military aide to the president (see Handy to Hodges, 21 September, 8 October 1932, Secretary's File, HHPL). I am indebted to David Burner for bringing the quote from Hodges's diary to my attention.

6. Hodges diary, 9 May 1930, HHPL.

7. Chicago *Defender*, 31 May 1930. This quote is almost exactly as Hodges recorded it.

8. Ibid.

9. Barnett to Akerson, 3 June 1930, CQ.

10. For another example of Hoover's failure to relate well to politicians, see Andrew Sinclair, *The Available Man: The Life Behind the Masks of Warren Gamaliel Harding* (New York: The Macmillan Co., 1965), pp. 184–85.

11. Rickard diary, 12 February 1925, ER Papers.

12. Barnett to Holsey, 20 July 1930, CAB Papers.

13. See n. 6.

14. Magdaline W. Shannon, "President's Commission for the Study and Review of Conditions in Haiti and Its Relationship to Hoover's Foreign Policy" (M.A. thesis, University of Iowa, April 1974), pp. 21–23. See also James Weldon Johnson, *Along This Way: The Autobiography of James Weldon Johnson* (New York: Viking Press, 1933), p. 360; Walter White, *A Man Called White* (New York: Viking Press, 1948), p. 116.

15. Arthur Ruhl to HH, 8 February 1930; Akerson to Ruhl, 11 February 1930, Foreign Affairs, Moton Commission File, HHPL.

16. Moton to HH, 20 February 1930; R. Barrows to Newton, 5 April 1930; Helen Cook to Newton, 15 April 1930, Foreign Affairs, Moton Commission File, HHPL.

17. See chapter 18, nn. 6–9.

18. Newton to Moton, 17, 23 April 1930, Foreign Affairs, Moton Commission File, HHPL.

19. Moton to Newton, 17 April 1930, ibid.

20. Moton to secretary of state, 7 July 1930, ibid. See also Shannon, "President's Commission," p. 51; George F. Garcia, "Herbert Hoover's Southern Strategy and the Black Reaction," (M.A. thesis, University of Iowa, 1972), p. 137; Richard B. Sherman, *The Republican Party and Black America: From McKinley to Hoover, 1896–1933* (Charlottesville: University Press of Virginia, 1973), p. 251.

21. Hurley to HH, 28 January 1928; HH to Mrs. Du Bois, 10 March 1930, Gold Star Mothers, HHPL.

22. See chapter 4, nn. 49–51.

23. See the evaluations in Garcia, "Hoover's Southern Strategy," pp. 133–34; Sherman, *The Republican Party and Black America*, pp. 246–49; George F. Garcia, "Black Disaffection from the Republican Party during the Presidency of Herbert Hoover, 1928–1932," *Annals of Iowa* 45 (Fall 1980): 469–70.

24. Trotter to Newton, 19 February 1930, Gold Star Mothers File, HHPL.

25. Philadelphia *Tribune*, 12 July 1930.

26. Tom Canty to Akerson, 30 May 1930, Gold Star Mothers File, HHPL.

27. Roy Wilkins to W. J. Rice, 29 September 1932, Politics, NAACP Papers; F. H. Payne to Richey, 25 October 1932, Gold Star Mothers File, HHPL.

28. HH to John H. Robison, 26 July 1929; Ray Lyman Wilbur to HH, 25 July 1929; Robison to HH, 31 July 1929, Interior, Bureau of Education, HHPL.

29. Moton to Newton, 27 July 1931; WHN [Walter Newton] File Memo, 29 July 1931, Secretary's File, HHPL; attorney general to HH, 26 February 1931; File Memo, 9 March 1931, Judiciary, U.S. District Judges, Illinois, HHPL. See also Barnett to Moton, 26 July 1929, RRM Papers.

30. Wilbur to HH, 26 July 1929; LR [Larry Richey] Memorandum, 29 July 1929, Interior, Bureau of Education, HHPL.

31. HH to Claudius Huston, 9 December 1929, District Commissioners, Recorder of Deeds File, HHPL.

32. Sinclair, *Available Man*, pp. 184–85; Joan Hoff Wilson, *Herbert Hoover: Forgotten Progressive* (Boston: Little, Brown and Co., 1975), pp. 123–25. On Hoover's worsening relations with Congress, see the excellent study by Jordan A. Schwarz, *The Interregnum of Despair: Hoover, Congress, and the Depression* (Urbana: University of Illinois Press, 1970), pp. 10–11, 18–22.

33. George B. Lockwood to HH, 2 February 1929; HH to Lockwood, 6 February 1929, Lockwood File, HHPL.

34. Henry D. Hatfield to Newton, 29 May 1929, District Commissioners, Recorder of Deeds File, HHPL; Hatfield to HH, 21 January 1930; 28 March 1931; HH to Hatfield, 22 January 1930; 16 March 1931; 6 April 1931, Henry D. Hatfield Papers, University of West Virginia, Morgantown, West Virginia.

35. James A. Hughes to HH, 17 June 1929; Hugh I. Shott to HH, 17 June 1929; John M. Wolverton to HH, 17 June 1929; Frank L. Bowman to HH, 9 June 1929; E. T. England to HH, 20 June 1929; William G. Conley to HH, 18 June 1929; Walter S. Hallanan to HH, 7 June 1929, District Commissioners, Recorder of Deeds File, HHPL.

36. Hallanan to HH, 7 June 1929; J. N. Harman to HH, 12 July 1929, ibid.

37. See file memo, n.d.; Larry Richey to Arthur Froe, 8 September 1930; Froe to Richey, 8 September 1930; Sen. Guy D. Goff to HH, 21 March 1929, ibid.

38. Arthur Capper to HH, 18 January 1929; Henry J. Allen to HH, 26 April 1929; Kelly Miller to HH, 17 June 1929; Capper to HH, 11 October 1929; HH to Capper, 14 October 1929, ibid.

39. Daniel O. Hastings to Newton, 11 August 1930; Newton to Mr. Forster, 16 September 1930; File memo, 15 September 1930, ibid.

40. File memo, 27 September 1930; Hatfield to Newton, 1 September 1930; message for Mr. Newton, 25 September 1930; Newton to Hatfield, 27 September 1930, ibid. See also Hatfield to HH, 21 January 1930; HH to Walter F. Brown, 22 January 1930; HH to William D. Mitchell, 22 January 1930; HH to Hatfield, 22 January 1930; C. E. Stewart to Sen. Guy D. Goff, 8 January 1930, CQ. See chapter 16, n. 41.

41. James A. Cobb to Walter White, 8 August 1930, Politics, NAACP Papers. Cobb kept the NAACP fully informed on all major black appointments.

42. Perry Howard to Newton, telephone message, 22 September 1930; James A. Cobb to Newton, 23 September 1930, District Commissioners, Recorder of Deeds File, HHPL.

43. Moton to HH, 6 February 1930; Akerson to Moton, 10 February 1930, ibid. See also Barnett to Walter Brown, 17 July 1930, Politics, CAB Papers.

44. Perry Howard to Newton, telephone message, 22 September 1930, District Commissioners, Recorder of Deeds File, HHPL.

45. Newton to Cobb, 26 September 1930, ibid.

46. Cobb to Newton, 23 September 1930, JAC Papers.

47. James W. Geater to James Watson, 18 July 1930; Watson to HH, 25 July 1930, CQ. Geater called for a national director of Negro welfare.

48. Scott to Newton, 9 October 1930, CQ.

49. Ibid.

50. John R. Hawkins to Scott, 3 January 1931, EJS Papers. See also press releases giving the names of those attending the April 1930 meeting and outlining the purpose of the league. Unfortunately the vast bulk of the Scott papers for the years 1928–32 are not in the collection. These papers appear to have been lost.

51. Washington (D.C.) *Sentinel*, 3 May 1930; Holsey to Barnett, 22 July 1930, Holsey File,

CAB Papers; Barnett to Moton, 22 September 1930, Barnett File, RRM Papers.

52. Barnett to Moton, 22 September 1930, Barnett File, RRM Papers.

53. Working copy, undated, memorandum for Mr. Robert H. Lucas in the C. H. Huston File, RRM Papers.

54. Barnett to Moton, 22 September 1930, Barnett File, RRM Papers; Rickard to Newton, 26 August 1931, President's Organization for Unemployment Relief, HHPL. Rickard sent Hoover reports from Francis E. Rivers, the administration's trusted Harlem political leader, and from Robert F. Leftridge who gathered black political intelligence for the party. The reports revealed the massive erosion of Republican sentiment among blacks and the vicious personal attacks on Hoover by Democrats who insisted that the president was antiblack.

55. Barnett to Akerson, 19 November 1930 and copy of Raleigh (N.C.) *News and Observer*, 14 November 1930, CQ.

56. See n. 55 and Barnett to Moton, undated memorandum, RRM Papers. This memo is a two-page report on Barnett's efforts to secure Brown's backing for an assistant attorney general.

57. Barnett to Akerson, 19 November 1930, CQ.

58. Barnett to Moton, 19 Novembeerr 1930, RRM Papers.

59. Holsey to Barnett, 6 November 1930, Holsey File, CAB Papers.

60. Barnett to Moton, 22 September 1930, Barnett File, and undated memorandum, Politics; Moton to Barnett, 10 November 1930, RRM Papers.

61. See information in Huston File, HHPL. See also valuable correspondence in RNC Papers, Miscellaneous File, 1930, HHPL. For the Norris-Hoover feud see Hoover, Muscle Shoals File, GN Papers; and George W. Norris, *Fighting Liberal: The Autobiography of George W. Norris* (New York: Macmillan Co., 1945), pp. 267, 280–82, 287–88, 293–307, 314–15; Richard Lowitt, *George W. Norris: The Persistence of a Progressive, 1913–1933* (Urbana: University of Illinois Press, 1971), pp. 405–8, 411–12, 486.

62. Philadelphia *Record*, 24 May 1930; "Hoover and Huston," *New Republic* 62 (2 April 1930): 178–79; Rickard diary, 3 April 1930, HHPL.

63. Rickard diary, 23, 31 May, 1, 8 August, 31 December 1930, HHPL; Walter Brown to HH, 31 January 1934, Brown Papers, Ohio State Historical Society, Columbus, Ohio; HH to Lucas, 15 August 1930, Treasury, HHPL; William Worley to Walter White, 6 July 1930, Politics, NAACP Papers. On the Lucas appointment see Robert H. Lucas Papers, HHPL.

64. Brown to HH, 31 January 1934, Brown Papers, Ohio State Historical Society, Columbus, Ohio. See also David James Ginzl, "Herbert Hoover and Republican Patronage Politics in the South, 1928–1932," (Ph.D. dissertation, Syracuse University, 1977), pp. 329–31, 339–41.

65. Some of the best information is in RNC Papers, Miscellaneous, 1930, HHPL. See also File memo, 13 August 1930, 4 November 1931, Mann File; Moton to Newton 28 July 1930; Josiah T. Rose to Newton, 17 November 1930; Newton to Lucas, 20 November 1930, in RNC, Miscellaneous, 1930, HHPL. See also *New York Times*, 12, 24 August 1930; Atlanta *Constitution*, 26 December 1930; and Newton, memorandum to postmaster general, 13 January 1931, Mann File, HHPL.

66. Scholars have also had some difficulty in evaluating the conflicting and thus at times confusing evidence. Paul Lewinson concluded that it was not possible in 1930 to determine if Hoover's policy in the South was lily-white or black and tan (see Paul Lewinson, *Race, Class, and Party: A History of Negro Suffrage and White Politics in the South* [New York: Russell and Russell, 1963], pp. 174–76). Garcia also recognizes the problem but argues the case for a lily-white strategy ("Hoover's Southern Strategy," p. 86). Ginzl accepts Garcia's analysis ("Hoover and Republican Patronage Politics," pp. 165–75, but especially p. 171).

67. Rowlands to Newton, 21, 22 March 1930; Newton to Rowlands, 31 March 1930, RNC Papers, Mississippi State File, HHPL. See also William D. Mitchell to HH, 30 April 1935, William D. Mitchell Papers, Minnesota Historical Society.

68. Paul Lewinson, *Race, Class, and Party: A History of Negro Suffrage and White Politics in*

the South (New York: Russell and Russell, 1963), p. 167. For a good summary of the Democratic counterattack see Garcia, "Hoover's Southern Strategy," pp. 109–24.

69. Ginzl provides a highly detailed state-by-state analysis of the internal feuding ("Hoover and Republican Patronage Politics"). Although Ginzl is careful in weighing the facts, the evidence is of such a partisan, conflicting nature that it is not always possible to determine exactly which faction is closer to the truth. Each faction invariably shaded the story. For example, he concluded that his attempt "to unravel the byzantine course of Florida Republican politics during these years is nearly impossible." See David J. Ginzl, "The Politics of Patronage: Florida Republicans During the Hoover Administration," *Florida Historical Quarterly* (July 1982), p. 18.

70. Walter W. Holmes to Frederic C. Walcott, 17 February 1930; Walcott to Newton, 24 February 1930, RNC Papers, Florida State File, HHPL.

71. See chapter 13, nn. 19–23.

72. See the voluminous evidence in the South Carolina and Mississippi state files. See also J. S. Johnson to HH, 9 October 1930; G. J. Cherry to Newton, 30 October, 15 December 1930 and newspaper clippings, RNC Papers, South Carolina State File. Howard's return to power will be discussed in chapter 21.

73. Rose to Newton, 12 February 1930; Rose to Brown, 20 February 1930; Rose to Newton, 19 March 1930; Dirrelle Chaney to Brown, 11 March 1930; Rose to Newton, 14 April 1930, RNC Papers, Georgia State File, HHPL.

74. Charles Adamson to Newton, 21 April 1930; Walter Akerman to Newton, 25 April 1930; Ben Davis to Newton, 4 August 1930, RNC Papers, Georgia State File, HHPL. See also Ginzl, "Hoover and Republican Patronage Politics," pp. 199–210.

75. Walter Akerman to Newton, 25 April 1930; Rose to Newton, 4 September 1930; Ben Davis to Newton, 4 August 1930; John B. Dove to HH, 4 August 1930, RNC Papers, Georgia State File, HHPL. See also Savannah (Ga.) *Morning News*, 30 July 1930.

76. Stuart W. Cramer to Newton, 18 April 1930, RNC Papers, North Carolina State File, HHPL.

77. Ben E. Davis to Newton, 10 October 1930; Columbia (S.C.) *Free Press*, 10 October 1930, Secretary's File, HHPL.

78. Herbert Hoover, *The State Papers and Other Public Writings of Herbert Hoover*, ed. William Starr Myers (Garden City, N.Y: Doubleday, Doran and Co., 1934), 1:395–401.

79. Ben E. Davis to Newton, 10 October 1930, Secretary's File, HHPL.

80. Greensboro *Daily News*, 28 September 1930. See also information in RNC Papers, North Carolina State File; Richey to Brown, 23 July 1931; Brown to Newton, 27 July 1931, Executive Department, Post Office, HHPL. Two excellent analyses are Elmer L. Puryear, *Democratic Party Dissension in North Carolina, 1928–1930* (Chapel Hill: University of North Carolina Press, 1962), pp. 21, 37, 44–46; and Richard L. Watson, Jr., "A Southern Democratic Primary: Simmons vs. Barley in 1930," *North Carolina Historical Review* 62 (January 1965): 21–46.

81. See n. 60.

20. Black Expectations and Designs of Oppression

1. Henry Patterson to Walter White, 12 May 1930; White to Roberts, 12 May 1930; White to Hoover, 13 May 1930; Roberts to White, 14 May 1930; White to Roberts, 21 May 1930, Politics, NAACP Papers; "Owen J. Roberts" in *Who Was Who in America* (Chicago: A. N. Marquis Co., 1966), 3:732. On Cardozo see White to Felix Frankfurter, 16 January 1932; James A. Cobb to White, 18 January 1932; White to Cardozo, 15 February 1932; White to L. F. Cole, 17 February 1932, Supreme Court, NAACP Papers. Cobb assured White that Hoover would not appoint anyone opposed by Negroes. See also Ira H. Carmen, "The President, Politics and the Power of Appointment: Hoover's Nomination of Mr. Justice Cardozo," *Virginia Law Review* 55 (1969):

616–59. Carmen is critical of Hoover for selecting an "ideological opposite" who "helped to undermine the constitutional philosophy that Hoover and his advisors regarded as the very foundation of a sound and stable political order." Carmen assumes that Hoover had wanted an ideological conservative. See especially pp. 654–59. Others who disagree with aspects of Carmen's interpretation are Justin J. Green and John R. Schmidhauser, "President Herbert Hoover and the Federal Judiciary," paper read at the Seminar on the Presidency of Herbert Hoover, August 1974, HHPL.

2. T. J. Woofter, "Industrial Background of Study of the Economic Status of the Negro," CQ; press release, Summary and Recommendations of the Economic Status of the Negro, 20 October 1930; press release, Associated Negro Press, 29 October 1930, CQ.

3. Moton to HH, 9 March 1931, General Correspondence, RRM Papers.

4. Melvin Chisum to Moton, 16 March 1931, ibid.

5. Richey to Mr. Newton, memorandum, 18 March 1931; Newton to Moton, 18 March 1931; Richey to Newton, 20 March 1931; Moton to Newton, 31 March 1931; HH to Moton, 3 April 1931, Moton File, HHPL; HH to Wilbur, 16 March 1931; Wilbur to HH, 16 March 1931, Wilbur Papers, Hoover Institution, Stanford University, Palo Alto, Calif.

6. Herbert Hoover, *The State Papers and Other Public Writings of Herbert Hoover*, ed. William Starr Meyers (Garden City, N.Y.: Doubleday, Doran and Co., 1934), 1:545–48. For angry white reaction see Elizabeth Weaver to HH, 20 April 1931, CQ.

7. Moton to HH, 22 April, 22 May 1931; HH to Moton, 15 April 1931; Newton to Moton, 30 January 1932, Moton File, HHPL. See also HH to Moton, 19 April 1930 in PP File, Negro Matters, HHPL. For Hoover's encouragement of other Negro organizations, see HH to John Hope, 16 July 1931, PP File, Atlantic University, HHPL; and letters in PP File, Negro Matters, HHPL; PP File, Negro Club, HHPL; PP File, National Negro Business League, HHPL; PP File, Fisk University, HHPL; and chapter 15.

8. James Jackson to Newton, 1 December 1930, CQ.

9. Jesse O. Thomas to T. R. Hill, 1 December 1931, Southern Regional Office Correspondence File, National Urban League Papers, LC.

10. Nancy J. Weiss, *The National Urban League, 1910–1940* (New York: Oxford University Press, 1974), pp. 238–39. For the protest see John R. Hawkins to HH, 21 August 1931; Perry W. Howard to HH, 21 August 1931; Emmett J. Scott to HH, 21 August 1931; Walter White to HH, 21 August 1931; Eugene Kinckle Jones to HH, 4 September 1931, President's Organization for Unemployment Relief, HHPL. Newton blamed the delay on the initial inability "to secure an agreement amongst the different groups of negroes as to someone who can satisfactorily represent them" (see Newton to Jones, 9 September 1931 and Rickard to Newton, 24, 26 August 1931, President's Organization for Unemployment Relief, HHPL).

11. Albert U. Romasco, *The Poverty of Abundance: Hoover, the Nation, the Depression* (New York: Oxford University Press, 1965), pp. 144–72.

12. White to J. E. Spingarn, et al., 5 March 1931, NAACP Papers. White and the leading officials of the NAACP apparently did not take the overture seriously. For the effectiveness of White's criticisms, see Howard C. Lawrence to Robert Lucas, 20 April 1931; Lucas to Newton, 23 April 1931, CQ; Detroit *Free Press*, 13 April 1931.

13. See chapter 18, n. 17.

14. See working draft of HH to J. E. Spingarn, 23 June 1931, in PP File, HHPL; and Rickard diary, 22, 25, 26 June 1931, ER Papers.

15. HH to J. E. Spingarn, 23 June 1931, and working copies in PP File, HHPL.

16. On opposition to Doak's appointment, see White to James A. Cobb, 21 January 1930; White to HH, 21 January 1930; White to Du Bois, 26 May 1930, NAACP Papers. White was convinced that Doak was "thoroughly dangerous" to the Negro, but the proof of his danger had been destroyed by a fire in the West Virginia state capitol. See R. R. Sims to White, 28 November 1930, and "Minutes of the Committee on Administration, December 1, 1930," NAACP Papers.

17. See, for example, the references cited in chapter 18, n. 93, and chapter 4, n. 86.

18. For an excellent analysis of White's speech, see the confidential report submitted by Robert F. Leftridge to Edgar Rickard, 7 July 1931, CQ.

19. See an excellent detailed report by Francis E. Rivers, "The New Approach Necessary to Save the Negro Vote For the Republican Party." Rickard sent the report to Newton (Rickard to Newton, 26 August 1931, President's Organization for Unemployment Relief, HHPL).

20. Hawkins to Newton, 31 August 1931, WDP Papers. On the war record of the Tenth Cavalry, see White to Hurley, 2 October 1931, CQ. The official explanation for the reduction is in Newton to Rickard, 15 September 1931, President's Organization for Unemployment Relief, HHPL.

21. Ibid. See also White to Frederick H. Payne, 1 September 1931; Trotter to HH, 8 September 1931; HH to Payne, 8 September 1931; Gen. Douglas MacArthur to De Priest, 1 September 1931, WDP Papers; NAACP press release, 4 September 1931, CQ.

22. Moton to HH, 31 August 1931, WDP Papers.

23. James G. Strong to Newton, 9 September 1931, ibid.

24. MacArthur to Newton, 3 September 1931, ibid. On MacArthur's tendency to insist on conspiratorial explanations, see Donald J. Lisio, *The President and Protest: Hoover, Conspiracy, and the Bonus Riot* (Columbia: University of Missouri Press, 1974), pp. 91, 216–17.

25. White to MacArthur, 10 September 1931, CQ.

26. Maj. Gen. George Van Horn Moseley to White, 21 September 1931, ibid.

27. NAACP press release, 25 September 1931, ibid.

28. Payne to HH, 9 September 1931; HH to Moton, 10 September 1931; Payne to Hoover, 6 October 1931; Hoover to Moton, 6 October 1931, WDP Papers..

29. Moton to HH, 18 September 1931, ibid. and n. 26.

30. Moton to HH, 27 October 1931; HH to Moton, 30 October 1931; HH to secretary of war, 30 October 1931, WDP Papers; White to Hurley, 2 October 1931; White to Colonel Roosevelt, 20 October 1931, CQ; George F. Garcia, "Herbert Hoover's Southern Strategy and the Black Reaction" (M.A. thesis, University of Iowa, 1972), pp. 134–36. For other examples of Hurley's cooperation with MacArthur to stymie Hoover, particularly when MacArthur disobeyed Hoover and drove the Bonus Army marchers out of Washington, see Lisio, *The President and Protest*, pp. 233–35.

31. Lisio, *The President and Protest*, pp. 209–19.

32. To prove that blacks had not been neglected, administration officials began compiling extensive patronage lists. See especially memorandum from John R. Hawkins, 2 March 1933, in J. S. Taylor-Richard Gates Collection, HHPL. Hawkins's list is complete with names, position, date of appointment, and salary. Attached is another useful document, "A Statement Concerning Presidential Appointments and Other Colored Men and Women Employed by the Federal Government."

33. Rickard diary, 4–8 September 1931, ER Papers.

34. W. C. Hueston to Brown, 10 October 1931; Klein to Newton, 3 July 1931, CQ.

35. Rickard diary, 4–8 September 1931, ER Papers.

36. Ogden Mills to Larry, 20 October 1931; Richey to Mills, 23 October 1931; Newton to Joslin, 6 August 1931; Charles S. Duke to HH, 11 November 1931, CQ.

37. Eugene Kinckle Jones to HH, 23 November, 6 October 1932, PP File, Negro Matters, HHPL. For Hoover's messages to black organizations in 1931 see n. 6.

38. Leftridge to Rickard, 23 November 1931; Newton to Rickard, 27 November 1931, CQ. Trotter had written Hoover several times in 1929. This correspondence is in the Racial Discrimination file, *Hoover Papers*, Hoover Institution, Stanford University, Palo Alto, California (see Trotter to HH, 1 July, 11 November 1929, 16 January 1932). Walter White coined the phrase, "the Man in the lily-White House." He recalled that it "gained considerable currency, particularly in the Negro world." See Walter White, *A Man Called White* (New York: Viking Press, 1948), p. 104.

39. Newton to Hawkins, 23, 27 November 1931; Ray Lyman Wilbur to Mordecai W. Johnson, 10 December 1931; Wilbur to Newton, 10 December 1931, CQ.

40. Rickard diary, 19 October 1931, ER Papers.

41. Carl Murphy to White, 20 October 1931; Cobb to White, 20 October 1931, CQ.

42. John R. Hawkins, "The National Negro Republican League—What It Is and What It Stands For," 25 November 1931, press release, CQ; Church to Hawkins, 9 January 1931, RRC Papers; Washington *Sentinel*, 3 May 1930.

43. See, for example, Robert H. Brisbane, *The Black Vanguard: Origins of the Negro Social Revolution, 1900–1960* (Valley Forge, Pa.: Judson Press, 1970), pp. 122–23; Richard B. Sherman, *The Republican Party and Black America: From McKinley to Hoover, 1896–1933* (Charlottesville: University Press of Virginia, 1973). Sherman recognizes the impressive list of Negro federal employees but argues that "not many were presidential appointees" and that Hoover "failed to restore Negroes to the number of positions in the Executive Departments that they had held before Wilson's presidency" (p. 234).

44. Hoover, *State Papers*, 1:15.

45. Monroe N. Work, ed., *Negro Year Book, 1937–1938* (Tuskegee Institute, Ala.: Negro Year Book Publishing Co., 1937), p. 112. Work did not record several important presidential appointments.

46. John Q. Tilson to Newton, 6 March 1931; Newton to Tilson, 17 March 1931, RNC Papers, Miscellaneous Correspondence, HHPL.

47. Newton to Hawkins, 27 November 1931, and numerous letters to Richey, 4–6 November 1931 from various department heads; Hawkins to Newton, 1 November 1931, CQ. The complete, detailed list of Hoover's appointments is attached to memorandum from John R. Hawkins, 2 March 1933 in the Taylor-Gates Collection, HHPL. See also n. 33.

48. See chapter 16, nn. 23–31.

49. See nn. 32, 45, and 48. George F. Garcia also defends Hoover's appointments record (see "Hoover's Southern Strategy and the Black Reaction" [M.A. thesis, University of Iowa, 1972], pp. 138–39).

50. One very short newspaper item had appeared in the Washington (D.C.) *Times*, 14 November 1930.

51. The best source on the National Nonpartisan League is in the December 1931 Politics file, NAACP Papers.

52. Memorandum, telephone message from Hawkins, 27 November 1931, CQ.

53. HH to Sam H. Reading, 9 August 1930, PP File, Lynching, HHPL; Hoover, *State Papers*, pp. 371–72; Newton to White, 20 August 1930, CQ.

54. White to HH, 3 October, 13 November 1930; Akerson to Strauss, 22 October 1930; Akerson to White, 21 October 1930, CQ. White believed the "chief reason" for the increase in lynching was "the reaction of the Bourbon South to the Parker victory" (see White to James Weldon Johnson, 22 August 1930, James Weldon Johnson Papers, Yale University, New Haven, Connecticut).

55. Trotter to HH, 4, 12 November 1930, 7 February 1931; Akerson to Trotter, 17 November 1930; Trotter to HH, 20 November 1930; Barnett to Akerson, 20 November 1930, CQ.

56. See numerous letters requesting that Hoover see Trotter's delegation in November File, 1931, CQ. See also Joslin to Dallinger, 1 December 1931; Ray to Larry, 10 November 1931; J. E. Andrews to HH, 4 December 1931, ibid. Andrews, president of the Women's National Association for the Preservation of the White Race, protested Hoover's meeting with the Southern Commission. See also copy of *Lynchings and What They Mean: General Findings of the Southern Commission on the Study of Lynching* in the same file.

57. HH to Mr. Attorney General, 31 December 1931, Prohibition Enforcement File, HHPL.

58. Mitchell to HH, 6 January 1932, CQ. See Theodore G. Joslin to Charles Curtis, 21 March 1932, ibid.

59. In 1928 the Republican platform stated, "We renew our recommendation that the Congress enact at the earliest possible date a Federal Anti-Lynching Law so that the full influence of the Federal Government may be wielded to exterminate this hideous crime" (*Official Report of the Proceedings of the Nineteenth Republican National Convention, 1928* [New York: Tenny Press, 1928], p. 131). The 1932 platform, which dropped the above pledge, is in the *Official Report of the Proceedings of the Twentieth Republican National Convention, 1932* (New York: Tenny Press, 1932). A copy of the 1932 platform is in the French Strother Papers, HHPL.

60. HH to White, 20 August 1932, CQ.

61. R. R. Church to HH, 6 November 1929, CQ.

21. Difficult Choices

1. There are numerous examples, but see specifically Emmett J. Scott to Newton, 12 February 1932, Reconstruction Finance Corporation File; Newton to Franklin Fort, 1, 11 October 1932; Newton to Holsey, 1 October 1932; Holsey to Newton, 11 October 1932, Federal Home Loan Bank Board File; Moton to HH, 25 August 1932; HH to Moton, 27 August 1932, National Conference of Business and Industrial Committees; James A. Jackson to Newton, 24, 26 August 1932; Newton to Jackson, 24 August 1932, CQ; Moton to HH, 1 February 1932, RRM Papers; Walter White to Charles E. Mitchell, 21 September 1932, Politics, NAACP Papers. On the problems with the Federal Farm Board, see correspondence in the Moton papers and Moton to Barnett, 24 February 1930, RRM Papers.

2. John M. Marguess to Congressman James M. Beck, 26 May 1932; Newton, to the Postmaster General, memorandum, 2 June 1932; Beck to Newton, 31 May 1932; Newton to Beck, 2 June 1932, CQ.

3. Charles H. Martin, "Negro Leaders, The Republican Party, and the Election of 1932," *Phylon* 32 (Spring 1971): 85–86.

4. Emmett J. Scott to Newton, 2 March 1932, RNC Papers, Mississippi File, HHPL. See also "Lily-Whitism," editorial in New York *Age*, 27 February 1932. Scott repeated his warning in May (see Scott to Newton, 17 May 1932, CQ); Requa to Newton, 28 April 1932, Hoover Institution, Stanford University, Palo Alto, California.

5. Barnett, "Memorandum for Mr. Saunders: The Attitude of the Negro Voters," n.d., CAB Papers.

6. Oral history, Alonzo Fields, HHPL. Fields was the White House chief butler. He overheard the conversation while serving refreshments. For the reference to "belligerent" black politicians in the preceding paragraph see chapter 20, n. 35.

7. See chapter 15, especially n. 11.

8. See chapter 20. Hoover's refusal to intervene in the Tenth Cavalry and Gold Star mothers disputes is a good example of his acceptance of segregation. See also U. S. Grant III to Newton, 3 September 1932, CQ. Grant justified racial segregation in the federal parks in Washington, D.C., on the grounds that "efforts to mix races . . . only leads to trouble here in Washington." Grant suggested that segregation was a "practical matter" necessary to protect Negroes against a hostile white majority. See also chapter 2, n. 41.

9. Glenn B. Skipper to Newton, 30 March 1932; Newton to Harry R. Hewitt, 15 April 1932; Hewitt to Newton, 4 April 1932, RNC Papers, Florida State File, HHPL; Tampa *Morning Tribune*, 28 March 1932 and Edgar Rickard diary, 12–16 June 1932, ER Papers. See also George F. Garcia, "Herbert Hoover's Southern Strategy and the Black Reaction" (M.A. thesis, University of Iowa, 1972), pp. 146–48.

10. HH, "Message to the 23rd Annual Conference of the National Association for the Advancement of Colored People," 18 May 1932, PP File, NAACP File, HHPL. See also White to Joslin,

19, 22 January 1932; "Memorandum from Miss Randolph, April 25, 1932," Walter White File, NAACP Papers; Ray Lyman Wilbur to French Strother, 3 May 1932, PP File, NAACP, HHPL.

11. HH, Commencement Address, Howard University, 10 June 1932, "The Importance of Training Leaders of the Negro Race"; White to HH, 5 March 1932, Interior, Howard University, HHPL; G. Lake Imes to Barnett, 7 March 1932, Tuskegee File, CAB Papers. See especially Wilbur to Abraham Flexner, 18 March 1932, Howard University File, Ray Lyman Wilbur Papers, Hoover Institution, Stanford University, Palo Alto, California; and Ray Lyman Wilbur, *The Memoirs of Ray Lyman Wilbur, 1875–1949* (Stanford, Calif.: Stanford University Press, 1960), pp. 557–58.

12. Rickard to Gibson, 25 June 1932, Gibson Papers, Hoover Institution, Stanford University, Palo Alto, California; *New York Times*, 14 June 1932; New York *Herald Tribune*, 9 June 1932; Garcia, "Hoover's Southern Strategy," p. 147.

13. New York *Herald Tribune*, 9, 11 June 1932.

14. Ray Benjamin to Newton, 8 June 1932, Secretary's File, HHPL.

15. Newton to Brown, 8 June 1932, Benjamin File, HHPL; Edgar Rickard diary, 12–16 June 1932, ER Papers.

16. New York *Herald Tribune*, 10 June 1932; *New York Times*, 11 June 1932.

17. *New York Times*, 14 June 1932.

18. New York *Herald Tribune*, 11 June 1932 and related documents in RNC Papers, Mississippi, HHPL.

19. See, for example, Howard to Church, 11 November 1931 in Perry Howard File, RRC Papers. See also Pittsburgh *Courier*, 25 June 1932; Memphis *World*, 21 June 1932; New York *Herald Tribune*, 11 June 1932; *New York Times*, 16 June 1932.

20. New York *Herald Tribune*, 13 June 1932.

21. Pittsburgh *Courier*, 25 June 1932; Memphis *World*, 21 June 1932; *New York Times*, 14 June 1932.

22. *New York Times*, 14 June 1932.

23. The voluminous correspondence on the Montgomery appointment is in the Justice Department, Mississippi State File, HHPL. See, for example, Rowlands to HH, 9 February 1931; and Rowlands to Newton, 17 November 1931.

24. Mary Booze to Newton, 17 November 1931, Justice, Mississippi State File, HHPL; Mary Booze to Walter White, 9 March 1931; White to Senator George Norris, 22 June 1932; NAACP press release, 24 June 1932, Politics, Montgomery File, NAACP Papers. The documents and correspondence on the Montgomery appointment are extensive but are concentrated in the two locations cited in this note.

25. For Hoover's efforts see the correspondence in PP File, Negro Matters, Booze, HHPL.

26. See n. 24.

27. See the forty-four page pamphlet "Before the Republican National Committee, Lamont Rowlands et al. vs. Perry W. Howard, et al., Contest for State at Large and Seven Districts Mississippi, Record and Brief of Contestors." See also the 158-page booklet, "Evidence Exposing the Fraud and Illegality of the Howard-Redmond Claim To Be Recognized by the Republican National Convention." Both of these documents together with a large broadside "Senate Report Shows Howard Faction Guilty of Sale of Public Offices" are in the Secretary's File, Lamont Rowlands File, and the Mississippi State File, HHPL.

28. See the highly detailed report by Claude Barnett, n.d., labeled "Mississippi" in CAB Papers. Although it is lacking in important sources and therefore interprets the entire contest differently one should see also David J. Ginzl, "Lily-Whites Versus Black-and-Tans: Mississippi Republicans During the Hoover Administration," *Journal of Mississippi History* (August 1980), pp. 208–11.

29. Rowlands to HH, 14 June 1932; E. M. C. Hawkins to Newton, 20 June 1932; Newton to

Hawkins, 23 June 1932, Mississippi State File, HHPL. See also Garcia, "Hoover's Southern Strategy," pp. 147–48. This correspondence is especially useful.

30. Ralph J. Bunche, *The Political Status of the Negro in the Age of FDR*, ed. Dewey W. Grantham (Chicago and London: The University of Chicago Press, 1973), p. 1187. See also Hanes Walton, *Black Republicans: The Politics of the Black and Tans* (Metuchen, N.J.: Scarecrow Press, 1975), p. 162. For angry lily-white reaction to Hambright's acceptance of the Negro delegates, see A. A. Gates to Newton, 4 May 1932, South Carolina File, HHPL. See also South Carolina State Convention Report, 8 March 1932 sent by Tolbert to HH, 25 June 1932. For NAACP efforts to help secure the appointment of federal officials sympathetic to Negroes, see extensive correspondence in NAACP Papers, Politics, and in Samuel J. Leaphart File, but especially White to James A. Cobb, 3, 16 March 1931 in Leaphart File, NAACP Papers. William T. Williams to NAACP, 30 August 1931; William T. Andrews to White, 10 September 1931; White to Andrews, 21 September 1931; N. J. Frederick to White, 31 January 1931, Politics, ibid.

31. *New York Times*, 15 June 1932; Claude Barnett, "South Carolina," n.d., CAB Papers.

32. C. B. Ruffin to Newton, 21 June 1932; Newton to Ruffin, 27 June 1932, South Carolina File; HH to J. C. Hambright, 1 July 1936, PP File. On Tolbert's unpopularity see New York *Herald Tribune*, 15 June 1932 and *New York Times*, 16 June 1932.

33. Louis H. Crawford to Walter Newton, 22 April 1930; Benjamin J. Davis to Newton, 4 August 1930; Newton to Rose, 5 August 1930; Rose to Newton, 7 August 1930; Rose to Newton, 4 September 1930, CQ; John M. Morrin to Newton, 12 September 1930, Georgia, Justice, HHPL. See also important correspondence in RNC Papers, Georgia, HHPL.

34. A. S. Anderson to Newton, 5 January 1931; Rose to Newton, 10 January 1931, RNC, Georgia; Rose to Newton, 12 January 1931; Rose to Charles P. Sisson, 12 January 1931; Walter Brown to Newton, 24 January 1931, Justice, RNC Papers, Georgia, HHPL.

35. Rose to Walter F. Brown, 7 March 1931; G. F. Flanders to Newton, 8 August 1931; Rose to Newton, 11 August 1931; Newton File Memo, 12 August 1931; Rose to Newton, 27 August 1931; Newton to Arch Coleman, 29 August 1931, ibid. See also informative correspondence in Justice, Appointments, United States Attorney, and United States Marshal, ibid. David J. Ginzl, "Patronage, Race, and Politics: Georgia Republicans During the Hoover Administration," *Georgia Historical Quarterly* (Fall 1980): pp. 280–93. Ginzl does not describe the administration's coalition efforts. He accepts the charge that the administration was pursuing a lily-white policy.

36. See chapter 20 n. 41 and Mrs. George S. Williams to Newton, 12 March 1932; Walter F. Brown to Williams, 21 March 1932; Newton to Williams, 31 March 1932, Georgia State File, HHPL. Ginzl, "Patronage, Race, and Politics: Georgia Republicans," pp. 288–91, but especially p. 289.

37. Barnett, "Georgia," n.d., CAB Papers.

38. Ibid. Ralph Bunche concluded that the lily-whites had captured control in 1932. Oddly enough he cited a 1939 interview with Benjamin Davis as the source for this conclusion (see Bunche, *Political Status of the Negro*, pp. 1182–83).

39. Oliver Street still controlled the Alabama delegation, and following the death of Walter Cohen in 1930 Ernest Lee Jahncke, the assistant secretary of the navy, took control of the Louisiana party. Jahncke included some blacks in his delegation, and protests from the politically disunited black factions were turned aside by the credentials committee. For an excellent account see Barnett, "Louisiana," n.d., CAB Papers, and the correspondence in RNC Papers, Louisiana, HHPL.

40. Republican National Committee, *Republican Party Platform, 1932*, in the French Strother Papers, HHPL; chapter 20, nn. 53–60. For the administration's failure to act against peonage, see Peonage Files, Department of Justice, HHPL. See also Martin, "Negro Leaders," p. 87.

41. Barnett to White, 24 June 1932, National Politics File, CAB Papers. For the efforts of the NAACP to influence the Republican platform, see White to Director, 6 June 1932; White to HH,

14 June 1932, and Press Release, 17 June 1932, Republican National Convention File, NAACP. See also Martin, "Negro Leaders," p. 87.

42. The best account is Frank Freidel, *F.D.R. and the South* (Baton Rouge: Louisiana State University Press, 1965).

43. In addition to the individual Southern state files of the Democratic National Committee, one should also consult FDR's personal correspondence, 1928–32, FDRL.

44. At the time of the furor over the De Priest tea at the White House, Governor Roosevelt demanded that Virginia Republicans retract the statement that he had invited Negroes to lunch (see FDR to Henry W. Anderson, 4 November 1929; Anderson to FDR, 7 November 1928 and FDR to Harry F. Byrd, 21 November 1929, ibid).

45. See the extensive correspondence between Farley and Jones in the Democratic National Committee, Georgia File, FDRL (hereafter the Democratic National Committee will be cited as DNC). See especially Farley to Jones, 18 January 1932; Farley to FDR, 23 February 1932; Farley to Jones, 23 February 1932; Farley to FDR, 22 March 1932, DNC, Georgia, FDRL.

46. John M. Callahan, "To the Delegates to the National Democratic Convention," 11 June 1932 and accompanying broadside reproducing the correspondence entitled "An Open Letter to Governor Franklin D. Roosevelt of New York Pertaining to Recent Suit Filed in Georgia Which Reveals Approval of Ku Klux Klan Activity in Behalf of His Presidential Candidacy in the South," 11 June 1932, in Politics, NAACP Papers. See also White to Callahan, 17 June 1932. White asked Callahan for fifty copies and requested him to supply additional copies to all Negro newspapers.

47. White to FDR, 20 June 1932; Guernsey T. Cross to White, 21 June 1932, Politics, NAACP Papers. Cross was one of FDR's secretaries.

48. White to Belle Moskowitz, 24 June 1932, Politics, NAACP Papers. Although the letters were authentic, FDR and Farley had no knowledge of efforts to recruit Klan support (see Claude N. Sapp to FDR, 18 June 1932; Sapp to Callahan, 18 June 1932; FDR to Sapp, 24 June 1932, DNC, South Carolina, FDRL).

49. White to Earl B. Dickerson, 20 June 1932; Robert F. Wagner to White, 22 June 1932; White to Robert J. Bulkley, 18 June 1932; Bulkley to White, 23 June 1932, Politics, NAACP Papers.

50. White to Ralph Harlow, 16 June 1932; Earl B. Dickerson to White, 25 June 1932; White to Dickerson, 24, 28 June 1932, ibid.

51. Martin, "Negro Leaders," *Phylon*, p. 90; Henry Lee Moon, *Balance of Power: The Negro Vote* (Garden City, N.Y.: Doubleday and Co., 1948), p. 17; Andrew Buni, *The Negro in Virginia Politics, 1902–1965* (Charlottesville: University Press of Virginia, 1967), p. 111; Harold F. Gosnell, *Negro Politicians: The Rise of Negro Politics in Chicago* (Chicago: University of Chicago Press, 1935), p. 32.

52. Mary Church Terrell to Norris A. Dodson, 12 October 1932; Campaign Speech, October, 1932; "Report on Philadelphia Meeting," 4 November 1932, in Mary Church Terrell Papers, LC.

53. Mary Church Terrell to Mrs. George Fitzgerald, 26 September 1932, Mary Church Terrell Papers, LC. See also Mary Church Terrell, *A Colored Woman in a White World* (Washington, D.C.: Ransdell, 1940), p. 413.

54. See nn. 50 and 55.

55. W. E. B. Du Bois, *The Correspondence of W.E.B. DuBois*, ed. Herbert Aptheker (Amherst: University of Massachusetts Press, 1973), 1:463–64.

56. Albon L. Holsey to Newton, 8 July 1932; Holsey to Brown, 8 July 1932; Newton to Holsey, 14 July 1932; James A. Cobb to Newton, 9 July 1932; Newton to Cobb, 14 July 1932, CQ. Newton denied Hoover's lack of concern and sent a copy of Cobb's complaints to Brown. See also Newton to Cobb, 14 July 1932, JAC Papers; and Moton to Barnett, 20 September 1932, RRM Papers.

57. Barnett to Moton, n.d., "Democratic Victory in Maine," ibid.

58. Moton to Barnett, 20 September 1932, ibid. Walter White agreed that FDR had not

appointed Negroes to major positions in New York (see White to Benjamin H. Fisher, 5 October 1932, Politics, NAACP Papers).

59. Moton to Barnett, 20 September 1932, RRM Papers.

60. See Melvin J. Chisum, "Dr. Baranca Will Line up the Masonic Order against Hoover," Baltimore *Afro-American*, 23 July 1932, copy in CQ. See also front-page article on Chisum's attack in the Louisville *News*, 27 August 1932, Hatfield Papers and Barnett to Moton, 28 July 1932, RRM Papers.

61. Moton to Barnett, 20 September 1932, ibid.

62. Robert R. Church to Raymond Benjamin, 25 May 1929; Church to Perry W. Howard, 11 May 1929, RRC Papers.

63. Andrew Buni, *Robert L. Vann of the Pittsburgh Courier: Politics and Black Journalism* (Pittsburgh: University of Pittsburgh Press, 1974), pp. 180, 194–97; Martin, "Negro Leaders," *Phylon*, p. 91. As a special assistant to the attorney general during FDR's first term, Vann quickly became disillusioned with the attitude of FDR's top advisers toward Negroes. See especially Robert L. Vann to Mr. Howe, 15 December 1933 with enclosure of Baltimore *Afro-American*, 16 December 1933; and R. B. Leanos to Colonel Howe, 4 November 1933, OF 93, Negroes, FDRL. For smears against Hoover employed by Vann and others, see Misrepresentations File, HHPL.

64. See especially chapters 1 and 2. For a succinct summary of Du Bois's numerous charges against Hoover, see Du Bois to Dear Proctor, 28 September 1932, in *DuBois, Correspondence*, 1:463.

65. *Crisis* 39 (November 1932): 362–63. See also Martin, "Negro Leaders," *Phylon*, p. 92.

66. Yost to Richey, 24 September 1931; Newton to Yost, 28 September 1931, CQ; Ogden L. Mills to T. Arnold Hill, September, n.d., 1932; Hill to Mills, 15 September 1932; Hill to HH, 16 September 1932; James A. Jackson to Newton, 13 September 1932; White to HH, 10 September 1932; Richey to White, 10 September 1932; Ferry K. Heath to HH, 4 October 1932, Government Contracts, HHPL; *New York Times*, 11, 15 October 1932.

67. Cobb to White, 11 May 1932; White to Francis E. Harmon, 16 May 1932; White to Helen Boardman, 1 July 1932; Helen Boardman report, "Investigation of Labor Camps in Federal Flood Control Operations," MFC File. See also Philadelphia *Tribune*, 1 October 1932; Newton to Ray Benjamin, 6 October 1932; Holsey to Newton, 14 October 1932, CQ; Newton to Travis, 5 July 1932, Everett Sanders File, HHPL; and Garcia, "Hoover's Southern Strategy," pp. 148–49.

68. White to Robert LaFollette, 9 August 1932; Robert F. Wagner to White, 10 September 1932, MFC File, NAACP.

69. White to Hurley, 22 August 1932, ibid. He sent the same letter to Hoover and Mitchell.

70. Lytle Brown to White, 31 August 1929; Royal S. Copeland to Hurley, 7 September 1932; Hurley to White, 31 August 1929; White to Hurley, 7 September 1932, ibid.

71. White to Spingarn, 7 September 1932, Walter White File, NAACP Papers.

72. White to Mary White Ovington, 12 September 1932, Walter White File; White to Will Alexander, 19 September 1932; White to Holt Ross, 23 September 1932; White to editors of the colored press, 24 September 1932; White to Charles E. Russell, 7 November 1932; and press releases, MFC File.

73. Newton to president, 24 October 1932; press release, 26 October 1932; U. S. Grant III to Newton, 8 November 1932; Grant to Newton, 6 December 1932, Newton File memo, 23 February 1933, Mississippi River Flood Control, HHPL; White to James Weldon Johnson, 13 October, 3 November 1932, James Weldon Johnson Papers, Yale University, New Haven, Connecticut.

74. Richey to Frederick Payne, 18 October 1932; Payne to Alexander, 19 October 1932, Will Alexander, Secretary's File, HHPL; Lytle Brown to secretary of war, 13 Feburary 1933; Hurley to Newton, 24 February 1933, and accompanying reports but especially the final report by 1st Lt. Charles G. Holle, "Report of Investigations of Labor Conditions—Flood—Mississippi," Mississippi River Flood Control, HHPL.

75. Hawkins to Newton, 24 May 1932, Foreign Affairs, Charles E. Mitchell File; Hawkins to Everett Sanders, 4 August 1932, Hawkins to Newton, 6 August 1932, CQ; Barnett to Robert H. Lucas, 26 July 1932; Barnett to Holsey, 27 July 1932; Holsey to Barnett, 27 September 1932, CAB Papers; Moton to Barnett, 14 October 1932; Barnett to Moton, 17, 28 September 1932, RRM Papers. Nancy J. Weiss, *Farewell to the Party of Lincoln: Black Politics in the Age of FDR* (Princeton, N.J.: Princeton University Press), p. 31. See also n. 56.

76. Robert R. Church, Jr., to the attorney general, 27 February 1934, Politics, RRC Papers.

77. Theodore Joslin to Eileen O'Connor, 28 July 1932, HHPL. Democrats believed that the photograph cost Hoover many votes in Florida. See Fred W. DeLancy to FDR, 11 October 1932; FDR to DeLancy, 18 October 1932, DNC, Florida State File, FDRL.

78. Philadelphia *Tribune*, 1, 13 October 1932. Both Moton and Church had refused to attend. See Moton to Barnett, 14 October 1932, RRM Papers. For the reaction of black critics see S. W. Green to Carl Murphy, 11 October 1932, and Walter White to Green, 24 October 1932, Politics, NAACP Papers. See also photographs and newspaper stories in the Barnett Papers and Moon, *Balance of Power*, pp. 113–14; Garcia, "Hoover's Southern Strategy," pp. 152–53.

79. Walter White to HH, 14 September 1932, CQ; James A. Cobb to Newton, 9 August 1932; Newton to Cobb, 16 August 1932, JAC Papers. See also White to FDR, 28 September 1932; White to Herbert H. Lehman, 29 September, 4, 11, 31 October 1932, Walter White File, NAACP Papers, and Walter White, *A Man Called White* (New York: Viking Press, 1948), p. 139.

80. Francis E. Rivers to Newton, 1 November 1932, Secretary's File, HHPL. Rivers believed that the "strongest arguments" were contained in the campaign pamphlet "An Appeal to Negro Voters for Clear Thinking." He enclosed a copy of the pamphlet in his letter.

81. Weiss, *Farewell to the Party of Lincoln*, pp. 30–31; Moon, *Balance of Power*, p. 18; Martin, "Negro Leaders," *Phylon*, p. 93; Garcia, "Hoover's Southern Strategy," pp. 154–55; Gosnell, *Negro Politicians*, p. 31; White, *A Man Called White*, pp. 114–15, 139; and White to Wilkins, 19 November 1932; Roy Wilkins to Eustace Gay, 23 November 1932, Politics, NAACP Papers.

82. Buni, *Robert L. Vann*, pp. 194–97; Weiss, *Farewell to the Party of Lincoln*, pp. 29–31.

83. Martin, "Negro Leaders," p. 93. Martin challenges older assessments, which credited Negroes with a larger Democratic vote than warranted. See also Richard Sherman, *The Republican Party and Black America: From McKinley to Hoover, 1896–1933* (Charlottesville: University Press of Virginia, 1973), pp. 244–46, 252–56; Moon, *Balance of Power*, pp. 18, 112–13; Walter White tended to exaggerate the number of Negroes voting Democratic as well as the degree to which black voters deserve credit for the defeat of pro-Parker senators. See, for example, F. B. Ransom to White, 28 November 1932 and NAACP press release, 18 November 1932, Politics, NAACP Papers. For the South see Ginzl, "Hoover and Republican Patronage Politics," pp. 366–75. In Chicago, Cleveland, and Knoxville Republicans increased their percentage among black voters (see Weiss, *Farewell to the Party of Lincoln*, p. 31).

84. On the positions of the Negro press see Martin, "Negro Leaders," p. 92.

22. Shattered Hopes

1. Moton to HH, 12 January 1933; HH to Moton, 17 January 1933, PP File, Moton, HHPL.

2. Moton to HH, 14 January 1937; Bernice Miller to Moton, 1 February 1937, PP File, Moton, HHPL. Moton's letter was forwarded to Hoover, who was traveling in the East, but there is no record of any reply.

3. HH to F. D. Patterson, 3 June 1940, ibid.

4. HH to W. Hardin Hughes, 15 January 1951, ibid.

5. Barnett to HH, 10, 12 October 1949, PPS, Colored, HHPL.

6. HH to Barnett, 17 October 1949, ibid. Hoover did not respond to Barnett's questions

concerning his record toward blacks (see Barnett to HH, 24, 27 July 1935). In 1943 Hoover again declined to respond to Barnett's repeated questions, but he did agree to talk to Barnett when the newspaper editor again visited New York City (Barnett to HH, 11 August 1943; HH to Barnett, 13 August 1943, PPS, Colored, HHPL).

7. HH to Arch N. Shaw, 31 July 1939; HH to Robert M. Hutchins, 30 July 1939; NBC transcript of broadcast, 30 July 1939; *Look*, 15 August 1939; HH to J. Yozell Guinter, 6 August 1939, in Colleges and Universities, University of Chicago, 1939 file, HHPL. The same charge was made by Henry L. Mencken, *Making A President* (New York: Alfred Knopf, 1932), p. 27.

8. HH to Barnett, 17 October 1949, PPS, Colored, HHPL.

9. The original typewritten copy of Woofter's study is in the President's Committee on Social Trends File, Hoover Papers, Hoover Institution, Stanford University, Palo Alto, California. The committee did not publish this study. Instead, on 14 April 1932 it released a short mimeographed condensation, which excluded Woofter's emphasis upon multiple forms of discrimination and exclusion. Barry Karl has noted that Edward Eyre Hunt, who had been appointed by Hoover as secretary of the Committee on Social Trends, had been highly critical of Woofter's manuscript, "possibly over the political implications of its position on racial issues." Hunt apparently wanted Woofter to rewrite his study, but another member of the committee, Howard W. Odum, succeeded in mollifying Hunt, and the manuscript remained unaltered. Nonetheless, it appears likely that the drastically shortened mimeographed release of 14 April 1932, which excluded Woofter's discussion of the multiple sources of racism, was the direct result of Hunt's pressure. In this respect, Claude Barnett's cynical remark about Hoover's scholarly studies of black problems seems appropriate. Barnett had little faith that anything meaningful could be expected from such studies. When the report on black housing needs was completed, he predicted that it would simply be forgotten "until some searcher with a doctor's degree digs it up twenty years from now." (See Barnett to William Pickens, 10 December 1931, Pickens file, CAB Papers. See also the excellent analysis by Barry Karl, "Presidential Planning and Social Science Research: Mr. Hoover's Experts," *Perspectives in American History* 3 [1969]: 393.) For the controversy over Woofter's conclusions on race see, for example, E. E. Hunt to Howard W. Odum, 28 July 1932 and Odum to Hunt, 4 August 1932, E. E. Hunt Papers, Hoover Institution, Stanford University, Palo Alto, Ca.

Bibliographical Essay

The most comprehensive body of Hoover manuscripts is in the Herbert Hoover Presidential Library at West Branch, Iowa, and this repository houses many of the additional manuscript collections that I consulted for this study. To reduce the length of this essay, only those collections vital to the understanding of Hoover's southern strategy and his encounters with racism are discussed. Others are cited in the notes. However, because the Hoover papers are at times incomplete, additional manuscript collections were essential in piecing together this complex story. Their importance has led me to intersperse discussion of them, topically, wherever appropriate.

Hoover made surprisingly few specific references to variations among races. What is known is cited in the notes to chapter 2. Evidence of his earliest contact with black people is widely scattered throughout the extensive Commerce Papers and among the papers of his secretary, George Akerson. When gathered together, this evidence establishes a gradual appreciation of black needs and aspirations. Several letters in the Negro File of the Hoover papers in The Hoover Institution on War, Revolution, and Peace at Stanford University, Palo Alto, California, are also useful in tracing this evolution. But the most enlightening single account is Claude Barnett's unpublished autobiography. The little-used but unusually valuable collection of Barnett Papers at the Chicago Historical Society is indispensable to any scholarly study of black Republican leaders and politics during the Hoover years.

The Mississippi Valley Flood Papers are among the most detailed at the Hoover Library in West Branch. In these documents one learns of Hoover's damaging sensitivity to criticism from the NAACP; his efforts to correct abuses uncovered by the Moton commission; his promise to help blacks combat peonage; his close personal relationship with Robert R. Moton, Jr.; and his first contacts with southern leaders who would later become enthusiastic supporters of his bid for the Republican presidential nomination. But scholars must not be tempted to assume that the entire story is contained within these voluminous files at West Branch. The records of the American Red Cross at the National Archives in Washington, D.C., have an informative Negro relations file, reports by individual members of the Moton commission, and evidence of the suppression of the Moton commission's criticism. In the Library of Congress the Mississippi Valley Flood Control File of the National Association for the Advancement of Colored People is an exceptionally valuable source for the emergence of a critical black perspective on Hoover. Claude Barnett's incisive reports and observations at the Chicago Historical Society, coupled with the smaller number of items in the excellent Robert R. Moton, Jr., Papers at Tuskegee Institute, Alabama, corroborate the NAACP criticisms. Evidence in the Barnett and Moton collections contrasts sharply with the impression of Hoover that emerges from the NAACP Papers. Instead of an ambitious politician trying to cover up the abuses against black people, they reveal his awakening to the obstacles to black progress and his personal desire to begin combating these obstacles, especially peonage. Oddly enough, each perspective had much to recommend it.

The crucial importance of the southern delegations in capturing the nomination becomes apparent in the papers of Hoover's campaign manager, Hubert Work. This collection of Work's papers was housed in the State Archives and Public Records in Denver, Colorado, and are currently in the process of being arranged by Dolores Renz at Denver University for eventual transfer to the Hoover Institution, at Stanford University, Palo Alto, Ca. They are identified in the

357

notes as HW Papers. This small collection dramatically illustrates Work's strategy of alternating between courting and pressuring the southern state leaders into early declarations designed to create a sense of irresistible momentum for Hoover. Work's political correspondence mysteriously ends in June 1928, yet it is sufficient to indicate the great stress that he placed on southern delegate strength and the fact that his political skills and influence during the drive to the presidency have been underestimated by scholars. Another smaller collection of Work Papers consisting mainly of his political scrapbooks is at the Hoover Institution. From the George Akerson Papers at West Branch, Hoover's awkward preconvention relationship with lily-white leaders in Mississippi illustrates his growing recognition of the political importance of his new white supporters in the South.

Second only to the Work Papers in assessing the importance of the southern delegations is the testimony gathered by the Senate Special Committee Investigation of Presidential Campaign Expenditures. These hearings forced into public view the frantic behind-the-scenes maneuvering of Hoover's campaign managers in the South, the use of money to pay convention expenses, Hoover's personal embarrassment, and the pragmatic strategy of courting both black-and-tan and lily-white delegations willing to support Hoover's nomination. Important testimony by Hoover, Rush Holland, Claudius Huston, James Good, Perry W. Howard, Benjamin Davis, and others provides crucial details on the prenomination southern strategy that are not available in any other source. Unfortunately the questioning was neither probing nor vigorously pursued. The senators seemed content to humiliate Hoover with proof of "bribes" to win southern delegate votes. None of these men except Hoover saved his papers.

The corruption issue has not been emphasized in analyses of Hoover's 1928 campaign. Indeed, Hoover's conviction of the urgent need to reform the southern state parties cannot be appreciated fully without an understanding of the impact of corruption charges on the candidate. Understandably he was proud of his good name and concerned at the damaging claims that he had bought the nomination. Like most Republicans, he was aware of the corruption problem in the South long before it touched him. Moreover, he had great respect for Christian A. Herter, who had once served him as private secretary and was by 1928 the crusading editor of the progressive magazine, the *Independent*. Demands for southern reform from the *Independent*, from Sen. George Norris, and from the *New York Times*, for example, made Hoover especially sensitive to corruption in the South and to the appearance of his own entanglement in it. Evidence in the Christian A. Herter file and in the Akerson Papers is helpful in focusing on this dimension of Hoover's nomination.

Even more useful on the corruption issue are the papers of Sen. George Norris at the Library of Congress and the extraordinary collection of Department of Justice documents in the Perry W. Howard File at the National Archives. Historians have not yet effectively utilized the Howard File, which is an invaluable case study of the nature of politics and of political corruption in the South. From this source one gains a greater appreciation of the complexities in the long history of the national Republican party's efforts to deal with allegations of corruption hurled by lily-white challengers against incumbent black and tans. Included are internal investigations conducted by the Department of Justice, numerous FBI reports, sworn affidavits, court records, newspaper clippings, extensive correspondence, and a variety of other useful documents. The Norris Papers at the Library of Congress supplement the Howard File by highlighting the crusading senator's battle to expose what he believed to be a massive cover-up of corrupt nomination politics by the Republican party's top officials. Yet more important still is the intense fervor with which Mabel Walker Willebrandt, Norris, and others pursued the issue. Without these corroborating collections historians would be unable to grasp the relentless zeal and sense of outrage felt by Norris and Willebrandt or Hoover's immediate decision to support her prosecution of Howard regardless of the political costs or appearances. There is no doubt either of Willebrandt's belief that Howard was guilty or of her disregard for the costly political repercussions. Her papers at the Library of Congress contain several important letters pertaining to the gathering of pro-Hoover southern delegations to the 1928 national convention, the second trial of Perry Howard, and her resignation.

Moreover, without a clear sense of the cumulative impact of these events upon Hoover many of his later speeches and actions concerning reform in the South are likely either to be discounted as mere rhetoric or, worse yet, interpreted as evidence of a lily-white racist strategy.

Another common interpretative problem arises from the retrospective assumption that the Hoover nomination bandwagon could not be stopped and that he captured the nomination with ease. Careful examination of the Campaign and Transition Papers, the Edgar Rickard diary, and the illuminating three-page report "The Lowden Dawes Strategy" at West Branch reinforces Work's earlier concern and heightens perception of the great fear among the Hoover campaign staff. This in turn enables one to reconstruct the frame of mind among the Hoover stalwarts on the credentials committee when they insisted on seating only pro-Hoover delegations from the South, whether black-and-tan regulars or lily-white challengers. With these delegations safely in the Hoover camp the tide turned increasingly in his favor until a first-ballot landslide became a reality. Without these sources one may well assume, as some black leaders did at the time, that Hoover's nomination was assured and that therefore the Hoover-controlled credentials committee was pursuing an anti-black or lily-white strategy.

The hitherto unused Jennings C. Wise Papers and, to a much lesser extent, those of Henry W. Anderson, both of which are at the Virginia Historical Society, are essential in understanding Hoover's campaign in the South. There has been a great deal of understandable doubt and confusion over Hoover's objectives in this campaign. The Wise Papers offer the conclusive evidence of the southern "revolution," which is only hinted at in the Hoover Papers or tantalizingly yet too vaguely suggested in an earlier article on Anderson in the *Literary Digest*. Evidence in the Wise Papers makes Hoover's later efforts to reform the state parties much more intelligible and much more in keeping with his penchant for tenaciously pursuing lofty, idealistic goals. It also highlights otherwise obscure yet very important evidence in other collections, but especially unclear references in the Hoover Papers at West Branch.

The role of Horace Mann in the southern campaign has been misunderstood, primarily because previous writers had been unable to find sufficient evidence and because they tended to accept speculations by newspaper reporters. Several rare letters by Horace Mann do exist, however, in the Gilchrist Stockton Papers at the Hoover Institution. These prove conclusively Mann's desire to eliminate all blacks from the southern state parties. (Mann did not preserve any papers.) But as Stockton acknowledges, Mann was not as influential as was assumed. At Memphis State University in Memphis, Tennessee, are the important recently opened papers of Robert R. Church, Jr. These papers demonstrate Hoover's repudiation of Mann and his assurances to Church that his policy was not antiblack and was not designed to drive blacks from the party in the South.

In the Campaign and Transition Papers at the Hoover Library and in the Barnett and Moton collections is proof that Hoover had explained his plan of recruiting new southern white leaders to the black members of his new Colored Voters Division, that he had received their endorsement, and that these black leaders initially cooperated with Mann. Monroe N. Work, editor of the *Negro Year Book: An Annual Encyclopedia of the Negro, 1931–1932*, is an excellent source on the growing black alarm over the degeneration of the southern campaign into a contest dominated by the bigots and racists of both parties. Nonetheless, there is little direct evidence to support the claim that Hoover actively managed the campaign in the South. What does exist suggests instead that he was prone to blame Democrats for the religious prejudice and appeals to racial fears while negligently allowing Work, Mann, Wise, Anderson, and his local southern allies free rein in combating them. Although not actively encouraging the bigotry, Hoover seriously damaged his reputation by remaining too high above it.

Prior to this study scholars were unaware of Hoover's effort to recruit a new black elite for his Colored Voters Division. Fortunately, members of this CVD preserved enough of their papers to permit an adequate although less than satisfying reconstruction of their activities. Most of the collections are disappointingly small. Both the James A. Cobb Papers at Howard University, Washington, D.C., and the Emmett J. Scott Papers at Morgan State University, Baltimore,

Maryland, contain several useful items. Whereas Cobb apparently did not save his correspondence, Scott systematically did so, but there is an inexplicable gap for the years 1927 to 1931. Because Scott was an experienced and skillful black politician, this gap is especially regrettable. The Cobb and Scott materials most useful in this study are in the Hoover Papers at West Branch. At the time I utilized the Robert R. Church Papers, they were not yet open to scholars and still in considerable disarray. The Lincoln League, 1928 campaign, the politics file, and the Perry W. Howard File were used in conjunction with the helpful volume by Annette and Roberta Church, *The Robert R. Churches of Memphis* (Ann Arbor: Edwards Brothers, 1974). Some important Church correspondence is also in the NAACP Papers and at West Branch. Still the sparseness of political correspondence in the Cobb, Scott, and Church collections, coupled with the absence of personal papers for John R. Hawkins is especially unfortunate because these men were among the few black political leaders with whom Hoover and his administration had close contacts. Few other black leaders appear to have had comparable status. Neither the James Weldon Johnson Papers nor the Walter White Papers, both at Yale University, contain materials of importance to this study. There is another big gap in materials on the De Priest tea. Congressman Oscar De Priest and his wife did not preserve their papers. Fortunately the Moton collection helps to bridge a number of these gaps and deserves to be ranked near the top of the collections utilized in this study. But the best single source on individual members of the black elite and on black Republican politics generally is the Claude Barnett Papers. His unpublished autobiography, memorandums, reports, scrapbooks, news releases, national convention notes, and campaign materials are invaluable. For example, from no other single source does one gain so clear an understanding of the great importance of black newspaper owners and editors or of the Hoover administration's consistently careless and damaging neglect of them.

The nature of southern Republican politics during the period from 1927 to 1933 presents special problems. Making sense of Hoover's complicated and seemingly contradictory reform of the southern state parties requires careful use of the voluminous files kept for each state by the president's chief political secretary, Walter H. Newton. Appointments (or patronage) files, organized separately under "Justice," "Post Office," "Treasury," and other appropriate designations, often contain additional material of value. Among the most important of the state files are Virginia, Louisiana, Georgia, Florida, Mississippi, and North Carolina. But these must be used in conjunction with the Wise and Anderson Papers and also with the Louis Strauss collection at West Branch. The William J. Howey Papers at Florida State University, Tallahassee, Florida have excellent newspaper clippings, which are valuable in unraveling the complicated Florida Republican squabbles. The Smith Brookhart investigation, Senate Report 272, "Influencing Appointments to Postmasterships and Other Federal Offices" is a storehouse of information, but this too must be used cautiously because it contains numerous allegations by rival southern politicians. Brookhart's spirited exchanges with the Texas boss R. B. Creager and his inclusion of documents detailing charges against Perry W. Howard are among the most noteworthy materials.

There are a number of special problems in utilizing the correspondence in the southern state files. As each of the factional leaders tended to shade the truth, or make assumptions based either on limited knowledge or mere suspicion, it is difficult, and, at times, impossible to determine the accuracy of the information. Thus extreme caution is required, most especially when the correspondence concerns patronage squabbles or leadership contests or both. Although the administration's instructions and admonitions to state leaders are usually clear enough, one should keep well in mind that rather than one strategy Hoover and his managers pursued several strategies simultaneously within his overall strategy of reform. Until now this has not been disclosed and thus has created much misunderstanding. Finally, the voluminous records at West Branch do not tell the whole story. It is essential that one consult all of the sources discussed in this essay and cited in the notes before a clear, comprehensive, and reliable understanding is possible.

Very few southern Republican leaders preserved their papers. After consulting the standard sources for locating manuscript collections I compiled a list of leaders in each state and wrote to the major repositories and other likely institutions requesting assistance. Manuscript librarians and archivists were kind enough to check their collections, but none of them uncovered the papers of Republican leaders in addition to those cited in this essay. Among those consulted were Auburn University, Birmingham Public Library, the State Department of Archives and History, and Stamford University in Alabama (the Oliver D. Street Papers are at the University of Alabama Library, Tuscaloosa, Alabama); Florida State University, University of Florida, Lakeland Public Library, Florida Historical Society, Jacksonville Public Library, Miami Public Library, and Rollins College in Florida; the University of Georgia, the Georgia Historical Society, Georgia State University, Emory University, the Georgia Department of Archives and History, the Atlanta Historical Society, and Atlanta University in Georgia; the Filson Club, the University of Kentucky, Western Kentucky University, Berea College, and the Louisville Free Public Library in Kentucky; Louisiana State University, Louisiana State Library, the Louisiana Historical Society, Tulane University, and Xavier University in Louisiana; the Johns Hopkins University, the Maryland Historical Society, and the Hall of Records of Maryland in Maryland; the University of Mississippi and the State Department of Archives and History in Mississippi; the University of North Carolina, Duke University, the State Department of Archives and History, and Bennett College in North Carolina; the University of South Carolina, Clemson University, the South Carolina Historical Society, and the State Department of Archives and History in South Carolina; the University of Tennessee, the Tennessee State Library and Archives, Southwestern at Memphis, Joint Universities Libraries, and the Chattanooga Public Library in Tennessee; the College of William and Mary, Virginia State Library, and the Virginia Historical Society in Virginia (the Bascom C. Slemp Papers are located at the University of Virginia); and the West Virginia University Library and the State Department of Archives and History in West Virginia.

Because Hoover's desire to help blacks usually lacked specific direction, his unsystematic and uncoordinated efforts must be gleaned from a variety of scattered sources. The records of the Commerce Department, the Interior Department, and the correspondence in the Colored Question are the most fruitful sources at the Hoover Library. The Ray Lyman Wilbur Papers at The Hoover Institution are also helpful. Hoover instructed his good friend Wilbur to sponsor studies of problems important to blacks and to appoint black experts to these study commissions. Reports on blacks are included in the published findings of the President's Research Committee on Social Trends, the National Advisory Committee on Illiteracy, the White House Conference on Child Health and Protection, the President's Conference on Home Building and Home Ownership, and an extensive study of Negro health, as well as educational surveys. Unfortunately, the absence of correspondence between Wilbur and the black experts who conducted and wrote the reports limits the value of his papers. Hoover's willingness to make more use of federal agencies to help blacks appears in the Moton Papers and in his correspondence with cabinet officers. For his numerous expressions of the need to work toward greater racial progress, see the oral histories of Carrie Butler Massenburg, Mrs. Leon Thompson, Ruth Fesler Lipman, and Alonzo Fields; the Augustus T. Murray papers; the President's Personal File—Negro Matters; the Commission on Interracial Cooperation; the Moton File; Hoover's numerous speeches and greetings to black organizations; and the notes in chapters 2 and 15.

Sources on black patronage are abundant. In the Presidential Papers at West Branch is the Principal Negro Officials Chart compiled by Emmett J. Scott. A compendium by John R. Hawkins is in the J. S. Taylor-Richard Gates Collection. Other valuable materials in the Presidential Papers are the Negro Appointments File; the Colored Question correspondence; the Justice Department files; and the District Commissioners, Recorder of Deeds file. An earlier list is in the Census Bureau files, Commerce Department papers. Also at West Branch are the Edgar Rickard Papers and his useful diary. The intense competition between the two major black factions on the Colored Voters Division is best understood in the revealing personal correspondence between Moton and Barnett. In addition there are useful items in the Church Papers and the Cobb Papers. Postmaster General Walter F. Brown's papers at the Ohio Historical Society are devoid of material dealing with the South or with black Americans. Walter Newton apparently incorporated all of his own correspondence into the Hoover Papers at West Branch.

There are three excellent sources for the Senate fight over the nomination of John J. Parker to the Supreme Court. Each of these sources tells a different yet essential side of the story. In the extensive John J. Parker Papers at the University of North Carolina, Chapel Hill, is the evidence of Parker's eventual decision to pursue his own southern strategy by rallying southern senators. The North Carolina State File and documents in the Judiciary File at West Branch attest to Hoover's surprise at the opposition, to his efforts to persuade opponents that Parker had sympathy for both the rights of labor and of black people, his stubborn retreat to the principle of the independence of the judiciary from special-interest politics, and his too little, too late effort to stave off defeat. But it was the supposedly ineffectual NAACP, with Walter White's incessant reiteration of a cynical, racist southern strategy and his whirlwind campaign to win over the border states and northern Republican senators against Parker, which kept the best collection of correspondence and documents. Of course, the sequence of events cannot be reconstructed without extensive research into each of these collections and several others as well. The Daniel E. Steck correspondence establishes that senators already believed that the nomination was political before the supposedly crucial Dixon letter was made public. Steck's letters are in the Verne Marshall Papers at the Hoover Library. The Arthur H. Vandenburg and W. B. Mershon Papers at the Bentley Historical Library, University of Michigan, Ann Arbor, explain Vandenburg's decision to vote against the nomination. Walter White's recollections in *A Man Called White* (New York: Viking Press, 1948), and *How Far the Promised Land?* (New York: Viking Press, 1955), are milder than is his correspondence in the NAACP Papers, while Hoover's Memoirs (New York: Macmillan Company, 1952) are generally unreliable and reflect poorly on him. The damage to Hoover's reputation is recorded with special emphasis in his *Memoirs*, in the diaries of Col. Campbell B. Hodges and Edgar Rickard at West Branch, and in Rickard's correspondence in the Hugh S. Gibson Papers at the Hoover Institution.

The 1932 campaign saw the abandonment of Hoover's ill-fated efforts to rise above racial politics and to reform the southern state parties. Most of the important sources are in West Branch, but several others deserve special mention. Correspondence in the Democratic National Committee, Georgia State File, in the Franklin D. Roosevelt Library at Hyde Park, New York and the 1932 politics file of the NAACP Papers establishes the growing fear of FDR among Hoover's most severe black critics. This fear of FDR's southern cohorts was utilized effectively by black Hoover loyalists such as Mary Church Terrell, whose papers are in the Library of Congress. By this time Moton and Barnett were disillusioned with Hoover, yet they too shared in the fear of the Democrats. Also pertinent to the 1932 campaign, Barnett's detailed notes on the dramatic counterattack at the national convention by the black-and-tan Republicans against Hoover's appointees are identified simply, and without dates, as Mississippi, South Carolina, Georgia, and Louisiana. They should be used in conjunction with the state files at West Branch. News reporters were keenly interested in the counterattack and provided important information that is lacking in the correspondence and documents. For Roosevelt's skill in dealing with southern politics one should consult the southern state files in his papers at Hyde Park and the perceptive analysis by Frank Freidel, *F.D.R. and the South* (Baton Rouge: Louisiana State University Press, 1965).

There are several scholarly studies on Hoover and black Americans from which I have benefited but with which I also differ on many points of interpretation. The first that I should like to acknowledge is a master's thesis written by George F. Garcia, "Herbert Hoover's Southern Strategy and the Black Reaction" (University of Iowa, 1972). His mentor, Ellis Hawley, has directed a number of excellent theses and dissertations on Hoover topics, and this one is no exception. Garcia later condensed his essay into two articles, "Herbert Hoover and the Issue of Race," *Annals of Iowa* 44 (Winter 1979), and "Black Disaffection from the Republican Party during the Presidency of Herbert Hoover, 1928–1932," *Annals of Iowa* 45 (Fall 1980). Another recent study is David J. Ginzl's unpublished dissertation, "Herbert Hoover and Republican

Patronage Politics in the South, 1928–1932" (Syracuse University, 1977) and his three published articles on Mississippi, Georgia, and Florida, which are cited in the notes. Ginzl concentrated on Hoover's efforts to reform patronage politics in the southern state Republican parties. His state-by-state analysis deserves the respect of scholars, but this emphasis on state patronage politics severely narrows his focus. Thus, he did not examine Hoover's attempt to create new elite leaderships or the complex interrelationships which developed between Hoover and national black leaders. His study is limited also by many of the previously mentioned special problems arising from an overreliance on the correspondence in the southern state files at West Branch. Still another unpublished study is Larry H. Grothaus, "The Hoover Administration and Blacks." By condensing his findings into thirty-seven typewritten pages, Grothaus has written the most succinct account to date, yet its brevity is also a shortcoming. Harshly critical of Hoover's 1928 campaign is Allan J. Lichtman, *Prejudice and the Old Politics: The Presidential Election of 1928* (Chapel Hill: University of North Carolina Press, 1979). An interpretation with a broader perspective is the pertinent chapter in Richard B. Sherman, *The Republican Party and Black America: From McKinley to Hoover, 1896–1933* (Charlottesville: University Press of Virginia, 1973). Yet in all of these studies, their understanding of Hoover's southern strategy differs significantly from mine. Each of them argues that Hoover pursued a single strategy designed primarily to eliminate blacks. Some of them actually consider Hoover a racial moderate but cannot reconcile that view with the lily-white strategy that they describe. In their indictment of Hoover they often rely too heavily on the materials at West Branch. None of them utilizes all of the major resources that are essential to a clear and comprehensive interpretation of Hoover's southern reform effort. I have cited them in the notes to acknowledge their contributions and to indicate the numerous places where my study differs from theirs in interpretation, emphasis, and resources.

Several general studies on Hoover have been of such value that they deserve special mention. I have benefited immeasurably from the Hoover scholarship of Ellis Hawley, David Burner, Joan Hoff Wilson, Barry D. Karl, and George H. Nash. Hawley's *The Great War and the Search for a Modern Order* (New York: St. Martin's Press, 1979) and his articles cited in the notes have left all Hoover scholars deeply in his debt. David Burner's standard one-volume biography, *Herbert Hoover: A Public Life* (New York: Alfred A. Knopf, 1979) brings together an impressive amount of evidence to argue convincingly that Hoover was a reform-oriented president who was liberal on many social issues. A similar theme is presented by Joan Hoff Wilson, *Herbert Hoover: Forgotten Progressive* (Boston: Little, Brown, 1975). Both of these studies compliment one another, and each in its own way adds significantly to our understanding of Hoover. For Hoover's early years the best account is George H. Nash, *The Life of Herbert Hoover: The Engineer, 1874–1914* (New York: W. W. Norton, 1983). One should also consult the scholarship of Gary Dean Best, *The Politics of American Individualism: Herbert Hoover in Transition, 1918–1921* (Westport, Connecticut: Greenwood Press, 1975); and his more recent two-volume study, *Herbert Hoover: The Postpresidential Years, 1933–1964*, 2 vols. (Stanford, California: Hoover Institution Press, 1983). I am indebted as well to Barry D. Karl's perceptive analysis, "Presidential Planning and Social Science Research: Mr. Hoover's Experts," *Perspectives in American History* 3 (1969): 347–409 and to his chapter on Hoover's use of social science research in *Charles E. Merriam and the Study of Politics* (Chicago and London: University of Chicago Press, 1974). A number of useful articles are in Martin L. Fausold and George T. Mazuzan, eds., *The Hoover Presidency: A Reappraisal* (Albany, N.Y.: State University of New York Press, 1974); J. Joseph Huthmacher and Warren I. Susman, eds., *Herbert Hoover and the Crisis of American Capitalism* (Cambridge, Massachusetts: Schenkman Publishing Company, 1973); Lawrence E. Gelfand, ed., *Herbert Hoover: The Great War and Its Aftermath, 1914–1923* (Iowa City: University of Iowa Press, 1979); and Ellis W. Hawley, ed., *Herbert Hoover As Secretary of Commerce: Studies in New Era Thought and Practice* (Iowa City: University of Iowa Press, 1981).

I have benefited as well from a number of excellent general studies of southern politics and black history. Perhaps the most useful has been Paul Lewinson, *Race, Class, and Party: A History of Negro Suffrage and White Politics in the South* (New York: Russell and Russell, 1963), originally published in 1932. Lewinson traveled throughout the South during Hoover's administration interviewing scores of leading southern politicians, both black and white. His discussion "White Politics in the South," with its lengthy analysis of the tactics of Democratic opponents, and the "Handicaps of Lily-Whitism," were especially valuable. William H. Chafe's insightful examination of black views about patronage, "The Negro and Populism: A Kansas Case Study," *Journal of Southern History* 34 (August 1968), helped me to appreciate more fully the crucial importance of patronage to black leaders and to recognize that this thinking had not changed, and may even have become more pronounced by the 1920s. Although I differ with her interpretation of Hoover, there is a useful chapter on black Democrats during the 1932 campaign in Nancy J. Weiss, *Farewell to the Party of Lincoln: Black Politics in the Age of FDR* (Princeton, N.J.: Princeton University Press, 1983). Other especially helpful studies are Andrew Buni, *Robert L. Vann of the Pittsburgh Courier: Politics and Black Journalism* (Pittsburgh: University of Pittsburgh Press, 1974); and *The Negro in Virginia Politics, 1902–1965* (Charlottesville: University Press of Virginia, 1967); Ralph J. Bunche, *The Political Status of the Negro in the Age of FDR* (Chicago and London: University of Chicago Press, 1973); Paul D. Casdorph, *Republicans, Negroes, and Progressives in the South, 1912–1916* (University, Ala.: University of Alabama Press, 1981); Pete Daniel, *The Shadow of Slavery: Peonage in the South, 1901–1969* (Urbana: University of Illinois Press, 1972); and *Deep'n As It Come: The 1927 Mississippi Flood* (New York: Oxford University Press, 1977); John Hope Franklin, *From Slavery to Freedom: A History of Negro Americans*, 3d ed. (New York: Alfred A. Knopf, 1967); Louis R. Harlan, *Booker T. Washington: The Making of a Black Leader, 1865–1901* (New York: Oxford University Press, 1972); Charles F. Kellogg, *N.A.A.C.P.: A History of the National Association for the Advancement of Colored People, 1909–1920* (Baltimore: The Johns Hopkins Press, 1967); V. O. Key, *Southern Politics in State and Nation* (New York: Alfred A. Knopf, 1949); Bruce Alan Lohof, "Hoover and the Mississippi Valley Flood of 1927: A Case Study of the Political Thought of Herbert Hoover" (Ph.D. dissertation, Syracuse University, 1968); Eugene Levy, *James Weldon Johnson* (Chicago and London: University of Chicago Press, 1972); David Gordon Nielson, *Black Ethos: Northern Urban Negro Life and Thought, 1890–1930* (Westport, Conn.: Greenwood Press, 1977); August Meier, *Negro Thought in America, 1800–1915: Racial Ideologies in the Age of Booker T. Washington* (Ann Arbor: University of Michigan Press, 1963); Wilson J. Moses, *The Golden Age of Black Nationalism, 1850–1925* (Hamden, Conn.: Arckon Books, 1978); Elliot M. Rudwick, *W.E.B. Du Bois: A Study in Minority Group Leadership* (Philadelphia: University of Pennsylvania Press, 1960); George B. Tindall, *The Emergence of the New South, 1913–1945* (Baton Rouge: Louisiana State University Press, 1967), and *The Disruption of the Solid South* (Athens: University of Georgia Press, 1972); Nancy J. Weiss, *The National Urban League, 1910–1940* (New York: Oxford University Press, 1974); C. Vann Woodward, *Origins of the New South, 1877–1913* (Baton Rouge: Louisiana State University Press, 1951), and *The Strange Career of Jim Crow*, 2d ed. rev. (Oxford University Press, 1966); Robert L. Zangrando, *The N.A.A.C.P. Crusade against Lynching* (Philadelphia: Temple University Press, 1980). Scarcity of primary sources limits the value of Hanes Walton, *Black Republicans: The Politics of the Black and Tans* (Metuchen, N.J.: Scarecrow Press, 1975), and *Black Political Parties* (New York: Free Press, 1972).

Index